# WOMEN VIETNAM VETERANS
## OUR UNTOLD STORIES

Donna A. Lowery

authorHOUSE®

*AuthorHouse*™
*1663 Liberty Drive*
*Bloomington, IN 47403*
*www.authorhouse.com*
*Phone: 1 (800) 839-8640*

*This book is a work of non-fiction. Unless otherwise noted, the author and the publisher make no explicit guarantees as to the accuracy of the information contained in this book.*

*Scripture taken from the King James Version of the Bible.*

*Published by AuthorHouse 10/27/2015*

*ISBN: 978-1-5049-1399-7 (sc)*
*ISBN: 978-1-5049-1400-0 (hc)*
*ISBN: 978-1-5049-1398-0 (e)*

*Library of Congress Control Number: 2015909219*

*Print information available on the last page.*

*This book is printed on acid-free paper.*

# CONTENTS

# DEDICATION

This book is dedicated to Precilla Landry Wilkewitz and Claire Brisebois Starnes. These women served in the Vietnam War with honor and distinction. They are among the most ardent supporters of all women veterans, and especially those who have served in combat zones. In 1999, they formed a non-profit: Vietnam Women Veterans, Inc.

The purpose of the Vietnam Women Veterans, Inc. is:

- to help foster, encourage and promote the improvement of the condition of the Vietnam women veterans;
- to promote physical and cultural improvements, growth and development, self-respect, self-confidence, and usefulness of Vietnam women veterans;
- to foster new attitudes toward Vietnam women veterans;
- to develop channels of communication which will assist the Vietnam women veterans to maximize self-realization;
- to enhance women veteran membership representation in veterans organizations;
- to create a more positive image of veterans in general; and,
- to assist the disabled and needy veterans, including, but not limited to, the Vietnam women veterans and their dependents, and the widows and orphans of deceased veterans.

While considering whether to take the time needed to research, gather stories, contact women and assemble that material into a book – tangible and published, Precilla asked the author, Donna Lowery, "If you do not take the opportunity to tell these stories, who will? We will not survive four more decades. It is past time."

In recognition of their many years of support and friendship, I dedicate this book to them. Thank you! ***Donna A. Lowery***

Who would have ever dreamed that a young red-haired Cajun girl from Louisiana, who joined the Women's Army Corps in 1966, would play a small part in reuniting women of military service who served in the Republic of Vietnam? Who would have thought that talking with my dear friend, fellow hootch-mate, Claire Brisebois Starnes, about how great it would be to have a reunion with the women who served in Vietnam – and it actually happened?

People often ask us, "How did Vietnam Women Veterans, Inc., come about?" It began with two of my roommates, Marilyn Roth and Claire B. Starnes, agreeing to meet up at the dedication of the Women in Military Service for America (WIMSA) Memorial at the gates of Arlington National Cemetery in DC/Virginia, October 18, 1997. I had three blue vests made with the dates of our service in Vietnam printed on the back. With the visibility of those vests, we connected with 13 other women who served in 'Nam who also were at the dedication. From then on, we wondered how many others were at the dedication that we did not have an opportunity to see. While at the hotel that last day of the dedication, we started recalling names of the women who served that we could remember. It was a good start!

People noticed our blue vests and the big white letters on the backs; plus, Claire being Claire, stood on a chair attracting attention. Oh, yes! Everyone could see us! The next day I was on the plane heading back to Louisiana. A lady seated across from me had a *Washington Post* opened to the page of the WIMSA dedication. And there, big as day, was our photo for the world to see, blue vest and all – the same blue vest most of our Vietnam Women Veterans (VWV) members wear to our reunions.

Now, the questions was, "How were we going to find all the women?" I knew that a Dr. Han Kang, director of Environmental Epidemiology Service, Veterans Administration, Washington, DC, had sent out a questionnaire letter to women who served in Vietnam asking about our health. So I knew he had some names. Claire contacted him, but he said, "NO," he could not give us the names, but maybe he could forward a letter from us to the names he had. That's all it took; Claire was turned loose. Thus began the massive, complicated search. Letters went out. She called family, friends and even neighbors until she found the women listed as having served in Vietnam.

We all owe Claire a world of thanks for all her years of searching and communicating with whomever to find the women. She gave birth to the VWV list of names. Then came, "Well, are we going to do a reunion?" and, "What do we have to do?" It would need money; we needed Articles of Incorporation, Tax ID number for donations, a name for the organization and a logo . . . and, who would be the President and Treasurer? I said, "Claire, you're the President and I'm the Treasurer because our paperwork must have those two officers listed to get started." Thus began VWV, Inc. The rest is history with the first reunion in Olympia, WA, November 11-13, 1999.

When I look back on my military service, especially Vietnam service, I see that all of the women who served in the US military in Vietnam made a difference. The military we knew allowed us to be the Rallying Force for future young women to make a difference in the Armed Forces. We unknowingly became models for those who would come behind us. We proved our mettle under fire. Witness today's women warriors' heroic actions. Our legacy through our stories of military service will become part of what our forefathers did for this great country.

They served when and where they were needed, and they gave their all toward that service, just as we did in Vietnam.

I often think back about VA entitlements not available to us upon our return from Vietnam; and again, I know we also have made a difference there. We had to step up and speak out about healthcare needs for women veterans. The VA finally has seen that the face of the veteran has changed; and, therefore, the VA is starting to meet those demands for healthcare for women veterans.

In closing, let me thank all the military women for their service to our country, our communities, VWV members and our veterans. Let us honor those living and deceased and remember those who suffer from Agent Orange-related cancers and other illnesses. I salute those who have worked hard to tell our story in the book put together by Donna Lowery and her team, and to perpetuate our military service in the Republic of Vietnam.

*Precilla Ann Landry Wilkewitz, Long Binh, Vietnam, January 5, 1968 to September 5, 1969*

We were from the World War I era through the Desert Storm era to October 1997. We came about 35,000 strong from Washington to California, from Maine to Florida. We converged on Washington, DC. The uniform of the day ranged from dress to jeans. We laughed. We cried. We slapped each other on the back. We hugged. We were from all the armed services . . . and we were all women!

No words adequately describe the feelings I experienced throughout the events celebrating the dedication of the Women in Military Service for America (WIMSA)Memorial, October 16-18, 1997. You had to live it.

I must admit that at the beginning I did not want to go. I don't particularly relish large crowds of people. Precilla Landry Wilkewitz, my "hootch" mate in Vietnam and godmother to my oldest son, talked me into going. Today, as I reminisce, I'm absolutely happy that she did.

All the speeches and the hoopla were great. However, the most precious memories I carry are the renewals of faded friendships that were born, oh, so many years ago in 1969 through 1971. There they were: Marilyn, Joyce, Teddi, Marty, Esther, Lucki, Donna, the twins — Charlie and Cathy, Ellis, Linda (Mac), Sonya, Lillian and others who I can't pull from memory as I'm writing this.

To make it easy for others to find us, Precilla had made vests with huge white lettering on the back that read "WAC-Army Long Binh Vietnam" and the years we spent there. The first tap on the shoulder became a face bearing a great big smile, and there was Joyce, our former supply and mail clerk! Still on active duty, she was now serving in the Air Force as chief master sergeant. Though she wore her Air Force uniform, she marched the Candlelight March commemorating our fallen sisters with us, her former Vietnam Army buddies.

Cries of joy, hugs and tears filled our little corner of the world as we found each other and caught up on 28-plus years. Our group representing the women who served at Long Binh was possibly the largest group present at 14. I later learned that there were more at the events, but, sadly, we never connected.

That Sunday, we had to say goodbye, knowing that many of us would not meet again. With that in mind, we somberly said our farewells as we promised each other we would someday get together again. As I was driving home to Northern Maryland, I thought of those who didn't come. I grieved for those who had passed on.

Once home, I called Precilla and we reminisced about the events we had just witnessed. We talked about the women with whom we had renewed our bond. We talked about a possible reunion. That conversation soon became, "Why not try to find as many as we can." In a matter of days, Precilla and I discussed including all services and all who served in Vietnam as staff and line officers and enlisted. Never did I realize what that latter conversation would entail. The spark that ignited at the WIMSA dedication led to a major effort to locate ALL the non-nurse women who served in Vietnam.

In early 1999, Precilla and I launched the Vietnam Women Veterans, VWV, Inc., and the search took over a great part of my life. It was difficult tracking these veterans. Incomplete records made it difficult to track these veterans. At that time, only the Navy and Marine Corps provided the names of their women and their time in country. Additionally, many of the women had married, and available records only listed their maiden names.

I traveled around the country, visiting veterans, looking at their pictures taken so long ago; meeting with people; and locating files and rosters to aid in the research. I developed detailed "search and found" lists with growing input from women veterans across the country, even from Wales, Australia and Panama. I became proficient in using the internet – though limited in 1999 – to conduct my searches. The VWV would not have been possible without the internet. With the help from so many, the search exceeded my expectations. By conference time, we had located about 700 of what we thought was 1,000-plus women who had served in Vietnam. The women were getting excited when they reconnected with one another as the search progressed.

We decided to have our first conference/reunion in Olympia, WA. With the assistance from Washington State, Olympia and dozens of volunteers, the "First Homecoming Conference" became a reality on Veterans Day, 1999. I want to thank fellow Vietnam veterans SGM Donna Lowery (USA, Ret), SFC Anita "Jinx" Wampach (USA, Ret) (deceased) and Capt Ruth Ellis Anderson (USAF, Ret) who were my boots on the ground in Washington State. Without them, the conference would never have happened.

My sincere gratitude goes to BG Evelyn "Pat" Foote (USA, Ret) and to Brig Gen Maralin Coffinger (USAF, Ret) who provided me with their expertise while guiding me through a myriad of Army and Air Force issues. I can't express my appreciation enough to COL Pat Jernigan (USA, Ret) who helped tremendously in the search in the Washington, DC, area. Special recognition goes to Army Vietnam veteran Patricia Babcock Schmauch for helping contact the women and helping me maintain the database as we were finding them. To everyone who helped me, especially the women veterans themselves who responded in overwhelming numbers, please accept my sincere thank you.

During the conference planning, Precilla and I talked about doing a "Memory Book" which would contain experiences of the women in their own words. In 2000, I was finally able to get it printed at a local printer. It wasn't fancy, but it did have "then and now" pictures with whatever story the women provided. It also included a short history of military women (other than nurses) who served in Vietnam, information about and pictures of the first conference (for the benefit of those who were unable to attend) and some "did-you-know" facts. That soft-cover book was for internal use – for the women Vietnam veterans. The book was made possible and published in record time with the assistance of Army Vietnam veteran Linda Barnes Poole and Marine Corps Vietnam veteran Sandra Spatz Wiszneauckas.

I want to acknowledge retired SGM Donna Lowery for expanding on that first book's information, and publishing a more formal book that will be available to everyone. I commend her team who worked long hours to locate more women, procure their stories and pictures, and ensure all Vietnam women veterans who were staff and line officers, medical non-nurses and enlisted are represented.

To all the Vietnam veterans, I say, "Welcome Home."

*Claire M. L. Brisebois Starnes, Long Binh and Saigon, Vietnam, February 1969 to July 1971*

# Acknowledgements

Many organizations and individuals worked to make this project a reality. More than two years of research, multiple trips to various museums and archives, and countless phone calls, emails and letters resulted in this collection of stories and information about the women who served their country in Vietnam. We are indebted to the following organizations and individuals in particular:

**Women in Military Service for America, Washington, DC:**
Marilla J. Cushman, LTC (USA, Ret), Director of Public Relations and Development

**US Army Women's Museum, Fort Lee, VA:**
- Dr. Françoise B. Bonnell, Ph.D., Director, US Army Women's Museum, Book Team Member
- Amanda Strickland, Museum Specialist-Archivist, US Army Women's Museum, Book Team Member

**Marine Corps History Division, Quantico, VA:**
- Dr. Charles P. Neimeyer, Director, Marine Corps History Division, Gray Research Center
- Dr. Fred Allison, Oral Historian, Marine Corps History Division
- Annette Amerman, Senior Reference Historian, Historical Reference Branch, Marine Corps History Division

**US Air Force:**
- The Historical Support Division of the Air Force History and Museums Program, Technical Support

Many others have provided information, encouragement and support along the way for which we are grateful.

- Everett Forbes, Photograph Restoration
- Joanne P. Murphy, Photograph Restoration, Book Team Member

- Charlene Kinsey Henry, Editorial Support
- Terry Blocher, Administrative Support
- Debbie Braun McFadden, Administrative Support
- Brian Russell, University of Idaho, Information Systems Program
- Pauline Cote Shaw, Administrative Support
- Ann W. Sublette, Administrative Support

Continuous love and support from my nephew, Second Lieutenant Nick MacKinnon, USAF, attending pilot training, Vance AFB, Enid, OK

For those women who served in Vietnam who we were not able to locate, we think of you and hope your stories are being told.

## Book Team Members

*Served in Vietnam:*
Carmen "Penny" Marshall Adams
Darlene K. Brewer-Alexander
Marion C. Crawford
Mary Glaudel-DeZurik
Glenda Storni Graebe
Marsha "Cricket" Holder
Pat Jernigan
Nancy Jurgevich
Joanne P. Murphy
Carol A. Ogg
Shirley M. Ohta
Patty Babcock Schmauch
Lyndell D. Smith
Jean Stallings
Claire Brisebois Starnes

*Served in other locations:*
Alfie Alvarado-Ramos
Françoise Bonnell
Dee McWilliams
Phyllis K. Miller

*Civilian Member*
Amanda Strickland

--I authorize all book team members and Precilla Landry Wilkewitz to have their own book signings and any other promotional events they may choose. *Donna A. Lowery*

# PREFACE

In gathering material for this book, we have relied to a large extent on the extraordinary record keeping that was done by the Vietnam Women Veterans (VWV) organization. Beginning with its database, the search was extended to the Services, Department of Defense (DOD), and archived public records.

Early in the planning stage, the decision was made to limit our stories only to those enlisted women and officers (other than nurses) who were assigned to the Republic of Vietnam, rather than all of Southeast Asia (SEA). There are several reasons for this decision. First, most of my book team served on the staffs of Military Assistance Command, Vietnam (MACV), United States Army, Vietnam (USARV), 7th Air Force Headquarters (7AF/HQ), and other combat-support organizations; we are most familiar with that dimension of the war. Second, books have been written and films produced about the extraordinary work of our nurses, but there is scant documentation of the some 1,200 of the rest of us. The third, and probably most compelling, reason is that our experiences are quite different from those who were not actually in Vietnam. While women who served in Thailand also put in very long hours and endured extremely harsh living conditions, they were not exposed to the combat environment of daily rocket attacks and the constant threat of Viet Cong (VC) incursions. Their contribution to the war effort was significant and their stories are also worthy of a book. I hope it will be written.

The war in Vietnam became a pivotal event in the history of women in the military. For the first time since World War II, a Women's Army Corps (WAC) Detachment was activated in a combat zone. General William Westmoreland, Commander of all US forces in Vietnam, recognized the need for administrative help from the WAC, and he needed help NOW. The problem was that after WWII a belief persisted that women did not belong in a combat theater, much less a combat zone. As a consequence, no programs existed for women to prepare for such assignments. In fact, the Director of the WAC, Colonel Elizabeth Hoisington, had actually eliminated Weapons Familiarization in basic training for the WAC. As MG Jeanne Holm stated in her book, *Women in the Military—An Unfinished Revolution*, "The women in the line had not the training, conditioning, clothing, or equipment to prepare them for deployment to a combat theater."

So it was! We were deployed in our dress uniforms complete with heels and nylons. Once there, however, we made an impression. It was obvious, even to the skeptics, that we could deal with the combat environment, with the intense heat, with the red, dusty clay and the monsoons – and that we excelled in our jobs. Soon after the WACs' arrival, Air Force, Marine and Navy women were deployed. Most of the initial requests were for women to fill traditional administrative positions, but as the war extended, military women were assigned to nearly all non-combat positions and to several locations throughout Vietnam.

There were many "firsts" amongst these women in positions no one thought would be or could be performed by women. Opening these assignments to military women in the combat zone paved the way for the true integration of women into the armed forces. We can now be found in nearly every specialty including some designated combat. That pivotal turning point began in Vietnam.

With few exceptions, the stories are in the women's own words. Be ready to cry, to laugh, to be totally amazed by these young, young women and the extraordinary sacrifices they made to serve their country alongside their military brothers. In addition to a chronological sequence of their names, dates served, and duty assignments, the book also includes chapters detailing our "Untold Stories."

One of these chapters tells about how a quilt came to be which had been inspired by events at our First Homecoming Conference, November 1999, in Olympia, WA. Yet another chapter gives the reader a glimpse into the heart and soul of the women in their time away from work. They share some hysterically funny stories, the importance of supporting and caring for the orphans in a nearby village, many photos of pleasant – some unpleasant – events and sights, and poems that cloud the eyes and create goose bumps.

Our deceased sisters are noted with a heart symbol (♥) next to their names and they are included in the virtual cemetery site on Find-a-Grave.com http://goo.gl/yTjo9t

# Chapter One

# THE STORIES WE WANT TO TELL

*For those women who served in Vietnam who we were not able to locate, we think of you and hope your stories are being told.*

Buried in an archive somewhere is the paperwork that would tell us exactly how many military women, not including nurses, served in Vietnam. But, we are still guessing because the best number that the Pentagon could give us was about 1,000 women on orders.

In 1964, shortly after General William Westmoreland approved two positions for WAC Advisors to the Vietnam Women's Armed Forces Corps, he decided that he wanted to have WAC stenographers as well. Eleven women arrived in 1965, including stenographers, advisors, and others; 27 arrived in 1966, and then the gates opened. Five of the 1966 arrivals served as cadre to establish the first WAC Detachment in a combat zone since World War II. The Army women were billeted at Tan Son Nhut Air Base, in a location named Tent City B, consisting of Quonset huts. The Air Force, Marine and Navy women who came later were billeted in hotels in Saigon. In 1967, the Army women moved to Long Binh into wooden two-story barracks located near Headquarters US Army Republic of Vietnam (USARV). In that year, 153 women (that we know of) arrived in country, officer and enlisted, from every branch except the Coast Guard. Many of them volunteered, but some, like the author of this book, were surprised to find themselves selected to serve.

Decades after the end of the conflict, the women who served in Vietnam are dying. They ranged in age from 62 to 93 as this book was being written. There are people who believe that no military women, other than nurses, served in Vietnam. They will tell you so outright. We are determined that these military women will have their place in history and have this opportunity to tell their stories.

Listed by year are all the women we could locate who served – the clerk-typists, the stenographers, the intelligence analysts, the translators, the communications technicians, the supply specialists, the doctors, the medical records clerks, the lab technicians, the dietitians and physical therapists, and all the other military women who deserve this recognition. Listed by their arrival date, each year contains first the women who do not have exact dates, then the women about whom we could find more information. If they submitted a story, it is included. Some gave us one line, some gave us five pages.

We have included a biographical chapter on the women who served as Advisors to the Vietnam Women's Armed Forces Corps.

We also have a collection of stories titled, "The Consequences of War?" Many of the women wanted to talk about their health issues, their children's health issues, and the problems they have with Posttraumatic Stress Disorder (PTSD). Some speak of problems encountered in Vietnam.

A collection of "Tales to Tell" is entertaining and sad, interesting and horrifying – the women were honest about many of their thoughts and experiences.

It took extraordinary effort to locate the women veterans for the first formal Homecoming Conference in November 1999. Eventually a database with 791 names was compiled – but only 124 of them could attend the conference. Out of that conference came the Vietnam Memory Book 2000. We were allowed to use all the pictures and stories from that effort and are grateful to Claire Brisebois Starnes and Precilla Landry Wilkewitz for that permission.

There were 81 women's names read for the Memorial Service at the first Homecoming Conference. Our Virtual Cemetery (http://goo.gl/yTjo9t) has 245 names as we prepare to submit this book for publication. That number will only increase. Additionally, we have a Sister Search List that contains many names of women who we believe served in Vietnam. We would like to locate them or at least find more information, especially the dates they were in country. They are listed in a second Virtual Cemetery –Sister Search at http://goo.gl/wCVcDk.

Providing a complete list of those we know about, and their services, and the history of each service's commitment to the effort seemed a fitting addition to our book. It is our hope that those who are looking for a specific veteran will find this section helpful.

And last, it should surprise no one that the author had a few things to say.

# Chapter Two

# EXPLAINING THE VIRTUAL CEMETERY AND LISTINGS

http://goo.gl/yTjo9t

*When asked to help Donna Lowery on this book project, I knew what my part would be before she said a word. I have been doing family research for nearly 10 years and www.findagrave. com has helped me so much. When I retired in 2010 and came back home, I found that the local cemeteries where the parents and grandparents of all my childhood friends are buried had not been recorded. The first two years of my retirement, I was always in the cemeteries taking pictures of headstones or on the computer recording burials out of the Cemetery books for the three counties around where I grew up. Now I am looking at every site I can for references to any deceased veteran and checking to make sure their lives are recorded on "Find a Grave" so their service to their country will not be forgotten. I created the Vietnam Women Veterans Virtual Cemetery where memorials created to honor our deceased sisters can be easily accessed. I am especially proud to do this for all the women who served their country. May their sacrifice for their country and place in history never be forgotten!!*
***~ Marsha D. "Cricket" Holder ~***

There is no way to adequately express gratitude to someone who routinely stays up until midnight, searching through files and internet pages, trying to locate women who served in Vietnam. The original list used for this book had 570 names. As the book gets ready to go to press, it has more than 1,000 women listed. It is a work-in-progress.

# ASSIGNMENT LISTINGS

Chronological listings of the women based on their arrival dates in Vietnam are in the following chapters, 1962 – 1972. Each woman is identified with four or more lines of information that detail her name(s), dates in country, highest rank in country, service and duty assignment(s) while there. The infographic shows the structure of the information. We hope future researchers and genealogists will find this useful. A few of the women were married when they arrived in Vietnam, but the majority of them were not.

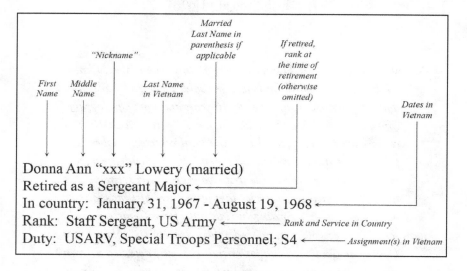

An Image Index lists credits and sources for the images used throughout the book. Many women sent pictures, but we are especially indebted to Vietnam Women Veterans, Inc.; the Women in Military Service for America Memorial Foundation Register; and the US Army Women's Museum for their contributions.

Throughout the chronological chapters listing the women, there are some *Memory Lane* and *Songs* entries. Sometimes a reference to music or what was happening in the States will evoke stronger memories of the time than simply seeing the year listed.

# ACRONYMS

All information related to a specific field has its own language, and this is especially true of the military. Where possible, terms and labels have been spelled out, but there are a few acronyms used throughout the book and they are listed here.

| | |
|---|---|
| AMSC | Army Medical Specialist Corps |
| BMSC | Biomedical Sciences Corps |
| BOQ/BEQ | Bachelor Quarters, both Officer and Enlisted |
| CQ | Charge of Quarters |
| Jl/G1 | Personnel |
| J2/G2 | Intelligence |
| J3/G3 | Operations |
| J4/G4 | Logistics |
| J5/G5 | Plans |
| J6/G6 | Communications-Electronics |
| MACV | Military Assistance Command, Vietnam |
| NAVFORV | Naval Forces, Vietnam |
| R&R | Rest and Recuperation |
| SEATO | Southeast Asia Treaty Organization |
| TDY | Temporary duty |
| USAHAC | US Army Headquarters Area Command |
| USARV | United States Army, Vietnam |
| USO | United Service Organizations |
| VC | Viet Cong |
| VFW | Veterans of Foreign Wars |
| WAFC | Women's Armed Forces Corps |
| WIMSA | Women in Military Service for America |

# Chapter Three

# WELCOME TO VIETNAM

*Compiled by Joanne Murphy*
*Second WAC Detachment Commander*

## Introduction

All work and no play makes Private "I 'borrowed' a jeep" Jones and Specialist "I clung for dear life to a McGuire lift" Smith very dull girls. The women worked 12-14 hour days, oftentimes seven days a week. Most of them were young, full of energy, and, even though tired from their long hours at the office, they wanted to drink in all that this unique assignment offered them. The following pages are a glimpse into their off-duty hours, their happy, fun-loving times, their love and respect for each other, the lifelong friendships made, their compassion for the orphans, and their deep concern for our fighting men. There are first-hand accounts of key events in the Vietnam conflict. The activation of the first WAC Detachment in a combat zone since World War II is discussed. Tet Offensive experiences are shared.

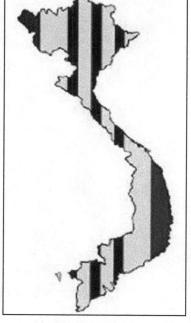

# Calendar of Events

## 1962

- MAJ Anne Marie Doering arrives, first WAC officer to serve in Vietnam

## 1965

- First WAC Officer and NCO Advisors to the WAFC arrive; first seven stenographers arrive

## 1966

- Additional women arrive and begin serving in staff officer jobs; first Navy Medical Service Corps women begin serving on USS *Repose* and USS *Sanctuary*
- March – Capt L. Jane Struthers, first Air Force line officer, arrives; first Army physical therapist, MAJ Barbara Gray, arrives
- May – First Army dietitian consultant, LTC Patricia Accountius, arrives
- October –1SG Marion C. Crawford, hand-picked to activate the first WAC Detachment in Vietnam and the first in a combat zone since WWII, and her Field First/Admin NCO, SFC Betty J. Benson, arrive
- October 31 – CPT Peggy E. Ready, handpicked to be the first Commanding Officer of the WAC Detachment, arrives
- November 1 – Groundbreaking Ceremony for the new WAC compound at Tan Son Nhut
- November – SSG Edith "Effie" Efferson, first WAC Detachment Supply Sergeant, arrives
- December 17 – Hank Snow Show – Mortar fire rages all around; the air is filled with the sound of B-52s bombing. Those in the audience stay pretty calm, but Hank can hardly sing! Can't help but notice that Hank's wife has her running shoes on! Nancy Sinatra, who accompanied Hank, changes the words of her big hit to "These boots were made for running!" Once the show is over, all the entertainers make a rapid exit.
- December 24 – Bob Hope Show – Accompanying Bob is his wife Delores, Phyllis Diller, Anita Bryant, Vic Damone and Joey

Heatherton. What a great show! Sitting in the sun for three hours meant blisters. Oooh! Pain! But, more than worth it.

- December 24 – Francis Joseph Cardinal Spellman, Archbishop of New York, celebrates an outdoor Mass. Cardinal Spellman supports US involvement in Vietnam
- December 27 – A Protestant Chaplain brings a small, standard size French poodle to the WAC Detachment. 1SG Marion Crawford becomes her owner and names her Ko-Ko. Unit mascot position filled!

## *1967*

- First Air Force Biomedical Sciences Corps dietitian, Capt Joan Kyllo, arrives in Vietnam
- January 12-17 – The first group of Army enlisted women arrive, 35 E4s. Two have just come off their honeymoons. Two women have spouses already in country.
- January 21 – Grand Opening, USARV WAC Detachment.
- March 12-15 – RED ALERT – The Viet Cong (VC) broke through the perimeter of Tan Son Nhut Air Base. The women are hurried into their bunkers – three nights without sleep!
- March 18 – MSgt Barbara Dulinsky, US Marine Corps, first woman marine to serve in a combat theater, arrives
- April 8 – 1SG Crawford organizes and trains a drill team; 27 women are eager participants
- May 14 – Women's Army Corps 25th Anniversary. The WAC Drill Team gives its first performance at the party. The USARV Combo provides live music for the party/dance, which lasts into the evening.
- June – LT Elizabeth G. Wylie, first Navy woman, arrives
- June 9 – Capt Vera Mae Jones, USMC, first woman marine officer, arrives
- June 17 – First five enlisted Women in the Air Force (WAF) arrive
- July 4 – Capt Grace Scruggs, first Air Force physical therapist, arrives
- July 13 – WAC Detachment relocates to Long Binh for greater safety
- October 18 – CPT Joanne Murphy arrives to replace CPT Peggy Ready as WAC Detachment Commander
- October 27 – Change of Command – CPT Ready turns the unit over to CPT Murphy

- December 12 – 1SG Marion C. Crawford is med-evac'd to Camp Zama, Japan; misses Christmas with her troops
- December 25 – Bob Hope Christmas Show with Barbara McNair

## 1968

- January 14 – 21 enlisted women of the first group, USARV WAC Detachment, rotate to the States; eight new women arrive; 29 en route
- January 30 – Tet Offensive begins
- January 31 – Ammunition dump at Long Binh is hit
- February 18 – Ammunition dump at Long Binh is hit again; rocket attack on Bien Hoa Air Base
- May 14 – Women's Army Corps 26th Anniversary. The mess hall provides a lavish feast; the women invite many guests for the dinner/dance. Music provided by the Special Troops Band.
- August – Maj Norma A. Archer is first WAF to give daily briefings of key air strikes to the 7th Air Force HQ staff
- October 16 – Change of Command ceremony. CPT Murphy hands the unit guidon to her replacement, CPT Nancy Jurgevich

## 1969

- January – Grand Opening of the new WAC Detachment, Long Binh
- Navy LCDR Barbara Bole is the first Navy woman awarded the Bronze Star with Combat "V" in the Vietnam conflict
- April – MSG Betty Grace Claus (Teager) arrives; upon promotion, only WAC Sergeant Major in country
- November – Army LTC Barbara Wirth (Colon), MD, arrives as physician in Saigon
- November 12 – CPT Shirley Ohta arrives to replace CPT Nancy Jurgevich as WAC Detachment commander

## 1970

- February – Army LTC Janice Mendelson, MD, arrives for duty as Chief Surgeon and Surgical Rehabilitation Advisor
- July 6 – Army COL Clotilde Dent Bowen, MD, the only black physician in the Army, arrives to be chief psychiatrist in Vietnam

- September – Army SP5 Joy J. Smith is first WAC assigned to Maxillo-Facial Team (Dental), 24th Evacuation Hospital
- November – Maj Barbara J. Thompson, USAF, is first female ever assigned to the Red Horse Squadron
- CPT Marjorie Johnson arrives to replace CPT Shirley Ohta as WAC Detachment commander

## 1971

- August 1 – Air Force Maj Virginia Schooler, Chief Dietitian, closes hospital at Cam Ranh Bay
- November 7 – Change of Command ceremony – CPT Marjorie Johnson to CPT Constance Seidemann, last commander of the WAC Detachment
- December 22 – Navy CDR Elizabeth Barrett, the first senior female Naval line officer to serve in Vietnam, arrives

## 1972

- February – Navy CAPT Mary Anderson (Shupack) assists in the closing of the Naval Air Facility in Cam Ranh Bay and is the last Navy woman to serve in Vietnam
- September 21 – USARV Special Troops WAC Detachment deactivates; remaining women move to MACV Saigon

## 1973

- February – Army Medical Specialist Corps 1LT Rebecca Shumate (Richardson) is the last physical therapist to leave Vietnam
- Army MAJ Frances Iaconi (Krilich) is the last dietetic consultant to leave Vietnam
- March – Army MAJ Georgia Wise is the last WAC officer to leave Vietnam
- March – CWO4 Ernestine Koch is the last USMC woman to leave Vietnam
- March 29 – last WACs leave Vietnam
- March 29 – 7th Air Force command moves to Thailand; all remaining Air Force women move with it out of Vietnam

## Our Lighter Moments

***Donna Loring:*** The photo with my story in 1967 is the only photo I had when I came back to the States because I lost my camera in Vung Tau. Betty Gant and I snuck away to this resort town to celebrate her birthday. Swimming in the South China Sea with our fatigues on and getting a ride on a McGuire Lift underneath a helicopter – now that was fun! All of a sudden, though, we had to make a quick exit from our day at the beach. Charlie was spotted heading our way. We got back to the detachment undetected, but not without having to bribe the security guard with a case of Bud! I'll never forget that day.

***Doris Denton:*** Fran Gonzales and I were roommates at the Medford Hotel. We were both reading on our bunks, when, all of a sudden, I saw movement out of the corner of my eye. I looked over to the wall next to Fran's bed and saw the biggest lizard I have ever seen. I told Fran to look. When she saw it, she jumped up and screamed. With that, the lizard jumped toward me. I jumped on Fran's bed. Next, the lizard jumped on our dirty clothes pile and turned the same color as our uniforms. The Army girls next door heard the commotion, came in with a broom, and chased the lizard out the door onto the balcony.

***Sue Schungel (Delk):*** My father, LTC Daniel F. Schungel, and I had the unique experience of serving in Vietnam at the same time in 1968. He was the Deputy Commander of the 5th Special Forces Group headquartered in Nha Trang. I was a Personnel Specialist at USARV HQ. One morning, in our very large and normally very noisy office, a sudden hush came over the entire office. I looked around. Everyone was staring at the door. Oh, my! There

stood my father wearing his Green Beret – tall, erect, tanned and handsome, and looking much younger than his 42 years. As tears rolled down my cheeks, he approached me with open arms. It was the first time I had seen him since arriving in country. I jumped into his open arms. It was one of the happiest and proudest moments of my life.

He wanted to take me to the Special Forces Command Liaison Office in Saigon for the remainder of the day and bring me back the next day. My boss gave his permission. He knew of my father and that everything was on the up and up. However, I still needed the permission of my company commander, CPT Joanne Murphy. She was a superb commander who deeply cared for her soldiers. She was particularly concerned about the safety and welfare of her girls and would never permit the possibility of one of us being in danger. My father and I went to the Orderly Room where Dad introduced himself to CPT Murphy and voiced his request. From the outset, I could tell that she was suspicious. After a lengthy discussion, a review of his ID card, and confirmation from other sources, she finally accepted that this young-looking, handsome man was, in fact, my father and not an admirer with other intentions. So, Dad and I proceeded to Saigon for a wonderful evening of steaks and conversation. As I think back, the event is so comical considering the lengthy details of the Orderly Room discussion. Thank you, Captain Murphy, for protecting and caring for us. I shall never forget those memorable days.

***Nora Lebron:*** One day Idalia Correa and I were resting against a railing outside of the 24th Evacuation Mess Hall waiting for the WAC bus to arrive. Suddenly, this handsome soldier came and stood by us. In Spanish, "Corrie" and I started talking about how handsome he was and how we wouldn't mind his putting his shoes under our beds. Much to our surprise and embarrassment, he turned to us and said that he would love that too. I don't know who was more embarrassed, "Corrie" or me. It turned out that he was Puerto Rican/German. We all started laughing and introduced ourselves. From that day on, we were a threesome until he went stateside. We invited him to all of the functions held at the WAC Detachment.

***Marion C. Crawford:*** During her briefing of the newly arrived women, Supply Sergeant Edith "Effie" Efferson showed them how to put on their emergency equipment – a backpack stuffed with essentials. She would put on all the equipment then collapse to her knees to show how heavy it was! That always gave the women a good laugh. Our dear departed Sergeant Effie was full of laughs.

***Patsy "Dianne" Hatley:*** When I first arrived at Tan Son Nhut and was assigned a room, I tried to get rid of all the geckos in my room. Geckos were everywhere – in the shower, latrine, locker, hanging from the rafters – as I said, they were everywhere! My friends told me that I should leave the geckos alone because they eat other critters. I should have taken their advice sooner.

One night when I was in bed, my left leg kept itching. Over and over again I kept rubbing it with my right foot. Finally, I threw back the covers, turned on the light, and found a very big cockroach in my bed. I got the cockroach on the floor, picked up one of my combat boots, and began hammering away at it. After that incident, geckos were welcome!

***Diana "Andy" Andrews:*** ". . . or the time my girlfriend and I caught a hop back from Thailand and the plane had no bathroom facilities. It only had a can which she would not use. The pilot radioed ahead to the tower at Bear Cat (his destination) to let them know he would be stopping at the end of the runway to let off two passengers to use the facilities there. It wasn't long before the whole base knew that two women were there. She had me guard the door for her. When she left the building, the tower guys announced over the base speaker system that she owed them a quarter for the use of the restroom."
*Source: Vietnam Memory Book 2000*

***Elizabeth "Dee" Barrett:*** Among a few amusing situations, there was the problem of getting my socks back from the laundry when I wore my field uniform. When down to my last pair, I drew a picture of a sock with a question mark and left it for my mama-san. It worked. I got all my pairs of socks back plus a bonus pair.

***Glenda "Stormy" E. Storni (Graebe):*** My first night in country wasn't funny then, but it is now. My arrival was a total surprise to CPT Ready. The only one who knew I was coming was my dear friend Jan Curtis (now deceased). Somehow, my orders didn't arrive to warn them of my arrival. I flew into Saigon in the middle of the night with many GIs. Once on the ground two very nervous sergeants had to find somewhere to put me because they didn't know there were women in country (other than) those going to a hospital for duty. They had no clue where the WAC Detachment was. I sat there for hours, waiting, watching and listening. The Vietnamese men were all over me, touching my red hair. I began to think that perhaps I was a little over-zealous for wanting to go to Vietnam. The sergeants finally found out that, yes, we had a WAC Detachment and, yes, I wasn't there by mistake. If memory serves me, SFC Benson and CPT Ready came to get me at about 3:30 a.m. Now that's what I call a first impression. I don't think I made too many points that night.

***Glenda "Stormy" E. Storni (Graebe):*** Everyone in our hootch was going out to a party, but I was running late. I intended to join the group a bit later. As I tried to leave, I was stopped dead in my tracks by this ugly green stick-like figure. It just stayed in the middle of the doorway. I moved to my left, it moved to its right. I moved to my right, it moved to its left. I finally gave up and decided to stay in for the night. Who was it that reminded me I was bigger than that praying mantis?

**Nancy Jurgevich (Third Commander):** About two months after I became Commanding Officer, we moved to a new barracks with air conditioning and a large covered patio for recreational activities, movies, local plays and bands. The rooms were about 20x20 with normally three women assigned to share each room. This was not a lot of space but not bad for a combat zone. A few weeks after moving into the new barracks, the air conditioner in the NCO barracks broke. The maintenance people determined that a new part had to be shipped from the States that could take some time. The women worked all over the base and were able to find out more information than I could ever find. Somehow, they found out the Generals' Mess Hall/Dining Facility had the same air conditioner that was in the NCO barracks. It took no time at all for them to determine that if they could borrow/steal that part from the Generals' facility, they could repair their air conditioner. Their solution was to sneak over there late at night and drop the smallest, skinniest NCO into the air conditioner and take the part. Not only could this make the Generals angry but also would endanger the safety of the woman being down there – what if the air conditioner went on? Thanks to 1SG Manning, who was alert and heard the women talking about their plan, for getting the NCOs together and telling them there would be no such action. This was a case of the young NCOs' ambition being greater than their maturity.

**Nancy Jurgevich (Third Commander):** The PINK BUS – actually, the bus was not pink at all, only on the front where a license tag is usually located. But that's what we called it. We had the bus and a driver assigned to take the women to United States Army Vietnam Headquarters and First Logistical Command Headquarters. The women's daily routine was reveille at 5:30 a.m., then breakfast at the 24th Evacuation Hospital. The bus arrived at 7:30 a.m. to take the women to their duty stations, brought them "home" for lunch, then brought them back to the WAC Detachment at the end of the workday. Oftentimes, though, the women asked him to detour to the Post Exchange before going "home." (Truth be told, there were far fewer women on the bus at the end of the day than in the morning – so many of them worked 12 to 14 hours a day; they had to call a military taxi.) Actually, the bus driver was not required to shuttle them around the post; he was just being a nice guy. All was well, until one day a couple of the women complained to 1SG Mary Manning that the driver was jerking the bus. Sergeant Manning called in the driver to find out what the problem was. As it turned out, yes, he was jerking the bus because his shoulder hurt. Seems the women were hitting his shoulder with their caps as they got on and off the bus as a friendly gesture. So Sergeant Manning had a little meeting with the women and told them to quit "beating up" the driver.

In a gesture of friendship, outgoing commander, CPT Joanne Murphy, offers Donna M. Loring her boot filled with champagne. They had many conversations in the CO's office! Today they are best friends.

With a rare afternoon off, these women couldn't wait for the pool to fill. It wasn't very large nor was it very deep, but it was a welcome opportunity to cool off from the intense Vietnam heat. The pool was donated by a stateside WAC Veterans organization.

*Amy Carter:* The guys I worked with pulled all manner of practical jokes on me. Jim Welling, otherwise known as "The Montana Mule," usually had something to do with these. One time he told me about a lizard a Vietnamese woman gave him. He said it looked up at him and died. I figured one way or another I would see that dead lizard. That night I received a very large orange envelope. I was expecting my travel orders for my leave in Taipei. I thought maybe the envelope contained these. I did not notice that there was nobody in the office except two colonels. I opened the envelope and didn't see anything until I looked at the bottom of the envelope. There was the lizard. I screamed or gasped, and threw the envelope toward the colonels. They looked at me with what I construed as disgust. I ran out of the room to the Kitchen Division. All the guys were there. I told Jim I was going to kill him. I was asked if I screamed. I think they saw the colonels and didn't dare stay though they would have paid money to see me open that envelope.

Another time, after Jim had gone on vacation to Taipei, I started to type and could not. Jim had put an elastic or rubber band over the keys within, immobilizing them.

We used chalk to cover erasures. Jim asked me for some chalk. I thought that was strange, as I believed he already had some, but I still looked in my desk drawer. There it was – a huge roach. In Vietnam, roaches fly. Its legs were trapped with a clamp to bind papers. I took the clamp off the roach's legs and called Joe, this guy across the hall I had a crush on. I asked him to put the roach in a trash can and carry it out. I didn't want it harmed or killed. I just wanted it gone.

The very worst thing Jim did involved a coke. Jim used to buy me cokes or I did. He'd open them for me as I didn't like the noise the opener made. I wanted to reimburse him by getting him a soda. He opened it, and it squirted all the way up his tall skinny body and down to his feet. I laughed so hard, I cried. The more he accused me of knowing the soda was frozen, the more I laughed, and the guiltier I looked.

I tended to drink my cokes just a little at a time and get back to them later. I saw some orange shavings on the top of the coke when I first drank it. I just thought it was pieces of the orange labels we had, and maybe Jim had done that. The coke tasted OK. Much later, I took a big swig of the now warm coke. It was horrible. We were given malaria pills every Monday, and I had experimentally tasted the quinine before and tried to drown out the taste with a coke. I knew what Jim had done as the taste was the same. Quinine gives some diarrhea, and that is from one dose. I didn't have that problem, but I wondered what would happen with another dose. I think it was Wednesday when I had my double dose.

I can't say I was a saint as I played some pranks as well. The guard shack was on the other side of our fence, but there was an opening towards the top of the shack. I pulled up a chair and stood on it. I pushed a broom handle through the opening and tapped the guard on the shoulder. He about jumped out of his skin, then he was very angry with me. He said I could have gotten myself shot if he had been one of the guys who worked in the field and very skittish. I was ashamed, and I never tried that one again.

# DRY TANK CITATION

**Specialist 4 Amy L. Carter** is about to be released from her protective custody cell and turned loose on the unsuspecting citizens of Massachusetts and California. Amy is probably the only SP4 in the Army who forced a Major to move out of his office and give it to her so he could remove himself from her constant chatter.

The word was passed up from Maintenance Division when Amy came to Services that if they wanted her, they would have to cut out their colorful language. With only one typist and 8 action officers, they were willing to comply. However, someone failed to pass the word along to POL where Amy acquired knowledge of an extensive Army vocabulary. Specialist Carter's decorative talents will be missed in the POL Branch. Where else was flower power so evident? Everything – the sign out board, file folders, doors signs – all decorated with Amy's flowers. Even the girls on the PM calendars did not meet with Amy's approval, so she made clothes for them. SP4 Carter with her devious ways and mischievous ways, on her last Sunday, inveigled a poor unsuspecting guide to take her into the Pearl of the Orient to see it in all its grandeur.

On the night of her farewell party, she blackmailed her guide to escort her through Monkey Valley back to her billets. Her main concern of that night was to arrive back at the WAC Detachment on time. According to the new curfew, one must be in by 2330, but Amy had the luck to arrive on or about the hour of 2345 or 2400. One question that arose was why it took so long to get back to her barracks. What monkey business went on in Monkey Valley? Little is known. This could be classified as one of the great mysteries of the Orient. On the serious side for a moment, Specialist Carter is one of the best typists in the division. The action officers were always being bugged about improper format, no mfr (don't ask) improper words, improper English, ad infinitum.

We will all miss her squeaks, squeals and oh's. The office will probably return to a dull military working unit. Bon voyage, Amy! Make all the girls in California beautiful for the dirty old GIs when they return from Vietnam.

SP4 Amy Carter was presented with a special citation as she prepared to leave Vietnam. The POL Branch was petroleum, oils and lubricants.

***Alice "Baby" Delgado:*** We HAD to laugh a lot! There was danger "out there" – everywhere! So we told each other jokes; some were raunchy, some really funny. For example: Two 'Nam soldiers became separated from their unit; found themselves surrounded by VC. One says, "Looks like we're about to get it, we'd best say a prayer." The other one says, "I don't know any prayers." His buddy said, "There was a Catholic church close to our house at home. They said prayers a lot – I'll try to say one for us." So they knelt and the soldier started his prayer: "Under the B – 15; under the O – 65; under the N – 38, etc." You have to be a BINGO player (or a Catholic) to appreciate that one. We laughed anyway. It was good to laugh!

My very best and most memorable humorous experience involved our Headquarters Chaplain, COL Jim Allen. What a super guy! To this day (2014), we still correspond with Christmas cards. Recently, we spoke on the phone. The Chaplain is now 98 years old, but he vividly recalls the day he invited me to his hotel room (can't remember the name of the hotel), to come watch the movie, "The Sound of Music." I had not seen it and they were showing it at his hotel. During this time, it was dangerous for us to travel at night due to VC activity. So he offered to give up his room so that I could leave work during the day and stay overnight in his room to watch the movie. Of course, the Chaplain was going to bunk-in with one of his buddies so I could have his room. However, the Vietnamese maid thought that the Chaplain and I would be sleeping together, so she put two pillows on the bed. She moved some of HIS things from the dresser drawer and gave me room to put my personal things in his drawer. The maids were very accommodating that way. The maid was terribly disappointed when she found out that we did not share the bed. The Chaplain once came with his wife to visit me years ago, and she got a big kick out of that story. To this day, we fondly remember that event, and we laugh!

Another humorous event that I recall had to do with the young and beautiful Vietnamese worker that was assigned to me in a somewhat secretarial position. I did not know how to type so I asked for help, and my boss, LTC Busse, sent me Miss Thu (pronounced TOO). She was truly beautiful. All the guys in the headquarters visited me A LOT! Of course, they simply wanted to see and talk with Miss Thu. I got a big kick out of this and made even more close friends from our unit.

## The Innocents

***Virginia "Gini" A. Griffith:*** A favorite and very special memory is of my trips to the orphanage in Bien Hoa. A group of us women joined a group of Air Force men who supported the orphanage by making improvements and playing with the children. It was a bit of a culture shock on my first visit, though. The little boys were wearing shirts but no bottoms. However, on our subsequent visits, they were wearing both shirts and shorts. Their living quarters were rather rickety, made mostly of corrugated metal. Yet, their temple with a sitting Buddha in the center was very ornate. During one of my visits, the woman who ran the orphanage asked me if I wanted to go grocery shopping with her. I considered her invitation quite an honor. Of course, I went with her. That was a unique experience! There was raw meat, plucked chickens hanging out in the open, and a tub of live squirming eels. It was something this woman was not accustomed to seeing. But it was their culture, and that was their way. I have often wondered what happened to the children and their caretakers when we left.

***Tanya Murphy (Hickman):*** My biggest reward while serving in Vietnam was working side-by-side with doctors, medics and enlisted personnel at the St. Vincent de Paul Orphanage run by nuns. The orphanage was in desperate need of medication/medical attention and supplies. The facility was run down and in need of much care. The surrounding grounds were overgrown with weeds. Lots of stray dogs hung around. The babies were suffering from malnutrition and lack of bedding, clothing and proper hygiene. Their little bodies lay on wire racks; their cribs had no mattresses. They had on diapers but had no shirts. Their little backs had sores that attracted the dogs and flies – lots and lots of flies.

***Glenda "Stormy" E. Storni (Graebe):*** My sister, who was a Girl Scout in Bakersfield, CA, and her troop sent 28 large boxes of clothing, which they had collected for the orphanage. It was a joy to see the faces of all those children when I started taking the clothing out of the boxes.

Children at the orphanage waiting to see what's in the boxes. SSG Janet Singer in the background.

Glenda Storni (Graebe) passes out dresses to some very happy little girls.

Clockwise, from top left: Marlene Bowen Grissett; Amy Carter and Kevin – the child adopted by Cathy Oatman; Ernestine Koch hands out school supplies to the children in a remote village; Ermelinda Salazar, USMC, at St. Vincent de Paul Orphanage during some off-duty time; Patsy "Dianne" Hatley; Below, holding hands with two of her young Vietnamese friends is BG (then Major) Evelyn "Pat" Foote in the village of Phuoc Thien. "The Village was attacked by the VC the night before our visit," said General "Pat." (June 1967)

***Karen Offutt:*** Someone told me about an orphanage that was downtown in Saigon. I started going there on my 1/2 day off. It was heart breaking to see so many children with shrapnel wounds, tiny babies there with no parents, kids without limbs. They slept on mats on flat table-like cots. Some babies were so small; they fit in what looked to be knitted hats. There was one little girl that I very much wanted to adopt, but I was told, as a single woman, that it would be pretty much impossible. I loved to spend time with them, but their faces have haunted me all these years. I wonder if they lived when Saigon fell. I wonder if any of them ever made it to the States. If you ever want to know what war does, look at the children.

Clockwise, from top left: Karen Offutt brings a bit of joy to this little orphan girl as they play on the swing; Karen Offutt playing with the orphan baby girl she wanted to adopt; Karen Offutt in the playground with the orphan boys. Note the boy on the left saluting the photographer.

***Joanne Murphy (Second Commander):*** Bien Hoa was only a short distance, perhaps about three miles, from the WAC Detachment and other units based at Long Binh. Exactly how the troops became aware of the school there and the orphanage is not clear. But, aware they were! Their fondness, attachment, and love for these children were infectious. The word spread. Many, many of them spent a great deal of their off-duty time with the children. A good number of troops had written family and friends asking for clothing, toys and other gifts to give the children. Once the new arrivals who replaced the first group of WACs were all settled in at the Long Binh detachment, the cadre invited children in the younger grades from the Bien Hoa school to a party at our cantonment area.

Note the sandbags in the middle of the photo, behind the children; the top of the photo shows a portion of the cargo parachute which served as the ceiling for the WACs' outdoor dayroom.

After refreshments, some of the women led the children in "Ring Around the Rosie." Tanya Murphy, in the patterned dress, is in the center of the circle. Directly behind Tanya is Reya Monte.

# Tet Offensive – January/February 1968

*Mary Glaudel-DeZurik:* Tet Nguyen Dan ("the first morning of the first day") is the most important holiday on the Vietnamese calendar. Tet is like our Thanksgiving, Christmas, Fourth of July and Easter all rolled into one. It is customary for the Vietnamese during this time to prepare special foods, visit friends, travel to a relative's home and general merry making. It had also been customary to have an informal truce in South Vietnam's long running conflict. This wasn't the case in 1968. On the eve of Tet, I was with some friends in the Plaza Hotel in Saigon. We had been watching a crowd of people in the street below who were celebrating and lighting firecrackers. Some of those would land on the ledge of the hotel windows. I remember being worried about my friend who was sweeping them off with his hand. I didn't understand why this was allowed so close to the hotel but it was their holiday and their celebration so I suspected an exception was being made. Early the next morning my roommate, Cpl Pauline Wilson, and I got ready for work as usual. We had to be in the lobby of the hotel by 6:30 a.m. to catch our military bus, which would take us to the MACV Compound in Tan Son Nhut. As we approached the lobby, we saw that the lights were out. We also noticed that there was no traffic, no people; no one was on the street. We went back to our room as instructed and waited for information. We soon found out that there were attacks going on in Saigon and Cholon (Chinese section of Saigon) as well as the rest of the country. We were told that we would be remaining in the hotel for an undetermined amount of time. I had already been in Saigon for six months and had adapted to the everyday precautions that needed to be taken in moving around the city. However if there was ever a time when I felt vulnerable, it was the first night of Tet when we could hear small-arms fire. We couldn't tell where it was coming from or where it was going, but hearing it so clearly made it close enough. At MACV, we had an attack plan and assigned bunkers but at the hotel we had no place to go. Again, that evening there was a loud blast that served as a reminder that there wasn't a front line in this war. No area could be considered completely safe. Since the Vietnamese employees would not leave their homes for days, it left us with a restaurant/club on the 6th floor that was not in operation. We were then issued C-rations and soon after, fatigues and combat boots. Not content with sitting in our rooms, some of the Women Marines headed for the sixth floor restaurant to help out by making sandwiches for troops coming in off the street and maintaining a mini mess hall. Within four days, the military buses were again running but this time with armed escorts, as well as an escort riding in the bus with us. It was quite an experience and one I'll never forget.

**Marion C. Crawford:** Upon my return to Vietnam after a month of hospitalization at Camp Zama, Japan, I still needed some convalescing time. So, my Field First/Administrative NCO, SFC Betty Benson, and I went on R&R to Sydney, Australia, for a week. What a wonderful week we had! We took in lots of entertainment, spent time lying on Bondi Beach taking in the sun and surf, went shopping and dined in some of Sydney's finest restaurants.

When it was time to fly back to Vietnam, we boarded our plane along with a couple hundred troops. Curiously, we landed in Northern Australia "for refueling," or so we were told. We sat there for hours. Finally the pilot told us that our destination was changed, that Tan Son Nhut was under attack and the American Embassy had been overtaken by the Viet Cong. We were being diverted to Cam Ranh Bay. Shortly after taking off, the pilot came on with another announcement. We couldn't land in Cam Ranh Bay either because that was also under attack. We were going to try for Bangkok, Thailand. All the fellows let out a huge cheer. When we landed in Bangkok, we were told that we could not have our luggage because they didn't know how long we'd be there and we had to be ready to take off for Vietnam as soon as the airport was secured. So we all checked into a hotel and were told to standby until further notice.

Betty and I were in shock because we were both very worried about our women. We immediately tried to get in touch with our unit, but to no avail. Later that evening our commander, CPT Joanne Murphy, got a call through to us and reported that they were all okay. She had been in the process of paying the women when all hell broke loose; everyone had to head for cover. CPT Murphy kept in touch with us for the next day or so. Knowing that all the women were okay, Betty and I were able to relax somewhat. What a terrible time to be away from our unit!

Something funny happened the next morning in Bangkok. Because we didn't have our luggage, we had washed out our lingerie and used a sheet to wrap up in to sleep. We ordered coffee the next morning from room service, and when the boy knocked on the door, I sent Betty to answer it. She was still half asleep and was trying to hold the sheet around herself. However, when she reached for the tray, the sheet fell around her feet. The look on the boy's face and Betty's face – priceless! I cracked up laughing, and I'm sure all the people in the hotel could hear me. Betty made me promise not to tell our troops about it. I couldn't hold back, though. During a training class I was holding soon after we were back at the unit, I just "happened" to spill the beans. When Betty realized what I was about to tell the women, she started jumping up and down and shaking her fist at me. The women sure enjoyed that story!

**RED ALERT**: Pay day, January 31, 1968. The WAC Detachment had been moved from Saigon to Long Binh in 1967 for greater safety. When the Tet Offensive began, many areas came under rocket and mortar attack. The ammo dump at Long Binh had been hit by mortar fire in the early hours of January 31. There were lots of black and blue marks on many of the women from getting tossed around from the concussion. Another attack occurred during the mandatory pay day formation. "Get to the bunkers," CPT Murphy yelled at the women, while trying to get under her desk, but the space was already occupied by a Red Cross lady – who wasn't even in the pay line. Interestingly, the 10 Quonset huts that were the original WAC Detachment in Saigon were totally destroyed.

*An aerial view of the WAC Detachment at Tan Son Nhut Air Base, known as Tent City B – there was no security fence separating the golf course from the area where the WACs lived – just a short fence, a row of tents for the engineers, the street, and the WAC Detachment, which was fenced.*

***Norma Busse:*** During the Tet Offensive, a 124mm rocket burst about 25 feet from the Headquarters – a near miss. All the ambulatory patients who were able and those in wheelchairs from the nearby evacuation hospital were issued weapons and were sent out on the perimeter of the grounds to guard the hospital. We were unable to return to the Rex Hotel, where we were billeted, to obtain clothing. We slept on the floor of the headquarters for the first week after Tet. Members of our enlisted staff who were trying to get to headquarters were ambushed and came under fire. One soldier was shot and fell off the APC (armored personnel carrier) as it backed off from the sniper fire. When the order to go forward came, the APC driver, unknowingly, drove over the soldier as he was lying on the ground. When we checked on him later at the morgue, we saw that he was completely flat from the waist down. We prayed his family wouldn't ask to view his remains when he arrived home. This event brought back memories of an attack on one of our Post Exchanges several months earlier when some of our civilian employees were killed.

***Marsha "Cricket" Holder:*** Spraying was done regularly. Where once there stood a grove of rubber trees to the right and around Headquarters, there was nothing – no trees and no grass. At the bottom of the hill was a small creek, and from that creek up to the end of our building, was concertina wire; the area had been sprayed by plane. To the left of where that truck is spraying is where the VC had come up from the creek and tunneled toward the officers' quarters. We weren't allowed to go to Headquarters for two days while the helicopters bombed the area; then they used napalm to burn any survivors out of hiding. Wasn't much left of the rubber tree grove after that!

A US Army truck sprays an unknown chemical around the USARV Headquarters buildings very close to the WAC Detachment.

**Ruth Ellis (Anderson):** During the Tet Offensive (1968), the Viet Cong breached the Tan Son Nhut Air Base in Saigon. Numerous rockets and mortars were lobbed into the area. One night a rocket hit the parking lot of the Vietnamese Air Force Chapel across the street from our living quarters. I sprang out of my second floor bed in my shorty pj's, ran to the stairs barefoot, and jumped the last few steps to land on concrete while rockets whizzed over my head. Two days later, I suffered excruciating shin splints, but I felt very blessed not to have been killed or wounded, as were so many others during that terrible time.

## Indelibly Imprinted

*CPT Joanne Murphy, WAC Detachment Commander:* One aspect of that unforgettable night, February 18, 1968, 0110 hours, has never left me. To some, it may seem quite insignificant. An indescribable concussion bolted me upright from a sound sleep. I cried out "Jesus!" Very quickly, I put on my boots, unlaced, and helmet, grabbed my robe, and ran down the stairs – my quarters were on the second floor of our Orderly Room building. I ran to the Orderly Room and asked CQ Lidia "Marty" Contreras if the Special Troops Officer of the Day had called. He hadn't. Immediately I called to find out what "condition" we were in. "Yellow Alert," was his reply. I wasn't convinced because explosions continued and we could see an unbelievably high tower of black smoke. Meanwhile, 1SG Crawford, SFC Benson, and SSG "Effie" were assisting the women with their mattresses and getting them situated behind our sandbags. Some of the women on the second floor of the barracks and some who were in upper bunks suffered scrapes and bruises. 1SG Crawford reported to me that all the women were safely behind the sandbags. Some were able to sleep; some just dozed on and off. Many of us stayed up all night.

One of the NCOs had just asked me if I would unlock the Lounge, which is when I saw a massive fireball heading our way. I replied, "No, I want everyone perfectly sober if we have to evacuate." (It's that brief exchange that has that night forever with me—the TiTi Lounge had been set up less than a week before for the NCOs. It was a place for them to let their hair down, to enjoy a soda, a cold beer, or whatever.) Then, I hurried to the Orderly Room and placed another call to the Officer of the Day. "I need some buses to evacuate the women. A fireball is headed straight for us." "No, ma'am, we're still in Yellow Alert," he said. "Well, you're not seeing what I'm seeing. It sure seems to me to be Red Alert. I need to evacuate the women." He was nonplussed and assured me he would call if the condition changed. I was furious. I never felt my responsibility for the safety of the women more acutely than that night. Though the explosions lasted until about 0600 hours, the women stood Reveille at the usual 0530 hours, had breakfast, and then boarded the buses for their duty sections.

The sound of the explosion was deafening when the ammo dump was hit that night. The cargo parachute canopy (over the WAC Detachment outdoor dayroom) was completely shredded from the concussion. A door from the second floor of one of the barrack buildings was blown off and tumbled down the stairs. The explosions lasted until 0600 hours. Smoke and the odor of gun powder filled the air all day.

***Sonia "Suni" B. Gonzalez Mendez:*** Well, did I ever get a good welcome that night (February 18)! We were about a mile or so from the ammo dump at

Long Binh, and Charlie (that was the Viet Cong, the enemy) decided to blow up the ammo dump. Seems it was about 2 a.m. We were all sleeping when the big bang went off. I raised my head just in time to see the door flying away and got a face full of sand. As I turned my head to the side, I saw a pink streak flying off the top bunk and running toward the back of the building. I called out, "Come back." (Earnestine) Dumas came back just as I was turning on the lights. "No," she said, "turn off the lights."

They all knew what to do, but I sure didn't. "Quick, put your uniform on; we have to go to the first floor for cover." Scrambling in the dark, I managed to get my issue (clothing) on. The boots were very uncomfortable, but this was no time to think of comfort. We ran down the stairs and dove under the first opening we could find – under one of the first few bunk beds. But, after a while, there were so many under the bed that the bed started to rise up off the floor. Then someone came in with a flashlight and told some of the girls to go down further to other bunks. We were there for some hours. I had to go to the bathroom – just couldn't wait any longer. Someone who had a light also had to go, so I asked to go with her. But, before I finished, someone called my friend with the light, and she left – with her light. I could not see a thing; it was so dark in there, and we were on noise-discipline. Now, I didn't know how to get back and was bumping into doors and walls until someone else realized I was gone too long and came with a flashlight. We stayed there until the next morning. A formation was called; and as roll call was being taken, everyone started laughing. My pants were on backwards; my uncomfortable boots pointed outward with the left boot on the right and the right boot on my left foot; my shirt was buttoned lopsided. I just looked like a mess.

That was the funniest thing that happened to me on my tour. After that night, I was no longer afraid. I wore my uniform proudly and took my work very, very seriously.

## Christmas Stories

One of the older women was pleading her case — trying to convince Santa that she had been a good "girl." Poor Santa! Betty Benson, Field First/Administrative NCO, on Santa Effie's lap, Christmas Eve, 1967.

Santa appears to be perplexed. Where is Santa's helper? There are lots of gifts to hand out to all the good girls. The Red Cross and other civic organizations sent gifts for each woman.

***Barbara Ebel:*** While I was on active duty, I had spent Christmas in Berlin, Turkey, West Point and several other stateside posts, but the most memorable was in Vietnam when Company Supply Sergeant Efferson dressed up as Santa.

SSG Margaret Trapp (l) and SP5 Carol Matisz help bring Christmas cheer to the barracks at Long Binh, 1967.

***Betty Jean Stallings:*** Christmas morning was on a Sunday in 1969. When I went to the dining facility for breakfast, someone asked if I was going to see Bob Hope. That was the first I knew he was coming; but he was to be there soon and it would be televised live.

In my office, whoever had the smallest TV went home to get it and we all watched the whole show. It was somewhat disappointing live, because not all of the acts are as good as the excerpts I had seen televised in late January in earlier years. Once when I had to walk down the hall, I realized the same TV show was coming out of every office; obviously not much work got done that day!

The next day, it was easy to see who had seen the show in person and who had watched on TV. Those who had watched in person were quite sunburned!

***Virginia "Gini" Griffith:*** For Bob Hope's final Christmas show at Tan Son Nhut Air Base, December 1972, Carol Urich was asked by CMSgt Jacobucci, the 377th Air Base Wing Senior Enlisted Advisor, to present a suitably inscribed BUFE (we'll forego the translation!), a small ceramic elephant, as a token of the Wing's appreciation. Prior to leaving for the show,

I jokingly mentioned to Carol that she should give Mr. Hope a kiss on the cheek from all the WAF. Yeah, she did it. That was the first time I had seen Bob Hope speechless and without a quick comeback. The show aired in the States before I returned so I don't know if that particular incident was included in the broadcast.

***Brenda Sue Eichholz (Caldwell):*** It was Christmas Day, 1969. I was supposed to be at work, but "Little Joe" (CPT Joseph J. Joyce, Jr.) pulled up in a jeep and told me to get in. We were going to the Bob Hope Show in Long Binh. We arrived at the show and met up with the guys from my office. We sat on a berm right behind the patients brought from the hospital, along with many thousands of other GIs. The show was fantastic! Neil Armstrong, the first man to walk on the moon, was there. So were Raquel Welch and Connie Stevens. The guys just swooned and drooled all over them. Then came the New Christy Minstrels. They were a variety act of young women and men. They could dance! They wore solid white – white skirts and blouses, white shirts, white vests, and TIGHT, WHITE pants with white shoes and white socks. I just couldn't help myself. I'm a 20-year-old female in country for 10 months who is accustomed to seeing fatigues, especially baggy fatigue pants. Never did I think it was possible for a female to lose it, but there I was, drooling all over myself. I just couldn't take my eyes off of those TIGHT, WHITE pants. The guys I worked with teased me unmercifully and never let me forget it. To this day, I still swoon just thinking about those TIGHT, WHITE pants.

Bob Hope Christmas Show, Long Binh, December 25, 1969.

Front (l-r) Theresa Graves, Connie Stevens and the incomparable Bob Hope; rear, the Gold Diggers.

US Ambassador Ellsworth Bunker chats with General William Westmoreland just before the start of the Bob Hope Christmas Show, December 25, 1967.

***Laurie A. Clemons (Parkerton):*** Armed Forces Vietnam (AFVN) had a number of civilian volunteers but by far the most memorable, and with whom I started a lifelong friendship, was Edie Weller. Born and raised in Germany, she and her husband Volker were stationed in Vietnam through Volker's employment with Pan Am. He was high up the food chain and as a result, they had a lovely home in Saigon. Their cook was of Chinese descent and she could cook any cuisine, be it Vietnamese, Chinese, Italian, German, etc., to absolute perfection. I spent many off-duty evenings in their home, but the most memorable was Christmas night. Edie invited me and a few other AFVN-ites for Christmas dinner. Volker had a large, honest to goodness pine Christmas tree shipped in. After dinner, we all gathered in front of the tree. The house lights turned off and the only illumination came from the dozens of lighted small white wax candles that peppered the tree. It held no other ornaments yet the tree was stunningly beautiful. Volker stood off to one side and in a quiet voice told us about how Christmas is celebrated in Germany. In the distance, I could hear the muted "thump" of what was probably rockets from a nearby battle, but in my mind it was the sound of distant B-52s dropping their loads. That moment in time seemed so surreal yet visceral. I was unaware that I was crying until my lap got soggy.

It was more than 30 years before Edie, Volker and I reconnected. We found one another through an AFRTS-Vietnam website. Edie and Volker became US citizens and retired in Florida. I have visited them once and will be returning for another visit soon.

***Norma Busse:*** For months prior to Christmas 1967, BG Albin Irzyk's secretary, an enlisted WAC specialist from near Augusta, ME, waxed nostalgic about Christmas in Maine and lamented the fact that no large trees were available in Saigon for a proper holiday celebration. The WAC decided to contact her state's governor and request a tree. Working with a commercial airline, the governor arranged for the state to buy and transport a large Maine fir tree to Saigon for the first Christmas celebration with ornaments that the Saigon area and the local Vietnamese had ever seen. Local troops were also amazed and unbelievingly overwhelmed to see and feel a taste of home thousands of miles away from loved ones.

***Joanne Murphy:*** While Norma's account is intriguing, it begged the question: who is this enlisted woman? When I made a plea to the book team members to help me find her, enthusiasm abounded. Patty Babcock (Schmauch) did a thorough search of our database. My dear friend Donna Loring, who still lives in Maine, got involved. Carol Ogg found a contact for BG Irzyk, the mystery woman's boss. General Irzyk, 97 at this writing, recalled the incident, not the woman's name, but he did remember that she worked for the State of Maine before entering the Army. That was an important piece to the puzzle. So Donna Loring was once again contacted; she enlisted the help of the Maine Legislative and Law Library. Eureka! An article with photo appeared in the *Sun Journal*, Lewiston, ME, December 11, 1967. Ida Colford (Willis) is a mystery woman no more.

Talk about serendipity! Carol Ogg has a friend who lives right next door to a relative of Ida. Through him, we located her. The following section is Ida's first-hand account of the event.

## The Christmas Tree

*Ida E. Colford (Willis):* It was November 1967. I had been in country since April – the only enlisted female stationed at US Army Headquarters Area Command (USAHAC) in Saigon. Christmas was fast approaching, and I was missing the traditions of a family Christmas in Maine. I knew that my family at home was getting ready to hang the evergreen wreath on the door, find and decorate a live balsam fir for the living room, and finish their Christmas shopping. I was missing these traditions, the "smell" of the evergreens, and the cold, snow-covered ground of Maine seemed far from the heat of Vietnam. It was about this time when my company commander came into the office bragging about the flag he received from his home state of Texas. A little research showed me that flags were often sent from the States to the soldiers stationed in Vietnam. Well, never one to settle, I decided it would be more appropriate to have a "real Maine Christmas tree" instead of a flag. I got lots of encouragement from my co-workers, and I began to search out how to go about getting this done. Since there didn't seem to be any precedent for my request, I decided that it wouldn't hurt to ask the top man in Maine.

I composed a letter to the Governor of Maine, Kenneth M. Curtis, requesting a tree – not just any tree, but a nine-foot tree with decorations. I said in my letter, "We at Headquarters Area Command need a tree. Since Maine grows the biggest and prettiest trees in the United States, I feel that a good gesture of Maine's concern for its citizens here in Vietnam would be to send a nine-foot "live" Christmas tree from the Pine Tree State, with decorations if possible, to Headquarters Area Command so that those of us from Maine, as well as others from many different States, can enjoy a touch of home at Christmas time. Incidentally, the New England States are very well represented at this Headquarters." Everyone at USAHAC supported my effort, but nobody believed anything would come of it.

On December 5, Governor Curtis responded to my letter. He stated in his letter that he had asked the Maine Department of Economic Development (MDED) to proceed with the request. He stated that the Maine Christmas Tree Association was enthused about the idea, and arrangements were quickly made for a tree to be cut and prepared for shipment. He also indicated that there was no difficulty with decorative materials because the Paragon Glass Company in Lewiston, probably the largest producer of Christmas ornaments, soon would be sending them under separate cover. However, the MDED encountered a problem in getting the tree from Augusta to Saigon in time for the holidays. Enlisting the Maine Adjutant General's help, it became apparent that no branch of the military services could transport the tree. The idea of the Army National Guard performing the transport was explored, but their regulations also prohibited the transport even if an aircraft were bound for Vietnam and empty of freight. Undeterred, the MDED then contacted a major airline to arrange to take the tree at a cost of $150.00. According to the letter, these arrangements seemed satisfactory and there was hope to get the tree to Saigon in time for the holidays.

Around December 8, I received a telegram from James K. Keefe, Commissioner of the MDED, telling me the tree and ornaments would be arriving in Saigon via Pan American Airways on December 10 or 11. My excitement was nearly uncontainable. However, around December 15, I received another telegram stating the tree and ornaments were delayed and would arrive on December 16 or 17. I was still very excited, but now a bit worried, as well. My worry was exacerbated by the doubts of my fellow soldiers. They were convinced that I would not get a tree for Christmas.

My joy was uncontrollable on that very same day, December 15, 1967, when the tree and decorations arrived in nearly perfect condition. As I stated in my thank you letter to Governor Curtis, "The tree was as fresh as though it had just come from the woods of Maine, and the decorations had only three balls broken in the whole box." There was much joy but a little confusion as we searched for the perfect spot for the tree. Finally, the tree was set up in the conference room, which had ceilings high enough to accommodate a nine-foot tree, to allow the branches to fall out properly.

The next day, we went to work decorating the tree with many hands involved; and with each Christmas decoration placed on the tree, came a thought of home. Once decorated, the tree brought daily visitors from within the Headquarters, as well as from surrounding companies, to look at and "smell" the Maine tree. The tree was more than a symbol of Christmas to the USAHAC community. It lifted the spirits of all of us so far from home and family, allowing us to enjoy Christmas the way we would if we were with them. It gave each person a piece of his Christmas tradition back home. My tree was the topic of conversation throughout Saigon, as well as many notations in letters to families back home. It was the best Christmas present ever!

Although the Vietnamese at USAHAC felt the tree was very beautiful, it did not mean the same to them as it did to the Americans. The tree was beautiful, but to me it was a link over miles of land and sea to my family and my home state of Maine. It proved to me that the folks back home cared how we, so far away, spent Christmas and were proud to support their soldiers.

Following Christmas, I received countless newspaper clippings about the tree from friends, family and even strangers. My favorite article had a photo of my dad and my sister with the Forest Commissioner and Governor sending off the tree.

(Ida still has the letters exchanged with Governor Curtis, copies of the telegrams, and the tags that came on the tree. Now, that really is the rest of the story.)

L to R: Anita Colford, Ida's sister; Forest Commissioner Austin Wilkins; Governor Kenneth M. Curtis; and Joseph Colford, Ida's father. The 9 foot Maine balsam fir is ready for shipping via Pan Am.

(Sun Journal, *Lewiston, ME, December 11, 1967.* Used with permission)

## Some Additional Stories

***Marion C. Crawford:*** A Protestant chaplain brought a small poodle to the WAC Detachment. Each of the senior cadre wanted Ko-Ko for their own. It was decided that each of them would make a bed for him to see where he'd go for the night. He examined all his choices and chose my room. When he wasn't patrolling the area or chasing unwanted canine visitors away, he spent his days under my desk. Ko-Ko was the unit mascot for the next 20 months. When I rotated to the States, Ko-Ko came with me; he lived out the rest of his days with me. The other dog in the photo is Tammy, SSG Effie's pet. Tammy also went back to the States when Sergeant Effie rotated.

Military regulations prohibited the possession of American money. Upon entry into Vietnam, all coins and currency were converted to Military Payment Certificates (MPC). Periodically, there was a "conversion day" in which all MPC were exchanged for new ones – totally different art work and color. A detailed account of "conversion day" by Patricia "Patty" Babcock (Schmauch), who worked in the Central Finance and Accounting Office, is in the 1969 chapter.

***Mary Joan Webb:*** Dang Thi Man worked at the 377th Services Squadron as the secretary to the commander, Lt Col Joseph Hotard. Her office was in the same area with the Airman's Club, NCO Club and the Base Theater. Her co-workers nicknamed her "Susie." Shortly after our arrival at Tan Son Nhut, my husband Austin, Betty Fowler and I met "Susie" as she was getting off work. That began our friendship. "Susie" recalls that about a week later Austin and I invited her to join us to see the movie "The Adventures of Huckleberry Finn." It was very enjoyable!

Years later "Susie" told me that she worked with hundreds of male USAF personnel and had numerous friends and acquaintances. But US female personnel were few in Vietnam at that time and it was very refreshing to have a female friend with a different perspective of things in general. When we left Vietnam, "Susie" and I shared addresses. When the Vietnam War was over in 1975, she was lucky enough to have escaped, came to the US and settled in Utah. In July 2011, "Susie" and her husband Glen Ahrens came to visit us in Yuba City, CA. We went to the Museum of the Forgotten Warriors in Marysville, CA, and had our picture taken together in the museum library.

Then                      Now

(l-r) Mary Webb, MSgt Austin Webb, my husband, (retired as SMSgt), Betty Fowler (retired as TSgt) and two children whose parents gave us permission to photograph them.

We enjoyed many visits to the Saigon Zoo. On one visit to the zoo, a man who, in just minutes, using a broken razor blade, did a silhouette picture of Austin and me. Over the years, I often wished I could have purchased razor blades and had known how to see the man again to give them to him. That was very special.

Betty Fowler had arrived at Tan Son Nhut just days before I did and we quickly connected. We shared a tiny cubicle space in a building created for the 15 non-nursing Air Force women who arrived at Tan Son Nhut in December 1970. It was a structure with screening around the top edge. We were fortunate to obtain a fan that ran all night. Betty and I have remained friends and in contact all these decades.

***Virginia "Gini" Griffith:*** There weren't enough of us enlisted females in Vietnam to form a WAF (Women in the Air Force) squadron so we had an advisor. Then Capt Pat Murphy served in that capacity in addition to her assignment as the base Personal Affairs Officer. I was "den mother" in the barracks. Somewhere I had read that during WWII company clerks and others who used typewriters (apparently the military used Remington typewriters) were referred to as "Remington's Raiders." It seemed perfectly natural to me that we WAF in support career fields call ourselves "Murphy's Marauders." It was all a play on words. We got together in the yard outside the WAF barracks on a Sunday afternoon, had a barbecue and took photos.

After I returned to the States, I located all but one of the women in the photo, sent the photo to them and got autographs. It's fading now but is still hanging on my "I love me wall" in the living room.

"Murphy's Marauders" (l-r) TSgt Virginia "Gini" Griffith, TSgt Margaret Buck, SSgt Carol Urich, Capt Patricia Murphy, Sgt De Ann Masters, SSgt Linda Bellard, Capt Jill Tate, SSgt Patsy "Dianne" Hatley

**Donna M. Loring:** Ordered a case of beer under a warrant officer's name. When the beer supply at the detachment was declared off limits to me, CPT Joanne Murphy, my commander, said I was going to be the "driest young lady in Southeast Asia."

(Note from Donna's commander, Joanne Murphy): She may well be the only soldier who served in Vietnam for one full year who left country as a Private (E2). Don't ask! But here's the rest of the story. Donna was appointed Aide-de-Camp with the rank of Colonel to Governor of Maine Angus King. She served as the Tribal Representative for her Penobscot Nation in the Maine State Legislature for 11 years.

(l-r) Governor Angus King, Donna M. Loring, Major General Earl Adams, Maine Army National Guard, looks on.

***Nancy Jurgevich (Third Commander):*** Working 12 plus hours a day, seven days a week, and being restricted to the base could get awfully boring, especially to 20 year olds, even with movies on the patio. So I felt I had to try to help get some variety to break the monotony. The WAC had advisors assigned to the Vietnam Women's Armed Forces Corps and to their training center in Saigon. The advisors decided it would be nice for the enlisted women at Long Binh to come to Saigon and see the Vietnamese Training Center. It sounded good to me. So, I spoke to my boss, the Troop Commander, and got his blessing. I called a Training Day, meaning the women were excused from work. We put a sign-up sheet for the women who desired to go for the day. Of course, everyone signed up. The motor pool provided us with four buses and the Transportation Detachment furnished two armed security guards for each bus. Now, how were two security guards going to keep rockets from coming in? I had to be out of my mind to agree to all of this, anything could have happened. The trip started out to be a half-day visit at the Training Center. Well then, we had to get the women to lunch. There were some great French restaurants in Saigon that I thought about, but those restaurants could not handle a group of 130 plus people. Our advisors came up with a place called Cheap Charlie's. With this name, how was I going to tell the women of this great treat we had in store for them? I just kept telling them that what was special in our culture was not always true of other cultures. Several Vietnamese military women guided the educational and very interesting visit to the Training Center. Some of them joined us as we motored to Cheap Charlie's, a big banquet room with bare walls, long tables with tablecloths and flower arrangements. The women were so happy to be off the post at Long Binh, to learn something about the Vietnamese women soldiers and to visit with them. Cheap Charlie's was also a treat, even with such a name. After lunch, we were escorted to the Saigon Zoo for the afternoon. Surprisingly, the zoo showed no sign of war, and the women really enjoyed the visit. After a few hours, we boarded the buses back to Long Binh. Of course, the women wanted to know if they could do it again. Not under my watch! Looking back, that could have been a very bad decision on my part because of the chance I took. I am so thankful to this day that there were no attacks.

In looking back, I can't believe that I also consented, along with the approval of my boss, to allow the women to get on helicopters to go down country to a pool party. A commander and first sergeant of a helicopter company came to see us and invited us to Sunday party at their compound. They would fly up to Long Binh, pick up the women, take them to the party and fly them back before dark. This would give the women an opportunity to ride in a helicopter, and we could have another Volunteer Training Day. Of course, 100 plus of the women signed up for the trip. When I look back at that, I question my sanity – my thoughts at the time were that it was good for the morale. Maybe this is why the military is made up of mostly young people.

### *Excerpts from* Fields of Fire, *a book by Carol Ogg*
### *The Young Boy*

He might be four or five, but I don't think much more. Barefoot, walking shorts and a ragged shirt. There is a stick in his hand. On his head, an Army green baseball cap with captain's bars.

I watch him closely; he hasn't spotted me yet. He squats down, drops the stick, and carefully sifts dirt through his hands. I look at my watch; it's 6:30 in the morning. The air is filled with the smell of urine; reminds me of cat urine. The open sewer ditch is swelling with morning use. The mopeds haven't started their daily trips up and down the street. Across the way, a Vietnamese guard lifts his cap, looks at us, replaces it, and tries to go back to sleep. His weapon leans haphazardly against the tower wall.

The young boy sees me now. He drops the dirt and slaps his hands against his shorts as he stands and faces me. He swaggers in my direction.

Little bastard! Been living among the GIs. Cute little shit! "Hey you, GI!" he calls out with confidence. I give no answer. "Me Di Wee." He points to the insignia on his hat. I throw him a mock salute.

"You got cigarette," he asks, squinting. "You're too young to smoke." "Give me cigarette." He grabs my arm with a tug. "Me Di Wee." "No!" "F--- you, GI." He grins as he throws me the bird.

He reaches in the pockets of his shorts, pulls out a Marlboro cigarette, places it in his mouth. He then takes a flip-top lighter and expertly cups his hand to protect the flame. With ease, he inhales deeply and proceeds to blow smoke in my direction.

He winks and walks away.

### The Casualty

Lydia leans over the edge of the roof scanning the skyline; she points in the direction of the street below. I follow the direction of her outstretched arm.

The bicycle rider carries bananas in a small bunch. All but one is tucked under his arm. Balancing with ease, pedaling with little effort, his hand holds the fruit; and he quickly peels the outer shell and stuffs the ripe banana in his mouth. With a graceful flick of his hand, the banana peel loops through the air and over the fence near the guard watchtower.

There is instantaneous movement from the guard tower. Lydia and I watch as the guard brings the weapon to his shoulder. Crack! It is like the sound of whip on a cold crisp morning. Time slows as the face of the bicycle rider looms before us in unreal dimensions. The eyes wide, his mouth opens without sounds, and a trickle of blood spills over the edge.

The rider loops backward off the bicycle, bounces, and skids into the ditch. The bicycle wobbles in forward movement then crashes in a heap.

Lydia and I turn to each other. Nausea makes us gag momentarily. Without words, we run to the stairwell, scramble down the stairs past the dayroom, and burst outside to the front of our hotel quarters. We stop. A Vietnamese police officer takes the arms of the bicycle rider and slowly drags him toward a waiting taxicab. A sandal falls away from the dragging foot. The rider's head hangs backward. His face is partially missing. Off by the ditch, another police officer is kicking dirt over the fresh pool of blood.

Lydia grabs my arm,  and her fingers dig into my flesh.

The cabdriver opens the door to the backseat of the vehicle. Together the officers stuff the body into the car. The cab moves away. The officers mount the moped and starts to drive away, hesitates, and then one of them reaches down and snatches up the lost sandal.

*Fields of Fire* is available at Amazon.com in both book and Kindle formats. It is also available from www.xlibris.com

**Mary Fran Draisker:** My memories include: General Jeanne M. Holm visiting us at Tan Son Nhut; meeting Yvonne Pateman, a female intelligence colonel who had been in the Women Airforce Service Pilots (WASP) during

World War II and who was still authorized to wear wings at a time when women in the Air Force couldn't fly; losing weight from 116 to 104, the skinniest I was as an adult; a fellow officer getting a sandwich at the Officers' Club with a cricket in it saying that he'd take it back, but they would charge him extra for the "delicacy"; my BOQ being across the street from the Vietnamese Air Force morgue; learning to eat peanuts with chop sticks; being told to put my valuables in my boot the two times I got off to go to downtown Saigon; going sailing for the first time in my life in Sydney harbor when I went there on R&R; saving up my combat pay and paying off my student loans early; trying to get a bronze star for the master sergeant in our branch and being told they were only for officers; staying awake all night playing bridge with two colonels and a major before my 4 a.m. check-in for my flight home, so I was sure I wouldn't oversleep and miss my flight; the flight home being low on fuel, landing at Seattle to refuel and keeping us on board – the "joke" passing from row to row was that we survived our 365 days in Vietnam only to die when the plane exploded during refueling.

## USARV Special Troops WAC Detachment

*Marion C. Crawford:* In October 1966, a friend, SFC Betty Benson, was selected to be my Field First or Administrative NCO, as some call the position. SFC Benson and I had been in basic training together some 17 years earlier. I was tickled pink to see her. We were the only women on the plane that was full of young, very quiet soldiers and some very somber officers and noncommissioned officers. None of us was excited about this dangerous adventure upon which we were embarking.

Some 24 hours later, we landed at the Saigon Airport, which was a scary adventure in itself. In order to avoid ground fire, the planes had to land in a very unusual way. The pilot had to get on top of the flight line and then plunge straight down as though in a dive. Let me tell you, we troops were hanging by our toenails and seat belts. Once my stomach had gone back to its normal position, I stood up with the others. We deplaned into sweltering heat. The airport was filled with our guys and Vietnamese soldiers, all in fatigues and carrying weapons. It was a frightening sight to Betty and me, and I guess also to our young fellow passengers. In that moment, the war became very real.

Sergeant First Class Benson and I were taken to the Ambassador Hotel in downtown Saigon that was to be our home for three or four weeks while our WAC Detachment was being completed. By Vietnam standards, the Ambassador was pretty nice, but to Americans, it was pretty much "roughing it." The very first night there, we were on alert. Explosions early in the morning threw both of us out of our beds and blew out the windows. By the time a jeep came to take us out to Tan Son Nhut Air Base (the Army had a section of the base called Tent City B), we were both basket cases. Every time one of those Vietnamese people raised a hand to do anything, I thought they were tossing a grenade into our jeep, which I had heard happened quite often. By the time we got to Headquarters USARV and reported to our battalion commander, I was shaking like a leaf. I was quite embarrassed because I was to be the leader of a large group of women, and I didn't want the colonel to think a mistake had been made in selecting me. He either read my mind or my body language because he said, "Don't worry, First Sergeant Crawford, it's so nice to see a little femininity over here." He sent someone to the dispensary to get me a tranquilizer.

The next day I met with the Commanding General of USARV, LTG Jean Engler, and the USARV Engineer, BG Thomas Cole. We went over the plans for the WAC Detachment. My only suggestion for change was to move the bathhouse/latrine to the center of the cantonment area. Ten Quonset huts were set up and surrounded by a 12-foot-high wooden fence. At the entrance to the cantonment was a house that formerly was the home of a French family; this became the orderly room, supply room and quarters for the cadre. All personnel entering the cantonment area had to enter through the orderly room building. The huts were in place, sod was on the ground, and the area was now ready in time for the first of our women to arrive.

On October 31, our commander, CPT Peggy Ready, arrived; the rest of the cadre, Company Clerk Ren Stoabs and Supply Sergeant Edith Efferson arrived a few weeks later. An incredible amount of work was done in a very short period to get the unit ready.

## Breaking Ground

Lieutenant General Jean E. Engler, deputy commander USARV, breaks ground for the new Women's Army Corps compound at Tan Son Nhut. Looking on are MAJ Shirley R. Heinze (center), assistant G1 (Enlisted Personnel Management) and CPT Peggy E. Ready who will command the first WAC unit in Vietnam. Ten prefabricated Quonset buildings will serve as quarters. Two frame buildings, already on the installation, will serve as quarters for the NCOs and the Orderly Room.

***Peggy E. Ready, first WAC Detachment Commander:*** My plane touched down at Tan Son Nhut Air Base outside of Saigon at midnight Halloween 1966. It was surreal. Jeeps with mounted artillery patrolled the airstrip. The hot, humid air assaulted me as I stood uncertainly atop the stair ramp in my Class B uniform. Finally, a young captain in jungle fatigues and flak jacket stepped to the bottom of the ramp and said, "Captain Ready? I'm your escort officer." The next morning at 0700 hours, I participated in the official groundbreaking ceremony for the quarters for members of the WAC Detachment, HQ Special Troops, USARV. It was there I met my senior NCO Cadre, 1SG Marion C. Crawford and Field First/Administrative NCO SFC Betty J. Benson. This was my first command. These are the women who played an enormous role in assuring the success of this first women's unit sent to Vietnam by Department of Defense. In so doing, they also assured my success as the first commander. These NCOs taught me to be a troop commander. The unit members honored me by being the perfect unit. It was such great fun.

## Grand Opening of the WAC Detachment, Saigon – January 1967

*Marion C. Crawford:* In early January, our first group of women had arrived. They were such an outstanding group that Detachment Commander CPT Peggy Ready and I were eager to show them off; so we invited the staff from HQ USARV and from the Special Troops Battalion to our cantonment area. I was so proud of our young commander; not only was she attractive, but also quite personable. I could tell that the male officers were duly impressed. A very large bouquet of flowers arrived from our battalion commander with the message, "Welcome, Ladies, you are a wonderful sight to our starved eyes." LTG Jean Engler, Deputy Commanding General of USARV, arrived along with COL Graham, Battalion Commander. They were briefed by CPT Ready. We had invited about 50 guests, but word of the Grand Opening spread throughout the post and hundreds showed up; many of the troops also wanted to welcome our women. Because the activities lasted into the dinner hour, LTG Engler called

the mess hall and had the evening meal sent over to our area so we could feed everyone.

Some of the fellows from the USARV Band played. To our delight and surprise, three of our women, SP4s Baker, Moore and Harris, got up and did an impromptu dance that looked very professional. As I was watching the dance, an Army photographer captured the look of  pride I had in my women. The photo was picked up by the Associated Press and was in many stateside newspapers.

The dancing three also should have been picked up. Despite the sound of incoming and outgoing mortar fire, it was an impressive day for everyone. We had a wonderful time, and the women were certainly made to feel welcome.

### 25ᵗʰ WAC Anniversary – May 14, 1967

*Marion C. Crawford:* All the officers and section chiefs were invited to help us celebrate the 25ᵗʰ Anniversary of the Women's Army Corps. The WAC Staff Advisor came in from Hawaii as did all the WAC officers stationed in Vietnam. The USARV band provided the music for the affair, and a wonderful large cake arrived to complete the celebration. The youngest enlisted woman was selected to assist CPT Peggy Ready in cutting the cake. The newly formed Drill Team, organized by the First Sergeant, performed for the guests and received many accolades. A photo of that event was picked up by the Army and the Associated Press, which was wonderful.

Our once very quiet, dignified women's compound became very noisy, and laughter abounded. In the middle of a combat zone, as small-arms fire could be heard all around us, the band played on. A dance was held, and the men and women of our command forgot for a few hours that they were in very dangerous surroundings.

*The Drill Team:* A youthful 27-member USARV Special Troops Women's Army Corps (WAC) Drill Team made its premiere performance Sunday, May 14, as part of the 25ᵗʰ Anniversary celebration of the Women's Army Corps. The eight-routine performance was the featured attraction of an afternoon open house.

The classy repertoire is set off by the sharp-looking dress of the unit. The young women wear their green cord uniform, white aiguillettes with gold tips, white scarves with the USARV patch in the center and black high heels.

"Unusual," their final routine, concludes with a salute to the reviewing officer. (That photo is on the front cover.) "Pin Wheel" is depicted in the photo below. The team is under the command of 1SG Marion C. Crawford, Sault Sainte Marie, MI. This vivacious lady first sergeant is no newcomer to drill teams. She organized and led similar teams when she was first sergeant of the WAC Detachment at Aberdeen Proving Ground, MD, and at the WAC Battery, Fort Sill, OK.

Sergeant Crawford organized this drill team more than two months ago and has been secretly training its members in the WAC dayroom. The young women rehearse for 40 minutes during their lunch hour on Tuesdays and Thursdays.

"We had no trouble gaining interest. With each practice we gain more enthusiasm," Sergeant Crawford said.

Gloria Grenfell (l) and Cheranne "Cheri" Asmus raise their glasses in a toast to the Women's Army Corps on its 25th Anniversary, May 14, 1967.

(l-r) Margaret Trapp and Ann Marie Lally enjoy a lighter moment with SFC Betty Benson at the 25th WAC Anniversary.

### New WAC Detachment, Long Binh, January 1969

Eagerly looking forward to the completion of the permanent home of the WAC Detachment at Long Binh, 1SG Marion Crawford and SFC Betty Benson checked the progress frequently. Both women extended their tours because their job wasn't finished until they could get the women settled into their new quarters. Unfortunately, the construction went well beyond the target date so they didn't see its completion.

At the entrance of the new and permanent home of the WAC Detachment, the Chaplain offers his blessing for the compound and the women who will occupy it, January 1969.

Let the celebration begin! The mess hall always provided the most beautifully decorated cakes for such special occasions. Making the first cut are (l-r) a representative of the Vietnam Women's Armed Forces Corps, the "twins" SP5s Charlene and Catherine Kahl, and LTC Lorraine Rossi.

CPT Ready's letter also included a detailed list of items to bring

DEPARTMENT OF THE ARMY
HEADQUARTERS, UNITED STATES ARMY VIETNAM
APO SAN FRANCISCO 96307

IN REPLY REFER TO

9 December 1966

SP4 C Asmus, WA8225378
Hq 3d Army
Ft. McPherson, Ga

Dear SP4 C. Asmus

    It is my pleasure as Commanding Officer of the WAC Detachment, USARV, to extend congratulations to you for having been selected to join us here in Vietnam.

    I would like to orient you in reference to our part in the conflict taking place here in this part of the world. First of all, rest assured that the US Army takes extra precaution where its women are concerned. All facilities which are needed are near the WAC Detachment.

    Our brand new detachment, dedicated 3 November 1966, consists of one building which houses the Orderly Room downstairs and BEQ upstairs. There are nine prefab "hutches" behind the Orderly Room and one building is used as the shower and latrine facility. The entire area is enclosed by a solid fence 12 feet high, an armed guard stands duty 24 hours a day at the only entrance to the compound. Nearby are such facilities as library, theatre, PX, snack bar, pool, the chapel, dental clinic, dispensary and golf course.

    A list of items you should bring with you that would aid you immensely is attached. Do Not—repeat—DO NOT ship any items as hold baggage that you will need within 60 days of arrival.

    My cadre and I are anxiously awaiting your arrival, and so that you can be properly received upon arrival in Saigon, do write us Air Mail giving us your port call, flight number and date of departure. In the event we are not waiting for you—go to the Red Cross counter in the air terminal and ask them to call Army 622.

55

Speaking of cadre, I thought you might be curious, so will give you a thumbnail sketch of each.

COMMANDING OFFICER: Captain Peggy E. Ready, Greenville, Miss. Graduate of Blue Mountain College, Miss. Was Production Editor of Fawcett Magazine, and worked around the world with the American Red Cross prior to accepting a commission of 1st Lt. in the WAC, 2Dec64. After WOBC, assignments included a tour with the College Junior Program and Executive Officer of Co C at the WAC Center, and Executive Officer of the WAC Company at Ft. Myer, Va. just prior to coming here to Vietnam.

FIRST SERGEANT: 1SG E8 Marion C. Crawford, Sault Ste. Marie, Mich. Entered the WAC 18 years ago right out of high school. Entire career spent in cadre and recruiting fields. Ft. Lee WAC Center 49-51, WAC Recruiter in Toledo, Ohio 51-53, in Canton, Ohio 56-59, and in Baltimore, Md 61-64, First Sergeant in Kaiserslautern, Germany 53-56, at Aberdeen Proving Ground, Md 59-61, and at the WAC Battery Ft. Sill, Oklahoma 64-66 prior to coming to Vietnam as "Top Kick."

ADMIN & TRNG NCO: SFC E7 Betty J. Benson, Cleveland, Ohio. Entered WAC 18 years ago (went through basic with 1SG Crawford) and was assigned after QM School, Ft. Lee, Va. and Veterinarian School, Chicago, Ill. to Ft. Devens, Mass. in 1950. Hanau, Germany 51-53, Ft. Ord, Cal. and Ft. Lawton, Wash. in 1954, Camp Zama, Japan 54-56, Ft. Myer, Va. 56-60, Recruiting tours in Albany, NY 60-64 and in Des Moines, Iowa 64-66 were last assignments prior to assignment here.

SUPPLY SERGEANT: SSG E6 Edith L. Efferson, Chicago, Ill. Entered WAC in Jun 52 at Ft. Lee, Va. and stayed there until May 54. Yokohama, Japan 54-56, Ft. Riley, Kan. May56-Dec56, Ft. McClellan, Ala. 57-59, Aberdeen Proving Ground, Md. 59-64, Ft. Ritchie, Md. May 64-Jan65, Ft. Meade, Md. Jan65-Jul65, and Ft. Lee, Va Jul65-Oct66 prior to coming to Vietnam.

DETACHMENT CLERK: PFC E3 Rhynell M. Stoabs, Winfield, Kansas. Entered WAC 13months ago, went to Personnel School, Ft. Knox, Ky and was assigned to Fitzsimons Gen. Hosp. Colo. prior to assignment to Vietnam.

Have a nice trip over, and look forward to an interesting year of hard work, but the rendering of invaluable service to the US Army in Vietnam.

SINCERELY,

PEGGY E. READY
CPT          WAC
Commanding

## Change of Command Ceremonies at the WAC Detachment

CPT Peggy Ready (l) passes command of the WAC Detachment to CPT Joanne Murphy, October 27, 1967, 1SG Marion Crawford looks on.

CPT Joanne Murphy (l) passes command of the WAC Detachment to CPT Nancy Jurgevich, October 16, 1968.

Photographs of two other change-of-command ceremonies could not be located: CPT Jurgevich passed command to CPT Shirley Ohta in November

1969. CPT Ohta passed command to CPT Marjorie Johnson in November 1970.

CPT Marjorie Johnson (l) passes command of the WAC Detachment to CPT Constance Seidemann, the last WAC Detachment commander in Vietnam, November 1971.

### WAF Sponsor Letter example

We have just learned that you have been alerted for a tour in Vietnam! Although there is no formal WAF sponsorship program, we feel that this information might be of some help to you in preparing for your year's "visit" here. If you are looking for an assignment with plush living conditions and all the modern conveniences, Vietnam is not your "thing." But if you are flexible and willing to adapt to a completely different environment and forego some of the stateside advantages to which you are accustomed and have taken for granted, welcome aboard! A tour in Vietnam is a challenge to one's initiative, sense of humor and patience, but we all seem to fare quite well. We find it a different and an interesting experience that none of us will soon forget!

You will be at the focal point of the Southeast Asia activity and will learn to understand the circumstances behind the events taking place here. Your attitudes toward Vietnam and our position here will be influenced when you actually are participating; making and seeing the "news" first hand. Now for some idea of what you can expect and how to expect it: Bear in mind that this information changes daily and living conditions are improving the longer women are assigned to Vietnam!

ASSIGNMENT: Some enlisted WAF are assigned to Headquarters Military Assistance Command, Vietnam. MACV is a joint service command composed of personnel from all military services and some of our allies from the Free World Military Assistance Forces (FWMAF). It is the senior US command here, commonly known as "Pentagon EAST." WAF Officers can be assigned to MACV, to units at Tan Son Nhut Airfield, or to Cam Ranh Bay in a limited number based on female billeting capacity. Both MACV and Tan Son Nhut (TSN) are located approximately five miles north of the center of Saigon. Cam Ranh Bay is located on the east coast of Vietnam about 180 miles northeast of Saigon.

WEATHER: Saigon is always hot and humid. The rainy season is from about April to November when it rains almost every day; anything from a brief shower to a tropical downpour. During this rainy season, the humidity rises to compete with the temperature, which varies from about 70 degrees to the high 90s. From December to March is usually the dry season, with temperatures still hot, but minus the rain and some evening breezes as close to cool as it ever gets to be here. The lack of rain makes everything very dirty and stirs up the dirt. Most prefer the rainy season, since the dirt and odors make it somewhat unpleasant during the dry season. During the rainy season, one must contend with, among other things, mud, swelling sewage streams, and other odors and indoor living. Often and everywhere, there is a fragrance of "Eaudo Nook Mom" (phonetically spelled), the national favorite flavoring sauce made of fermented dried fish. Some adventurous Americans like Nook Mom on Vietnamese food but few enjoy the Eau de aroma.

QUARTERS: Enlisted MACV WAF live in an Army operated BEQ and a few in downtown Army hotels. Two or three occupants per room is usual, with WAF, WACs, Lady Marines or WAVEs sometimes sharing rooms together. Since July 1970, WAF enlisted personnel assigned to units on Tan Son Nhut Airfield are quartered in a non-air-conditioned WAF barracks (hootch) on Tan Son Nhut Airfield. WAF officers and nurses assigned to units at TSN live in BOQs consisting of small single rooms measuring about 9x10. There are community bath facilities, some with tubs and the lack of privacy. Everyone here showers, so remember to bring shower clogs and cap. WAF officers assigned to MACV live in Army operated BOQs with dual occupancy in a room with bath. The WAF/AF Nurse (integrated) BOQ is two adjoining buildings numbered 146 and 148 on TSN. Between them is a parachute-covered, hard surface BBQ cookout area with picnic tables. There is a screened mini-gym with Ping-Pong tables and some indoor exercise machines; and within the compound a basketball hoop and volley ball/badminton court to assist in the "whittle-down" weight program while here. (PS. Most lose weight while here!)

AIR CONDITIONING: The BOQ rooms are not air-conditioned but are merely equipped with an overhead fan. However, in this climate, an air conditioner is not considered a "luxury." It has been the practice for rotating personnel to "sell" their air conditioner to someone forecast inbound (along with other personally acquired and useful "creature comforts" such as dishware and bedspread, etc). One's adjustment to Vietnam will be much easier and the entire tour more comfortable if one's sponsor can arrange to "buy" the room of someone departing about the time you arrive or shortly after. If an air-conditioned and outfitted room is not to be available, we strongly recommend that you buy an inexpensive window air conditioner from a stateside firm and mail it to your APO so that it might be here when you arrive. Receipt of such items takes about six weeks en route because of weight and package bulk. The box is usually too heavy to come by PAL or SAM and must come by boat/surface transportation. Since the rooms are comparatively small, a rectangular window model with 6000 BTUs in 110 voltage is more than adequate. Installation of a new one is a minor problem with all the "gentlemanly Yankee ingenuity and talent" available around you. Officially, Civil Engineers discourages the installation of each new one since they do not approve of additional ones being added to the already overburdened and archaic electrical power source we inherited from the French (and for various other reasons). Most duty sections and clubs are air-conditioned. One's issued sweater can be a most welcome possession at time in some overly A/C offices. Overall, HAPPINESS is keeping our COOL over here.

FURNISHINGS: Generally, the BOQ rooms have single quarter-type beds; a three-drawer wardrobe that doubles for a desk; a chair; a mirror (wall type); a five-drawer chest; a small night table; a metal wall locker (GI); a mattress and a pillow. Bookcases and table lamps can be drawn from Housing Supply on a waiting list basis. You will be issued one set of linen when you clear billeting (try to ask for two sets for emergencies – rain, etc.) With your limited allowance for accompanied baggage, do not try to bring anything with you to improve your room. Standard passenger baggage weight on MAC contract flights is 66 lbs. If you desire an excess allowance, you must request your CBPO to state it in your orders before checking in for your flight. The excess can be increased to 1001 lbs total. Items can be ordered later from the States if necessary. But, many items are available on the local economy: lamps, etc. The floors are covered in GI linoleum. Some rooms have small rugs left by former occupants.

The WAF enlisted (hootch) women's quarters at TSN Airfield are two standard "hootches" converted for a recommended capacity of 15 total female occupants. Converted means "joined" by a newly constructed inside community lavatory. The hootch is not air-conditioned but has overhead fans and louvered side screens; none are private rooms – merely partitioned. The furnishings from housing supply are similar to the BOQs and by some clever furniture arranging and spacing, both privacy and ventilation can be achieved. We have many improvements in the mill still on order or underway but considerable improvement has been made to the facility since we recently converted it and moved in on 2 January 1971. One can be quite comfortable here really, by prowling the exchange for new items, buying from others or just using plain "Yankee" initiative, imagination and improvisation. One does not spend much time in one's room with the usual 12-hour duty day for 6-7 days a week while here.

MAID SERVICE: All quarters have maids who clean daily and do laundry for less than the equivalent of $5-$6.00 per month. The going monthly wage varies from 800 to 1,000 piasters plus two boxes of soap, spray starch, if desired, and a can of black shoe polish – all available in the Base Exchange (BX) periodically. The maids are hard on clothing but with the long duty hours you will be glad to have their services. Some do very fine work and now have discovered ironing boards instead of the floor. Their primary job is keeping your room clean and your uniforms washed, ironed and ready. They do other tasks if time permits but should be compensated for special favors (dishes, pots and pans, etc.) They have many to care for and in fairness to them and others, we must limit "special" chores. (Might suggest "iron on" name tags since the maids wash all together and "ink" your clothing with your room number to identify later. The maids sometimes place the room numbers in an "embarrassing" location on your clothes!) Female quarters at TSN now have washers and dryers. Some wash is done by hand and some should be. Training one's maid is "interesting" and individual preferences should be conveyed to the maid when necessary.

COMMISSARY: Located in downtown Saigon (Cholon) and not readily accessible. As with the exchange, stocks are limited and selection is limited. The commissary is presently controlled by the Army and not open to private individuals (you or me) but sells only to "large units" such as the various clubs, messes and to units for "official functions." This is to keep the items off the "black market" which does nothing to help stabilize the economy in Vietnam. Snacks are available in the BX – crackers, instant coffee, canned soups, peanut butter, potato chips and the like, but not on a readily available basis. Somehow, familiar food like steak, chicken and fresh vegetables are available and show up on our table. We manage! And there are always the very welcome "care packages" from home!

CLUBS AND MESSES: Some downtown Saigon billets (MACV) have dining rooms and cocktail lounges in the same building. Officers use the TSN Officers Open Mess, the Army messes and clubs in the area, and the TSN consolidated Field Ration Mess; NCOs have their own club, plus they use the TSN Field Ration Mess. Airmen use the Airmen's Club and TSN Field Ration Mess. All messes are field ration and in addition, there are some cafeterias around the base whose food is BX-sponsored, not gourmet, but filling. All grades may use the Vietnamese Air Force Officers Club, which is a short distance from the quarters (a "Hop-Tac") ride away of about five minutes, and with an international menu considered quite good locally, if a little expensive. Often, we WAF/Nurses pool and collect our hoarded goodies for cookouts on our BOQ patio and whip something up on room appliances in our BOQ hootches.

FINANCES: In military facilities and government operated agencies, Military Payment Certificates (MPCs) are the medium of exchange. Vietnamese piasters and dong (275 piasters/dongs to one dollar is the current official rate) are used on the local economy. All are required to convert all stateside "green" and declare any other dollar negotiable currency (Travelers Checks, etc.) upon arrival at the Port of Entry. MPCs must be converted to piasters at a government authorized conversion office before one can shop on the local economy. MPCs cannot be used on the economy nor paid to a local national. While you are here, you will receive some extra pay: hostile fire – $64 per month; Income Tax Exemption of all pay for Enlisted and $500 per month for Officers. To be sure that you start off right, try to have a minimum of $75 in cash with you on arrival. Arrangements should be made for direct deposit of your pay to a stateside bank when you clear your last station as pay records are not maintained in country.

APPLIANCES AND CONVENIENCES: Electrical: All the quarters where WAF now live have 110 volt current, but with that limited weight allowance, remember to mail any room appliances you may need. There are two outlets and one refrigerator/air conditioner outlet in each room. Radio: This is a MUST! It is important to have a FM reception since military alert and emergency announcements are made on FM. Outlets are limited and the electricity not the most sophisticated, so a transistor or a transistor/plug-in combination is advisable. Frequently, the exchange has AM-FM radios in stock and they are also available through PACEX (Pacific Exchange) order. Radios are a rationed item in the exchange. Electric Cooking Items: Hot plate, toaster/broiler, coffee pot, electric skillet, saucepan, etc. – though nice to have, should not take up your precious 66 accompanied baggage allowance. Some of these are occasionally available in the exchange or you can borrow or buy one from someone rotating after you arrive. Tape Recorder: "Letter writing" home by tape is a widely used means of communications here. Small cassette recorders are often available in the exchange. Alarm Clock: Bring a standard hand-wound alarm clock with you. They are seldom available at the BX

MISC. ITEMS: Linens: Bedspreads are not provided and have seldom been available in the exchange. Sometimes a lightweight cover is needed with air conditioning but many survive with just a top sheet. Pillows are GI issue but the exchange occasionally has foam rubber pillows for sale. Towels and facecloths are not supplied. Bring some with you, but remember that the maid washes daily so a large supply is not needed. You may want to bring an "emergency" set of personal linen. Housing or unit supply will issue a blanket if you request one but it will normally not be needed. Shower cap, clogs and robe: Bring a cap and clogs for the shower since these items are not overly abundant nor often in the exchange. A lightweight robe or shift is advisable to travel to and from the community bathroom (via the outside corridor for BOQ residents.) Bring something sensible, i.e. nylon or cotton, drip dry, COOL but a cover up. Camera: You will certainly want to take pictures over here. History is being made all around you and some of the things you see and experience are not believed, nor soon forgotten. No one will believe you back home without pictures. Beauty Shops: An exchange concessionaire beauty shop operates within a five-minute walk of the WAF/Nurse BOQ at TSN and about eight minutes from the WAF BEQ.

UNIFORMS: SEA- (Southeast Asia) women have been testing a suitable uniform since the first WAF arrived in Vietnam! Currently, the uniform recommended and most worn in the jobs that WAF perform here is the two-piece blue-and-white striped polyester/Dacron – DACs. The DACs can be worn quite comfortably year-round and withstand the harsh laundering rather well with some instructions to the maids. The second most worn, but harder to maintain than the DACs, is the super blue A-line skirt with the light-blue tabbed blouse (without the jacket – do not even bring the jacket for it will not be worn here and will rot and mildew from the heat and humidity. One is issued two sets of the SEA ("grunt") green jungle fatigues, boots, helmet and flak jacket, etc., by one's unit during processing. Some WAF wear this uniform on a daily basis that is frowned upon by the command for it should be worn only for those duties requiring its wear. On Seventh Air Force installations, the Commander has made the wear of hats/headgear optional for all USAF women with any authorized Air Force uniform. While here, females are permitted to wear the Navy (WAVE) blue and white overseas cap with the DACs. This hat is not available here but can be purchased at any WAVE or Navy clothing supply store in the States before coming. The beret, WAF flight cap, WAVE overseas cap or the WAF dress hat with white cover can be worn here. Even though the headgear is optional for wear on 7th AF installations, there will be occasions when it will be required so bring a hat with you. One must be worn traveling to and from Vietnam. And, for some official TDY inter-country and intra-country travel, a hat may be required. Bring enough uniform items to last you for a one-year tour considering that the duty week for most is seven days, and that the cleaning facilities are almost non-existent and laundry methods are harsh and certainly not up to stateside quality. Shoes are not available in Vietnam; either bring a year's supply of comfortable plain, black, calf pumps or arrange with a stateside source to have them sent to you. Important to note that since the transportation is limited and one walks almost everywhere, shoes wear out faster than in the States. The rainy season and the mud do not help either.

CIVILIAN CLOTHING: Expect Saigon to be like July in Alabama or Louisiana – hot, sticky and muggy. Select loose, sensible, lightweight, easy-care clothing that requires no dry cleaning. You will wear civilian clothing in your limited off-duty time and on your R&Rs. Uniforms must be worn off base in most instances. Bring enough lingerie and hose to last you. Very limited supply in the BX.

LEAVE AND R&R: Each military member on a normal one-year tour in Vietnam is entitled to one out-of-country R&R. An R&R is permissive temporary duty without per diem and not chargeable as leave. A "space required" seat is furnished on an R&R aircraft round-trip. The out-of-country R&R sites currently available are: Hawaii, Sydney, Hong Kong, Taiwan and Bangkok. Bring some clothes for the climate you are interested in visiting for civilian clothing is permitted for R&R. You are also eligible for a 14-day leave while here, but if you travel by military air, it will be on a space-available basis or at your own expense, if commercially. Recently, directives have been changed to allow CONUS leave not to exceed 14 days total and at one's own expense.

# Chapter Four

# 1962

*Memory Lane: John Glenn is first American to orbit the Earth.*
*Song: "I Can't Stop Loving You" by Ray Charles*

♥**Anne Marie Doering**
**Retired as a Lieutenant Colonel**
**In country: March 30, 1962 – April 1963**
**Rank: Major, US Army**
**Duty: MACV, US Military Assistance Advisory Group, Combat**
**Intelligence Officer, Saigon**

The first member of the Women's Army Corps to serve in Vietnam was Major Anne Marie Doering. She had the unique distinction of being a native of North Vietnam (known as French Indochina at the time) and of speaking both French and Vietnamese as her native languages. She was born October 5, 1908, in Quang Yen near Haiphong. Her father, a French officer, died when she was six. Her mother, who was German, subsequently married an American who worked for the Standard Oil Company. Young Anne Marie was educated in French Catholic schools in Haiphong and Saigon before moving to Texas in 1924 to live with relatives. She had a facility for languages and quickly learned English. Following high school, she graduated from Southwestern University in Georgetown, TX, and worked for several years in New York City before returning to Texas.

Anne Marie enlisted in the Women's Army Auxiliary Corps in March 1943. Commissioned in May, she served briefly in the US before being assigned to New Guinea. As the war progressed, she was reassigned to Manila in the Philippines. She was discharged in 1946, but kept her commission in the Reserves, returning to active duty in 1950. While a civilian, she lived and worked in Japan. With the start of the Korean War in 1950, many WAC officers were asked to return to active duty; she was likely part of that recall. Her assignments included posts in the US and Europe before she was selected for assignment to Vietnam with the US Military Assistance Advisory Group in Saigon. She arrived March 30, 1962, to be the first and at the time the only WAC officer to serve there. It was the first time she had returned to her native country since leaving as a teenager.

Then a major, she was one of three military women in country (the other two were nurses) at a time when the US presence in Vietnam totaled only 5,000 US service members. Her assignment was to the Intelligence Division where she served as chief of the Military Assistance Command, Vietnam Liaison Branch; her military occupational specialty was 9301, Combat Intelligence Officer. She was fluent in French and took the opportunity to resume studies of Vietnamese. In a 1962 interview she noted that Saigon was "very quiet (and) peaceful." Asked how she came to be assigned to Vietnam, she said she didn't know, though she was always reticent about her assignments and duties. Returning to the US in April, 1963, she was briefly assigned to the WAC Center, Fort McClellan, AL, and Fort Bliss, TX, before being reassigned in 1965 to the Pentagon, Washington, DC.

Her experiences in Vietnam were put to work as a member of the Office of the Deputy Chief of Staff, Operations group charged with developing the Army study titled, "A Program for the Pacification and Long-Term Development of South Vietnam" (short title PROVN). She was the only woman officer to participate in the study. Initially briefed to senior officials, the study then fell into obscurity. Later analysis of the report shows that many of the issues identified in Vietnam as problem areas were discussed, but were never implemented on the ground. It's likely that she visited Vietnam while working on the PROVN study. A cousin reported seeing her near Da Nang around 1966 or 1967, but further details concerning these trips are unknown.

Her last active duty job was in the Office of the Chief of Staff, Intelligence, as a member of the Foreign Liaison Office (a natural given her language capability). Promoted to lieutenant colonel, Anne Marie retired in March 1967. She lived initially in Georgetown, TX, and later in San Antonio, TX. She was active with the Salvation Army and the YWCA as well as other organizations. She died in San Antonio, TX, June 6, 2001, and is buried at the Fort Sam Houston National Cemetery.

(Information for this article comes from the files of her namesake, Ms. Anne Marie Jamison, Houston, TX, as well as from other internet resources. Note on awards: Bronze Star (awarded in 1945 presumably for service in the Philippines) and overseas service bars indicating two years in a combat zone. She would have earned two more bars for her Vietnam service.)

*Sources: Documents and information provided by Doering family member, Ms. Ann Jamison. Article written by COL Pat Jernigan, USA Retired.*

# Chapter Five

# 1965

*Memory Lane: President Johnson announces his program to create Medicare; gas costs 31¢ a gallon.*
*Song: "(I Can't Get No) Satisfaction" by The Rolling Stones*

**Theresa A. Catano**
**Retired as a Sergeant First Class**
**In country: 1965 – Date of departure unknown**
**Rank: Specialist 6, US Army**
**Duty: MACV, Executive Administrative Assistant**

**♥Louise M. Farrell**
**Retired as a Master Sergeant**
**In country: 1965 – Date of departure unknown**
**Rank: Sergeant First Class, US Army**
**Duty: MACV, Executive Administrative Assistant**

**♥Nana Bertha Wathaw (McDaniel)**
**In country: 1965 – Date of departure unknown**
**Rank: Specialist 5, US Army**
**Duty: MACV, Executive Administrative Assistant**

**Janet May Ellis (Ziegler)**
**Retired as a Lieutenant Colonel**
**In country: 1965 – 1966**
**Rank: Major, US Army**
**Duty: Personnel Staff Officer**

**♥Rebecca Jurel Fourth**
**In country: 1965 – 1966**
**Rank: Specialist 5, US Army**
**Duty: MACV, Executive Administrative Assistant**

**♥Anne S. Frantz**
**Retired as a Staff Sergeant**
**In country: 1965 – 1966**
**Rank: Specialist 6, US Army**
**Duty: MACV, Executive Administrative Assistant**

**♥Betty Lee Adams**
**Retired as a Sergeant Major**
**In country: January 15, 1965 – December 3, 1965**
**Rank: Master Sergeant, US Army**
**Duty: MACV, Joint Staff, First NCO Advisor to the Vietnam Women's Armed Forces Corps**

In 1964, the situation in Vietnam had intensified, and the Republic of Vietnam was organizing a Women's Armed Forces Corps (WAFC) and wanted US Women's Army Corps to assist them in planning and developing it. General William Westmoreland, Commander of Military Assistance Command, Vietnam, authorized one officer space and one enlisted, and the requisitions were submitted to the Pentagon to Colonel Emily Gorman, Director of the Women's Army Corps.

The requisition for the enlisted woman was a first, and she was to be chosen for excellence in leadership, training, administration and recruiting. On January 15, 1965, Sergeant First Class Betty Adams stepped off an airplane in Saigon and into the advisory position for the WAFC. Upon her return to the United States, she related a couple of "close calls" that had occurred while she was away. She stated, "The closest I ever came to actual combat was during a visit to a field hospital when word was received that the area was soon to be overrun by the Viet Cong. It was under the protection of mortar rounds that my party and I boarded a plane waiting for us with the engines running."

She was promoted to Master Sergeant on July 30, 1965. On December 3, 1965, she left Vietnam at 5 p.m. and arrived in San Francisco at 9 p.m. the same day, her birthday. "It was the longest birthday I ever had – 38 hours long." The next day she took TWA Flight 42 to Kennedy International Airport. It was just before landing that the 707 she was flying in was involved in a midair collision with an Eastern Consolation flight. Her plane lost 30 feet of wing but landed safely. She stated, "Believe me. I never had as anxious a moment in Vietnam as I did in the final five minutes of the flight into New York." Her next assignment was back to Fort Myer, VA, with duty at the Military Personnel Center, Washington, DC.

This job in personnel led to her promotion to Sergeant Major and to another first. Lieutenant General Walter Kerwin, Jr., Deputy Chief of Staff for Personnel, administered the oath of reenlistment to SGM Adams at a ceremony at the Pentagon. SGM Adams reenlisted for assignment to the Army General Staff as an action officer, a unique event in that she was the first enlisted woman to serve as an action officer on the General Staff.

*Excerpt from the* Anniston Star, *January 29 – January 30, 2012*

♥**Kathleen "Kitty" Iris Wilkes**
**Retired as a Lieutenant Colonel**
**In country: January 15, 1965 – December 3, 1965**
**Rank: Major, US Army**
**Duty: MACV, Joint Staff, First Senior Officer Advisor**
**to the Vietnam Women's Armed Forces Corps**

♥**Betty Eloise Reid**
**Retired as a Master Sergeant**
**In country: October 1965 – February 1969; November 1970 – November 1972**
**Rank: Sergeant First Class, US Army**
**Duty: MACV, Personal Secretary to MACV Commanding General William Westmoreland; Joint US Public Affairs Office**

**Jane Carol Szalobryt**
**Retired as a Master Sergeant**
**In country: November 1965 – November 1966; March 1968 – March 1969**
**Rank: Master Sergeant, US Army**
**Duty: MACV, Joint Staff, Second NCO Advisor to the Vietnam Women's Armed Forces Corps; MACV, Awards and Decorations Branch**

**Florence "Flo" I. Woolard (Lovensheimer)**
**In country: November 17, 1965 – June 8, 1968**
**Rank: Specialist 6, US Army**
**Duty: MACV, J3, Executive Administrative Assistant**

At the time I was ordered to Vietnam, I was living in the barracks (southern part of Arlington, VA) that was later torn down and turned into the south part of Arlington National Cemetery. I was assigned to the Pentagon. The way I found out that I was going to Vietnam was through the WACs at the barracks where I was living. I was in shock. When I returned to my assigned duties at the Pentagon, I was formally informed that I had been chosen to go to Vietnam.

That was when the Army first sent in troops, plus a few WACs. We had no training, no briefing before we left, just orders to go. When we arrived at Saigon, Vietnam, we were included with all the male troops in an entrance briefing. The briefer had no idea that there were females included with the males for this briefing. Until then, it was strictly male and believe me there were some embarrassing moments when the briefer looked over the crowd and saw a couple of females. I was told I was the seventh WAC to be in Saigon at that time. There were also Red Cross women, known as Donut Dollies, and nurses.

We were driven to the hotel because there were no barracks at that time. The only roll call was when we arrived at our office. This was a time of the buildup – very exciting. The Navy was in charge of all administrative things that went on in Saigon – the lodging, food for the troops, roll call, etc. When the Army took over, things changed. Everything was in a confusing situation.

I was fortunate enough to arrive at a time when I saw everything. I witnessed the move from the old MACV headquarters building from downtown Saigon to the new MACV headquarters building near Tan Son Nhut. I went all over Saigon with my Vietnamese friend. I was fortunate enough to see the people as they were. The actual radio station depicted in the movie "Good Morning, Vietnam" was located just across from the hotel where we WACs were billeted.

Then our hotel got hit and our luck ran out – we were in turmoil! The only way our office knew where we were was when we did finally show up at our workstations. I could go on and on, but it would take volumes of paper. Anyway, we were there one year before anyone else showed up (female Marines or Air Force). Then a year later, I believe they built the WAC barracks at Long Binh; I never saw Long Binh.

I was in Vietnam during the 1968 Tet Offensive. It was not pleasant. I have a few pictures of that also, but not the bad ones. At that time, we were not allowed to take pictures of some of the things we saw and experienced. I am fortunate enough to have pictures of everything I am writing about.

Betty Reid and I did pal around with each other. Most of the women went their own way. Anyway, she was the one to nominate me to go to Berlin, Germany. I went to Berlin where I met and married my husband. We were married for 41 years. He died in 2010, and I moved back to Kentucky where we had enlisted years before. He is buried in Kentucky Veterans Cemetery across from Fort Knox, which is where I will be buried with full military honors.

Right now (2014), I have a beautiful Vietnamese family living across the street from me and we are friends.

**Audrey Ann Fisher**
**Retired as a Colonel**
**In country: December 31, 1965 – December 1966**
**Rank: Major, US Army**
**Duty: USARV, G1, Chief of Morale Branch**

I left for Vietnam just after Christmas 1965. I was the first WAC officer assigned to US Army Vietnam. The headquarters was fairly new and our offices were scattered around the Tan Son Nhut Air Base. The G1 had offices in a low wooden utility building without bathrooms or water. A few months later, a new building was constructed to hold most of the headquarters staff. A second WAC officer, Major Shirley R. Heinze, arrived; she was also assigned to G1. Then a month or so later, enlisted cadre arrived to assist with the establishment of a WAC Detachment. More and more WAC officers arrived during the latter months of my tour. I left Vietnam in December 1966 just before US Army Vietnam moved its headquarters to Long Binh.

There are two memories I've never forgotten. The Vietcong "blew up" a building near my office building. It was being used to house GIs awaiting flights home. To my best recollection, many flights were cancelled. The second memory was hearing the cries of a soldier being told he would lose his leg. I was in a nearby space recovering from minor surgery.

Saigon was still a beautiful city while I was there. We had access to downtown where MACV Headquarters was located. During this time, the war was growing from the Delta to the coast and up country. Buddhists were setting themselves on fire, and there were many large protest groups. This was all done against the current regime. As the protests increased and I had business at MACV, I was assigned a jeep and an armed driver. I was a bit nervous after a bomb was discovered in the furnace room of my BOQ.

We worked 12-hour days. Sightseeing was limited. We endured monsoon rains and very high temperatures. Morale was good, though.

# Chapter Six

# 1966

*Memory Lane: First episode of the sci-fi TV series Star Trek; "How the Grinch Stole Christmas" is shown for first time on CBS.*
*Song: "Sounds of Silence" by Simon and Garfunkel*

**♥Maxene Monetta Baker (Michl)**
**Retired as a Colonel**
**In country: 1966 – 1967**
**Rank: Lieutenant Colonel, US Army**
**Duty: MACV, USAHAC, Saigon**

*Marsha "Cricket" Holder:* Colonel Maxene Michl was one of the Women's Army Corps' finest leaders. She worked as a food chemist before enlisting in the Women's Army Air Corps in September 1942 during World War II. She continued to serve during the Korean conflict and in Vietnam, retiring in March 1972. Her primary specialty was logistics. Among her many awards was the Legion of Merit for her Vietnam service as Secretary of the General Staff, Headquarters Area Command, Saigon. After her tour in Vietnam (1966-1967), she was the WAC Staff Advisor to the Fourth Army (1967-1968) and WAC Center Commander (1968-1969), Fort McClellan, AL. In 1968, Colonel Michl was among the first six WACs to achieve the rank of colonel in the US Army. She was the first WAC Center Commander to hold that rank. Many changes were made at the WAC Center during her command including adding drug abuse and race relations courses to the WAC basic training program. Prior to retiring in 1972, she was the Department of Defense Food Program coordinator and deputy commander of the Army's Natick Laboratories in Natick, MA.

Of her military accomplishments, Michl was most proud of having established the Women's Army Corps Foundation in 1969, to provide funding for the Edith Nourse Rogers Museum at Fort McClellan, Anniston, AL. The museum contained WAC memorabilia and chronicles women's military involvement throughout history. (Note: It is now the US Army Women's Foundation, and the museum was relocated to Fort Lee, VA, and is now the US Army Women's Museum). She also obtained approval from the Department of the Army to publish the *WAC Journal* (now the *Flagpole*) to provide news and information of career interest to WAC officers and enlisted women.

Colonel Michl retired to Sanibel, FL, became active in numerous groups and organizations and was renowned for her fund-raising ability. Colonel Michl was born in Mattoon, IL, and until her death had owned and managed a 204-acre corn and soybean farm in Illinois. *Sources:* The Women's Army Corps 1945-1978, *Bettie J. Morden; and article "Island activist Maxene Michl dies,"* Sanibel Captiva Islander, *Tuesday, March 24, 1992*

♥Thelma Alberta Merrill (Morse)
**Retired as a Chief Warrant Officer 4**
**In country: 1966 – 1967**
**Rank: Chief Warrant Officer 4, US Army**
**Duty: MACV, Counterintelligence Technician**

♥Ann Wansley
**Retired as a Lieutenant Colonel**
**In country: 1966 – 1967**
**Rank: Major, US Army**
**Duty: USARV, Office of the Judge Advocate General**

Lieutenant Colonel Ann Wansley was one of the first five WAC officers at USARV. She was part of a five WAC officer singing group called "The Bootleggers of Old Long Binh." She co-wrote the Long Binh songs, located in the Songs and Poems collection in this book.

**♥Ann M. McDonough**
**Retired as a Chief Warrant Officer 3**
**In country: 1966 – 1968**
**Rank: Chief Warrant Officer 3, US Army**
**Duty: MACV, Counterintelligence Technician**

Chief Warrant Officer 3 Ann McDonough's military career began in 1949 when she joined the US Women's Army Corps. She received intelligence analyst training and broke the gender barrier by being the first enlisted student in the Counterintelligence Corps Basic Agents Course, from which she graduated with honors. She was also the first woman assigned to the Counterintelligence Corps in 1952 and later to Internal Affairs at the Intelligence Center, Fort Holabird, MD.

After studying French in 1956 at the Defense Language Institute at the Presidio of San Francisco, CA, she again broke new ground by serving in the 66th Military Intelligence Group as the first female special agent assigned overseas. For the next five years, she completed several covert assignments in East and West Germany, in addition to attending the German Language School in Oberammergau.

In 1963, Chief McDonough was appointed a warrant officer. She again opened new areas to women in the counterintelligence field by being the first woman to attend Polygraph School at Fort Gordon, GA. She added Vietnamese to her linguistics qualifications.

She was then assigned to Military Assistance Command, Vietnam from 1966 to 1968. There she traveled throughout South Vietnam working as a polygraph examiner. She wrote, "I used my polygraph training to assist the South Vietnamese in their investigation of suspected double agents."

She retired in 1974 due to a medical condition. Her awards include: Bronze Star Medal (for meritorious service in Vietnam), Army Commendation Medal, Army Good Conduct Medal, Army of Occupation Medal, National Defense Service Medal, Armed Forces Expeditionary Medal, Vietnam Service Medal, Vietnam Campaign Medal, Vietnam Cross of Gallantry, and Meritorious Unit Commendation.

Chief Warrant Officer 3 McDonough was inducted in the Military Intelligence Hall of Fame in 1988. She died in 1994 and is buried at Arlington National Cemetery.

On April 29, 2012, the 902nd Military Intelligence Group, Fort Meade, MD, dedicated its new headquarters and Army Counterintelligence Center complex to Chief Warrant Office 3 Ann M. McDonough. The decision to name the new building after Chief McDonough came after a process that solicited input from the entire 902nd MI, the US Army Intelligence and Security Command historian and the US Army Intelligence Center of Excellence historian. Chief McDonough is considered a legend in the counterintelligence community.

Thomas McDonough, nephew to the Chief, was guest speaker at the ribbon-cutting ceremony. In the speech, he said, "My aunt's accomplishments in her distinguished military career were a result of her ability and her belief that she could do whatever she set her mind to. Being first in her field was merely another challenge, not a permanent obstruction."

*Excerpt from April 26, 2012 issue of* Soundoff! *Fort Meade, MD*

**♥Judith Christian Polk Bennett**
**Retired as a Colonel**
**In country: January 1966 – December 1966**
**Rank: Lieutenant Colonel, US Army**
**Duty: MACV, Joint Staff, Second Senior Officer Advisor to the Vietnam Women's Armed Forces Corps**

***Charlotte Phillips:*** Judy Bennett and her sister, Grace, joined the Women's Army Auxiliary Corps (WAAC) in 1942. Judy went through Officer's Candidate School (OCS) class #2 at Fort Des Moines, IA. Her sister went through class #3, making them the first sisters to become WAAC officers.

Judy transitioned to the Women's Army Corps, formed in September 1943. She loved to tell stories about her family and her World War II experiences. She liked to tell how her father reacted to customers during WWII when they discussed with him how lucky he was to have girls so his children did not get drafted and go off to war. To which he replied, "Both my girls are in the Army."

She established the WAC Detachment at Finschhafen, New Guinea, and often told stories about their experiences. While sailing for New Guinea, she cordoned off a section of the deck with canvasses when it rained. The women were able to take showers and wash their hair in fresh water as the boat rolled. She was also responsible for censoring the letters home, and more than a few stories were about how homesick the women were. Being blessed with a seamstress in the unit, they worked together to make their clothing more utilitarian.

WWII ended, so Judy left the service as a Captain in early 1946 and started studying under the GI Bill at the University of Alabama. She joined the Army Reserve to supplement the GI bill payments. Almost instantly, the Army began encouraging her to return to active duty. The Army wanted her back during the Korean conflict, but she did not return until 1950, after earning a Master's Degree in Business from the University of Alabama.

She attended the first Women's Army Corps Advanced Course and served in a wide variety of unit commands, both command staff and advisor assignments. In 1966, Lieutenant Colonel Bennett was assigned to Military Assistance Command, Vietnam, Joint Staff, as the second Senior Officer Advisor to the Vietnam Women's Armed Forces Corps, and her first challenge, prior to her arrival in Vietnam, was to learn the language. The exam was multiple-choice and she said she guessed well, as she received high marks. The Vietnamese were expecting an individual who was fluent in their language. However, she spoke the language very minimally and understood the writing even less.

Lieutenant Colonel Bennett was a non-drinker and a "picky" eater, but she was in a position where she was expected to consume liquor and eat different foods with military and civilian leaders. When the situation required her to drink liquor, she situated herself near a plant or where there was a hole in the floor, so after making the pretense of taking a drink, she would pour the drink away, either in a plant or between the floorboards.

However, the food was an even greater challenge. As an example, the head of the chicken was a prize piece of meat, and the blood of the chicken was used in preparing the dishes for the meal. She was expected to eat what was given to her.

Her duties required her to travel around Vietnam and she was even in a plane that was shot at. For these trips she was also required to carry a pistol;

a practice that was not common for women. However, again her stability and outstanding leadership in handling challenges made this just another job to be done. One of the interesting stories about her travels is in the section on WAC and WAF Advisors to the Vietnam WAFC.

After Vietnam, she was assigned as WAC Staff Advisor, US Army Pacific, and then as the first WAC officer at STRIKE Command at MacDill Air Force Base, FL, and finally as a full colonel to Fort Sam Houston, San Antonio, TX. She retired in 1971.

As a retiree, she led a very busy life – learning to build and repair houses for Habitat for Humanity, repairing bicycles for a big children's Christmas project in San Antonio, working at the Fort Sam Houston Hospital as a "pusher" along the long corridors, and working at the Fort Sam Thrift Shop. I believe she was proud of the job she did in Vietnam.

She died January 5, 2011, and is buried at the Fort Sam Houston National Cemetery, San Antonio, TX.

**Barbara A. Tarczynski**
**In country: January 12, 1966 – December 17, 1966**
**Rank: Specialist 6, US Army**
**Duty: MACV, Logistics Specialist**

My normal workday was 12-14 hours. I was the only female American soldier working in the Cholon Compound to which I was assigned. I commuted to work by military bus or staff sedan. There was an 11 p.m. curfew. If duty required working past curfew (often), we were provided an escort for the return to the hotel. We were not issued weapons unless leaving the city. I did carry a .45 caliber pistol (belonged to our General) when leaving the city. Socialization with other female Americans was a rarity and with the exception of my two roommates, reduced to one during my tour of duty, I very seldom saw them. I did, however, make Vietnamese friends, and even though I had a language problem, we managed to understand each other. I think sign language is universal.

I was often considered an anomaly by the Vietnamese because of my stature (5 feet tall). They thought all Americans were big.

One of my amusing stories involves a Navy Captain who was a member of the J4 staff. He had a spinal problem and did sit-ups each morning before coming to work. He had rigged a rope to the ceiling over his bed and he would use the rope as an "assist" in his exercise routine. Unfortunately, his maid thought he had planned suicide since the rope design he chose was a hangman noose. She took the rope and wouldn't give it back. (We did resolve the problem by having our Vietnamese driver explain everything to the maid.)

**Pauline D. Wireman (Edison)**
**Retired as a Sergeant First Class**
**In country: February 1966 – July 1967**
**Rank: Specialist 7, US Army**
**Duty: MACV, Executive Administrative Assistant**

**Loretta Jane Struthers**
**Retired as a Major**
**In country: March 1966 – September 1966**
**Rank: Captain, US Air Force**
**Duty: Headquarters 7th Air Force, Intelligence Staff Officer**

Major Struthers was the first Air Force line officer in Southeast Asia.

**Barbara Dickinson Gray**
**Retired as a Colonel**
**In country: March 1966 – March 1967**
**Rank: Major, US Army Medical Specialist Corps**
**Duty: 44th Medical Brigade, Long Binh, Physical Therapist Consultant; 17th Field Hospital, Saigon, Physical Therapist**

I volunteered to serve in Vietnam. I was the first AMSC officer assigned to a combat zone. My job included recommending assignments of physical therapists and physical therapy specialists to all Army surgical, field and evacuation hospitals in the country. This was an important job because before that time, soldiers with ankle sprains and other non-serious injuries were relocated to Okinawa, Japan, Korea and Hawaii.

I really enjoyed skydiving before I went to Vietnam and in June 1960, I was selected as the first woman member of the US Parachute Team. I finished 12th out of 50 of the nation's top skydivers in tryouts to make the team. In

August 1960, the World Championship of Skydiving took place in Sophia, Bulgaria. Unfortunately, I broke a bone on my second jump.

I never thought about being a pioneer for military women. I really enjoyed doing my job as a physical therapist in the Army.

"Physical Therapy has finally been recognized as a necessity for early treatment of combat wounds and has received full status as a medical team member with the 44th Medical Brigade. . . . Physical Therapy treatment administered to the patients after surgery by trained Physical Therapy personnel would restore patients to duty more quickly." *Major Barbara D. Gray, Staff Advisor on Physical Therapy to the Commanding Officer, 44th Medical Brigade, US Army, Vietnam. Quoted in "Activities Report, 17th Field Hospital, Mar-Dec 1966."*

**Grace J. Wright**
**Retired as a Sergeant First Class**
**In country: March 1966 – September 1967; November 1968 –**
**August 1969**
**Rank: Sergeant First Class, US Army**
**Duty: MACV, Executive Administrative Assistant**

**Ruby Rose Stauber**
**Retired as a Colonel**
**In country: April 1966 – April 1967**
**Rank: Major, US Army**
**Duty: MACV, Information Office**

**♥Patricia Lee Accountius**
**Retired as a Colonel**
**In country: May 1966 – May 1967**
**Rank: Lieutenant Colonel, US Army Medical Specialist Corps**
**Duty: 3rd Field Hospital, Saigon, First Dietetic Consultant**

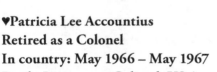

Patricia Accountius graduated from the University of Ohio and was commissioned as a second lieutenant in 1952 in the Women's Medical Specialist Corps, which was later designated in 1957 as the Army Medical Specialist Corps.

She was assigned to Walter Reed Army Medical Center and served in hospital and staff positions in the US and overseas. She completed the Dietetic Intern Program at

Walter Reed. In 1966, she was the first Army dietitian assigned to Vietnam where she did groundbreaking work establishing the hospital food service program.

"I was the first Army dietitian assigned to Vietnam, even though there was no such slot (open position). I was assigned first to the 3rd Field Hospital in Saigon, then to the 68th Medical Group at Long Binh, then to the 44th Medical Brigade as consultant for the three medical groups in country. I was then assigned additional duty as consultant for the Surgeon, USARV. I rewrote the menu for Vietnam as a cyclic menu for MACV. When I arrived in country, I was covering eight hospitals; when I departed, I was covering 18 hospitals. Upon my departure, dietitians were assigned to brigade, each medical group and the 3rd Field Hospital."

Colonel Accountius served as Chief of the dietitian section for the Office of the Surgeon General and to the Health Services Command in San Antonio, TX.

Colonel Accountius was buried with full military honors at the Fort Sam Houston National Cemetery, San Antonio, TX.

**Renee Estelle Lippman (Priore)**
**Retired as a Lieutenant Colonel**
**In country: May 1966 – June 1967**
**Rank: Major, US Army**
**Duty: MACV, USAHAC, Office of the Adjutant, Saigon**

**Marcia A. Galbreath**
**Retired as a Chief Warrant Officer 4**
**In country: May 1966 – December 1967; December 1969 – December 1970**
**Rank: Chief Warrant Officer 3**
**Duty: USARV; MACV, Counterintelligence Technician**

**Memorable experiences:** When I was appointed a Warrant Officer (WO), there were only 16 female WOs on active duty. I met General William Westmoreland at Headquarters Field Force Vietnam in 1966; he called me "Mr." Galbreath. At that time, the Officers' Guide stated that all WOs were called "Mister."

*Courtesy of Women's Memorial Foundation Register*

**♥Shirley M. Rowell Heinze**
**Retired as a Colonel**
**In country: June 1966 – August 1967**
**Rank: Major, US Army**
**Duty: USARV, G1, Personnel Staff Officer**

Shirley Heinze entered the Army in September 1951. Her career would span 30 years and include many "firsts." Shirley Heinze was one of the first five staff officers assigned to Long Binh. She was present for the groundbreaking ceremony for the first WAC Detachment in a combat zone since WWII. She assigned the first WAC arrivals to their positions in USARV. Her work as a Personnel Staff Officer included the basic study, design and implementation of the special combat soldier promotion system adopted by Department of the Army.

Sarah F. Niblack, Evelyn "Pat" Foote, Alice Hampson, Ann Wansley and Shirley Heinze formed a group called "The Bootleggers of Old Long Binh." They named themselves that because they wore jungle fatigues and boots and the boots left marks on their legs. Here is the song they wrote about their friend, Shirley, sung to the tune of "Cockles and Mussels":

> In old Long Binh city,
> The WACs don't dress pretty.
> They all have to wear jungle boots and fatigues.
> The fellows make light of
> The terrible plight of
> These ladies, sad ladies,
> Done in by intrigues.
>
> ~~~~
>
> Yet the Red Cross and DACs*
> Do not wear OD slacks.
> They wear dresses or skirts,
> Heels and hose, use cologne.
> But to us Tabor said,
> Feminity's dead,
> WACs are one of the boys
> While in this combat zone!
>
> ~~~~

The inequity of it
Makes all of us covet
The different status of Red Cross and DACs.*
But we will persevere
Col Heinze, never fear.
Baggy pants, muddy boots,
We're still proud to be WACs.

~~~~

At the Army War College,
Colonel Heinze will excel.
She'll convince all them fellers,
She knows strategy well.

~~~~

Multilateral treaties,
Militarily viewed,
Will not scare this WAC leader.
They'll be cranial food.

~~~~

For she loves knotty problems,
Controversy adores.
Likes to bait stodgy thinkers,
Can expound on all wars.

~~~~

She's conversant on Russia,
China, Poland and France.
All those fellers won't snow her,
With their male song and dance.

~~~~

They'll be awed by her wisdom,
Overcome by her charms.
Sure they'll make her a member,
Of their own combat arms.

~~~~

And when she's graduated,
I'm sure no one will laugh.
When she's quickly appointed
FIRST-WOMAN-CHIEF-OF-STAFF!

*DACs: Department of Army Civilians

The complete song list with lyrics is in the Songs and Poems chapter. Shirley Heinze has the distinction of being one of the first two WAC officers to graduate from the Army War College. She was the WAC officer responsible for enlisted assignments in Vietnam. Colonel Shirley Heinze passed away February 14, 2015. *(Photo and song courtesy of US Army Women's Museum)*

**Doris L. Caldwell**
**Retired as a Colonel**
**In country: July 1966 – July 1967**
**Rank: Major, US Army**
**Duty: MACV, Administrative Officer**

**Joy J. Jacob (Kent)**
**In country: July 1966 – May 1968**
**Rank: Captain, US Army**
**Duty: USARV**

**♥Paula Cecilia Towle**
**Retired as a Lieutenant Commander**
**In country: October 1966 – October 1967**
**Rank: Lieutenant Commander, US Navy Medical Service Corps**
**Duty: USS *Repose* (AH-16), Pharmacy Officer**

**June P. Dohnal**
**Retired as a Lieutenant Colonel**
**In country: October 1966 – November 1967**
**Rank: Major, US Army**
**Duty: MACV, J2, Strategic Intelligence Staff Officer**

**Betty Jean Benson**
**Retired as a Command Sergeant Major**
**In country: October 1966 – June 1968**
**Rank: Sergeant First Class, US Army**
**Duty: USARV, Special Troops, WAC Detachment, Field First/**
**Administrative NCO**

***Marion C. Crawford:*** What do you say about a woman who served longer than any other enlisted woman in the Army at that time? After 3l years of serving, Betty went out kicking. She never wanted out of her beloved Army. In fact, as her mandatory retirement neared, Betty was often heard to say: "If I have to, I'll start World War III."

Betty enlisted in the Army in 1949 and went through basic training at Fort Lee, VA. Following basic, some of her assignments included: Murphy General Hospital, Fort Devens, MA; US Naval Hospital, Portsmouth, NH; Hanau, Germany; Fort Ord, CA; Camp Zama, Japan; Fort Myer, VA; and the US Army Recruiting Command, Hampton, VA.

In 1966, she and I arrived in Vietnam together. Her assignment was as the Field First Sergeant/Administrative NCO for the WAC Detachment. One of her favorite activities was acting as the unit "medic." She told the women: "If you have a minor ailment and don't want to go on sick call, come see me." She kept a footlocker near her desk in the orderly room and many a troop came in to get something for headaches, cramps, toothaches, etc. And, many a band aid was applied, too.

After Vietnam, Betty went to Fort Monroe, VA, as the First Sergeant. From there, she went back to the Recruiting Command. In January 1973, she became the first female to attend the newly established Sergeants Major Academy, Class #1. Upon graduation in June of that year, she received the AUSA Award for "Excellence in Leadership." Her illustrious career continued with her promotion to Command Sergeant Major (CSM) and she was assigned as CSM, Headquarters Battalion, WAC Center and School, Fort McClellan, AL, former home of the Women's Army Corps.

Another first: CSM Benson was the first female assigned as a Post Sergeant Major in an overseas command, the 8th Support Group, Camp Darby, Italy. Fittingly, at Fort McClellan, AL, Betty served as CSM, 2nd Basic Training

Battalion, US Army Military Police School and Training Center, where she remained until retirement in June 1980.

Though retired from the Army, Betty was not about to rest on her laurels. She was elected President of Chapter 62 of the WAC Veterans Association in Anniston, AL. She was also the President of the Animal Welfare League, which she activated and operated for seven years until her health made it impossible to continue.

The entire time we spent in 'Nam, there were many funny incidents that happened in the unit and while we were on R&R; she made me promise not to tell the troops about these happenings. I'd say, "Sure, sure, Betty," and at the first opportunity back at Company meetings, I'd tell them everything. Off to the side, she would jump up and down flailing her arms trying to get me to stop.

Those times when we came under attack, she would hold her little finger out the doorway saying she wanted the Purple Heart but she didn't want to lose anything too valuable. I had many a laugh at her expense. She was such a good soldier. We all love her.

**Marion Cecelia Crawford**
**Retired as a First Sergeant**
**In country: October 1966 – June 1968**
**Rank: First Sergeant, US Army**
**Duty: USARV, Special Troops, WAC Detachment, First First Sergeant**

In February 1949, I realized a childhood dream. I enlisted in the Army as the first woman in Michigan to join the peacetime Women's Army Corps. At age 10 to 11, I had been a WAAC (Women's Army Auxiliary Corps) mascot at Fort Brady, MI, 501st WAAC Operations Company. *The Detroit Free Press* had my photo in the paper that read, "Former WAAC mascot realizes her dream as she becomes the first woman in the state to join the peacetime Women's Army Corps."

My Army career began with basic training at Fort Lee, VA, followed by Leadership School and Administration School. My first assignment there was at Headquarters and Headquarters Company. In order to get started in achieving one of my goals – travel – I volunteered for recruiting duty. In 1953, I was the WAC recruiter in Toledo, OH. During my two years of covering all of northwest Ohio, I was promoted twice. I was one of two top recruiters of WACs in the country. I was promoted to the rank of Master Sergeant at age 23.

My next assignment was in Kaiserslautern, Germany, where I became the First Sergeant of the unit in 1955. While in Germany, I seriously took up fastball softball pitching. After Germany, I was once again assigned to recruiting duty, this time in Cleveland where I covered all of northeastern Ohio and later on to Canton. Then, it was to Aberdeen Proving Ground, MD, for two years. Following that duty, it was back to recruiting duty covering all of Maryland and part of West Virginia.

Fort Sill, OK, was my next duty station where I was the First Sergeant of the WAC Battery. I started up a drill team there which traveled touring the country (sponsored by the Army Recruiting Service). It was while at Fort Sill that I was placed on orders for Vietnam in 1966. I activated the first WAC Detachment in Vietnam. After six months at Tan Son Nhut, the detachment was relocated farther north to Long Binh. My drill team performed at both locations. I extended for another tour of duty in country, as did my entire cadre. In June 1968, I left Vietnam and was assigned to Fort Sheridan, IL, as the First Sergeant of a 500-woman unit. I organized a drill team there, as well.

Even though I was about to be promoted to be the seventh Sergeant Major in the WAC, I retired from my beloved Women's Army Corps in July 1969. As luck would have it, I did come out on orders on January 22, 1970 – SIX MONTHS AFTER RETIRING. Funny!

I retired from the Army but I didn't really retire. I became the first female JROTC instructor in the nation with the Indianapolis School System, where I remained for three years. Later, Hampton, VA, became home where I was the office manager for the Burroughs Corporation of Newport News. For eight years after that job, I was once again in Ohio. While there, I was active with the Humane Society, wrote a newspaper column about animals, and did adoptions for homeless animals out of my home.

My next move put me where most WACs went in those days – to Alabama, near Fort McClellan, home of the Women's Army Corps. I lived there for 18 years and was a Realtor. As a very serious RV enthusiast, I became co-owner of the American Heritage RV Resort in Williamsburg, VA. Finally, I moved to Florida and bought a home on Lake Eustis in 1992 and another home in Blairsville, GA, in 2013. Now, retired!

My blood still runs red, white and blue and with many hints of moss green and gold (our WAC colors) even though I have reached my 85th year.

**Peggy Elizabeth Ready**
**Retired as a Colonel, USAR**
**In country: October 31, 1966 – November 1, 1967**
**Rank: Captain, US Army**
**Duty: USARV, Special Troops, WAC Detachment, First Commander**

My plane touched down at Tan Son Nhut Air Base outside of Saigon at midnight Halloween 1966. It was surreal. Jeeps with mounted artillery patrolled the airstrip. The hot, humid air assaulted me as I stood uncertainly atop the stair ramp in my Class B uniform. Finally, a young captain in jungle fatigues and flak jacket stepped to the bottom of the ramp and said, "Captain Ready? I'm your escort officer." The next morning at 0700 hours I participated in the official groundbreaking ceremony for the barracks for members of the WAC Detachment, Headquarters Special Troops, USARV. It was there that I met my senior NCO cadre, First Sergeant Marion C. Crawford and SFC Betty J. Benson, Field First/Administrative NCO. This was my first command. These are the women who played an enormous role in assuring the success of this first women's unit sent to Vietnam by DOD. In so doing, they also assured my success as the first commander. These NCOs taught me to be a troop commander. The unit members honored me by being the perfect unit. It was such great fun.

But it did present unusual challenges. For example, it taught us to stamp the hands of invitees with the WAC Detachment stamp for all monthly parties. It was also a lot of work. Everything required thought, initiation and coordination. I spent many days setting up support for medical care and treatment, mess facilities, and Post Exchange products. For example, even though there were about 500 nurses in country, there were no feminine hygiene products available. The women relied upon care packages from home. When USARV Headquarters, with all supporting units, moved to Long Binh in July 1967, the women were finally out of class B uniform and wore jungle fatigues. This is where Supply Sergeant Edith "Effie" Efferson's coordination and rapport with other supply NCOs paid off. All women's jungle fatigues arriving in country were mysteriously diverted to the WAC Detachment for distribution. Effie kept all her trading material in a big tent at the back of the WAC cantonment area. I never looked in her tent. I just told her, "Sergeant Efferson, just don't get me hanged." She could acquire anything the unit needed by trading.

It cannot be overstated what that year meant to me and my career. I served in other capacities as the "first woman" throughout my military and civilian careers. After nine years, I left active duty, joined the US Army Reserve and served another 24 years before I retired having achieved the rank of Colonel. During this time, I received my law degree at the University of South Carolina then moved to Florida. On the military side in 1987, I was appointed first woman commandant of a USAR school in Jacksonville, FL (one of 92 such schools nationwide). In 1989, Florida Governor Bob Martinez appointed me, from among 12 applicants, as the first woman judge in St Johns County. I retired in 2000 after serving 10 years, unopposed, on the bench.

Little did I know that hot, humid Halloween so long ago that I was stepping into the pages of history.

**♥Edna Elizabeth "Mickey" McCormick**
**Retired as a Lieutenant Commander**
**In country: November 1966 – November 1967**
**Rank: Lieutenant Commander, US Navy Medical Service Corps**
**Duty: USS *Repose* (AH-16), Blood Bank Specialist**

Edna McCormick enlisted in the USNR (WR) on October 2, 1942, at Tacoma, WA. She was commissioned in September 1943, was released to inactive duty in 1945, recalled in October 1950 and retired May 1, 1968. Lieutenant Commander McCormick was a graduate of Bowling Green College in Ohio and a registered Medical Technologist with the American Society of Clinical Pathologists. She served as a Blood Bank Specialist aboard the hospital ship USS *Repose* (AH-16) for 18 months during the Vietnam War.

**♥Mary E. "Phill" Phillips**
**Retired as a Master Sergeant**
**In country: November 1966 – November 1967**
**Rank: Master Sergeant, US Army**
**Duty: MACV, Joint Staff, Third NCO Advisor to the Vietnam Women's Armed Forces Corps**

"Phill" served in the US Army from September 17, 1949, to December 1952. She had a 10-day break in service, after which she served until June 30, 1973. She was stationed at Fort Mason, CA; Heidelberg and Sandhofen, Germany; Fort Buckner, Okinawa; Presidio of San Francisco, CA; Fort Ord, CA; Recruiting Duty, Los Angeles, CA; and at the Recruiting Command, Hampton, VA. Phill was a member of the American Legion, Veterans of Foreign Wars, Retired Enlisted Association, WAC Veterans Association, Heritage Chapter 62, Vietnam Veterans Association, Chapter 502; League of Animal Welfare, National Association of Realtors, Alabama Association of Realtors, and Calhoun County Board of Realtors.
*Source: Vietnam Memory Book 2000*

**LTC Frances Chaffin (Gannon):** Mary was short in stature, the size of her Vietnamese trainees who were all very small women. She was definitely a hands-on advisor: drilling, checking barracks, keeping an eagle eye on the details. She trained (the Vietnamese women recruits) in the US Women's Army Corps' way of doing things.

**♥Beverly Eileen Ridley**
**Retired as a Chief Warrant Officer 3**
**In country: November 1966 – November 1967**
**Rank: Chief Warrant Officer 2, US Army**
**Duty: USARV, 525th Military Intelligence Group (attached to II Field Force), Imagery Analyst**

## ♥Edith L. "Effie" Efferson
## Retired as a Sergeant First Class
## In country: November 1966 – June 30, 1968
## Rank: Staff Sergeant, US Army
## Duty: USARV, Special Troops, WAC Detachment, first Supply Sergeant

***Marion C. Crawford:*** Sergeant Effie and I first met in 1959 when I was First Sergeant of the WAC Detachment at Aberdeen Proving Ground, MD. She was not cadre but a very good NCO in the Company. She spent all her off-duty time fishing. In fact, CPT Murphy gave her some fishing equipment as a farewell gift when it was time to leave Vietnam. She was my Dad's and Mother's favorite troop; they met her while visiting me in the States.

In 1973, at the age of 53, Effie adopted Angela, age 5 and Michele, age 6. I met the children when I visited Effie at Fort Meade, MD. They were older then, probably early teens, and nice girls being raised right by our dear Effie. One thing she told me that had me laughing like mad was that she would train them before she died to drink beer and CC (Canadian Club whiskey). Some of you might remember that was Effie's drink of choice.

When the Pentagon briefed me about my Vietnam tour, I was told who my cadre was going to be. I was tickled pink that not only did I know Betty Benson, but also when they told me that my Supply Sergeant was to be Edith Efferson, I whooped and hollered! One of the things I particularly remember is her trip by the Orderly Room, part of her daily routine, trying to round up the rest of the cadre for cocktail hour. She'd go by singing "Salty Dog, Salty Dog." It never failed to crack us up. When we got to the cadre lounge, she was usually bent over with her head in the refrigerator, and I would always jab her, which sent her screaming, head first deep into the fridge, cussing me out the whole time, "Top, I'm going to kill you." Included in her briefing to the new arrivals was that they would learn to sleep like she did – one eye open, one eye closed.

Whenever there was an incident, such as the ammo dump explosions when we all thought our time had come, I had to assign Betty to take charge of Effie while I looked out for the remainder of the company. Effie almost turned white every time we came under attack! Oh, and she was an expert at exchanging chickens for steaks and lobster tails from the General's Mess and "borrowing" Army trailers and painting them WAC colors to put beer and soft drinks in for our Company parties. SIGNS OF A GREAT SUPPLY SERGEANT!

Sergeant First Class Efferson died December 22, 1982, and is buried in the Maryland Veterans Cemetery, Crownsville, MD.

**Phyllis Arlene Puffer**
**In country: December 1966 – December 1967**
**Rank: Captain, US Army**
**Duty: MACV, 519ᵗʰ Military Intelligence Battalion, Intelligence Officer**

I arrived in Saigon in December 1966. I don't remember the exact date but it was before the Bob Hope show. I'm a country girl and really don't like cities very much. Ever since my arrival in Saigon, I had one burning objective – get out of the city and see some of the countryside. As a member of the Women's Army Corps, I knew I was doing good even to get to Vietnam at all. Very few of us ever made it there during the whole war. Not only was I one of the first, as far as I have been able to determine, but when I arrived as the only woman in my unit of several hundred men, I was the only one of "us" I knew of in the whole country. Shortly after I settled in, other WACs began arriving, and eventually we were able to have a get together of around 25 or 30.

On the whole, American women were a scarce commodity on the scene, and finding a date was never a concern. My goal was to find a date who could get transportation to get out of the city to look around. In those days, the Army was overly protective of its women, especially compared to these days when women soldiers go everywhere and are armed. Then, we were not allowed anywhere near dangerous areas, and outside the city was dangerous. You had to get a ride on some form of military transportation – jeep, plane, truck or all three. That was just not all that easy – vehicles were in demand to haul humans and supplies – tourists were not welcome.

On New Year's Eve, my date and I went to one of the large clubs where Americans congregated. I thought he was a little boring, but then he might have thought I was the boring one. After a couple of hours it seemed to me that he began drinking rather a lot and more rapidly. I thought he was probably gathering his forces to make his big move. I had no fear. I was prepared with centuries of small-town morality behind me and ancestry straight back to the Puritans.

We went to a smaller club. Few people were there, six men to be exact, sitting together at a table. The men clearly were American military, probably soldiers or marines. They had crew cuts and a scrubbed, clean-cut look. They all wore well-ironed dress shirts, well-ironed dress summer slacks, belts, ties and well-polished shoes. They were quiet, calm, alert and athletic, each sitting over a drink.

My date and I chose a small table nearby. After a time, he left to visit the men's room. Probably the extra drinks were taking effect. The scene remained quiet as I sat alone, the goal of getting out of the city filling my thoughts and giving me patience in fulfilling my part of the bargain. Tranquility reigned for approximately three minutes after the total disappearance of my date. It became apparent that the group of six had been closely studying the situation. Opportunity had appeared. One of the men came to my table and asked for a dance. We danced a few steps and the others lined up. They actually lined up one behind the other. After a few steps, the man would leave and another took his place. Then the next and the next. My date eventually returned. The six went back to their table, and everything returned to the way it had been before.

My date took me back to the hotel, which had been turned over to US military personnel for the war. Unfortunately, I neglected to set a day and time for his part of the bargain. I never saw that man again. I could not locate him through his unit even after several tries. You might like to know that I did get a day in the country much later. This time I had found a date of sterner stuff, and we had a really good time.

## Rhynell M. "Ren" Stoabs (Karr)
**In country: December 1966 – July 1968**
**Rank: Specialist 5, US Army**
**Duty: USARV, Special Troops, WAC Detachment, first Company Clerk**

In Vietnam, when you flew into or out of an airport, you flew in contracted airplanes. The pilot flew in high and dove down to the tarmac to avoid being hit by mortars. This is a very scary way to land. About the time the plane had landed you were wondering, "What am I doing here and how do I get back home?" You knew your life had taken a very drastic turn. Takeoffs were

no better; the wheels cleared the ground, and you were in a steep ascent to get out of range.

The flight to Vietnam was 18 hours through five time zones. I was exhausted when I arrived. That night I prepared for bed and was deep asleep when Staff Sergeant Efferson woke me. We were under attack. I got dressed, into my shoes, ID in my pocket, money, shot record, etc. I had it all. Time went by and still exhausted, I once again went to bed. This scenario was repeated several times. When the incoming rounds came, I was this little blonde streaking to the bunker – no shoes, no ID, no money, just me and my nightgown!

One night while in Saigon, a Conex container (huge shipping box that could be lifted from an 18-wheeler or train onto a ship) was hit by a mortar round at the Tan Son Nhut Airport about three miles from us. The mass of tear gas was invisible but got in our eyes and lungs as it drifted over. I remember thinking that I was going to die. The fear was so real because you knew if you could smell gas, your gas mask was useless. We did not know, of course, that it was only tear gas.

I was "chosen" to go to Vietnam as the company clerk of the first and only WAC Detachment in a combat zone since World War II. I was in the advanced party who prepared the detachment for the 100-150 women coming later. This consisted of the commanding officer, the first sergeant, the field first/administrative NCO, the supply sergeant and me. Policy was established. We did loads of typing, dealt with the logistical mess of getting enough beds, linens and all other items needed to house us. This was new territory for us all.

I roomed with Staff Sergeant Efferson, the supply sergeant, who had a deathly fear of the many, many lizards that climbed on anything not moving. It was very entertaining to watch one particular gecko that loved her – always above her head on the ceiling. Wherever she would move, it followed, even into other rooms.

When asked what I did in Vietnam, I tell everyone that, if they watched *M\*A\*S\*H\** on TV, I was a female Radar. I made distribution runs every day, and often I would get somewhere and they would require the Company Commander's signature. Rather than returning miles to the Detachment, I would go around the block, sign the Captain's name and return to do business. I got a lot of funny looks – but always got what was needed. Just like in *M\*A\*S\*H\**, the captain would ask if she signed something or had I.

The WAC Detachment in Tan Son Nhut eventually became part of a fenced compound referred to as Tent City "B." These tents housed incoming

GIs until they were shipped to their assigned in-country units. Every fifth tent was a cold-water shower. For "combat" showers, you get wet, turn off the water, soap up and then rinse very quickly. The first time I made the distribution and mail run (the second day I was in country), I was mortified because the shower tent sides were rolled up for ventilation: I saw *everything*! No one expected a 19-year-old American woman to be walking through the compound. The next day the tent flaps were down!

Those showers were also our laundry rooms where the mama-sans cleaned our clothes. Imagine my brand new Vanity Fair lingerie on the cement, scrubbed with a brush. The pretty pastels were soon dirty brown. Well, they didn't last long either.

The Army, in its infinite wisdom, sent us to Vietnam in our Class B uniforms – polyester cords that had to be starched and ironed. Dresses in a war zone!! We had no ironing boards – but wait – you could buy a million ironing board *covers* in the Post Exchange. One day I passed a trash pile with the top of an ironing board showing. In our orderly room, I asked to have the ironing board with legs on it. Soon delivered in a familiar shade of pink, it was the only ironing board in the Detachment for a long time.

Our main mode of transportation was the back of a pickup or deuce-and-a-half (a 2.5-ton truck). Try getting in a huge truck wearing a straight skirt. My solution was to grab a couple of GIs, one on each side. I would walk my feet up into the truck and the GIs would then push me up into the truck bed.

We soon learned that women are the stronger sex; we seemed to be able to cope with the daily fear that was our constant companion. The men asked how we could act so normal and joke around like we did. How do you explain that those *were* our coping skills? A guard was assigned to protect us in the bunkers. What was one lonely GI going to do if security was breached? I felt then, and I still feel, that he was assigned to be sure that we were not taken captive. Sometimes we could hear the strap of his weapon rattle; he was more afraid than we were. Many things happened in those bunkers. We played cards, polished our nails, drank beer and ate. We were really good at drinking beer. God forbid that we would sit on the ground – critters lived there. More than one mattress was dragged out. One at a time, we would sneak in and retrieve something that we *had* to have.

USARV Headquarters was relocated to Long Binh about 27 miles from Saigon. Prior to building our billets, the jungle was defoliated with Agent Orange. The land was cleared; not one blade of grass remained. Temporary buildings with louvered sides were built much like the one in Saigon. We worked 12-14 hour days, seven days a week. Many times, we partied after that because it helped us forget the realities of war.

When making mail runs or going to the field hospital mess hall about a mile away, often I saw many bodies in their body bags lined up on the ground waiting to be processed. Nearby, there was an ever-ready stack of crates for them to be sent home in. You never forget a sight like that.

The 1968 Tet (Vietnamese New Year) Offensive was a really bad time; every night, we were under constant fire. The ammunition dump, a half mile away, was hit one night and three pads exploded at the same time. Each pad had enough ammo to fill a train car, with one side open so trucks could pull in, load, and get out in a hurry: Drivers did not want to be there long. When the dump exploded, I was at the top of the stairs heading to the bunker. I threw my arms up to protect my face and could feel dirt and sand hit my arms, face and hair; I have no idea how I got to the ground. I can still close my eyes and see that explosion. It was horrifically beautiful and the most frightening thing I have ever seen. Once again, I thought I was going to die.

Imagine being a girl and needing to go to the bathroom in a war zone. At best, the bathrooms were outhouses. Every morning a detail pulled the barrel from under the outhouse, poured in jet fuel and set it on fire to burn off the contents. The smell was awful. The outhouse sidewalls were constructed with louvers about half way up and the rest screened. There was little room for modesty as anyone could see you. Just when I thought I would explode I would yell, "I'm coming in!" Then I would grab a couple of GIs and make them stand guard to keep other GIs out. Most GIs paid no attention, until inside. At that point, I really didn't care who saw what; I was going to the bathroom somewhere.

One time, three of us were returning from R&R. We flew into Cam Ranh Bay, well north of where we were supposed to land. I talked our way onto a flight to Saigon. We were on a C-130 cargo flight so loaded that the only place to sit was in the cockpit. Being night, we could see light flashes on the ground and knew we were being shot at. Once in Saigon, I talked our way onto another flight. This one was to Bien Hoa Air Base, near Long Binh.

From Bien Hoa, a GI driving a jeep offered us a ride (instead of waiting for a bus) if we could fit. We sat on our duffle bags and stuff. My head was bent over so it wouldn't rub the jeep's canvas top. I told the driver to make the jeep fly because I was terrified of sniper fire. What kept us from crashing I don't know, because we were going so fast and jeeps roll so easily. The next day, we learned that the first bus carrying the incoming GIs had hit a land mine and four people were killed. We would have been on that bus if we had not ridden in the jeep. Only the weight and different wheelbase had saved us.

All the jeeps and other vehicles had a tall center post with wire that went across the hood to each side. This was to keep a person from being beheaded. This is just one of the things we lived with on a daily basis. Fear was our constant companion. At night, we would lie in bed knowing that you never hear the mortar round that gets you.

The PX carried female items for us and the men could not shop in that section. This was to keep our items from making their way to the black market. When we first arrived, we saw bras and panties. How nice, if only they had not been large enough to fit an elephant!

On a whim, I went to a photograph studio in Saigon and had a portrait done as a gift to a GI I was dating back in the States and to my mother. My hair was very blonde and made quite a hit with the Vietnamese people. The next time I passed that shop, my photo, huge, filled the entire window. Then, it was all over Saigon, and guys from up-country, when they saw me, said they had seen my photo in shops all over Vietnam. Soldiers came up to us with tears in their eyes because they had not seen "round eyes" or American women in months.

# Chapter Seven

# 1967

Cadre photo: Standing (l-r): PFC Rhynell "Ren" Stoabs, Company Clerk; CPT Peggy Ready, Commander; SFC Betty Benson, Field First/Administrative NCO; and SSG Edith "Effie" Efferson, Supply Sergeant; 1SG Marion C. Crawford, seated, activated the unit.

The first WAC Detachment in a combat zone since World War II had its beginnings in January 1967. The unit was located at "Tent City B" part of Tan Son Nhut Air Base, Saigon. It consisted of 10 Quonset huts, all of which were destroyed during the Tet Offensive of 1968.

**♥Sophia Adele Dziadura**
**Retired as a Major**
**In country: 1967 – Date of departure unknown**
**Rank: Captain, US Air Force**
**Duty: 7ᵗʰ Air Force, J2, Intelligence Officer**

In 1944, Sophia Dziadura enlisted in the Navy, where she served for 12 years. She then received a commission in 1956 with the Air Force, where she spent another 14 years. In all, she served during World War II, the Korean Conflict and the Vietnam War.

As an intelligence specialist, Major Dziadura was one of the first female Air Force officers to be sent to Vietnam, which was followed by tours of duty in Africa, Latin America and Eastern Europe. Following her discharge from the military in 1970, she continued her devotion to those who served by remaining active with Military Family Services – an organization geared to helping families with parents on active duty.

**Phyllis J. DeLong**
**In country: 1967 – Date of departure unknown**
**Rank: Specialist 4, US Army**
**Duty: USARV, Clerk-Typist**

**Emma Jean Clark**
**In country: 1967 – 1968**
**Rank: Specialist 5, US Army**
**Duty: USARV, Clerk-Typist**

**♥Elizabeth J. Hamilton**
**Retired as a Colonel**
**In country: 1967 – 1968**
**Rank: Lieutenant Colonel, US Army Medical Specialist Corps**
**Duty: 36ᵗʰ Evacuation Hospital, Vung Tau, Physical Therapist**

**Joan B. Kyllo**
**In country: 1967 – 1968**
**Rank: Captain, US Air Force, Biomedical Sciences Corps**
**Duty: Dietitian**

♥Jacqueline "Jackee" M. Lavin
Retired as a Major
In country: 1967 – 1968
Rank: Major, US Army Medical Specialist Corps
Duty: 71st Evacuation Hospital, Pleiku, Physical Therapist

Ida Richard
Retired as a Lieutenant Colonel
In country: 1967 – 1968
Rank: Major, US Army Medical Specialist Corps
Duty: 55th Medical Group, Qui Nhon, Dietetic Consultant

♥Lois May Steelman
Retired as a Lieutenant Colonel
In country: 1967 – 1968
Rank: Major, US Army
Duty: MACV, G4, Supply Staff Officer

# JANUARY

*Memory Lane: US astronauts Gus Grissom, Edward Higgins White, and Roger Chaffee are killed when fire breaks out in their Apollo spacecraft during a launch pad test; the first Super Bowl played between Green Bay Packers (Win 35-10) and the Kansas City Chiefs.*
*Song: "I'm a Believer" by The Monkees*

Mary E. Rutledge (Fish)
In country: January 1967 – March 1967
Rank: Specialist 4, US Army
Duty: USARV, Signal Corps, Clerk-Typist

I was at Fort Gordon, GA, when I was selected for Vietnam and was definitely surprised. That was in December 1966. So, I went on leave to New York to tell mom, dad and my husband the news. Dad was the only one who was excited. We flew out of Romulus Army Depot, NY, to Oakland then went to Vietnam via Hawaii and Guam. There were about 25 women on the plane! In Hawaii, we laid over for three days because two of the plane engines went out. Then it was to Japan for fuel, then to Guam, then Tan Son Nhut. We got off the plane into sweltering heat and lots of jungle. One girl was praying her rosary – she was a wreck! I can still see her when I close my eyes. We went by bus straight to the WAC Detachment which was Tent City B. I was assigned to Signal Corps, Compound B, and reported there to work as a clerk typist with six male officers.

Two months after my arrival, I discovered I was pregnant. The officers put a note up on the board that said – Rutledge – assignment Baby Production. I kept getting sick and one of the officers finally said, "You are pregnant! I've got five kids and I know pregnant!"

The WAC Detachment gave me a baby shower. I did not stay long enough to see my replacement come in. I was really sad to leave the other women and my career. I landed in Oakland and reported to be discharged, which was mandatory in those days, and all I did was sign a form and hand over my ID card. It was just a routine, cold handover with no ceremony. I had a ticket home to Houston, TX. I took a cab to my apartment and told my husband that evening that I was pregnant.

♥**Bernice Ann Kearschner (Guion)**
**In country: January 1967 – April 1967**
**Rank: Specialist 4, US Army**
**Duty: USARV, Plans and Operations,**
**Clerk-Typist**

**Carol A. Williams (Harris)**
**In country: January 1967 – May 1967**
**Rank: Specialist 5, US Army**
**Duty: USARV, Clerk-Typist**

Little did I know when I joined the Army that I would be in the first group of non-medical women in Vietnam. Six months after I got married, I found out that I was on levy for Vietnam!

The 18-hour trip to Vietnam was surreal. The stopover in Hawaii was nice but not long enough; the fresh pineapple was quite a treat. We also stopped in the Philippines which was hot and full of cockroaches! The entire trip, I was in shock and thought that at any point I would wake from a nightmare. We arrived in Vietnam at Bien Hoa Air Base. The temperature was excruciatingly hot, heavy with the smell of vegetation.

I worked in an air-conditioned office with Colonel Benner as his secretary. Needless to say, the men in the outer office were jealous. I also enjoyed the marching drills, even though I got holes in the soles of my shoes. There were so many activities and exotics that I would go on all day mentioning them. The most memorable is while on base, one of the soldiers had a spider monkey on a leash. Some of the men were teasing him so the owner let him off the leash and of course it was I who was bitten.

Headquarters USARV was at Tan Son Nhut, close to Saigon. My new home was in a Quonset hut, next to the bunker. In the cadre office was the locked gun cabinet in case of emergency. On occasion, the huts would shake when the surrounding area was bombed.

I even had a mama-san (maid) who would sweep, make the beds and clean our clothes – all for only 12 dollars a month! However, I dreaded having to take the quinine pills to prevent malaria; they always gave me bad stomach cramps. Because of that, I almost landed in the hospital with dehydration from the dysentery. My friend Margaret and 1SG Marion Crawford nursed me back to health. Thank you, both, again, many years later.

My brave adventure off base to Cholon Commissary was different. I rode in a jeep with a skirt, nylons and a girdle (NO pantyhose then.) We were instructed to inspect the jeep very carefully in case of a bomb. Upon arrival, a small Vietnamese boy looked at my legs, smiled and said, "Number one" – a grading scale used a lot in Vietnam; "one" meant the best.

As promised, I was promoted to SP5 (Specialist 5). I did miss the monsoon rains, as I got a compassionate reassignment because of my husband's health. When the kids used to tease, "Your momma wears combat boots" – I DID!

I was proud to wear my uniform and join the fight for freedom. I now support the American Legion, AmVets, the Elks, and Disabled American Veterans (DAV).

Thank you for asking me to share my story! God Bless America!

**Evelyn "Pat" P. Foote**
**Retired as a Brigadier General**
**In country: January 1967 – December 1967**
**Rank: Major, US Army**
**Duty: USARV, Public Information Office**

I had tried earnestly to be sent to Vietnam. The Director of the Women's Army Corps in 1965-66 twice turned down my request to be assigned in Vietnam. She informed me that women replaced men so that they could serve in combat. I felt very strongly about serving anywhere, the same as my male counterparts. Fortunately, the Director was about to send me to the Advanced Course and gave me a choice – either the Women's Army Corps Advanced Course or the Adjutant General Corps Advanced Course. I chose the latter, as I felt that if I did go to the AG Corps I would be sent to Vietnam, and indeed, I was.

**♥Jo Ann Hoyer**
**In country: January 1967 – January 1968**
**Rank: Specialist 5, US Army**
**Duty: USARV, Clerk-Typist; MACV**

I graduated from high school in Louisville, KY, and talked with a few recruiters over the next few months. I decided that the Army had more places where women could be stationed, and that was behind my decision. I arrived for basic training at Fort McClellan, AL, on December 28, 1965. After clerical training at Fort Jackson, SC, I was stationed at Fort Monroe, VA. The man I was dating was reassigned to the Pentagon, and after several trips back and forth, we decided to get married. That was December 3, 1966. We took some leave and travelled to Missouri to meet his family. One day the phone rang, and the person was asking for Specialist Hoyer. My husband answered and then said they wanted me. I was astounded to hear my commander tell me that I had been selected to go to Vietnam. My husband got back to his unit and volunteered to go also.

In January 1967, I flew out of California with five other women on our way to Vietnam. We had medical reviews before we got on the plane, and the medic said I needed some shots, so of course, I got them on the spot. Then, the men were loaded on the plane first, and the women were last on. We did not get to sit together and the shots made me very sick, so I was constantly running for the bathroom on this huge cargo plane. I was embarrassed.

The plane stopped at Guam, and I thought I would go into the terminal and get a coke or something that might make me feel better. But, there were so many roaches in the building that I just left. We also stopped in the Philippines.

We landed at Bien Hoa Air Base and all the lights of the plane were turned off. A man and a woman came onto the plane with flashlights and told us to exit rapidly, stay stooped low and to run for the buses waiting to transport us. I remember thinking, "I just got here and am not going to live through the night!"

They took us to a small building where there were dirty mattresses and lots of dust and gave us sheets and pillows. It was the first time I had ever seen a mosquito net.

We went by bus to Tan Son Nhut and caused quite a stir. There were almost no women there and we were billeted in a Quonset hut. Mud and dirty water came out of the spigots.

My work was mostly just typing reports and troop movements. After two months, I applied to work in Saigon where my husband was assigned. The Army does make every effort to assign married couples together, but we were the first ones they had to deal with, I believe. We were finally put in this old French hotel. I don't really remember any of the women from the first two months and they don't remember me either. I did go to the second reunion of the Vietnam Women Veterans organization in San Antonio. My grandmother sent me a newspaper article from Louisville, KY, that had the headline, "WAC Leaves Husband for Vietnam while on Honeymoon."

I spent 13 months in country but can't say that I really saw the war. I did see the wounded.

There were orphans everywhere. They would sleep on the streets and sidewalks in these drawstring bags that looked like laundry bags. One shoeshine boy wanted to shine my shoes at a bus stop. When I wouldn't let him, he cussed me out in very specific American cuss words!

It became obvious to us that something was going to get blown up that night when all the Vietnamese workers would leave the area early. They all seemed to know, and as a result, it was hard to trust any of them.

We were able to come back to the States on the same flight. Going to Vietnam changed our minds about making the military a career. We didn't tell very many people that we had been there either.

I hope that the Vietnamese people finally have peace in their lives after so many decades of war.

*Jo Ann Hoyer Collection, (AFC/2001/001/6992), Veterans History Project, American Folklife Center, Library of Congress*

**Frances Virginia Chaffin (Gannon)**
**Retired as a Colonel**
**In country: January 1967 – July 1968**
**Rank: Lieutenant Colonel, US Army**
**Duty: MACV, Joint Staff, Third Senior Officer Advisor to the Vietnam Women's Armed Forces Corps**

*From a telephone interview with Phyllis Miller:* One of the interesting things about the assignment as Advisor to the Vietnam Women's Armed Forces Corps was that there was no real structure to the job. No one was quite sure what it would involve because the WAFC was growing rapidly, and the role of the Advisors changed as new challenges arose. The role was evolving daily. My NCO Advisor, MSG Mary Phillips, was invaluable. She was involved in the daily, hands-on training. The WAFC Director, Colonel Huong, and I spent many weeks travelling in country, making sure the women were serving in appropriate roles.

**Sherian Grace Cadoria**
**Retired as a Brigadier General**
**In country: January 1967 – October 1969**
**Rank: Major, US Army**
**Duty: USARV, Provost Marshal Administrative Officer; Qui Nhon Support Command, Protocol Officer**

I arrived at the Bien Hoa airfield in January 1967. As the senior officer (Captain) on board the flight with 149 men, I was told I was responsible for making sure we all arrived for duty. That was fine had we not refueled in Hawaii, where it took all my prayers and coaxing to get three of the men to reboard the aircraft because they had decided that perhaps staying in Hawaii was better than going to Vietnam. We arrived at night, and I counted off all 149 men. Then I heard someone say, "One straggler." I immediately said, "Oh no, all the men are accounted for." However, I was told, "you are the straggler." Since they didn't know what to do with me, they brought me to the nurses' compound and turned me over to the lieutenant colonel in charge. The next day I was picked up by two military policemen (MPs) and taken to Headquarters, US Army, Vietnam (USARV) Provost Marshal's Office at Tan Son Nhut (that's a story all by itself), where I served as the Administrative Officer for BG Harley Moore. I was housed in the BOQ with the senior officers and roomed with the commander of the WAC Detachment. USARV Headquarters was moved to Long Binh during my sixth month of service in that position, and I was housed with the WAC Detachment.

Because Headquarters USARV was still under construction when we moved to Long Binh, my office had no windowpanes. That changed rapidly when a soldier passing by the building saw me sitting at my desk and jumped through the window opening. One compelling shriek and every MP including the general surrounded the young man who was too frightened to move.

In February 1968, I was assigned as Protocol Officer for the Qui Nhon Support Command and remained there until my return to the States in late October 1969. I was housed with the doctors and nurses in the hospital area. A reporter dubbed me "Woman of the North." I reconned the areas where I would be taking the VIPs, and ensured sufficient security was provided for every visit. Having learned to fire weapons with the MPs, I rode shotgun when we picked up the VIPs, and my commanding general said I was the best secret weapon he had because visitors were more afraid of me than the VCs (Viet Cong, South Vietnamese who sympathized and fought with the North Vietnamese Army). I was promoted to major while serving in that position.

**Emma L. Thornton (Henderson)**
**In country: January 10, 1967 – May 1967**
**Rank: Specialist 4, US Army**
**Duty: USARV, Clerk-Typist**

I joined the Army in November 1965. My clerical training was at Fort McClellan, AL, and then I was assigned to Fort Benning, GA. I was honored to be among the first large group of WACs to be selected and deployed to Vietnam. As a single woman of 19, this was an adventure of a lifetime. During my short stay in Vietnam, I gained valuable experiences and learned a lot as I procured supplies for the men on the front lines.

Today, I continue to work on my book detailing some of my experiences and I thank God for a safe return and for 68 years. It was an honor to serve my country.

**♥Donna Kay Van Deventer (Turpen)**
**In country: January 10, 1967 – December 1967**
**Rank: Specialist 4, US Army**
**Duty: USARV, Engineer Division, Clerk-Typist**

**Cheranne "Cheri" Asmus (Halsey)**
**In country: January 10, 1967 – January 9, 1968**
**Rank: Specialist 5, US Army**
**Duty: USARV, Communications and Electronics, Clerk-Typist**

My time "in country" began with a steep descent to the runway at Bien Hoa Air Base, a greeting by cadre and a bus ride to temporary overnight quarters. I remember noting the broken, wired windows on the bus and the armed guards; but what bothered me most was that we couldn't brush our teeth because there was no safe water.

We were spoiled at our fenced WAC Detachment USARV compound in Tent City B at Tan Son Nhut Air Base on the outskirts of Saigon. Our new Quonset huts were named for Las Vegas casinos. We had "mama-sans" to do our laundry and keep things neat. And, no floors to buff! We had a guard at the gate, our own sandbag bunker and mosquito netting over our cots. Memorandum for Record (MFR): steel helmets were **not** designed to fit over curlers!

The sound of mortar rounds exploding and the view of tracers in the sky became routine. While at Tan Son Nhut, we also took advantage of the opportunity to explore the city of Saigon. We'd walk uphill along a golf course, past a local beer stand and catch little taxis to and from town. One of my most vivid memories of that time was the juxtaposition of fear and humor on one return from a night in town. The golf course was considered "Charlie Territory" at night. That particular evening, we heard the unmistakable sound of a "lock and load." As a group (men and women), we dropped and covered. I prayed. For what seemed an eternity, it was silent. Then, a voice with a distinctive southern drawl, announced, "Y'all hurry back! There's a Yellow Alert." I remember a prayer of thanks for a safe return and also that my underwear was dry. MFR: death or injuries were accepted risks of service. I was most afraid of being taken as a prisoner of war.

About midway through the year, all of Headquarters USARV moved to Long Binh. The workdays seemed longer but probably because of the bus rides to/from work and mess. Class B uniforms were gone, replaced by jungle fatigues and boots. Unit clubs and parties replaced Saigon night clubs. No more weekly Headquarters parades. MFR: I'm still glad "Charlie" never sighted between those water towers on Tuesday mornings and hit the parade ground.

The dearest and most lasting memory from my time in Vietnam is my late husband. We met there and married when we returned to the "World." We shared 20 wonderful years and two children. After our Army days, we settled in the San Diego area where he became a city police officer and I later went to work for the United States Navy. Someday, we, and our service, will be remembered together again at Fort Rosecrans National Cemetery in a spot that overlooks the city he always swore to serve and protect.

I look forward to reunions with the outstanding women I served with so long ago. I am both humbled and proud to remember my Army service and my time in Vietnam. I am proud that we did our jobs well, earned many promotions and that we were part of that time and place. I'm especially proud of those who completed careers in the Army. Yet, I am humbled by all the women who serve today. Their opportunities, achievements and sacrifices are just awesome. I hope in some small way our collective honorable service in Vietnam helped to advance the roles of women in the military. Today, military women are going into far harsher places, further into harm's way and more and more side-by-side with their male counterparts. More women are coming home maimed in body and spirit, and certainly more have died. They deserve our salutes, our thanks and our support. MFR: If there was a job for me and I was asked to go to war again, my answer in a heartbeat would be, "YES!"

**Christine "Cookie" Baker**
**In country: January 10, 1967 – January 9, 1968**
**Rank: Specialist 5, US Army**
**Duty: USARV, 1ˢᵗ Aviation Brigade, Clerk-Typist**

**Martha Duncan (Jackson)**
**In country: January 10, 1967 – January 9, 1968**
**Rank: Specialist 5, US Army**
**Duty: USARV, Surgeon's Office, Clerk-Typist**

***From a telephone interview:*** I joined the WAC when I was 20 years old. I lived in Memphis, TN, at the time and I wanted to go to college, but there was no money to do it. The GI bill sounded like a good deal.

My mom reluctantly signed the papers. She had 12 children; three of the boys had joined but I was the only girl who joined.

My basic training was at Fort McClellan, AL, and I had some training at Fort Benjamin Harrison, IN, before I was stationed at Fort Lee, VA.

I did not volunteer for Vietnam. I was one of the first big group of women to be selected to go and I took a lot of teasing when I first got my orders.

Getting off that plane in Vietnam was surreal; I had never been outside of Tennessee, so it was actually kind of exciting to look around and see Saigon on the ride to the barracks. We were in open barracks, so I had lots of roommates although I don't remember too many of them. We had freedom to move around, sightseeing and riding in taxis in the city. I don't have any really bad memories from that time. The poverty was awful.

One of the bad things I encountered was a Vietnamese woman who looked a lot like me. She had a black GI father and I talked with her briefly. The biracial children and adults were horribly ostracized in Vietnam.

I came back to the States and processed out because I had changed my mind about reenlisting. Back in Memphis, TN, I looked around and saw that there was no work, and after staying home for about a month, I told my mother I wanted to leave. I went to Washington, DC, with a friend who said she had a job there and I got a job working for an insurance company. I met my husband and we got married in 1969. I have three children, and three grandchildren.

**Gloria J. Grenfell (Fowler) (Leigh)**
**In country: January 10, 1967 – January 9, 1968**
**Rank: Specialist 5, US Army**
**Duty: USARV, Office of the Adjutant General, Comptroller,**
**Clerk-Typist**

I was stationed at Fort Leonard Wood, MO. I was called to the commander's office, hoping it was news about my transfer to Georgia. Not to be! I remember her words, "You have been chosen."

My thoughts about why/when didn't matter, only how was I going to tell my family. They handled the difficulty of the situation with dignity/pride. I departed from Oakland, CA. Many protesters made it scary/confusing for all. Hugs/kisses/tears – we said goodbye. I walked away and turned around for one last look. When I reached the plane, my thought was, "Please let me come home to my family."

It was a long flight with several stops, wearing dress greens/heels. When we arrived in Vietnam, it was dark and being bombed – fear was real! We departed the plane and ran to a bus that took us away. Our first pit stop was a camp full of guys, and we had the pleasure of using their outdoor latrine. Finally, we arrived at our new home. We met 1SG Crawford, who was great. She showed us dignity, courage, fun, taking on challenges and kicking butt. She and our commanders took good care of all of us.

My strongest memories:

- Saigon - dress greens/heels
- Long Binh - fatigues/combat boots/helmets
- Our welcome party in Saigon
- Visiting the hospital

- Drill team
- Being assigned to the Bob Hope show
- Promotion in rank
- Helicopter ride
- Rest and Relaxation to Kuala Lumpur and Hong Kong
- Most importantly, the wonderful women I met who became an important part of my life, friends forever
- Politics of war - reality

Coming home to the US would be one of the most difficult experiences of my life; there was no support/dignity, especially for the wounded and those who perished. It is **still** a silent heartbreak for me.

I was thankful to return and have a fulfilling life.

I support all veterans.

**Vicki Ann Heydron**
**In country: January 10, 1967 – January 9, 1968**
**Rank: Specialist 5, US Army**
**Duty: USARV, G2, Clerk-Typist; US Army Engineer Construction Agency, Vietnam**

> **Athena and I**
> The dark night wind of Fate
> Howls now about my chimney.
> It carries the rain of blood lost in war,
> Of death and pain
> Suffered in defense of me
> And of my heritage.
> I listen and weep
> For the strong arms now still,
> Arms that once held me,
> Caressed me softly.
> But I do more than weep,
> For within my house
> There abides another;
> Together we endure
> Heartbreak, uncertainty,
> And the knowledge,

Loud in the howling wind,
That we have helped
To kill.

At dawn we stand ready,
Athena and I,
To fight in bitter loneliness
A war of patience,
Using as our weapons
The skill in our hands,
The alertness of our minds,
And the power in our hearts –
Women's hearts –
To love our country
And its men
And bear all things
For their sakes.

SP4 Vicki Heydron, WAC Detachment, USARV (1967)
*Source: US Army Women's Museum*

**♥Carol J. Matisz (Miller)**
**In country: January 10, 1967 – January 9, 1968**
**Rank: Specialist 5, US Army**
**Duty: USARV, Communications and Electronics, Clerk-Typist**

*This is a reprint in part of a letter received in September 1997 from Carol's brother, Martin Matisz, Jr. These are his words:*
Growing up as Carol's little brother in Pennsylvania, I heard many stories of her exploits in the Army, and particularly about her service in Vietnam. She had many fond memories of her sister soldiers, and thought of you all often. As a former Vietnam-era Marine, I know what it is like to be a member of a band of brothers. To this day, I know I was once part of something bigger than myself. Regardless of the circumstances or relative popularity of our efforts, we stuck by each other through it all, with our heads held high and our honor

intact. I know this is how Carol felt about her service and her friends. *Source: Vietnam Memory Book 2000*

Carolyn L. Mitchell      Carolyn A. Moore
(Wiggins)

**Carolyn L. Mitchell (Wiggins)**
**In country: January 10, 1967 – January 9, 1968**
**Rank: Specialist 5, US Army**
**Duty: USARV, G1, Clerk-Typist**

**Carolyn A. Moore**
**In country: January 10, 1967 – January 9, 1968**
**Rank: Specialist 4, US Army**
**Duty: USARV, Information Office, Clerk-Typist**

**Beverly "Bev" Mounter (Evans)**
**In country: January 10, 1967 – January 9, 1968**
**Rank: Specialist 5, US Army**
**Duty: USARV, G4, Ammunition Division, Clerk-Typist**

**Comments and Memories:** Carol Matisz, married Miller, and I always found this story quite funny. We both arrived in Tan Son Nhut about the same time. She was chosen as our "Bay Sergeant." Her area was right next to mine. We couldn't stand each other! I wanted to keep a wild parrot and had received permission from our commander to do so. Carol had a fit! She hated birds. I had the parrot  about a month, but since he had bitten my mama-san, I let him loose in the wild. Carol came in from work that night and sarcastically asked where my bird was. I told her that I didn't know; that it must be in the barracks somewhere. She went berserk! I started laughing while she screamed at me,

"Mounter! You'd better find that bird by the time I get back!" Finally, I told her I let it go. God! We hated each other. About two to three weeks later, we had both just come in from work, and she asked me if I wanted to join her for a couple of drinks. Since that time, we have been good friends, even after returning from Vietnam. We communicated at least twice each year until she passed away. I miss her so much. She always worried about my health, since I had developed cancer. She was supposed to outlive me! Her heart was made of gold. She was genuine and true to her friends. I love her so much and miss her more! *Source: Vietnam Memory Book 2000*

Lillian Sampson    Holly A. Smith    Dianne P. Tipton
(Grasham)                              (Turbyfill)

**Lillian Sampson (Grasham)**
**In country: January 10, 1967 – January 9, 1968**
**Rank: Specialist 5, US Army**
**Duty: USARV, G2, Clerk-Typist**

I had my 20th birthday in Vietnam and was with my best friend, Dianne Turbyfill.

**Holly A. Smith**
**In country: January 10, 1967 – January 9, 1968**
**Rank: Specialist 5, US Army**
**Duty: USARV, G1, Clerk-Typist**

Member of the WAC Detachment drill team.

**Dianne P. Tipton (Turbyfill)**
**In country: January 10, 1967 – January 9, 1968**
**Rank: Specialist 5, US Army**
**Duty: USARV, G2, Clerk-Typist**

**Patricia "Pat" L. Brooks (Hildebrand)**
**In country: January 10, 1967 – August 1968**
**Rank: Specialist 5, US Army**
**Duty: USARV, G3 and G4, Clerk-Typist**

**Janet F. Singer**
**In country: January 10, 1967 – August 1968**
**Rank: Staff Sergeant, US Army**
**Duty: USARV, Adjutant General, Clerk-Typist**

**Reya Monte**
**In country: January 10, 1967 – October 1968**
**Rank: Staff Sergeant, US Army**
**Duty: USARV, G3, Clerk-Typist**

Reya Monte was promoted to SSG while in Vietnam. She served in the military for eight years. Reya shared this story: "One scary thing that happened was when the ammo dump blew up and I was thrown out of the top bunk." Reya loved playing with the Vietnamese children. A picture of her playing "Ring Around the Rosie" with the children from the nearby village is in another section of this book.

**Loretta J. Bohlke (Meredith)**
**In country: January 11, 1967 – January 10, 1968**
**Rank: Specialist 4, US Army**
**Duty: USARV, Engineer Division, Clerk-Typist**

Member of the WAC Detachment drill team.

**Virginia Pearl Dubics (Pimental)**
**In country: January 11, 1967 – January 10, 1968**
**Rank: Specialist 4, US Army**
**Duty: USARV, Adjutant General, Clerk-Typist**

**Penelope "Penny" L. Lewis (Wilcox)**
**In country: January 11, 1967 – January 10, 1968**
**Rank: Specialist 5, US Army**
**Duty: USARV, Engineer Division, Clerk-Typist**

**Juliette Anita Dortch (Coleman-Hallman)**
**Retired as a Chief Warrant Officer 4**
**In country: January 11, 1967 – March 1968**
**Rank: Specialist 5, US Army**
**Duty: USARV, G4, Clerk-Typist; First Guidon Bearer**

I was chosen to serve in the first WAC Detachment in a combat zone since WWII. When another female soldier and I were ordered to the commander's office for congratulations on our selection, I asked "Why me?" Well, the Oath of Enlistment says, ". . . if called to defend against enemies foreign or domestic. . ." I had committed and now I was to complete. Was I scared? Yes and no. I was young, 19, and had not been too far from home.

I went on military leave to break the news to my family who, at first, did not believe that this could be happening to me. We departed Travis Air Force Base on a C-140 cargo plane, and flew sitting backwards with sack lunches of bologna and cheese on white bread. We arrived at Tan Son Nhut Air Base, Saigon, in January 1967 – very long trip. We were met by the WAC Detachment cadre members, (among the best cadre throughout my career, against which I often measured others.)

We were billeted in Quonset huts; each named after a hotel in Las Vegas. They did not look like them at all (smile). But they were safe, clean and livable, and we had each other.

I became a logistics clerk at Headquarters, USARV. I liked my job. I was fully aware of the number of casualties to our soldiers. I actually saw the lists and the home areas of the United States of the soldiers. I saw the names of at least two persons I went to school with because Graves Registration came under Logistics.

I was the first Guidon Bearer for the USARV WAC Detachment. I was always afraid of hitting the commander, and she would say, "Now, do not hit me or let it drop." I took this responsibility seriously. 1SG Marion Crawford formed a Drill Team, and we performed at reviews, parades and special occasions as protocol dictated. We visited orphanages and interacted with the children.

In the monsoon season, it was wet for months. It rained so much our beds were floating along with most everything that was not anchored down. Everything smelled, the mud was red, and it got into everything. Yes, I grew up with red clay in Alabama and now I have it in Georgia – just cannot get away from the red earth. But the heat, mugginess and rain in Vietnam was not like Alabama.

About halfway through my tour, USARV Headquarters moved to Long Binh, 27 miles north of Saigon. My R&R trips were to Tokyo and Thailand – very educational and I needed the rest. I could sleep and get up when I wanted. Wow!

The 24th Evacuation Hospital at Long Binh received in-country wounded personnel prior to their being transported to the States. Our assigned dining facility (mess hall) was with the hospital staff, patients and soldiers. We were blessed with having some closeness with our soldiers. We assisted with writing letters and visited sometimes just to talk and encourage them.

There were times, upon returning to the States wearing my USARV Patch, I was told to take it off, and that I should be ashamed. Never was I asked if I was authorized the wearing.

I continue to suffer and hurt. I tend to become very anxious and want to hide away; it sometimes gets very bad. But, I press on, working it out by staying very busy (volunteering, gardening, baking, etc.) and doing things for others.

I stay as close to the military as I can, as it has been a major part of my life. Working with soldiers in the US Army Reserve, I stress that they maintain discipline to understand the reality of being called up to support wars – as I experienced at an early age.

After 9/11 and the mobilization of some of my unit members, some have said to me, "I now understand what you were trying to explain to me, Chief. I now know that you cared and just wanted me to be able to make it." My life has taught me that preparation is the best approach. At age 19, I was not ready for what was to come.

The lessons I learned from Vietnam, the Army and from my parents, Mr. and Mrs. Goodman (Josephine) Dortch, Sr., pushed me to always do my best in everything I did. You never know when you will be on the receiving end of your involvement.

My brother Buddy was severely injured in Vietnam the year after I returned. Siblings were not supposed to be deployed into hostile areas at the same time, so after I returned he was deployed and later wounded. That was very hard for us all, especially him. He continues to battle because of his injuries. I am blessed to have him still through all of his health issues. There are many like him. I have learned much from his non-bitterness and humbleness. His wounds are visible; others are not, but they are there.

I would like to thank everyone for making this book possible for us. Your selfless involvement is truly an attribute to be admired and appreciated. I salute you. I pray God's bountiful blessings for you and yours. And, to my fellow Women Vietnam Veterans I thank you for your loyalty and service to our country. I am proud to be counted among you and I call you Sisters in Arms.

**Delores Ann Bala (Liederbach)**
**In country: January 11, 1967 – August 1968**
**Rank: Specialist 5, US Army**
**Duty: USARV, 1st Aviation Brigade, Clerk-Typist**

**Donna J. Dear**
**Retired as a Sergeant Major**
**In country: January 11, 1967 – August 1968**
**Rank: Staff Sergeant, US Army**
**Duty: USARV, G4, General Materiel Division, Clerk-Typist**

I was at the WAC Detachment, Fort Hood, TX, when I was selected to serve in Vietnam. I did basic and advanced individual training at Fort McClellan, AL, and then was assigned to Fort Hood, TX.

I hoped that I would get to see my brother who was serving in Vietnam. He would probably want to come home when I got there. My mother had really mixed emotions about having two children in Vietnam. I flew out of Oakland, CA, with a stop in Hawaii. I was the only woman on the plane. We landed in Bien Hoa and I stayed overnight in a very small wooden building with black curtains. I was the only one in this small building and it was a room with bunk beds. 1SG Marion Crawford and Field First Betty Benson picked me up and we drove to Saigon, Tent City B. I was assigned there for five months. I was a clerk-typist in G4 Logistics.

Public Affairs did a story on my brother and me because we were the first brother-sister team in Vietnam. We went throughout Saigon taking pictures with another WAC (Peggy Sigley) and another GI and they took pictures of us at the market, at the palace and several other locations.

One morning I woke up to find a rifle round lying on my pillow. It didn't dawn on me until much later that day that the round could have hit me! I still have it.

The whole headquarters relocated to Long Binh where I worked for 13 months. We were less than a quarter mile from the ammo dump, which was hit by the Viet Cong. Everybody was on their way to work and one of the civilian women hid beneath the First Sergeant's desk! It was a tremendously loud explosion.

We spent many evenings on the patio at the WAC Detachment under a large parachute. We finally got a little blow-up wading pool that we enjoyed.

When I got ready to board the plane to return to the States we were at Bien Hoa and came under sniper fire. We had to return to the terminal until things calmed down. I remember thinking that it was time to go home and we couldn't even get on the plane. When we finally got on the plane, there was just a silence – no one said anything until after we were airborne. At 30,000 feet, we all cheered and finally felt safe and knew we were on our way home. We felt safe for the first time since we arrived.

I went to Fort Monroe, VA, for my next assignment and I worked in Personnel. I spent 27 years in the service.

## Linda K. Ostermeier (McDermith)
**In country: January 12, 1967 – January 11, 1968**
**Rank: Specialist 4, US Army**
**Duty: USARV, G4, Clerk-Typist**

Stationed at Fort Sam Houston, TX, I told my Sergeant Major I was volunteering for duty in Vietnam. I was young and fearless. I can see her expression when she told me, "The stench over there is so bad, you will not like it." My Mom's disbelief came in her calm response, "Oh, you are not. Of course, it would be nice if you were going to Hawaii."

Oh, so-o-o many memories from the backward-facing ride to Vietnam with numerous fellow soldiers in the open belly of that huge plane. I helped serve the on-board meal. I wonder how many of those soldiers made it back home.

Our first WAC home was Tent City B, where we lived in Quonset huts. My two-foot stuffed black gorilla with red lips was kept at the foot of my bed. In the dark, one bed-check patrol was concerned as to what it was. This gorilla traveled with me during my three years of active duty. (My car license plate is GORILLA.)

The Bob Hope Show Tour was coming to our area. The WAC Drill Team was to perform, but the stage was not big enough, so we were canceled.

One evening, a flare landed in our WAC compound. A bit frightened, we didn't know what it was until it landed. I pulled a fellow WAC (Mary S) away from it.

Once, some male soldiers pushed a drunken soldier over our compound fence; I'm certain they got in trouble for that stunt.

Our detachment's move to the newly built Long Binh compound was an adventure. We now lived in nice two-story wooden buildings. We were near a hospital and would constantly see and hear helicopters bringing in the wounded. I sometimes visited them.

We could hear explosions. On one payday, when cash was routinely being distributed outside, vibrations from explosions blew the cash off the table!

I was taken to Headquarters at night to frisk Vietnamese women, but we found nothing hidden on them.

On August 13, 1967, while working at my desk at USARV Headquarters, my co-workers and I heard a loud explosion. We ran to the windows and saw nothing, but back at my desk, the light fixture above had a cracked covering with a bullet in it. Wow! This was the noise we heard! Later, to my pleasant surprise, the office colonel and my commanding officer presented me with a plaque, "Lucky Thirteen Linda."

Vietnam left me with an overall experience I will always remember, along with little things like appreciation for having water to drink.

Today (2014), I am 67 and recently retired after 43 years with the State of Illinois in addition to working two off-and-on part-time jobs I enjoyed. I have a 44-year-old son and a 10-year-old granddaughter. I am blessed with no health issues. I have a strong faith and know God has been good to me.

**Sharon A. Ridout**
**In country: January 12, 1967 – January 11, 1968**
**Rank: Specialist 4, US Army**
**Duty: USARV, Engineer Division, Clerk-Typist**

## Linda S. Pritchard (Woolm)
### In country: January 13, 1967 – January 12, 1968
### Rank: Specialist 5, US Army
### Duty: USARV, Provost Marshal's Office, Clerk-Typist

I remember getting my orders for Vietnam while I was stationed at Fort Dix, NJ. Somehow, I knew I would be going as part of the large group that was to be sent to Vietnam in 1967. I shared my premonition with a friend just a week before I actually received my orders. Still, when I received my orders I was in shock and wondered if this was really something I could do. I took two weeks of leave to visit family and friends before my departure. When I arrived in California to catch my plane, I was told they had forgotten to manifest me on the same flight with the rest of the women heading to Vietnam. I was put up in a motel that night and departed the next day on a flight that consisted of all men with the same destination. This, too, was very intimidating because I did not know how I would be treated. At this point, I considered going AWOL. Actually, they were kind of concerned that I was going to a war zone. The trip was long and exhausting, riddled with fear of the unknown. When I arrived in Vietnam January 13, 1967, I was greeted by SFC Betty Benson and whisked away to the WAC compound.

During my time in Saigon, I had both good and bad experiences as I am sure everyone did.

Good Experiences:

Some of my good experiences were going into Saigon shopping and eating at the Continental Palace, walking around the city and going to the zoo. I also made many good friends with whom I enjoyed spending time. We had very little free time. During my time in Vietnam, I went on two R&Rs, both to Thailand. Thailand is a beautiful place and the people were very friendly and treated us very well. Shopping was amazing and exciting in trying to get the best price for whatever it was you wanted to buy. I went on some tours and I remember the elephants and how majestic they were, and the oriental dancers were beautiful and elegant. I also took the floating market tour and visited Buddhist temples. These days were memorable and gave us a break from the reality of war, allowed us to sleep in a real bed, eat good food, go swimming and generally enjoy the better side of life.

Another good experience was attending the Bob Hope USO show. We also were the only American group ever allowed to tour the South Vietnamese President's Palace (President Nguyễn Văn Thiệu). The Palace was very elegant, filled with beautiful art work much like you would see in a museum.

Bad Experiences:

1. Military men treating us like we were sent to Vietnam to service them. Whenever we would leave the WAC compound, they would yell obscene things to us and treat us as though we were their property.
2. Living in such cramped quarters with fear that something would happen to us and we would not see our family again.
3. Eating at the 24th Evacuation Hospital and seeing the toll on American soldiers who would be brought in after a mass casualty event.
4. Monsoon season when the water would be up to the bottom of our cots and all kind of debris floating through our living area.
5. "Red Alerts" when I prayed I would survive this tour and make it home.

Once I was safe at home, watching on TV all the caskets of fallen soldiers who lost their lives during the Tet Offensive and not being able to control my crying for them and their families.

**♥Janice Gwen Curtis**
**In country: January 13, 1967 – January 12, 1968**
**Rank: Specialist 5, US Army**
**Duty: USARV, Adjutant General, Clerk-Typist**

Janice was 26 and had been a secretary before she entered the Army. She was one of the young women who volunteered for Vietnam. During that time, she wrote, "I wanted to come to Vietnam because I just wanted to do as much as I could in this war. Vietnam has many problems and I would like to see this country settled in peace. The problems can only be solved slowly. It can't be done overnight no matter how much the people back home might wish for it. The dirt and dust is depressing sometimes but the girls seem quite happy. We all get along beautifully, more so than in the States. In fact, I love the new fatigues. They are cool and comfortable."

Janice intended to travel "just anywhere in the United States" after she got home.

*This information comes from an old and battered document. The document does not have a title or an author.*

**Joeanne "Jo" Harris (Burr)**
**In country: January 13, 1967 – January 12, 1968**
**Rank: Specialist 5, US Army**
**Duty: USARV, G4, General Materiel Division, Clerk-Typist**

**Comments and Memories:** I was on CQ (Charge of Quarters) duty one night and someone called to report that we were on Red alert. I didn't report to the officer in charge and only alerted the hootch I stayed in. I completely forgot to report to anyone else. *Source: Vietnam Memory Book 2000*

**Patricia "Pat" A. Wilcoxon**
**Retired as a Sergeant First Class**
**In country: January 13, 1967 – February 1968**
**Rank: Specialist 5, US Army**
**Duty: USARV, 1ˢᵗ Signal Brigade, 69ᵗʰ Signal, Clerk-Typist/Switchboard Operator**

Initially assigned to Tan Son Nhut, there was no switchboard slot available for me and I worked as a clerk-typist. When the WAC Detachment moved to Long Binh, I was assigned to the post switchboard and eventually became its Chief Operator.

**Rosario "Rosie" Bermudez (Tinsley)**
**In country: January 15, 1967 – August 1968**
**Rank: Specialist 5, US Army**
**Duty: USARV, Surgeon General's Office, Clerk-Typist**

**Comments and Memories:** On my way to Vietnam, I was the only female on the Air Force plane. One of the soldiers asked if I was a stewardess. When I said no, he then asked if I was a Girl Scout leader. I thought that was pretty funny! *Source: Vietnam Memory Book 2000*

**Faye S. Conaway**
**In country: January 16, 1967 – January 15, 1968**
**Rank: Specialist 5, US Army**
**Duty: USARV, G1; TDY USO in Pleiku, Chu Lai, Phu Bai, Saigon**

For three months I trained and rehearsed for a performance called "Show Boat Jamboree" – and after an opening performance at the officers' club, I got the word. I was on a levy to Vietnam. I found myself in Vietnam, being driven through Saigon to join the troops at Tan Son Nhut.

The heat, the smells, the erratic driving in and out of lanes, and yet the most overwhelming surprise was the Vietnamese women screaming to me as we drove by calling out, "Soul Sister, Soul Sister."

I was among the first 45 women assigned to the newly activated WAC Detachment in the first such unit established in a war zone since WWII. There were many things that were hard to take: the malaria pills, the 24/7 assignment in un-air-conditioned offices (and quarters), the men who mostly ignored my presence, openly scratching crotches. The men, including the officers in charge, were obviously displeased having a woman assigned to their unit. I was assigned to Headquarters USARV, G1, and there were some hard-nosed colonels who went out of their way to make it unpleasant for me. I had never known direct discrimination in my entire life. I was 19 years old. I would go home to my barracks and cry every night. The other female troops were both inquisitive and supportive. Finally, I went to talk to my company commander, Captain Peggy Ready, to discuss my situation. I tried to tell her, diplomatically, what the problem was – I *couldn't* tell her they hated me – but I just cried like a baby and put my head down. When I looked up, Captain Ready was also in tears. Somehow, at that moment I knew that everything was going to be all right. I was going to make it. 1SG Marion Crawford and Captain Ready were like mothers to me and the other women in our detachment. I will forever be grateful for their support.

Sometime after that, I was interviewed about performing in USO shows. I was trained to escort movie stars as they would arrive. Then I was practicing with an enlisted USO Rock 'n' Roll band and going on tours with them. I would return to the barracks each night and go on to my office assignment the following morning as a clerk-typist. I performed with the "Black Patches," and "Faye and the Rogues." We entertained troops of our WAC Detachment and men throughout South Vietnam and, it was not only for the Army, but the Navy, Marines and Air Force as well. Other WACs were also with me and we not only entertained, but we were members of the WAC Detachment Drill Team, too. We went by escorted jeeps to all the bases and besides singing, we danced and had drinks and meals with the men. One night during monsoon season, I was running to the outhouse and lost my way. I tried running toward voices I heard, but fell into a ravine and hurt my neck and back. (I began to show signs of this accident about ten years ago – bulging discs and pinched nerves.) I'm currently in the medical program at the VA Medical Center in Kansas City, MO. My benefit is for Agent Orange Diabetes.

I am now out of the Army and a retired teacher. I have taught K-12 students, private students, sang and directed choirs in many churches and look forward to the next chapter in my life.

**Mary Ann Stedman (Vasas)**
**In country: January 21, 1967 – January 19, 1968**
**Rank: Specialist 5, US Army**
**Duty: USARV, G4, Clerk-Typist**

We were all so very young when we arrived in Vietnam. Our cadre was only a few years older than we were, and they did a wonderful job being our parents away from home.

Some of us suffered homesickness, and others like me took a few weeks to adjust to the climate. We worked long, hard hours, mostly six and a half days a week.

The work bus picked us up at the WAC compound and took us to breakfast at the mess hall then on to our workstations. The same routine happened for lunch, dinner and home at night after our day at work.

One of my fondest memories was at Christmas time when Penny Freeman and I decided to decorate General Plouger's office while he was in the field. Well to make a long story short, he came back early. We weren't done with the decorating. He caught us in the act. We told him how sorry we were; he told us that we made an old general's heart glad. I still have my thank-you note that he gave me.

**Donna Ann Lowery**
**Retired as a Sergeant Major**
**In country: January 31, 1967 – August 19, 1968**
**Rank: Staff Sergeant, US Army**
**Duty: USARV, Special Troops Personnel, Personnel Records Clerk; S4, Noncommissioned Officer in Charge**

Late in 1966, the women in my unit at Fort Monmouth, NJ, were told that someone would be selected to go to Vietnam as part of the first WAC Detachment assigned there. I had no interest in going because I had a great job, a wonderful boyfriend and loved being stationed in New Jersey. I didn't pay much attention. However, several weeks later and much to my chagrin, my 1SG called me into her office and said I was hand-selected for the Vietnam assignment! My initial orders were delayed. I arrived three weeks later than the first group of women. I was the only woman coming off that Braniff Airlines plane on January 31, 1967. We had to circle for 45 minutes due to ground fire. I could not have imagined then the significance of actually being assigned to that WAC Detachment, the changes the assignment would make in my life and the attitude and the place that the unit would take in history. The friendships I made from that assignment have lasted for more than 45 years. They mean the world to me.

Until I served in Vietnam, I had no interest in a military career. Somehow, I went from being a "scatterbrained" woman, as my friend Precilla Landry

Wilkewitz says, to a committed leader. In retrospect, I believe several things influenced me. I was the first in our unit to be promoted to Staff Sergeant. At the age of 21 in Vietnam, I was tasked with supervising men and later a woman as part of my responsibilities. I found my passion and commitment in leading them. I went from Vietnam to Germany, where at age 21, I was the youngest first sergeant in the Army, outside of combat. I went on to have three more companies. I loved being the First Sergeant of each and every one of them! I was also greatly influenced by 1SG Marion Crawford and SFC Betty Benson. They are truly two of the best leaders I encountered in my 26 years in the Army. I have always felt close to them.

Although I was sent over as a clerk-typist, I had actually graduated from personnel school at Fort Leonard Wood, MO. While in-processing at Tent City B, one of the men suggested I ask to be assigned as a personnel records clerk. I did and got the job. Initially, I was the only woman working in the Special Troops personnel office in Saigon. When we were at Tent City B in Saigon, it was just a short walk to work. After the WAC Detachment moved to Long Binh, I took a military taxi because I was about five miles or so away from where everyone else in the unit worked; the rest of the women took the bus. When Long Binh was overrun during the 1968 Tet Offensive, I was at the personnel office and remained there during the hostilities. The other women had all returned to the Detachment on the bus. The defense plan for those of us women at the barracks was to hide in a particular ditch. If the Viet Cong got near, we were to jump up and kill the enemy. Of course, the enemy had weapons and we did not! I was very young and too naïve at the time to really process everything. Today, as I look back, I cannot believe we were sent over in Class B uniforms, wore heels and nylons, and did not have any weapons. But, we had a beautician in our compound because that is what our Director insisted we have. All I can say today is, OMG!

I was not required to eat at the 24th Evacuation Hospital like so many of the women. I am thankful I did not see most of the wounded and the deceased. I know some of my friends have PTSD and terrible nightmares about what they saw. Many of them quit going to the mess hall and ate snacks from the Post Exchange to get them through.

I really enjoyed working with all of the men in both the Personnel and S4 offices of Special Troops. The man who recommended that I ask to be assigned to Personnel was Larry Thompson. We dated all of 1967. We lost contact more than 40 years ago. I believe he was from Gardena, CA, which is in the Los Angeles area. I would love to be able to find him and see how his life has turned out. Mine has been pretty great!

# FEBRUARY

*Memory Lane: The Twenty-fifth Amendment to the US Constitution, establishing the succession to the Presidency, is enacted; the American Basketball Association is formed.*
*Song: "Kind of a Drag" by The Buckinghams*

**Anne Marie Lally**
**In country: February 1967 – June 1967**
**Rank: Specialist 5, US Army**
**Duty: USARV, G1 and G4, Clerk-Typist**

It became necessary for me to depart from Vietnam after a little more than five months of duty. A tropical disease got the better of me and I was sent to Hawaii for the last year of my enlistment.

I have been a Sister of Saint Joseph, Brentwood, NY, for the past 37 years. Presently, I am the Chairperson of the Religious Studies Department and Campus Minister in an all-girls Catholic high school. It is always with great pride that I share my military experience with my students, most especially my time in Vietnam.

When I was a young woman, I joined the Women's Army Corps with the hope of being of some service to the United States of America. My enlistment soon took me to the war in Vietnam of which I knew little. I learned many lessons on respecting life during that time. Once I arrived in Vietnam and settled in, myself and several of our WACs volunteered during our free time to assist in a local Vietnamese orphanage. Never before had I seen such poverty. Groups of ten very small children sat in a circle while a bigger child, maybe ten years of age, fed each little one using one spoon and one bowl of food until the bowl was empty. I learned an important lesson from that experience: respecting the gift of living in America where I never had to worry about where my next meal was coming from or would there be enough food for me.

When we American women first arrived at USARV headquarters, we worked from 7:30 in the morning to 7:30 at night, seven days a week. Fresh fruit was not available to us in the mess hall. One day word was out that a cargo of fresh fruit from America had arrived. When I went on my supper break that day, I received a bright, fresh orange. I was amazed at how a piece of fruit could mean so much. As I was returning that evening to the barracks, I passed the barbed wire fence that separated the military post from the local people. I began to notice how the people just quietly stood there watching us as we walked next to the fence. Then I realized, they too had heard of the fresh fruit. On that day, I was given an opportunity to do some good. Respecting life also meant that I share what I have been given with those who have not. I watched in awe as every American service woman I walked with put her hand through the barbed wire fence and gave away her fruit, just as I had.

**♥Penny "Tex" Arlene Freeman (Choiniere)**
**In country: February 1967 – February 1968**
**Rank: Specialist 5, US Army**
**Duty: USARV, G4, Office of the Inspector General, Clerk-Typist**

**Comments and Memories:** Seeing Captain Peggy Ready, the commanding officer, when I arrived in Vietnam. We recognized each other at once. We first met during my basic training at Fort McClellan, AL. During a night march, an infiltrator entered our platoon; as the last member of the platoon (the shortest one, of course), it was my duty to capture the infiltrator. The infiltrator turned and began running; I gave chase, as instructed. Suddenly, the infiltrator stopped. There was so much momentum, I couldn't stop, so I jumped on the infiltrator's back and grabbed her around the neck. The infiltrator was led away by our platoon leader. The next morning, 1LT Peggy Ready came in to inspect our tent. As she stood in front of me, I noticed angry red marks on her neck. It was at this point that I realized who the infiltrator had been! She gave me an "I know who you are, and I know what you did" look before moving on. When she saw me arrive at the WAC Detachment in Vietnam, she looked at the other members of the cadre and said something about packing their bags, because the war would be over in a couple of weeks. Yes, I was embarrassed by that one, but we laughed about it when we saw each other on March 5, 1999.
*Source: Vietnam Memory Book 2000*

***Donna Lowery:*** Penny and I met in Vietnam. We became close friends after she moved from Florida to Washington. She was so impressed with the services she received from the Washington State Department of Veterans Affairs at the 1999 Homecoming Conference that she moved to Washington. She became active in the local American Legion Post 94. Penny was widowed and had three daughters. Penny served in the Army from July 1965 – June 1969. She served in the Navy from January 1976 to December 1978. Penny had a Bachelor of Arts in Psychology from Eastern Connecticut State University and was a member of Psi Chi Honor Society for Psychology Students. After residing in Washington for a number of years, Penny moved back to Florida where she died in 2012.

**♥Janet Elise Lupher**
**In country: February 4, 1967 – November 1968**
**Rank: Staff Sergeant, US Army**
**Duty: USARV, G1, Clerk-Typist; MACV, G4**

Janet enlisted in the Air Force after high school. She served for four years, and when her term of enlistment was finished, she joined the Army. Her service included tours in Germany and Vietnam.

**Hester "Peanut" E. Miller**
**In country: February 6, 1967 – November 1968**
**Rank: Specialist 5, US Army**
**Duty: USARV, G4, Clerk-Typist**

As a projectionist at Long Binh, while showing a movie one night, I went into the booth to change over to the second projector and realized the first reel had broken. There was film from the floor almost to the ceiling. I never realized how big a mess it was and how much "fun" it was to rewind the tape on the reel. *Source: Vietnam Memory Book 2000*

**Donna K. Bramley**
**In country: February 10, 1967 – January 9, 1968**
**Rank: Specialist 5, US Army**
**Duty: USARV, G2, Clerk-Typist**

Instead of waiting for the WAC bus to go get our shots (like we were supposed to), we got a ride in a deuce and a half (2.5-ton truck). We all hopped on the back and as soon as the driver pulled off, it threw us all on the ground. I think I probably got it the worst. I had no skin on my knees, elbows and face; plus all those areas were full of gravel. The doctor cleaned out all the wounds and I was on my way. I thought I got by with that one until I was offered a Purple Heart. Naturally, I refused it and 1SG Marion Crawford wasn't happy when I had to tell her the entire story.

**Lauren F. Collins**
**In country: February 10, 1967 – February 9, 1968**
**Rank: Specialist 5, US Army**
**Duty: USARV, G1, Clerk-Typist**

**Patricia A. Ogg**
**In country: February 10, 1967 – February 9, 1968**
**Rank: Specialist 4, US Army**
**Duty: USARV, G2, Clerk-Typist**

**Mildred "Moth" A. Park**
**Retired as a Master Sergeant**
**In country: February 10, 1967 – February 9, 1968**
**Rank: Staff Sergeant, US Army**
**Duty: USARV, G1, Administrative NCO**

♥**Edith "Edie" Ann Powell**
**In country: February 10, 1967 – February 9, 1968**
**Rank: Specialist 5, US Army**
**Duty: USARV, 1ˢᵗ Aviation Brigade, Clerk-Typist**

### Why are the WACs in Vietnam?

"Why are the WACs in Vietnam?" men ask.
"Why are they sent to do men's tasks?"
Women have no use on a battlefield.
While in a place like this, they could be killed.

As the war struggles on from day to day,
Danger increases in every way.
Their lives, their minds and their hearts are at stake.
At any moment, death can overtake.

We're here, because like you, we heard a call.
A merciful cry for freedom to all.
We give our hearts and lives to cease this cry.
Somewhere in the near future, peace will lie.

And until we see that glorious day,
We'll help and support you in every way.
*Source: US Army Women's Museum*

**Judith L. Rathman**
**In country: February 10, 1967 – February 9, 1968**
**Rank: Specialist 5, US Army**
**Duty: USARV, Communications and Electronics, Clerk-Typist**

**Ruth E. Riter**
**In country: February 10, 1967 – February 9, 1968**
**Rank: Specialist 5, US Army**
**Duty: USARV, Adjutant General, Clerk-Typist**

**Janet A. Smith**
**In country: February 10, 1967 – February 9, 1968**
**Rank: Staff Sergeant, US Army**
**Duty: USARV, Special Troops, S4**

**Kathleen E. Stoner (DeCollo)**
**In country: February 10, 1967 – February 9, 1968**
**Rank: Specialist 5, US Army**
**Duty: USARV, Inspector General's Office, Clerk-Typist**

While stationed at Fort Sam Houston, TX, in 1967, I received my orders for Vietnam. I was not happy, but duty called. I was the second group of 15 to be picked by a computer (so I was told). After the initial 30, the rest of the women volunteered, and so my friend Gwen Faught joined us. I have great memories of the year. I worked for the IG where I met my future husband. It was truly an experience I will never forget. I look forward to the book.

**Luretha Taylor**
**In country: February 10, 1967 – February 9, 1968**
**Rank: Specialist 4, US Army**
**Duty: USARV, Engineer Division, Clerk-Typist**

**Margaret "Marge" T. Trapp (Jones)**
**In country: February 10, 1967 – February 9, 1968;**
**December 1969 – December 1970**
**Rank: Staff Sergeant, US Army**
**Duty: USARV, G4; 1ˢᵗ Aviation Brigade,**
**Administrative NCO**

**Phylis A. Wahwasuck (Thomas)**
**In country: February 10, 1967 – February 9, 1968**
**Rank: Specialist 5, US Army**
**Duty: USARV, G4, Clerk-Typist**

I was born in Oklahoma City, OK, April 13, 1947. When I was 18, I joined the Army. My parents were quite supportive of that, but my older sister was not. I did basic and advanced training at Fort McClellan, AL, and I stayed at McClellan and provided clerical support to the emergency medical technicians at Noble Army Hospital.

I volunteered for duty in Vietnam; I felt it was the patriotic thing to do. My company commander wished me well and I was on my way.

Bien Hoa arrival – it was hot and stinky in Vietnam on February 10, 1967. 1SG Marion Crawford was about the first person I met. Years later, at a job in Michigan, I found out one of the guys I worked with was Marion's brother!

I worked in G4, providing support to other personnel in country and it felt like a necessary and worthwhile job. I was also a member of the drill team.

I remember standing on a balcony and watching tracers lighting up the night in the distance and thinking how beautiful and, of course, how deadly.

It always amazed me and still seems very strange that the women were sent to Vietnam and could not carry weapons. We had some weapons training in basic training at that time. It wasn't right.

One of my most profound and vivid memories is flying in a Huey over the Delta around Vung Tau – it curled and rolled around through the most beautiful greenery and I felt bad for all the destruction.

I also fell in love with the children at the orphanage.

I brought home a small piece of blue and white silk – maybe a yard of it. I still have it but just can't figure out what to do with it and don't want to get rid of it either.

My husband and I flew home together February 9, 1968, landed at Oakland and were discharged right there. No ceremony, nothing. We flew to Denver and then to New York City. I remember going to the local VFW and being told that it didn't matter that I had served in Vietnam; women could only join the Auxiliary so I left and haven't been back since.

It has always bothered me that none of us who served there could really talk about it with a sense of pride. Compared to the young people coming back now, we really were not treated well and it left many of us bitter.

**Joyce "Twanna" P. Trumpet**
**In country: February 10, 1967 – May 1968**
**Rank: Specialist 4, US Army**
**Duty: USARV, Clerk-Typist**

**Comments and Memories:** The time I jumped from the motor vehicle into a ditch to keep from being hit by an incoming missile and was stuck there for hours with the driver. *Source: Vietnam Memory Book 2000*

**Margaret "Peggy" M. Sigley (D'Onofrio)**
**In country: February 10, 1967 – September 9, 1968**
**Rank: Specialist 5, US Army**
**Duty: USARV, G2, Clerk-Typist**

**Comments and Memories:** Slogan while in Vietnam, "I'm Checking Out of This Hotel." *Source: Vietnam Memory Book 2000*

**Linda M. Bruns (Moore)**
**In country: February 10, 1967 – October 1968**
**Rank: Specialist 5, US Army**
**Duty: USARV, Adjutant General, Staff Message Control, Clerk-Typist**

**Michele T. McCarthy**
**In country: February 11, 1967 – February 10, 1968**
**Rank: Specialist 5, US Army**
**Duty: USARV, Adjutant General's Office, Clerk-Typist**

**Joanne B. Manger (Willaford)**
**In country: February 12, 1967 – September 1968**
**Rank: Specialist 5, US Army**
**Duty: USARV, Surgeon General's Office, Clerk-Typist**

**Diana M. Reed**
**In country: February 14, 1967 – February 13, 1968**
**Rank: Specialist 5, US Army**
**Duty: USARV, Engineer Division, Clerk-Typist**

**Nancy M. Wooten (Thorne)**
**Retired as a Sergeant First Class**
**In country: February 14, 1967 – March 10, 1968**
**Rank: Specialist 5, US Army**
**Duty: USARV, G4, Personal Effects Division, Clerk-Typist**

I entered the US Army June 14, 1965, a year after graduating from high school. After basic training and advanced individual training at Fort McClellan, AL, I was assigned to Fort Jackson, SC, as a clerical technician at the US Army Hospital.

During the fall of 1966, I received orders for Vietnam. I left the US on Valentine's Day 1967. I was assigned to the Personal Effects Division.

In late January of 1968, I went to Japan for R&R, which I really enjoyed. The day I departed Japan, there was a bad snowstorm; I made it out just in time.

A few days back in Vietnam, here came the Tet Offensive. I admit I was really afraid. I had extended just one month so that with less than 90 days left on my enlistment, I could be discharged when I returned to the States. I began to worry if I had done the right thing.

March 10, 1968 was my big day – and the longest day of my life. I had to travel by helicopter to the point of departure. It took all day for me to process. I prayed "Charlie" wouldn't send a mortar round and kill me. I was only able to relax when I heard we were on the island of Guam. When we landed at Travis Air Force Base in Northern California, I was one happy sister.

During my exit physical, the doctor discovered a lump or cyst in my right breast. I was sent to Letterman General Hospital for a week.

I returned home, worked a little while in New York, then returned home again. I went to Business College, then a year or two at the University, and guess what – enlisted in the National Guard and later the Army Reserves where I retired with 21 years.

I'm dealing with PTSD and the effects of cancer, but I am grateful I'm still here. I am proud to have served my country, including in Vietnam.

**Sherry E. Saunders (Howard)**
**In country: February 15, 1967 – February 14, 1968**
**Rank: Specialist 5, US Army**
**Duty: USARV, Staff Judge Advocate, Clerk-Typist**

**Dorothy Smith (Gardner)**
**In country: February 15, 1967 – February 14, 1968**
**Rank: Specialist 5, US Army**
**Duty: USARV, Comptroller, Clerk-Typist**

My first assignment after advanced training at Fort McClellan, AL, was the Stockade at Fort Meade, MD, in 1966. After a few months, I decided I wanted to go to the Army Language School at Fort Ord, CA. I submitted the paperwork three times to the Department of Defense (DOD); each time it was rejected saying they did not have facilities for women. But, before I could put the request in the fourth time, I received orders for Vietnam. I thought I received the orders because each time I requested, I stated that I was willing to serve anywhere in the world. That was all that DOD read. I talked to my first sergeant about my situation. She explained that I would have to tell the Army how Vietnam would affect me mentally. I knew there was life after that one year, and I did not want that on my record.

I arrived in Tan Son Nhut in February 1967. Home was a Quonset hut. I worked as a typist in a Quonset hut for the Comptroller along with soldiers and one WAC (Earnestine) and two Vietnamese women typists (Ms. Hon and Ms. Loc). I was a member of the drill team.

Not long after my arrival, my father passed and I returned to the States for his funeral. Then I returned to Vietnam. I was told that Tan Son Nhut had been overrun by the Viet Cong (VC). The Detachment had moved to Long Binh where the women were housed in large two-story wooden barracks. The shower was on the outside ground level, and one was often greeted by the sound of a large frog sharing the shower. There was a large outside area for watching movies where we often found ourselves getting up off the ground after not too distant mortar attacks. The word was out that if the VC overran Long Binh, the Captain was supposed to shoot us. We always heard mortar fire day in and day out.

I went to Thailand on R&R. We flew over on a commercial jet. We returned on a helicopter gunship with the machine gunner sitting in the open door as we flew over the trees. That was not a good feeling.

There were days when I would stand on the second floor porch and watch the traffic as it drove by. Thousands of bicycles and too many people on tiny little buses until the weight would cause the bus to flip over and the chickens would run everywhere. My saddest time on that second-floor porch was seeing large flatbed trucks go by with shiny aluminum boxes stacked high and wide. I told my sergeant at the office about them and he told me that they were our soldiers being sent home.

I returned to Fort Monroe, VA, and met Specialist Billy D. Gardner. We married in January 1969 and decided upon military careers. I had a career change, though, in April 1969, due to the pregnancy of my first of three sons. I went on to have a 33-year career with the Cincinnati Police Department.

**Barbara A. Ebel (Flaaen)**
**Retired as a Sergeant First Class**
**In country: February 19, 1967 – April 1968**
**Rank: Specialist 5, US Army**
**Duty: USARV, G3, Clerk-Typist**

Like most of us in the first Company, I was 19 when I received my orders. I turned 20 just before leaving the States and turned 21 during the Tet Offensive in 1968. I did some special projects for the SGS (Secretary to the General Staff) and was privileged enough to meet all of the General officers at our headquarters, including General William Westmoreland. I worked for Colonel George S. Patton, Jr. While on active duty, I had tours in Sinop, Turkey; West Point; Christmas in Berlin; and several other stateside posts. As a proud WAC, meeting WAC Director Colonel Elizabeth Hoisington in Long Binh, of all places, was a highlight of my tour.

## Glenda "Stormy" E. Storni (Graebe)
**In country: February 20, 1967 – September 19, 1968**
**Rank: Specialist 5, US Army**
**Duty: USARV, Adjutant General, Clerk-Typist**

Indiana loves her veterans. "Welcome Home" is heard throughout the land. Nestled in the country, in the small town of Lexington, the peace and quiet shadows the memories of Vietnam. Enjoying the changes of the season, Summer while tending the vegetable and flower garden, and Fall with vivid colors of yellow, orange and red, the beauty of snow in winter, and Spring when everything is new. Families of geese, chipmunks, squirrels and rabbits running around the yard like it's their private playground. Ahhh, how retirement suits me well.

Several things brought me great satisfaction during my 18 months in Vietnam. I didn't object to working long hours and 6½ days a week most of the time. It was such a joy in finding and bringing to Headquarters some of the fellows I grew up with and went to school with. They really appreciated having a warm shower and warm mess hall food. Other than my time spent at the orphanage, perhaps my greatest satisfaction came from my trips to the field evacuation hospitals where I read to and wrote letters for the wounded who could not be moved.

Truthfully, I wasn't aware of the actual danger we were in. There's a lot to be said about "young and dumb." The ammo dump explosion was my biggest memorable event. I landed on my face with one of the girls "protecting my back." When the concussion from the blast hit her back, down we went face first onto the floor. I came up with a few scrapes but found it to be "adventurous." One other dangerous moment was when I was with a male friend in a truck headed for Bien Hoa to the Air Force club. We were caught in a crossfire while going through the rubber tree plantation. The front of the truck was hit. I was handed an M-16 to shoot back, but didn't know if I hit anything. On our trip back "home," we positioned ourselves in between a convoy for protection.

**Judith Diane Nickloy (Jones)**
**In country: February 22, 1967 – February 18, 1968**
**Rank: Specialist 5, US Army**
**Duty: USARV, G3, Clerk-Typist**

It took me 15 years to get enrolled with the VA. For the past 20 years, I have been trying to get the VA to test me for Agent Orange. I get boils on my face and tailbone (three or four at a time) and my 28-year-old son gets them also. He is totally blind in one eye due to what I suspect is from my exposure to Agent Orange. His father (my ex) also came in contact with Agent Orange.

# MARCH

*Memory Lane: Jimmy Hoffa begins eight-year prison sentence.*
*Song: "Love is Here and Now You're Gone" by The Supremes*

**Anita Flores (Massey)**
**In country: March 1967 – November 1967**
**Rank: Specialist 5, US Army**
**Duty: USARV, Clerk-Typist**

**Patsy June Robinson**
**Retired as a Lieutenant Commander**
**In country: March 1967 – February 1968**
**Rank: Lieutenant, US Navy Medical Service Corps**
**Duty: USS *Sanctuary* (AH-17), Laboratory Division, Medical Technologist**

**Mary Sandra Hall (Van Bebber)**
**Retired as a Colonel**
**In country: March 1967 – March 1968**
**Rank: Major, US Army Medical Specialist Corps**
**Duty: 85th Evacuation Hospital, Qui Nhon, Physical Therapist**

**Jolene Kay Tomlan**
**In country: March 1967 – March 1968**
**Rank: Captain, US Army Medical Specialist Corps**
**Duty: 24th Evacuation Hospital, Long Binh, Physical Therapist**

"I became interested in the Army's physical therapy program after hearing a former Army physical therapist speak at a career guidance meeting during my college freshman year. In the summer of my junior year, I attended the Army Summer Practical Program that allowed me to spend three weeks living on an Army post. I became a member of the Army Medical Specialist Corps in July 1964, shortly after I received my Bachelor of Arts degree. . . .

"My major of physical education and my profession of physical therapy are similar. They both involve working with people and the teaching of skills. Instead of sport skills, a physical therapist teaches the activities of daily living. I am especially indebted to my professors in the department of physical education for women who taught me to think, to analyze and to see beyond myself."

Captain Jolene Tomlan arrived at the 24th Evacuation Hospital in March 1967. She was immediately faced with the problem of creating a physical therapy program under the disadvantages of a still growing hospital complex, which lacked basic physical therapy equipment.

"Once I organized my daily visits to the intensive care post-operative wards, I managed to obtain three machines that could be used on my patients to reduce pain in their healing injuries. . . .

"One of my other needs was a machine on which soldiers could perform therapy exercises. Really, several machines consisting of weighted pulleys and tension springs would be needed. Instead of waiting for supply to obtain the equipment, I designed and helped build a machine on which several patients would exercise at the same time. It's crude but functional."

Captain Tomlan's day is spent in the hospital's post-operative and intensive care wards.

"Many of the patients in the intensive care wards are recovering from severe head injuries. Muscle weakness usually accompanies this type of wound. It's my job to provide therapy to maintain range of motion and thereby prevent secondary disability to the patients can recover in the fastest time possible."

Some patients are unable to speak because of brain injury. Captain Tomlan must give them shoulder, arm, hand and leg exercises while keeping up a one-sided conversation.

"How's that arm doing today, Joe? Let's bend it a little bit . . . that's it . . . concentrate on keeping that shoulder loose. . . ."

More than two-thirds of all American soldiers treated at the hospital are returned to duty within 30 days. Those that are evacuated to Army hospitals out of the country for further treatment have already begun this therapy thanks to CPT Tomlan.

Captain Tomlan's off-duty hours are divided between a correspondence course in mechanical drawing, the chapel choir, Bible-study classes and reading.

This is the spirit which characterizes Jolene Tomlan. The desire to heal through daily, progressive care. In her words, ". . . the ability to see beyond myself."

*Excerpts from an article titled "Jolene Tomlan B.A. '64 – A Dedicated Young Woman From Newton, Iowa, Brings Hope To the Wounded in Vietnam," written by SP5 Evan L. Thomas, published in* The Alumnus *by the Alumni Association of the University of Northern Iowa, February 1968.*

**Mary "Derb" Frances Westhoven**
**Retired as a Colonel**
**In country: March 1967 – March 1968**
**Rank: Lieutenant Colonel, US Army Medical Specialist Corps**
**Duty: 17ᵗʰ Field Hospital, Saigon; 3ʳᵈ Field Hospital, Physical Therapist Consultant**

***Telephone interview with Phyllis Miller, 12/1/2014:*** I had just finished college and decided I wasn't too interested in teaching. In August 1950, $200 a month sounded great and the Army was a good opportunity. My family was mostly okay with it, and I was assigned to a variety of hospitals in my first 17 years of service, including Hawaii and San Francisco. When I was at Fort Bragg, NC, I was selected to go to Vietnam. I arrived in March 1967, replacing Barbara Gray.

The first few months, I was in Saigon at one of the hotels and lived on the seventh floor in a building with no elevator. That was good exercise! Then I was assigned to the 3ʳᵈ Field Hospital and the physical therapists were in the same type of villas that the nurses had for living quarters.

One of the other physical therapists under my supervision was Elizabeth Hamilton who was stationed at Vung Tau. She got lots of supervision from numerous people because it was one of the most beautiful beach areas in Vietnam.

I had two R&Rs, one to Thailand and one to Singapore. About the only souvenir I brought back was one of those elephants but I don't have it anymore.

**♥Imogen Elaine Averett**
**Retired as a Colonel**
**In country: March 1967 – April 1968**
**Rank: Lieutenant Colonel, US Army**
**Duty: MACV, USAHAC, Secretary to the General Staff**

***Donna Lowery:*** Colonel Imogen Averett was a veteran of World War II, Korea and Vietnam. She was in the first group of WAC officers selected for promotion to colonel after the law limiting such promotions for women was abolished. She enlisted in the Women's Army Auxiliary Corps (WAAC) in 1942. She became a personnel officer at Fort Des Moines, IA. There, she was tasked with locating qualified women to work with atomic scientists in New Mexico during World War II. She also worked on the Marshall Plan Recovery Program for Greece in the Military Attaché Office in London. Imogen was handpicked to be the personnel officer for General Dwight D. Eisenhower when he was appointed Chief of Staff of the US Army; she maintained that position for subsequent Chiefs. Her decorations include two Legions of Merit, the Presidential Unit Commendation Medal, the Bronze Star and the Army Unit Commendation Medal. While she was in Vietnam during the Tet Offensive of 1968, she worked on the Secretary General Staff. Colonel Averett was an extraordinary woman.

**Juana "Jenny" Christina Felix**
**Retired as a Sergeant First Class**
**In country: March 8, 1967 – October 8, 1968**
**Rank: Specialist 5, US Army**
**Duty: USARV, 1st Aviation Brigade Safety Office, Clerk-Typist**

I went into the Women's Army Corps after high school graduation in 1965. My recruiter assured me I would not go to Vietnam because women were not being sent there. I assured my parents of this, as well.

After training, I was stationed at Fort Sheridan, IL, where I joined the Fifth Army Headquarters basketball team in 1966. Returning from a tournament, I was called to report to the Commanding Officer. (I thought I was in trouble.)

She said, "Specialist Felix, I have orders for you to go to Vietnam." Flabbergasted, I exclaimed that I had requested to go to Hawaii, Japan or Okinawa as my overseas assignment. She said, "I am sorry." I naively stated that the recruiter told me women were not being sent to Vietnam. She said a new general order stated that 65 women with clerical skills between the ages of 18 and 25 were selected, and I was among them. How quickly, I realized, regulations and policies can change in the military and in life.

I knew nothing about why we were fighting in Vietnam, learned very little about the war while there, or even after I left. I knew we were trying to stop the spread of Communism – something I was surely against from what I learned in school. But, most of us were young and did not concern ourselves with politics. We served with pride in support of our country and went wherever we were told.

Being in Vietnam was a learning experience. I felt I had the best job in the world and certainly one of the most rewarding while in the military. My job was to take reports on all helicopter accidents, incidents, forced landings, precautionary landings, combat damages, combat losses and human error involving helicopters throughout Vietnam.

I also drew "Snoopy" (the Red Baron), and typed and published the magazine *HQ USARV Aviation Safety Magazine* with input and proofreading from my pilot officers, a bunch of loving, understanding, charming gentlemen whom I adored. (I learned a lot from them.)

We worked 13-hour days, 13 days straight, with one day off every two weeks. On days off, we would go to the NCO club or into Saigon with whatever male friend had transportation. On the way back from our first Saigon visit, the jeep driver drove into a deep ditch. The two soldiers with us tried to pull it out, with no luck. The other two ladies and I stood on the side of the road out of the way. No military vehicles stopped and, without fail, the men passing would yell in amazement, "Look, round eyes," while pointing at us. We women finally got so angry we yelled at them to look beyond the round eyes and help us get the jeep out of the ditch. Finally, that worked and help came to our aid. Late returning to the WAC Detachment, we got in trouble.

After I left Vietnam, I seem to have stored my experiences in the back burner of my mind. In 1988, at a convention for Women in the Military held by the Governor of New Mexico, I started getting vivid memories while listening to MAJ Jacqueline Rhoades, an Army Nurse who served in Vietnam. She talked about her experiences, men she treated and bodies she handled.

As I was listening, I thought of all the men that I had been acquainted with who died in Vietnam, and about friends who lost their lives in country not as a result of direct combat. I also thought about six men friends who died while back in the States (what a waste).

I also remembered several 18-year-olds Reya Monte and I met on a plane when we were returning from leave in Puerto Rico for our second tour in Vietnam. From Puerto Rico and the Virgin Islands, these young soldiers had finished infantry training and had less than a year of service. Many were in tears. As MAJ Rhoades spoke, I started to cry uncontrollable sobs that I did not even know I could muster.

## Susie Mae Stephens (McArthur)
**Retired as a Sergeant Major**
**In country: March 10, 1967 – March 9, 1968**
**Rank: Specialist 5, US Army**
**Duty: USARV, G4, Communications and Electronics, Clerk-Typist**

In early 1967, I was notified I had been *selected* (I did not volunteer) to go to Vietnam; I was devastated as was my family. I did not know what the war was about or why women were sent there. To avoid going I was given two choices: get pregnant or get married. Then the Army would remove my name and process my discharge. Go figure.

This miserable trip was my first flight: Atlanta to California to Japan and finally to Vietnam. We deplaned to the most awful stench, loaded onto a bus and went to the WAC Detachment on Tan Son Nhut Air Base. We were welcomed by the Cadre with smiles and promised we would be okay – on with in-processing and all the "Do's and Don'ts." Assigned to my 10- to 12-hours-a-day job (G4), Communications and Electronics Division, I was an excellent typist and fast became the typing pool's go-to typist.

My four close friends and I really enjoyed visiting the off-limits entertainment places. The GIs we met or traveled with treated us with respect – like their little sisters or daughters – and were very protective.

Memorable moments: Seeing the WAC Drill Team perform – they were super – watching movies in the dayroom (military term for unit lounge) and drinking beer (which was plentiful). After moving to Long Binh – watching the ammo dump explosion and dealing with the many alerts.

In the 1968 Tet Offensive, I thought we in the WAC Detachment surely were gone. I remember we were told to hit the floor and cover with a mattress.

A male friend, SSG Carrol Johnson, was killed in an accident after coming for a visit one Sunday; he was the only person I knew personally who was killed in Vietnam. My circle of friends and I were devastated.

Field First Betty Benson could be counted on to come to our rescue including our being late for curfew. The cadre was caring and tolerant of my attitude and defiance which, later in my career, I truly came to appreciate.

After my first three years in service and after leaving Vietnam, I decided to reenlist for a career. I retired June 1991 with 26 years of active service.

After the Vietnam years, my most enjoyable assignments were three tours in Germany. My most rewarding assignment was as Drill Sergeant and as a Cadre at the Drill Sergeant School, Fort Jackson, SC.

My husband, Sergeant Major Eddie McArthur (Retired), and I live in Tampa, FL. I am active with veterans' organizations, the local VA hospital, my community and church, and avidly support local homeless women veterans. I still enjoy traveling, entertaining and visiting my military friends. I claim one daughter, two sons, and six grandchildren. I am blessed and thank God each day for directing me to choose my Army career path.

**♥Gwendolyn "Gwen" Kay Faught (Wakolee)**
**In country: March 10, 1967 – May 1968**
**Rank: Specialist 5, US Army**
**Duty: USARV, Office of the Inspector General,**
**Clerk-Typist**

**♥Anita Marie "Jinx" Wampach**
**Retired as a Sergeant First Class**
**In country: March 10, 1967 – June 1968; April 1971 – March 1972**
**Rank: Staff Sergeant, US Army**
**Duty: USARV, G4, Plans and Operations; MACV, J3, Surface Operations**
**Division, Administrative NCO**

*Donna Lowery:* "Jinx" was one of the most incredible human beings I have ever met. She made a difference in so many people's lives. She could have been a stand-up comic; she always had everyone laughing, uncontrollably at times. I have always been envious of her great sense of humor. Behind that beautiful face and gorgeous white hair was a truly mischievous, child-like person. She had a smile that told you she was up to something or about to share with you one of her "adventures." For "Jinx" there was only one unit of enlisted women in any service in Vietnam. It was the Army unit, WAC Detachment Special Troops, United States Army Republic of Vietnam (USARV). While at USARV, "Jinx" worked 12-14 hours a day. She had one Sunday per month off. Somehow, she arranged to "borrow" a jeep, which she somehow used "sometimes" as her means of transportation. Apparently, she considered the uncovered jeep only a minor inconvenience during the rainy season. No one knew about this until 1999, when we had our First Homecoming Conference in Olympia, WA. Jinx went back for a second tour where she served at MACV. In 1999, "Jinx" wrote this about that tour: "I sent myself back to CONUS assigning myself to Oakland, CA, pending further assignment. I had 11 months in country and decided it was time to go back. Had to call DA for an assignment." That is the Jinx we all knew and really loved. I don't know anyone else who would either think to do that, much less actually do it. She was the most generous person I have known; she truly would give you the shirt off her back. Well educated, she had both a Master of Arts in Counseling and a Bachelor of Arts in Psychology. She worked as a Mental Health Therapist helping children. That was her calling, and she was very good at it.

**Joanne E. Fenninger**
**In country: March 15, 1967 – December 4, 1967**
**Rank: Captain, US Army Medical Specialist Corps**
**Duty: 3rd Field Hospital, Saigon, Physical Therapist**

Brigadier General Pat Foote and I were stationed at Fort McClellan, AL, at the same time. Later we met up again in Vietnam and decided to take a boat ride. Unfortunately, the motor died and we drifted toward the opposite shore which, I was told, was VC territory. Luckily, we were rescued and towed back by the "White Mice" (Saigon police).

**Nancy A. Meyer (Elliott)**
**Retired as Colonel, USAR**
**In country: March 18, 1967 – August 3, 1967**
**Rank: Captain, US Army Medical Specialist Corps**
**Duty: 43rd Medical Goup, Nha Trang, Dietetic Consultant**

**♥Barbara Jean Dulinsky**
**Retired as a Master Sergeant**
**In country: March 18, 1967 – October 1968**
**Rank: Master Sergeant, US Marine Corps**
**Duty: MACV, Marine Corps Personnel Section**

Barbara was the first US Marine Corps woman to serve in a combat theater. She requested the assignment to Vietnam. On March 18, 1967 (after an 18-hour flight), she arrived at Bien Hoa Air Base where she was billeted overnight. The next morning she was taken by bus and an armed escort to Koeppler Compound in Saigon.

During the Tet Offensive, she commented in a letter dated February 9, 1968, "We are still on 24-hour curfew, with all hands in utilities. MACV personnel (women included) were bussed down to Koeppler compound and issued three pairs of jungle fatigues and a pair of combat boots. Right now, most of us don't look the picture of "the New Image." Whew! Hardly! I can't determine at night if I'm pooped from the work day or from carrying around these anvils tied to my feet called combat boots."

*Written by Mary E. Glaudel DeZurik with information from* A History of The Women Marines 1946-1977, *Colonel Mary V. Stremlow, US Marine Corps Reserve, published by the History and Museums Division Headquarters, US Marine Corps, Washington DC 1986.*

# APRIL

*Memory Lane: In San Francisco, 10,000 march against the Vietnam War; Muhammed Ali refuses military service and is stripped of his boxing title.*
*Song: "Happy Together" by The Turtles*

♥**Alice I. Hampson**
**Retired as a Major**
**In country: April 1967 – April 1968**
**Rank: Captain, US Army**
**Duty: USARV, G1, Adjutant for General William Westmoreland**

**Beverly K. Huber (Roberts)**
**Retired as a Major**
**In country: April 1967 – April 1968; March 1972 – March 1973**
**Rank: Major, US Air Force**
**Duty: USAF Postal Services, Tan Son Nhut; Social Action, Tan Son Nhut**

♥**Lillian Mildred Lewis**
**Retired as a Lieutenant Colonel**
**In country: April 1967 – April 1968**
**Rank: Major, US Air Force**
**Duty: 7th Air Force, Administrative Staff Officer**

**Norma V. Busse**
**Retired as a Lieutenant Colonel**
**In country: April 1967 – May 1968**
**Rank: Major, US Army**
**Duty: MACV, USAHAC, Deputy Director for Personnel**

On January 31, 1968, we were awakened by gunshots and tracers from helicopters in Saigon proper. We were billeted in the Rex Hotel right in town, and all hell had broken loose. We, COL Prentice, G4; LTC Imogen Averett, Office of the Secretary of the General Staff; and I, Deputy G1, dressed quickly and crept out slowly to our vehicle parked about 500 feet away in an open area with a number of other cars. Our driver, a corporal, was 1,000 feet away in the enlisted quarters. Shots from snipers had been flying all around us. Then, suddenly, all was quiet and calm. As the junior officer, I had to walk from the car to the enlisted billets to get the driver who had the car keys. At 5'11", I had no way to disguise myself nor was I able to huddle into doorways. My slow walk to the driver's billets had me sensing any minute that I would be shot down, but I made it safely. Once we were all in the vehicle and on the way to headquarters, we were pinned down at the American Embassy for a couple of hours until we were rescued by our military policemen.

**Ida E. Colford (Willis)**
**In country: April 1967 – July 1968**
**Rank: Specialist 5, US Army**
**Duty: MACV, USAHAC, Secretary to BG Albin Irzyk**

I enlisted in the Women's Army Corps in August 1965, completed my basic training at Fort McClellan, AL, and went on to Fort Leonard Wood, MO, for advanced individual training as a Personnel Specialist. My first assignment was at the US Army Personnel Center (USAPERSCEN) in Oakland, CA, as a stenographer because of my high school training in shorthand and my civilian job before entering the Army. USAPERSCEN was a frozen post and nobody went anywhere unless somebody in Washington decided. Many folks had volunteered for Vietnam to no avail, but I decided to try when my "boss" the Secretary to the General Staff, LTC Imogen Averett, got orders for

Vietnam. I made the request, which was denied all the way to the Pentagon. But somebody must have helped me out, and I found myself on the plane to Vietnam in April 1967, wondering what I had done. Originally assigned to Military Assistance Command, Vietnam (MACV) where some of the enlisted women were but most of them were at USARV Headquarters, I was reassigned upon arrival to US Army Headquarters Command (USAHAC) as secretary to the commanding general. I was the first and only enlisted woman assigned to USAHAC. That, in itself, was interesting, but proved to be fun, exciting and scary throughout my tour. I met my husband of 45 years in Vietnam, and, interestingly enough, he was assigned to MACV Studies and Observation Group. I have fond memories of the people I met during my three years in the Women's Army Corps, and although I have had no contact with any of them, I think of them often with great affection.

**♥Kathleen "Katie" Frances Sabo (Grassmeier)**
**Retired as a Major**
**In country: April 1967 – November 1968**
**Rank: Captain, US Air Force**
**Duty: 7th Air Force, 8th Aerial Port, Transportation**
**Staff Officer**

**♥Roberta "Robby" Bozman**
**In country: April 5, 1967 – April 4, 1968**
**Rank: Specialist 5, US Army**
**Duty: USARV, G3, Clerk-Typist**

**Patricia C. Pewitt**
**In country: April 24, 1967 – November 1968**
**Rank: Specialist 5, US Army**
**Duty: USARV, Special Troops, WAC Detachment,**
**Mail Clerk and Company Clerk**

**Barbara M. Maine**
**Retired as a Master Sergeant**
**In country: April 25, 1967 – May 1968; December 1969 –**
**November 1970**
**Rank: Staff Sergeant, US Army**
**Duty: USARV, Office of the Adjutant General, Clerk-**
**Typist; MACV, G5; MACV, 1ˢᵗ Logistical Command/**
**Saigon Support Command, Administrative NCO**

**Linda Jean Garrigan**
**In country: April 27, 1967 – April 26, 1968**
**Rank: Specialist 5, US Army**
**Duty: USARV, Special Troops Personnel, Personnel Specialist**

Author's Note: I have searched for Linda for more than 10 years, but have never been able to find her although I found five articles in the Joplin, MO, newspaper when she was a little girl.

**Mary Eliza Hay (Wilson)**
**In country: April 30, 1967 – April 29, 1968**
**Rank: Specialist 5, US Army**
**Duty: USARV, G1, Clerk-Typist**

When I reached the WAC barracks at Tan Son Nhut Air Base, having traveled from California through Hawaii, Guam, Okinawa and the Philippines to reach Vietnam, I was a bedraggled 19-year-old in a withered class B uniform with holes in my stockings. My new First Sergeant Marion Crawford looked at me with glee and said, "I have at last gotten my tall gal in to join the drill team." That opening salvo to which she would later repine, "You will never march in a formation again."

General William Westmoreland was due at the headquarters for an inspection of stationed troops. The WAC Detachment was ordered to be present. I had marched in basic training and in advanced training. Always the first on the right hand side as units are arranged by height, so that was where you would always find me, as I am 6'2". Each successive row (also on the right hand side) is the person to keep the unit straight on the field and always, always eyes are straight ahead – presumably, so that I wouldn't march us into a bog or march off the field. Everyone else in the company is "eyes right." On that particular day of the inspection, I decided I needed to look right and got my first and only glimpse of General Westmoreland. Of course, Sergeant Crawford with eyes in the back of her head saw the exchange and so I NEVER marched again – especially not on her drill team!

# MAY

*Memory Lane: Elvis Presley marries Priscilla Beaulieu; "Mister Rogers' Neighborhood" debuts on NET (now PBS)*
*Song: "Groovin'" by The Young Rascals*

**Anna A. McPherson**
**In country: May 22, 1967 – May 21, 1968**
**Rank: Specialist 5, US Army**
**Duty: USARV, Adjutant General, Clerk-Typist**

# JUNE

*Memory Lane: Solicitor General Thurgood Marshall is nominated to be the first Black justice of the US Supreme Court*
*Song: "Respect" by Aretha Franklin*

**Elizabeth "Betsy" Gordon Wylie**
**Retired as a Captain**
**In country: June 1967 – July 1968**
**Rank: Captain, US Navy**
**Duty: NAVFORV, Command Information Center**

"I was the first woman Line Officer assigned to Vietnam from 1967 – 1968."

Captain Elizabeth Wylie was the first US Navy woman to serve in Vietnam. She reported to the staff of the Commander of Naval Forces in Saigon in June 1967.

She worked in the Command Information Center, which prepared various kinds of reports, including briefings to visiting journalists and politicians. She spent three to six days each month in the field gathering information and taking pictures.

"I'd go back if I had the chance," she later told a newspaper reporter. "The opportunity to see the heart of the Navy at work is unique and rewarding." She did not want "to glorify what I did in Vietnam. I never was under hostile fire or anything like that."

Speaking of the women with whom she shared quarters in Saigon she said, "The only difficulties encountered were the same as the men. We were all away from home, families, and not in a particularly pleasant situation." *Excerpt from* Women in the Navy, *Jean Ebbert, former Lieutenant (Junior Grade), US Navy, and Marie-Beth Hall*

**♥Vera Mae Jones**
**Retired as a Colonel**
**In country: June 9, 1967 – June 5, 1968**
**Rank: Captain, US Marine Corps**
**Duty: NAVFORV, Marine Corps Personnel Section**

Captain Vera Mae Jones was the first Woman Marine officer to be sent to Vietnam. She was the only Woman Marine to attend Vietnamese language school, and while there taught English to women and children and also a class to Vietnamese policemen.

On February 3, 1968, Captain Jones wrote a letter to the Woman Marine Director, Colonel Barbara Bishop, about what it was like to experience the Tet Offensive. She wrote, "It's hard to believe that a war is going on around me. I sit here calmly typing this letter and yet can get up, walk to a window, and watch the helicopters making machine gun and rocket strikes in the area of the golf course which is about three blocks away. At night, I lie in bed and listen to the mortar rounds going off. The streets, which are normally crowded with traffic, are virtually bare."

*Written by Mary E. Glaudel DeZurik with information from* A History of The Women Marines 1946-1977, *Colonel Mary V. Stremlow, US Marine Corps Reserve, published by the History and Museums Division Headquarters, US Marine Corps, Washington, DC, 1986.*

**Ruth M. Fulton**
**Retired as a Sergeant First Class**
In country: June 15, 1967 – July 10, 1968
Rank: Specialist 5, US Army
Duty: USARV, G2, Clerk-Typist

**Marie I. Dube (Gross)**
In country: June 16, 1967 – July 1968
Rank: Specialist 5, US Army
Duty: USARV, G1, Clerk-Typist

Leaving Vietnam was as tense as during the Tet Offensive. Russia was trying to hijack troop aircrafts so the time and where I was going to leave from in Vietnam wasn't told to me until the last moment. I spent the whole time watching out of the window. I was discharged from the Army and flew to Fort Gordon, GA, to meet my future husband, who I met in Vietnam. We married in July 1968. We have two boys; one was born in 1972 and the other in 1973. I have been a housewife and mother. I am now the grandmother of three. My husband retired from the Army. I am retired and enjoying making quilts. I am still married. It is going on 46 years.

**Mary Louise Cook (Curry)**
**Retired as a Master Sergeant**
In country: June 17, 1967 – April 27, 1968; November 7, 1968 – November 1, 1969; April 18, 1971 – May 3, 1972
Rank: Sergeant First Class, US Army
Duty: MACV, J2, Executive Administrative Assistant

Initially, I believe I was the only female soldier serving with her husband (SGM Arthur J. Curry) in MACV Saigon. The female lieutenant colonel advised that I should not be allowed to live with my husband since the male soldiers were separated from their wives. The MACV J2 (my boss, Major General P.B. Davidson) intervened and we were eventually allowed to live together. I believe the name of the old hotel where most of the female soldiers (me and hubby included) was called "The Mayflower." I could be wrong about that.

Originally, there were seven of us in MACV (Army and Air Force) all serving in an administrative capacity. Betty Reid was the receptionist in General William Westmoreland's office.

The female military at MACV were treated very well.

I can remember trying to barter with a supply sergeant for a lobster tail. The outcome was that he could get me "a case of them" but not "one." Everyone in the hotel ate lobster for a couple of days.

I was there in Saigon (MACV) during the 1968 Tet Offensive. We were not allowed to leave Headquarters MACV for three days. As I recall, the biggest problem we had was to get the door off the PX (post exchange) so we could get toothbrushes.

The only time my boss, the general, got angry with me was when he left the office early leaving a big orange on his desk. The temptation was too great and I ate his orange. Upon his arrival the next morning, he was not amused to find his orange gone, but I fessed up.

I later served for the same general in the office of the Secretary of Defense at the Pentagon. I also served in the office of Lieutenant General Edward Rowny in the Joint Chiefs of Staff during the Strategic Arms Limitation Talks.

June 17, 1967 – The first five enlisted women in the Air Force (WAF) and the fourth WAF officer to be assigned to Vietnam arrive at Tan Son Nhut Air Base, South Vietnam. The women (l-r) are: LtCol June H. Hilton, A1C Carol J. Hornick, A1C Rita M. Pitcock, SSgt Barbara J. Snavely, A1C Shirley J. Brown, and A1C Eva M. Nordstrom.

**June H. Hilton (Augustine)**
**Retired as a Lieutenant Colonel**
**In country: June 17, 1967 – June 16, 1968**
**Rank: Lieutenant Colonel, US Air Force**
**Duty: MACV, J1, Personnel Staff Officer**

I was in charge of the section that made arrangements for the men and women to go on R&R to Hawaii. If married, we made arrangements for the family to be with them in Hawaii. (Everyone in country was granted R&R every six months.)

**Carol J. Hornick (Gilmour)**
**Retired as a Technical Sergeant**
**In country: June 17, 1967 – June 16, 1968**
**Rank: Staff Sergeant, US Air Force**
**Duty: MACV, J4**

I was one of the first five Air Force enlisted ladies to be assigned to MACV. After our arrival and all of the picture taking, Eve Nordstrom and I got separated from all the others. The taxi driver we were given did not understand us and took us to several different hotels before finally getting us to the Ambassador. Eve and I had no idea where we were or even where we were supposed to go. There was no air conditioning in the taxi.

The other memory would be when Tet started in 1968. I was in my room getting ready to go to work. I was told to stay in the hotel and was there for three days before going to work. We were taken to work in armed bus convoys and went through bombed out areas of Saigon. We were pretty much restricted to our hotel and work after this.

I remember bits and pieces from being there, but don't think about that time in my life very much.

**Rita Pitcock (Gilchrist)**
**In country: June 17, 1967 – June 16, 1968**
**Rank: Staff Sergeant, US Air Force**
**Duty: MACV, Judge Advocate General**

In October of 1963, I signed up for eight weeks of basic training at Lackland Air Force Base in San Antonio, TX. There, it was decided that Administration would be my career field. After basic training, I was assigned to Travis Air Force Base in California for four years.

The Air Force wanted five enlisted WAF in the Administration field to volunteer for Vietnam. It was 1967 in the heat of the war protesters, drugs and hippies. I wanted to be one of the five! My family freaked out when I was accepted and said yes. I was scheduled to get out, but instead extended for a year in order to accept the assignment.

In June 1967, five enlisted WAF (including myself) and Lt Col June Hilton landed at Tan Son Nhut Air Base in Vietnam.

I was assigned to the War Crimes Division of the Staff Judge Advocate Office, downtown Saigon, and was later moved to the new MACV Headquarters at Tan Son Nhut. We worked 12-hour days for the first few months. I spent any off time working with the nuns and the kids at the local orphanage.

Downtown Saigon was inhabited by civilians and there were places to shop and to eat. We were aware of the combat zones and certainly felt like we were in the heat of battle at times, but we were not as exposed as the men in the field. We lived in the Palace 'hotel', two to a room, right in the middle of town.

Tet is the Vietnamese New Year and the most important Vietnamese holiday. In late January 1968, during the Tet Offensive as it's been dubbed, we awoke to men yelling, "Saigon is under attack." We could hear the incoming mortar rounds, machine guns, bullets hitting the wall. There was no way we were leaving there alive! When the convoy got to us, nothing made sense, men sobbing, the carnage, the fires and fear.

Tet changed the way we worked and the way we lived, much as 9-11-2001 did. One day you are surrounded by coworkers and friends, the next day they are gone.

Our plane touched down in California to the protesters spitting on us and yelling baby killers, murderers, dope addicts go back to Vietnam. We in turn kissed the ground we had left the year before. I felt sorry for the protesters; they had no idea how lucky they were.

My tour of duty in Vietnam touched my life forever, for the better. I can stand and say I'm proud to be an American and even more proud to be one of the first administrative Women in the Air Force to serve in Southeast Asia.

**Barbara J. Snavely**
**Retired as a Master Sergeant**
**In country: June 17, 1967 – June 16, 1968**
**Rank: Technical Sergeant, US Air Force**
**Duty: MACV, J3, Operations, Administrative Specialist**

"One of the things I like about being stationed in Vietnam is having the opportunity to learn the customs and language of the Vietnamese people. I hope to go home better informed about the Asian way of life." *(Quoted from an article about the first five enlisted WAF assigned to South Vietnam that appeared in* Airman (the official Air Force magazine) *sometime between September 1967 to March 1968).*

One thing I can say about MACV (J3) was that I did not have time to do much sightseeing! J3 was the Operations Division within MACV Headquarters.

My average workday was 12-14 hours, 7 days a week. I was actually doing the work of three other military slots that had not yet been filled, plus my own work. Those slots started filling in April 1968. The ride to my billets after a long day was normally in one of the General's vehicles.

The thing I did enjoy was the camaraderie of all the officers in my duty sections. Their main concerns were their jobs, but they also insured this female from Michigan was well taken care of. My officers were Army, Air Force and Navy.

As the vacant administrative slots began to fill, I was strongly urged to take an R&R. I went to the Philippines with another WAF where we enjoyed some much needed rest and relaxation. In May 1968, I was sent to Bangkok, Thailand on TDY (temporary duty). Very soon after that, I returned to the States. My final duty station was at SHAPE Headquarters, Belgium.

I volunteered for Vietnam but I became strongly disappointed as to why we were there. To this very day, I grieve for the 58,000 names on the Vietnam Wall.

Shirley J. Brown      Eva Marie Nordstrom

**Shirley J. Brown**
**In country: June 17, 1967 – Date of departure unknown**
**Rank: Staff Sergeant, US Air Force**
**Duty: MACV, Executive Administrative Assistant**

**♥Eva Marie Nordstrom**
**Retired as a Senior Master Sergeant**
**In country: June 17, 1967 – Date of departure unknown**
**Rank: Staff Sergeant, US Air Force**
**Duty: MACV, Executive Administrative Assistant**

**♥Bonnie Jean McWilliams**
**Retired as a Lieutenant Colonel**
**In country: June 17, 1967 – June 16, 1968**
**Rank: Major, US Army**
**Duty: MACV, USAHAC, Engineers, Personnel Management Officer**

**Pamela J. Forbing**
**In country: June 26, 1967 – June 25, 1968**
**Rank: Specialist 4, US Army**
**Duty: USARV, G3, Clerk-Typist**

# JULY

*Memory Lane: Race riots spread – Newark, NJ; Plainfield, NJ; Minneapolis, MN; Detroit, MI and Milwaukee, WI.*
*Song: "Windy" by The Association*

**Juanita R. Cox**
**Retired as a Major**
**In country: July 1967 – July 1968**
**Rank: First Lieutenant, US Air Force**
**Duty: 7th Air Force, Intelligence Officer, Political Analysis, Indications and Warning Division**

**Comments and Memories:** Riding "side saddle" on a motorcycle in the rain (of course) with mud splattering on my nylons and black shiny high heels while in my uniform, blouse and skirt.

Being serenaded after curfew hours by co-workers who bribed the guard with a couple of cigarettes. The complex was never the same as they woke up everyone, including five full colonels.

*Source: Vietnam Memory Book 2000*

**Sara "Skip" N. Harris**
**Retired as a Lieutenant Colonel**
**In country: July 1967 – July 1968**
**Rank: Lieutenant Colonel, US Air Force**
**Duty: Headquarters 7th Air Force, Executive Officer**

**Comments and Memories:** Flight line fellows found an orphaned pup and brought him to me. I named him VC. (VC was short for Viet Cong, the enemy.) Shortly after the Tet 1968 Offensive, VC strayed from my hootch. I began a vigorous search among the barracks yelling, "VC, VC." When the barracks emptied and the bunkers filled, I realized I had made a grave mistake by giving him that name.
*Source: Vietnam Memory Book 2000*

**Carmen Esther Oliveras (Martinez)**
**Retired as a Sergeant First Class**
**In country: July 1967 – July 1968**
**Rank: Specialist 6, US Army**
**Duty: USARV, Administrative NCO**

**Catherine J. MacBride**
**Retired as a Master Sergeant**
**In country: July 1967 – July 1968**
**Rank: Master Sergeant, US Air Force**
**Duty: MACV, J1**

**Agnes M. Carlin**
**Retired as a Major**
**In country: July 1967 – January 1969**
**Rank: Major, US Army**
**Duty: MACV, USAHAC**

**Grace E. Scruggs**
**Retired as a Major**
**In country: July 4, 1967 – July 4, 1968**
**Rank: Captain, US Air Force, Biomedical Sciences Corps**
**Duty: 7ᵗʰ Air Force, 12ᵗʰ Tactical Wing, 12ᵗʰ USAF Hospital, Cam Ranh Bay, Physical Therapist**

I received orders to report in July 1967 to the USAF Hospital at Cam Ranh Bay, South Vietnam. The base was on a peninsula shared with US Army and Navy units. When we landed, I recall someone saying it was the Fourth of July.

I wondered how this assignment in a "war zone" would differ from the "normal" ones. What did I expect? Certainly not a complete hospital! Well, what I found is that my treatment work was similar wherever I go. My faith is strong; I don't recall ever feeling afraid. I was good to go.

The Physical Therapy (PT) Clinic held regular clinic hours. On our own time, a few things I enjoyed were singing in the (men's) chorus. Three of us girls practiced and sang with them. We were filmed and later told that we had been on TV in the USA on New Year's Eve! One day we heard that Martha Raye was coming, so we prepared a welcome for her with "Hello, Martha!" (as in Dolly). She loved it.

I was happy to join our MEDCAP (Medical Civic Action Program) team on two trips. Trucked out into a village, crews set up temporary clinics. The team – doctor, dentist, nurse, med tech and anyone else who would or could help – worked steadily all day. It reminded me of mothers at home caring for a simple bump, sting, wound or scrape. After cleaning and treating, we would give the patient (or parent) soap and a washcloth and tell them to keep the area very clean. Busy all day, we were happy to return to base for food and rest.

Miss Johnson, a 72-year-old lady Baptist missionary, lived on the mainland about 10 miles from the airbase. Our Base Chaplain, with armed guard, would go check on her each week. He frequently asked if I could get away to go with him. I did, often, as my outstanding NCOIC could handle most anything in the PT clinic. Also at the mission, Army, Navy and Air Force volunteers went one night a week to teach classes. Having taught high school English, I also taught it there.

In February 1968 during Tet, fighting went on around the mission station, but nothing happened to the mission or Miss Johnson; they were specifically protecting her. The in-country Mission Board told her to leave. She complied but in a few months was right back on the job. We met her needs – she had lost most belongings in travel – as best we could from base personnel and the base exchange.

A Vietnamese child, treated in our hospital, needed a brace. At my suggestion, our Hospital Commander sent me to Tachikawa Airbase, Japan, and with just a week's temporary duty, we delivered the needed brace.

A very interesting year for me: enjoyable and happy, sad and glad, learning and fun travel. The day I left, I noted that it was the Fourth of July 1968. Going home!

**♥Shirley "Stretch" Larsen**
**Retired as a Master Sergeant**
**In country: July 11, 1967 – July 10, 1968**
**Rank: Sergeant First Class, US Army**
**Duty: USARV, G2, Counterintelligence Division, Intelligence Analyst**

My Commander, CPT Joanne Murphy's quarters were just above mine. When it poured rain, it would flood her area, come through her floor and onto my bed. Most of the time, my poncho was used to cover my cot. Me, I stayed wet.

After she retired, Stretch volunteered at the public library, shelving and sorting books. In addition, she delivered meals-on-wheels. Stretch was a member of the WAC Veterans Association. *Source: Vietnam Memory Book 2000*

July 13, 1967 - The temporary WAC Detachment opens in Long Binh. It was very muddy and the women lost the standard allowances for cost of living and separate rations – a total of $152 per month which was significant in 1967! They were housed 28 in the small bay and 54 in the larger bay, double bunked, and separated by wall lockers. The outside walls had alternating wood slats and wire, which meant that any rainfall came into the building, and when it was dry, the red dust/dirt drifted in constantly.

## Tanya L. Murphy (Hickman)
### In country: July 21, 1967 – November 1968
### Rank: Specialist 5, US Army
### Duty: USARV, G2, Clerk-Typist

 On my way to Vietnam I was the only woman on a troop plane. Though a long trip, I was well taken care of, but when I got off the plane it was very scary. Off we marched, the men to one area and I to another. I waited forever, it seemed to me, for a ride. It seems I wasn't expected, so it took a while before I got a ride. Finally, I arrived at quarters and was issued a bunk. My bunkmate wasn't sure she liked me, but I had no problem with her. So my life began.

My job was clerk-typist helping to give clearances to people who needed them.

I have always liked and am drawn to animals. When First Sergeant Marion Crawford learned I had groomed poodles at home, she let me groom her poodle, and Sergeant Efferson had a little dog, too. A supply depot guy gave me a pup from his litter. I couldn't think of a name for her and liked Captain Peggy Ready, my company commander, so I named her "Ready." As it turned out, she didn't mind.

We were invited to an orphanage at Bien Hoa and from then on, I was hooked. I loved kids even more than dogs. We would go once a week and cleaned babies and played with them if they were able.

I went to church and even sang a solo once. I made friends with a Lieutenant. I think she was a nurse, but can't remember. She played piano and sang in church.

Once I ended up in the hospital. We were standing in line to get flu shots, and I was sicker than a dog with really bad chills. Instead of the flu shot, I was sent to the hospital. They kept asking questions; I could hardly remember my name. Put in a cubicle, I was told to lie there until they could process me. I was covered with coats and blankets. Later they admitted me.

I was given a bed and found that the bathrooms were outhouses across the street. After going to the bathroom, I came out the door, and it felt like the ground came up to smack me in the face. I had passed out, and next thing I know, I'm back in my hospital bed.

Back in the detachment, I was told I had a visitor. I couldn't think who it might be. I went to the office and found my cousin Wendel. He invited me to spend some time with him in Saigon. He had a driver and we had a lot of fun. After our visit, while they were returning to their base, the driver was killed. He was pretty young, too.

A major at my job never liked my dog Ready. When I became a "short timer," he told me that when I left he was going to feed her to the VC (Viet Cong). I said, no he wasn't, that I was taking her with me. Then I had to figure out how to make that happen! Jokingly, I said I was going to take a collection to send her home. The idea snowballed and many small donations added up to $180 to help send her home. I was very lucky with my driver (wish I could remember his name) because he knew Saigon and was a real help in getting where we needed to pick up the paperwork for Ready to leave the country.

Ready arrived in Moab about a week before I got back. My Dad picked her up and took care of her until I came home. He brought her to the airport to pick me up. When she saw me, she went nuts; it was good to see her again.

# AUGUST

*Memory Lane: Jimi Hendrix's debut album, "Are You Experienced?" is released in the United States.*
*Song: "Light My Fire" by The Doors*

**♥Mary Armstrong (Kelso)**
**Retired as a Lieutenant Colonel**
**In country: August 1967 – July 1968**
**Rank: Lieutenant Colonel, US Army Medical Specialist Corps**
**Duty: 43rd Medical Group, Nha Trang, Dietetic Consultant**

During World War II, Mary was commissioned as a dietitian in the Army Medical Service Corps and served aboard hospital ships. She was recalled to active duty during the Korean Conflict and served until her retirement in 1970. Lieutenant Colonel Kelso died September 3, 2006, and is buried at the Fort Sam Houston National Cemetery. *(From obituary published in the Austin American-Statesman, September 8, 2006)*

**♥Mary Jane Grimes**
**Retired as a Colonel**
**In country: August 1967 – July 1968**
**Rank: Major, US Army**
**Duty: USARV, G1, Personnel Staff Officer**

***Dorene J. Steklasa:*** Mary Jane Grimes entered military service from Darlington, IN, in 1951. She served in a variety of WAC positions and personnel assignments as an Adjutant General officer. Her overseas assignments included duty in Vietnam from August 1967 to July 1968. She was assigned to USARV Headquarters in the office of the Deputy Chief of Staff for Personnel.

Other assignments included First Recruiting District, Fort Meade, MD, Personnel Support Command, Fort Bragg, NC, and Assistant Executive Officer, Department of the Army Inspector General.

Her WAC assignments included Company Commander, Co A, 1st WAC Training Battalion followed by assignment as the battalion Adjutant. She returned to Fort McClellan, AL, to serve as the Commander, 2nd WAC Training Battalion from 1974 to 1976. She was promoted to Colonel April 1, 1976. Her final assignment was the Director of Training, US Army Military Police School and Training Center. She retired in 1979.

***Evelyn "Pat" Foote:*** I knew Jane most of my Army career. She was the complete professional officer, always placing duty before self. USARV Headquarters had relocated to Long Binh by the time Major Jane Grimes arrived in August 1967. She replaced COL Shirley Heinze in USARV Personnel. We had a very close-knit group of women officers at Long Binh who dubbed themselves "The Bootleggers of Old Long Binh," and Jane fit right in. Members included Shirley Heinze, Sarah Niblack, Alice Hampson, Ann Wansley, Jane and me.

When then COL Hoisington, Director of the Women's Army Corps and LTC Leta Frank (WAC Staff Adviser, USARPAC) visited Long Binh in 1967, Jane was the project officer. When that visit ended, I went with Jane, COL Hoisington and Leta Frank to Tan Son Nhut Airbase to see the officers off to Hawaii. Their airline tickets had been cancelled in error and COL Hoisington was vowing not to leave the airport until tickets were obtained. Jane and I left the colonels in the VIP Lounge, engineered first class tickets for both ladies, paying the price difference ourselves. We definitely wanted the two of them on their way! (We were reimbursed later.)

**Beverly Ann Salisbury (Suafoa)**
**In country: August 1967 – July 1968**
**Rank: Specialist 6, US Army**
**Duty: MACV, US Joint Public Affairs Office**

**Cynthia H. Little**
**Retired as a Colonel**
**In country: August 1967 – March 1969**
**Rank: Captain, US Air Force**
**Duty: 7th Air Force, 377th Combat Support Group**

How do WAF get along with the Vietnamese? Many of the officers have Vietnamese employees, both men and women, working for them. The enlisted WAF frequently rubbed elbows as they worked alongside Vietnamese women clerks. Captain Little, an administrative officer, put it this way: "The Vietnamese people are kind, conscientious, considerate and polite, but also somewhat shy and withdrawn." "One of my Vietnamese clerks won't speak to her first," said another officer. "But then, her background has taught her that I'm the boss, and she is not supposed to speak to the boss. Otherwise she is quite pleasant and a diligent worker. I'm sure things would be different if we knew each other socially rather than occupationally. *Source:* Airman, *May 1969*

**♥Barbara Mae Sweeney (Pratt-LeMahieu)**
**Retired as a Lieutenant Colonel**
**In country: August 7, 1967 – August 1968**
**Rank: Lieutenant Colonel, US Air Force**
**Duty: 7th Air Force, Administrative Management Officer**

**Mavis "May" D. Schmidt**
**In country: August 8, 1967 – September 7, 1969; June 1971 – May 1972**
**Rank: Specialist 6, US Army**
**Duty: USARV, G2; MACV, General Abrams' secretary; Joint US Military**
**Advisory Group as Executive Administrative Assistant**

I came to Vietnam after working as a clerk-typist, having the good fortune to be working for General Harold K. Johnson, Chief of Staff of the Army, Vice Chief of Staff General Creighton W. Abrams, and Secretary to the General Staff Brigadier General Charles Corcoran. I volunteered to go through a stenographer course at Fort Benjamin Harrison, IN, then go to Vietnam from there, which I did – myself and 200 other GIs landed at Tan Son Nhut Air Base, were bused to Long Binh Post, USARV, and billeted at the WAC Detachment – lots of stories there.

I worked for Secretary Joint Staff, General Abrams' office, for two years, and went through the Tet Offensive in Saigon – tons of stories there also. In this job, I had the privilege of working for and meeting many high-powered and famous people.

Then I had a break in service. Back in the US, I missed my friends so joined up again and went back to Saigon, working at Joint US Military Advisory Group compound this time. After my year in Vietnam, I returned to the US, stationed at Fort McPherson, GA, and then to Albuquerque, NM, whereupon I left the Army with an Honorable Discharge. I took some college courses and had several jobs, winding up back home in Iowa, where I raised my daughter Melody. I have two wonderful grandchildren to spoil and enjoy.

I shall be writing a book about my experiences in the military, about some of the high-powered and famous people I met in Vietnam, and some civilian jobs I've had, some good and some bad. But, I wouldn't trade anything for my experiences and the pleasure of being with friends as we went through lots of "survival times," at the least! I hope that I will be sharing some "good" memories for the most part. Weren't we all still quite young and learning all about life, too? I've learned a lot, as anyone does as they go through their lives.

Since living in Iowa, I've had numerous jobs, including truck driving, trying to pay bills and raising my daughter. I've also been in several car accidents and one truck accident. Severe carpal tunnel limits the use of my wrists – I'm barely getting this sent – and lots of drunks running into my cars. So, it has been difficult.

**Ruth M. Ellis (Anderson)**
**Retired as a Colonel**
**In country: August 11, 1967 – March 6, 1969**
**Rank: Captain, US Air Force**
**Duty: Headquarters 7th Air Force, Assistant Chief of Staff for Intelligence, Director of Plans and Programs, Intelligence Officer**

A recent graduate of the Air Intelligence School, off I went to steamy Vietnam clad in a two-piece, skirted uniform undergirded by a garter belt, nylons, and high heels. Hours later, I hobbled into the terminal at Tan Son Nhut, swollen ankles overflowing the new shoes. Eighteen months later, we were wearing a more utilitarian skirt and blouse but never anything more appropriate for the duty or the climate. The first few weeks I was living with a superior female officer in a hotel in Saigon while the barracks at Tan Son Nhut were being completed. Once we moved there, we each had our own non air-conditioned room and shared a floor bathroom.

I envied my colleagues who worked in air-conditioned buildings because ours was quite dirty with high open screens where windows would have been, providing the perfect habitat for beetles and other insects that skittered about our desks or flew into our faces. When the Tet Offensive of 1968 occurred, somebody decided we should be sandbagged, a particularly unhealthy business when the bags inside our office leaked, assaulting our sinuses and leaving us perpetually grimy. But we complained quietly for we weren't tramping around the jungle, or being tortured in a prisoner of war camp.

My work was most interesting—documenting the air war both in and out of country. The officers reporting on downed aircrew members worked a couple of desks over, and as they locked their safes every evening they would say, "Goodnight, guys. Take care wherever you are." I had to publish the results of their findings, of how many people we had lost throughout the region, and how successful or not we had been during the week. It was often heart rending. Maybe I wasn't nursing dying guys, but none of us who served were untouched by the reality of the conflict.

Prior to Tet 1968, we enjoyed going downtown on our rare days off to shop, or enjoy the hotel restaurants. After Tet 1968, we could no longer go to Saigon, which I missed. From that time, we were essentially cut off from the people we were there to save, and the war became another assignment, albeit a more dangerous one. (That said, in 1981 I was thrown to the ground when the Bader Meinhoff terrorist gang bombed Ramstein Air Base, Germany. In Vietnam we were prepared for sudden danger; in Germany we were caught unaware.)

I am probably the only American who cried when leaving Vietnam. It was time to go for my parents' peace of mind and for my career. But, I had good friends still serving there, and I really missed the intensity once I reached my next assignment in Germany. In 1973, the United States walked away from the war. We didn't lose it, we left it. In the fall of 1968 when President Johnson announced we wouldn't bomb the north any longer, I was angry, and began to believe we weren't serious enough to win the war. Unfortunately, this proved to be true.

The liberation of military women may be the only positive result of the Vietnam War. We proved we could shoulder our responsibilities without requiring undue care and attention. In that regard, like our predecessors, we helped pave the way for the next generation of women who have nobly fought our wars beside their male counterparts. I'm proud of today's military women, and I'm eternally grateful that I had the opportunity to serve the greatest nation on earth.

**Betty Ann Patterson (Pope)**
**Retired as a Lieutenant Colonel**
**In country: August 15, 1967 – August 15, 1968**
**Rank: Major, US Air Force**
**Duty: 7th Air Force, Out of Country Defense Division**

The year I served in Vietnam proved to be the most memorable in my long lifetime. Of many noteworthy events, the most unforgettable was the Tet offensive in January and February of 1968.

Visible tension hung in the air that first morning as the smoke from the 122mm rockets fired by the Viet Cong drifted upward. Eight-foot deep craters near the Air Force women officers' billet and the Intelligence Branch Office where I worked testified to the deadly intent of the attack. Luckily, none of our Air Force women line officers, nurses (who shared our billet) or men in my office (all protected behind sandbags during the worst of the attack) was injured. Since both our billet and my office were near the flight line, we were in the direct line of rocket fire.

During the following week, no one was permitted on or off Tan Son Nhut Air Base which meant that our small 8x10 rooms had to be shared with all those unfortunate male officers who lived off base but had been on duty that evening. They also shared our central bathrooms (one for each floor) and housekeeping chores (e.g., sheets washed in the bathtub by us instead of Vietnamese maids who were prevented access). During that time, a fellow officer in the Intelligence Division on night shift shared my quarters during the day, a truly memorable event.

NOTE: In light of the current reporting of rape and other offenses and indignities suffered by military women, I must comment that nothing of that nature occurred to me during my year in Vietnam or during my entire 22 years of military service. No lewd remarks were directed my way and objectionable language was quickly curtailed when I arrived in the area.

During the early days after WWII which I well remember, one of the arguments used in a vain attempt to prevent women from serving in the military was that they would be vulnerable to the offenses currently being reported. That sort of thinking lingered for a number of years. Air Force women were not accepted in Vietnam (a combat zone) because critics said many airmen would be required to guard the quarters removing them from important guard work on the base perimeter. Eventually, after diligent efforts by USAF Major General Jeanne Holm and others, Air Force women line officer volunteers were assigned to the combat zone.

Now that women have achieved significant number and stature in all the services, I am not surprised that this grizzled monster has resurfaced. In spite of our many accomplishments, we are still not welcomed by a certain element in the military establishment. We're making headway, but we're not there yet.

**Pauline "Polly" W. Wilson**
**In country: August 17, 1967 – March 2, 1969**
**Rank: Corporal, US Marine Corps**
**Duty: MACV**

## Mary Elizabeth Glaudel-DeZurik
**In country: August 28, 1967 – August 15, 1968**
**Rank: Sergeant, US Marine Corps**
**Duty: MACV, Adjutant General, Mail and Distribution Section**

On August 28, 1967, after a very long flight, I arrived at Tan Son Nhut Air Base. Like everyone else who takes that first step out of the plane, the heat draped over me like a wet blanket. I was taken to the Ambassador Hotel in Saigon. I was greeted by Marine MSgt Barbara Dulinsky and settled in. The next day I received my work assignment at MACV Headquarters. I was assigned to the Adjutant General Mail and Distribution Section.

My job was to receive classified documents, reports, maps and correspondence sent from various Pacific commands. All materials marked "SECRET" had to be recorded, tracked and signed for. Most came with a distribution list but if there wasn't one, or if there were extra copies, I had to determine which office in the Headquarters should receive the material. The workdays were long, 10 to 12 hours, and time off was limited to one day a week, at least until the Tet Offensive. There was a definite "before" and "after." After Tet, everything changed.

At the end of October 1967, we had moved from the Ambassador to the Plaza Hotel. For the rest of 1967, life was as normal as it could be for living and working in a combat zone. Normal meaning going to work in a military bus with grates on the window; watching out for cabs that had no door handles on the inside and the "cowboys" who sped around the city streets on their mopeds. I had my watch stolen off my arm before I could even react. Lesson learned – no expandable band on a watch. On Christmas Day, a group of us from the office picked up some children from Go Vap Orphanage and took them to the Saigon Zoo. I don't remember seeing many animals as the zoo was in poor condition but it was a nice outing for the children. We finished the day with supper at a BEQ (enlisted quarters) and treats for the kids.

Then came the Tet Offensive. January 31, 1968, was a very noisy night. There were many firecrackers going off from the street crowds celebrating their new year. The next morning I got up and got ready for work as usual. Polly (Cpl Pauline Wilson, USMC), my roommate, and I headed toward the main lobby to catch our military bus for work. As we approached the lobby we saw that the lights were out and there were no vehicles or people on the street. We were told to return to our room and wait for information and instructions. Within a short time, we were told that not only Saigon and Cholon, but most of the country, was under attack. We knew we wouldn't be going anywhere for an undetermined amount of time. The top floor of the Plaza was normally a club where you could order food and drinks but it was now turned into a mess hall. We worked there making food for the troops coming in off the street and washing dishes, serving and clearing tables. We all wanted to stay busy as being confined to a small hotel room got old very quickly. Those first few nights of the Tet Offensive, I could hear small-arms fire that seemed to be coming from nearby rooftops. There was one explosion that caused me to fly off my bed. It probably wasn't that close but it was loud! I thought it was then a good time to go across the hall and visit two friends, Cpl Nola Makinster, USMC, and SSG Beverly Salisbury, US Army. It took five days before we were able to get back to work at MACV. The planes were still not landing at Tan Son Nhut Air Base and it would be two weeks before they did. This was my calm before the storm since my incoming mail came from those deliveries. Once the mail started coming in I was swamped with work and time off became a memory. It would be the end of April before I had a day off when I was able to take my R&R. Our uniform of the day became fatigues and combat boots. Due to my short stature (I am 4'11") there was difficulty in finding fatigues that fit. Every set was too long and too big. Finally, someone at the Marine Liaison Office made a trade with the Vietnamese Marines for three pairs of fatigues. They were comfortable and practical but I had to get used to carrying only a few things in my pockets. It wasn't long before we made another hotel change. This time we moved to the Billings BEQ in Tan Son Nhut and much closer to MACV. As my tour was ending in late August 1968, I decided to extend my time to match my EAS (end of active service) date. My request was approved but I had to rescind it shortly after as I heard that my father was very ill. Although I had really wanted to stay, it was the right decision to make as he passed away a month after I returned. My time in the Marine Corps was completed at Marine Corps Recruiting Depot, San Diego, CA. I will always be grateful for the time I spent in Vietnam as it showed me just how lucky I am to live where I do and enjoy the freedoms that I have. And, the Marine Corps? Well, they are my other family. Semper Fidelis!

Update: I married Peter DeZurik in 1973. We have four children and nine grandchildren. I was a stay-at-home mom until my youngest was in preschool. I started working at the Minnesota State Environmental Agency in 1988 and retired January 15, 2013, after 25 years.

# SEPTEMBER

*Memory Lane: Jim Morrison and The Doors defy CBS censors on The Ed Sullivan Show, when Morrison sings the word "higher" from their #1 hit "Light My Fire," despite having been asked not to.*
*Songs: "You Can't Hurry Love" by The Supremes; "Ode to Billie Joe" by Bobbie Gentry*

**Jacqueline M. Salisbury**
**Retired as a Sergeant First Class**
**In country: September 1967 – September 1968**
**Rank: Sergeant First Class, US Army**
**Duty: MACV, J3, Operations**

My arrival in Saigon, Vietnam was a little culture shock. I spoke a little French and when I was asked by the American University to join the Orphanage Society, I was delighted to do so. The staff and children were a delight. Some of the kids couldn't walk and some were so malnourished they had to be fed with an eye dropper. We cut their hair, wrote to friends to send clothes and toys as well as hygiene items.

My most vivid memory was the beginning of Tet as I was worried for my older brother, Charles, who came in December 1967. He assured me he was ok. We weren't allowed out of the hotel for five days. The staff (especially kitchen workers) did all they could before we took over making coffee, cleaning tables and floors and finding something for everyone to eat (including those who were on R&R). Finally, the Vietnamese head chef sneaked in with food.

My younger brother, Dick, came over a couple of months later, so we got to see each other.

We marveled at the older kids taking care of the younger, even to the point of sleeping on the sidewalk with the little ones between them. The people who worked in our office often showed up with loads of bananas, other fruit and sweetened rice wrapped in banana leaves.

**Elisabeth "Lisa" A. Schattner**
**Retired as a Major**
**In country: September 1967 – September 1968**
**Rank: Captain, US Air Force**
**Duty: 7ᵗʰ Air Force, Intelligence Photo-Radar Officer**

**Frances Talley (Symes)**
**Retired as a Lieutenant Colonel**
**In country: September 1967 – April 1969**
**Rank: Captain, US Air Force**
**Duty: 7ᵗʰ Air Force, 12ᵗʰ Reconnaissance Intelligence Tech Squadron**

"What spare time?" She echoes the comment of many of the WAF. The photographic interpreter is assigned to the 12ᵗʰ Reconnaissance Intelligence Squadron at Tan Son Nhut. "My days, seven of them in every week, run to 14 and more work hours. Most of us are fortunate to have a few moments to write a letter or two before turning in every night."

The WAF have virtually no outside activities and spend their limited off-duty time reading, listening to music or, as Lieutenant Talley does, writing letters or making tapes to send home. Rarely do they get off base to shop and browse through local stores. *Source:* Airman, *May 1969*

# OCTOBER

*Memory Lane: US Navy pilot John McCain is shot down over North Vietnam and becomes a POW; tens of thousands of Vietnam War protesters march in Washington, DC.*
*Songs: "Purple Haze" by Jimi Hendrix Experience; "The Letter" by The Boxtops*

## Jeanette I. Hensley (King)
**In country: October 1967 – April 1968**
**Rank: Sergeant, US Marine Corps**
**Duty: MACV, J3, Administrative Specialist**

My time in Vietnam was quite a memory that I wish at times I did not have, but I was there during the beginning of the Tet Offensive, so that itself was a scary ordeal. With sniper fire and mortar going all around, everyone feared for their life. I was told before I went to Vietnam that Saigon was the pearl of the Orient. I think my commander must have gotten that very wrong.

## Dona R. H. Hildebrand
**Retired as a Lieutenant Colonel**
**In country: October 1967 – December 1968**
**Rank: Lieutenant Colonel, US Air Force**
**Duty: Headquarters 7th Air Force, Personnel Division, Executive Officer**

## ♥Mary Van Ette Bender
**In country: October 1967 – May 1969; September 1970 – August 1971**
**Rank: Chief Warrant Officer 2, US Army**
**Duty: MACV, 525th Military Intelligence Brigade, Counter Intelligence Technician**

*CW3 Dave Mann:* Mary was a sergeant, like I was at the time, when I first met her. I was doing background investigations while I was serving at the Pentagon. You can imagine that (she) and I had lots to talk about when we would meet up in Vietnam. Usually, I would handle the setting up of the wired mikes and the photo coverage in the areas where she was conducting examinations. I spoke to her about applying for a warrant appointment, and she told me straight away that I should do it, "that I would make a good one." I retired as a CW4 in 1988. We really hit it off as friends; she was a close-in-age mentor, so to speak. Chief always found the time to chat.

Our longest working association came in mid-1968 when she came up to Da Nang to (investigate) an involved sabotage case. The case involved three soldiers who deliberately sabotaged the fire control circuits on helicopter gunships' turret guns. Chief, along with three or four other poly people were brought up from Saigon and Okinawa, and a couple of CID (Criminal Investigation Division) warrants from Japan. We were able to identify the individuals, draftee soldiers who were members of an anti-war underground group.

One thing I noticed right away – how somber she was when she was usually a joker and lively. During an off-time (gathering), we were having a bull session and the conversation turned to the events of Tet. She said in general terms how the NVA had basically come knocking on their doors, and she was stuck with "only the ****** thirty-eight (special agent's .38 snub nose pistol) and some old carbine left over from World War Two!"

She was incredibly fortunate to have survived those three days and nights. I received the distinct impression from the bull session and later conversations with other guys from the 525th MIG (Military Intelligence Group) Tech Shop in Saigon that she performed some very heroic actions. She was responsible for saving the women hiding in that side of her BOQ (bachelor officers' quarters). Except for one WAC major, the women were either non-combatants or nurses, none of whom could effectively use a weapon. Chief was billeted in the Meyerkord. Women were located on the third floor.

I know one thing. As a former infantryman, I would not want to be stuck in a stairwell for three days with just a lightweight M1 carbine – especially with no electricity, shooting going on all around, no food, no water, etc., and wondering if the next thing you saw coming around the corner of the lower landing was a VC (Viet Cong) with an AK-47 on full auto.

***From her own statement:*** Much of the area surrounding the hotel was burnt to the ground from incoming mortar rounds. There was small-arms fighting around the hotel perimeter, and the enemy was making an effort to capture the hotel, needed as a strategic position to launch an attack on the Presidential Palace. I left my room with flak jacket, helmet and carbine. A male officer asked me to get the women out of their rooms so they would not be fired upon through their windows. The male residents were defending the hotel from the roof and balconies. The MPs (military policemen) guarding the building had been killed almost immediately. I was then asked by another male officer to guard the stairwell to the third floor. He then gave me grenades and instructed me to blow up the stairwell in the event that the Viet Cong were able to take the bottom two floors. I laid on the floor at the top of the stairwell. I could hear bullets ricocheting off the walls from the floor below. At some point someone yelled, "They're on the first floor.

"In discussing this with another agent who served with her at a later point in her career, he states that she had eliminated several VC in that stairwell."
*~CW3 Dave Mann*

For her actions, CW2 Bender was recommended for the Silver Star, but was denied. She did, however, receive two Bronze Stars. Her other awards include the Army Commendation Medal, Meritorious Unit Ribbon with Oak Leaf (525th Military Intelligence), the Good Conduct Medal, the Vietnam Service Medal with 10 campaign stars and the Vietnam Campaign Medal with '60 device.

In January 2002, Mary Bender died alone and homeless. After a hard fight by her son and others, the person who once interrogated Viet Cong prisoners and had fought so hard to defend her hotel mates in 1968 was finally embraced by the Army after having been cast aside for pregnancy. On February 1, 2002, Mary Bender was inurned at Arlington National Cemetery with full military honors.

**♥Gloria "Toni" Ann Walker**
**Retired as a Master Sergeant (USAR)**
**In country: October 1967 – November 1969**
**Rank: Specialist 6, US Army**
**Duty: MACV, Annex, Food Service Specialist; USO Shows**

Gloria Walker joined the Army at the end of 1964. After basic training at Fort McClellan, AL, she completed advanced training as a Food Service Specialist in May 1965 at Fort Knox, KY. She volunteered and in October 1967, she arrived in Vietnam where she was assigned to the MACV Annex with duty in the mess hall. While in Vietnam, she also performed in some USO shows. She was asked to sing on stage as opener to the Bob Hope Christmas Show in 1968. She returned stateside in November 1969 and left active duty when her enlistment was up. Specialist 5 Walker transferred to the Army Reserve in late 1972 where she soon made Specialist 6. She retired in 1991 with the rank of Master Sergeant. MSG Walker died April 25, 2006.

**Doris "Lucki" Ida Allen**
**Retired as a Chief Warrant Officer 3**
**In country: October 1967 – September 1970**
**Rank: Specialist 7, US Army appointed to Warrant Officer**
**Duty: USARV, Army Operations Center, Senior Intelligence Analyst; 1st Logistical Command, Security Plans and Operations, Security Division, Supervisor; MACV, 519th Military Intelligence Battalion, Combined Documents Exploitation Center, Translation Branch**

*Excerpt from The Military Intelligence Corps 2009 Hall of Fame.* SP7 Allen reported to Vietnam and served as the Senior Intelligence Analyst, Army Operations Center, Headquarters, US Army at Long Binh, Vietnam. While in Vietnam she started her second tour and held the position of Supervisor, Security Division, Office of the Assistant Chief of Staff, Security, Plans, and Operations, Headquarters, 1st Logistical Command, Vietnam. In the spring of 1970, she would be appointed as a Warrant Officer. She was then one of only nine female warrant officers in (Military Intelligence) and one of only 23 in the entire Army at the time.

WO Allen began her third consecutive tour in Vietnam in March 1970 as the Officer in Charge of the Translation Branch, Combined Document Exploitation Center-MACV, Saigon, Vietnam. Despite not being able to speak Vietnamese, WO Allen supervised approximately 40 South Vietnamese nationals employed in the translation of the large amount of captured enemy documents brought to the center on a daily basis. Her loyalty, diligence, and devotion in all of her assignments in Vietnam earned her the Bronze Star with two Oak Leaf clusters.

*Excerpt from the article titled "Unarmed and under fire: An oral history of female Vietnam vets," November 11, 1999, Salon online magazine. Used with permission.*

Returning to the US from Vietnam in September 1970, she would serve as an Instructor for Prisoner of War Interrogations, Army Intelligence Center and School, Fort Holabird, (MD) and moved with the school in 1971 to Fort Huachuca (AZ).

"I worked in the operations center. There were 300 men to every woman on the Long Binh post. Run that around in your mind. I started (doing) intelligence analysis in USARV, the Army Operations Center. Every intelligence report, every information report that had to be written down from all over Vietnam, came across my desk. Usually they would throw them out. (The report) would say Charlie crossed the street last night. Another report, way down, would say Charlie walked down the street and he went into the third house . . . I was the one who sat there and said, "Hmm hmmm," and put it together. The reports would come in saying Allies had five killed and 20 wounded and three enemy killed and 81 wounded. Most of the time we did better than they did, because all you can say is I think I killed them. It got so bad that down in My Tho one of the commanders told his troops, "When you come back here you bring an ear and I will know that he's dead." And, that's when they started calling them "apricots" in order to prove that somebody had died.

I got there in October of 1967. Tet Offensive was January 31 of 1968. Thirty days prior to that happening, I turned in a report called "50,000 Chinese." I knew a major offensive was coming from all that I had read. There couldn't have been that many Viet Cong in the world. The report was a page and half. I took it to my supervising officer and he said, "Take it to Saigon." It was that important – he believed in me. I took it to Saigon. I took it to MACV (Military Assistance Command in Vietnam). I talked to the bigwigs. I was thinking, 'you better disseminate this.' They said, "No. I don't think we can do this." I asked myself why they weren't listening. I just came up recently with the reason they didn't believe me. They weren't prepared for me. They didn't know how to look beyond the WAC, black woman in military intelligence. I can't blame them. I don't feel bitter. That's just people, baby. When you aren't prepared for something, you just aren't prepared. I came back to the States with no guilt. I had sadness; I saw those names on the wall, but I kept doing my job.

*(Note:* Three Days Past Yesterday: A Black Woman's Journey Through Incredibility, *by Chief Warrant Officer 3 Doris I. "Lucki" Allen (US Army Retired) is available at amazon.com, barnesandnoble.com, tower.com. Paperback only.)*

**Alice "Baby" J. Delgado**
**Retired as a Colonel**
**In country: October 12, 1967 – October 1968**
**Rank: Major, US Army**
**Duty: MACV, USAHAC, Education Officer**

I wholeheartedly agree with the concept of the book we are attempting to produce. I'm willing to share as much of my story as I can, psychologically and emotionally, in support of this effort. I feel strongly that not one soldier, past or present, can ever really reveal the depth of their experiences. Nevertheless, I decided to share something good, something humorous and something bad.

The very good part of my year in Saigon was truly the friendships that grew from this tour, both in country and even years after leaving Saigon. There were several co-workers with whom I continued to correspond. There were many co-workers who touched my heart and whose names I can't recall, but their faces, however, are indelibly imprinted in my mind and heart – especially those who tragically lost their lives in the line of duty. We worked hard together; we laughed and joked; we ate and drank a lot; we knew we had a mission to accomplish together. Even now, so many years later, how GOOD it is to remember dear friends.

Then there is the bad part of my tour in Vietnam. I was there during the Tet Offensive. From the rooftop of my hotel we saw the American Embassy attacked. How foolish we were to be exposed like that. Things got worse – daily bombings, random small arms firing, and news of possible kidnappings. A bomb exploded right outside our headquarters, shattering the huge glass window just behind me while I sat at my desk. How I didn't get all cut up is a miracle.

Then there was a fire in my hotel. I still suffer from that experience. Worst of all: the picture in my mind of a truckload of dead bodies, from our own headquarters people remains with me – and will forever. Every day was awful after that. It was hard to laugh; we just drank a lot more. My heart was heavy; my mind and soul became numb. It's hard to write anything else . . . The BAD was VERY BAD.

*(Note: Colonel Delgado received the Army Commendation Medal for heroism for preventing a fire disaster at the Rex Hotel BOQ in Saigon. She also received the Bronze Star for meritorious service during her tour in Vietnam.)*

**Joanne "Murph" P. Murphy**
**In country: October 18, 1967 – October 17, 1968**
**Rank: Captain, US Army**
**Duty: USARV, Special Troops, WAC Detachment, Second Commander**

"No, select one of the other two. I don't want to go over there. There's a war going on" was my response to the 5th Army WAC Staff Advisor when she told me I was one of three officers being considered to replace CPT Peggy Ready. Well, I was the one selected, and I couldn't be happier with the decision. My eight years, nine months, and fourteen days were among the happiest of my life. I was in the Women's Army Corps. And, the happiest year of all was that of being the Commanding Officer of the finest unit the Army ever had. What a privilege to serve with these women! I was scared every day for their safety, but they gave me strength to be what I never thought I wanted to be – a Commanding Officer. Now that we're in our twilight years, I'm so happy to say that many of these women have become very dear and lifelong friends.

# NOVEMBER

*Memory Lane: US Secretary of Defense Robert McNamara announces his resignation to become president of the World Bank. This action is due to President Lyndon B. Johnson's outright rejection of McNamara's early November recommendations to freeze troop levels, stop bombing North Vietnam and hand over ground fighting to South Vietnam.*
*Songs: "Soul Man" by Sam and Dave; "To Sir With Love" by Lulu*

**Dale R. Ford (McGlynn)**
**Retired as a Staff Sergeant**
**In country: November 1967 – November 1968**
**Rank: Staff Sergeant, US Air Force**
**Duty: MACV, Protocol, Administrative Specialist**

**Comments and Memories:** Trying to walk with a .45 caliber pistol secured around my waist because they had run out of M-16 rifles. *Source: Vietnam Memory Book 2000*

**Evelyn J. Ford**
**Retired as a Master Sergeant**
**In country: November 1967 – November 1968**
**Rank: Master Sergeant, US Army**
**Duty: MACV, Joint Staff, Fourth NCO Advisor to the Vietnam Women's
Armed Forces Corps**

I remember landing in country at night. After a 24-hour flight with no sleep, I was handed bedding, a towel and wash cloth and told to go down a road to a building which was at the end. When I got there, the door was locked. Someone was in the building, but had locked all the doors. After pounding and pounding on the door, I finally got into the building and at last, got some much-needed sleep.

I had not been in country long, when the Tet Offensive happened. For days, we were all in lock down at the hotel where we lived in Saigon.

I can remember going to the Vietnamese Headquarters where they had bodies in pine boxes. They were not airtight. To this day, I can still smell the odor of rotting bodies lined up in the hot sun. There were other smells that, after all these years, I can still remember. The smells were the open fish market and the piles of trash in the streets.

There are other memories that are more pleasant. I traveled throughout South Vietnam – anywhere that the Vietnam Women's Armed Forces Corps were stationed. Lieutenant Colonel Frances Chaffin and I visited places like Nha Trang, Da Nang and Da Lat. I swam in the South China Sea. Vietnam had some of the most beautiful beaches. I can remember thinking, what a wonderful tourist area it could be.

I have many memories of my tour, some good and some not so good.

## Glenda F. Jones (Hamlin)
**In country: November 1967 – November 1968**
**Rank: Sergeant, US Army**
**Duty: USARV, 1st Signal Brigade, 160th Signal Group, Staff Supervisor**

Sergeant Jones had a baby pink telephone on her desk. As the staff supervisor at the telephone exchanges in the Saigon/Long Binh area, she was responsible for the collection and analysis of the control office and the switchboard traffic data for the 160th Signal Group. The pink phone was a perk although no one was sure where it came from.

## ♥Rita A. Lawler
**Retired as a Lieutenant Colonel**
**In country: November 1967 – November 1968**
**Rank: Major, US Air Force**
**Duty: Headquarters 7th Air Force, Personnel Staff Officer**

## Donna M. Loring
**In country: November 1967 – November 1968**
**Rank: Private (E2), US Army**
**Duty: USARV, 1st Signal Brigade, 44th Signal Battalion, 60th Signal Group, Communications Specialist**

I remember exactly when this photo was taken. That day was one of the highlights of my time in Vietnam because the photo was taken by a fellow member of the Penobscot Indian Nation, my friend Terry Lolar. He had just returned from spending three months in the jungle. He happened to pick up the current issue of *Stars and Stripes* and spotted a picture of me and the article "Comm. Center Has New Line – 3 WACs" about my duty assignment. The paper published the story because it was unheard of at the time for enlisted women who were attached to the WAC Detachment to be working at other than USARV Headquarters. I was assigned to the 1st Signal Brigade, 44th Signal Battalion which was a combat support unit. Though there were other women in combat support units throughout the country, it was a big deal for me to work at 1st

Signal because everyone else at the WAC Detachment was assigned to USARV Headquarters. I worked in the Communications Center where we processed all the casualty reports for Southeast Asia. Terry was just up the road from our detachment. Still with jungle mud on his boots and fatigues, he came right over to see me. I was really happy to see another tribal member. Terry passed a few years ago, and this photo reminds me of that very special day.

*Suggested reading:* In the Shadow of the Eagle *by Donna M. Loring available at Amazon.com*

**Carmen "Penny" P. Marshall (Adams)**
**In country: November 1967 – November 1968**
**Rank: Lieutenant, US Navy Reserve Medical Service Corps**
**Duty: USS *Repose* (AH-16), Officer in Charge, Laboratory and Blood Bank**

Flying into Da Nang airspace, we circled the field as tracers and flares lit up the night sky – a firefight near Red Beach. Deplaning onto the metal-sectioned landing pad wearing a winter dress uniform with high heels in 90% humidity helped form my first thought, "What the hell am I doing here?" I spent the first night at the Naval Hospital, Da Nang, in unfinished nurses' quarters surrounded by the red dirt that was South Vietnam.

I was assigned to the Naval Hospital Ship, USS *Repose* (AH-16). The *Repose* sailed up and down the coast off I Corps, a big white target with lighted red crosses on the sides. Following the Geneva Convention rules made it easier for the choppers to find us as they brought casualties directly from the field. They also brought emergency blood, general supplies and much awaited mail while we were on the line.

Our mission was to provide trauma care in a fully equipped hospital; my primary duty was Laboratory and Blood Bank Officer. Developed for mass casualties, our on-board system for blood transfusions was unique. The big problem was the time needed to prepare the blood for use. We could do five units at a time, but it took two people. Our entire staff of nine ran the lab 24/7, if you included the pathologist, the morgue technician and me. Out of necessity, we determined that extending the expiration date of stored blood was the better solution. On the line for 61 days, this extension got us through Khe San, Battle of Hue City, and Pegasus as we struggled to handle all the casualties. We were stationed just below the DMZ, only going into Da Nang harbor to transfer patients and receive supplies – as quickly as possible – to be back on the line by dark.

I was also on rotation as Administrative Watch Officer for the hospital, which, when on duty, required my presence for all helicopter landings from 8 p.m. to 8 a.m. Other administrative duties included counting drugs in the pharmacy, inspecting food in the enlisted mess and checking the ambulatory patients berthing area. Because this area was all men, a male duty officer did that for me. Some nights I was both Lab Officer and Admin Officer. I took "power naps" at my desk in the lab because it was close to the flight deck – not that I was allowed out there! No place for a woman, the "Old Navy" sailors would mumble: "Women didn't belong on ships," but there we were.

We had showers, hot food, real milk and ice cream. We had John Wayne war movies and, once in a while, a comedy. We took patients to the Philippines for transfer to stateside hospitals, 300 or more at a time. It wasn't a pleasure cruise, but better on the way back. We traveled to Manila or Baguio for a few days leave, which meant beauty shops, restaurants, and shopping (another story). It was a real break from the war and much needed by all.

For the first five months of my tour, the only time the women could leave the ship was when we docked in the Philippines. Even in Da Nang, we could leave only with a male carrying a gun. That was so he could shoot us if there was any chance that we (women) might be captured. Only when the gunners mate went did I go; he knew how to shoot. It was a year of constant work, often as heartrending as it was rewarding.

Returning home, it took a while for me to wind down. We were doing the same job, but things weren't so frantic; duties were more limited. And, working with staff who had also been in Vietnam made it easier. We had worked independently and now had to answer to all and sundry for our actions. The pace was slower with eight-hour shifts the rule. We were back in the world!

I can still hear a helicopter before most people. I've forgotten most of the names of my shipmates, but I will always remember the experiences of Vietnam, though they bring tears to my eyes.

**Regina "Gina" M. McGuiness**
**Retired as a Colonel, USAFR**
**In country: November 1967 – November 1968**
**Rank: Captain, US Air Force**
**Duty: Headquarters 7th Air Force, Joint US Public Affairs Office, Information Officer**

At the 7th Air Force Information Office staff meetings, someone always cracked a joke, or said something humorous about a meeting item. *Source: Vietnam Memory Book 2000*

**Patricia M. Dean (Rourk)**
**In country: November 1967 – April 7, 1969**
**Rank: Staff Sergeant, US Air Force**
**Duty: MACV, J2, J3 and J4, Administrative Specialist**

**Memorable experiences:** Vietnam was made memorable and worthwhile by providing, at least for a time, a sense of hope, love and caring to Vietnamese children. The Saigon Orphans Christmas party in 1968 was special and saw tremendous support and contributions from home. *(Courtesy of Women's Memorial Foundation Register)*

**♥Sarah Fairly Niblack**
**Retired as a Lieutenant Colonel**
**In country: November 1967 – September 1969**
**Rank: Lieutenant Colonel, US Army**
**Duty: USARV and MACV, Logistics Officer**

## Nola Evon Makinster (Wilcox)
**In country: November 1, 1967 – September 1968**
**Rank: Sergeant, US Marine Corps**
**Duty: MACV, J2, Directorate of Intelligence Production, Record Keeper**

I arrived in Vietnam November 1, 1967. I had orders to go to USARV Headquarters, but ended up at MACV in J2 Intelligence Production. I was the record keeper of intelligence of all before, during and final activities of 2,000 intelligence gathers. I did a lot of typing for J2 and making of charts.

I had a large group of intelligence officers. They were a great group of men. And being a rather naïve young woman, I was the brunt of a lot of gags and teasing. All of it was in fun and broke the tension.

Saigon was a beautiful city going in and fairly safe, but, after the Tet Offensive and 2,000 refugees coming into the city and with a lot of mortar fire, the city was a garbage dump when I left.

I didn't do much but work while there. The people in the country were great and were having hard times. It was a great opportunity to see how other people lived and ate. I still love eating Vietnamese food here in Arizona.

One story that happened was when General Phillip Davidson stole my live Christmas tree that my folks had mailed. I had it in my office so everyone would enjoy it. I came in one morning and it was gone. I went all over MACV Headquarters looking for it. The last place I went was to General D's office and asked him if he saw it. As I was leaving his office, I noticed it behind his desk on top of the safe. I gave him a hard time about it as he was going to Guam for Christmas with his family. He had a great laugh over the whole thing. As I said earlier, I was great entertainment for the guys in J2.

I did receive the Joint Service Commendation Medal, but when I got out of the service, the Marine Corps didn't recognize it. I was one of the first five women marines sent to Vietnam. It is one of my greatest accomplishments while I was in the Marine Corps. Semper Fi!

# DECEMBER

*Memory Lane: Soul singer Otis Redding, 26, and band members killed when their airplane crashes into Lake Monona, WI.*
*Songs: "I Heard it Through the Grapevine" by Gladys Knight & the Pips; "Daydream Believer" by The Monkees*

**♥Catherine Louise Dismuke**
**Retired as a Major**
**In country: December 1967 – December 1968**
**Rank: Major, US Air Force**
**Duty: Headquarters 7ᵗʰ Air Force, Office of the Deputy Commander**

Major Dismuke was a graduate of the University of Georgia, Air Force Squadron Officer School, Communications-Electronics Staff Officer School and Department of Defense Command and Control School. She served in Air Force units in Europe, Southeast Asia and throughout the United States. Her service awards include the Bronze Star, the Meritorious Service Medal, the Air Force Commendation Medal and the Vietnam Service Medal.

**Donna Dutton**
**In country: December 1967 – January 1969**
**Rank: Specialist 6, US Army**
**Duty: MACV, J6, Studies and Observations Group**

**♥Betty Mae Davis (Smith)**
**In country: December 1967 – February 13, 1969**
**Rank: Specialist 5, US Army**
**Duty: USARV, G4, Clerk-Typist**

**Therese "Terri" E. Harnden (Peters)**
**In country: December 1967 – March 1969**
**Rank: Specialist 5, US Army**
**Duty: USARV, Surgeon's Office, Administrative Specialist**

**Comments and Memories:** One night Wanda Baker sprayed starch instead of bug spray all over her cubical. One other day, another girl woke up petting a rat. *Source: Vietnam Memory Book 2000*

**♥Mary Elizabeth Pritchard (Lennon)**
**Retired as a Master Sergeant**
**In country: December 1967 – December 1969**
**Rank: Sergeant First Class, US Army**
**Duty: USARV; MACV, Operations,**
**Administrative NCO**

**♥Carolyn Ann Carmack (Robinson)**
**In country: December 1967 – February 1970**
**Rank: Staff Sergeant, US Army**
**Duty: USARV, Special Troops Personnel, Personnel Specialist**

*Peggy Hilton:* From day one, Carolyn Carmack and I were friends. We were roommates until the new barracks was built and we moved into it. I left Vietnam in September of 1969 and didn't see "Carely" again until 1975. I lived in Chicago and she was going to school at Fort Ben Harrison, IN, and from there going to Germany. While in Germany, she married and was reassigned to Fort Ord, CA. She had a daughter who was "her life." We wrote and called one another. And, in 1996 while I was in Alabama and when she was on her way to Florida, she and her daughter stopped by for a day and we visited. In 1998, I moved to Las Vegas and we lost touch with one another. Then in 2010 she found me and we started writing and calling. We made plans to meet but she got sick and it just went out the window. Later her husband called me and told me that Carolyn was bad off and I had just had knee replacement surgery so I was unable to go to see her. She improved for a few days and then just passed away. She is a friend I will never forget.

This makes the motto of the Women's Army Corps come to life: "SERVICE TOGETHER, FRIENDS FOREVER"

**♥Miriam G. Marsh (Felty)**
**Retired as a Staff Sergeant**
**In country: December 1967 – July 10, 1970**
**Rank: Staff Sergeant, US Army**
**Duty: MACV Annex, Saigon, Personnel, Career Counselor; Armed Forces Courier Service, Tan Son Nhut; Joint US Public Affairs Office, Saigon**

*Telephone interview with Claire Starnes, May 9, 2015:* Miriam Marsh (Felty) remembers arriving in Vietnam late in December 1967. She was at the WAC Detachment in Long Binh for only a few days before being assigned to the Personnel Office at the MACV Annex in Saigon. During the first 18 months she was in Vietnam, she served as a career counselor and traveled throughout Vietnam delivering official papers to units where soldiers were reenlisting. At times, she also filled in as receptionist for GEN Creighton Abrams. In August 1969, she began working at the Armed Forces Courier Service at Tan Son Nhut Air Base. Her responsibilities of delivering classified documents took her to Thailand, the Philippines, Hawaii and Alaska, with an immediate turnaround to Vietnam. For a few months prior to her departure, she worked at the Joint US Public Affairs Office, dealing with civilian correspondents covering in-country events.

Note: Miriam Marsh (Felty) was surprised to hear from anyone about this book. She said it had been at least 40 years since she had spoken with anyone she served with in Vietnam. She died June 4, 2015.

# Chapter Eight

# 1968

♥Harriet Grace Albers
In country: 1968 – 1969
Rank: Staff Sergeant, US Army
Duty: Administrative NCO

Varina A. Albers
In country: 1968 – 1969
Rank: Staff Sergeant, US Army
Duty: Administrative NCO

♥Apolonia Patricia Atayde
Retired as a Command Sergeant Major
In country: 1968 – 1969
Rank: Sergeant First Class, US Army
Duty: USARV, Special Troops

♥Jacqueline R. Chappell
Retired as a Lieutenant Colonel
In country: 1968 – 1969
Rank: Major, US Army
Duty: USARV, Management Analyst

Mary Patricia Dwyer
Retired as a Lieutenant Colonel
In country: 1968 – 1969
Rank: Major, US Army Medical Specialist Corps
Duty: 68th Medical Group, Long Binh, Dietetic Consultant

Betty J. Ferguson
In country: 1968 – 1969
Rank: Specialist 4, US Army
Duty: USARV, Clerk-Typist

♥Gabrielle M. Goulet
Retired as Staff Sergeant
In country: 1968 – 1969
Rank: Staff Sergeant, US Army
Duty: USARV, Personnel Specialist

Paulette B. Hill
In country: 1968 – 1969
Rank: Specialist 4, US Army
Duty: USARV, Administrative Specialist

Patricia E. Keefe (Miyaji)
In country: 1968 – 1969
Rank: Specialist 5, US Army
Duty: USARV, Still Photographic Specialist

♥Estill Vilate Latimer
Retired as a Lieutenant Colonel
In country: 1968 – 1969
Rank: Major, US Army Medical Specialist Corps
Duty: 3rd Field Hospital, Saigon, Physical Therapist

Christine Marie Matthews (Blocksidge)
In country: 1968 – 1969
Rank: Staff Sergeant, US Army
Duty: Unit Supply Specialist

Bonnie G. Moscatelli
In country: 1968 – 1969
Rank: Captain, US Army Medical Specialist Corps
Duty: 43rd Medical Group, Nha Trang, Dietetic
Consultant

♥**Mary Sue Ozburn**
**Retired as a Colonel**
**In country: 1968 – 1969**
**Rank: Major, US Army Medical Specialist Corps**
**Duty: 36th Evacuation Hospital, Vung Tau, Physical Therapist**

**Dorothy Peek**
**In country: 1968 – 1969**
**Rank: Technical Sergeant, US Air Force**
**Duty: MACV, Personnel Management Division**

♥**Mary Rachel Preston**
**Retired as a Colonel**
**In country: 1968 – 1969**
**Rank: Lieutenant Colonel, US Army Medical Specialist Corps**
**Duty: 44th Medical Brigade, Long Binh, Dietetic Consultant**

Since I have arrived, I have visited the 3rd Field, Saigon; 18th Surgical, Quang Tri; 22d Surgical, Phu Bai; 95th Evacuation, Da Nang; and 24th and 93d Evacuation, Long Binh. I go by U21 (aircraft), helicopter, jeeps, trucks, ambulances, sedans, or any other transportation that is available. The 94 Foxtrots (Hospital Food Service Specialist) have really proved themselves over here. And I do hope that Charlie continues to operate outside the perimeter. *From a letter to LTC June E. Williams, Chief, Dietetic Section. US Army Center of Military History, AMSC historical files.*

Lieutenant Colonel Preston died July 7, 1992.

**Judith L. Roberts**
**In country: 1968 – 1969**
**Rank: Specialist 4, US Army**
**Duty: Executive Administrative Assistant**

♥**Julia Ann Neale Rosengreen**
**Retired as a Colonel**
**In country: 1968 – 1969**
**Rank: Lieutenant Colonel, US Army Medical Specialist Corps**
**Duty: 68th Medical Group, Long Binh, Dietetic Consultant**

**♥Bonnie Jane Stewart (Hurst)**
**Retired as a Lieutenant Colonel**
**In country: 1968 – 1969**
**Rank: Lieutenant Colonel, US Air Force Biomedical Sciences Corps**
**Duty: 7ᵗʰ Air Force, 12ᵗʰ Tactical Wing, 12ᵗʰ USAF Hospital, Dietitian**

I am Bonnie Stewart and this is Cam Ranh Bay, Republic of Vietnam, home of the 12ᵗʰ Tactical Fighter Wing. The 12ᵗʰ USAF Hospital, second largest in the Air Force, currently operates 675 beds. The hospital started with 10 beds in September 1965 and grew to its present size in less than three years. The dining hall was completed and occupied in July 1968. It consists of 9,900 square feet of floor space. The dining room seats 200 and is quite lovely, I think. Draperies, brass vases and flowers for the tables were bought in Hong Kong. We framed and hung pictures of airplanes. We have 12 food carts to serve 18 wards and, when the hospital is full, it's a dicey situation serving all the wards. All the kitchen machines are Hobart which delights me. The Groen tilting braising pan is our pride and joy and it is used constantly.

The kitchen floor is painted metal and most of the non-skid paint has worn off. The metal rusts and is slick when wet, which is most of the time. We have a project started to paint the floor, which, I suspect, will be a continuing thing.

The drainpipes are black plastic, and the sealer used to glue the connections is water-soluble. We have a difficult time keeping the leaks fixed. Water stands under the building for weeks, after a leak is discovered and we walk through water at the loading dock because the building is lower than the road. Sealant has been applied to the roof seams several times to stop ceiling leaks. The last typhoon we experienced prompted a remark by one of my sergeants after violent rain all night. He came into the office and said, "The building must be water-tight; it holds 10,000 gallons."

We have many distinguished visitors come through the hospital and, even with all our problems, we are proud to show our dining hall. It was interesting to watch the cooks react to the (Air Force) Chief of Staff, General John McConnell. They didn't pay nearly as much attention to Gypsy Rose Lee when she was here.

*Excerpt from* Vietnam Talk, *Capt Bonnie Stewart, Retired Air Force Dietitians Association Newsletter, Winter 1993-94. Used with permission from the Retired Air Force Dietitians Association.*

Lieutenant Colonel Hurst retired in 1982. She died in 2011.

♥**Betty Mae Stone**
**In country: 1968 – June 1969**
**Rank: Specialist 4, US Army**
**Duty: USARV, G2, Clerk-Typist**

♥**Ann R. Johnson**
**Retired as a Lieutenant Colonel**
**In country: 1968 – 1970**
**Rank: Lieutenant Colonel, US Air Force**
**Duty: Headquarters 7th Air Force, Administrative Management Officer**

# JANUARY

*Memory Lane: Rowan & Martin's Laugh-In debuts on NBC; the Green Bay Packers defeat the Oakland Raiders (33-14) in Super Bowl II; The Tet Offensive begins as Viet Cong forces launch a series of surprise attacks across South Vietnam. Song: "Hello Goodbye" by The Beatles*

**Joan L. Barnes (Barco)**
**In country: January 1968 – March 1969**
**Rank: Captain, US Army**
**Duty: USARV, G4; 1st Aviation Brigade, Support Management Officer**

When I was a junior at Florida State University (FSU), the Army had what was called the college junior program. I applied and was accepted. You were sent to Fort McClellan, AL, and underwent six weeks of training. Back in the 1960s, women were not allowed into ROTC, so this was the next best thing. Upon graduation from FSU, I was commissioned a second lieutenant along with the ROTC boys. I was sent back to Fort McClellan and entered Officer Basic Training. Upon graduation, we were given our first assignments as Army officers. Wouldn't you know it, I was assigned to be an instructor for the WAC basic recruits. I laugh now because that is why I joined the

Army – to get out of teaching school. The big difference was the recruits had to listen to you whereas the junior high kids would ignore you.

A year of teaching and then I was assigned to WAC Headquarters in the logistics field (Supply Officer under the S4). I was sent to Fort Lee, VA, for Quartermaster training. At this point the Quartermaster (QM) branch picked me up and assigned me to Walter Reed Army Medical Center as the S4 (Supply Officer).

No longer under the control of the WAC branch, I came down on a levy for the Quartermaster branch with orders for Vietnam. I couldn't believe it since WAC officers had to volunteer for assignment to Vietnam. Since I was under the control of the QM, I had to go. I left for Vietnam in January 1968 and arrived in country right before the big Tet offensive. I arrived in country only to discover I was assigned to a line unit out in the field. The replacement depot couldn't believe I was a female. Remember the old mimeograph orders? I'm sure they thought Joan was John when they saw the QM branch. They would not send me home, but said they "would find me a job." I was assigned as an administrative officer at USARV Headquarters, G4 at Long Binh. When I told them I didn't know anything about administration, that I was quartermaster trained, their reply was, "That's OK. You are a woman." During those six months, I would in-process all new officers assigned to USARV Headquarters, G4. I sat in an air-conditioned office and could watch air strikes out the window. Barney (my husband to be) was one of those officers. His first comment, "This is a hell of a war to have a female captain as my escort officer."

I stayed with USARV G4 for six months and continually looked for a quartermaster job. With Barney's help, I found a job with the 1st Aviation Brigade as their supply officer. I was the first woman ever assigned to the brigade.

When I first arrived in country, I was assigned to a two-story wooden building that housed mostly enlisted women and civilians. In a few weeks, I was moved to newly constructed concrete billets for officers. I met a female civilian worker and we became good friends. Since the concrete billets were lonely, we asked to be moved into a trailer together. With two women in a trailer surrounded by numerous trailers full of male officers, we became the place to "hang out." We never lacked for food or entertainment despite the long hours of working.

**Regenia Feltner (Sizemore)**
In country: January 1968 – July 1968
Rank: Specialist 5, US Army
Duty: USARV, G2

**Patricia K. Coder (Humeumptewa)**
In country: January 1968 – November 1968
Rank: Specialist 4, US Army
Duty: USARV

**Cathy L. Brock**
**Retired as a First Sergeant**
In country: January 1968 – January 1969
Rank: Staff Sergeant, US Army
Duty: USARV, G3, Force Development Division, Equipment Branch

    **Comments and Memories:** The payday morning when the ammunition dump was blown and the scene of Captain Joanne Murphy, our commander, doing the 'Duck Walk' out of her office as she buckled on her helmet while we're all laying on the ground. *Source: Vietnam Memory Book 2000*

**Fannie M. Brooks**
In country: January 1968 – January 1969
Rank: Specialist 5, US Army
Duty: USARV

**Judith Karen Chorak (Greathouse)**
In country: January 1968 – January 1969
Rank: Specialist 5, US Army
Duty: USARV, Signal Group, Administrative Specialist

**Barbara F. Chorak (Ballas)**
In country: January 1968 – April 1969
Rank: Specialist 5, US Army
Duty: USARV, G1, Administrative Specialist

**Camilla L. Wagner**
**In country: January 1968 – January 1969**
**Rank: Captain, US Air Force (Purple Heart Recipient)**
**Duty: 7ᵗʰ Air Force, 377ᵗʰ Supply Squadron, Supply Operations Officer**

If the WAF in Vietnam are ever afraid for their own personal safety in the middle of a war, they do not show more than passing concern. Many are almost disdainful of personal harm. Captain Wagner, an accounting officer, is the only WAF in Vietnam to be awarded the Purple Heart. She was injured when an enemy combatant threw an explosive device into a bus in which she was a passenger. But, she lightly dismisses her wound: "It was a fluke. I don't think I would be in similar jeopardy again for a thousand years." *Source:* Airman*, May 1969*

**Sandra Emily Wainwright (McGowan)**
**In country: January 1968 – January 1969**
**Rank: Specialist 4, US Army**
**Duty: USARV**

A book about WAC service in the Vietnam War. What a wonderful idea! Mostly what I remember is working very long hours, seven days a week, with time off for church, if wanted. Good friends – like Julie Hollis, Judy Chorak, Mary Nichols, Chris Matthews, Pat Landry. I remember always feeling like I was a part of something bigger than myself and contributing in a small way to something noble and important. I am still very grateful for the intelligent and compassionate leadership we had. What a job it must have been to keep that mass of young women in line – much worse than herding wild cats.

**Marian J. Wells**
**In country: January 1968 – January 1969**
**Rank: Specialist 5, US Army**
**Duty: USARV, Executive Administrative Assistant**

**Cheryl L. Connor (Ainsworth)**
**In country: January 1968 – January 28, 1969**
**Rank: Staff Sergeant, US Air Force**
**Duty: MACV, Staff Judge Advocate's Office, Administrative Specialist**

**Sally Louise Bostwick**
**Retired as a Commander**
**In country: January 1968 – February 1969**
**Rank: Lieutenant, US Navy**
**Duty: NAVFORV, Operations Analyst**

When I see and hear what today's women in service do, my time in Vietnam seems so simple and safe. I arrived around Tet 1968. I first stayed in the McCarthy Hotel and then the Navy moved us to the officers' quarters at the Li Qui Don Hotel.

All US Navy personnel in Saigon and ship riders with the Vietnam Navy were housed there. Because it was small, officers above lieutenant commander (04) were moved to a hotel in downtown Saigon – I was a Navy lieutenant at the time. My professional background was operations research/systems analysis/computer modeling.

Now a memory – the one I have chosen deals with civilians I knew. Where they are now I don't know. I used a bakery across from NAVFORV Headquarters for croissants each day. The lady baker invited me to visit her home. I asked another Navy lieutenant to accompany me. One Sunday we took a cyclo (a three-wheel bicycle taxi that had a double seat supported by the two front wheels, with the driver sitting behind) to the baker's home (near the Newport Bridge on the road to Long Binh.) The home was a combination farm and chateau. Chickens, goats, pig, etc., all around. They also operated a mill for flour. The baker's husband worked for the US Army in logistics in Saigon. Her English was excellent. As we enjoyed tea and pastries, her husband talked of the necessity for quality control! I looked out and saw chickens walking in the flour. I almost cracked up. They were gracious to us. I do not know what happened to them after the fall of Saigon but memory of a friendly, funny Sunday remains.

I had the advantage of going from I Corps (northernmost provinces of South Vietnam) to IV Corps (southernmost provinces) giving me the opportunity to see the beauty of the country and people in very difficult times.

**♥Gabrielle "Gabe" Brancato**
**Retired as a Sergeant First Class**
**In country: January 1968 – February 1969; July 1971 – August 1972**
**Rank: Staff Sergeant, US Army**
**Duty: 24th Evacuation Hospital, Long Binh, Medical NCO**

When *The Overseas Weekly – Pacific Edition* did an article on the WAC Detachment in May 1972, Staff Sergeant Gabrielle Brancato had been in the WACs for 11 years. Her assignment at the 24th Evacuation Hospital gave her the opportunity to spend her day off in the operating room, observing surgery.

"I've seen patients come in next to death's door and pull out of it. The people here work very fast." She is planning to receive additional medical training at Fort Sam Houston, TX. "My greatest satisfaction is observing the devotion to duty of the doctors and nurses here, their patience and teamwork."

*Excerpt from "The women behind the concertina barricade,"* The Overseas Weekly – Pacific Edition, *May 8, 1972, publication defunct 1975*

**Emily Ellen "Em" Embree**
**In country: January 1968 – February 28, 1969**
**Rank: Specialist 5, US Army**
**Duty: USARV, Office of Preventive Medicine**

I want people to know that my life is best described in the spaces between the lines that are the lives of my friends. I am the mortar that holds the bricks together. Nobody ever says, "Oh, how pretty the mortar." But, many people say, "See the pretty brick homes." I help in the building of people's lives.

**Comments and Memories:** Martha Raye's visit to the WAC Detachment at Long Binh. Painting the benches green and having the monsoon rain wash them clean. *Source: Vietnam Memory Book 2000*

**Norma S. Hamm**
**Retired as a Command Sergeant Major**
**In country: January 1968 – April 1969**
**Rank: Staff Sergeant, US Army**
**Duty: USARV, Administrative NCO**

**Lee N. Wilson**
**In country: January 1968 – June 1969**
**Rank: Specialist 5, US Army**
**Duty: USARV, Engineer Division, Facilities Service Section,**
**Administrative Personnel**

**Comments and Memories:** We all grew up so fast and came home so old. It's taken me a lifetime to accept my time and youth lost to Vietnam. Hitching rides on tanks and choppers. Laughing with Vicki and Marilyn. Watching the men watch us. And most ironic, watching the war from a bunker. *Source: Vietnam Memory Book 2000*

**Esther M. Gleaton**
**Retired as a Sergeant First Class**
**In country: January 1968 – August 1969**
**Rank: Specialist 5, US Army**
**Duty: USARV, Administrative Specialist**

**Virginia S. Green**
**Retired as a Staff Sergeant, USAR**
**In country: January 1968 – August 1969**
**Rank: Specialist 5, US Army**
**Duty: USARV, Administrative Specialist**

**Betty "Fran" F. Gant (Kinney)**
**Retired as a First Sergeant**
**In country: January 1968 – August 1969**
**Rank: Specialist 6, US Army**
**Duty: MACV, US Agency for International Development**

**Doris L. Lewis (White)**
**Retired as a Command Sergeant Major**
**In country: January 1968 – January 1970**
**Rank: Specialist 4, US Army**
**Duty: USARV, G2 Intelligence, Administrative Specialist**

**Maryna "Marty" Lee Misiewicz**
**In country: January 1968 – March 1970**
**Rank: Staff Sergeant, US Army**
**Duty: USARV, G4, Services Division; US Army Engineer Command,**
**Administrative NCO/Attaché Specialist**

I was at Fort Sill, OK, when I got my orders, assigned to the Field Artillery School working in the office. I had volunteered for Vietnam. I got my orders about a month after volunteering. My mother was in the hospital, and I had to borrow a friend's car to go see her and tell her.

I was nervous and excited and felt like I was following in my stepdad's footsteps going to serve my country. It felt very patriotic.

Our plane landed at Tan Son Nhut Air Base in the middle of the night at the time the Tet offensive was underway.

They moved me to an NCO barracks and I spent about five days there. During the day, I was searching the mama-sans when they came into the buildings and helped with KP (kitchen police) in the mess hall. I had my cord uniforms and a sergeant gave me a set of fatigues to wear during the day. I got a helicopter ride from Saigon to Long Binh.

I was an administrative assistant in the services division of G4 at USARV. That was my first year. We covered petroleum supply, food service and mortuary affairs. One of the things I remember was a major doing inspections of the morgues and I could see how that affected him. We had one instance of a body being sent back. Another soldier had a similar name and the body went to the wrong family. This caused a congressional investigation. We were not happy to have the mix-up and were sorry to have caused so many problems for the families.

During my off-duty hours, I was one of the movie projector operators for the WAC Detachment. I visited the orphanages a few times. For those of you who did that on a regular basis, I give you a lot of credit for giving of yourself that way.

On Christmas 1968, Ruth McKenney and I went up to the helipad at USARV Headquarters, and we got to go on a helicopter ride with Richard Cardinal Cushing.

I extended twice; the first time was the same day I was supposed to fly home. I just wasn't ready to leave my friends and I felt that what I was doing was important. So, I was given a new assignment for the top engineer in Vietnam, working for MG John Dillard, Jr., who was killed about two months after I left Vietnam. I went to his funeral and also the funeral for SGM Griffith Jones who was also on the helicopter. I have visited the wall to look at their names.

Three of my high school friends, one woman and two men, died in Vietnam shortly after I arrived there, but my parents did not tell me about it until I returned to the States.

My first year home I had a Christmas celebration that spanned both years – my parents had left the tree up and my presents under it.

In 1972 the Army asked me if I wanted to go to Germany or to Belgium. I didn't like any of the choices, so when they asked if I wanted a tour in Cambodia at the US Embassy, I said yes. That assignment changed my life because I adopted my son and it gave me a different priority. The Khmer Rouge was actively operating offensively so it was a scary assignment.

I spent 10 years on active duty and 5 years in the Reserves. After 10 years in the Army, I became a civilian again. I retired from the telephone company and worked three years for our local school district. Thanks to my military service, I was able to be hired as the first Superintendent for the Veterans' Assistance Commission of Stephenson County (VACSC). Daily I am humbled by the assistance our VACSC provides our veterans in need of shelter, heat, water, electricity, food, clothing and transportation.

When I think back on my time in Vietnam, I remember:

- The old wooden barracks, the big parachute tent, the movie projector shack, the swimming pool, the wooden walkway (which was really needed during the rainy season).
- Having a mama-san to do my laundry and polish my boots.
- The bus with the pink sign that picked us up to take us to work.
- The heat, the rain, more heat, more rain.
- The USO shows, celebrities such as Bob Hope, Ann Margaret, Rosie Greer.
- The Billy Graham performance, getting to sing on stage in his choir.

- Moving from the "old" barracks to the "new" barracks.
- The bunkers and the hours and nights we spent hunkered down waiting for the all clear.

But most of all, I remember the faces of those I worked with, those I lived with, my fellow WACs. I also remember those I knew who lost their lives in Vietnam such as General Dillard, Sergeant Major Jones, and my classmate Allen Mummert and fellow Lanark High School graduates Chuck Olson and Michael Wittevrongel. The latter three were killed in action in 1968 while I was in Vietnam, although I did not find that out until I had returned to the States.

I was blessed and honored to serve my country overseas in Vietnam and Cambodia. I gained a son, Michael Vannak Misiewicz, which changed my life in ways I never would have imagined. Michael is such a success story having graduated from the US Naval Academy and going on to command the destroyer USS *Mustin*. I am so proud of him.

There are so many memories, good and bad, of my time in country. The best part, the very, very best part, is the lifelong friends I made from having served in that "hazardous duty zone."

To my fellow Vietnam women veterans, I say with pride: ***thank you for your service*** and ***welcome home***!

**Grendel Alice Howard**
**Retired as a Sergeant Major**
**In country: January 1968 – October 1970**
**Rank: Sergeant First Class, US Army**
**Duty: 1ˢᵗ Logistical Command, Journalist**

***From a telephone interview:*** In 1956, I was 23, had been married and divorced, and I was living with my brother in Philadelphia. In four days, I had had four flat tires and had to change them myself, dressed in business clothes, on my way to work. That fourth day, I decided to join the Army and specifically the Transportation Corps. My brother was not pleased, but I knew it was time for a change. I went to Fort McClellan, AL, for basic training and stayed in for six years. But you couldn't get promoted, so I got out of the Army and went to work for a company in Denver, CO, and went back to school at night. That was hard. The company I worked for had a retirement plan, but it required you to work to age 60 or for 30 years, and I decided the Army life looked pretty good. In 1965, I reenlisted. I had to go back to Fort McClellan, AL, but not for full basic training.

In January 1968, I volunteered to go to Vietnam and was on orders right away. When we landed, I was scared to death. It was night. They put us on a bus, and I eventually got to the WAC Detachment.

Doris "Lucki" Allen was one of my closest friends. There were so many restrictions on the women in Vietnam. We weren't supposed to be out in vehicles on our own, or fly in aircraft. Well, Lucki was in Intelligence, and I was a journalist, and we would get jeeps and go places when we needed to which seemed reasonable to us. We also went on R&R together to Hong Kong, Kuala Lumper and Japan.

My tours in Vietnam were actually good duty. There was great job satisfaction, in spite of some of the restrictions, and we felt like our work had value.

I always felt sorry for the nurses, many of whom would come over to our detachment during their time off because we had air conditioning and they didn't.

I know many people complained about how they were treated in the airports back in the States, but the most hostility I saw was in Japan.

I retired in March 1985. One thing I have noticed over the years is that no one talks about the women who served in Vietnam. If you bring the subject up, they just look at you in bewilderment.

***Donna A. Lowery:*** In 1971, a new Army regulation had an ambiguity in it that allowed single military women to adopt children. SFC Edith "Effie" Efferson was probably the first military woman to take advantage of this change, adopting two children. SGM Grendel Howard was mostly likely the second single woman in the US Army to adopt a child. Both women were stationed at 1st Army Headquarters, Fort Meade, MD. With support from the command, their requests were approved within weeks of each other. SGM Howard adopted a 4-year-old boy named Jason. The permission to approve an adoption for a single WAC was granted by individual court-martial authorities. There were no centralized records on this issue. I am proud of the leadership of Fort Meade, which gave these two Vietnam veterans the gift of motherhood.

**Precilla "Pat" Ann Landry (Wilkewitz)**
**In country: January 5, 1968 – September 5, 1969**
**Rank: Specialist 5, US Army**
**Duty: USARV, Office of the Inspector General, Investigations and**
**Complaints, Inspection Division**

Precilla Landry Wilkewitz is a co-founder
of the Vietnam Women Veterans, Inc.
organization

They didn't issue us weapons in Vietnam. At basic training in Fort
Benning, GA, we trained with M-16s and M-14s. We had to do marksmanship
and be in foxholes and we had to do mounted and dismounted attacks. But,
they didn't issue women weapons (in country). One night we had a human
mass attack on all four corners at Long Binh. We had mortar attacks that
could have landed on our compound and killed all of us. Did we have
anything to protect us? No, all we had was prayer. And I did a lot of that.

All women had to eat at the 24th Evacuation Hospital. So, when we went
there we had to eat with the patients. Some of them had missing arms, legs,
eyes, and had IVs sticking out and all these little gadgets hanging from that
walking thing. There were only two redheads there in the first place. I would
sit down with the patients and they would start crying. Many, many of them

asked me if they could touch my hair, because they saw very few round-eyes, and everybody who was there had an aunt or a friend or schoolmate who was redheaded. It was so traumatic that I quit going. I don't think I ate 20 times in the mess hall because they would cry. How can you sit there and eat while these soldiers are crying?

When I got back, I had lost 40 pounds by nerves and improper diet. My sister used to say, "You just ignore things." Petty things didn't mean anything to me. People would say to me, "Don't you think (that woman's) dress is short?" and I thought that was ignorant. I had been to Vietnam. Those were not things that you thought about. If you did not have hot water that night, that was not important. What I couldn't get over was color. In Vietnam, everything was brown and dirty and there wasn't any color. I came home for Christmas. And, that first night when I came home, my mother found me asleep underneath the Christmas tree. Because of the lights, I couldn't get enough."

*Excerpt from the article titled "Unarmed and under fire: An oral history of female Vietnam vets," November 11, 1999,* Salon *online magazine. Used with permission.*

**Ladina L. Moore**
**Retired as a Command Sergeant Major**
**In country: January 6, 1968 – January 5, 1969**
**Rank: Specialist 5, US Army**
**Duty: USARV, G4, Plans and Operations**

I had known since the 8th grade that I wanted to go into the military, but it took me until October of 1966 to convince my dad to sign the papers. Back in the day, it was extremely rare for women to enter any branch of service. Most of us, though, had a family history of service – parents, aunts, uncles, cousins. We felt a need to honor their service and also felt an obligation to serve our country.

My tour in Vietnam began January 6, 1968. I arrived at Long Binh late at night and was a little concerned about what I had gotten myself into. I was a Specialist 4, 19 years old and had just a little over a year in the Army. My tour as a clerk-typist at Headquarters, USARV, in the Office of the Army Chief of Staff, G4, consisted of many long days, usually seven days a week. I had lots of company, though, since the other clerks, noncommissioned officers and officers were right there alongside me. We developed some excellent friendships, some bonds that last to this day. As simple as my job was, I saw some results of my section's efforts and believed that I was helping make things a little better for some soldier in the field. I felt fortunate not only for that but also for being in a relatively safe environment.

The places I lived and worked felt safe to me because of the leadership at the WAC Detachment and because of the combat arms units around and near Long Binh. The commander and first sergeant at the Detachment looked after the women entrusted to their care. Regardless of what was going on, they always had a calm demeanor. Whether we were standing in a pay line when an attack on the compound occurred or sitting in a bunker because of a threat, their presence seemed to say, "It's okay. We've got this."

I left Vietnam late at night January 5, 1969, as a Specialist 5, 20-year-old. While traveling through the San Francisco airport, I was treated much the same as my male counterparts – followed around, taunted, called names. I could not imagine how hard that must have been for those who had truly been in harm's way and had given so much for their country.

After spending almost a month at home on leave, I reported to Fort McClellan, AL. It wasn't long before I began wishing that I had extended my tour and stayed in Vietnam. That feeling lasted for about a year. The people I admired were those who stayed or who went on assignments to other Southeast Asia countries in support of our efforts there. I admired those who got involved with the communities and did things to help people recover. I admired those who sponsored families or who adopted children.

**Lidia "Marty" M. Contreras**
**Retired as a Sergeant First Class**
**In country: January 9, 1968 – January 6, 1969**
**Rank: Specialist 5, US Army**
**Duty: USARV, Office of the Judge Advocate General, Legal Specialist**

I saw my service in Vietnam like a mystery novel – filled with intrigue and uncertainty. Each day I was there, I would turn the page, the plots would thicken, and the players were my fellow WACs. There to do a job in the most extraordinary of circumstances, we discovered a lot about ourselves, our strengths and weaknesses as we dealt with life and death situations.

The stars we saw at night were tracer bullets, and we counted the explosions as we lulled ourselves to sleep. The next day another page was turned and another memory began. In the back of our minds, we collected and stored our memories. Yes, there were some good times, dances and such, and listening to AFN on the transistor radio. But, those times were rare.

At the end of our journey, or tour of duty, when the last page was turned, we returned home. There was sadness as we hugged and waved goodbye to our friends, remorseful that we were leaving them behind to finish the job. Little did we know that our lives would never be the same. Could we ever tell this story to anyone? No, not really. Who would believe it? We served with honor and pride in a country so far away, VIETNAM!

**Linda D. Jankowiak (Pride)**
**In country: January 15, 1968 – July 13, 1969**
**Rank: Specialist 5, US Army**
**Duty: USARV; MACV, Administrative Specialist**

**Margaret F. Bevill**
**Retired as a Master Sergeant**
**In country: January 22, 1968 – February 21, 1969**
**Rank: Sergeant First Class, US Army**
**Duty: USARV, Central Finance and Accounting Office,**
**Finance Senior Sergeant**

***Dawn Brown, family member:*** During the 1968 Tet Offensive, Margaret Bevill was at Long Binh during both the VC/NVA (Viet Cong/North Vietnamese Army) attacks and when the large ammunitions storage area exploded due to enemy fire.

Shortly after Tet, Margaret was visited at the WAC Detachment by her nephew, Lieutenant Edward E. Bevill, now Colonel, USA Retired, who at that time was an Infantry Platoon Leader in the 101st Airborne Division.

Margaret was very good friends with Betty Benson, who was the WAC Detachment's Field First/Administrative NCO when Margaret arrived in country. Betty Benson was the first female graduate of the Sergeants Major Academy at Fort Bliss, TX.

**Judy "Sam" Ann Jacque**
**Retired as a Master Sergeant**
**In country: January 31, 1968 – February 27, 1969**
**Rank: Staff Sergeant, US Army**
**Duty: USARV, G3 Classified Documents, Administrative NCO**

I arrived at Bien Hoa Air Base during the Tet Offensive of 1968. Our baggage was unloaded and the plane left. We stood wondering, "What are we doing here?" We were loaded on a bus with barbed wire around the windows and a machine gun on the front hood. It finally sank in – we were really in Vietnam. After we arrived at the Long Binh WAC Detachment, I was assigned a temporary room upstairs facing air-conditioned civilian trailers; it seemed far away from everyone. During the night, the ammunition depot was attacked and bombed. The night lit up like day, and I stood in my room doorway not moving. Someone grabbed me and shoved me under the bed, a safer place to be. The WAC Detachment was surrounded by barbed wire, and the perimeter was patrolled during alerts. This was not a nice start to my year tour, and many times I was just plain scared.

I was assigned to USARV Headquarters, G3 Classified. Three enlisted women and a lieutenant (male) worked there, staffed 24 hours a day, 7 days a week. One enlisted woman covered the 12-hour night shift. At night, walking the headquarters' empty halls to pick up documents was daunting. Our office was a vault sitting on top of another vault and I thought, if the building was attacked or overrun, I'd be sitting in a vault two stories up.

It seemed I was always working so I had no time to eat at the dining facility. I'd buy food items at the exchange or snack bar and, ever so often, made it back to the barracks to enjoy a cookout. I grew to like the little cans of food with the sterno on the bottom to warm them. No wonder I never lost a pound while there.

I was lucky to be assigned a lower, end room next to an out-of-the-way bunker. On alert, not many used it. I wasn't so afraid anymore; my main concern was losing sleep.

During the monsoon season, it seemed as if the rain never ended and I needed a poncho over me at night to keep dry. We kept everything off the floors and flooding was not uncommon. I remember standing in my room doorway and watching a young rat float by on a piece of wood. We had to keep everything in our lockers, closed tightly, so the rats couldn't get in. As long as they didn't disturb my sleep, I was fine. We moved to a new permanent barracks shortly before I left. I missed my slatted-wall room at the other end of the old barracks.

After my tour, we landed in California and were told to change to civilian clothes because picketing and riots were going on in opposition to the Vietnam conflict. No one said, "Welcome home" or "Thank you" for serving; being spit on was more common.

In May 2010, I attended "12 Lambeau," a tribute ceremony at the Green Bay Packer Stadium. This three-day event welcomed home more than 25,000 Wisconsin Vietnam Veterans, their families, and friends. For many, it provided closure and a long overdue "Thank you."

**Peggy R. Hilton**
**Retired as a Sergeant First Class**
**In country: January 31, 1968 – September 6, 1969**
**Rank: Staff Sergeant, US Army**
**Duty: USARV, Administrative NCO**

What can I say? A tour in Vietnam is something that I will never forget. I liken it to one big family – in the barracks and at work. We worked 10 hours a day, 7 days a week and never complained. I spent 18 months there and when I came back stateside, I was very lucky and was assigned just four hours from my mother's home. I put 22 years in the Army.

I then worked for the US Postal Service for 15 years. I have lived in Las Vegas now for 13 years. There is no place like it!

# FEBRUARY

*Memory Lane: The 1968 Winter Olympics are held in Grenoble, France; a civil rights protest at a white-only bowling alley in Orangeburg, SC, is broken up – three college students are killed.*
*Song: "Chain of Fools" by Aretha Franklin*

♥**Annette M. Drumming (Douglas)**
**In country: February 1968 – January 1969**
**Rank: Specialist 5, US Army**
**Duty: USARV**

**Julie E. Hollis (Bumpas)**
**In country: February 1968 – January 1969**
**Rank: Specialist 5, US Army**
**Duty: USARV, Surgeon General's Office**

♥**Priscilla Katharine Gilchrist**
**Retired as Lieutenant Colonel**
**In country: February 1968 – February 1969**
**Rank: Lieutenant Colonel, US Army Medical Specialist Corps**
**Duty: 3rd Field Hospital, Saigon, Physical Therapist**

When World War II broke out, Priscilla Gilchrist was studying at the University of New Hampshire, majoring in physical therapy and English. After completing accelerated studies, as so many others did at that time, she wanted to join the Army. She received her commission after completing training at O'Reilly General Hospital, Springfield, MO, and Rhodes General Hospital, Utica, NY. During the war, she practiced her craft on those wounded at the Battle of the Bulge.

An oversea tour of duty took Captain Gilchrist to the 1st Station Hospital in Quan Su, Korea, and later to the 382nd Hospital in Ascom City.

She left the Army in 1948 but rejoined two years later. "I was invited back. I missed it," she explained in an interview for the *The Citizen* newspaper of Laconia, NH.

Between 1950 and 1967, she served in various stateside hospitals and in Germany. In 1968, she went to Vietnam with assignment to 3rd Field Hospital, Saigon. "I arrived during the Tet Offensive. It was the Gilchrist luck," she said.

In Vietnam, she was chief of staff of Physical Therapy clinics and consultant to the Surgeon General. She had 12 therapists under her command and was responsible for 13 hospitals.

What she saw in Vietnam were some of the worst casualties she ever treated. The wounds, she explained, were not like the horrible burns, bullet wounds or shrapnel from World War II. "Land mines were the biggest bugaboo. There were also lots of wounds from mortars and sharpened bamboo sticks," she said.

She traveled from base to base via helicopters. She also had the opportunity to work in a triage area of a field hospital.

She remembered one wounded man who was more concerned about his "buddy" than himself. The soldier's best buddy was his dog. The soldier was the point man whose dog led the soldiers along the jungle trails. He had to be told that the explosion which wounded him had killed his dog.

Part of the job of a physical therapist in these conditions was to tell the wounded soldiers what would happen to them once a leg or arm was amputated. They would explain how the prosthesis would be fitted and how it worked once they got used to it.

Lieutenant Colonel Gilchrist saw lots of firefights between soldiers and Viet Cong. Many of these were all around the base where she was. She learned to tell the differences between incoming mortars and rockets. "A rocket would click. A mortar would boom," she said.

After one year, she came home expecting to be taunted by anti-war demonstrators. She had been advised not to wear her uniform while traveling. Defiantly, she said, "I was proud to wear my uniform. I never experienced any problems. If I had, they would have heard from me!"

Lieutenant Colonel Gilchrist, who was promoted in Vietnam on September 29, 1968, went on to become the Chief of the Physical Therapy Unit at Walter Reed Military Hospital and consultant to the US Surgeon General. She retired in 1971 after treating wounded soldiers from three wars.

Lieutenant Gilchrist died December 12, 2012. She is buried at the Franklin Cemetery, Franklin, NH.

*Based on information from article "Priscilla Gilchrist: a member of the greatest generation," by Gordon D. King, staff writer,* The Citizen, *Laconia, NH, February 18, 2000. Used with permission.*

**Lynn F. Gormley (Christian)**
**In country: February 1968 – February 1969**
**Rank: First Lieutenant, US Air Force**
**Duty: 7ᵗʰ Air Force, 3ʳᵈ Aerospace Rescue and Recovery Group, Administrative Officer**

**Susan F. Hamilton (Cusson)**
**Retired as a Lieutenant Commander**
**In country: February 1968 – February 1969**
**Rank: Lieutenant, US Navy**
**Duty: NAVFORV, Historical Section**

Two years after my promotion to full lieutenant, I was honored to be one of the first three women line officers assigned duty in Vietnam. I was the first woman, officer or enlisted, to attend SERE (survival, evasive and resistance education) training in preparation for service in country. I reported to COMNAVFORV (Commander Naval Forces Vietnam) within a week of Tet 1968 just as the NVA (North Vietnamese Army) stepped up its hostile actions in Saigon.

My duty assignment was that of Naval Historian. One of my very memorable experiences was the shelling of our BOQ one morning just before dawn. My roommate and I both rolled out of our beds and crawled into our bathroom for coverage. There were no injuries and very little damage, except for our jangled nerves.

I retired in 1983, after 20 years of service, as a lieutenant commander. During my retirement years, I have enjoyed being a part-time bookkeeper and a beach bum.

**♥Nancy Jolene "Johnny" Johnson**
**In country: February 1968 – February 1969**
**Rank: Specialist 5, US Army**
**Duty: USARV, Administrative Specialist**

**Sandra F. Phipps**
**In country: February 1968 – February 1969**
**Rank: Specialist 5, US Army**
**Duty: USARV**

**♥Barbara Jean Stearns**
**Retired as a Lieutenant Colonel**
**In country: February 1968 – February 1969**
**Rank: Lieutenant Colonel, US Army Medical Specialist Corps**
**Duty: 6th Convalescent Center, Cam Ranh Bay, Physical Therapist**

**Willella "Billie" T. Taylor (Williams)**
**Retired as a Sergeant Major**
**In country: February 1968 – February 1969**
**Rank: Staff Sergeant, US Army**
**Duty: USARV, G4, Ammunition and Aviation Division**

**Nancy K. Wiltshire**
**In country: February 1968 – February 1969**
**Rank: Specialist 4, US Army**
**Duty: USARV, G4**

**Doris L. Denton**
**Retired as a First Sergeant**
**In country: February 1968 – March 1969**
**Rank: Staff Sergeant, US Marine Corps**
**Duty: MACV, J5, Administrative Clerk**

 When I arrived in Vietnam, everyone was still on high alert. I was met by an Army person with double bandoliers of ammunition draped over his chest and holding his weapon. I was told they were expecting an attack any moment. If it came, we were to get under the nearest table; but, if we got a direct hit, we would not have to worry anymore. I spent the first night at the end of the airport in a room by myself. During the middle of the night, I heard loud booming noises and people outside my room yelling, "Get down! Incoming!" I got under my bunk, pulled the mattress over my head and tried to dig a hole in the cement floor.

The next day I was taken into Saigon to the Ambassador Hotel – again, in a room by myself. This was on the weekend; I had no idea where to go for food or anything else. I spent two days drinking water and taking vitamin pills until Monday when I was taken to the weeklong indoctrination for new people. Capt Jones and MSgt Dulinsky picked me up for lunch, and, boy, did I eat! I had served with them before on the drill field.

My assignment was in the J5 section of the MACV Headquarters where we did the battle plans for operations up country. I was also in charge of the classified material. We worked 12-hour days and many times 24 hours. We endured attacks on the headquarters on several occasions by mortar and sniper fire.

General Raymond Shaffer awarded me the Joint Service Commendation Medal. After 20 years of active service, I retired with the rank of First Sergeant.

**Diana Jean "Sam" Symanowicz (Reedy)**
**In country: February 1968 – May 1969**
**Rank: Specialist 5, US Army**
**Duty: USARV, G2, Office of the Deputy Chief of Staff for Logistics**

**Earnestine Dumas (Barkers)**
**In country: February 1968 – July 1969**
**Rank: Specialist 5, US Army**
**Duty: USARV, Clerk-Typist**

**Sheron L. Green**
**In country: February 1968 – July 1969**
**Rank: Specialist 5, US Army**
**Duty: USARV, 1ˢᵗ Aviation Brigade; MACV, USAHAC, Executive Administrative Assistant**

**♥Christa "Crystal" Maria Grayer**
**Retired as a Master Sergeant**
**In country: February 1968 – May 1970**
**Rank: Sergeant First Class, US Army**
**Duty: USARV, G4, Administrative NCO**

**Marsha "Cricket" Dale Holder**
**In country: February 2, 1968 – April 7, 1970**
**Rank: Specialist 5, US Army**
**Duty: USARV; 1ˢᵗ Logistical Command, Administrative Specialist**

When I graduated from high school in 1966, I had two options, factory work or college. My older brother had joined the Marine Corps in March 1966, so I joined the WAC September 1966 and was stationed at Fort Hamilton, NY, after basic training. Christmas 1967, my brother and I were both home for the holidays; he told me he had  volunteered for Vietnam to get away from the sand fleas in South Carolina. I wanted to get away from the two feet of snow we always seemed to have in Brooklyn that winter. When I got back to Fort Hamilton, I volunteered for Vietnam and had orders within three weeks. My flight to Vietnam was delayed two days because of Tet 1968 but I arrived February 2, 1968. When the plane landed, flak jackets were brought on board for the officers. When they saw that there were WACs on board, they told us to go first. We could still hear gunfire in the area. The other girls and I decided we would let the officers go first. We exited the plane with all those GIs around us. I was thinking Vietnam was like Mississippi in midsummer – hot and dusty. I was in for a shock too when I saw the barracks with no solid outer walls, just cheesecloth stapled on the inside of the studs to keep out the dust and boards on the outside at an angle to allow air circulation and to keep the rain out. Another shock was the open barrack like in basic training. It was known as the E4 barrack. The E5s and above had rooms.

My next big shock came just over two weeks later when the ammo dump blew up in the middle of the night. Dust in the cheesecloth went everywhere; the doors at both ends of the upstairs barracks blew off, and mirrors hanging on wall lockers hit the floor. This was my first experience in the bunkers, but when we could still hear the ammo exploding throughout the night, we were happy to have them. When we finally got back to the barracks, everything was red with dust. What a mess!

By August 1968, my brother had arrived in Vietnam but he was all the way up in Da Nang. For me to call him, I had to go through two or three switchboard operators. I figured if he was just getting started on his tour, I might as well stay another six months so we would be going home about the same time. I went home for the month of December 1968, and, while I was gone, the WAC Detachment moved into the new barracks. We had solid walls but we still had the dust and heat. By the time my first extension was about to end, my younger brother had joined the Marine Corps and was not doing well in the training school. The Marine Corps gave him the option of doing better or going to Vietnam – he did better. In the meantime, my father's younger brother and two first cousins were sent to Vietnam. My enlistment was going to be up in September 1969, so I extended that six months and volunteered for another six-month tour. I was discharged April 7, 1970.

I had several jobs while in Vietnam. With each extension, I asked for a new assignment. My first job was in the G4 typing pool. When I extended the first time, I came back to a job working for General David S. Parker, commander of the Engineering Troops in Vietnam. I logged all his correspondence and kept his files. I have heard that he didn't like having women in Vietnam but he was always nice to me. My next job was at the 1ˢᵗ Logistical Command. We typed up orders for troop movement and had boxes on the wall for all the units in the area. That was my favorite job because I met a lot of people and got to talk a lot which, if you know me, you know I like to talk.

My military career didn't end when I left the Army. I joined the Mississippi National Guard where I was a Flight Operations Dispatcher for a Huey helicopter unit. Following that, I went to work for the US Army Corps of Engineers. I had several jobs over the next 28 years including Civil Engineering Technician on the Tennessee-Tombigbee Waterway and on a dredge on the lower Mississippi River, Construction Inspector on a Red River lock project and finally, Lock Operator on the Tennessee River. I retired January 1, 2010, with more than 32 years federal service.

I am living in my beloved Mississippi now and taking care of my 88-year-old parents. I enjoy researching my family history, photographing headstones and recording local cemeteries on Find a Grave, and enjoy spending time with my classmates each month at BHS Buddies lunch. I am also the proud aunt of nine nieces, two nephews (both Marines) and 19 great nieces and nephews.

*Author's Note: Marsha "Cricket" Holder is the creator of the Virtual Cemetery that honors our deceased women Vietnam veterans.*

**Sonia "Suni" B. Gonzalez Mendez**
**Retired as a Master Sergeant**
**In country: February 14, 1968 – October 1969**
**Rank: Specialist 5, US Army**
**Duty: USARV; MACV, Clerk-Typist**

In 1966, I had completed basic training and was assigned to the Pentagon, Washington, DC. I was so proud of myself! Being a size two in clothing, everyone thought I was just too cute in my uniform.

My first year at the Pentagon was coming to an end when my supervisor informed me that I had to be reassigned because they only kept clerk-typists for one year then they had to move on. What a shock! During that same time all my friends were volunteering for Vietnam. I thought they were crazy.

One day during lunch, I told them what my supervisor had told me. "Bingo!" they said, "Come with us to Vietnam." "What? Don't you know there is a war over there?" I said. They went on to tell me how there was a WAC Detachment, and we would be guarded all the time, but I would not volunteer. My friends did not give up, however. Every time I met one in the hallway, they would ask if I completed the paperwork for Vietnam. My brother was already in Vietnam; he told me never to volunteer for anything.

I did finally volunteer, though. The next shock was that none of them was selected, only me. I was the only clerk-typist in the group, and that is all they needed at the time. So there I was, the only female on the plane with 200 men.

It was a smooth flight until we reached the airport. We had been singing and telling stories and just having a good time until the pilot announced that the airport was under attack and we could not land. The lights in the airplane were turned off and a blanket of silence came over us. One by one, the young soldiers took turns sitting next to me and holding my hand. It was like confession for some; others just wanted to sit next to the last American female they would see.

It seemed like we were never going to hit the ground. We could see all the fireworks from the windows. Finally, we had no choice but to land because we were running out of gas. After receiving strict orders, we quietly did a fall-and-crawl to the terminal with a shower of bullets overhead. Oh, mama, what did I get myself into? I was in my Class B uniform and high heels. Whoever wrote that a Class B uniform was required for travel to a war zone was kookoo.

I spent the night at the airport and felt very protected. The next morning, I was taken to WAC Detachment Special Troops where I was issued my jungle fatigues and boots, but they did not have a helmet for me. I went to my assigned bunk on the second floor of a long wooden building that looked like a two-story chicken coop, but it was clean and I was right next to the door. Everyone looked sharp and healthy, so I started feeling better, knowing that we were properly cared for. My roommate had gotten a care package from home – pink rollers, pink gown, all the nighty things in pink.

**Dorothy "DJ" J. Rechel**
**Retired as a Sergeant Major**
**In country: February 15, 1968 – February 21, 1969**
**Rank: Sergeant First Class, US Army**
**Duty: USARV, Office of the Adjutant General, Administrative NCO**

I was very fortunate to have been accepted to go to Vietnam and reap the priceless ticket punch that went with it. Other benefits: I lost 15 pounds, sucked up a ***bunch*** of Scotch, and brought home a pregnant cat, which would otherwise likely have been someone's dinner!

I suspect that younger women – maybe on a second enlistment – will have been more struck by events than those of us who were already halfway to a career. The closest memory to indelible I have is the taste of steaks cooked (fire started with some kind of fuel oil) at gatherings to which we were invited because we were women. Oh, come to think of it, those may have been the last steaks I've ever eaten. When I came home, I ate salads and broccoli and apples and celery and anything green! And still do.

**♥Marie Sylvia Knasiak**
**Retired as a Lieutenant Colonel**
**In country: February 26, 1968 – February 10, 1969**
**Rank: Lieutenant Colonel, US Army**
**Duty: MACV, USAHAC, Secretary General Staff, Personnel Staff Officer**

On February 26, 1968, Lieutenant Colonel Knasiak arrived in Saigon, where she was assigned as Secretary General Staff, US Headquarters Area Command, Military Assistance Command, Vietnam. Saigon was experiencing heavy enemy fire at that time. This was the Tet Offensive of 1968 and she was involved as no one would have expected.

During one attack, Marie was running down the street attempting to reach her duty station, when she came under small-arms fire. She pulled her .45 caliber pistol and returned fire. For her actions during Tet and for her service in Vietnam, she was awarded the Bronze Star Medal. She left Vietnam February 10, 1969, for some leave time and her next assignment.

# MARCH

*Memory Lane: My Lai massacre takes place – story will not become public until November 1969; President Lyndon B. Johnson announces he will not seek re-election.*
*Song: "(Sittin' On) the Dock of the Bay" by Otis Redding*

♥**Betty Jane Fuller (Legleiter)**
**In country: March 1968 – June 1968**
**Rank: Specialist 5, US Army**
**Duty: USARV, Administrative Specialist**

**T. Elaine Palmer**
**Retired as a Sergeant First Class**
**In country: March 1968 – February 1969**
**Rank: Sergeant First Class, US Army**
**Duty: USARV, 1ˢᵗ Logistical Command, Administrative NCO**

It was an honor to be assigned to the 1ˢᵗ Logistical Command in Long Binh, Vietnam.

My memories of the WAC Detachment are special. At first, I wondered why any young woman would volunteer for this? The look of the land and the sounds I heard on arrival at Bien Hoa Air Base were evidence of the war in progress – and maybe of how geographically close it was. I de-boarded to a loud boom! The landscape was red, unappealing, and there was an overwhelming stench everywhere. Living quarters at the cantonment area, though above ground and structurally pretty sound, were rough and crude; shower stalls weren't too inviting and shower curtains revealed bugs the size of a school bus clinging to every curtain hem (I checked them all)! The bugs collected on the curtains and looked like twice-chewed tobacco and simply stayed and accumulated! The bunkers invited me down on my first or second night there, and I wondered what critters shared them with us? Working hours were extremely long and sometimes one arrived back to the detachment very late, tired, and alone – the area would be at sleep. Looking out from an upstairs balcony, it could be lonely down below. But like everything in life, there was an upside tucked inside this cantonment area.

In it was a collection of women soldiers of varying ages and experiences, who were friendly, sensitive, and always with eager greetings and smiles. An unspoken, but undeniable surround of understanding hearts, were ready to help with the adjustments of arrival and any individual matters that might arise in the course of a Sister's tour. I never learned the names of all of these women, but I had special moments of fellowship and conversations with many of them.

I remember reporting to morning formations – everyone was ironed and starched, well presented (usually fully dressed!) and ready to begin the new day. Field First Betty Benson went to great effort to make sure all was well with everyone and, by her very nature, she sent a special signal of comforting recognition and unconditional approval to each one of us. I thought how unique and positive her leadership skills and her sensitive brand of humor were. Sometimes I reported too close to formation time I think, and she would say, "Here she comes, Miss America!" At first, I was embarrassed, but then I caught on – she simply had a special endearment for everyone! She could not accept an empty space/a missing face in the formation lines; we often waited for every line to complete. I'm not sure I smiled much, but I certainly remember their smiles at the sight of Betty each morning as they fell in formation and as cantonment morale was refreshed for another day! I had a roommate for a short while (she'll know who she is), and I could not always convince her it was bedtime. She stood watch for "Charlie" on our hootch balcony and did so as earnestly as any sentinel!

The full Company staff (original and successors) was always available to us and kind. The Orderly Room was on top of everything – nothing was forfeited in terms of professionalism, expectations of decorum from us, personnel matters and records, and the responsibilities assumed for our welfare and safety. Make no mistake when I speak of morale (and smiles). Those were not smiles of fun and games, but true smiles of pleasure from 'bumping in' to a Sister soldier when paths crossed. Like morale, regard for one another was high. Working hours began early; conveniences were provided, but with minimal adequacy; personal adjustments from duty in the States to duty in Vietnam were NOT minimal. The privilege for being selected to support the combat troops and related elements of combat was 'the only deal' for these 'strictly' volunteer women soldiers. I think it made one smile at the other because 'we got there' and could do what we were doing to help. Sometimes we were very tired, but we wished we could do more. I was always pretty sure that occupational proficiency outgrew everyone's expectations by the Vietnam experience. So, for me, it is much easier to speak of the camaraderie than to speak of anything remotely contradictory.

One night coming back from the mess hall, some of us cut through the hospital tent. One young soldier in bed with his injuries raised up and shouted, "OMG, I think I'm dying!" Of course, we stopped and turned our attention over to him. The soldier smiled and simply said aloud, "I saw blonde curls for a second and thought I must be dying!" That was a tender moment that validated our (unauthorized) presence. I wish we had gone back to actually visit. I think there were three of us, and I hope someone else remembers that moment too.

We had the NCO (noncommissioned officer) lounge where we came together as Sisters and friends, where we learned about each other and the contributions we might each make, where we hashed out the day, sometimes shed tears and fed on awful snacks (Oh God, the music!), and where we celebrated birthdays and promotions and each other. I was a new sergeant first class. Before Vietnam, I would rarely reach out and socialize at all. I remember Effie Efferson (so enjoyed and respected by everyone), Lucki Allen (the same), DJ, Sergeant B and others (not named) that I admired and respected. The personality dynamics, strengths and attitudes among the NCOs were strong and impressive. It was a special mix, for sure. I remember the 'dating cage' that tiny little space with a tiny little lopsided table and four tiny little chairs (right outside the Orderly Room), where one could entertain a guest in the presence of three other couples and be observed from a balcony above (and expect occasional flyovers of popcorn from above!) Sometimes a second little table with some more little chairs would be squeezed in that tiny little space, and more guests would be in there at one time! It was very funny! We celebrated a beautiful WAC Anniversary under our 'campus' tent – that was a huge success. We dressed UP(!) Everyone was beautiful – the cadre in authentic Vietnam dress; the invited (male) guests attentive and delightful (some even wore a tie). The simple elegance of fellowship, dress, music and dancing under night-lights and stars remain a major part of my visions – no protocol specialists needed there! CPT Joanne Murphy, 1SG Marion Crawford, Field First Betty Benson and others provided a commendable celebration setting. I was one who met and escorted Martha Raye to the detachment, and we enjoyed her stories and questions long into the night! I rescued a puppy named Calee that the command and first sergeant allowed to remain in the cantonment area with me. I planned to fly her back to my home in Maryland. Calee quickly became a mascot during her short life with us. (I have the cutest picture of her sitting beside Lucki, each on their own chair). Our new 1SG Katherine Herney loved Calee and became her daytime caretaker. I think Calee followed her everywhere! Then there was the iguana – that's an awful long story. A sizable and good-looking guy iguana slept under my bed for weeks during Monsoon, making only unidentifiable soft, shuffling sounds. Although I heard the sounds, even swept my floor (and under my bed) a number of times, he never showed up until the rains were over and I opened my door for a full day! He finally walked (simply took his good old time) out of the room, made it as far as the sandbag surround, jumped up and sat there for a number of hours in the sun, then disappeared forever. What a guy!

As I write these things, I wonder about the memories our women are bringing back from combat now? Our days ended with some intended or unintended diversion almost every day and with the knowledge that a huge number of people were looking after us. I would not want anyone to take my revelations lightly. Duty, honor, country and personal strengths were front and center in this organization of women. It was a serious undertaking for each one, and we simply did the best and the most that we could do within the scope of our training, abilities, and experiences. Imagine, though, what more we might have done. Though service in a combat area is much different for women now, the footprints of friendship and camaraderie are natural gifts from one soldier to another (gifts that tend to be everlasting), and anyone who survives a combat tour will have reflections and memories of special people like those mentioned here. They will be so thankful for every friend on combat location and the memories created together. Though gratitude follows us around, sometimes it does not land on our hearts exactly when it should. I thank Donna Lowery for this opportunity to recall these faces and these occasions in our WAC Detachment home. I reboarded for home at the same airport and to the sound of another loud boom. I can't remember the exact date, but it was near the end of December 1969. I spent that last night in a command bunker under fire! I also sprained my ankle getting there!

I was sure that when I did rotate back to the States that nothing would ever be the same for me. It took quite a while before I would land an assignment where I would again feel worthy, qualified, included and acknowledged. And I was right. My tour in Vietnam was blessed by opportunity and trust (offered by soldiers of magnificent character) and, if some tainted events arose, it is still the camaraderie of leadership and friendships that blessed me the most. I have pictures that would tell this story better than I can and that depict the Anniversary celebration and times spent with friends I've truly missed and regret losing touch with. I hope everyone of them are well, happy, and beautifully blessed – Gabe Brancato, Frances Black, Reya Monte, Ginny Hanley, Donna Dear, a gal named Peggy, and others not named but not forgotten. I treasure my time with them and the memories of the friendship they offered.

I retired from the Army in 1981 at Fort Knox, KY.

### ♥Victoria Ann "Vicki" Lapinski (Lennert)
**In country: March 1968 – March 1969**
**Rank: Specialist 5, US Army**
**Duty: USARV, Facilities Service Division, Administrative Specialist**

*Marsha "Cricket" Holder:* Vicki Lapinski was one of those people you could never forget. She seemed to always be smiling and it was contagious. Vicki married a fellow Vietnam veteran before her discharge from the Army and they had 8 children. She got a degree in education from Temple University. Sadly her husband passed in 1995 and Vicki passed in 2007.

### Marsha L. Mossing
**Retired as a Sergeant First Class, USAR**
**In country: March 1968 – March 1969**
**Rank: Specialist 5, US Army**
**Duty: USARV, Surgeon's Office, Clerk-Typist**

I had the end bunk by the door on the second floor of the barracks. One day, after showering, with the towel still around me, I happened to look out the door and saw a couple of GIs in a jeep driving ever so slowly past our compound. They were looking up at the second floor barrack entrance. Hmmm! I wondered if SSG Effie could do me a favor. I asked her if a piece of plywood could be placed at the end of my bunk. Ever resourceful, she got the job done and privacy prevailed. The plywood was perfectly plain and smooth so my bunkmates and I decided to put a design on it. Snoopy was the result.

**Comments and Memories:** One of the noncommissioned officers (blonde and always very neat) made the mistake of telling 1SG Marion Crawford that she didn't have enough troops to throw her into the swimming pool (1SG "C" and this NCO were standing on the second-floor porch overlooking the pool). 1SG "C" yelled to us in the pool, "Did you hear that, girls? Sgt _____ doesn't think I have enough troops to throw her into the swimming pool!" Dutiful troops that we were, we all got out of the pool, marched up the steps, grabbed Sgt _____, carried her down the steps and dunked her! *Source: Vietnam Memory Book 2000*

**Jane C. Vickery**
**Retired as a Lieutenant Colonel**
**In country: March 16, 1968 – March 16, 1969**
**Rank: Major, US Army Medical Specialist Corps**
**Duty: 24th Evacuation Hospital, Physical Therapist**

Vietnam was both tedious and satisfying. I have always been appreciative of that experience.

**Jane E. Gierhart**
**Retired as a Colonel**
**In country: March 1968 – June 1969**
**Rank: Major, US Army Medical Specialist Corps**
**Duty: 85th Evacuation Hospital, Qui Nhon/Phu Bai; 29th Evacuation Hospital, Can Tho/Binh Thuy, Physical Therapist**

**♥Wanda Lee Baker**
**In country: March 1968 – October 1969**
**Rank: Staff Sergeant, US Army**
**Duty: USARV, Surgeon General's Office, Administrative NCO**

**Frances I. Gonzales (Shore)**
**Retired as a First Sergeant**
**In country: March 1968 – October 1969**
**Rank: Staff Sergeant, US Marine Corps**
**Duty: MACV, J3, Classified documents**

I arrived in Vietnam shortly after the Tet offensive. Everyone was still under 24-hour curfew. We were bused to and from work. I was issued a green field uniform from the Army that two people could fit into; we had to have them altered to fit. I was assigned to the hotel where the nurses were for a few days (there was a cookout every night on the roof). After that, I moved to a hotel not far from Headquarters MACV where I still had bus service.

At noon, we would get brave and go to Tan Son Nhut Air Base for lunch. That did not last long after we saw the rats just walk under the table to eat whatever they found. They were like pets. They did not run from you. Wow. We went back to the mess hall.

Once curfew was lifted, we were able to move around and view the area. We visited the orphanage and helped move the young children around. It was very sad to see their living conditions – four or five to a bed. Sanitary conditions were not the best, but the smiles were there.

In October, I took over MSgt Barbara Dulinsky's job with classified documents at MACV. Turnover was fast and the MSgt was ready to go home.

In November, we cooked two turkeys with all the trimmings and invited everyone to come to the hotel and enjoy the festivities. A good time was had by all.

**♥Karen J. Dillaman (Scott)**
**In country: March 1968 – December 1969**
**Rank: Specialist 5, US Army**
**Duty: USARV, G1, Administrative Specialist**

**♥Deloris Lee Browning**
**Retired as a Major**
**In country: March 1968 – 1970**
**Rank: Major, US Army**
**Duty: USARV, Adjutant General's Office, Chief of Personnel Actions**
**Division**

*By Marsha "Cricket" Holder:* Deloris Lee Browning first enlisted in the Marine Corps Women's Reserve Battalion, Camp LeJeune, NC, in 1945 before the end of WWII. In April 1949 before the Korean War, she enlisted in the Marines in which she served for the next nine years. In September 1958, because of an age restriction in the Marines, she enlisted in the Army to get a commission. Deloris Browning served in the Army September 1958 to June 1970. She was stationed at Long Binh, Vietnam, working at the USARV Adjutant General's office. She retired as a Major after serving during WWII, Korea and Vietnam. Major Browning died May 29, 1998, and is buried in Arlington National Cemetery.

**Doris Olheiser (Davison)**
**In country: March 5, 1968 – March 2, 1969**
**Rank: Specialist 4, US Army**
**Duty: USARV, G1**

**Comments and Memories:** My very best friend was Diane (Sam) Symanowicz. She kept me very busy doing fun and crazy things. Yes, we are still in touch with each other. I wish we did not live so far apart! *Source: Vietnam Memory Book 2000*

## Natalie E. Moody (Summers)
### In country: March 5, 1968 – March 4, 1969
### Rank: Specialist 4, US Army
### Duty: USARV, Engineer Division, Message Center, Clerk-Typist

I remember one of the times when the ammunition dump blew up. I looked around and everyone was acting unusually uneasy. I decided to go to bed. In the morning, everyone was shocked that I slept through the whole thing. I now have a loss of high pitch hearing from Vietnam.

## Jeanne L. Francoeur (Bell)
### In country: March 21, 1968 – October 18, 1969
### Rank: Sergeant, US Marine Corps
### Duty: NAVFORV, Marine Corps Personnel Section

I enlisted in the Marine Corps June 6, 1966. After basic training and school, I was stationed at Headquarters Marine Corps in Washington, DC, working at the Navy Annex in Congressional Correspondence. After 18 months, a notice asked for volunteers for Japan, Hawaii, Okinawa, or Vietnam. I didn't want to go to Vietnam, but the other places were inviting. I signed up and got orders to Vietnam. This was a good lesson for me: To this day, I do not gamble, even if the odds are good.

I arrived in Saigon March 21, 1968. Oh my God! What a place! I was in winter greens (uniform) and it was hot. I quickly learned that a pungent odor that you never get used to was due to the country's lack of sanitation.

Vietnam was a very poor country where life was expendable. Saigon was dirty, overcrowded, and clouds of pollution could be seen until noon. The river water was brown. The people lived on the street or on sampans with several families to a home. One family lived at the local zoo in the elephant quarters.

We lived in quarters that were like hotels in the 1950s, old, rundown, cold water, a fan, but we had stateside toilets and toilet paper. We had mess halls but few used them. The VC (Viet Cong) would mortar or use C-4 explosives to blow up anywhere American soldiers would gather. We ate on the economy, cooked one-pot meals, and, of course, had access to C-rations. Cigarettes were 10 cents a pack and whisky $1.50 a bottle, when available.

I worked at Naval Forces, Vietnam. My job was to go to Tan Son Nhut Air Base to transport marines that were attached to us. We provided in-country support for the advisors to the Vietnamese Marine Corps. We took them to get their helmets, fatigues, combat boots, weapons, mess kit, etc. At Koeppler Compound they learned about Vietnamese money, customs, and the "Do's and Don'ts." while in country.

A lot of what I saw and experienced in Vietnam was sad, frightening and just cruel.

Sometimes we had fun. In the evenings, we played cards for money; we seldom slept. Every now and then, we went to the Zoo for an hour. A four-lane bowling alley served hot dogs. We drank the local beer, though awful. Everywhere, men and women soldiers were comrades.

Of course, the best time was to sit and talk about America – the foods we would eat when we got home, the places we would go, and the peace to worship without fear and thank God for helping us come home. Thousands of men and eight women paid the ultimate price in Vietnam. Many, many more were wounded, and those without physical wounds suffer in silence, for our country knows not that the war for some of us will never be over.

# APRIL

*Memory Lane: Martin Luther King, Jr. is shot dead at the Lorraine Motel in Memphis, Tennessee. Riots erupt in major American cities, lasting for several days afterwards; President Lyndon B. Johnson signs the Civil Rights Act of 1968. Song: "Honey" by Bobby Goldsboro*

**Lois A. Main**
**Retired as a Master Sergeant**
**In country: April 1968 – February 11, 1969**
**Rank: Staff Sergeant, US Army**
**Duty: MACV, Office of the Adjutant General**

**Janet M. Brusseau (Munger)**
**In country: April 1968 – March 1969**
**Rank: Specialist 6, US Army**
**Duty: USARV, Judge Advocate General's Office**

**♥Joan Mae Crawford (Blakeley)**
**Retired as a Chief Warrant Officer 4**
**In country: April 1968 – April 1969**
**Rank: Chief Warrant Officer 3, US Army**
**Duty: USARV, 1ˢᵗ Signal Brigade, Cryptographic Custodian for**
**Communications Center**

**Highlights of memorable experiences:**

- Serving around the world as the only WAC Warrant Officer serving with the Signal Corps and one of only 17 WAC Warrant Officers in the Army
- Living with the people and cultures of other countries through six tours, nearly half my career, assigned to Germany, Italy, Vietnam and Thailand
- Incoming mortar attacks on the compound and exposure to enemy fire and Agent Orange residues when taking crypto codes to communications outposts in Vietnam
- 22 years of service, and decorations including the Bronze Star Medal, Meritorious Service Medal, and Army Commendation Medal with two oak leaf clusters

**Henrietta E. Florido**
**In country: April 1968 – April 1969**
**Rank: Specialist 4, US Army**
**Duty: USARV, Clerk-Typist**

**Madelene L. Hall (Showers)**
**In country: April 1968 – April 1969**
**Rank: Specialist 6, US Army**
**Duty: USARV, 1ˢᵗ Aviation Brigade, Personnel Specialist**

**Mary A. Marsh**
**Retired as a Brigadier General**
**In country: April 1968 – April 1969**
**Rank: Captain, US Air Force**
**Duty: MACV Detachment 10, Air Force Advisory Group, USAF WAF Staff Advisor to the Vietnam Women's Armed Forces Corps**

The saga of Capt. Mary Marsh in Vietnam began when the Vietnamese Air Force (VNAF) asked the US Air Force if they could provide a woman advisor to "assist" them in building a VNAF Women's Component of the Armed Forces. The task went to Brigadier General Jeanne Holm (WAF Director at the time) to find the woman officer who would be the "first AF female advisor to the VNAF." The woman selected was none other than Capt. Mary Marsh.

Getting qualified on weapons was a basic requirement, but posed no problem as she and her husband were avid clay pigeon and trap shooters. But, Capt. Marsh, being a practical person posed the question of "What am I to wear?" At that time, there were no Air Force combat uniforms for women. General Holm told her to get a hold of the WAC (Women's Army Corps) Colonel over there and see if "she can fix you up." So, except for ceremonial and photo op purposes, Capt. Marsh wore WAC fatigues and a Navy overseas cap, which she still has today. Orientation was pretty basic: find a good strong nail, hammer it on the back of your dorm room door; hang your flak jacket and helmet on the nail; have a pair of flip flops on the floor, always at the ready. And, when you hear the sirens, grab your helmet and flak jacket, put something on your feet and take cover. "Well, the first time that siren went off, I put my helmet on my head, put my flak jacket on, and bent down to put on my shoes. Well, that helmet slid right off my head and almost broke my toes! The next time the siren went off, the helmet went on after the shoes!"

Captain Marsh had an office in the VNAF Headquarters building and her duties took her all over South Vietnam traveling with the Vietnamese Air Force. The Vietnam Women's Armed Forces Corps (WAFC), was a single organization from which the women would be sent out to the various branches. Her job was to establish a dedicated female unit for the VNAF. As the only US woman assigned, it was a real challenge. She had learned some of the language and learned fairly quickly that to get things done you needed to make the Vietnamese think it was their idea. She succeeded in setting up "the first female unit of the VNAF," established standard administrative and personnel procedures, designed the uniforms, and almost got them to wear shoes – preferring flip flops, they would often say, "Shoes hurt feet, no shoes."

Mary Marsh was always a doer and was a professional entertainer before entering the Air Force, and she put those skills to good use in Vietnam. Before Christmas of 1968, the Tan Son Nhut chapel choir wanted to perform Handel's Messiah. Not one to pass up a challenge, she agreed to "give it a go." She said, "We have an organ and organist, 60 men, but only 8 women, so you women must sing louder!" Come Christmas the performance was standing room only. Morale was flying high by the end of the show, for both audience and performers. There were no rocket attacks that night – a truly joyous night!

*Taken from an interview with BG Marsh by BG Patricia Hinneburg and SMSgt Sharon Young*

**Karen McClung (Feher)**
**In country: April 1968 – April 1969**
**Rank: Specialist 5, US Army**
**Duty: USARV, IG; Engineer Division**

**Patricia C. Patterson (Smith)**
**In country: April 1968 – April 1969**
**Rank: Specialist 4, US Army**
**Duty: USARV, 1ˢᵗ Logistical Command, Clerk-Typist**

My experience was very ordinary. I did my tour and enjoyed my time but don't have anything in particular to brag about. I came back from Vietnam, and according to my DD214 (Certificate of Release or Discharge from Active Duty), I did 2 years, 8 months and 24 days and got a Vietnam early out.

**♥Joan A. Peck**
**Retired as a Master Sergeant**
**In country: April 1968 – April 1969**
**Rank: Sergeant First Class, US Army**
**Duty: USARV, Personnel, NCO Records and US Army Headquarters Area Command, Personnel, NCO Records, Personnel Sergeant**

Master Sergeant Joan Peck was an active contributor to many organizations. She was a member of VFW; Disabled American Veterans; Humane Society of US; National Parks and Conservation Association; and the American Society for Prevention of Cruelty to Animals. *Source: Vietnam Memory Book 2000*

**♥Marilyn Roth**
**Retired as a Sergeant First Class**
**In country: April 1968 – April 1969**
**Rank: Specialist 5, US Army**
**Duty: USARV, Administrative Specialist**

**Comments and Memories:** The night the Viet Cong tried to take over Long Binh. While I was grabbing for my helmet, pistol belt and canteen on the top of my wall locker, a stereo speaker fell on my hand. I started running around screaming, "I've been hit. I've been hit!" I really thought I had been hit by a mortar round. Everyone had a good laugh the next morning when we saw the stereo speaker on the floor. *Source: Vietnam Memory Book 2000*

**Carol S. Bessette**
**Retired as a Lieutenant Colonel**
**In country: April 1968 – May 1969**
**Rank: Captain, US Air Force**
**Duty: Headquarters 7th Air Force, Intelligence Applications Officer**

"The very nature of our job considerably restricts our personal lives." An intelligence expert, she's a career officer with nearly nine years' service. Her husband, Capt. John F. Bessette, is assigned to the 3rd Special Operations Squadron at Bien Hoa Air Base, about 30 miles from Saigon. "Those of us in intelligence may not travel into the countryside. Consequently, my husband can only visit me; I cannot visit him." Carol considers her work and her assignment a challenge and one of the real opportunities to put her training to its fullest use. *Source:* Airman*, May 1969*

**Patricia "Pat" A. Givens**
**Retired as a Master Sergeant**
**In country: April 1968 – May 1969**
**Rank: Specialist 5, US Army**
**Duty: USARV, Protocol**

**Pilar L. Magallon**
**Retired as a Sergeant First Class**
**In country: April 1968 – May 1969;**
**June 1970 – July 1971**
**Rank: Specialist 5, US Army**
**Duty: USARV, Staff Judge Advocate; MACV, Staff Judge**
**Advocate, Legal Clerk/Court Reporter**

**Charlotte E. Phillips**
**Retired as a Colonel**
**In country: April 6, 1968 – July 4, 1969**
**Rank: Major, US Army**
**Duty: USARV, G4, Reports Officer**

One hot sticky Thursday afternoon in September 1967, I packed up my personal belongings and headed for Atlantic City, NJ, to attend the Miss America pageant and join my crazy friend Kay Linton. My last free time for nearly two years.

When I returned to work at Fort Lee, VA, I was told by our personal staff that I had been chosen to serve in Vietnam leaving next spring. I was also told to write a letter volunteering to go to the Republic of Vietnam (RVN). Although I was a captain, I had never thought about serving in Vietnam. I knew that was where the action was and that any officer should be proud to serve in RVN.

I had no idea what serving in RVN really meant, except there was a war going on there. I was assigned to Cam Ranh Bay to work in the G4. I also had heard on the TV and read in the paper how the Tet offensive in 1968 was a real setback for the Americans. To prepare for this assignment I had to make many personal decisions, like what to do with my nice convertible, my house, the new fur stole I had just bought, and the camping trailer I owned. Well, I stored the camper, put the stole in fur storage and sold the red convertible and rented the house.

After the usual preparation processing procedures – trying to learn the language and getting lots of shots – I left for a short leave, before flying to Vietnam. I left my home in Vermont April 5, 1968, the day after Martin Luther King was murdered. For some unknown reason, I had purchased a full fare ticket. That was in the days when military could fly stand-by for a reduced rate. I flew into Washington, to see it burning, and then experienced mob scenes as college students tried hard to get seats on the airplanes. And, I thanked God I had bought a full-priced ticket for the airline.

Three days later, I arrived in Vietnam, still not realizing how my life was going to be affected by this assignment. Once we were on the ground at Tan Son Nhut Air Base, the airplane took off in a hurry. Apparently, some planes had been attacked if they remained too long on the ground.

I went through in-processing, and was told I was not going to Cam Ranh Bay, but I was to be assigned to G4 Supply and Services at Long Binh.

That decision was not so bad; I was assigned half a trailer with great air conditioning and a housemate, Jackie Chappell. She was a great gal; I knew her from our basic training class.

I quickly found out that my job was to be the AR 711-5 reports preparation person for the command. What did we do? We requested a listing of all the equipment the various units had on hand. Our job was to compare authorizations to on-hand status, consolidate the unit reports and send that report on to higher headquarters. The report was prepared quarterly. To assist in the report preparation, a staff of three sergeants and two people from the Army Materiel Command (AMC) worked to make the report accurate and complete. We spent hours going over unit reports – comparing the input from the units between quarters, and reviewing the combat loss reports. We all visited units either randomly or after a request from a unit that they were having problems. These visits helped us evaluate how accurate the reports were and what better instructions we could give the units.

The reports became the planning guide for AMC to plan shipment of equipment to Vietnam. Later this report was used as a planning document for shipping equipment from the units back to the USA as the war was drawing down.

Of course, the computer report had to be carried by me to our next higher command, US Army of the Pacific. This meant I got to go to Hawaii three times during my tour in Vietnam.

I planned to extend for six months and take advantage of 30 days free leave, but the Women's Army Corps (WAC) had other ideas. They felt, since I was one of the few logistical WAC officers with experience in Vietnam, I had to come and instruct at the WAC school for officers. So I returned to the United States in July 1969.

Among lasting impressions are: the shock about the relationships that formed between Vietnamese women and our married officers and enlisted men; how fragile life was, even when assigned to a secure area – like stray rockets hitting officers' living areas and killing them instantly; and that free time did not mean one could go where they wanted when free. Most of our freedom was deciding to go to the officers' club for the evening or back to work. When we returned to evening work, we often watched – outside our offices – the aerial spraying of Agent Orange.

Lastly, I believe that men while going to the bathroom talked more than they should to fellow officers. Why do I center on the bathroom? There was nearly always a group of Vietnamese women, who kept our offices clean, gathered around the drain in the bathrooms chattering. I believe those women were spying and passing along the information they gathered to our enemies.

I am proud I served in Vietnam, but the experiences of seeing how the Americans lived, versus the way the Vietnamese people lived, still haunts me.

**Penelope "Peny" H. Hill (Radebaugh)**
**In country: April 16, 1968 – April 13, 1969**
**Rank: Specialist 5, US Army**
**Duty: USARV, Engineer Division, Administrative Specialist**

One day a giant (human fist-sized) bee visited our morning formation. Captain Joanne Murphy, our commanding officer, dismissed formation, ran back to her office and slammed the screen door. We troops scattered for cover faster than when the ammunition dump was blown by the enemy.

*Specialist 5 Hill received the Army Commendation Medal for meritorious service in support of allied counter-insurgency to the Republic of Vietnam.*

**♥Velma "Pee Wee" M. Calcio**
**Retired as a Sergeant First Class**
**In country: April 29, 1968 – Date of departure unknown**
**Rank: Sergeant First Class, US Army**
**Duty: USARV, Special Troops, WAC Detachment, Supply Sergeant**

Tet Offensive 1969: We started getting incoming mortars around 2:00 a.m. I was on duty in the Orderly Room and LTC William Dickey, Special Troops commander, came in. He had on his boots, unlaced, soft cap and his .45 caliber pistol. He wanted to know how the women were. I told him we were in the bunkers. Later, he returned, this time with his boots laced and wearing his steel helmet and flak jacket. He wanted to know how the women were. He came a third time, again checking on us. That night he was killed. He was so loved and respected that a black cloud hung over Special Troops. When I left a week later, it was that way still.

The men from Special Troops who were guarding the perimeter heard the WAC Detachment had been hit. A mortar hit a Conex container behind the Finance building. They made a truck driver drive to the WAC Detachment, get out and check on us. What's so remarkable is that they had only two hours to get more ammo, eat and sleep. Still, they had to know if we were okay.

Some other supply sergeants picked me up early one Sunday morning to go look at a trailer for the company commander. It was delivered in a couple of days and the commander moved in. I also got an ice-cube-making machine, but someone later gave it away. *(As told to SFC Mary "Connie" Koster)*

Sergeant First Class Calcio was also a trumpet player in the 14th US Women's Army Corps Band.

## Mary "Connie" Constance Koster
**Retired as a Sergeant First Class**
**In country: April 29, 1968 – March 3, 1969**
**Rank: Sergeant First Class, US Army**
**Duty: USARV, 1ˢᵗ Aviation Brigade, Administrative NCO**

Staff Sergeant Edith Efferson, our supply sergeant, had a small dog named Tammy, who was always so friendly and loved to be petted. One morning while I was waiting for the bus, I saw Tammy in the doorway of the Supply Room. I walked over to her, bent down, and said, "Tammy, how're you doing?" She growled at me! I asked SSG Effie, "What's wrong with Tammy?" "She hasn't had her coffee yet," was her reply.

On the bus one evening as we were on our way back to our billets, we started to get some incoming mortars. The bus driver sped up just as we were going down a hill. As we were making a left turn, the bus leaned to the left, then it righted itself. When this happened, I slid across the aisle and landed in SSG Marty Contreras' lap. She wasn't any more surprised than me!

During the Tet Offensive 1969 – we were in the bunkers, and we almost always sat in the same places, so when I turned around to talk to someone, I noticed she wasn't there and neither was her roommate. I said, "I'll go look for them." It was really dark. I went up the stairs to the first landing and started up the next set of stairs. I heard a really loud helicopter, looked off to my right, and suddenly there was a really bright light that lit up the big field behind the WAC Detachment. The light went off as quickly it appeared. I could hear debris hitting the roof. I was holding the railing with my right hand when I was blown into the air and spun around in slow motion, hit the building, and then in regular motion, blown down the stairs to the landing. I was trying to run, but I was turned around, and facing the railing, so close I was afraid I would go over. I pushed back from the railing toward the building. I fumbled around and found one shower clog and then felt my way in the dark back up the stairs to find the other one. About that time, one missing woman came running. I asked her where her roommate was and she said she was right behind her. Apparently they had stopped to get dressed! We all went down the stairs and into the bunker. My feet felt funny the whole time we were in the bunker and when daylight came a few hours later, I saw that I had the shower clogs on the wrong feet! The next day we heard that the enemy had breached the perimeter in three places and almost made it to the WAC Detachment. The next daily bulletin emphasized that there was to be no stopping to get dressed when the alert sounded.

**Kathleen "Kathy" E. Kennedy (Fontana)**
**In country: April 29, 1968 – April 28, 1969**
**Rank: Specialist 5, US Army**
**Duty: USARV, G5**

Volunteering for Vietnam, I expected military conditions would be different from stateside. At 0600 hours, "GOOD MORNING VIETNAM!" resonated loudly from radios throughout the barracks, indifferent to what had occurred during the night. Everyone in Vietnam started a new day, some luckier than others to be able to hear the greeting again. I liked my job at Headquarters USARV, and that was fortunate because 12 hours a day, 7 days a week was normal working hours. Most of all I liked the people I worked with. Colonel Mundy was my favorite boss. The cadre at our WAC Detachment was wonderful, always seeking to make living easier for us in a war situation: parties under the parachute (food was mostly meat, everything else from a can), and visits from celebrities like Martha Raye in uniform.

Vietnam was not a popular war; it was called a "conflict." Mentioning service in Vietnam could produce a lot of negativity. In the years that followed Vietnam, what most surprised me was that military women like me who served in Vietnam became nonexistent information in textbooks. The nurses, civilian women and USO girls were recorded, but no uniformed women in other occupations. In 2003, the faculty of a high school near me invited veterans to come to an event with their military mementos and pictures. I went because it was part of my job as a veterans' representative to be involved with community events. I sat with other veterans, with my combat boots and picture in front of me, talking to students, when the teacher in charge interrupted and called me a fraud. He was so angry with me and told me to leave, but I did not leave. Everyone around me heard him, even the German who sat next to me, who had swum from the Bismarck and had been picked up by a US ship. The teacher believed him, but did not believe me. About

20 minutes later the teacher came back and apologized for having become so angry. He informed me that Vietnam history had already been written and there was no mention of any uniformed armed forces women having been in Vietnam, only nurses. This book is important to pass on our experiences of Vietnam. We were really there!

**Mary J. Nicholls**
**In country: April 29, 1968 – December 4, 1969**
**Rank: Staff Sergeant, US Army**
**Duty: USARV, Communications and Electronics, Administrative NCO**

In 1968 at Fort Ord, CA, I received orders for Vietnam. I had no idea what to expect. It turned out I was stationed on a large Army post (Long Binh) about 27 miles north of Saigon. Except for nightly rocket attacks, it was relatively safe if one had to be in a war. A downside was witnessing helicopters flying the wounded to the nearby evacuation hospital.

I worked in an administrative capacity for the Army chief of staff for Communications and Electronics at Headquarters, USARV. I worked with a great group of men (and have kept in touch with several over the years). A rocket hit USARV headquarters once during my 18-month tour. Of all the top-secret facilities at Headquarters, that one rocket hit the post office. Because it was at night, no one was injured, but there was a big hole in the wall.

We traveled by military bus, jeep or helicopter for occasional trips to Saigon and one very nice trip to Vung Tau, a beach community on the South China Sea. I also had R&R trips to Hawaii, Japan and Australia. Because I extended my tour six months, a grateful government gave me 30 days free leave and a flight anywhere in the free world. A friend also extended and we chose to visit Europe, touring eight countries. We also stopped in Guam and Anchorage, AK.

After Vietnam, I left the military, lucked into a job at the Pentagon, and loved every minute of the 28 years I served there. I always knew what was happening anywhere in the world, and worked with interesting people involved in interesting things.

Retired in 1998, I was living in northern Virginia that awful day in September 2001. I tried to contact friends I knew at the Pentagon; thankfully, they were spared. My heart was broken knowing human beings could be so selfish, so cruel, as to take so many innocent lives.

I moved to Rockford, IL, in December 2004 to be near my family. Over time, I joined three veterans' organizations. We march in parades, participate in ceremonies for those who died in service to our country, to remember those yet missing, to send young men and women off to war and, even better, ceremonies to welcome them back home.

# MAY

*Memory Lane: The US and North Vietnamese delegations agree to begin peace talks in Paris later this month. The formal talks began on May 10.*
*Song: "Tighten Up" by Archie Bell and the Drells*

The monsoon season in the southern part of Vietnam is normally from May to September. Here is SSG Donna Lowery modeling the latest in olive green ponchos. Also shown is the pile of sandbags, getting ready for the monsoon. In front of the Personnel Office, where SSG Lowery worked, there was a 5-foot deep ditch – it was completely filled with rainwater, as was the entire area.

♥**Mary Lavinia Crosby**
**Retired as a Lieutenant Colonel**
**In country: May 1968 – April 1969**
**Rank: Major, US Air Force**
**Duty: Headquarters 7th Air Force, Operations, Personnel Staff Officer**

In 1979, Lieutenant Colonel Crosby received the "Military Woman of the Year" award at Los Angeles Air Force Station. She was previously awarded five Air Force commendation medals for meritorious service, as well as, the Bronze Star, the Republic of Vietnam Gallantry Cross, and the Republic of Vietnam Campaign Medal. She was a member of the Charleston Post of the Veterans of Foreign Wars.

**Christine Almanza (Sampley)**
**In country: May 1968 – May 1969; September 11, 1970 – April 3, 1972**
**Rank: Specialist 5, US Army**
**Duty: USARV, Casualty and Medical Evacuation Division; MACV, US Army Security Agency, 509ᵗʰ Radio Research Group, Administrative Specialist**

I joined the Women's Army Corps in September 1966. Basic training was at Fort McClellan, AL. To a California girl who had never been outside of the state, Alabama was quite a cultural shock, especially the food. To this day, I still can't eat grits. My first permanent duty station was at Fifth Army Headquarters, Chicago. I was assigned to the Casualty Reporting and Survivors Assistance Branch. We were billeted at the Del Prado Hotel. It didn't take long to get used to that lifestyle, but all too soon, we were moved to Fort Sheridan, IL. It was mentally challenging as well as heartbreaking taking all the reports of soldiers, missing, wounded or killed. Vietnam seemed so far away. I don't know what made me volunteer to go there, not too many women wanted to go. In September 1968, I left for Vietnam. There were mixed feelings from my family, I being the youngest of 10 children.

I was assigned to the Casualty and Medical Evacuation Division, at USARV Headquarters in Long Binh. It was a 24/7 day operation. I was the first woman assigned to this unit and it was very intimidating working with all men. I'm sure we all heard rude remarks from the men regarding "women in the military." For those of us who were in Long Binh, the compound where we were billeted had high walls and topped with concertina wire. That was to make us feel safer. I won't go into details of my job. We ate meals at the 24ᵗʰ Evacuation Hospital alongside the ambulatory wounded soldiers. The sound of helicopters coming and going was ceaseless. We spent many a night in bunkers. After one night in particular after we had incoming, I went to work the next morning and was informed that one of the officers in the office next to ours had been killed. Upon arrival in Vietnam, I was given a short-timer calendar – 365 days, I was so happy when I became a "one-digit midget!" Readjustment to life stateside was not easy. For months, I had trouble sleeping and kept hearing the thumping sound of helicopters in my sleep.

I didn't realize that so much of life had passed me by. I was twenty years old going on Forty! My perspectives on life had changed so much. My friends at home hadn't changed. Vietnam was just something they saw on TV. I did go out with them once, but left realizing that we didn't have anything in common anymore. So, I put in to go back to Vietnam. For another year and a half, I was with the 509th Radio Research Group outside of Tan Son Nhut Air Base. Life after Vietnam was never the same. My last duty station was with the Army Security Agency in Arlington Hall Station, VA.

My husband is a retired Army sergeant major who served for 24 years and is also a Vietnam veteran. In October 2014, we will have been married for 41 years. We have two wonderful children. I presently work for the Veterans' Administration as a Medical Support Assistant.

**Zulma I. Cruz (Martorell)**
**Retired as a Sergeant First Class**
**In country: May 1968 – May 1969;**
**September 1970 – April 1972**
**Rank: Specialist 5, US Army**
**Duty: USARV, G4; USARV, Inspector General/**
**Adjutant General, Administrative Specialist**

**Eleanor Elaine Filkins (Davies)**
**Retired as a Colonel**
**In country: May 1968 – May 6, 1969**
**Rank: Major, US Marine Corps**
**Duty: NAVFORV, Marine Corps Personnel Section, Administrative Officer**

Unfortunately, in that time frame, women marines were sent to Vietnam with no weapons training. But to my good fortune, I met a number of male Marine Corps staff NCOs who determined that someone without any weapons savvy was a danger. Hence, they spent two days with me at a range in Hue. I shot every weapon in their arsenal, to include a grenade launcher.

I made Major while in country. My assignment while there was as administrator (a glorified commanding officer) to all marines not formally attached to a division or smaller unit. The units

247

under that responsibility included Advisor to the Vietnamese Marine Corps and the ARVN (South Vietnamese) Army, Communicators with Defense Communications Agency, Southeast Asia Command (DCA SAM), Radio and TV personnel with Armed Forces, Vietnam Network, COORDS personnel, MACV marines, RungSat Special Zone marines, and a highly classified spook group in Da Nang (these Marines and Navy personnel told me that if they revealed to me what they did in Vietnam they would have to kill me – ha ha). These are just a few of the units that I served. My office was responsible for about 750 to 850 marines. We were located in an eight-story building without an elevator, so arrival at work began with a climb up eight flights of stairs. Once at work, we didn't leave during the day except to go to a noon meal or to our quarters after a day's work.

I shared a room with a lady naval officer at the Le Que Don, a motel-type facility, a terrible place, without dining facilities. As a result, I ate my main meal at the Embassy Restaurant, often at noontime. The rest of my food was either obtained from vendors off the streets of Saigon, or food we were able to find at the commissary. We ate a lot of rice and jello. Those two things are not in my current diet.

One of my most vivid memories was when I was invited as the guest of honor to lunch with the recruits at the Vietnamese boot camp. They were so proud to serve me a hot meal of meat and potatoes. I found out later that I had dined on dog and monkey. It was a good thing I didn't know at the time what was being served.

While I was there, John McCain was a POW. His father was an Admiral. Naval Forces Vietnam (NAVFORV) invited the Admiral and Mrs. McCain for a two-week visit. I was privileged to have been Mrs. McCain's military escort during their visit. That was truly a highlight of my tour.

My worst memory was that one of my responsibilities was to ID all killed-in-action marines from any unit assigned to my office. Often this had to be done using only their service record book (SRB). Luckily, this was not a duty that was performed often, since very few NAVFORV/MACV marines were killed during my time there.

Sergeant Jeanne Francoeur Bell worked for me while stationed in Vietnam. I talked with her recently. When I called her, she answered the phone and said, "I would know that voice anywhere." You must understand, we were in close quarters in our office seven days a week, as much as 15 hours a day. We all got to know each other pretty well!

On my return to the USA, I was stationed at 29 Palms, CA, where I met and married a wonderful Marine Major by the name of Larry Davies. We both retired as Colonels. I was the senior Marine Corps Colonel for nearly two years (until my retirement in 1988). I am now almost 80 years old and live in a log home on a 50-acre ranch in Montana.

**Ann D. Fritsch**
**Retired as a Colonel**
**In country: May 1968 – May 1969; May 1970 – November 1971**
**Rank: Major, US Army Medical Specialist Corps**
**Duty: 8th Field Hospital, Nha Trang, Physical Therapist; MACV Surgeon's Office as the Rehabilitation Advisor for the Vietnamese Army**

 In Vietnam, my first assignment was 8th Field hospital, Nha Trang. We were the community medical center for an Air Force Base, Special Forces, and several support units. We also cared for battle injuries and children who were brought from local orphanages. Traveling by helicopter or Air Force cargo planes, I also served two or three days a week at an evacuation hospital at Phu Hiep. The patients were primarily those with combat-related conditions.

The Physical Therapists would begin the rehabilitation process of the injured, sometimes within a few hours after injuries were incurred. This made a difference in the outcome, both physically and in the soldier's acceptance of his or her wounds.

During a second tour, I worked out of Saigon with MACV as the Rehabilitation Advisor for the Army of the Republic of Vietnam (ARVN) Medical Service. I organized and taught six courses in exercises, primarily for amputees and patients with fragmentation and chest wounds. The courses, a month in length, were given for nurse aides who worked on orthopedic wards. One or two students came from each ARVN hospital for each course. We had lectures in the morning and practice on the wards in the afternoon. I used films and demonstrations and worked with an English-speaking physical therapy aide. Between courses, I visited the hospitals to work with the students in their own setting and with their physicians.

Both tours provided exceptional professional experiences that could never be repeated, and I was fortunate to have these assignments. There were some rough times but my greatest memories are the positive changes we made in the care of the ARVN soldiers and their families.

**Louise Haselrig**
**In country: May 1968 – May 1969**
**Rank: Staff Sergeant, US Air Force**
**Duty: MACV, Force Development, Administrative Specialist**

Here's an Air Force woman (WAF) who found Vietnam a not unpleasant surprise. "Vietnam wasn't at all what I had expected it to be. I wasn't disappointed by conditions at all, and I was surprised that accommodations for WAF in a war zone were as good as they are." General George S. Brown, Seventh Air Force commander, expects to see many more WAF like Sergeant Haselrig and the others serving in the combat zone. WAF are serving in South Vietnam with dedication and professionalism. "I have only high praise for their performance. As additional adequate quarters become available in Vietnam, we may see more WAF stationed here in an ever-increasing number of assignments, with commensurate increase in responsibility and contribution to the overall Seventh Air Force mission." *Source:* Airman, *May 1969*

**Comments and Memories:** One night, sniper fire broke out and all the lights in the hotel were turned off (blackout) to avoid being hit. We're standing around in the dark and all you could see were small red glows here and there. Turns out that some people were smoking. All a sniper had to do was aim for the smokers! *Source: Vietnam Memory Book 2000*

**Jane E. Helms (Vance)**
**Retired as a Major**
**In country: May 1968 – May 1969**
**Rank: Captain, US Air Force**
**Duty: 7th Air Force, 377th Combat Support Group,**
**Computer Systems Programming**

♥**Velma Frances Reid**
**Retired as a Master Sergeant**
**In country: May 1968 – May 1969**
**Rank: Staff Sergeant, US Air Force**
**Duty: MACV, J12, Personnel Management Division**

**♥Marilyn J. Schmechel**
**Retired as a Colonel**
**In country: May 1968 – May 1969**
**Rank: Lieutenant Colonel, US Army Medical Specialist Corps**
**Duty: 44th Medical Brigade, Long Binh; 3rd Field Hospital, Saigon, Dietetic Consultant**

**♥Phyllis Arlyne Williams (Palmer)**
**In country: May 1968 – May 1969**
**Rank: Specialist 4, US Army**
**Duty: USARV, Administrative Specialist**

*Claire Brisebois Starnes:* When I arrived in Long Binh in February 1969, Phyllis was Vietnam-tested and nothing seemed to faze her. She was much too willing, along with Teddi Gitman and Precilla Landry, to play a prank on me, which landed me on the floor. Teddi describes this quite well in her write-up. Phyllis and I became steadfast friends after that incident. She was the quieter one of the bunch, but always ready for a good laugh. I searched many years for her, and was delighted when I finally found her. I spent several hours speaking with her son who was more than willing to bring me up to date on Phyllis' life. Rest in peace, my friend.

**♥Katherine E. Herney**
**Retired as a Sergeant Major**
**In country: May 1968 – May 15, 1969**
**Rank: First Sergeant, US Army**
**Duty: USARV, Special Troops, WAC Detachment, Second First Sergeant**

*Linda Earls:* 1SG Katherine Herney arrived at the WAC Company in mid-May 1968, about two weeks after my arrival so she was my First Sergeant during most of my tour. I have many fond memories of her. One of the first was that I was working in a division which had no slot for me and wasn't in my MOS. I talked to her and she said she would see what she could do to help me get in a slot, which made me feel better.

As time went on, she was always friendly and helpful. I moved into another room in the barrack and wanted some excess furniture moved out. I asked her about it and she had it moved. Later when we moved to the new barracks and I was promoted to staff sergeant (SSG) she kept a space in my room open until my friend made SSG so we could room together. She often came to our room and ate with us and played Yahtzee. Sometimes she just stopped by to talk or watch TV. She was always concerned about the welfare of the women, and was a very kind and caring person. One day, a number of us went to a party at another unit. That evening when we arrived back at the barracks there was our first sergeant waiting for us to make sure we were safely "home." At night when we had to "hit the bunkers," she made sure that the dog, Otto B., got in one also. She gave me my first opportunity to be in charge of a platoon and to be a barrack sergeant, which was the foundation of my later being a drill sergeant and first sergeant. She could "hang out" with us but she never lost her status as First Sergeant and was always respected. She went out of her way to do the little things that meant so much to women far from home in a combat situation.

♥**Betty J. Bailey**
**Retired as a Sergeant First Class**
**In country: May 1968 – June 1969**
**Rank: Sergeant First Class, US Army**
**Duty: MACV, Studies and Observations Group; J2, Air Reconnaissance, Intelligence Analyst**

**Janice A. Kluge (Fountain)**
**Retired as a Master Sergeant**
**In country: May 1968 – December 1969**
**Rank: Specialist 5, US Army**
**Duty: USARV, G1, Communications and Electronics, Personnel Specialist**

**Olivia "Ellie" J. Ellis (Favre)**
**In country: May 1968 – December 1969**
**Rank: Specialist 4, US Army**
**Duty: USARV, IG, US Army Engineer Construction Agency, Vietnam, Administrative Specialist**

♥**Marjorie Ann Brzozowski**
**Retired as a Master Sergeant**
**In country: May 1968 – June 1969; June 1969 – July 1970**
**Rank: Sergeant First Class, US Army**
**Duty: USARV; MACV J2, Intelligence Analyst**

**Helene Gotch**
**Retired as a Senior Master Sergeant**
**In country: May 1968 – June 1971**
**Rank: Senior Master Sergeant, US Air Force**
**Duty: MACV, J4, Logistics**

**Linda "Lyn" S. Earls**
**Retired as a First Sergeant**
**In country: May 1, 1968 – May 15, 1969**
**Rank: Staff Sergeant, US Army**
**Duty: USARV, Comptroller, Budget Division**

Among my memories of my year in Vietnam, two events stand out as highlights for me. The first was my promotion to Staff Sergeant on Christmas Eve 1968. The First Sergeant called my office and asked that I be released early to come back to the WAC Company. When I got there, I found three other women had been called too. We reported to the commander and received our promotions. What a great Christmas present that was!

Second was Christmas day 1968. Some friends and I were looking for something to do and decided to go to the USARV helipad and see if we could catch a ride somewhere. There was a chopper that was taking Terence Cardinal Cooke, the Military Vicar, back to Bien Hoa. We got to meet him and ride along with a tour of Long Binh on the way. He gave each of us little cards. Our ride went on to a couple of other places then back to USARV. We had a really exciting Christmas day and I loved the adventure.

During my year, I wrote 145 letters to my mother and she saved them. I didn't think about them for years but when I did and mentioned them to others I realized they are history and should be in print somehow. With a lot of encouragement from my aunt and my friend, I started to put them on the computer. It took two years but I did get them published as a book, *Vietnam- I'm Going!* The title comes from my first letter to my mother when I got orders.

I was so excited and I wrote, "I'm going!" The book is a day-by-day account of the life of a young WAC in a war zone. It has a mostly positive outlook and has many descriptions of places and activities. Anyone who was there will find something familiar in the book, and those who weren't will find a historical account of that year. The book is available in hardback, paperback and eBook at Amazon.com, BarnesandNoble.com and from the publisher, Xlibris.com

**Linda M. Barnes (Poole)**
**In country: May 13, 1968 – July 17, 1969**
**Rank: Specialist 5, US Army**
**Duty: USARV, Inspector General's Office, Administrative Specialist**

I thought how strange it was that I was the only girl on a plane going to Vietnam and that the entire crew was men. I remember that one of the guys on the plane said that I must have made a mistake because the destination was Vietnam. I told him no that I had orders for Vietnam. That's when reality hit. My God! I was going into a war zone.

When I arrived in Vietnam I was picked up and taken to Long Binh WAC Detachment. That night, rounds came in and I didn't know what to do. I was not assigned any gear yet (most importantly – no helmet). I followed everyone outside where there was a wall of sand bags and ducked down. I remember thinking: What about all of those guys I was on the plane with? Did any of them get killed on their first night in Vietnam? Yes, their base camp had incoming and I found out that some of the men were killed. When everything settled down, I was assigned my gear and bunk. There were no windows; we had screens (for natural air conditioning). Being on the top bunk, I would later experience the effect of my first monsoon. I would get wet because I was next to the screened window. We had mosquito netting over the bunk, and I would cover myself with the poncho at night to keep dry but still would get wet.

I do have many good memories of being in Vietnam. We were a small group of women who had to stick together to support each other (they will always be my sisters). But, things happen when you have been in a war zone. I have been going to VA counseling and have been diagnosed with Posttraumatic Stress Disorder (PTSD). I could go on with more incidents while I was in Vietnam, but at this point in my life, my VA counselor is the one helping me to adjust.

I have never regretted going to Vietnam. I wanted to serve my country. Yes, I can now say I am a Vietnam veteran and served my country with pride.

**Comments and Memories:** Our area in Long Binh was hit during Tet of 1968. To rush my going to the bunker, I grabbed the shirt of Earnestine Dumas since she was the fastest runner around. She could have qualified for the Olympics! She couldn't figure why she was slowed down. But, we were still the first ones in the bunkers! Coming down from the second floor, our feet never touched the steps. *Source: Vietnam Memory Book 2000*

# JUNE

*Memory Lane: US presidential candidate Robert F. Kennedy is shot at the Ambassador Hotel in Los Angeles, CA.*
*Song: "Mrs. Robinson" by Simon and Garfunkel*

**Karen S. Linley (Anderson) (Kamm)**
**In country: June 1968 – August 1968**
**Rank: Specialist 4, US Army**
**Duty: USARV**

I had married prior to being sent to Vietnam. My husband was also in the process of going to Vietnam. He was stationed at Bien Hoa. We found out we were unable to be stationed together. Shortly after arrival, I found I was pregnant and was sent home. He stayed for the duration of his duty.

**Grace "Marti" M. McAlister (Gallo)**
**In country: June 1968 – June 1969**
**Rank: Staff Sergeant, US Air Force**
**Duty: MACV, Adjutant General's Office, Administrative Supervisor**

I was the oldest of six girls (no brothers) and chose to join the United States Air Force after graduation from high school in part because my own dad was so proud of his military service (US Navy) during WWII and in part to serve my country.

When the opportunity came to volunteer for Vietnam I jumped at the chance for the same reasons – to honor my

dad, his service to our country, and commit to our shared belief that freedom belongs to everyone.

I hesitate to write or share my experience in Vietnam because of the many horror stories I've read over the years shared publicly by women who served. The truth is that I had a positive experience in the year I served. I was treated with respect by everyone I worked with, officers and enlisted, men and women. I worked hard and was awarded the Bronze Star at the end of my tour in recognition of that hard work.

I remember camaraderie and lots of good-natured teasing but I do not recall comments or conversations that ever stepped over the bounds of decency. I certainly never felt sexually harassed or that I wasn't an equal member of a cohesive team. I made good friends and felt safe.

I was Air Force enlisted and assigned to the MACV Adjutant General's office, a joint service command. I worked in an office, not in the field, so perhaps the level of decency increases in accordance with the environment. When I came home, I was not subjected to harassment, snide remarks or negative reactions when people learned I had served in Vietnam. My friends and most certainly my family were supportive and proud of my service.

I can honestly say that, in the seven years I served in the military, there was only one incident where I felt an individual acted in an inappropriate sexual manner toward me. I went straight to the colonel (male) I worked for, and the matter was handled immediately and to my satisfaction. It is a shame that every female in the military cannot work with and for the men (and women) I was lucky enough to know and serve with, especially in Vietnam.

Please do not believe for a minute that I do not sympathize with the military women who suffered from sexual or mental abuse from those persons with which they served. I am extremely blessed to not be one of those stories.

**Grace M. McAlister:** In spite of the discomforts, hardships, long hours, occasional masculine rebuffs and, although they seem to ignore it, the ever-present danger inherent in a Vietnam assignment, these women feel their accomplishments will influence the Air Force to further expand both the number of WAF in Vietnam and the amount of their responsibility.

Sergeant McAlister says, "Of course it will be good to go home again when my tour is up this summer, but I would seriously consider volunteering to return to Vietnam again – or anywhere else where I feel that I could work in such a meaningful situation." *Source:* Airman, *May 1969*

♥**Cora "Pete" Dexter Reynolds**
**Retired as a Lieutenant Colonel**
**In country: June 1968 – June 1969**
**Rank: Major, US Army Medical Specialist Corps**
**Duty: 29th Evacuation Hospital, Can Tho/Binh Thuy, Physical Therapist**

**Mary L. Himes**
**In country: June 1968 – June 24, 1969**
**Rank: Specialist 5, US Army**
**Duty: USARV, Clerk-Typist**

**Sharon Miller Murry**
**Retired as a Lieutenant Colonel**
**In country: June 1968 – June 1969**
**Rank: Captain, US Air Force**
**Duty: 7th Air Force, 619th Tactical Control Squadron, Administrative Officer**

Sharon is one of some half dozen of the ladies who have a special reason for being in Vietnam. She is married to Army Major William V. Murry, an artillery commander. Though stationed some miles apart, they see each other once or twice a month. "To understand what the service is really like, one must come to a theater where we're doing what we've been practicing in the US. Over here, it is quickly understood why military people feel the way they do about the service and why so many of them spend as much as 35 years of their lives devoted to it. After seeing first-hand the good that we're doing here, it will be much easier for me to go home and stand up to those who disagree with American involvement in Vietnam." *Source:* Airman, *May 1969*

**Patricia M. Powell**
**Retired as a Chief Warrant Officer 3**
**In country: June 1968 – June 1969**
**Rank: Specialist 4, US Army**
**Duty: USARV, G3, Training Aid Illustrator**

**Comments and Memories**: I remember being put in the wall locker by my friend Teddi and the pool parties. *Source: Vietnam Memory Book 2000*

♥**Martha Jane Provo**
**Retired as a Chief Warrant Officer 4**
**In country: June 1968 – June 1969**
**Rank: Chief Warrant Officer 3, US Army**
**Duty: USARV, Personnel, Personnel/Administrative Technician**

**Eileen T. Seelman (Meredith)**
**In country: June 1968 – June 1969**
**Rank: Specialist 6, US Army**
**Duty: USARV, Operations, Executive**
**Administrative Assistant**

**Janis G. Horvat**
**In country: June 1968 – June 1969**
**Rank: Specialist 4, US Army**
**Duty: USARV, G4, Clerk-Typist**

**Ruth "Ruthie" Ann McKenney**
**Retired as a Sergeant First Class**
**In country: June 1968 – January 1970**
**Rank: Staff Sergeant, US Army**
**Duty: USARV, Adjutant General, Administrative NCO**

I joined the military because I love my country. Going to Vietnam was important to me. I felt we as women needed to be there to support the fellows. I am thankful I was never raped in the military. I am so ashamed of what has been going on now in the military.

Maybe some of the women went in to find a man; but, I believe most of us went in to serve our country. I didn't do much other than work six days a week. My claim to fame was running the projector for us so we could watch movies at the WAC Detachment.

**♥Lorraine A. Rossi**
**Retired as a Colonel**
**In country: June 1968 – January 11, 1970**
**Rank: Lieutenant Colonel, US Army**
**Duty: MACV, Joint Staff, Fourth Senior Officer Advisor**
**to the Vietnam Women's Armed Forces Corps**

**♥Susan "Sky" M. Commons**
**Retired as a Sergeant First Class**
**In country: June 1968 – March 1970**
**Rank: Specialist 5, US Army**
**Duty: USARV, Administrative Specialist**

Sergeant First Class Susan Commons was likely the only enlisted woman to have served in Vietnam and as a member of the Old Guard at Fort Myer, VA. Her career began in the Women's Army Corps and ended as an Active Duty Reservist.

Susan M. Commons joined the Women's Army Corps on February 28, 1966. In June 1968, then SP4 Commons requested and was granted reassignment to the US Army Republic of Vietnam Headquarters at Long Binh, (Vietnam). Having served 18 months in Vietnam, SP5 Commons returned to the States and served the last 10 months of her enlistment at White Sands Missile Range, NM.

Specialist 5 Commons entered the US Army Reserve in September 1975. In May 1979, SFC Commons reentered active duty as a Private First Class, taking her second Basic Training at Fort Leonard Wood, MO. She completed AIT as a Power Generator/Wheeled Vehicle Mechanic in October 1979. In March 1981, SGT Commons requested reassignment to Co E (Honor Guard), 3rd Infantry (The Old Guard), Fort Myer, VA, where she served as NCOIC of the Female Detachment and as a member of the First Presidential Marching Platoon until her term of service ended on May 24, 1983.

In November 1983, SSG Commons reentered the US Army Reserve. On June 11, 1999, Sergeant First Class Susan M. Commons retired from the Army Reserve Personnel Command, St. Louis, MO. *Photo and obituary, Kansas City Star, November 17, 2011.*

## Carole "Teddi" A. Gittman
**Retired as a Sergeant First Class**
**In country: June 1968 – May 1970**
**Rank: Staff Sergeant, US Army**
**Duty: USARV, Engineer Division, Administrative NCO**

So many memories! Among the ones that really stand out are my many nights under the canopy. I called it our beer tent. Our canopy was a huge silk camouflage parachute. Don't ask! In the States, this area would be called the den, the family room or the living room. It was our multipurpose open-air dayroom. When we could get a small band, we invited fellows from a near-by unit to come to our "dance hall." When SSG "Effie" got us cases of chicken and steaks – don't ask! We fired up our grill then served in our "dining room." Or, on nights when nothing particular was going on, we just visited with one another in our "rec room" – cold beer or soda in hand. And, let's not forget the green beer we had on St. Patrick's Day. Gotta love it! Those evenings under the canopy are when my lifelong friendships with Peanut and Marty were forged.

Oh my! Then there was Martha Raye! Not enough can be said about her devotion to our soldiers. She went to the farthest outposts, to the thickest jungles to entertain the fellows. A special treat was the day she came to our WAC Detachment for a visit.

Every once in a while enough of us got an afternoon off. So, our first sergeant, a tremendous athlete, organized a softball team for us. "Top" was our fastball pitcher. There weren't many of those days, but what we had were really special.

On the other hand, and also on the other side of one of our fences, were barracks for the RMK contractors (principal Vietnam contractors). One day I heard a volleyball game being played. I thought nothing of asking "Top" if I could join the fellows. I was so sure she'd say "yes." Guess what? I snuck over there anyway. I was having a really good time 'til Top caught me. A memory with mixed emotions – yet, a memory.

**Comments and Memories:** When SP5 Claire Brisebois arrived in country in February 1969, she was tired and went to sleep in a top bunk. I yelled, "INCOMING." She fell out of her top bunk straight to the floor. I was only joking. She got initiated to Vietnam WELL! My roommates and I have had many laughs over that stunt. *Source: Vietnam Memory Book 2000*

**♥Margaret Elizabeth Gold**
**Retired as a Sergeant First Class**
**In country: June 1968 – June 1970**
**Rank: Staff Sergeant, US Army**
**Duty: USARV, Special Troops, WAC Detachment, Field First/**
**Administrative NCO; US Army Engineer Construction Agency,**
**Vietnam**

A veteran of 19 years in the Army, Staff Sergeant Margaret Gold, Grand Rapids, MI: "I wanted to see firsthand what was going on. When I first came into the service, I worked with Korean casualties, and that gave me an interest." *Source: US Army Women's Museum – from a press release in article titled "A Chance to Serve" by First Lieutenant Carol Johnson, USARV Information Office*

*In a letter dated July 1, 1968, to CPT Patricia H. Jernigan, SFC Gold writes:* We arrived at Bien Hoa Air Base two days later (after we left the US). The first sergeant, two military policemen with an armed jeep came to pick me up. The town of Bien Hoa is off limits at night and very dangerous. (I) was told to keep low (wearing a flak jacket), and if anything was thrown into the jeep to grab it and throw as far as possible. We drove at high speed thu [sic] the town. Even tho [sic] I was dead tired, I stayed very much alert.

I am assigned as the Field 1SG or Admin NCO, which is only one of many additional duties. I do get to travel where most of the enlisted women haven't been off post since arriving 8-10 months ago.

I've made two trips to Saigon, two into Bien Hoa (only certain on-limit areas) and an overnight trip by helicopter to Vung Tau. This trip was exciting. We flew at 3,000 feet. The doors were open and I sat next to the gunner. I prayed the seat belt would hold and the gunner wouldn't have to go into action.

It has been quiet here since the ammo dump was hit. I'm getting used to hearing the bombers and helicopters day and night. Every night we can hear the mortar and see flares in the distance.

Next week the Special Troops Sergeant Major is going to take 1SG Katherine Herney and me to one of the perimeters, so we can see the claymore mines, rockets, etc. set up at the bunkers. This should be interesting.

# JULY

*Memory Lane: The semiconductor company Intel is founded.*
*Song: "This Guy's in Love With You" by Herb Alpert*

**♥Barbara Jean Ivey (Riddle)**
**In country: July 1968 – February 1969**
**Rank: Specialist 5, US Army**
**Duty: USARV**

**Diane R. Matthews**
**In country: July 1968 – June 1969**
**Rank: Sergeant, US Air Force**
**Duty: MACV, 1131ˢᵗ Special Advisory Group, Administrative Specialist**

**Ida Imani Betts**
**In country: July 1968 – June 25, 1969**
**Rank: Specialist 4, US Army**
**Duty: USARV, Administrative Specialist**

Sappy, maybe, but I owe my more than 37 years in education to my military training – especially the year I spent in Vietnam. My military benefits completely paid for my college education. I am very proud of my two careers.

**Charlotte Clark**
**Retired as a Lieutenant Colonel**
**In country: July 1968 – July 1969**
**Rank: Major, US Army**
**Duty: USARV, G1, Personnel Staff Officer**

**Peggy Pruitt**
**In country: July 1968 – July 1969**
**Rank: Specialist 5, US Army**
**Duty: USARV, G4**

**Constance L. McVey**
**Retired as a Captain**
**In country: July 1968 – August 1969**
**Rank: Second Lieutenant, US Air Force**
**Duty: 7ᵗʰ Air Force, J2, Intelligence Officer**

"All of the American WAF – even the non-volunteers – would recommend, almost without reservation, that other WAF volunteer to serve in Vietnam. The sense of accomplishment, of being a part of this great undertaking, is the most satisfying and personally rewarding task I have ever done."

Another puts it in even stronger terms: "I would urge even my sister to come to Vietnam. I've done just that with some of the WAF with whom I formerly served." *Source:* Airman, *May 1969*

**Jean M. McLintock (Smith)**
**In country: July 1968 – September 1969**
**Rank: Captain, US Air Force**
**Duty: Headquarters 7ᵗʰ Air Force, Computer Programmer**

My most memorable experience in Vietnam was not directly related to the war.

My husband and I were involved in a combined choir which consisted of singers from Protestant and Catholic chapel services on base, plus Seventh Day Adventist and Southern Baptist missionaries from the USA and two tenors from the South Korean Army. This ecumenical group performed major portions of Handel's Messiah, along with other selections, in several performances on base and at both missions. Although I cannot remember the names of any of the other singers, I remember that our accompanist was an Air Force Chaplain named White, who I believe was a Major at the time. In addition to accompanying the choir and soloists, he also played several piano solos. One of my favorite memories is of his trying to explain to Vietnamese children, through an interpreter, what Leroy Anderson's Sleigh Ride was supposed to represent (including describing snow).

A couple more memories: There was a lot of trading, often a bit bizarre. The strangest one I overheard was trading a fire engine for a ride to the

Philippines. We cooked in our room, or on the balcony, most of the time, and ate "on the economy" often. We were not very careful – had ice in our drinks, etc., and never suffered any ill effects. But, we ate Thanksgiving dinner in the mess hall and both got food poisoning! (Go figure!)

**Marcia Lou Rinkel**
**Retired as a Colonel**
**In country: July 19, 1968 – January 1970**
**Rank: Major, US Army**
**Duty: USARV, 1st Logistical Command, Personnel Staff Officer**

**Patrice Maureen McKeone**
**In country: July 26, 1968 – July 25, 1969**
**Rank: Specialist 5, US Army**
**Duty: USARV, Adjutant General, Personnel Specialist**

Specialist 5 Patrice McKeone was responsible for maintaining the personnel records for the ranks E1-E9, including 5th Special Forces Group.

**Doris W. Gustafson**
**Retired as a Lieutenant Colonel**
**In country: July 26, 1968 – February 18, 1970**
**Rank: Captain, US Air Force**
**Duty: 7th Air Force, 377th Transportation Squadron,**
**Transportation Officer**

Lucy, on my lap, full-grown here, was given to me in Vietnam as a six-week-old pup. She stayed with me and lived to the ripe old age of sixteen.

The uniform I had to wear in Vietnam was a test. It was a baby blue top, wrap-around dark blue skirt and blue sneakers. For a hat, we had a female Navy hat. Liked the hat! The uniform not so much! I felt like the target of the day. The guys all wore that dark green color and so did the Army women. I was very surprised Colonel Jeanne Holm didn't do something about it.

My 18 months in Hawaii at PACAF (Pacific Air Force) Headquarters was very interesting and lots of hard work. The very long hours and six days a week conditioned me for the seven days a week, 10 hours a day in Vietnam. It was routine for me.

I was the only woman in the squadron, but the three commanders I had treated me well. The airmen working in all the sections of the squadron were very helpful as well. I really didn't need to be looked after, but they looked after me anyway. I was invited to all the parties in the squadron and the Vietnam Transportation Squadron also invited me to their parties.

When I look back on all my assignments, it suddenly dawned on me I was generally the only military woman in the unit, and very quietly and subtly all the men who worked with or for me looked after me. My time in the Air Force was full of ups and downs, but I prefer to remember the ups and not the downs. I am still in touch with some of the women with whom I went through basic training. Over the years, some of us have managed to get together as well.

# AUGUST

*Memory Lane: Richard Nixon is nominated for US President; Spiro Agnew for US Vice President; The Medal of Honor is posthumously awarded to James Anderson, Jr., the first black US Marine to be awarded the Medal of Honor. Song: "Hello, I Love You" by the Doors*

**Gwendolyn E. Caton (Doty)**
**Retired as a Major**
**In country: August 1968 – February 1969**
**Rank: Captain, US Army Reserve Medical Service Corps**
**Duty: 93rd Evacuation Hospital, Long Binh; Regional Clinical Lab, Saigon, Clinical Laboratory Officer**

**Emma F. Rides Bear Adams (Core)**
**In country: August 1968 – June 1969**
**Rank: Specialist 4, US Army**
**Duty: USARV, Aviation Safety Office, Clerk-Typist**

**Norma A. Archer**
**Retired as a Lieutenant Colonel**
**In country: August 1968 – July 1969**
**Rank: Major, US Air Force**
**Duty: 7ᵗʰ Air Force, 600ᵗʰ Photo Reconnaissance,**
**Audio-Visual Staff Officer**

Major Norma A. Archer's assignment in Southeast Asia (SEA) gave her a front and center view of the air war in Vietnam. As Operations Officer for the 600ᵗʰ Photographic Squadron, she was key to the photographic documentation of Air Force activities in SEA. She saw what our fighter pilots saw through the collection of still photos and motion pictures recorded on gun cameras and aircraft camera blisters and pods, and strip photos taken of air strikes from fighter and bomber aircraft. Shortly after arrival at Tan Son Nhut Air Base, Major Archer was tasked to narrate the showing of the previous day's recording of air strikes to the Command element of 7ᵗʰ Air Force. She must have done an excellent job as that became one of her daily duties . . . big FIRST for a woman. *Source:* Airman, *May 1969*

**Bessie L. Fickel**
**Retired as a Lieutenant Colonel**
**In country: August 1968 – August 1969**
**Rank: First Lieutenant, US Air Force**
**Duty: Headquarters 7ᵗʰ Air Force, Intelligence Officer**

**Sally Jane Moore**
**In country: August 1968 – August 1969**
**Rank: Specialist 4, US Army**
**Duty: USARV, 1ˢᵗ Aviation Brigade, Flight Records, Clerk-Typist**

I enlisted in the Women's Army Corps nine days after my 18ᵗʰ birthday. I lived on a small farm most of my life and this was a great change. Experiences were almost daily for me in my new environment. When I went through basic training we were told we were ladies. Ladies did not handle weapons, so here we were in Vietnam with no weapons, but we had our fingernails and, unfortunately, I bit mine in those days. This was in the years 1968 and 1969.

There were three major events that stick out prominently in my mind. I was assigned to USARV Headquarters in Long Binh where I worked for Officer Flight Records in Aviation. One day I was waiting at the gate for a shuttle bus to take me to work, when I chanced to look at the armed guard at our gate. He looked familiar so I spoke to him. "Where are you from?" I asked. That was a usual question to ask anyone there. He said "Indiana." That was a surprise to me as I was raised in Indiana. "Where in Indiana?" I asked. "Auburn," he responded. That was even more astounding to me. "Where did you go to school?" I asked. His reply was "Eastside High School in Butler, Indiana." It was then that I remembered where I had seen him before. We had graduated from high school together. His name was Steve Culler. A most unusual event to me.

We were being shelled one night and, of course, we had to run to our designated sandbagged bunker. At that time I was living on the second floor in a room almost directly over the Commander's office. I couldn't find my glasses, without which I am lost, but I ran anyway, grabbed my helmet, canteen, gas mask and whatever else we were required to take with us. Unfortunately for me I was in pajamas, a robe and slippers. I went shooting out of my room and took the stairs I normally would take every morning when leaving for work. I ran past the commander's office and CQ (Charge of Quarters) area and my robe was flapping in my hurry to get to a safer place. My robe got caught on the spigot of the water cooler that was between the orderly room and supply room. I didn't stop or care at that moment and gave it a jerk. The water cooler hit the deck and shattered. Sometime later, the first sergeant came along and asked, "Who broke the water cooler?" I said, "I did first sergeant. My robe got caught on the spigot but I kept on running." No more was said about the cooler. Around 2 or 3 in the morning, we were allowed to leave the bunkers and someone noticed I was walking with a limp. I realized my feet were hurting and ran my fingers along the sole of one foot and found I was bleeding. I went to the first sergeant and told her my feet were bleeding. She carefully extracted glass from both my feet and did a great job. To this day I still have a scar on my left foot. I also have a phobia about losing my glasses, and each night I make a mental note of just where my glasses are before I go to sleep.

We were once again in our bunkers during Tet 1969. We were getting really hammered by "Charlie" and his NVA (North Vietnamese Army). Every time we were under fire and in the bunkers, a platoon of men would arrive and station themselves around our small compound. Most would be on the outside but others would be guarding the inside perimeter. This particular night, the VC (Viet Cong) got through the major perimeter and onto our installation. The men were whispering on the line around us in the dark and word was the VC had broken through. I snuck out of the bunker I was in and surveyed the men in the dark. I saw a man who looked like he had been in the field and knew what it was like. You could usually tell the ones who had been in the field and those who hadn't. I slipped up to him and asked, "Promise that you won't let them take me." He looked at me strangely and I added "You know what I'm asking, don't you?" He nodded his head and whispered, "I won't let them take you." The VC was finally pushed back and as the sun came up, we were allowed out of our bunkers to walk around but they were still fighting on the perimeter. We could still hear the guns firing, helicopters flying and see smoke on the horizon. We were finally allowed back to our rooms to get dressed for work although we were all going to be late. The next day photos were being circulated of the dead bodies of the VC. I saw one or two photos but refused to look at any others. They were carrying can openers because they had been promised all the C-rations they could carry. Today I tell myself that if only I had known they were hungry I would have given them all the C-rations they wanted. After all, that is not home cooking. In my years of service, both Active and Reserve, I only ate C-rations when it was absolutely necessary.

After Vietnam, I worked several office jobs and in 1972, I joined the 601st Military Police Battalion, Indiana Army Reserves at Fort Wayne, IN. I was the Supply Sergeant and a SFC when I resigned in 1983 for medical reasons.

**Nancy C. Young**
**In country: August 1968 – August 1969**
**Rank: Specialist 4, US Army**
**Duty: USARV, Administrative Specialist**

**Linda L. Pilcher**
**In country: August 1968 – March 1970**
**Rank: First Lieutenant, US Air Force**
**Duty: Headquarters 7th Air Force, Intelligence Officer**

**Rose "Jackie" M. Jackson (Johnson)**
**Retired as a Sergeant First Class**
**In country: August 1968 – November 1970; March 1971 – April 1972**
**Rank: Staff Sergeant, US Army**
**Duty: USARV, Engineer Division; Saigon Transportation**

**Comments and Memories:** The day following Tet, everyone in our bunker the night before was restricted to the barracks. The captain wanted to know why everyone in our bunker was laughing so hard. We had been listening to those who had just returned from R&R in Singapore describing Singapore's "Ladies of the Night." *Source: Vietnam Memory Book 2000*

**Penelope "Penny" A. Ormes (Price)**
**In country: August 1968 – November 1970**
**Rank: Staff Sergeant, US Army**
**Duty: USARV, 1st Aviation Brigade; Adjutant General**

It is so hard to remember that many years ago. These are the happenings I do remember. I knew many that were at the reunions but my closest friends were Phyllis Bertram, Jessie Gregory and Lizzie Freaney. It saddens me to know they are no longer with us.

My good memories were of seeing Bob Hope, "Tex Ritter" singing at the club, and Billy Graham. These are well-known, loved men, but those most important to me were those who I worked with. They treated me like a sister even though I was their noncommissioned officer in charge. My job was very important to me and for that reason I extended my tour twice. I have five brothers and hoped that would keep them from having to go. However, one did and has many problems. He was awarded the Silver Star, but not until 2010. My brother that had to go was with the 82d Airborne. When he was able to visit me, his first sergeant always made sure he had a clean uniform and good boots.

My parents and three brothers are veterans so I grew up loving my country. When I returned home on leave for the first time, my flight landed at Travis Air Force Base and then I was told to change to civilian clothes before continuing because service members were being treated horribly. It was not safe to wear the uniform in my own country.

**♥Frances Juanita DeLee (Taylor)**
**Retired as a Major**
**In country: August 1968 – March 1971**
**Rank: Major, US Air Force**
**Duty: 7th Air Force**

Major Taylor graduated from Claflin University in Orangeburg, SC, and enlisted in the Air Force in 1954. She was a flight stewardess and drill instructor as an enlistee and then rose to the officer rank. She served in Spain, Vietnam and Hawaii. At Bolling Air Force Base, Washington, DC, she was base traffic manager before becoming a member of the inspector general's team that inspected bases in Asia and the Pacific. She retired from the military in 1974, with a Bronze Star among her awards.

*Excerpt from obituary on Virtual Cemetery.*

# SEPTEMBER

*Memory Lane: 60 Minutes debuts on CBS; 21 killed by hijackers aboard a Pan Am jet in Karachi, Pakistan.*
*Song: "People Got to be Free" by The Rascals*

**Constance "Sue" S. Schungel (Delk)**
**In country: September 1968 – July 1969**
**Rank: Specialist 5, US Army**
**Duty: USARV, Adjutant General, Personnel Specialist**

It was 1968. I was a 20-year-old enlisted woman, Specialist Four, stationed at the Pentagon and working for Brigadier General Elizabeth Hoisington, the first general of the Women's Army Corps. Several times a week, I walked to the basement of the Pentagon and pestered the sergeant in OPO (Office of Personnel Operations) to get me on a levy for Vietnam. My father, LTC Daniel F. Schungel, was the Deputy Commander of the 5th Special Forces Group headquartered in Nha Trang and I wanted to serve in Vietnam too.

After several months, I received the much-awaited call. I was on a levy for Vietnam. I was elated. My mother, Adeline M. Schungel, living in Carlisle, PA, with my three younger siblings (Danny, Laura, and Georgia) did not share my elation. Not only did she have to worry about her husband, my father, but also about her oldest daughter. After a teary farewell, I found myself seated on the plane next to another young enlisted woman, Judy Fisher. We ultimately became roommates at the WAC Detachment in Long Binh.

After what seemed like days, we arrived, were processed in country, and loaded on little buses with bars on the windows with the dozens of male soldiers on our flight. With illumination exploding all around, it was an eerie ride through the hot and steamy countryside and small towns before arriving at our destination. The new WAC Detachment had not been completed yet so Judy and I were taken to the old one. There were bays, not rooms, and a large community latrine. As we were being escorted to our bay, a huge rat ran in front of us. Judy and I seemed to be the only ones distressed by that event. We were each assigned a bunk bed with plenty of mosquito netting. I'll never forget the feeling I had as I laid on my top bunk with the mosquito net covering me, listening to the buzz of insects, remembering the sight of the rodent in the latrine, and thinking, *"What have I done!"* And yet, a year later, after it was all said and done, and I was standing in line in the pouring rain waiting to board our flight home, I was deeply saddened to be leaving the many wonderful people who had become my family in Vietnam. In spite of how eager I was to see my family at home, the moment was truly bittersweet.

**Judith "Judy" A. Fisher**
**In country: September 1968 – September 1969**
**Rank: Specialist 4, US Army**
**Duty: Personnel Specialist**

**Judith "Judy" M. Adelman (Eason)**
**In country: September 1968 – August 1969**
**Rank: Captain, US Army Medical Specialist Corps**
**Duty: 71ˢᵗ Evacuation Hospital, Pleiku, Physical Therapist**

**♥Virginia "Ginny" Elizabeth Hanley**
**In country: September 1968 – September 1969**
**Rank: Staff Sergeant, US Army**
**Duty: USARV, 1ˢᵗ Logistical Command, Administrative NCO**

**Rosemary Hanson (Miller)**
**In country: September 1968 – September 1969**
**Rank: Specialist 5, US Army**
**Duty: USARV, 1ˢᵗ Logistical Command and Provost Marshal Office,**
**Administrative Specialist**

**Carrie M. Latimer**
**In country: September 1968 – September 1969; October 1970 –**
**October 1971**
**Rank: Specialist 5, US Army**
**Duty: USARV, Executive Administrative Assistant**

**Mary P. Lowery**
**Retired as a Lieutenant Colonel**
**In country: September 1968 – September 1969**
**Rank: Major, US Army Medical Specialist Corps**
**Duty: 67ᵗʰ Medical Group, Da Nang; USARV Surgeon's Office, Dietetic**
**Consultant**

**Gloria "Sandi" A. Sondra Olson**
**Retired as a Colonel**
**In country: September 1968 – September 1969**
**Rank: Major, US Army**
**Duty: MACV, Public Affairs Office, Information Officer**

***www.macoi.net:*** Sandra "Sandi" Olson enlisted in the Women's Army Corps in September 1953. Following WAC basic training at Fort Lee, VA, she received a direct commission in March 1954 and completed WAC Officer Basic Course three months later. She was assigned to public affairs duty.

By May 1967, she was at the Pentagon where she served as Deputy Chief of the News Branch in the Department of Defense Public Affairs Division. In November 1968, as a Major, she was sent to Vietnam where she served in the MACV Office of Information as Deputy Chief of Command Information. In this position, she traveled extensively throughout the country.

Back in the United States, MAJ Olson reported to Fort Meade, MD, as Chief of the WAC branch of the Army's First Recruiting District. In this capacity, she traveled to cities in her assigned area on publicity and recruitment missions until her retirement as a Colonel with 23 years of service to her country.

Her hobbies, over the years, have included photography, writing and breeding champion boxer dogs. Colonel Olson has also funded a scholarship at her alma mater, Oswego Teachers College, which is now the Oswego branch of the State University of New York. The Gloria A. S. Olson '51 Scholarship is open to new freshmen at the institution who can demonstrate financial need and a commitment to education. "I am giving back what Oswego gave me. It gave me so much," she said.

**Helga I. Rubnich**
**In country: September 1968 – September 1969**
**Rank: Staff Sergeant, US Army**
**Duty: MACV, Operations, Administrative NCO**

**♥Mary P. Walsh (McDermott)**
**Retired as a Gunnery Sergeant**
**In country: September 4, 1968 – September 1, 1969**
**Rank: Staff Sergeant, US Marine Corps**
**Duty: MACV, Top Secret Control Officer**

**Mary E. Baker**
**Retired as a Lieutenant Colonel**
**In country: September 4, 1968 – September 4, 1969**
**Rank: Captain, US Air Force**
**Duty: MACV, J2, Intelligence Data Handling System, Computer Systems Programming Officer**

I was sent (to Vietnam) as an Information Systems Analyst to the Military Assistance Command (MACV) Headquarters in Saigon. In the build-up after the January 1968 Tet Offensive, I served in a joint command unit at the Intelligence Data Handling Center at MACV J2. My unit was kept very busy upgrading computing equipment from IBM 407 accounting machines to IBM 1401 and 1410 main frames (and associated plotting and digitizing systems) for supporting J2 intelligence information analysts and MACV commanders.

Along with top notch IT professionals from IBM, and pioneer data automation technicians from the Army, Navy, Marine Corps and Air Force, we worked in liaison with South Vietnamese allies, and operated under the command of Lieutenant General Phillip Davidson, and subsequently, Major General William Potts, successive J2s under General Creighton W. Abrams, MACV commander. I was most proud to serve there from September 4, 1968 to September 4, 1969. After reports of the passing of Ho Chi Minh on September 2, 1969, I spent my last evening in Saigon with my fellow officers to help the populace celebrate (as a welcome contrast to the prevailing mood when we all first arrived there!).

**Carol F. Bruckerhoff (Reynolds)**
**In country: September 19, 1968 – September 1969**
**Rank: Specialist 4, US Army**
**Duty: USARV, US Army Engineer Construction Agency, Vietnam, Executive Administrative Assistant**

I was a girl with big dreams and I was going to travel and try to bring honor to my family and country. After all, I had never been anywhere; that is when I discovered the military. They really seemed to want to help me meet my goal. So, I left for the Army right after graduation from high school, September 1967. After basic training, I attended AIT (Advanced Individual Training). My MOS (Military Occupational Specialty) was then 71B30 (clerk-typist) and 71C30 (stenographer.) My first job in that specialty was at Fort Devens, MA, where I worked in the Military Court System as a court recorder. I still wanted to do something that would make a difference and about that time, I met another Army woman by the name of Linda Ostermeier from Springfield, IL. She had come to Fort Devens from Vietnam. She was beautiful and very reserved. I thought she had achieved every goal she had, and they were the goals that I set for myself. She said she never regretted her service. I thought there was no better way to show my commitment to my country. So I volunteered for an assignment to Vietnam.

I arrived at Bien Hoa Air Base in the early hours of September 19, 1968. That first night I pulled back my blankets on my cot to discover a snake beat me there. Nice welcome!

My assigned job was at USARV for the office of the US Army Engineer Construction Agency, Real Estate Division. We negotiated contracts with local nationals and built billets for soldiers. We had offices in Long Binh and Saigon. I started to know why Linda O. hadn't seemed to want to talk about life in Vietnam, but still, she had no regrets. It's hard to experience what we all saw but we knew it was necessary in order to do our job – no different than what our male counterparts experienced as well as the thousands of nurses who served at this difficult time.

When my tour of duty was over, I left Vietnam and landed in California where I was spit on, called a whore, and asked, "Did you kill babies like the male soldiers did?" This was shocking and scared me to my soul. We had no idea our country felt this way and did not support us. Here I thought I had done the right thing and found out upon returning that some did not think it was a good idea. It took me a long time to deal with this. I still get angry when I hear things like the abuse we took from our own people.

My children paid for my service over there. Both of them have suffered debilitating abnormalities that are a direct result of my exposure to Agent Orange.

Making my story end on a high note, I just want to say that there is no country in this world like the USA. What happened to us in the 1960s is not what they are doing to our soldiers coming home now. So given time, everyone makes the right choices.

**Sandra Lynn Spatz (Wiszneauckas)**
**In country: September 20, 1968 – September 12, 1969**
**Rank: Sergeant, US Marine Corps**
**Duty: NAVFORV, Marine Corps Personnel Section**

Traditionally, Tun Tavern in Philadelphia, PA, is called the birthplace of the United States Marine Corps. I grew up 50 miles from Philadelphia, keenly aware of Philadelphia's place in our country's history. On 30 September 1966, after having *"successfully passed the required mental, moral and physical examinations,"* I was processed through the Marine Corps Recruiting Station in Philadelphia and *"accepted for enlistment in the USMC."*

I was 19 years old, a high-school graduate, and a Licensed Practical Nurse, with experience working for a year on a medical-surgical unit at Community General Hospital in Reading, PA.

The Marine Corps used my nursing background well.

From August 1967 to September 1968, I was assigned to the Marine Corps Liaison Office at National Naval Regional Medical Center, Bethesda, MD. I met with Marine casualties evacuated from Vietnam and admitted to Bethesda Naval Hospital, giving administrative assistance to and helping them transition from the war zone to the States.

In the 1960s, the USMC was calling upon women marines to volunteer to serve in Vietnam. In September 1968, I responded and was sent to serve with Headquarters, United States Naval Forces, Vietnam. The office I was assigned to tracked US marines serving in Vietnam, the wounded, missing and killed.

In performing official duties, I traveled to Da Nang with my immediate commanding officer, Captain Elaine Filkins, to update and audit the service records of marines. On one trip, the helicopter in which we flew was fired on as we landed and we ducked, dodged and raced from the landing site.

The compound in Da Nang where we began our audit came under thunderous, ground-shaking rocket fire that sent everyone diving under metal desks for protection or reaching for their weapons and running to their posts. Times like these, underscored my sense of vulnerability.

I carried, in my handbag, a loaded .45 caliber pistol that was unofficially procured and given to me shortly after I arrived in Vietnam. I had never fired a gun and only knew how to release the safety lock on my concealed one. But I was thankful I had it to carry with me and always felt safer with it.

I live hoping and praying that my service advanced the cause of freedom.

*Excerpts from memoir of Sandra Lynn Spatz, USMCR, September 30, 1966 – November 28, 1969*

# OCTOBER

*Memory Lane: The Detroit Tigers win the 1968 World Series of Baseball, defeating the St Louis Cardinals 4 games to 3; Jacqueline Kennedy marries shipping magnate Aristotle Onassis.*
*Song: "Hey Jude" by The Beatles*

**♥Carol Alpha Adsit**
**Retired as a Captain, US Navy**
**In country: October 1968 – September 1969**
**Rank: Lieutenant Commander, US Navy**
**Duty: MACV, Computer Systems Analyst**

I spent New Year's Eve 1968 at Red Beach, a Seabee camp outside of Da Nang on the shores of Da Nang Bay. It was a beautiful beach with miles of white sand – right out of a resort poster – only for as far as the eye could see, there were coils and coils of barbed wire. The Seabees had built a small club and we gathered there for happy hour. I took my drink out onto the lanai to enjoy the breeze and view, barbed wire notwithstanding. Flashes of light caught my eye from the nearby hills – they were flashes of gunfire and you could hear the echoing of the gunfire and mortars. And, as I stood there with my drink, I realized that there were people – human beings – up on that hillside killing each other and I was overwhelmed by the feeling of the incongruity of it all. It is a memory I shall not soon forget. ~Carol A. Adsit, Da Nang 1968

*Compiled by Captain Georgia Clark Sadler, US Navy (Ret)*

Captain Adsit earned the Vietnamese Navy Staff Service Medal 1st Class, the Republic of Vietnam Campaign Medal and the Vietnam Service Medal with four bronze stars for her service in Vietnam.

**Alaine K. Ivy (Thomas)**
**In country: October 1968 – September 1969**
**Rank: Sergeant, US Marine Corps**
**Duty: NAVFORV, Marine Corps Personnel**
**Section, Administrative Specialist**

**♥Mary "Chief" Lou Hootman**
**Retired as a Chief Warrant Officer 4**
**In country: October 1968 – October 1969**
**Rank: Chief Warrant Officer 3, US Army**
**Duty: MACV, 525th Military Intelligence Group, Personnel/**
**Administrative Technician**

A Day in Vietnam: The sun had not yet appeared on the horizon when I was awakened by the sound of short, sporadic rifle fire outside in the street. Hopefully this would be another routine day and, best of all, one day closer to the time I'd finish my tour in Vietnam and be on my way home. I say hopefully because in Vietnam one never knows from one minute to the next, let alone from day to day, what is going to happen. Death, yours or somebody else's, seems always to lurk just around the corner or down the street a piece. But, fear is so futile that I turned to more pleasant thoughts of finishing my tour here and going home. Vietnam isn't the ideal place for a woman.

Quietly I slipped out of bed and started to put on my fatigues. By this time, I had grown quite accustomed to fatigues and the heavy jungle boots we were required to wear. In a few minutes, I would meet John, the major next door, for an early morning run around the jogging track at Tan Son Nhut. Strange that we should feel a necessity to keep in good physical condition while in a combat zone. Possibly, it is the desire to stay alive that makes you even more conscious of the need to maintain a high degree of fitness. If all went well we would run our usual mile, drive back to the quarters, shower, dress, pick up our gear, then meet in the mess hall for breakfast. Many would still be in bed while we were enjoying hot biscuits, ham and fresh eggs cooked to order. Why we chose to get up so early I'm not sure. Maybe we felt that getting an early start gave us a few more minutes of life before going out into the streets to meet possible death.

Though the morning had started routinely, it ended rather abruptly as we ran the last lap around the track. The whine of a bullet in the air brought us quite suddenly to the realization that we were not on a college track preparing for the Olympics. We were in a combat zone and anything could happen. There was no other cover in the area, so we ran to our jeep to take advantage of what little cover it would provide. As soon as John determined that there were no Viet Cong snipers in the area, we drove back to the barracks. Thank goodness, that bullet didn't have either of our names on it.

In the safety of the compound, I turned to thoughts of a refreshing shower and breakfast. The aroma of ham floated out of the mess hall window. That food was going to be especially good this morning. I jumped from the jeep and rushed to the barracks to shower quickly and try to beat John to the mess hall. It was a silly game we played each morning and one that I never won. I'm not really sure I tried very hard to beat him. He always seemed to enjoy teasing me about being such a slowpoke.

Breakfast each day was an enjoyable experience. The food was fresh, well prepared, and the conversation light and cheerful. It seemed each day that new faces arrived from the States to replace those going home. There was never any trouble sorting out the happy faces of those who had completed their tour and were about to go home. Having been in Vietnam for several months, I felt sad for the newly arrived, happy for those departing and, secretly, envious that it was not time for me to be going home. Every day in Vietnam seemed to me to be an eternity.

I worked on the far side of the city in a section called Gia Dinh. This area was quite hectic and had heavy lanes of traffic trying to go in different directions at the same time without the aid of traffic signals. Traffic on this particular morning was relatively light, though, and I was able to make the entire trip in about 20 minutes. It took much longer on most mornings. When traffic is as heavy, as it usually is in that area, people tend to become impatient and then accidents happen. Strange, I had been here all of those months and yet I couldn't get used to seeing the mutilated bodies lying in the street. But, there were no accidents this morning, so there was no need to worry about avoiding the sight of bodies in the street. At last, the office building loomed in the foreground.

When I arrived at the office, one of my sergeants reported that we had had no casualties during the night. I breathed a little prayer and proceeded to my desk. Mentally I was hoping for a quiet day as I had just gotten a new correspondence course in the mail and was anxious to start working on it. It seemed important to prepare for the future for I was hoping even then that the Army could one day send me back to college to finish my degree.

The morning passed very quickly; lunchtime came and went; I signed the reports for the day and then it was finally time to go back to the barracks. All I had to do was successfully maneuver through the traffic one more time and that day would be over. A day in Vietnam – one day closer to home! *Source: US Army Women's Museum*

**Comments and Memories:** I remember the day the MACV WAC Staff Advisor called my command and told them I couldn't carry a weapon. It was command policy that all officers carry a pistol and rifle. I carried a .45 caliber pistol and a .30 caliber rifle. We all had a good laugh, and I continued to comply with command policy. I am rated marksman in both weapons. *Source: Vietnam Memory Book 2000*

**Rita C. Minogue**
**Retired as a Colonel**
**In country: October 1968 – October 1969**
**Rank: Major, US Army Medical Specialist Corps**
**Duty: 6ᵗʰ Convalescent Center, Cam Ranh Bay, Physical Therapist**

Rita Minogue was one of those physical therapists who volunteered to serve during World War II. Upon her return to the United States after the war as a First Lieutenant, she left the military but was recalled to active duty during the Korean Conflict. Then, in the fall of 1968, she began service in a third conflict, this time in Vietnam. She is one of the very few who served in three wars. *(US Army photo, 1954, Korea)*

**Michele "Mich" A. Yacura (Fennimore)**
**In country: October 1968 – October 1969**
**Rank: Staff Sergeant, US Army**
**Duty: USARV, Personnel, Administrative NCO**

**Martha A. Cessna**
**In country: October 1968 – October 10, 1969**
**Rank: Staff Sergeant, US Air Force**
**Duty: MACV, Surgeon's Office, Administration Supervisor**

♥**Shirley Molohon Barnwell**
**Retired as a Lieutenant Colonel**
**In country: October 1968 – May 1970**
**Rank: Lieutenant Colonel, US Army**
**Duty: USARV, Personnel Management Officer**

**Ermelinda "Ermie" Salazar (Esquibel)**
**In country: October 1968 – October 5, 1970**
**Rank: Staff Sergeant, US Marine Corps**
**Duty: MACV, Staff Judge Advocate Office, Administrative Specialist**

Staff Sergeant Ermelinda Salazar (later Esquibel), who touched the lives of Vietnamese orphans, was nominated for the 1970 Unsung Heroine Award sponsored by the Veterans of Foreign Wars Auxiliary, and was immortalized in a painting by Marine artist Cliff Young. During her 15 months in Saigon, Staff Sergeant Salazar essentially took over a MACV civic action project involving the St. Vincent de Paul orphanage.

In a letter dated 10 September 1969, to Gunnery Sergeant Helen Dowd, she wrote:

"I don't remember if I mentioned to you that I had been working with the orphanage supported by MACV. It is not a big one – only 75 children ages from a few weeks old to about 11 or 12 years of age. They are precious and quite lively. This whole orphanage is taken care of by two Catholic sisters. One of them is rather advanced in age (about in her 60s) and the other is quite young and active. Still and all, Gunny, these two souls work themselves to death. The two sisters are Vietnamese who speak no English at all. And me? I know a limited number of broken phrases and words in Vietnamese. Since I've been working at the orphanage, I've had to overcome much repugnance. There's a lot of sickness and disease here in Vietnam. So, when I say the orphanage it doesn't have the same connotation that it does back in the States where the children are well fed and healthy for at least they have medical facilities and medicines available. These children have nothing! If the women marine company is wondering about any projects for Christmas, here is something you can think about. Anything and everything is needed."

Staff Sergeant Salazar personally contacted Marine units for contributions, arranged a site and bus transportation, enlisted interested people to help, and wrapped gifts for each child.

*This article titled "Woman Marines in Vietnam" is an excerpt from* A History of the Women Marines 1946-1947 *by Colonel Mary V. Stremlow.*

**Nancy "CPT J" J. Jurgevich**
**Retired as a Lieutenant Colonel**
**In country: October 14, 1968 – November 1969;**
**December 1969 – December 1970**
**Rank: Captain, US Army**
**Duty: USARV, Special Troops, WAC Detachment, Third Commander;**
**1st Logistical Command, Long Binh; Deputy Chief of Staff for Personnel,**
**Saigon Support Command, Long Binh**

Upon arrival at Bien Hoa Air Base, I was met by Captain Joanne Murphy in her fatigues and field boots, who was appropriately dressed, and there I was in my Army Green Cord uniform (skirt and top) and heels. It did not take any time for me to know I was in the wrong uniform in this dusty and dirty area. The Director of the Women's Army Corps led me to believe that everything was clean and air-conditioned and that the women should be wearing the Army Green Cord uniform and heels. I disagreed with the Director's guidance and my new Green "Cords" were in the mail back to the States.

One of my first questions to Joanne Murphy was: What are those little things that had entryways and sand bags all around? Of course, they were bunkers and I would be spending time in those quite often. When the alert siren went off, we were supposed to put on our helmet, grab our canteen and get to the bunker. The women were pretty good at this but they also would drag their belongings with them, cameras, tape recorders, even frying pans. One night someone was yelling, "I forgot the paper plates." On another occasion, one woman was complaining she was thirsty (they were supposed to put fresh water in their canteens every Monday), and so 1SG Mary Manning gave her canteen to the woman. The woman drank the water and afterward complained the water was old. Can you imagine? The women hated the bunkers, and I can't say that I blamed them. They were not very comfortable but they were a safe haven, and a necessary one. As soon as they did not hear any activity they wanted to get out of the bunkers, but we had to wait until the all-clear siren went off. We had NCOs assigned to each bunker to make sure the women stayed in until they were released.

During my 26 years in the Army, I consider my assignment as the WAC Detachment Commander to be an honor and the highlight of my career. It was a lot of responsibility, but also very rewarding. The women, who were volunteers, were young, smart, dedicated, loyal women who were honored to be there and it was a joy to work with them.

**Wilma L. Vaught**
**Retired as a Brigadier General**
**In country: October 18, 1968 – October 26, 1969**
**Rank: Major, US Air Force**
**Duty: MACV Headquarters, Saigon**

 More than 40 years have passed since I served in Saigon at MACV Headquarters. I think often about that year spent in country. Recollections of the sights and smells and especially the sounds can pop into my thoughts at the oddest moments. While I was stationed in Saigon, I lived at the Meyerkord BOQ Hotel. It was about three blocks behind the President's Palace and was frequently used by USO and Red Cross members passing through. The US Embassy, also about three blocks away, came under rocket attacks from time to time as did the Central Market about two blocks away from our hotel. I well remember one Sunday morning about 5:30 a.m. as I was getting ready to go to MACV when I heard several ssss-booms. I thought, "That sounds just like the stories I remember from World War II. It must be a rocket attack." Before I could go to the rooftop to see what was happening, the sound ended. That and a rocket attack on the embassy when I was walking about two blocks away was the closest I came to combat!

When I arrived, a woman who was getting ready to rotate back to the States told me that I should take her room, which was on the third floor. It was fairly large and she told me that it came with additional security. As it turned out, a drawer in the room contained a rifle and an AK-47. Although the Air Force had given me no training in the use of weapons, my brother-in-law had, and I felt that I could use them should the need arise. I never used either of them and turned them in when I departed country. Today's military women are trained in the use of weapons as part of basic training. Not so when I deployed.

The daily uniform for me was cords, a polyester blend uniform with skirt that was reasonably comfortable in the heat and humidity. Fatigues (which I wore once) were not uniform for military women at the time. A uniform like our cords would be totally unacceptable as a uniform in a combat zone in today's military with its battle dress uniforms.

Six and a half days a week, 12 hours a day, I worked at MACV Headquarters where I was a management analyst in the Comptroller Directorate. On Sunday afternoons, which we frequently had off, I joined friends to visit the Saigon Zoo, stores, or having a meal at some restaurant or hotel in the center of the city.

We weren't permitted to give anything to the Vietnamese people we came in contact with, but there was a family that I saw daily as I returned from work who lived on the sidewalk about half a block from our hotel. Somehow, many of us seemed to just drop things as we walked by them. Another child, a 9-year-old boy, slept in one of the jeeps every night. He did not have a family to go to.

There were only four military women assigned to MACV when I was there, an Army lieutenant colonel, an Army major, myself then a major, and an enlisted Army woman. The Army major, assigned to Logistics, and I visited a live-in school for blind female children. The Vietnamese director had studied at the Massachusetts Institute of Technology and did a tremendous job particularly considering her lack of funding, equipment, adequate building and furniture, etc. We were able to get a used refrigerator for the school and a church in the United States sent clothing for the children. I often wonder what happened to the school and the children after the war came to an end.

My balcony overlooked an alley and one of the businesses in the alley was a massage parlor. It was not unusual to see people visiting that establishment. As a matter of fact, I went once. The highlight was a massage with the Vietnamese girl giving the massage walking on my back. That's the only time in my life I ever had that treatment.

In a larger sense and beyond the more personal memories, I view my service there and our country's involvement in other ways. I feel today, as I felt then, that as a member of the US military I couldn't have done anything but serve in Vietnam – it was my duty. I also believe that America was right in being there. Communism was, indeed, a threat to democracy; the horrors it wrought upon the people of Vietnam compelled our involvement. And lastly, with the many changes in Vietnam of the past few years, I have concluded that our defeat there was only temporary – Vietnam is entering the modern, global community.

While the loss of so many lives is still difficult to reconcile, I firmly believe their sacrifice was not in vain. And, as the years pass, I realize even more the meaningful contribution each of us from that era made to our military, our nation and our society.

# NOVEMBER

*Memory Lane: Richard M. Nixon wins the US Presidential election; Yale University announces it is going to admit women.*
*Songs: "With a Little Help From My Friends" by Joe Cocker; "Love Child" by Diana Ross and The Supremes*

**Betty Leigh K. Nemyer (Shellenberger)**
**Retired as a Chief Warrant Officer 3**
**In country: November 1968 – November 1969;**
**September 1971 – August 1972**
**Rank: Chief Warrant Officer 2, US Army**
**Duty: 92nd Finance, Cam Ranh Bay; USARV, 1st Aviation Brigade, Personnel/Administrative Technician**

**Mary Lee Welch**
**Retired as a Lieutenant Colonel**
**In country: November 1968 – November 1969**
**Rank: Major, US Army Medical Specialist Corps**
**Duty: 68th Medical Group, Long Binh, Dietetic Consultant**

The 68th Medical Group was one of three medical groups comprising the 44th Medical Brigade, Vietnam. This was the largest medical brigade ever established in the history of Army Medical services.

The 68th covered III and IV Corps tactical zones and contained 10 hospital units. The food service operations of these units were the primary responsibility of the Food Service Section, 68th Medical Group of which I was a member.

Travel was the first problem a dietitian faced in Vietnam. This was especially true of the 68th Group because of the large geographical area covered. Four of the units in our section were located on Long Binh Post. The rest were spread from the 45th Surgical in Nay Ninh, located in northern III Corps, near the Cambodian border, to the 29th Evac in the Mekong Delta region in central IV Corps.

Our chief mode of transportation was by medical evacuation helicopters, most commonly known as "Dust Offs." Flights were not regularly scheduled and you might receive a 5- to 10-minute notice to be at a helicopter pad if you wanted to catch a flight to a certain unit. This at times made for gray hairs, but it was all part of the job.

Other means of air transportation included the C-130 Caribous, the C-123 Providers and the Army gunships and "slicks" of the combat arms troops.

Most admittedly, I preferred Dust Off. My face had become all too familiar to any Dust Off pilots and crewmembers. When they saw me they commonly asked, "Where are you going this time?"

Other problems faced by dietitians in Vietnam were the very same faced stateside: sanitation, availability of subsistence, supply items, equipment and personnel. Only they were seemingly magnified ten times and coupled with peculiar quirks because of the support situation in a combat zone.

Local Vietnamese were utilized in all units as kitchen police. The problem was training them in the simple principles of personal hygiene and kitchen sanitation. In the larger units, LVNs (licensed vocational nurses) were used in patient ward food service.

The most lasting memory I have of my tour in Vietnam is probably the sound of the "whop-whop" of the rotor blades of the Dust Off helicopters that I used to get from Long Binh to all the 68th Medical Group's outlying hospitals. I flew courtesy of Dust Off nearly 90 times during my tour. Even now, some 45 plus years later, I always stop when I hear a "chopper" fly overhead. Oh yes, I still say "incoming" to myself when I hear a loud bang.

♥**Mary Joe Hinton**
**Retired as a Sergeant Major**
**In country: November 1968 – September 11, 1970**
**Rank: Master Sergeant, US Army**
**Duty: MACV, Joint Staff, Fifth NCO Advisor to the**
**Vietnam Women's Armed Forces Corps**

♥**Charlotte Josephine Hall**
**In country: November 17, 1968 – November 16, 1969**
**Rank: Major, US Army**
**Duty: MACV, Joint Staff, First Junior Officer**
**Advisor to the Vietnam Women's Armed**
**Forces Corps**

**Lois L. Westerfield**
**Retired as a Lieutenant Colonel**
**In country: November 29, 1968 – October 30, 1969**
**Rank: Major, US Army**
**Duty: MACV, J4, Logistical Staff Officer**

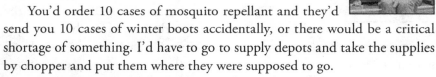

"I was selected to go to Vietnam from 1968 – 1969 as the supply support officer in J4 MACV, and my primary duty was to support and monitor the supplies to all the field units, especially the mobile advisement teams.

The climate was so humid and the computers malfunctioned.

You'd order 10 cases of mosquito repellant and they'd send you 10 cases of winter boots accidentally, or there would be a critical shortage of something. I'd have to go to supply depots and take the supplies by chopper and put them where they were supposed to go.

I learned so much about the supply systems of all the services, and they're all different. For my service there, I got a bronze star because I was in a combat zone – Vietnam. There aren't too many women who can say that."

*Excerpt from an article by Lois Westerfield as told to Abby Weingarten, which appeared in* The Sarasota Herald-Tribune.

# DECEMBER

*Memory Lane: US spacecraft Apollo 8 enters orbit around the Moon. Astronauts Frank Borman, Jim Lovell and William A. Anders become the first humans to see the far side of the Moon.*
*Song: "I Heard it Through the Grapevine" by Marvin Gaye*

## Clara "Chris" C. Johnson
**Retired as a Major**
**In country: December 1968 – June 1969**
**Rank: Major, US Air Force**
**Duty: 7ᵗʰ Air Force, 377ᵗʰ Combat Support Group, Management and Procedures, Supply Staff Officer**

"I've never been discriminated against because I am a Negro, but I have occasionally met firm resistance from men in the service because I am a woman. However, I've had no such trouble in Vietnam, neither from the men for whom I work nor from those who work for me."

Major Johnson is exceptionally well liked by the several hundred men who work for her. She heads Supply Management and Procedures at Tan Son Nhut Air Base, where 7ᵗʰ Air Force is located. Under her direction, in 12-hour shifts, 24 hours a day, seven days a week, the unit handles, in one way or another, the entire US Air Force supply operation at Tan Son Nhut. *Source:* Airman, *May 1969*

**Comments and Memories:** Taking cover in a bunker with the Baltimore Colts football team. I was holding up a picture of Buba [sic] Smith, who was crying and said, "Please God let me live and I will go to church every Sunday when I get out of Vietnam." *Source: Vietnam Memory Book 2000*

## Maria M. Abrahante
**Retired as a Master Sergeant**
**In country: December 1968 – November 16, 1969**
**Rank: Staff Sergeant, US Air Force**
**Duty: MACV, J4, Logistics, Administrative Specialist**

What motivates a woman to volunteer for duty in Vietnam? "I wanted to accomplish something," said Air Force Sergeant Maria M. Abrahante of New York City, a clerk typist at MACV. "I volunteered for Vietnam duty because this is where it is – this is what it's all about." Maria is originally from Puerto Rico, but now claims New York City as her home. She's an administrative specialist at MACV Headquarters and had arrived from Barksdale Air Force Base, LA, just a few weeks before, but her adjustment to combat life was rapid. "Of course, I was somewhat shocked by conditions when I arrived, but everyone was so helpful in helping me to get settled down, that I quickly overcame any misgivings I had. Now I feel that it's the greatest assignment in the Air Force." *Source:* Airman*, May 1969*

**Carolyn K. Boston (Bright)**
**Retired as a Staff Sergeant**
**In country: December 1968 – December 7, 1969**
**Rank: Specialist 5, US Army**
**Duty: MACV, J3, Operations, Administrative Specialist**

**Geraldine Young**
**In country: December 1968 – December 1969**
**Rank: Specialist 5, US Army**
**Duty: USARV, Administrative Specialist**

**♥Marjorie "Jean" J. Freeman**
**In country: December 1968 – February 1970**
**Rank: Specialist 5, US Army**
**Duty: US Army Engineer Construction Agency, Vietnam; USARV, 1ˢᵗ Logistical Command, Administrative Specialist**

# Chapter Nine

# 1969

♥Dorothy Jean Artioli
Retired as a Sergeant First Class
In country: 1969 – 1970
Rank: Sergeant First Class, US Army
Duty: USARV, Administrative NCO

♥Phyllis J. Bertram
In country: 1969 – 1970
Rank: Specialist 5, US Army
Duty: USARV, Administrative Specialist

♥Barbara Bole
Retired as a Commander
In country: 1969 – 1970
Rank: Lieutenant Commander, US Navy
Duty: NAVFORV, Training, Planning and Program Officer

Commander Barbara Bole was one of several Navy women officers stationed in Vietnam. She became the first Navy woman awarded the Bronze Star with Combat "V" in that conflict.

Beverly L. Brooks
Retired as a Command Sergeant Major
In country: 1969 – 1970
Rank: Specialist 5, US Army
Duty: USARV, Personnel Specialist

Verna M. Clark
In country: 1969 – 1970
Rank: Staff Sergeant, US Army
Duty: USARV, Adjutant General's Office, Awards Section, Personnel
Specialist

Frances Ernestine "Ellie" Ellwanger
Retired as a Sergeant First Class
In country: 1969 – 1970
Rank: Sergeant First Class, US Army
Duty: USARV, Data Service Center, Data Analysis Specialist

♥Jo Ann Fremont (Patterson)
In country: 1969 – 1970
Rank: Specialist 5, US Army
Duty: USARV, Clerk-Typist

♥Ellen "Fran" Frances Garvey
In country: 1969 – 1970
Rank: Sergeant First Class, US Army
Duty: USARV, Administrative NCO

Wera F. Grammer (Damhauser)
Retired as a Technical Sergeant
In country: 1969 – 1970
Rank: Staff Sergeant, US Air Force
Duty: 377th Air Base Wing, Staff Administrative Specialist

♥Pinkie Bell Houser
Retired as a Sergeant First Class
In country: 1969 – 1970
Rank: Staff Sergeant, US Army
Duty: USARV, Personnel Staff NCO

Beatrice Ashley Howard
Retired as a Lieutenant Colonel
In country: 1969 – 1970
Rank: Lieutenant Colonel, US Army
Duty: USARV, Public Information Office, Information Officer

♥**Barbara J. Wilson (Jack) (Norman)**
**Retired as a Chief Warrant Officer 3**
**In country: 1969 – 1970**
**Rank: Chief Warrant Officer 2, US Army**
**Duty: MACV, Signal Battalion, Cam Ranh Bay and Saigon, Personnel/**
**Administrative Technician**

 *Ann Kelsey, DAC, Army Special Services-Libraries, Vietnam 1969-1970*: Even though it is almost 30 years ago, I still remember Barbara Jack. From my point of view, a 23-year-old just out of library school, she was the essence of "together." Her starched and pressed fatigues and spit-shined boots seemed impervious to the sandy humidity of Cam Ranh Bay. I didn't know exactly what her job was (most of us women had only a vague idea of what the others did), but it didn't matter. Her dedication and sense of purpose was clearly evident. I admired and, I think, tried to emulate her stability and calm demeanor, especially during those many times when instability and craziness seemed to be the normal state of affairs.

I didn't realize then that Barbara Jack, a black female warrant officer assigned to Vietnam duty, was very likely a pioneer in every sense of the word. She is remembered and admired, I'm sure, by many, but certainly by this young civilian librarian who had the good fortune to share a billet with her in the sands of Cam Ranh Bay so many years ago. *Source: Vietnam Memory Book 2000*

**Doris Oliveras**
**In country: 1969 – 1970**
**Rank: Specialist 5, US Army**
**Duty: USARV**

**Marjorie D. McLain**
**In country: 1969 – 1970**
**Rank: Specialist 5, US Army**
**Duty: USARV, Clerk-Typist**

Many people talk about the atrocities of the war in Vietnam. Countless words have been written about My Lai. WAC SP5 Marjorie McLain, who just returned from a tour of duty in Vietnam, is appalled that so little attention is given to the other side of the American GI.

"I have seen the GIs in Vietnam with the children there. American men are so fond of children. The soldiers are doing a great deal for orphanages in Vietnam and they spend a lot of time with the children."

What people back home can't seem to realize, though, is that a common age for the Viet Cong soldier is 12 to 13 years old," she continued.

She feels that much of the criticism directed toward the Army is based on a "lack of understanding" of the situation in Vietnam by the people back home.

Should we be there? SP5 McLain thinks we should. "The fighting men extend in Vietnam because they think there's a cause worth fighting for. If they think we need to stay there until this thing is cleared up, how can people back here who know so little about the war sit in judgment?" The specialist said that morale is good in Vietnam in spite of the long, hard hours – 12 to 14 hours a day, six and a half days a week for WACs – and the perilous and thankless duties of the fighting men.

"Accounts of demonstrations and anti-war rallies at home hurt and disgust the guys, but it doesn't harm their morale too much."

SP5 McLain said that the worst morale-slump occurred during the postal strike. "During the strike everybody was pretty low. The most important thing to the people serving in Vietnam is a letter from home.

"My father didn't want me to go so far away from home and of course, Mother thought it was too dangerous. Now that I'm back and safe, I think they're glad that I went," she said.

The specialist, who was awarded the Bronze Star Medal for meritorious service with the 1st Logistical Command at Long Binh, wanted to go to Vietnam to do something which she felt was important. "It's hard sometimes to think of typing as being important, but combined with the terrific job that everyone else is doing there, it becomes important.

"And in many ways I think the war is a paper war. There is a continual flow of paperwork that never stops. There are no holidays there – we worked through Christmas and New Year's Day just like any other day."

Getting the job done leaves WACs in Vietnam with little free time, however there's little to do with the free time they have. "We aren't allowed to go off-post except on official business. Then we have to go in a military sedan," she said.

In spite of the inconveniences and the hard work, the specialist said she doesn't regret having gone to Vietnam. SP5 McLain is assigned to the Operations Branch of the US Women's Army Corps School.

*Excerpt from a press release from the Information Office, Fort McClellan, AL, 1970*

♥**Lillian Ruth Ogburn**
**Retired as a Master Sergeant**
**In country: 1969 – 1970**
**Rank: Sergeant First Class, US Army**
**Duty: USARV, Administrative NCO**

♥**Betty "Penny" Frances Whitmire (Freeman)**
**In country: 1969 – 1970**
**Rank: Specialist 4, US Army**
**Duty: USARV, Clerk-Typist**

**Jo Ann Gasmund (Dowdy)**
**Retired as a First Sergeant**
**In country: 1969 – 1971**
**Rank: Staff Sergeant, US Army**
**Duty: USARV, G2, Intelligence Analyst**

♥**Rena "Dee Dee" Darlene Hurley**
**Retired as a Master Sergeant**
**In country: 1969 – 1971**
**Rank: Staff Sergeant, US Army**
**Duty: USARV, Special Troops, WAC Detachment, Supply Sergeant**

# JANUARY

*Memory Lane: The New York Jets defeat the Baltimore Colts (16-7) in Super Bowl III; an explosion aboard the USS Enterprise near Hawaii kills 27 and injures 314. Song: "Hooked on a Feeling" by B.J. Thomas*

**♥Ann Bernardette Healy**
**Retired as a Technical Sergeant**
**In country: January 1969 – December 31, 1969**
**Rank: Technical Sergeant, US Air Force**
**Duty: MACV, J2, Administrative Supervisor**

**♥Marian E. Thompson**
**Retired as a Colonel**
**In country: January 1969 – January 1970**
**Rank: Lieutenant Colonel, US Army Medical Specialist Corps**
**Duty: 3rd Field Hospital, Saigon, Physical Therapist**

**Rayneta Diane Kinne**
**In country: January 1969 – February 1970**
**Rank: Staff Sergeant, US Army**
**Duty: MACV, Intelligence**

**Iva J. Wallace**
**Retired as a First Sergeant**
**In country: January 1969 – February 1970; January 1972 – February 1973**
**Rank: Specialist 4, US Army**
**Duty: USARV, Surgeon's Office, 44th Medical Brigade; MACV, Intelligence**

**Augustina R. Jones (Foster)**
**In country: January 1969 – June 1970**
**Rank: Specialist 5, US Army**
**Duty: USARV, Central Finance and Accounting Office, 7th Finance Disbursing Section, Finance Specialist**

**Doris Anne Denny**
**Retired as a Major**
**In country: January 1969 – July 7, 1970**
**Rank: Staff Sergeant, US Army**
**Duty: USARV and MACV**

**Louise J. Hartley (Rather)**
**In country: January 1969 – August 1970**
**Rank: Sergeant, US Army**
**Duty: USARV, G1, Administrative NCO**

**♥Joann Hastings**
**Retired as a Lieutenant Colonel**
**In country: January 1969 – September 1970**
**Rank: Major, US Army**
**Duty: USARV, 1ˢᵗ Logistical Command, Food Advisor**

**Susan C. Hicks (Franklin)**
**In country: January 1969 – September 1970**
**Rank: Staff Sergeant, US Army**
**Duty: USARV, Plans and Operations, Personnel Staff NCO**

**Susan J. Haack**
**In country: January 4, 1969 – January 5, 1970**
**Rank: Specialist 5, US Army**
**Duty: USARV, G1; US Engineer Construction Agency, Vietnam, Administrative Specialist**

I was in New York working one day in 1967 when my brother called and said, "Sis, I just got drafted. I'm going to Vietnam." I said, "I'll be there." Two hours later, I was signing up to join the Army. We were very, very close. Our birthdays are a year and three days apart. I got through my test and they said, "You passed everything but you flunked mechanics." I said, "Good. Then I don't have to get dirty nails." I went to basic training at Fort McClellan AL. Of course, I was one of the first mouthy ones there. I had to use a toothbrush to clean the tile floor in the bathroom because I was chewing gum. You know, I'm 18.

I got on-the-job training at the Pentagon Annex. By then I was a private E2, administrative specialist. I worked for Major General Edwin Burba, Sr. He had four sons, and he used to say I was the daughter he never had.

Enlisted women couldn't go to Vietnam unless they were E4 or above, so I put in for Vietnam as soon as I was a Specialist 4 in early 1968.

Then in November 1968, General Burba called me into his office. "Sue, sit down. You're going to Vietnam," he said. "But your job there is only going to be six months, because the guy who had it before you had ten days left in Vietnam and went outside the hootch and shot himself." He must've known more than he let on. All I knew was that I was going to US Army Vietnam (USARV) Headquarters in Long Binh, and that I would be assigning privates through staff sergeant, within Vietnam.

While I was at the Pentagon, I had made a good friend, Sue Schungel. She'd been in the Army longer than me, and in July 1968 she went to Vietnam. When I finally got to Nam in January 1969, Sue said to me, "Where the hell have you been? I've been waiting for you." I said. "I couldn't get here any faster!"

My brother, who was in the 9th Infantry Division, had left Vietnam in 1968, so I didn't get the chance to serve with him after all.

Sue and I were the only women in our office with 26 guys. We got an hour and a half for lunch, so Sue and I'd run home to tan. Sue and Sue. We weren't supposed to leave the WAC Detachment, but, one time we stole a general's jeep and got busted because we each had a bottle of champagne. I thought I was being nice by filling up the gas tank, but, I put diesel fuel in it. "Well, we'll sit here and drink our champagne while you empty it out," I told the sergeant at the station. We also hitchhiked, which was totally, totally not cool.

A guy named Gary and I were picked to do the processing of the KIAs – and send the letters home. It sounded easy at first. I used a form letter – just added a name to it on my typewriter. Mr. and Mrs. John Doe, you know. Then it was signed by the government. But it got harder and harder to do.

**Joyce I. Harker (Saitta)**
**Retired as a Chief Master Sergeant, US Air National Guard**
**In country: January 17, 1969 – January 17, 1970**
**Rank: Specialist 5, US Army**
**Duty: USARV, Special Troops, WAC Detachment, Company Clerk, Mail Clerk, and Supply Clerk**

I was at William Beaumont General Hospital in El Paso, TX, and had volunteered but had to battle with them to get orders for Vietnam. I went in as a medic but as soon as I got to El Paso they told me that only men were medics in Nam. So, I said I was no longer interested in being a medic so I ran the PCS (permanent change of station) housing, the BOQ and the post hotel while I was waiting for orders – and I was a private E2 at the time.

I arrived in El Paso in June of 1967 and departed for Vietnam in January 1969. I went over unassigned under limited duty because I had had surgery on my feet (hammer toes) both feet at the same time.

I was the only military female on the plane and was a surprise to the officer checking off names. We flew into Hawaii and they would not turn on the lights in the terminal, so we had to keep the bathroom doors open so we could see to use the facilities.

We landed at Bien Hoa Air Base and then they bused us over to the barracks. Got there about mid-morning and by afternoon I was playing softball. The next day they told me I would be the company clerk. I was the Company Clerk, Mail Clerk, Supply Clerk, beer and pop runner, and whatever else was needed.

Besides softball, I also enjoyed going to the Loon Foon restaurant and usually at least once a month on Friday afternoon would go down there and order a plate of egg foo yung. It had beautiful black mushrooms and it was a great yellow, and I would order sweet and sour sauce to put on it.

It always annoyed me that we had male soldiers to guard the area instead of issuing us weapons to guard ourselves. I wanted to be there and did what I could while I was there to make people's lives good and don't regret the service.

One of my worst memories is from near the chopper landing place where the medics would cut clothes off the guys – there was a huge pile of clothing and it didn't seem to get smaller. And, I remember the triage stations – not good memories.

On my return, I landed at Travis Air Force Base and was bused over to Oakland. From there I went to Colorado and served with the Colorado Air National Guard. I was three years active duty and 37 years in National Guard. I retired as a Chief Master Sergeant E9.

**Catherine "Cathy" Mary Kahl**
**Retired as a Command Sergeant Major**
**In country: January 22, 1969 – January 18, 1970**
**Rank: Staff Sergeant, US Army**
**Duty: USARV, Adjutant General, Congressional Section, Administrative NCO**
       **and**
**Charlene "Charlie" Mary Kahl (Kennedy)**
**Retired as a Command Sergeant Major**
**In country: January 22, 1969 – January 18, 1970**
**Rank: Staff Sergeant, US Army**
**Duty: USARV, Adjutant General, Release From Active Duty Section, Administrative NCO**

We requested to go to Vietnam and did not hear from the Department of the Army. We called the Adjutant General branch and were told that they did not have our request for orders to Vietnam. Apparently it was lost, so we sent the request through again and received orders soon after.

We had nine days of leave – we were stationed at Fort Belvoir, VA – so we went home to spend some time with our parents. It was in January; our parents did not really want us to go.

We were the only two women on the plane and flew out of San Francisco, CA, with stops in Hawaii and Guam. On arrival at Tan Son Nhut Air Base, we couldn't land immediately and had to circle because of small-arms fire on the ground. Finally, we went into the terminal building and then on to the WAC Detachment.

Nancy Jurgevich was commanding officer at the time and her replacement was Shirley Ohta.

We remember nightly movies shown on the patio under a huge parachute.

We were in Vietnam for a year and wanted to extend six months, but when we called home, our Mother cried the entire time we were on the phone, so we did not extend.

We spent a lot of time with Joyce Harker like the "3 amigos." We even took a two-week vacation with Joyce and went to Colorado to meet her family.

Major Deloris Browning, USARV Adjutant, could not tell us apart. So upon our arrival, she split us up in her large AG office. Cathy went to the Congressional Section on the "right" and Charlie went to the Release from Active Duty Section on the "left."

When our mama-san didn't show up to do laundry or polish boots, or when we pulled CQ, we always seemed to receive incoming rounds by the Viet Cong – two evenings in a row.

During one alert we remember hitting the bunkers and finding Cathy "missing in action." We had to go get her once roll call had been taken. We found her sound asleep in her top bunk, cutting zzz's under her camo blanket.

We had two very enjoyable R&R trips to Tokyo, Japan and to Sydney, Australia.

We remember kissing the ground when we arrived back in the States. Fort Huachuca, AZ, was next for duty and we spent our first 11.5 years in the Army together. The assignments branch worked at keeping us together. The one time we asked to be separated, we both hated it, so assignments got us back together at Fort Monroe, VA.

Charlie retired March 31, 1992. She has two sons and three grandchildren; she loves to visit with them.

Cathy had additional assignments to Valdosta, GA, then to Fort Eustis, VA, where she retired January 31, 1996.

Cathy has a daughter born on our first tour in Europe – Frankfurt, Germany (1977). After three tours in Germany, Cathy's daughter stayed there as a German exchange student, receiving her PhD in 2013 at a ceremony which Cathy attended.

# FEBRUARY

*Memory Lane: The Boeing 747 makes its maiden flight; Operation Barrier Reef begins in the Mekong Delta, Vietnam.*
*Songs: "Proud Mary" by Creedence Clearwater Revival; "Everyday People" by Sly and The Family Stone*

**Jessie Stuart Brewer**
**Retired as a Colonel**
**In country: February 1969 – January 1970**
**Rank: Major, US Army Medical Specialist Corps**
**Duty: 67ᵗʰ Medical Group, Da Nang; 68ᵗʰ Medical Group, Long Binh, Dietetic Consultant**

As a dietitian, I was assigned to the 67ᵗʰ Medical Group Headquarters in I Corps (northern most part of South Vietnam). I was responsible for servicing all medical units from the DMZ to Chu Lai. There were six hospitals: the 18ᵗʰ Surgical at Camp Eagle near the DMZ; the 22ⁿᵈ Surgical and 85ᵗʰ Evacuation in Phu Bai; the 95ᵗʰ Evacuation in Da Nang; and the 312ᵗʰ Evacuation, replaced by the 91ˢᵗ Evacuation, the 27ᵗʰ Surgical and one ambulance dining room in Chu Lai. Later the 2ⁿᵈ Field Hospital moved into buildings vacated by the Marines in Quang Tri.

My chief responsibility was to be an advisor to the assigned personnel and command concerning menus, food supply, diets, equipment and sanitation for each of the food services.

All the units prepared food on TO&E field equipment, i.e. field ranges with little refrigeration. Patient delivery system consisted of food carts containing bulk food containers. Meals were served on paper plates. Plastic eating utensils were also provided. Food Service warrant officers, noncommissioned officers, cooks and delivery personnel were not trained in hospital food service diet preparation, delivery and how to communicate with nursing personnel. There was no blender or baby food to use in preparing tube feedings. This made preparation more difficult when needed for the patients.

It was my responsibility to solve these problems. I worked with the dietitian consultant in USARV Medical Command, who coordinated with the 44ᵗʰ Medical Brigade to direct hospital trained personnel to the medical units. I was able to coordinate with US Agency for International Development to obtain baby food. I traveled to all our units to offer advice and recommendations to the food service personnel and commanders. Ground transportation was not safe therefore I "hitch hiked" on Dust Off choppers, Marine helicopters, Army fixed-wing planes and any other air transportation I could find to get to the units. I also traveled all over the country to depots to find food service equipment to replace the field equipment. I arranged for the equipment to be shipped to northern locations to service our units.

During the last month in country as medical units began to leave, I moved down to III and IV Corps 68th Medical Group, to orientate the new dietitian there. My mission was complete.

**Eva B. Schmaing (Pederson)**
**In country: February 1969 – January 1970**
**Rank: Staff Sergeant, US Army**
**Duty: USARV, 1st Aviation Brigade**

**Lawanda E. Allen**
**In country: February 1969 – February 1970**
**Rank: Specialist 5, US Army**
**Duty: USARV, Engineer Division,**
**Administrative NCO**

**Katie Mozelle Clark**
**In country: February 1969 – February 1970**
**Rank: Captain, US Air Force**
**Duty: 7th Air Force, 377th Combat Support Group, Administrative Management Officer**

**Carol Lynn Johnson**
**In country: February 1969 – February 1970**
**Rank: Captain, US Army**
**Duty: USARV, Public Information Office, Information Officer**

I was in the Public Information Office. We had a funny story. A woman from Georgia wanted to send her husband a watermelon! Pan American Airlines decided this was good PR.

They flew the melon to Vietnam. A Pan Am employee and I met in Saigon and went by chopper out to his firebase.

One time I decided to have a pizza party for the crew. I had an entire suitcase full of the mix when I came back from Japan. Got some smiles and looks when I went through customs.

**Sally Ann McCandless**
**Retired as a Lieutenant Colonel**
**In country: February 1969 – February 1970**
**Rank: Major, US Army Medical Specialist Corps**
**Duty: 24ᵗʰ Evacuation Hospital, Long Binh, Chief Physical Therapist**

I have never witnessed death so close as I saw the ravages of the war, and realized peace is better!

**♥Linda Sue Neblock (Plumm)**
**In country: February 1969 – February 1970**
**Rank: Specialist 5, US Army**
**Duty: USARV, Secretary General Staff, Administrative Specialist**

**Barbara C. Reid**
**Retired as a Lieutenant Colonel**
**In country: February 1969 – February 1970**
**Rank: Captain, US Army Medical Specialist Corps**
**Duty: 67ᵗʰ Evacuation Hospital, Qui Nhon, Physical Therapist**

It was February 1969, I was 25 years old, a Captain in the Army Medical Specialist Corps and I had been a staff Physical Therapist for 18 months at the 106ᵗʰ General Hospital, Yokohama, Japan. I flew from Tachikawa, Japan, to Saigon, Republic of South Vietnam. After landing early in the morning, I was sent to Long Binh for in processing. The Vietnamese Tet Offensive was underway and my vehicle had machine gun armored escort vehicles. I had traveled in my summer uniform and remember wearing high heels and lugging my duffle bag, briefcase and a purse. I processed in and received two sets of combat fatigues and boots and then was sent to a barrack and given a room. There was no one else in the barrack. I had a map noting the mess hall for meals. I changed into my new boots and fatigues and felt more comfortable to deal with my new world.

At nightfall, an enlisted man reported that he was assigned to guard the barrack and me for the night. I was awakened by the sirens of a Red Alert – incoming rounds and perimeter penetrated. The private said that I should go to the bunker next door. Within minutes they filled the bunker with all the

Vietnamese "mama-sans" who had been housed for the night. I sat in the dark, on a long bench seat surrounded by 30 non-English speaking women, and my guard outside was armed with only a nightstick to protect us. The night was long, and the woman sitting next to me urinated. My thought was, "I hope she didn't mess up my new boots." For the next four days and nights I spent my days traveling back and forth to the Saigon airport, waiting for flights and "cat napping" on the concrete floor using my duffle bag for a back and head support. I spent my nights trying to sleep in various above and below ground bunkers at the Long Binh compound. I ended up having to fly up country to Da Nang and be rerouted on another flight back south to Qui Nhon.

I was exhausted by the time I processed in to my new duty station at the 67th Evacuation Hospital. The hospital was located on the airfield. I was escorted to my new quarters and met my "roommate" a second lieutenant Army nurse who worked in the triage area. Together we shared a bathroom with two other nurses. The following day, I was introduced to my two enlisted Physical Therapy (PT) technicians who had been holding down the fort until I could arrive. I was now the Chief PT of a small clinic located in a Quonset hut located on the backside of the 67th Evacuation Hospital next to the main road that traversed the airfield and compound. The clinic had recently been air-conditioned, walls had been torn down to give us more room and had been painted, all of which was marvelous. One of the first personal things I did was to cut my hair short, which was done by a Vietnamese barber in the compound. No more time for hair rollers at night and fancy hair do's. The "Red Alerts" were a nightly event, and we had to be ready to wear our helmet and flak jacket. My mother was terrified to hear on the nightly news that the ammo dump in Qui Nhon had been blown up shortly after I arrived. The "mama-sans" washed and ironed our uniforms and spit shined our boots on a daily basis, making sure we looked sharp.

Prior to the Vietnam War, physical therapy had never been performed in a combat zone. We were pioneers and limited only by our imaginations. The earlier the intervention the quicker the results would be. With limited supplies, therapists throughout the hospitals were very resourceful and innovative in their approaches to building equipment or modifying equipment to meet their needs. I used portable IV poles for upper extremity exercises. I used scrap metal to make splints and ground the edges off on the concrete floor of my clinic. Lead shot created weight bags for strengthening. I even built standing platforms for bilateral leg amputees to become vertical and regain their trunk balance and arm strength. We worked 12-hour days and had one day off a week. The PT clinic was manned seven days a week. We performed more than 100 treatments a day. We treated a multitude of injuries, and often I would venture into the operating rooms at night to view surgeries on the newly incoming casualties. This gave me insight into their injuries and allowed me to initiate treatment plans on the soldiers the following day. We treated many patients in the clinic, but about 10 a.m., we would move to the wards and treat the patients in ICU, orthopedics and surgical wards. Then we would return to the clinic at 1 p.m.

We had two whirlpools where we did all the burn debridement followed by exercises. There were lots of amputees, head injuries, chest and abdominal wounds, fractures and spinal cord injuries. The trauma and injuries were horrific, and it was hard to believe these young men could survive, much less, ever heal from these very complicated injuries. The human spirit and the divine spirit would kick in and miraculous events took place. Our soldiers were young, strong and healthy. We taught many breathing exercises for chest and abdominal wounds and got many patients up on crutches for beginning ambulation. The techs would take a weight cart around the wards for strengthening exercises for the bedridden to maintain their good extremity strength. Our work was exciting, rewarding, challenging and I loved being able to serve our soldiers and my fellow humanity. We also treated POWs during their postoperative period. I usually saw them on the wards and they were always under guard. One day I had a revelation as I was working on this young POW. He worked hard each day and was motivated to make progress. I thought to myself, he is young and believed he was doing what was right for his country. He was no different from the American soldier in the bed next to him. I was able to treat and help him with love and compassion. My heart was opened to serve unconditionally. All the POW patients were transferred down the road to the POW hospital. On occasion, I would be sent there to perform some follow-up programs. Treating the POWs made a big shift in my consciousness.

Not only were we treating wounded and ill American GIs, but we saw many civilian patients, as well. The Save the Children's Hospital was in Qui Nhon, and children of all ages were shuttled back and forth for surgery and follow-up PT. Often I would go to their hospital and instruct the nurses in exercise programs. The Canadian Rehabilitation Center was in town, and patients with combat injuries and polio would be seen, operated on, treated with PT and then returned to the Rehab Center for continued follow up. They were making orthotics and prosthetics for Vietnamese military and civilians. Treating post-polio patients who had never had care was a new frontier for me. I learned much about muscle substitution patterns and how readily the body can adapt to perform function. I filmed many children to analyze their gait patterns.

Outside of Qui Nhon on the southern coast was the Quy Hoa Leprosarium which was run by the French Benedictine nuns. Mother Superior had been there for 40 years. She spoke English, Vietnamese, French and German. She always knew where the Viet Cong were, and if the road was not safe, she would radio in and tell us to come by chopper. I loved coming by chopper; it was thrilling to fly in and land on the coconut-lined beach, jump out with supplies and be met by several nuns and patients. It's one of my favorite images, like a scene from some famous movie. These MEDCAP (medical civic action program) activities would send teams out usually on Saturdays to treat and operate on patients. The Leprosarium had its own hospital and operating rooms. Our Chief orthopedic surgeon performed many Syme (amputation of the foot at the ankle joint) amputation operations on the terribly infected feet. The nuns used bamboo to carve out prosthetic limbs, and old tires to make sandals. They were very kind, devoted and loved all the patients. Many times the hospital could not send an operating room nurse so the surgeon trained me to be his assistant. It was exciting for me to learn another skill and add to my professional knowledge.

After surgeries and ward rounds, we would be served a nine-course French meal with B&G Chateauneuf du Pape. With our bellies full, we could spend the afternoon swimming at their famous Quy Hoa beach. This became a favorite day off. Today if I find myself in a fancy wine shop and see B&G Chateauneuf du Pape many wonderful images waif forth from the beautiful colony by the sea. This was a mountain-sea refuge for us, a day away from the war and casualties, calmed by nuns, a first-class meal, and a leper colony.

On occasion, I could slip away for an afternoon where I learned to sail a Rhodes 19 in the South China Sea. After I treated the II Corps General for knee surgery, I was often invited for a cruise on the General's motor yacht where we had beer and goodies to eat. I even got to take the helm as we cruised Qui Nhon Bay before sunset. I had been dating a naval officer who had a jeep so we had found freedom and new adventures. Other escapes were snorkeling in the waters off nearby islands and making a run on a naval vessel to the 12 Mile Island. There were lots of parties and drinking. My worst hangover was from drinking too much sake at a going away party for a visiting General. I took my leave and returned to Japan for a week's vacation. My R&R was spent meeting my twin sister Jean and her husband in Australia. They were both in the Army stationed in Hawaii. Jean was a PT also, and stationed at Tripler General Hospital. We saw the famous show "Hair." It was delightful. When I was stationed in Japan, I started taking Hatha Yoga classes. I would do my routine every day and started to teach myself meditation by repeating the mantra "Om" to myself. These practices gave me much relief from the stresses of working in a combat zone. I always say these practices saved my life.

A group of the nurses and I had met several of the pilots at the airfield as they ate at our mess hall. On occasion, we got to fly to several other cities like Dalat and Pleiku for lunch. When I was transferring out of country, the guys decided they would fly me and several friends to Saigon. We had a clear day and I got to take the controls and fly the plane myself for about an hour. It was my last great adventure in country.

As I write this in January 2015, I am now 71 years old. I departed Vietnam 46 years ago. I am grateful for the fact that I volunteered to go to Vietnam and served my country and our wounded soldiers. I received a Bronze Star for meritorious service. I retired in 1985 with 20 years of service and obtained the rank of Lieutenant Colonel. I believe war is a horrible way to address conflict between countries. It destroys lives and wounds our service men and women both mentally, emotionally, spiritually and physically. It saddens me to this day that our veterans of Afghanistan and Iraq wars were repeatedly sent for multiple deployments and every day someone resorts to suicide. One deployment is difficult enough to recover from and I often wonder if one ever does completely recover. War changes one's life. We return different from when we went.

**Frances Weir**
**Retired as a Colonel**
**In country: February 1969 – February 1970**
**Rank: Lieutenant Colonel, US Army**
**Duty: USARV, 1ˢᵗ Logistical Command,**
**Personnel Staff Officer**

**♥Evelyn L. Lozano (Roussos)**
**In country: February 1969 – March 1970**
**Rank: Specialist 4, US Army**
**Duty: USARV, Clerk-Typist**

**Susan "Sue" E. Wudy**
**Retired as a Staff Sergeant**
**In country: February 1969 – May 1970**
**Rank: Specialist 6, US Army**
**Duty: MACV, J3; USARV, Entertainment Branch,**
**Executive Administrative Assistant**

**Comments and Memories:** First quarterly briefing I recorded was in Da Nang (I Corps). At lunch, I went to the latrine, which was filthy, and decided to sneak out to the nearest tree. A Marine captain stopped me and said he would take me to the senior officers' hootch. Little did I know this entailed a chopper trip, and the pilot (you guessed it!) decided he'd show this prima donna a thing or two. Though I loved the trip, it was a bit dangerous at times. The captain must have explained this was not at my request because my return trip was very tame. *Source: Vietnam Memory Book 2000*

**Claire M. L. Brisebois (Starnes)**
**In country: February 1969 – July 1971**
**Rank: Staff Sergeant, US Army**
**Duty: US Army Engineer Construction Agency, Vietnam,**
**Administrative Branch; Headquarters MACV, Office of Information,**
**Photojournalist** *(MACV Observer)*

Claire M. L. Brisebois (Starnes)
is a co-founder of the Vietnam
Women    Veterans,    Inc.
organization

LIFE IN LONG BINH: The biggest fear was to be taken prisoner. Can you imagine what kind of nightmare in terms of public relations it would have been? What a coup for North Vietnam! Apparently in 1968 military intelligence had gotten a document off a North Vietnamese that they were offering a $25,000 reward for a white American female. Our own government gave us life insurance, which was worth only $10,000. We laughed about it, because we were worth more to the North Vietnamese.

COMING HOME: It was the trip from hell. There were some parts that I don't remember because of the stress. I was in the northern part of South Vietnam. At my hotel, the Medford, I was in the fatigues from the day before. Mama-san came up to the fourth floor and told me, "The chaplain's downstairs." I knew just what it was. When I saw the chaplain, I told him, "My mother died, right?" He said, "You need to leave right away, we've started the paperwork." I went up to headquarters for my emergency orders while my roommate was packing my things. I was told to immediately go to the International Airport in Saigon, which was in Tan Son Nhut. I was told, "You'll have time to change at Travis Air Force Base (CA) when you get to the States."

I get on the plane and 22 hours later, I arrive at Travis. No time to shower or change as my flight out of San Francisco was soon leaving. I finally get to Frisco and they are holding the plane up. I hadn't slept, I was really tired. I looked like hell and probably smelled like hell, too. Now I'm in airport and running to the gate. All of the sudden I hear, "Hey Sarge, how's the war going, kill any babies lately?" I looked back at these guys and I said to myself, "Screw 'em." I kept on going, but they kept following me. I saw the gate and at that point, my blood was boiling. I told myself, "That's it, I've had enough." I turned around. I said, "You want a piece of me? Come on, let's go." The attendant at the gate is in the process of closing the gate door and is yelling at me to hurry. So I headed straight for the door. I sat down and thought, "Jesus I don't want to be here."

I sat down next to this girl and thought, "Oh, no." I knew what a peacenik looked like, and this girl had long, straight hair and wore large, horn-rimmed glasses. I thought, "She's one of those hippies from Frisco." I was totally wrong about her as she was very interested in what was happening in Vietnam. With mixed emotions, my thoughts kept returning to Vietnam. Life there was not always safe, but there was a war going on. It was expected. But, here in my home country? I'm supposed to be safe, but I didn't feel that way.

*Excerpt from the article titled "Unarmed and under fire: An oral history of female Vietnam vets," November 11, 1999,* Salon *online magazine. Used with permission.*

**Comments and Memories:** My tours in Vietnam made me realize how good we have it in this country. Though we returned to a not-so-good reception, I will never regret having volunteered. I only regret that all women who served in Vietnam, military and civilian, were not recognized sooner for their selflessness and courage.

I don't recall the exact date, but it was in early 1969 at Long Binh. We had just settled in for a good night's rest after a long day when all hell broke loose. One of my roommates, Pat Landry, who was always calm and cool, made sure we all made it to the bunkers. While trying to calm my nerves, I searched for Pat (Landry-Wilkewitz.) There she was near the bunker's entrance, doing the sign of the cross just as fast as she could. I knew then that if God was listening to her pleas, we'd all be okay. We laughed about it later, but we sure prayed a lot that night!

Also, I remember the time there was a fire in a Vietnamese hamlet immediately behind our "hotel" in Saigon. For many weeks, we had not slept because of a pig that snorted all night long. When the fire broke out, we all wondered what had happened to the pig. Seems the Vietnamese firefighters had been more concerned in saving the pig than the people. One of our own female members, Karen Offutt, had repeatedly gone into the inferno saving the children. Not knowing that the pig had been rescued, we thought we would have a restful night after the fire. Wrong! Upon the first snort, many of us wanted to go in the ashes and "kill" that pig. But then, Tet came and the pig disappeared. *Source: Vietnam Memory Book 2000*

**Carol F. Johnson**
**In country: February 1969 – November 1971**
**Rank: Specialist 5, US Army**
**Duty: USARV, G2, Administrative Specialist**

**♥Catherine Louise Oatman**
**Retired as a Staff Sergeant**
**In country: February 1969 – May 1972**
**Rank: Staff Sergeant, US Army**
**Duty: USARV, Data Processing Unit; MACV, Data Analysis Specialist**

Most of the groups over there sponsored an orphanage one way or another. And, we went into the Tam Mai orphanage. It was a little town. It was right off of Bien Hoa Air Base. I got attached to one little boy there and I started paying a lot of attention to him. One day we had a staff picnic at the barracks, and we'd go out and get the kids and keep them there in the barracks with us for the day. When it became time for them to go home, my commanding officer asked me, "What are you going to do about Kevin? If you don't get started you won't be able to get that baby out of country."

So I went to work on getting the paperwork going. I got him out of the orphanage and he stayed with me at the barracks for about a month. The orderly room would babysit while I went to work – the rest of the time he was in my room. I always laugh about it because when I had him at Long Binh and I would take him out at night, the other women in the barracks would say, "Get him out of the night air." And if I didn't take him out, they would say to me, "Take him out. Quit keeping that baby locked up." He had so many mothers it wasn't funny.

Then I decided I didn't want to raise him by himself, so I thought, "I'll have to go find me another one." I come from a big family myself and I just couldn't imagine a kid being raised on its own. I went to World Vision and I found my daughter there, Kimmy. They had a little hospital there. The Vietnamese government would bring their babies with medical problems to World Vision to get help. But, the orphanages would try to take them back when it came time, because the Vietnamese government paid the orphanages by the number of children they had in their charge.

Well, when I decided on Kim, I asked one of the ladies who worked there, "What are we going to do? When they come to take her back to the orphanage, I'm not going to get her back?" So I found a Vietnamese lawyer who could speak English, and I got the paperwork and I let him take over. He got the birth certificate and everything. The military changed the rules real quick after that, changed the policy on single parents adopting kids while you're in the military. Now, you can't do it.

I extended my time by another six months because it took a while to get this done. My next step was to go to the American Consulate and get them on the visa list. If I had been married, they could have immediately left country as soon as their paperwork was finished. But, because I was single, they had to wait for a visa. I was frustrated. When I went in with Kevin, to get him on the list, the vice consul just fussed over him and she thought it was wonderful that I was doing this. I went back in and said, "I'm taking another one." She couldn't believe it. But what I found out later is that she put Kimmy on the list at the same time she put Kevin. It was so they could leave the country at the same time.

Kevin is now 30 and Kim is 29. I used to wonder about whether either of my kids had any desire to go back to Vietnam. In the town we used to live in, there was a little Vietnamese lady who used to run the alterations shop. And Kim went in there one day, and the lady asked her if she ever wanted to see her real mother. And she pointed out to the car to me, and said, "That's my real mother. That's the only mother I know." I realized I didn't have anything to worry about.

*Excerpt from the article titled "Unarmed and under fire: An oral history of female Vietnam vets," November 11, 1999,* Salon *online magazine. Used with permission.*

**Nora Hilda Lebron (Encarnacion)**
**Retired as a Sergeant First Class**
**In country: February 4, 1969 – February 5, 1970**
**Rank: Specialist 5, US Army**
**Duty: USARV, G3 Operations, Clerk-Typist**

I remember walking across the field in the mornings going to the 24th Evacuation Hospital Mess Hall for breakfast and smelling that awful smell of burning body parts, and those times when the WAC bus was stopped at the helipad when the helicopters landed with the dead and wounded. So sad. But, there are many happy memories. There were times when we did not have running water and we washed our hair with beer. I remember the time when we went on helicopters to a party and we were gassed. The Bob Hope Show was wonderful. Another memory was the trip to Saigon where we met the Vietnam female soldiers. What a treat it

was to go with the officers of the G3 section of the Dog Training Battalion and seeing the dogs being trained. I enjoyed eating at the Chinese restaurant (Loon Foon) down the road. I also enjoyed staying up all night on CQ duty and talking with the overseas operators and getting to talk to the folks back home on those occasions. Going to Hong Kong is really a fun memory.

**Lana H. Clark (Majewski)**
**In country: February 26, 1969 – February 22, 1970**
**Rank: Specialist 5, US Army**
**Duty: USARV, G1, Clerk-Typist**

Specialist 5 Clark's job was to assist the G1 Executive Officer, LTC Charles Nash, with the assignment of all colonels within USARV.

**Brenda Sue Eichholz (Caldwell)**
**In country: February 28, 1969 – March 10, 1970**
**Rank: Staff Sergeant, US Army**
**Duty: USARV, Army Officer Reassignments, Personnel Staff NCO**

To get to a meal, I had to walk to the nearest hospital where the mess hall was located. The best route was walking next to the helipad where the wounded were brought in. I had to walk through the emergency room. After a battle, the wounded were brought in groups. Triage, a medical strategy which determines the level of care to the wounded, was readily practiced. Quick assessments were made, and those who would not survive, were pushed aside on a gurney.

The average age of a soldier was 19, my age at the time. I walked past these gurneys and most soldiers would be moaning in pain. Many wanted to talk, so I stopped and listened. Many times, I tried to comfort them by holding their hand. I watched many die. When I came back to the World, I brought these men back with me. Every day they flash before my eyes. They were my comrades. Someone needs to remember them.

# MARCH

*Memory Lane: Former general and President Dwight D. Eisenhower dies following a long illness.*
*Song: "Dizzy" by Tommy Roe*

**Ruth Marleen Neeley (Cremin)**
**In country: March 1969 – January 12, 1970**
**Rank: Staff Sergeant, US Army**
**Duty: USARV, Special Correspondence Section; MACV Command Section, Administrative NCO**

Right after high school graduation, Debbie Chaney, a friend since girlhood, and I moved to Amarillo, TX, to seek our fortunes. An Army recruiter bugged the life out of us to join up. Finally, we enlisted, and in January 1968, away we went to Fort McClellan, AL – on our first plane ride and first time away from home.

You already know what awaited us in basic training – fun, fun and more fun. Upon graduating, I became a private E2 and went to Fort Sam Houston, TX, for Clinical Psychology School. I soon realized this wasn't the field for me, and asked to change my MOS.

Meantime, I was sent to assist a second lieutenant in the Medical Library. For the record, I did NOT join the Army for the men! This lieutenant followed me around like a stag in rut; finally, I asked him to leave me alone! The next day I was told to report to Brooks Burn Center (San Antonio, TX) mail room. Oh, bother! After sorting, I hand delivered mail to the patients, seeing them as persons and not as their wounds. I visited with them, reading letters to those unable to manage.

Later, I was sent to Fort Knox, KY. After completing the Army Communications Course and testing, I asked to stay there to work. The E5 looked at me as if I were demented; the E8 gave me a six-week trial run. I fixed up an office, and things went swimmingly. I was the gofer for lunch sandwiches. Finally, I got a jeep, did other errands, and went to driving school. I was a well-cared-for and gently treated family member of the cadre at the school.

Promoted to E3 and E4 within a few months, I was then told I would go before the E5 board. I made E5 early and, in quick succession, E6 all before my first year was completed.

I was busy and made good friends, but caught a WAC hiding something in my room before inspection. I told the first sergeant my suspicions and worked with the CID (Criminal Investigation Command agents) at Fort Knox to uncover a drug ring. The JAG (Judge Advocate General) reneged on its "confidential informant" promise, and I contacted my congressman. No sooner had I been questioned by the post commander than I had orders to Vietnam.

The only female on the plane besides the flight attendants, when we landed, I was transported to Long Binh, and after sleeping for a day and a night, taken to the mess hall in the 24th Evacuation Hospital. The sidewalks were wooden over dirt and tents were everywhere. Patients in wheelchairs sat outside in the sun.

Our eggs and milk were reconstituted powder. We had an NCO (noncommissioned officer) Club where Filipino bands played and girls sang. Our fare was hamburgers, rusty-tasting cokes, and French fries of powdered potatoes smashed through a sieve and fried. The young men were so dear and polite. I wore Estée Lauder Youth Dew, and the men usually said I reminded them of someone at home.

In Long Binh only a few months, I interviewed with General Creighton Abrams' staff for a position. As we were finishing, General Abrams walked in and said, "Welcome." What an adventure! I worked in a reception area outside his offices. I lived the life of a fairytale princess or was bored into a coma and worked on classes by mail. I met my husband-to-be, aide to the Air Force commander, and we married at the Embassy with the Village Chief. I still lived in the hotel and Jack in his trailer at Tan Son Nhut Air Base.

After I found I was expecting a "bundle from Heaven," General George Brown had us accompany him to the US to have a church wedding. On return to Vietnam, bombings escalated in Saigon, and WACs could not be mothers, so I was discharged to the States to await my husband's return and what the future held. That future held another 24 years as an Air Force family. My husband, Jack, was a fighter pilot and finished his career as the NORAD (North American Aerospace Defense Command) Space Inspector General. We have two wonderful sons, a daughter-in-law and a precious granddaughter. My military time often seems like a book I read, a chapter in an unbelievable life.

♥**Jessie Marguerite McGraw**
**Retired as a Lieutenant Colonel**
**In country: March 1969 – March 1970**
**Rank: Major, US Air Force**
**Duty: 7th Air Force, 834th Air Division, Personnel Staff Officer**

**Sharon "Wink" Dawn Weikel**
**Retired as a Sergeant Major**
**In country: March 1969 – March 1970**
**Rank: Staff Sergeant, US Army**
**Duty: USARV, Office of the Adjutant General, Administrative NCO**

I remember an aviation group that invited the WACs to a swimming party, flew to Long Binh to get us and flew us to their company area. Also, in 1969-1971, "us ladies" could not go to Saigon without an escort, so the Evacuation Company arranged a trip.

**Comments and Memories:** Three of my brothers, James, Jerry and Milton (deceased), US Marine Corps, served in Vietnam approximately the same time I did in 1968-1969. *Source: Vietnam Memory Book 2000*

**Patricia L. Hill (Shoum)**
**In country: March 1969 – September 1970**
**Rank: Specialist 4, US Army**
**Duty: MACV, Executive Administrative Assistant**

**Ella "Doc" L. Netherton**
**In country: March 1969 – September 1970**
**Rank: Sergeant, US Marine Corps**
**Duty: MACV, Strategic Plans Division (J52),**
**SEATO Division, Administrative Specialist**

**Adelina "Dee" Diaz (Torres)**
**Retired as a Master Sergeant**
**In country: March 1969 – October 1970**
**Rank: Gunnery Sergeant, US Marine Corps**
**Duty: MACV, Strategic Plans Division (J52), SEATO Division,**
**Administrative Specialist**

I was born and raised in Silver City, NM. I joined the US Marine Corps in January 1960 and retired in January 1980. I served at Camp Lejeune, NC; San Diego, CA; Los Angeles, CA; Parris Island, SC; Saigon, Vietnam; Camp Smith HI; and Camp Pendleton, CA. While at Parris Island serving as a drill instructor, I was asked if I wanted to serve in Vietnam and I jumped at the chance. While in Vietnam, I was assigned to Headquarter, MACV (J52) SEATO Division along with Doc Netherton, another Woman Marine. My duties were mostly administrative. Once a month I traveled to Da Nang and other small Marine Corps units with the officer in charge assigned to visit the marines and deliver their payroll. It was then that I was given the opportunity to see the beautiful country of Vietnam.

While in Saigon, we lived at the Medford Hotel, a four-story building. There were two to a room and we shared a bathroom with four other females. All of us rushed after work to be the first to use the showers because of the lack of hot water. There were Army, Air Force and Marine Women plus some male soldiers residing there. The Medford Hotel was located about a mile from MACV Headquarters.

My first memorable moment was arriving in Tan Son Nhut Air Base right after the Tet Offensive and seeing military guards with rifles pointing everywhere. It was scary and exciting at the same time. Another moment was making tacos for about 20 people along with Ermie Salazar (my roommate). Took us a while in the small kitchen but we fed everybody. We made do with what was available at the commissary (taco shells that came out of a can). To us they were delicious. Another was visiting the orphanages and playing cards to all hours of the night. Serving in Vietnam was a memorable experience, one that I will treasure always, meeting so many wonderful people especially Sergeant Donna Hollowell (Murray) who has since passed away.

**Lynda K. Jacobs (Michalik)**
**In country: March 1969 – January 1971**
**Rank: Specialist 4, US Army**
**Duty: USARV, Administrative Specialist**

# APRIL

*Memory Lane: First human eye transplant performed; Paul McCartney says there is no truth to rumors he is dead.*
*Song: "Aquarius/Let the Sunshine In" by The 5th Dimension*

**Idalia "Corrie" Edna Correa**
**In country: April 1969 – February 1970**
**Rank: Specialist 5, US Army**
**Duty: USARV, G4, Administrative Specialist**

**Lois J. Bertram**
**Retired as a Chief Warrant Officer 4**
**In country: April 1969 – April 1970**
**Rank: Captain, US Marine Corps**
**Duty: NAVFORV, Marine Corps Personnel Section, Administrative Officer**

*Mary Glaudel-DeZurik:* Chief Warrant Officer Lois Bertram arrived in Vietnam in 1969 as the replacement for Major E. Elaine Filkins (Davies). While in Vietnam, she resided at the Le Qui Don and Rex hotels in Saigon. She retired after 30 years of service.

**Alice I. Champagne (Littlejohn)**
**Retired as a Major**
**In country: April 1969 – April 1970**
**Rank: Captain, US Air Force**
**Duty: MACV, Detachment 10, Air Force Advisory Group, USAF WAF**
**Staff Advisor to the Vietnam Women's Armed Forces Corps**

I arrived at Tan Son Nhut Air Base in April 1969 and was introduced to the two areas where I would spend most of my time. My quarters were a small room in a two-story sandbagged building which housed American female officers, primarily nurses. My office was on the second floor in the Vietnamese Air Force (VNAF) headquarters; it was shared with four Americans assigned to the advisory group.

I set out to encounter the reason for my being there – the VNAF women who were housed in a small building at the end of the VNAF compound. They had two primary training officers: a female captain who was on maternity leave and a lieutenant who spent her mornings teaching English in the MACV language school and arrived on her motorcycle in the afternoons. She was very enthusiastic about her job, explained a major concern about the adequacy of housing for the enlisted women, and became my traveling companion. Working from her excellent rapport with the VNAF officers, we examined the problem and concluded that we should travel to multiple sites. We flew with the Vietnamese from Nha Trang in the north to Binh Thuy in the south when space was available; it was usually transport provided to Vietnamese personnel making assignment moves with their families – the wives, the children and the household animals. With help from the US Army advisor, my travel uniform became small-size male green fatigues with bloused combat boots, my required .38 weapon, and my Vietnamese insignia (Dai Uy – Captain – worn with all uniforms between the second and third buttons). I quickly learned that a "building" consisted of four walls and a roof; all other amenities, doors, shutters and especially outdoor trench latrines, were to be negotiated. Fortunately, Vietnamese base commanders were anxious to have the women on their staffs and were welcoming and helpful.

The year passed quickly. The Vietnamese were learning how to operate computers. Vietnamization was underway.

**Judith P. Lewis**
**Retired as a Master Sergeant**
**In country: April 1969 – April 25, 1970**
**Rank: Staff Sergeant, US Army**
**Duty: MACV, Command Staff and J1**

My husband and I were together in Vietnam. Joe went back in Special Forces after returning to Fort Bragg, NC. He was in Vietnam three times and had to go back every 13 months.

We have been married 46 years, almost 47.

While we were in Vietnam in 1969 – 1970, he was with the Vietnamese Training School.

**Carol A. Mellen (Lincoln)**
**In country: April 1969 – April 1970**
**Rank: Sergeant, US Army**
**Duty: USARV, 1ˢᵗ Signal Brigade, 34ᵗʰ Signal Battalion,**
**Communications Center Specialist**

WAC Comcenter Specialist Has Important Viet Role
by Spec 5 Dick Ierardi *(staff writer for MACV Observer)*

**Long Binh, Vietnam (Special)** – Sgt. Carol Mellen has been a waitress, a lithography operator in a factory, a hospital dietary aide, a chef in a pizza parlor and a department store Easter Bunny.

Now she's the only US Army woman communications center specialist in Vietnam.

The petite brunette WAC tends a UNIVAC 1004 computer in the US Army Vietnam Communications Center at USARV headquarters here. The Worcester, Mass., native helps handle the more than 300 messages a day that come into the ultra-secure center from throughout Vietnam. The computer which she supervises receives and transmits at the rate of 1,200 words a minute.

As one of 90 communications center specialists at USARV, Sgt. Mellen has a crucial role in the war effort. The comcenter here is the focal point in the communications network that blankets the country.

Incoming messages are relayed by her computer to teletypewriters. Outgoing messages are typed by the operators and sent out over the wires by the computer.

She joined the Army in 1967, attended signal school at Ft. Gordon, Ga., later that year, volunteered for duty in Vietnam and arrived here in April. She was previously assigned to the Strategic Air Command-Pentagon Telecommunications Center in Washington. *Source:* MACV Observer, *August 3, 1969*

**Rejeanne "Jean" Cecile Marie Tellier (Ridgeway)**
**Retired as a Master Sergeant**
**In country: April 1969 – September 1970**
**Rank: Specialist 5, US Army**
**Duty: USARV, Staff Judge Advocate; 1ˢᵗ Logistical Command**

**Comments and Memories:** When Webb and I accompanied Betty Freeman to visit her boyfriend (who she later married) to a unit lounge, there were no female facilities. Betty nudged her beau to stand guard at one of the three-sided outdoor latrines. I couldn't find the cone because it was dark and my whole leg went in. From then on, I could never get a shine on that boot. I certainly didn't want my boyfriend, Webb, who I had just started dating, to find out what had happened. Betty and I would giggle every time we looked down at that boot. Webb finally told me sometime later that he had known all along. It was quite embarrassing. *Source: Vietnam Memory Book 2000*

**♥Melba "Lin" Sue Lindsey**
**Retired as a First Sergeant**
**In country: April 1969 – October 1970**
**Rank: Specialist 5, US Army**
**Duty: USARV, G4, Administrative Specialist**

 While in Heidelberg, Germany, 1SG Lindsey volunteered for and was sent to USARV Headquarters, Vietnam, in March 1969. She was assigned as Classified Documents Supervisor, G4. Upon completion of her one-year tour of duty, she extended her tour and remained at USARV until October 1970 when she was assigned to Fort McArthur, CA. *Source: Vietnam Memory Book 2000*

**Paulette S. Luxford (Isabell)**
**In country: April 1969 – October 1970**
**Rank: Specialist 5, US Army**
**Duty: USARV, Central Finance and Accounting Office, Clerk-Typist**

**♥Betty Grace Claus (Teager)**
**Retired as a Sergeant Major**
**In country: April 1969 – October 1970**
**Rank: Sergeant Major, US Army**
**Duty: USARV, Casualty Medical Evacuation Division**

Betty Teager has the distinction of being the only WAC of Sergeant Major rank to serve in Vietnam.

**Julianne "Julie" Kubeczko (Viduya)**
**In country: April 1969 – November 1970**
**Rank: Specialist 5, US Army**
**Duty: USARV, Clerk-Typist; US Army Engineer Construction Agency, Vietnam, Administrative Specialist**

Teresa M. Romero
Retired as a Staff Sergeant
In country: April 1969 – November 1971
Rank: Staff Sergeant, US Army
Duty: USARV; US Army Engineer Construction Agency, Vietnam, Administrative NCO

Ruth "Tiger" Arlene Conrad
In country: April 1969 – June 1972
Rank: Staff Sergeant, US Army
Duty: USARV, Central Finance and Accounting Office, Finance Specialist

Edith "Nikki" I. Hayhurst
Retired as a First Sergeant
In country: April 1, 1969 – December 1971
Rank: Specialist 5, US Army
Duty: USARV, 1ˢᵗ Aviation Brigade; Office of the Adjutant General, Administration for POW/MIA/KIA, Clerk-Typist; Special Troops, WAC Detachment, Company/Mail/Supply Clerk

I was stationed at Long Binh, Vietnam, from April 1969 to December 1971. My first assignment was with Aviation/AG where I handled all reports of POW, MIA and KIAs for the region. My first trip in a helicopter with my warrant officer and colonel was a flight over the Saigon River. The pilot took a sharp turn over the river, and I thought I was going to fall into the river because there were no doors where I was sitting. They laughed at me, but I thought I was going to die in the Saigon River!

Our Sundays (only day off) we would go to the orphanage hospital to care for the little children. I remember cleaning this little girl (just a few days old) when the nun told me not to waste my time because the child wasn't going to make it. I kept cleaning up this little girl, holding her close. Not long after I finished, this special little girl died. It was such a hard time for me.

In Vietnam, I had a dog named Mesquite. When I got ready to leave Vietnam, it cost me my whole paycheck to send him back home, but I decided I was not going to leave him behind. I was afraid the Vietnamese would eat him.

Other positions I held were company clerk, postal clerk and supply clerk.

## Barbara J. Rubenstein (Acee)
**In country: April 15, 1969 – January 15, 1970**
**Rank: Specialist 5, US Army**
**Duty: 24th Evacuation Hospital, Long Binh, Clerk-Typist**

My flight to Vietnam was long and silent, and everyone was deep in her or his own thoughts. After arriving and deplaning, I immediately felt a stifling heat. I was directed to an open-air tent lined with beds on either side and told to wait for someone to pick me up. As I entered, I saw another girl heading towards the tarmac; perhaps I was replacing her.

After the ride to Long Binh, I was assigned to and billeted at the WAC compound where I shared a room with three other girls. Initially, I worked in the intelligence area where I contracted pneumonia and was sent to the 24th Evacuation Hospital. During my recovery, I was approached and asked to request assignment to the hospital as the secretary there. My request was granted and I happily worked long hours. I reveled in the idea of helping save lives and loved what evolved into a family atmosphere.

I learned, after the fact, that Army policy restricted assignment of women in Evacuation Hospitals to commissioned nurses. I consider myself unique as an enlisted woman to have had this experience.

I visited the wards in the evenings and recall a Jewish soldier, a quite badly injured patient that I befriended, being Jewish myself. I would stop by his bed and make small talk just to cheer him up a bit. One day he asked me to write a letter to his parents for him. I did that and was heartbroken when the very next day I was typing his death certificate. I wrote a letter to his parents telling them how brave he was. To this day, it is the most poignant memory I carry with me when I think of my time in Vietnam. I'm also very proud that towards the completion of my tour I was awarded the Army Commendation Medal for meritorious service for my work at the hospital.

I spent time off enjoying delicious Chinese dinners at a restaurant (Loon Foon) that had opened near our barracks – or even more likely, at the NCO Club where I was always running into people I had met along my journey in the Army.

In the process of leaving Vietnam, I was dropped off at the same open-air tent where I had arrived, and remember thinking that this girl I just passed is coming to replace my presence somewhere in Vietnam – a little déjà vu.

**Norma Jean Thelen**
**In country: April 30, 1969 – May 29, 1970**
**Rank: Specialist 5, US Army**
**Duty: USARV, 1ˢᵗ Aviation Brigade, Administrative Specialist**

The WAC Detachment in Long Binh actually had air-conditioned rooms. My brother Bob was stationed in Da Nang and visited me prior to his leaving. When he got home, he told my parents no need to worry because I was living in the "Taj Mahal" of Vietnam luxury.

I had great roomies, and they decided to teach me the facts of life. I grew up on a farm in a small, rural town in Minnesota and was really quite naïve. They were great about watching out for me, and I really appreciated them. One time I smuggled two bottles of cognac into our room; of course, the first sergeant found out. We all got restricted because none of my roomies would squeal. She took the cognac but we had some stashed Seagram's which we polished off. I was really hung over the next day; all we had for food was Spam. I have not eaten Spam since, although I still enjoy Seagram's.

I worked in the USARV Aviation Headquarters my entire time in Vietnam. I really did enjoy my work and the people. Whenever an Army aircraft went down, it was called into my group. I took the downed aircraft information and typed up the investigation reports to be sent to Fort Rucker, AL. We worked long hours, usually 12 hours a day, 7 days a week. I would be told by male GIs that my being there meant another man had to go to the field, but I always thought that perhaps another GI got to stay home.

When I first arrived in Vietnam, I was fitted with boots about two sizes too large because of the swelling from the heat and humidity. So I got tagged with the nickname "Boots" and my work group actually gave me a pair of combat boots for my birthday.

Every afternoon they would blow up old ammo. One afternoon it startled me from a nap; I jumped up and went running across the compound toward my bunker rather than the nearest one. Unfortunately, I was wearing only my bikini bottoms because I had been tanning in the sun; after all, I did not want tan lines from the bikini top. Well, that got a few chuckles.

I hated taking the malaria pill, so I figured if I took just a portion of the pill, I would not get malaria; and I would not get an Article 15 because it would still show up in my system.

Running for the bunker seemed to be part of our daily routine. One day the shelling came close to our building. As I went running for the bunker, I saw a newly arrived lieutenant under his desk. Being an old hand at this by now, I grabbed him and we ran to the bunker. After the shelling, we found shrapnel right outside our bunker; but the building was intact.

# MAY

*Memory Lane: Apollo 10 transmits first color pictures of Earth from space; Walt Disney World construction begins.*
*Song: "These Eyes" by The Guess Who*

**D. "Dee" Ann Sims (Antomattei)**
**In country: May 1969 – October 1969**
**Rank: Specialist 4, US Army**
**Duty: USARV, G2, Clerk-Typist**

In 1967, my first permanent duty station was at Fort Hood, TX. I worked in G2 Military Intelligence. I was proud to be a member of the Armed Forces of the United States!

After hearing the stories from a woman who recently returned from Vietnam, I was certain right then and there that I wanted to volunteer. I didn't get orders right away, though. First, I went to an Air Force base in Colorado. My orders for Vietnam came through about eight months later, and my supervisor recommended that I take some leave first. I spent some time with my family in TX. My Dad, a WWI veteran who served in France, was quite proud of me! Despite some severe anxiety attacks, I felt that I would do fine in Vietnam because of my strong faith in GOD!

Conversation on the plane was practically nonexistent – it was a quietness that was eerie to say the least! Arriving at Bien Hoa Air Base, we were greeted by a sun that was so HOT that my first thought was, "This is what hell must feel like!" Arriving at Long Binh USARV WAC Detachment, everything and everyone came across to me as unorganized. A couple of days later, I was aware that I might need to locate myself a work site. I remember asking around if there was a military intelligence unit on post. I went there and discovered the unit was short on staff personnel, asked if I could work there, and was warmly greeted and accepted as a co-worker.

There were four women assigned to a barracks room, twin-sized type beds, a wall or footlocker at the end of the bed, perhaps a dresser with a mirror shared by all four roommates. So thankful that we ladies had air conditioning! Felt really sad for the men on post who were billeted in hot "hootches!" I noticed that my skin tone became a deep, deep, dark tan, with blisters and wrinkles from dry skin and the effects of exposure to the extremely hot sun. I remember glancing in the mirror and at times, not recognizing my own face!

Mail was very important to us. The commanding officer of the WAC Detachment sent letters to all parents, informing and encouraging family members and friends to write as often as possible. Whenever a WAC received a goody box of snacks from the States, everyone at the Detachment knew about it, and the contents of the box were shared by all!

We each had a mama-san whose duties were to clean our fatigues and boots. I adored my mama-san. I made sure at the mess hall that I acquired some fruit for her to eat. I knew she was always hungry and didn't have adequate food. She ate beetles, bugs, rats, whatever she came across crawling! Mama-san's only income was from cleaning for the military.

Day-to-day life was repetitious – a few hours of sleep at night, waking early to dress and go to the mess hall to eat breakfast before work. Long hours meant coming back from working, showering, and then usually too worn out physically to even go to dinner in the mess hall, so spending an hour or two in conversation with my roommates before we shut our eyes to sleep. We had an enclosed patio area on the compound where movies were shown. But, because we were tired all the time, we seldom ever ventured out to the patio.

While in Saigon, I remember going into a tailor shop and ordering three traditional Vietnamese dresses. I even had an oil painting done of me in uniform by a professional Vietnamese painter.

Another time while in Saigon I was accompanied by a co-worker and we ate dinner at a Vietnamese restaurant, later went to the Saigon Zoo.

When there were incoming mortar rounds, we went to bunkers which were surrounded by sandbags. After being in Vietnam for several months, stress began to take a toll on me physically and mentally. Whenever I became distraught or deep depression set in, I pulled on my hair and rubbed the edges of my temples often until I made my head bald in that area. I knew I had to get away to somewhere, anywhere, before I completely lost my mind. I decided to take R&R. I went with three other WACs to Hong Kong, China. This seven-day trip was what we all needed to get our grip back on life. Vietnam was a life-changing experience like no other, a place in Asia where only a small percentage of military women can proudly say that they served! I will always cherish the memories of serving in the military of the greatest country in the world – the United States of America!

**Barbara J. Devlin**
**Retired as a Lieutenant Colonel**
**In country: May 1969 – April 1970**
**Rank: Captain, US Army**
**Duty: USARV, Long Binh Army Depot, Stock Control Division**

I graduated from East Stroudsburg State College in 1960 with a Bachelor of Science degree in Health and Physical Education, and a General Science minor. From 1960-1963, I taught Physical Education and General Science, coached softball, basketball and field hockey at Fairfield Jr/Sr High School in Fairfield, PA. I also taught First Aid for the American Red Cross.

From 1963-1966 I was Assistant Director of the Physical Education Department at Penn Hall Prep School and Junior College in Chambersburg, PA, teaching P.E., Athletic Theory, Anatomy and Physiology, and coaching field hockey, basketball and softball.

In May 1966, I was sworn into the US Army as a first lieutenant and served until I retired as a lieutenant colonel in August 1986. Among my career assignments were: Assistant Chief Firepower, Mobility Branch, Stock Control Division at Long Binh, Vietnam; WAC Recruiting Officer for Eastern PA, Delaware and South Jersey; Army Logistics Division with the National Guard Bureau, Pentagon; Assistant Chief of Staff for Services in Taegu, Korea; and Chief of the Supply, Maintenance and Services Division, 2nd Army Headquarters, Fort Gillem, GA, working with all Army Reserve and National Guard units in the southeastern US, including Puerto Rico and the Virgin Islands. Over my career, I received the Bronze Star Medal, the Meritorious Service Medals and the Army Commendation Medals.

The Army provided me with opportunities to travel to other countries including Sidney, Australia; Okinawa; and the Philippines. I have also traveled and camped in the mainland US and Alaska, as well as Canada. In January 1999, I went to Honduras with a church group to rebuild houses after Hurricane Mitch.

**Connie F. Conlin**
**In country: May 1969 – May 1970**
**Rank: Specialist 4, US Army**
**Duty: USARV, Administrative Specialist**

***Marsha "Cricket" Holder:*** Connie Conlin was one of my many roommates at the WAC Detachment and the only one I have been unable to locate. She was a spunky lady with red hair and always laughing and having fun. Don't think she took anything seriously, even being in a war zone. Don't remember where she was from or even where she worked at USARV.

**Janie R. Miller**
**Retired as a Lieutenant Colonel**
**In country: May 1969 – April 1970**
**Rank: Major, US Army**
**Duty: USARV, 1ˢᵗ Logistical Command, Personnel Staff Officer**

In early 1969, I was completing two and half years at Third Army Headquarters, Fort McPherson, GA, and it was time to fill out my preference sheet for my next assignment. I don't recall what I listed as my preference for a stateside assignment; but, when I got to the overseas preference, I listed Europe, specifically Germany, because I had been in Heidelberg as an enlisted woman and wanted to return. My second choice was Vietnam because  my boss at Third Army had spent two tours there and kept telling me that's where the action is and you need to get that on your record. Well, the ink was not dry when I got orders for Vietnam!

I was surprised and excited about the assignment and quickly made arrangements for someone to care for my little dog. There was a Tet Offensive just prior to my departure, which made me a little nervous, but everything was under control when I arrived at Long Binh in May 1969. I was assigned to Saigon Support Command, a subordinate unit of 1ˢᵗ Logistical Command. My boss was LTC Frances Weir, the Assistant Chief of Staff for Personnel. I was her deputy. We were the only two military women in the command. My primary job was to assign new officers arriving in the command.

I had several secondary jobs, one of which was Graves Registration Officer. One incident has remained very clear in my memory. The mortuary was at Tan Son Nhut, several miles from Long Binh. I had to make a trip there to assess the personnel needs of this facility. On my initial visit, helicopters were arriving with soldiers killed in a recent firefight. I watched as they unloaded these young men, placed them on one of the stainless steel tables for processing, and finally placed them in black body bags for shipment home. I made many trips to that facility and could always smell the formaldehyde long before we arrived. My driver and I always wore flak jackets on these trips, and he was always armed. He would say to me, "Major, hang on because we're not stopping for nothing!" as we barreled down the highway and through the streets of Saigon.

We had frequent rocket attacks and quickly learned the difference between the sound of incoming and outgoing rockets. We usually dived under our bunks or desks instead of going for the bunker. It was quicker. Besides, when the siren sounded, it was too late anyway because the attack was over.

There were fun times as well. I had my own jeep for transportation, and although we were on duty seven days a week, 12 hours a day, we got together in our compound after hours for cocktails and stories of the day. Female officers lived in very old house trailers that were surrounded by revetments to protect from shrapnel. We scrounged parachute canopies and erected them over big electrical cable spools for an outdoor picnic area. Long Binh had been scraped bare of any vegetation so there was red dust in the air and on everything. There were a few palm trees along a small stream that crossed the road on the way to USARV Headquarters and a family of monkeys made it their home.

I completed my tour in April 1970 and returned to the States on a plane full of GIs. When we landed at Travis Air Force Base, CA, the cheers were deafening. Some of the guys kissed the tarmac! When I got to the airport in San Francisco to catch a flight to Atlanta, there were hippies sprawled all over the place glaring at those of us in uniform. Nobody appreciated our service in those days – things are different now in 2014.

I retired in May 1975 with 25 years of service with the rank of Lieutenant Colonel. I would do it all over again!

♥**Beatrice Elizabeth Thompson**
**Retired as a Colonel**
**In country: May 1969 – May 1970**
**Rank: Lieutenant Colonel, US Army Medical**
**Specialist Corps**
**Duty: 8ᵗʰ Field Hospital, Nha Trang, Physical Therapist**

Colonel Beatrice Thompson received a Bronze Star for her service in Vietnam.

♥**Mary E. Manning**
**Retired as a First Sergeant**
**In country: May 1, 1969 – July 2, 1970**
**Rank: First Sergeant, US Army**
**Duty: USARV, Special Troops, WAC Detachment, Third First Sergeant**

**Comments and Memories:** Mary arrived in Vietnam May 1, 1969. She left July 2, 1970, and returned to Kentucky. She was assigned to Fort Knox, Armor School as the NCOIC of Officer Records. She ended her military career there, retiring in May 1973. In 1978, Mary enrolled in Jefferson Community College. She received her Associate in Arts degree in April 1982. She continued her education at the University of Louisville in the Nursing Program. She graduated Magna Cum Laude and a member of Phi Theta Kappa. She was an active volunteer with hospice of Louisville as well as other charitable organizations in the area. She never stopped doing her favorite activities: fishing, boating and taking annual trips to Las Vegas. She maintained her sense of humor and her zest for living during her illness. She died August 14, 1995, due to complications of a stroke suffered earlier.

Written by Colonel Shirley Ohta for the Vietnam Memory Book. *Source: Vietnam Memory Book 2000*

♥**Lillian Emily Baker**
**Retired as a Lieutenant Colonel**
**In country: May 20, 1969 – May 19, 1970**
**Rank: Major, US Army**
**Duty: MACV, Information Officer**

# JUNE

*Memory Lane: Warren Burger confirmed as US Chief Justice; "Johnny Cash Show" debuts on ABC-TV.*
*Song: "Spinning Wheel" by Blood, Sweat & Tears*

**Barbara D. Bacon**
**In country: June 1969 – June 1970**
**Rank: Specialist 5, US Army**
**Duty: USARV, Special Troops, WAC Detachment, Unit Supply Sergeant and Mail Clerk; USARV Management Analysis, Unit Supply Sergeant**

**Comments and Memories:** I had a six-month break in service upon returning from Vietnam, and when reenlisting, needed mommy and daddy to sign for me, as I was not yet 21. I may be the only Vietnam vet with that experience.

I served in Vietnam at the same time my older brother, Dan, did and visited with him four times in country. He may have been the only man to spend the night inside the WAC compound (supply room.)

One night a landing helicopter caused a huge picture to dislodge from its hook, slide down the wall and crash on my metal bed frame. The glass shattered into a million pieces and fell onto my face in the middle of the night while I was sleeping. Didn't seem funny at that time. *Source: Vietnam Memory Book 2000*

**Susie L. Carter (Houston)**
**In country: June 1969 – June 1970**
**Rank: Specialist 5, US Army**
**Duty: USARV, G1, Clerk-Typist**

♥**Linda Camille Honor**
**In country: June 1969 – June 1970**
**Rank: Specialist 5, US Army**
**Duty: USARV, Administrative Specialist**

**Catherine "Cathy" A. Martin**
**In country: June 1969 – June 1970**
**Rank: Specialist 5, US Army**
**Duty: USARV, Central Finance and Accounting Office,**
**Finance Allotment Clerk**

**Comments and Memories:** During my transition years, I was fortunate to work at several occupations that gave me truckloads of satisfaction and pleasure but very little money. But, you can't have everything, can you? Well now that I have also completed my terminal degree, I would like to report that I have a job that gives me truckloads of satisfaction and pleasure but still very little money.

I am happy to have had the opportunity to serve in Vietnam with a great group of women. It was an experience I will treasure forever. May God continue to bless us.

My funniest memory was the evening I was kissing my boyfriend while sitting on a bunker across the street from the WAC Detachment. I fell off the bunker, skinned my elbow, and tried to get a Purple Heart for being wounded in the line of duty! *Source: Vietnam Memory Book 2000*

**♥Neely Elizabeth Scott**
**Retired as a Technical Sergeant**
**In country: June 1969 – June 25, 1970**
**Rank: Technical Sergeant, US Air Force**
**Duty: MACV, Communications-Electronics Directorate, J6,**
**Administrative Supervisor**

**Betty Jean Stallings**
**Retired as a Lieutenant Colonel**
**In country: June 1969 – June 1970**
**Rank: Major, US Army**
**Duty: USARV, 1ˢᵗ Logistical Command, Plans and Operations, Supply Office, Logistics Officer**

Christmas morning was on a Sunday in 1969. When I went to the dining facility for breakfast, someone asked if I was going to see Bob Hope. That was the first I knew he was coming but he was to be there soon and it would be televised live.

In my office, whoever had the smallest TV went home to get it and we all watched the whole show. It was somewhat disappointing live, because not all of the acts are as good as the excerpts I had seen televised in late January in earlier years. Once when I had to walk down the hall, I realized the same day TV show was coming out of every office; obviously not much work got done that day!

The next day, it was easy to see who had seen the show in person and who had watched on TV. Those who had watched in person were quite sunburned!

My roommate had gone on R&R. I heard a loud noise when I came home from work. I looked around the trailer; saw lots of shrapnel in the bathtub, and other evidences of damage. In my room, the mirror flew off the wall and the light fixture jumped out of its usual position. I heard the siren and went to where we were supposed to go for safety. I was the only woman so I made sure I chatted quite a bit so the men would watch their language (which they did).

The next day someone found the remains of a rocket in my back yard. I eventually turned that over to the Women's Corridor in the Pentagon, where it occasionally comes out on display.

**Marcia B. Jones (Snow)**
**Retired as a Colonel**
**In country: June 1969 – July 1970**
**Rank: Captain, US Army Medical Specialist Corps**
**Duty: 71ˢᵗ Evacuation Hospital, Pleiku; 67ᵗʰ Evacuation Hospital, Qui Nhon, Physical Therapist**

Kathleen "Katie" Kabler
**Retired as a Master Sergeant**
**In country: June 1969 – July 1970;**
**August 1972 – January 1973**
**Rank: Specialist 5, US Army**
**Duty: USARV, Special Troops, Personnel; MACV, US**
**Army Security Agency, 509th Radio Research Group,**
**Personnel Records Specialist**

♥Aida "Rootsie" Ruiz
**Retired as a Sergeant First Class**
**In country: June 1969 – October 1970**
**Rank: Specialist 5, US Army**
**Duty: USARV, G2 Intelligence, General's Staff,**
**Personnel Management Specialist**

**Comments and Memories:** In the morning, you smelled like a rose – uniforms nice and starched. By noon, you smelled like a skunk, looked like a raccoon. After all, mama-san had washed the whole detachment's uniforms in the same water, never took the time to rinse them out! *Source: Vietnam Memory Book 2000*

Annie E. Whitman (White)
**In country: June 23, 1969 – June 22, 1970**
**Rank: Staff Sergeant, US Air Force**
**Duty: MACV, Administrative Specialist**

Patricia "Patty" Vera Babcock (Schmauch)
**In country: June 26, 1969 – June 24, 1970**
**Rank: Specialist 5, US Army**
**Duty: USARV, Central Finance and Accounting Office, Finance Specialist**

Conversion Day (C-Day) occurred periodically, but we never knew when. It was a tedious but necessary task that we didn't especially look forward to because it meant our lives would come to a screeching halt. We couldn't leave the Finance Center until the job was done, some 24

hours later. We had to count every bill of the old MPC (Military Personnel Currency) series and redistribute an exact outgoing amount with the new MPC series. Boy, talk about dirty money! The MPC looked very much like the popular Monopoly game money and the same size. The purpose of this periodic conversion was to keep the VC from getting their hands on our "greenbacks."

One bright, sunny, calm October morning, I was enjoying my walk to the Finance Center, which was just around the block from the WAC Detachment. This was a "calm before the storm" moment. As I approached the entrance, two of our male finance clerks were standing in front of the main entrance. I greeted them with a "good morning, fellas." They blocked me from entering. One asked, "Did you bring your money?" "What?" I asked. I thought they were just joking around. He repeated, "Did you bring your money?" I said, jokingly, "Do we have to pay to come into work now?" "Don't you know it's C-day?" Oh, no! The day I had dreaded arrived. No Vietnamese were allowed on post – no mama-sans, no beauty shop beauticians, no maintenance workers in the Finance Office – darn! It was as though half the population of Long Binh was not there. Hell had just arrived for the next 24 hours!

Hours were spent verifying the count of every bundle of 100 bills in denominations of $1, $5, $10 and $20's, then the bundles were banded into a "brick." We counted this money by hand and also with a money counting machine; it was a great nail trimmer if you lost your concentration as the money passed through the wheels – ouch! How many times can you count to 100 and not go crazy trying to remember where you were in the count? We verified stacks of bricks, which totally covered the surface of a cafeteria-sized table and almost over my head, and there wasn't a crack between the bricks for a cockroach to slip through.

The Finance Office was a beehive of activity. The hours were excruciating and fast-paced. There was a steady stream of officers from on-post, outposts, and front line units, with their guards as they carried out their responsibility of exchanging the 'old' for the 'new' MPC. Some of them looked like they hadn't slept for days. Their camos and boots were covered in red mud, had unshaven faces and hair that probably hadn't seen shampoo for a while. They came directly from the front lines. I prayed for their safe return to their units.

As this continued until late into the night, some of us got a reprieve and were sent back to our barracks. I don't even remember the walk back to the

WAC Detachment; thank goodness it wasn't very far. I had signed in, went directly to my room and promptly fell onto my bunk. I don't know if I had slept for minutes or an hour, when I was awakened by the sounds of sirens and incoming. I didn't want to get up, but I knew I'd be in big trouble with the commanding officer if I didn't head for cover. So, okay, being very groggy, I made my way to the bunker. As I was entering the bunker, I heard someone yell, "Babcock, Babcock, where is she?" Someone replied, "She's probably still at the Finance Center," but I answered, "Present and somewhat accounted for." The bombs kept coming. They fell as close as a city block from our WAC Detachment. As I sat on the bench, resting my head on the sidewall, I remembered my dad always saying, "It'd take a bomb to get you out of bed." He would have loved to have been there to see it for himself.

The following days weren't as intense, but the transition to a new series of "monopoly money" was, at times, humorous and then again, not so humorous. We watched the MPs (military policemen) come and go because some of the soldiers, as well as some of the Vietnamese, tried to exchange large amounts of old MPC for the new MPC. This money usually belonged to some of the Vietnamese who worked on post and were really fencing it for the Vietcong. The soldiers who participated were arrested and eventually let go with an Article 15 or worse. But, this time, Conversion Day, caught the VC with millions of unusable old MPC. Oh, golly darn – our bad!

# JULY

*Memory Lane: First men on the Moon, Neil Armstrong and Edwin Aldrin Jr. from Apollo 11.*
*Song: "In the Year 2525" by Zager and Evans*

**Frances "Frankie" Ann Earle**
**In country: July 1969 – February 1970**
**Rank: Specialist 5, US Army**
**Duty: USARV, Staff Judge Advocate, Legal Specialist**

***From a telephone interview with Phyllis Miller:*** I joined the Army in November 1967 and went to basic training at Fort McClellan, AL. I am one of 10 children. After basic training, I was assigned to Fort Lewis, WA, and worked as a clerk typist in the Judge Advocate General's office. I have heard conflicting stories about Vietnam and our role there, but I considered myself 150-percent patriotic American and I volunteered to go. I wanted to serve my country and that seemed like the best place to do it.

My parents were not happy about it and were very worried about me the whole time I was there. My brother was in Vietnam when I got my orders, but he came home the week before I left.

My flight went out of Travis Air Force Base, CA, through Hawaii. We changed planes in Hawaii so we were there for about 15 minutes! I was the only woman on the plane. When we landed in Saigon, and got off the plane, and I immediately thought that I had made a mistake. To make it worse, I was in dress uniform with nylons and heels and some drill sergeant type immediately got in my face and started yelling that I was in the wrong uniform and I needed to get changed into my fatigues. Of course, I didn't have any fatigues.

The first night I spent in a small building and I had an Air Force woman roommate. She spent the evening imagining all the bad things that were going to happen. The next day, a jeep took me to Long Binh to the WAC Detachment. I have to admit I was taken aback. A guard shack with two guards and barbed wire and fencing? Not what I expected. My first sergeant was Mary Manning. I had three roommates but I don't really remember them – one was Susie.

I worked at the Staff Judge Advocate Office, and there was another clerk typist there, a civil service woman named Linda Wilson. We handled the paperwork for many, many Article 15s (non-judicial punishment for minor offenses; normally administered by a commanding officer). The first sergeants of the units would send up dozens on the privates in their companies – and I have to say that the privates were very disrespectful, especially to the older Vietnamese people. In fact, some of our soldiers were just as badly behaved as we said the enemy was.

During my time in Vietnam was when charges were brought for the My Lai massacre and cover-up. The stories about that were awful!

No doubt I had led a sheltered life, but even with the bad things, I remember how wonderful the Vietnamese people I met were and I don't regret that tour. It was a great experience but it has left me with some serious health issues. I have high blood pressure, chronic depression, and I am being treated for PTSD (Posttraumatic Stress Disorder). You can't see people get their faces blown off and not keep seeing it. I also had to have a hysterectomy, and I heard that several of the women who served there had them. In addition, I have vitiligo – a loss of skin pigmentation – affecting mostly all the skin on my legs.

**Janie M. Brown (Cole)**
**In country: July 1969 – April 1970**
**Rank: Specialist 5, US Army**
**Duty: USARV, Central Finance and Accounting Office, Finance Specialist**

**Marcia Lou Turpin (Beasley)**
**In country: July 1969 – April 1970**
**Rank: Major, US Army Medical Specialist Corps**
**Duty: 43rd Medical Group, Nha Trang; 68th Medical Group, Long Binh, Dietetic Consultant**

I joined the Army in 1959 as a private in my senior year of college at Purdue University under the Army's college student dietetic program. The following year, I served as a Second Lieutenant at Walter Reed Medical Center in Washington, DC, in its dietetic internship program. Upon graduation, I was promoted and went to Fort Riley, KS, and served the two-year payback time as Assistant Food Service Director at the hospital.

I separated from the military and took a position on the faculty at Kansas State University as a director of food service at one of the residence halls. I returned to the Army Medical Specialist Corps and again served at Walter Reed Medical Center, received a master's degree in hospital administration from the Army-Baylor University program, and did my residence at Valley Forge General Hospital (now closed) before my tour in Vietnam.

In July 1969, with the rank of Major, I flew into Vietnam, landing at Bien Hoa. I was greeted by LTC Julia Rosengreen, AMSC, who was the ranking dietitian of the five who were serving at the time in Vietnam. (That was also the maximum number of dietitians who served in Vietnam at any one time.)

Aside from the one dietitian assigned to the hospital at Saigon, our mission was to visit each of the hospitals/medical units monthly, as consultants, addressing their food service and diet therapy services. The country was divided into three sections; I was assigned to the largest, the central section, at the 43rd Medical Group located at the 8th Field Hospital in Nha Trang. As such, I was assisted by one other dietitian, CPT John Harper. I assigned him to our northern area from Quin Nhon to Pleiku. He was stationed at the 85th Evacuation Hospital there. I served the southern area to Cam Ranh Bay but also made visits to our units in the northern area. Each of our 13 units was visited every month by one or both of us.

We each were supported by a Food Service master sergeant, and I also had a Food Service advisor, Warrant Officer Elmer Weishapl. The food service divisions at all our six hospitals were managed by warrant officers and the seven medical detachments by NCOs. Most of the warrant officers had had some experience in hospital food service operations stateside, but their background was limited. It became apparent to me that bringing all the hospital warrant officers together to share successes and problems could be of benefit to all.

I arranged and held the first (and possibly the only) Hospital Food Service Training Conference for food service warrant officers in Vietnam during the fall of 1969. All six of the warrants were able to attend. The two-day/one-night conference included training and sharing sessions, as well as a brief tour of the special features of the city. The warrants were very pleased with being able to share their hospital experiences with others in the same positions.

The dietitians assigned to Vietnam also met in September 1969 and held a conference at the central mountainous village of Dalat. There was an exceptionally fine "farmers" market there. This was also the village where the military worked with the locals, training them to grow vegetables for the troops with the use of appropriate and safe fertilizers. Less than a year later the hotel where we had stayed in Dalat was destroyed in a rocket attack by the Vietcong.

When visiting the units in the northern section of the Group, my staff and I would take food items to the Leprosarium located on the coast at Quin Nhon and operated by Catholic nuns. The nuns would serve us a bowl of soup for lunch, and we would take a short swim before returning to our base. My assistant, CPT Harper, and his master sergeant would often drive a jeep across country to visit the hospital at Pleiku. It was a dangerous road and they would have to take rifles with them for defense. Fortunately, they never encountered any trouble.

The Army treated some local Vietnamese, although the menu was not adjusted to the customary local diet. Our chief dietitian, LTC Julia Rosengreen, did secure and provide us one item that was a staple of the Vietnamese diet. Nuoc mam (sauce), made by fermenting raw fish until the flesh disintegrated, contributed a significant quantity and quality of protein to their diet. One can only imagine the smell of this fish product. The hospitals' nursing staffs were not pleased when we introduced the product to the Vietnamese patients' diet. Just removing the lid from a bottle of nuoc mam caused a most undesirable stench throughout the entire ward.

I took two R&Rs while stationed in Vietnam; one was to the Philippines and one to Australia. The vast majority of my travel in Vietnam was via the medical evacuation (Med Evac) helicopters. This mode was considered the safest. Once we did have to set down over night on an airfield north of Nha Trang due to engine problems, and another time we landed at the edge of our airfield in Nha Trang to learn the hydraulic system on the new chopper we were riding in had just failed.

When I first arrived in country I had to stay at an in-town villa with 43 other Medical Group officers (all men) until a room became available in a villa on the hospital compound where our 43rd Med Group was located. After only a few days, the officers in the villa received notice one evening of a possible attack near the Group headquarters and that they were going to return to the base and that I should stay at this villa in town. That was a tense evening, because I had no transportation to the base or knowledge of how to get back to the headquarters, nor could I speak any Vietnamese to communicate with the Vietnamese who I assumed were at the villa. Other than those small incidents, I had no "near calls" of which I am aware. I was in country during the rocket attack on the 6th Convalescent Center at Cam Ranh Bay, but I was not visiting that medical unit at the time.

In about late January or early February 1970, I was transferred to the 68th Medical Group located at the 93rd Evacuation Hospital in Long Binh as part of the initial drawdown of troops, and our 43rd combined with the 93rd Medical Group. But, shortly before I was transferred, I was hospitalized for a couple of days due to dehydration. In order to drink the highly chlorinated water, we added "Tang" (an orange-flavored concentrate that was developed in the early 1960s for the space mission). This flavoring made the water bearable, but we still did not drink as much as we needed. Milk was not a healthy substitute for water, as the milk was very high in saturated fat from the palm oil used to fabricate the milk.

Upon my departure from Vietnam, I was awarded the Bronze Star for my service there. I transferred directly to Germany with a short leave in the States.

I served in the Army Medical Specialist Corps for 20 years, retiring as a Lieutenant Colonel.

**♥Mary Elizabeth Dowd**
**Retired as a Captain**
**In country: July 1969 – July 1970**
**Rank: Captain, US Air Force**
**Duty: 7th Air Force, 600th Photo Squadron, Administrative Officer**

***Carol Martin Timar:*** Captain Mary Dowd and I met some years back. I've enjoyed her wonderful cooking and hospitality many times in her home in Dolen Springs, AZ. We also served together on the American Legion council and the same for the VFW. She was in Dolen Springs and I was in Kingman, AZ. Mary started out as an enlisted WAF and earned a commission the hard way. We will always remember her as a hard taskmaster but fair. She was never one to speak of her tour in Vietnam. She received the Bronze Star during that tour. I don't remember what the citation said, but I want the sisters to know this. She always had the best to say about everyone. I am very proud to have served with Mary. *Source: Vietnam Memory Book 2000*

**Kathryn A. Dwyer (Feltz)**
**In country: July 1969 – July 1970**
**Rank: Specialist 5, US Army**
**Duty: USARV, Eyes, Nose and Throat Specialist**

**Meredith L. Freeman (Nakabayashi)**
**Retired as a Technical Sergeant**
**In country: July 1969 – July 1970**
**Rank: Technical Sergeant, US Air Force**
**Duty: MACV, Clerk**

**Helen Ruth Gilmore**
**Retired as a Chief Warrant Officer 4**
**In country: July 1969 – July 1970**
**Rank: Chief Warrant Officer 4**
**Duty: USA Support Command, Saigon Army Depot, Personnel/**
**Administrative Officer**

**Linda A. Lesser (White)**
**In country: July 1969 – July 1970**
**Rank: Specialist 5, US Army**
**Duty: USARV, Special Troops Personnel, Personnel Specialist**

**Jeanne R. Moran (Gourley)**
**Retired as a Colonel**
**In country: July 1969 – July 1970**
**Rank: First Lieutenant, US Air Force, Biomedical Sciences Corps**
**Duty: 7th Air Force, 12th Tactical Wing, 12th USAF Hospital; 483rd USAF**
**Hospital, Cam Ranh Bay, Dietitian**

The hospital started with 10 beds in September 1965. The dining facility was completed and occupied in 1968. By 1969, there were 18 wards and 675 beds.

"We have regular rocket attacks once a year," I was told by one of the dietitians serving in Cam Ranh Bay before I volunteered. The first week in country, I flew off the top bunk when sirens alerted us of a rocket attack. There were certainly more than this one during my tour. I never had to touch a weapon in Vietnam, although Strategic Air Command required that I pass through Hamilton Air Force Base, CA, for M-16 training prior to Vietnam departure. I was the only female in the training; there were 84 men.

On August 7, the Cam Ranh Army Convalescent Center was attacked. A number of casualties were treated at 12th USAF Hospital. We later learned that some USAF newspapers identified the event as happening at the Cam Ranh Bay Hospital, not identifying that it was the Army facility. I received a form letter from a dietitian friend to check a block if I was injured or a block if I was OK and a letter of concern from my parents. No fast communication in 1969!

Our hospital kitchen had some great equipment – mixers, meat slicer, meat saw, steam-jacketed kettles and a dishwasher. Ambulatory patients who came to the dining room were often seen staring in awe at a choice of foods on the hot and cold serving tables and milk in a dispenser (although it was milk produced in Vietnam by combining powdered milk, coconut oil and water). There were a lot of challenges for the dietary staff to provide these meals. The dining room was air-conditioned; the kitchen was not. (Think of very high temperatures outside the building and adding heat in the kitchen with ranges and kettles). Getting a vehicle to pick up foods from the Army Procurement Center – miles away – was always difficult. Sometimes food was not even available, i.e., bread did not arrive. Even the most basic therapeutic diets could not be guaranteed. The dining facility was in a modular building with an 8-foot ceiling; thus, the dishwasher was only seven inches off the floor making it hard to clean under. The doors into the tanks did not go up all the way because of the low ceiling. When the dishwasher was broken, we had a paper goods inventory, but there was always the worry that the supply would run out before the dishwasher was repaired.

We usually felt a sense of accomplishment about providing good nutrition to aid in the healing process. Smiles and light-hearted conversation were often exchanged with patients. However, we were sometimes saddened by the realization that our food and smiles could not heal the mental anguish of some. One young sergeant had a birthday a few days after he arrived. The dietary staff baked a birthday cake and, along with some of the ward staff, sang happy birthday to him. This young soldier could not enjoy the moment. Witnessing the loss of a number of men in his platoon and the responsibility he felt deprived him of joy on this birthday and would probably haunt his memories for years to come.

A real Christmas tree arrived for the hospital in December 1969. Four stewardesses on a Seaboard World Flight were injured in turbulence on a flight in July and were patients for a few days before returning to the US. They sent the Christmas tree (decorations included) on a December flight to Cam Ranh Bay as a thank you gift. The tree was placed in the Hospital Dining Room. The harsh reality of war juxtaposed with normalcy sometimes seemed odd.

**Comments and Memories:** The hospital had a refrigerated van. It went into Transportation for repair on August 6, 1969. We got it back February 25, 1970. The storeroom personnel took it that day to pick up rations. The van broke down at ration pick-up and was taken back to Transportation. I never saw it the rest of my tour! *Source: Vietnam Memory Book 2000*

**♥Yvonne "Pat" Celeste Pateman**
**Retired as a Lieutenant Colonel**
**In country: July 1969 – July 1970**
**Rank: Lieutenant Colonel, US Air Force**
**Duty: 7ᵗʰ Air Force, Chief Warning Center, Intelligence Staff Officer**

***Martha N. Stanton:*** Lieutenant Colonel Pateman's story begins with her service in WWII. "I lived for flying." A few weeks after her first flying lesson, she saw a newspaper article describing the Women Airforce Service Pilots (WASP), a new civilian program under the direction of Jacqueline Cochran, the nation's top female pilot. With male military pilots needed in the war zones, qualified women pilots were being sought to ferry the fighters, bombers and transport planes from manufacturers to military bases within the US. The program gradually would expand to include towing targets for anti-aircraft gunnery practice, flying as engineering test pilots and performing other flying tasks. Some 25,000 women applied for the WASP training program; only 1,830 were accepted. Of those, 1,074 earned their wings, of which Pat was one. Her assignment ranged from ferrying aircraft to overseas shipping centers to performing "check rides" on aircraft that had undergone repair. She loved the flying and her job.

In December 1944, after Congress decided the service of the women pilots was no longer needed, the WASP program was disbanded. Pat went home, reluctantly, to return to her job in New Jersey in a General Electric Plant. She told *Airman* magazine in 1991 that she recalled that "I couldn't stand the idea," so she took off for California where she landed a job pumping gas at an airport, and shortly thereafter took on a job ferrying civilian aircraft from factories to buyers, and she became a flight instructor.

In 1949, she accepted a US Air Force Reserve commission as a first lieutenant and was assigned to a Volunteer Air Reserve Squadron. Called to active duty during the Korean War, Pat was assigned to the 78ᵗʰ Fighter-Interceptor Wing at Hamilton Air Force Base as an intelligence officer rather than flight crew since the Air Force did not have women pilots at the time. She served in the Philippines and Japan as an Intelligence Officer.

During the Vietnam War, Lt Col Pateman was assigned as chief of the 7ᵗʰ Air Force Warning Division at Tan Son Nhut Air Base in Saigon. She was responsible for providing intelligence for warning of enemy status/

advancement, particularly monitoring the Ho Chi Minh Trail and assigning targets to F-4 pilots.

Before her 1971 retirement, she was chief of the China Air and Missile Section of the Defense Intelligence Agency. "Pat Pateman had a path-breaking career in both aviation and the military, fields not traditionally open to women during World War II, the Korean War or the Vietnam conflict and not in a desk job or 'a ground-pounder or waffle-butt' as Pat was apt to say," said Deborah Douglas, Curator of Science and Technology at the MIT Museum in Cambridge, MA.

She was an outstanding leader, a gentle and compassionate lady, along with a refreshing sense of humor. In off-duty time, she was considered "a life of the party."

♥Dorcas Ann Stearns
Retired as a Lieutenant Colonel
In country: July 1969 – July 1970
Rank: Lieutenant Colonel, US Army
Duty: USARV, 1ˢᵗ Logistical Command, G4; G1
Support Command, Cam Ranh Bay, Personnel
Staff Officer

Eileen C. Ward (Rossi)
In country: July 1969 – July 1970
Rank: Captain, US Air Force
Duty: 7ᵗʰ Air Force, Intelligence Photo-Radar Officer

Frances "Fran" D. White (Marks)
In country: July 1969 – July 1970
Rank: Specialist 4, US Army
Duty: USARV

Ruth C. Minutoli
Retired as a Lieutenant Colonel
In country: July 1969 – July 27, 1970
Rank: Major, US Army
Duty: US Army Depot, Cam Ranh Bay

**Carmen M. Perez**
**In country: July 1969 – September 1970**
**Rank: Specialist 5, US Army**
**Duty: USARV, Personnel Specialist**

**Gloria "Chico" May Chicoine**
**Retired as a Sergeant Major**
**In country: July 1969 – September 1971**
**Rank: Staff Sergeant, US Army**
**Duty: USARV, Personnel NCO**

**Karen Irene Offutt**
**In country: July 18, 1969 – June 10, 1970**
**Rank: Specialist 5, US Army**
**Duty: MACV, Executive Administrative Assistant**

July 18, 1969, I went to Oakland, CA, with my parents and brother to catch a flight to Vietnam. I didn't have a clue where it was. I had been assigned to the Pentagon and it was while there that I decided I needed to find out what this war was about. There were protests going on and our men were being killed daily. I didn't think it was fair that only the men were risking their lives, so why not me? At Oakland I don't remember being worried or scared. I was excited and proud to be serving my country. I really didn't think it strange, for me, a woman, to be going. When I got on the plane, however, I realized that I was the only female, other than the stewardesses. That seemed a bit odd to me.

We landed at Bien Hoa Air Base, after stopping in Hawaii. I remember the heat and the red mud. Mostly, I remember so many soldiers, outside the plane, cheering. I thought they were cheering for us, but soon figured out that they were cheering because they were leaving the country.

Someone told me to get on a bus, so I did. Windows were covered with chicken wire and I asked an older guy about that. He said it was to deflect the grenades. I recall looking backward, toward the plane, to see if I might be able to get back on it.

The bus took me to Long Binh. I was supposed to have gone to Saigon. I had no clue what to do. I had no uniform, was in the wrong place and the monsoon rains were in full swing. The first night was hell. We were hit all night with rockets and mortars. The place looked like something from the TV show "F Troop." We had several girls in each room and the roof was leaking everywhere, rain plunking into pots and pans. One girl told me that if the incoming got really bad, we'd go to the bunker. I didn't know what a bunker was or where it was. I recall lying there, immobilized, basically paralyzed with fear, knowing that I was going to die my first night in country, as I listened to the concert of war sounds.

I tried to get someone to listen to me about how I was supposed to be in Saigon. I was told I was too young. I was 19 years old. I was not assigned to any unit in Long Binh, so they gave me jobs like wading in their doughboy pool to scoop out giant bugs from the green water. Somewhere in my memory, it seems we passed a medical unit when we went to the mess hall. I recall awful smells and saw people burning things, which I was told were body parts. By the time I reached the mess hall, I wasn't hungry. I really felt that I had been sent to Hell and I wanted out. One day, I wandered down the road and entered a nice, official looking building. I didn't know what it was, but I went in and asked someone if they could call Major General Raymond Conroy's office at MACV (Military Assistance Command, Vietnam). I asked them to tell him that I was in Long Binh and that they wouldn't let me leave. I believe it was that afternoon or the next day that a sergeant major came to the WAC office and asked for me. The women in charge told him that I couldn't go to Saigon because of my age. The sergeant major looked at me and said, "Get your gear!" I got my duffle bag and he put me in a black sedan. We headed for Saigon.

Saigon was a completely different experience. The smells were terrible. There were odors that I thought would never leave my nose. Houses were made from flattened beer cans and cardboard. Children were half-naked, playing in red mud. The poverty was blinding. Children and teens would touch my eyelashes and feel my skin, everywhere I went. Small kids would be out in the streets, trying to sell time with their sisters and mothers, to our soldiers.

In Long Binh, we had officers and sergeants in charge of us. It was more structured, as in the US. Not so in Saigon. No one knew where we were, where we went or when we got in. I was staying at an old hotel, the Medford, next to Third Field Hospital. Women had the top two floors and men had the bottom two. We had a fence in front that looked like the kind you would see behind a catcher in a baseball game. It was to deflect grenades also. We had a one-legged, tiny, old Vietnamese man who slept out front and whose job was to keep the generator going. I was told that, after I left, a grenade did make it over and killed him. Every so many yards, there was a guard station with a small Vietnamese soldier. I thought it ridiculous to think that one of them could ever protect any of us.

I worked six-and-a-half days a week, 12-15 hours a day. It was grueling; but, really, there wasn't much else to do anyway. I first worked for MG Conroy, who was a wonderful man. Sometimes the Secretary of Defense or Secretary of State would be there and I'd have to serve tea from this beautiful silver service. I would get nervous and often spilled it. I never got in trouble though. They all thought it was funny. During my time at MACV, I worked for various generals. Most were pleasant.

A few months after I arrived in Saigon, I was approached by the *MACV Observer* newspaper, to be a "Bunker Bunny," which meant they wanted me to pose for a pinup picture. I did not want to do it, but they kept telling me how much it meant to the troops, to keep up their morale, etc. It wasn't important what I was going through. They wanted me to be a soldier, risk my life, work nearly every hour of the day and also keep up the morale of the men. I finally did the photo shoot. They took pictures of me in a dress, at a zoo. Then, they took me to a TV station and had me put on a large camo top, with just my panties and I was to hug a huge TV camera. I was so embarrassed! When it came to picking the picture, I chose the one in a dress!

In January 1970, there was a fire in the hamlet, next to our hotel. I believe I was home, sick. I had shorts on and was barefoot, but when I smelled the fire, I started yelling for everyone to get out, as I didn't know, at first, if it was our hotel that was burning. I looked out a screened window and saw that it was the hamlet (behind our hotel) that was on fire. This hamlet had cardboard/beer can, 3-sided houses that were on opposite sides of a long alley. The top that joined the houses, from one side of the alley to the other, was made of a thatch-like roof. I went running outside and saw women and kids running back down the alley to get their possessions, pigs, etc. I just started grabbing them and hauling them out to the street. I was only about 120 pounds but I just did it. I believe about 80 families were involved. It made the newspapers back in the States. Eventually, a fire unit came and took over. I went back to my room. It was just another day in Vietnam. Several weeks later, a long declaration from the hamlet chief came to my boss. He had found out who I was and wanted me to be awarded something for what I did. I was put in for the Soldier's Medal, for heroic action. When the time came for me to receive the medal, they told me that it wasn't usually given to women. They gave me a Certificate of Achievement for Heroic Action instead. I didn't care. I didn't think I had done anything big anyway. I just did what my instincts had told me. More than 30 years later, I was finally awarded the Soldier's Medal, in Florida! I was very moved. I was told that I was the 10th woman in history to receive it. I'm not hugely impressed by medals, but it has given me a platform to speak out about veterans' rights, so I'm appreciative.

My constant companion was a parakeet named Perky that I bought in Vietnam. I worked and worked with Perky to teach him/her to talk, but he wouldn't say anything. One day, I told a mama-san that he just wouldn't talk. She told me that he talked all day! Then she told me that he spoke Vietnamese! I cracked up. Perky just wasn't bilingual. I put Perky in quarantine before I left Vietnam and he flew home before me.

# AUGUST

*Memory Lane: Manson family commits Tate-LaBianca murders; Woodstock Music & Art Fair opens in NY State (Max Yasgur's Farm); Hurricane Camille strikes US coastline, kills 259 people.*
*Song: "Honky Tonk Women" by The Rolling Stones*

**Connie McDonald**
**In country: August 1969 – June 1970**
**Rank: Specialist 5, US Army**
**Duty: MACV, 4th Psychological Operations Group; USO Show**

**Carol J. Baker**
**Retired as a Master Sergeant**
**In country: August 1969 – July 1970**
**Rank: Sergeant First Class, US Army**
**Duty: MACV, Administrative NCO**

**♥Carol Anne Martin (Timar)**
**Retired as a Major**
**In country: August 1969 – July 1970**
**Rank: Major, US Army**
**Duty: 24th Evacuation Hospital, Long Binh, Supply**

**Ruth Marie Black**
**Retired as a Lieutenant Colonel**
**In country: August 1969 – August 1970**
**Rank: Major, US Air Force**
**Duty: 7ᵗʰ Air Force, Intelligence Staff Officer**

**Phyllis Rae Egermeier**
**Retired as a Chief Warrant Officer 2**
**In country: August 1969 – August 1970**
**Rank: Chief Warrant Officer 2, US Army**
**Duty: USARV, 1ˢᵗ Logistical Command, 524ᵗʰ Military Intelligence**
**Detachment, G2, Counter Intelligence Technician**

**Comments and Memories:** As the lowest ranking officer in the unit, I had all the miscellaneous titles and jobs, i.e., Morale Officer, Voting Officer, Mail Officer, Historian, Security, Pay Officer for Vietnamese employees, etc. My duties included travel to our other field offices with several trips to Da Nang, Qui Nhon, Cam Ranh Bay, Pleiku and monthly trips down to MACV in Saigon.

Funniest memory: None. I found very little to smile about while there. I was the only female in my outfit and the men did not want a woman there to spoil their fun. It was a lonely war. *Source: Vietnam Memory Book 2000*

**Mary J. Johnson**
**Retired as a Sergeant First Class**
**In country: August 1969 – August 1970**
**Rank: Staff Sergeant, US Army**
**Duty: USARV, Administrative NCO**

## Sylvia Maria Rodriguez
**Retired as a Major**
**In country: August 1969 – August 1970**
**Rank: Captain, US Air Force, Biomedical Sciences Corps**
**Duty: 7ᵗʰ Air Force, 12ᵗʰ Tactical Wing, 12ᵗʰ USAF Hospital,**
**Chief Dietitian**

To me it was a blessing to serve my country in Vietnam. As the hospital Chief Dietitian it was my desire to prepare the best meals possible with what we had available and to have pleasant surroundings. While making rounds in the hospital I saw young soldiers wounded, some with missing limbs, others emotionally disturbed. It was very sad – a time to comfort, a time to hide tears, a time to pray. To me it was very emotional.

I remember one evening when one of our pilots did not return from his assigned round and all the base was still, waiting, praying for his return. It was like family.

I was to check all our female employees, and many times I found plates, silverware even cups hidden under their clothing. Checking around the department building, I found little pouches of marijuana. One day I entered the ladies' restroom and saw one of the employees cutting her face close to the eyebrows and she explained to me she had a headache and was taking the demons out. That way of belief was sad to me.

The beach close to the base was very nice and the sea life was beautiful. Jeannie and I attended services every week and sometimes we visited the Orphanage with the Chaplain. There were many mixed babies, beautiful, that no one wanted. I was very happy when many were brought to the USA.

Had the opportunity to take some helicopter rides with the army dietitians and observed the beautiful vegetation and countryside.

Heard that some people have returned and said the country of Vietnam has progressed a lot and has beautiful tourist resorts. I would like to visit.

**♥Elizabeth "Liz" Ellen Moore (Jones)**
**In country: August 1969 – September 1970**
**Rank: Specialist 4, US Army**
**Duty: USARV, Central Finance and Accounting Office,**
**Finance Specialist**

**Comments and Memories:** My funniest memory is of Casey and I running through the trees by the barracks when all of a sudden she disappeared. She had fallen in a hole. She was unhurt, and we both laughed so hard we almost got sick. *Source: Vietnam Memory Book 2000*

**Marcella "Toni" F. Trujillo**
**In country: August 1969 – September 1970**
**Rank: Staff Sergeant, US Army**
**Duty: USARV, G1, Administrative NCO**

**Joan G. Pekulik**
**Retired as a First Sergeant**
**In country: August 6, 1969 – April 5, 1972**
**Rank: Master Sergeant, US Army**
**Duty: MACV Annex, Headquarters and Headquarters Company,**
**34th General Support Group, Senior Supply Sergeant**

I was in the 34th General Support Group (GSG), the aircraft supply division. The 34th GSG had 600 people in the group, with three battalions, three companies in each battalion and two depots. There was no WAC Detachment. The Group repaired and supplied all rotary and fixed wing aircraft with parts.

The men in my division were all pilots, so I got to fly all over Vietnam. Our 166th Maintenance received a Cobra helicopter from the States and put it together. It became time to test fly it to include different maneuvers. Captain Dirska was supposed to go, but he was not in at the time the pilot called, so I asked if I could go. He said, "Be here in 15 minutes."

So, I grabbed my helmet and drove the jeep to Tan Son Nhut Air Base. To make a long story short, the pilot is behind you; you are in front. By the time we got through the maneuvers, especially diving 500 feet straight down 3 to 4Gs, it scared me to death. A "g" is short for gravity. That means that my body was subjected to 3 to 4 times as much force of gravity than I would normally feel. I thought we would never come out of the dives. When we landed, I walked over to the jeep and threw up.

**Gail Nelson**
**Retired as a First Sergeant**
**In country: August 31, 1969 – December 15, 1972**
**Rank: Specialist 5, US Army**
**Duty: USARV, 9ᵗʰ Army Communications Center; MACV General's Staff, Communications Center Specialist**

First, I would like to thank the United States Government, the US Army and the Signal Brigade for allowing me to serve my country in support of the SEATO Treaty (South East Asia Treaty Organization.)

My first battle as a new Specialist 5 started about six months before I arrived in the Republic of Vietnam (RVN). The Retention NCO at the Presidio of San Francisco kept saying my MOS (military occupational specialty) was tactical, not fixed station. On July 15, 1969, I told him that I worked with a warrant officer and a sergeant first class that served with women in communications centers in Vietnam. He called the Department of the Army, who then called 'P' Signal Brigade, who said, "Send all you've got." Three days later, I had an assignment to Long Binh.

After I arrived, while waiting for my clearance to come through, I did details in the WAC Detachment. One day, SP5 Barbara Bacon told me that Captain Nancy Jurgevich and First Sergeant Mary Manning thought I was a keg of dynamite looking for a place to explode. I still laugh about that.

I was assigned to 1ˢᵗ Signal Brigade. The first three years I worked in the Communications Center as a sergeant, 72B, Communications Supervisor, in support of the USARV Headquarters. I served with SGT Ruth, SGT Linda McClenahan, and SP5 Cynthia Baker. We handled most Army communications to notify the rest of the world to include casualty, Red Cross and logistics. If we did not communicate correctly, the troops did not have chow, ammunition or equipment.

On the WAC anniversary of 1971, I invited one of each rank from private to the Signal Brigade commanding general to a party at the Detachment. I liked messing with the orderly room so I did not inform them I would be having Brigadier General Wilburn Weaver as a guest. I am not sure if Captain Shirley Ohta was upset or not.

On my sixth extension, I was accepted on the General's staff in Operations at MACV and became the noncommissioned officer in charge of nine Army Communications Centers. We received and provided reports up and down the chain of command and ensured directives from Defense Communications Agency were complied with. I worked with SP5 Sandra Torrens who was the secretary for the General.

In September 1972, I was honored to be the enlisted member of a team of two (one officer, one enlisted, normally a command sergeant major) to carry the 1st Signal Brigade colors to Korea. Once the colors left the Republic of Vietnam, 1st Signal Brigade became US Strategic Command (STRATCOM) Southeast Asia.

In October 1972, I attended a mandatory joint service meeting on troop withdrawals. I believed I was just riding shotgun for Major Sharff, but in the meeting a question was raised on Communications Center requirements and he asked me to address the subject to the group.

The 1st Signal Brigade moved to MACV Headquarters. The last mission I completed after 40 months in Vietnam was to prepare a message to all Communications Centers directing them on how to ship or destroy classified equipment/materials upon withdrawing.

It was an honor and a privilege to serve with all of those men and women who provided outstanding communications support.

I completed 23 years of active service and retired as a first sergeant. My last assignment was the First Sergeant of Headquarters, Communications-Electronics Installation (CEI) Battalion, Fort Huachuca, AZ. I had a multitude of specialties and assignments between Vietnam and retirement, but Vietnam was the longest. Overall, I had a very rewarding career.

# SEPTEMBER

*Memory Lane: The first automatic teller machine in the US is installed in Rockville Center, NY; first broadcast of "Marcus Welby, MD" on ABC-TV.*
*Songs: "Give Peace a Chance" by Plastic Ono Band; "Sugar, Sugar" by The Archies*

## Karie Lee Ennis (Clark) (Robertson)
**In country: September 1969 – March 1970**
**Rank: Specialist 5, US Army**
**Duty: USARV, 1ˢᵗ Logistical Command; MACV, 4ᵗʰ Psychological Operations Group, Personnel Specialist**

I joined the Women's Army Corps in July 1967, right out of high school. My father was in the Army and was not happy with my decision. But as the oldest of six children, and having just enough money for essentials and little else, my mother thought it was a great idea.

I went to Fort McClellan, AL, for basic and advanced training where I learned how to type. After AIT, I was sent with the first group of WACs to be assigned to the 2ⁿᵈ Psychological Operations Group, JFK Center, Fort Bragg, NC. I was young, naive and very innocent. Though I had little self-confidence, I was a hard worker. I volunteered with my best friend, Connie McDonald, to go to Vietnam.

At Fort Bragg, I packed Army drab-green wooden footlockers of what seemed like millions of brown personnel file folders of young soldiers en route to Vietnam. I didn't know what the war was about or why I was going except that I felt that if they were all going, so would I.

Before I left, I married a Vietnam veteran who I worked with. My volunteering for Vietnam and upcoming departure made him volunteer to return a second time. We flew to Vietnam together in September 1969.

I was assigned to the WAC Detachment at Long Binh and worked at Headquarters, 1ˢᵗ Logistics Command. I saw my husband a few times before he left to go to Tay Ninh as a company commander. When he was shot, I hopped a helicopter that a friend of mine was flying and flew out to see him in his tent. We had about an hour as I recall.

In the New Year, I was able to transfer to Saigon, 4ᵗʰ PSYOPs, where I worked with my friend Connie, who had already been in the city for six months. In March, I returned to the US at my husband's request, and left the Army.

I served about three years in the military. I had learned to type, which served me well in my future careers as a paralegal/legal secretary, judicial assistant. I used my GI Bill to get a degree in psychology, which helped me get a job as a care coordinator/outreach worker with HIV/AIDS clients.

At 50, after two marriages and two divorces, both to Vietnam veterans, I was ready to see the world. I was accepted into the US Department of State, Foreign Service, where I worked as the executive assistant for a variety of Ambassadors and Consul Generals in many different countries: India, Sri Lanka, Pakistan, Uganda and Afghanistan. My favorite tour, though, was as the first Executive Assistant at the newly opened US Consulate in Ho Chi Minh City (still referred to as Saigon by those of us who were there during the war). I spent three years in Vietnam from 2003 to 2007. I learned so much from the Vietnamese and met wonderful and forgiving locals, some of whom were sent to reeducation camps in the city after the war and returned to work with Americans.

I am retired now and enjoy every day. I look back on my life in awe and often in disbelief that I have accomplished so many things in my lifetime. My life is full now. I have many memories; some are painful, most are pure joy. I learned and experienced many things along the way on my journey through life.

**Alice Faye Anderson**
**Retired as a Senior Master Sergeant**
**In country: September 1969 – August 1970**
**Rank: Technical Sergeant, US Air Force**
**Duty: MACV, Surgeon's Office,**
**Administrative Supervisor**

**♥Christine M. Marx (Head)**
**In country: September 1969 – August 1970**
**Rank: Staff Sergeant, US Army**
**Duty: 18th Military Police Brigade, Administrative NCO**

**Velma A. Anderson (Davis)**
**In country: September 1969 – September 1970**
**Rank: Specialist 4, US Army**
**Duty: USARV, Central Finance and Accounting Office, Finance Specialist**

**♥Linda M. Brackett (Grasso)**
**In country: September 1969 – September 1970**
**Rank: Staff Sergeant, US Army**
**Duty: USARV, Administrative Supervisor**

**Linda J. Eagleson (Dodge)**
**Retired as a Sergeant First Class**
**In country: September 1969 – September 1970**
**Rank: Staff Sergeant, US Army**
**Duty: USARV, G2, Administrative NCO**

**Rhoda C. Hay (Blitch)**
**In country: September 1969 – September 1970**
**Rank: Specialist 5, US Army**
**Duty: USARV, 1ˢᵗ Aviation Brigade**

**♥Agnes "Scottie" Shirley McLennan**
**In country: September 1969 – September 1970**
**Rank: Staff Sergeant, US Army**
**Duty: MACV, General Abrams' secretary**

***Claire Brisebois Starnes:*** Scottie, as everyone knew her, was short but had a lot of spunk. We called her Scottie because her mother was from Scotland where, once, she took a hop on a diplomatic plane to visit her. She carried a British passport. As General Creighton Abrams' secretary, she had little free time to herself. And, when she did, she liked to read. She would occasionally join some of us in our small kitchen on the fourth floor of the Medford Hotel when she smelled something cooking. I remember one evening when a group of Aussies showed up for a special dinner we were making. After much spirit and good cheer, they could not go back to their barracks. Scottie hosted them in her room, and she slept elsewhere. We had become good friends; she and I went together to Taiwan on R&R. Scottie got her wish of being assigned to embassy duty (Uruguay) after Vietnam.

Elaine James remembers that when Scottie left for embassy duty, her household goods were packed, crated and shipped. When the crates arrived and were opened, somewhere along the way, all her household goods had been stolen, and the crates filled with rocks.

***Anna Hildalgo Dennett:*** I remember (Scottie) as an extreme perfectionist. She'd literally jump over furniture to answer the general's phone right away. She always sat up perfectly straight in the car so as not to wrinkle her uniform blouse! The only time she got off was when the general went to Bangkok to visit his family, or to Washington, DC. I also recall that she loved the Aussies.

Her roommate remembers having maybe 15 or so Aussies racked out on the floor one night.

**Queenola Nelson**
**In country: September 1969 – September 19, 1970**
**Rank: Specialist 4, US Army**
**Duty: USARV, Clerk-Typist**

Delores E. Reid

Margaret "Peggy"
E. Walker

Kathleen "Dee"
Deschamps (Poole)

**Delores E. Reid**
**In country: September 1969 – September 1970**
**Rank: Staff Sergeant, US Army**
**Duty: USARV, Personnel NCO**

**Donna L. Stephens**
**Retired as a Sergeant First Class**
**In country: September 1969 – September 1970**
**Rank: Staff Sergeant, US Army**
**Duty: USARV; MACV, Office of the Adjutant General, Administrative NCO**

**♥Margaret "Peggy" E. Walker**
**In country: September 1969 – October 1970**
**Rank: Specialist 5, US Army**
**Duty: USARV, Office of the Secretary General Staff, Administrative Specialist**

**Kathleen "Dee" Deschamps (Poole)**
**In country: September 1969 – November 1970**
**Rank: Specialist 5, US Army**
**Duty: USARV, 1st Logistical Command, 18th Military Police Brigade, 8th Military Police Group (CID), Personnel**

**♥Doris Darleen Fuller**
**Retired as a Sergeant First Class, USAR**
**In country: September 1969 – November 1970**
**Rank: Specialist 5, US Army**
**Duty: USARV, 1st Logistical Command, Office of the Inspector General;**
**USARV Provost Marshal Office, Executive Administrative Assistant**

**Comments and Memories:** As I was coming into the compound one afternoon, we started to get bombed. One landed right next to our building. I knew Cathy Messer was off that day, so I ran to find her (we had been stationed together at Fort Myer, VA). She was in the shower. So, while she was getting out, I ran to get her equipment. When we got into the bunker, I noticed she still had soap all over her face, legs and arms. I asked her about it, and she said, "It's all over my body and it's drying. It's making me very itchy!" The bomb had struck our water supply. When it was safe to leave the bunker, Cathy jumped into the pool to rinse off. She later stood under the eaves during a rainstorm to get the residue from the pool and the rest of the soap off. *Source: Vietnam Memory Book 2000*

**Elizabeth "Gail" G. Meyer (Tullis)**
**Retired as a Lieutenant Colonel**
**In country: September 1969 – December 1970**
**Rank: Captain, US Army**
**Duty: MACV, J2, Counterintelligence Officer**

**Gayle B. Neave**
**In country: September 1969 – March 1971**
**Rank: Captain, US Air Force**
**Duty: Headquarters 7th Air Force, Historical**
**Division, Administrative Officer**

**Kimberly Y. Taylor (Johnson)**
**Retired as Chief Master Sergeant**
**In country: September 1969 – March 1971**
**Rank: Sergeant, US Air Force**
**Duty: MACV Headquarters, Office of the Deputy Chief of Staff**

Applying for a worldwide assignment and getting assigned to Saigon, Vietnam, was one of the best decisions I could have made and I believe set me on the path for the very successful career I had in the Air Force. I was fortunate to work for the Deputy Chief of Staff for MACV Headquarters, an Air Force General Officer who taught me so much and pushed me toward getting my college degree.

I arrived at Tan Son Nhut in September 1969 without a clue of what to expect as far as the job, the country and the people. I returned to the States 18 months later with a whole new mind set of working with Joint Services personnel, civilian personnel and the local Vietnamese citizens. The many acquaintances met during this time in my life will never be forgotten and remain vivid in my mind although there has been no contact in more than 25 years. The opportunity to meet dignitaries, such as Bob Hope and his USO groups, Neil Armstrong after his famous walk on the moon, and the loveable and adorable Martha Raye is priceless. And, of course, who could ever forget the gruffy, yet big teddy bear, MACV Commanding General Creighton Abrams who promoted me to Sergeant (E4) on my 21st birthday. The good ole days!

**Helen June Varden**
**In country: September 1, 1969 – August 14, 1970**
**Rank: Sergeant, US Marine Corps**
**Duty: NAVFORV, Administrative Specialist**

**Diane L. Potter**
**In country: September 1, 1969 – August 30, 1970**
**Rank: Corporal, US Marine Corps**
**Duty: NAVFORV, Marine Corps Personnel Section,**
**Administrative Specialist**

## Mary Frances "Fran" Draisker
**In country: September 3, 1969 – September 3, 1970**
**Rank: Captain, US Air Force**
**Duty: 7ᵗʰ Air Force, Out Country Intelligence, Intelligence Officer**

Out Country Intelligence had responsibility for reporting all military and political information on all countries in Southeast Asia except South Vietnam; that was In Country Intelligence's responsibility. For example, not only did we report on Hit and Downed aircraft, Missing in Actions, Search and Rescues, Killed in Actions, Surface to Air missile firings, Antiaircraft firings, and radar pings outside of South Vietnam, but also troop and supply movement to South Vietnam through Laos and Cambodia and political leanings of China and the other countries surrounding Vietnam.

My "normal" work week was 7 a.m. to 7 p.m. Monday, Wednesday and Friday; 11 a.m. to 11 p.m. Tuesday, Thursday and Saturday; 9 a.m. to 4 p.m. Sunday (an hour off in the morning to go to church services); and on-call any hour. The reason for the non-regular schedule was because the colonel in charge of the unit didn't want a female on duty at night when he wasn't there and the major in charge of my branch had to finagle hours between a male captain (who could brief the generals) and myself (then a first lieutenant, who didn't get to brief the generals – because she was female and the colonels didn't "think" the generals would want a female briefer). About halfway through my tour, I did get to take over the Saturday morning weekly wrap up for colonels and below, after a female from In Country Intelligence briefed the generals when there was no male briefer available and the generals didn't complain. Also, because I got off at 11 p.m. and had to be back at 7 a.m., one time when there was a rocket attack on the base I slept through it! I knew the noise wasn't my alarm and I wasn't about to get up until it was time to go back to the office.

Carrying a side arm and going out by the perimeter to burn classified material was "interesting." The most memorable event, however, was a three-day Search and Rescue (SAR) effort. My branch had to keep the "Hit and Downed Aircraft" and "Missing in Action/Killed in Action" statistics, so we got all the reports on these sorties. When they were going on, we hung around the office as many hours as our bodies would do without sleep. The result of this three-day SAR effort was the loss of an A-10 support aircraft and its pilot, but the recovery of the two-man jet fighter crew.

Other brief memories: Major General Jeanne M. Holm visiting us at Tan Son Nhut; meeting Yvonne Pateman, a female intelligence colonel who had been in the Women's Auxiliary Ferrying Squadron (WAFS) during World War II who was still authorized to wear wings at a time when women in the Air Force couldn't fly; losing weight from 116 to 104, the skinniest I was as an adult; a fellow officer getting a sandwich at the Officers Club with a cricket in it saying that he'd take it back, but they would charge him extra for the "delicacy;" my BOQ being across the street from the Vietnamese Air Force morgue; learning to eat peanuts with chop sticks; being told to put my valuables in my boot the two times I got off to go to downtown Saigon; going sailing for the first time in my life in Sydney Harbor when I went there on R&R; saving up my combat pay and paying off my student loans early; trying to get a Bronze Star for the master sergeant in our branch and being told they were only for officers; staying awake all night playing bridge with two colonels and a major before my 4 a.m. check-in for my flight home, so I was sure I wouldn't over sleep and miss my flight; the flight home being low on fuel, so it landed at Seattle to refuel and they kept us on board and the "joke" passed from row to row was that we survived our 365 days in Vietnam only to die when the plane exploded during refueling.

# OCTOBER

*Memory Lane: Hundreds of thousands in antiwar demonstrations across the US; Wal-Mart incorporates as Wal-Mart Stores, Inc.*
*Song: "Hot Fun in the Summertime" by Sly and The Family Stone*

♥**Carrie Minette Gray (Richmond)**
**In country: October 1969 – March 1970**
**Rank: Specialist 4, US Army**
**Duty: USARV, G1, Finance Specialist**

**Gwendolyn L. Mitchell**
**In country: October 1969 – March 1970**
**Rank: Specialist 4, US Army**
**Duty: USARV, 1st Logistical Command, Clerk-Typist**

**Donna P. Baldwin**
Retired as a Sergeant Major
In country: October 1969 – October 1970
Rank: Staff Sergeant, US Army
Duty: MACV, US Army Security Agency, 509th Radio Research Group, Personnel NCO

**♥Louise Jenny Giacomuzzi**
Retired as a Sergeant First Class
In country: October 1969 – October 1970; October 1971 – February 1972
Rank: Staff Sergeant, US Army
Duty: USARV, G1, Personnel; Tactical Headquarters, Administrative NCO

**♥Jessie Ann "Greg" Gregory**
Retired as a Master Sergeant
In country: October 1969 – October 1970;
October 1971 – October 1972
Rank: Staff Sergeant, US Army
Duty: USARV, G4; Long Binh Army Depot,
Inventory Control Center, Unit Supply; Special
Troops, WAC Detachment, Supply Clerk

**♥Margaret Mary Jebb**
Retired as a Lieutenant Colonel
In country: October 1969 – October 1970
Rank: Lieutenant Colonel, US Army
Duty: USARV, Engineer Division, Real Estate Officer

**♥Bernice "Bonnie" A. Myhrwold**
Retired as a First Sergeant
In country: October 1969 – October 1970
Rank: Sergeant First Class, US Army
Duty: USARV, Special Troops, WAC Detachment,
Field First/Administrative NCO

**Peggy Lou Patterson**
Retired as a Major
In country: October 1969 – October 1970
Rank: Staff Sergeant, US Army
Duty: USARV, 1st Aviation Brigade, Personnel NCO

♥Patricia L. Schlaht (Ernst)
Retired as a Major
In country: October 1969 – October 1970
Rank: Major, US Army
Duty: MACV, Support Command, Protocol Officer, Qui Nhon

♥Patricia "Pat" Jane Whalen
Retired as a Staff Sergeant
In country: October 1969 – October 1970
Rank: Specialist 6, US Army
Duty: USARV, G4, Firepower/Mobility Section,
Illustrator

**Aurora Gibson (Toth)**
In country: October 1969 – November 1970
Rank: First Lieutenant, US Air Force
Duty: 7th Air Force, Tactical Reconnaissance Squadron,
Administrative Officer

**Oneta "Pat" Arlene Harrington**
Retired as a Sergeant First Class
In country: October 1969 – November 1970
Rank: Staff Sergeant, US Army
Duty: USARV, 1st Logistical Command, Transportation, Personnel NCO

It was the responsibility of some of us to take the early bus to open our offices. The bus would stop by the company and then go around the hospital mess hall and back by the company and continue on to USARV 1st Logistical Command. This one morning, I was on the bus coming back to the company. I had a feeling I should get off the bus. I tried to get Dobbie aka Sylvia Dobson and the rest of our

friends to get off. They thought I was crazy so they planned to stay on the bus until they reached the golf course. The mortars started to come in and the young driver didn't stop. He turned right and then left toward USARV and the medical unit. Thank God it was early. There were no troops out yet. The medical unit took a hit. The injured driver finally stopped. The bus was slightly on its side so Dobbie and the rest of our friends were able to climb out. But after the all clear, Dobbie really let me have it! I did get her attention though.

**♥Barbara "Bobbie" Ann Cramer**
**Retired as a Staff Sergeant**
**In country: October 1969 – April 1971**
**Rank: Staff Sergeant, US Air Force**
**Duty: MACV, J4, Logistics and Pacification, and Civil Operations and Revolutionary Development Support (CORDS), Administrative Supervisor**

Upon arrival in Vietnam, I shed my Air Force clothes for Army green fatigues and went to work as assistant administrative supervisor for Civil Operation and Rural Development Support (CORDS) at MACV. In other words, I worked for the US Foreign Service and CIA under American Ambassador William Colby on a monthly nationwide survey of rural Vietnamese people. When the National Security Advisor, Henry A. Kissinger, arrived every third month, I was assigned as his personal typist.

While assigned to MACV CORDS, I had the occasion to see my baby brother again. He was grown up by then and served as an Army Personnel Officer at Bien Hoa, about an hour's drive from where I lived. Once a month, I got out of Saigon via medical helicopter to visit small hamlets and assist in the treatment of the sick and injured.

Saigon had a bad pollution problem from the mopeds, diesel trucks, military vehicles and especially the garbage piles that dogs, cats, bats, women and children rummaged through for food. My eyes were always feeling gritty, and the exhaust and pollution made breathing difficult. The nights made me uneasy. I could hear scattered gunfire from the surrounding area. Military quarters were always on the alert for a hand grenade, which we had once, but no real damage done, but sure caused a lot of noise and scared people. After curfew began (2300 hours), the black nighttime sky became daylight from the flares. We could hear the distant thunder of the artillery fire. Our quarters [the Medford] were under the [3rd Field Hospital] flight pattern, and the medical helicopters would constantly fly the seriously wounded men from the battle areas.

One night on the roof [of the Medford] during a party, we came under sniper fire, and all of us hit the deck on our tummies and crawled to the wall. We (men and women) held hands during the duration of about 40 minutes. The best part? Not one of us spilled our drinks when we hit the deck!

**Comments and Memories:** I thought my tour in Germany prepared me for Vietnam. WRONG! When I stepped off that plane at Tan Son Nhut, the odor and heat almost knocked me to the tarmac. What an acclimation I needed! *Source: Vietnam Memory Book 2000*

**Virginia Grant**
**Retired as a Master Sergeant**
**In country: October 1969 – May 5, 1971**
**Rank: Specialist 4, US Army**
**Duty: USARV; MACV, Logistics, Administrative Specialist**

**Rebecca R. Carlson (Gardner)**
**Retired as a Command Sergeant Major**
**In country: October 1969 – June 1971**
**Rank: Specialist 5, US Army**
**Duty: USARV, Executive Administrative Assistant**

**Mary M. Cartwright**
**Retired as a Major**
**In country: October 1969 – July 2, 1971**
**Rank: Captain, US Army Medical Service Corps**
**Duty: 12th Evacuation Hospital, Cu Chi; MACV, Surgeon's Office, Clinical Laboratory Technician**

**♥Mary Ellen Johnson**
**Retired as a Sergeant Major**
**In country: October 1969 – October 1971**
**Rank: Sergeant First Class, US Army**
**Duty: USARV, Personnel NCO**

## Mary Virginia Parker
**In country: October 1969 – December 1971**
**Rank: Specialist 5, US Army**
**Duty: Long Binh Army Depot and Cam Ranh Bay Army Depot**

*Telephone interview, October 25, 2014:* I joined the Army when I was 21 years old. Originally I had planned on joining the Air Force, but I thought the Army offered women more opportunities. I did basic training at Fort McClellan, AL, and advanced training at Fort Jackson, SC. Then it was back to Fort McClellan as cadre in either Company B or Company D. My parents weren't too happy when I got orders for Vietnam. When I arrived, the first night was spent in a small billet, by myself, and I had no instructions on what to do if anything happened. Sure enough, there was a mortar attack. I was really scared!

My orders said to report to the Depot at Cam Ranh Bay, but when I got there, they told me only female officers could be assigned there and I was sent to the WAC Detachment at Long Binh. After a few months, Mary Darr and I went back to Cam Ranh Bay. We were billeted in a small building that had four bedrooms, a sitting area, small kitchenette and a communal shower/toilet area. There were only three of us in the building so we had our own rooms. As one of our duties, we did pat-downs of the Vietnamese female workers. One of their common tricks was to conceal stolen padlocks in their rolled up hair. They disliked having to take it down when we thought there might be a problem.

I went on R&R by myself to Thailand, and had one trip back to the States. My favorite souvenir from my Vietnam tour is a crossbow I got from a Montagnard soldier. From Vietnam, I went to an assignment in Korea and when I returned, it was to an assignment at Fort Knox, KY. It was very different after the Women's Army Corps was dissolved in 1978 and I did not like it, so in 1981, I left military service.

## ♥Rosemary Lee Davis
**Retired as a Major**
**In country: October 27, 1969 – October 1970**
**Rank: Major, US Army**
**Duty: MACV, Joint Staff, Second Junior Officer Advisor to the Vietnam Women's Armed Forces Corps**

# NOVEMBER

*Memory Lane: US President Richard M. Nixon addresses the nation, asking the "silent majority" to join him in solidarity with the Vietnam War effort, and to support his policies.*
*Songs: "Come Together" by The Beatles; "Wedding Bell Blues" by The 5th Dimension*

♥**Barbara "Bobbi" Ann Duerkop (Biermeier)**
**In country: November 1969 – November 1970**
**Rank: Specialist 5, US Army**
**Duty: USARV, Central Finance and Accounting Office; Office of the Inspector General, Administrative Specialist**

*Patty Babcock (Schmauch):* Bobbi and I were best of friends during our time in Vietnam. Bobbi arrived in November 1969, five months after I got there. Her first job was in administration at the Central Finance and Accounting Office for about five months. She then transferred to the "Hill," USARV Headquarters, until she left in November 1970.

We would go the Finance enlisted and Post enlisted clubs often, and we were always treated with respect. Whenever Finance had an occasional party at the club, Bobbi and I were designated to decorate for the occasion. We did the Valentine's Day party, with a 5-foot red heart painted on the wall. Pictures were taken of us with Colonel Ledford, Finance commanding officer.

We were hostesses for the Bob Hope Show in December 1969. We didn't get to meet Bob Hope himself, but we did have enjoyable moments with Connie Stevens and the Gold Digger Dancers.

For R&R, we went to Hong Kong, in May 1970 – my second trip to the area. We really enjoyed all the sightseeing and shopping. My fiancé went to Australia. Darn. When we got back to Long Binh, I had less than a month left in country. Bobbi had about six months to go.

Bobbi was the "sister" I never had. My family was Mom, Dad, seven brothers and me. If I had a sister, I wished her to be like Bobbie. She always had a smile for everyone, always had kind words and was a good friend to anyone she met and mostly a joy to be around. God bless you, Bobbi, may you be resting in peace.

**♥Rosalie Ann Fleshman**
Retired as a Sergeant First Class
In country: November 1969 – November 1970
Rank: Sergeant First Class, US Army
Duty: USARV, Materiel Control and Accounting Specialist

**♥Vera "Gordie" I. Gordon**
Retired as a Master Sergeant
In country: November 1969 – November 1970
Rank: Staff Sergeant, US Army
Duty: USARV, Unit Supply Specialist

**Janet P. Jolin**
Retired as a Lieutenant Colonel
In country: November 1969 – November 1970
Rank: Major, US Army Medical Specialist Corps
Duty: 68th Medical Group, Long Binh, Dietetic Consultant

**♥Shirley Jane Marney**
In country: November 1969 – November 1970
Rank: Captain, US Army
Duty: USA Support Command, Saigon Army Depot

**♥Madeline V. Miller**
Retired as a Chief Warrant Officer 2
In country: November 1969 – November 1970
Rank: Chief Warrant Officer 2, US Army
Duty: MACV, 525th Military Intelligence, Counterintelligence
Technician

Madeline Miller first enlisted in November 1943, again in March 1953 and served until March 31, 1974. She was enlisted until June 27, 1969 when she got her commission to Warrant Officer 1. She was promoted to CW2 while in Vietnam. She was a veteran of WWII, Korea and Vietnam and is buried at Arlington National Cemetery, Arlington, VA.

**♥Sylvia Mae "Dobbie" Dobson**
**Retired as a Sergeant Major**
**In country: November 1969 – December 1970**
**Rank: Specialist 5, US Army**
**Duty: USARV, 1ˢᵗ Logistical Command, Comptroller Office**

I remember the mortar attack on March 2, 1970. I had taken the 0600 hours bus to work, had opened the office, made coffee and opened all the top-secret safes. Soon I heard mortar falling very close to my office. In fact, they had blown up the dispensary about 50 yards behind my office. I quickly unplugged the coffee machine, locked all the safes and laid down on the floor in the hallway across from the little chapel across from my office. As I was laying there certain I was going to die, I heard the telephone ring. Guess who? It was Fran Garvey whispering in the telephone. I asked, "Where are you?" She replied, "Under the desk." That made me laugh, and I asked, "Why are you whispering?" She replied, "Don't want them to know where I am!"

The dispensary was totally destroyed with health records blown all over. I really don't think they were aiming at the dispensary but rather the USARV Headquarters and they missed. Really lousy shots they were.

One thing that was hard was having to eat at the 24ᵗʰ Evacuation Hospital. To reach the mess hall, we had to pass all the body bags stacked on top of each other waiting to be transported back to the States. *(Personal email to Claire Starnes, dated August 3, 2000)*

**Sharon "Tommiie" Thomasina Acierno**
**In country: November 1969 – January 1971**
**Rank: Specialist 5, US Army**
**Duty: USARV, Logistics, Administrative Specialist**

There was a big party the night before for all the people leaving at the same time I was. We played cards, talked about all the things we would do back in the States. I had $400 in one of my pockets, but somehow I managed to lose it! Got on that plane anyway and headed back home without any money.

## Dr. Barbara Wirth (Colon), MD
**Retired as a Lieutenant Colonel**
**In country: November 1969 – October 1971**
**Rank: Major, US Army Medical Corps**
**Duty: Surgeon, 3rd Field Hospital, 218th Medical Dispensary,**
**Commanding Officer**

*Telephone interview with Claire Starnes:* Major (Dr.) Barbara Colon volunteered for and arrived in Vietnam in late 1969, and was immediately assigned as commanding officer of the 218th Medical Dispensary in downtown Saigon. She remained in that position until she left Vietnam in late 1971. When she returned to the US, she resigned her commission, renewed her board certification in family medicine and opened a private practice providing comprehensive medical care for families and individuals suffering from all types of illnesses, disorders, conditions and diseases. She operated her practice for 10 years in Howard Beach, NY. In 1989, she joined the US Army Reserve and went to work for the Veterans Administration at the Ainsworth Army Health Clinic at Fort Hamilton, NY, as a contract doctor. On October 1, 2013, the Fort Hamilton/Ainsworth Health Clinic no longer contracted to have a physician on site. She finally retired at 80 years old. Today, she wishes she were still working, saying, "I smell the roses when I'm working – helping people." She fondly remembers her time in Vietnam, but admits she was somewhat disappointed with her assignment as she was hoping to work actively at a hospital.

## ♥Betty Jean Elliott
**In country: November 1969 – November 1971**
**Rank: Staff Sergeant, US Army**
**Duty: Saigon Support Command, 3rd Ordnance Battalion, Civilian Personnel Office, Administrative NCO**

**Comments and Memories:** There were so many funny moments while in Vietnam. We were cooking in our room and incoming rounds had begun. Ruthie and I stretched extension cords from our room to the bunker and continued cooking. *Source: Vietnam Memory Book 2000*

**Marjorie Theresa Rinke**
**Retired as a Sergeant First Class**
**In country: November 1969 – December 1971**
**Rank: Sergeant First Class, US Army**
**Duty: USARV, Special Troops, WAC Detachment, Supply Sergeant**

*Loretta Kornuszko, family member:* In January 1955, Marjorie enlisted in the Woman's Army Corps at the age of 23. Her basic training was at Fort McClellan, AL. She was awarded the Bronze Star Medal for her outstanding efforts and achievements; the National Defense Service Medal; Vietnam Service Medal with one Silver Star; Republic of Vietnam Campaign Medal; and the Sharpshooter Qualification Badge

"Rinke" as she is known to her friends, is very outgoing and fun loving. She enjoyed participating in most sports.

Her last assignment was in Japan. Marjorie enjoyed Japan – its people and culture. Marjorie was stationed there for three years. She retired in January 1978.

*Joyce Oakes Poole:* When I met "Rinkie" – Sergeant First Class Marjorie Rinke – I had just arrived at the WAC Detachment at Long Binh. She was filling in at the orderly room for someone. I would think the first sergeant because of her rank. Rinkie was always upbeat – a happy person. She knew everybody. She was always telling us about going for helicopter rides with her buddies in other units. She wore a piece of chain on her wrist that one of her buddies had given her. She said it came from one of the belts that fed bullets to the machine gun on a gunship. Rinkie usually volunteered to chaperone us on our trips outside the WAC compound. She was older and had more rank than any of us. We got to go on a boat trip that way and to see Saigon. I remember her as a friend to everyone.

**Lillian "Lil" Sanchez**
**Retired as a Staff Sergeant**
**In country: November 1969 – February 1972**
**Rank: Specialist 5, US Army**
**Duty: MACV, J3, Combat Operations, Clerk-Typist**

I worked downstairs in the bunker at MACV Saigon. My job was to move little markers with unit names and numbers across the map, as the units entered Cambodia, and I brought back the markers as they returned to Vietnam. It was a very exciting experience.

**♥Adrienne "Andy" Lee Schamp**
**In country: November 1969 – April 1972**
**Rank: Specialist 5, US Army**
**Duty: USARV, Central Finance and Accounting Office; MACV, 7th Finance Group, Finance Specialist**

**Comments and Memories:** My tours in Vietnam were a defining time in my life. At the request of a friend, I kept a journal during the first year I was in Vietnam. I was recently encouraged to work on it, and now have a short memoir titled, *My Sister Wears Combat Boots.*

One funny memory is being on the patio of the WAC compound watching a movie. Of all things, they sent us "Green Berets." Of course, the movie has a lot of bombing, shooting, etc. While we were sitting there watching the movie, drinking and relaxing, First Sergeant Mary Manning came running out, shouting at us to get in the bunkers. We were quite confused. It turns out we hadn't heard the incoming rounds because of the sound track of the movie. She was upset but understood when we explained what had happened. We all had a good laugh. *Source: Vietnam Memory Book 2000*

**Martha "Marty" N. Stanton**
**Retired as a Major**
**In country: November 4, 1969 – November 4, 1970**
**Rank: Major, US Air Force**
**Duty: MACV, Military History Branch, Field Reporter**

During a tour in Vietnam, 1969-1970, I was a field reporter for the Military History Branch at Headquarters Military Assistance Command, Vietnam (MACV). In this position, I was responsible for preparing authentic historical accounts of activities of Headquarters MACV, the US Service Components, Free World Military Assistance Forces, and Republic of Vietnam Forces.

Specifically, I contributed to the annual MACV Command Histories (1969 and 1970) with classified chapters covering the progress of South Vietnamese Forces in "Vietnamization" of the war. "Vietnamization" was a term applied to the Agreement between South Vietnam President Thieu and US President Nixon in July 1969.

> *The name "Vietnamization" came about accidentally. At a January 28, 1969, meeting of the National Security Council, General Andrew Goodpaster, deputy to General Creighton Abrams and commander of the Military Assistance Command, Vietnam, stated that the Army of the Republic of Vietnam (ARVN) had been steadily improving, and the point at which the war could be "de-Americanized" was close. Secretary of Defense Melvin Laird agreed with the point, but not with the language: "What we need is a term like 'Vietnamizing' to put the emphasis on the right issues." Nixon immediately liked Laird's word.*
> *Source:* Ending the Vietnam War: a History of America's Involvement and Extrication From the Vietnam War, *Kissinger, Henry, Simon & Schuster, 2003*

**Memorable Events:** My memories were all involved with my work. It was serious business that I couldn't talk about or share with other Air Force personnel. Other memorable events, other than events of war, were the two one-week R&Rs – one to climb/hike Mt. Fuji in Japan and the other to Bangkok, Thailand.

**Carol E. Lester**
**In country: November 5, 1969 – October 20, 1970**
**Rank: Staff Sergeant, US Marine Corps**
**Duty: NAVFORV, Marine Corps**
**Personnel Section, Personnel Chief**

**Ruth Evelyn Pitts**
**Retired as a Sergeant First Class**
**In country: November 6, 1969 – February 5, 1971**
**Rank: Staff Sergeant, US Army**
**Duty: 1ˢᵗ Logistical Command, G1; 18ᵗʰ Military Police Brigade,**
**Personnel NCO**

**Comments and Memories:** I flew into Cam Ranh Bay. On arrival, the plane was met by a sergeant about 6'6" tall (I'm 4'11"). As I stepped from the plane, he took one look at me and said, "What the hell are you doing here?" He found me transportation out of Cam Ranh Bay in a hurry. I was flown to Tan Son Nhut in one of those camouflaged planes. I thought we were going to fall into the bay before that plane could get fully airborne. On my arrival at Tan Son Nhut Air Base, I was told I was "on my own" from then on. I was dumbfounded when I learned I had to "thumb" my way to the WAC billet in Long Binh. What a ride. And, yes, I can laugh about it now, but it was not funny at the time it was happening to me. *Source: Vietnam Memory Book 2000*

**Shirley M. Ohta**
**Retired as a Colonel, USAR**
**In country: November 12, 1969 – November 8, 1970**
**Rank: Captain, US Army**
**Duty: USARV, Special Troops, WAC Detachment, Fourth Commander**

I was stationed at Edgewood Arsenal, MD, in early spring 1969, when I first learned that I would be heading for Vietnam.

I left the States, bound for Vietnam on November 11, 1969, from San Francisco, California, a young captain both in age and in military experience. My

previous assignments had been a commander at Edgewood Arsenal, and an administrative officer at Fort Lewis, WA.

I boarded the plane, the only female in a group of combat-ready soldiers, they in their fatigues with full packs, helmets, weapons – me in my Class B uniform which consisted of a green skirt and jacket, hose and heels. I sat there quietly wondering, "What's wrong with this picture?" at one point and "What have I gotten myself into?" the next.

About 25 hours later, we landed in Saigon. I was met by my first sergeant, Mary Manning. I asked her, "How much longer are you going to be here?" because I was hoping we wouldn't have to work together too long. She was scary and intimidating. We drove back to Long Binh to the WAC Detachment. I don't remember how far it was, but the ride seemed like an eternity. After arriving, I was shown to my quarters (a two-bedroom trailer house), and changed into fatigues. We had a change of command ceremony and the previous commander, Captain Nancy Jurgevich left, leaving me as the Fourth Commander of the WAC Detachment at Long Binh.

One of my strongest memories is my first night in the bunkers. I was awakened from a sound sleep, the sirens going off and we had to head for the bunkers. My knees were shaking, my hands were shaking. I put on part of my clothes and grabbed the rest and ran as fast as I could, half-dressed. When I arrived, I was at one end of the bunker, still trying to get dressed and tie my boots. At the other end of the bunker were the rest of the group assigned to this location and then I noticed – they had brought frying pans full of fried chicken, bottles of beer, and were obviously ready for a party. I seemed to be the only one who was holding down those feelings of panic and fear.

At my previous assignment at Edgewood Arsenal, Sergeant First Class Edith Efferson convinced me we needed to get involved in sports. We started a softball team that competed against other teams in the 1st Army. We had fun, they let me play 2nd base, but we never won a single game. When I got to Long Binh, I was pleased to see that the softball team there consisted of all of the women who had been on those teams that had beat us so badly at Edgewood; so now, as their commanding officer, I could finally be on a winning team. And they let me play – still at 2nd base. We played on Sundays against the nurses at the 24th Evacuation Hospital and they never had a chance against our team. I knew how they felt.

Thankfully, I was not awarded the Purple Heart while I was there; but, my trailer did receive it from some of my detachment; I still have a photo of the large Purple Heart mounted on the outside of it. What happened was that some of the Vietnamese maintenance workers came to fix my stove and they failed to turn off the gas. There was an explosion, but the trailer survived.

I turned over command to Captain Marjorie K. Johnson in November 1970, and headed for my next assignment at Fort McClellan, AL.

**Linda "Sgt Mac" J. McClenahan**
**In country: November 15, 1969 – November 12, 1970**
**Rank: Sergeant, US Army**
**Duty: USARV, 1ˢᵗ Signal Brigade, 44ᵗʰ Signal Battalion, Communications Center, Communications Supervisor**

Growing up in Berkeley, CA, in the Sixties, just a few miles from the UC Campus, was very exciting and confusing. While attending Holy Names High School, I made a decision to enter the convent after graduation to become a Sister. But in November of my senior year on the way home on the bus, we were re-routed due to anti-war protests on the campus. Looking down Telegraph Avenue, I could see a police car overturned and on fire. It was that moment when I revised my plans and decided that before I gave my life to God, I would give three years of my life to my country. When I graduated in June 1967, I entered the US Army WAC (Women's Army Corps). I was a "spit and polish troop" and was promoted to sergeant in March 1969 with less than two years in the service. In November of 1969, I received orders for Vietnam. I was assigned to the 1ˢᵗ Signal Brigade on Long Binh Post and billeted at the WAC Detachment a half block away from the 24ᵗʰ Evacuation Hospital. My military occupational specialty (MOS) was 72B, a fixed station communications supervisor, and I worked at the USARV Headquarters Communications Center with one other woman, Gail Nelson, and about 50 men. We worked 12-hour shifts from 6:00 a.m. to 6:00 p.m. six days a week for a month, then switched to nights for 30 days from 6:00 p.m. to 6:00 a.m. Our office mostly processed all the casualty reports (they were the worst), troop movements and battle information. I often tell some of the guys I met that I probably knew more about some of the battles they were in than they did because we were getting the information from every unit involved. On Long Binh Post that year, things were relatively quiet. The whole year I was there we only came under attack maybe six or eight times. One attack in March 1970 was at the medical clinic near USARV Headquarters. I had just gotten off work and was heading to the clinic when I decided to go home and sleep instead. Less than five minutes after I turned around, incoming rockets hit the clinic. I would have been in the waiting room if I had kept going. I was also in a vehicle that picked up some sniper fire one night. I was proud of my service and felt like I was contributing well helping my brothers and sisters in the military do their jobs.

In the summer of 1970, I experienced three traumatic events that changed my life forever. The first involved a wounded orphan who I met when one of the orphanages came to the WAC Detachment to visit for a day of fun. The second was seeing a severely burned soldier come in to the 24th Evacuation Hospital while on my way to our mess hall. The third was being gang-raped by a friend of mine named Tony and two friends of his who were with the 212th Military Police Company. Afterwards, I was dumped out of the jeep Tony was driving like garbage discarded on the roadside and walked in a great deal of pain back to the WAC Detachment and told Captain Shirley Ohta about what had happened. She was wonderful. However, the men's commander refused to cooperate and nothing came of it. He had threatened to ruin my military record and besides, "What did you women expect trying to be part of a *man's* war?" After that time, I started drinking very heavily, kept myself away from people, and just waited out my time to leave. I even stopped going to Mass, because I no longer believed in God.

Coming back home was miserable. People were rude at best and violent at worst. Someone once called out, "Hey look, there goes one of Uncle Sam's whores." I was also with a paraplegic veteran friend who was pushed over in his wheel chair one day. I truly believed I was crazy because of the thoughts and emotions I had and the fact that I was angry all the time. But, I didn't want anyone to know so I acted okay during the day at work (although I was written up for "anger issues" more than once) and at night would drink myself into oblivion. When the term Posttraumatic Stress Disorder (PTSD) came on the scene, I was relieved to know I wasn't crazy. I became part of a women veterans' therapy group at the Vet Center in Concord, CA, which helped greatly, as well as individual counseling. It took a LOT of years and tears for me to feel somewhat "normal." I also found my way back to God. Actually, I formed a new relationship with God as I realized that it wasn't that I no longer believed in God, I just didn't believe in the God of my childhood. My own spiritual relationship with God is good.

I still thought about becoming a Sister at times but thought that no convent would want me with what I had done and what I had been through. I was wrong and in 1992 joined the Dominican Sisters of Racine, WI, an order known for its work with justice issues. I have been a co-facilitator of free retreats for veterans on healing from Posttraumatic *Spiritual* Disorder since about 2003, and give speeches on "Women in Military Service: from the American Revolution to Afghanistan and still forgotten in history."

I still suffer from PTSD, but am much better at responding to triggers and am at some peace with it all. I am proud to have served my country in a very difficult time and proud to be a Vietnam Veteran. I do, to be honest, still hold a little bit of resentment for how we were treated, but mostly I am okay.

**Audrey M. Bergstresser**
**Retired as a Sergeant Major**
**In country: November 26, 1969 – January 25, 1972**
**Rank: Staff Sergeant, US Army**
**Duty: USARV, G3, Administrative NCO**

I was in Belgium in 1967 when I received orders for Vietnam after submitting several volunteer requests. I was trying to keep a younger brother from having to go over. By the time I was approved for Vietnam, my brother was already there and I was within a few weeks of getting out of service, so I declined to reenlist to take the tour. The reenlistment NCO managed to amend my original enlistment contract from three years to four years, and I agreed to take the tour.

After a short leave in Pennsylvania, I proceeded to Fort Lewis, WA, then to Anchorage, AK. We had to deplane for refueling and when we got back on the plane, I was the only woman on the plane. We flew to Yakoda, Japan, to refuel and then flew into Cam Ranh Bay. There was no WAC Detachment there and the personnel clerks could not decide what to do with me. I got a few hours of sleep; then in the middle of the night, they put me on a C-130 into Saigon. After in-processing, they put me on a bus to Long Binh and I eventually wound up at the WAC Detachment. My commander was Captain Shirley Ohta.

I was a clerk for a unit called ACTIV – Army Combat Team in Vietnam. It was a research and development testing program – I spent all day typing reports. Things like night vision goggles and protective vests. After eight months, I went to the G3, which was USARV Operations.

There were always off-duty gatherings on the patio at the WAC Detachment, but I didn't drink because I didn't like the taste, so I took the far, far eastern University of Maryland college classes! I took Speech and Psychology classes among others.

My brother was a medic, and medics and officers were special targets of the Viet Cong. I kept extending my tour so that my brother did not have to return to Vietnam and my younger brother could not be assigned either. I also felt a tremendous sense of "contributing" my efforts.

It was 126 degrees Fahrenheit on the day I flew out of Saigon. I remembered we all cheered as the plane left the ground. We landed in San Francisco where we were not well received! I went home for 30 days of leave, flying into Pennsylvania. It was 35 degrees Fahrenheit and I refused to leave the terminal until someone in the family went out and warmed up the car! I went to recruiting school at Fort Benjamin Harrison, IN, and I spent eight years as a recruiter. It was hard to get reassigned out of recruiting duty. The paperwork kept getting lost! I retired in 1989 as a Sergeant Major.

**Nancy Lynn Comer (Lesher)**
**Retired as a Lieutenant Colonel**
**In country: November 28, 1969 – November 1970**
**Rank: First Lieutenant, US Air Force**
**Duty: 7th Air Force, 16th Tactical Reconnaissance Squadron (TRS) and 12th TRS, Intelligence Photo-Radar Officer**

I arrived at Tan Son Nhut Air Base the day after Thanksgiving 1969. Two weeks later, I noticed that the two large radar domes had been decorated with Christmas lights. As the radar inside the domes moved, the lights on the domes would light up. Unfortunately, later that same night, the base received several incoming rockets. It was the only time while I was there that the base was attacked. The shells landed in the Vietnamese housing area causing some damage. While some of the girls in our housing area scrambled to ground floor rooms, I slept through all the noise and confusion.

# DECEMBER

*Memory Lane: US holds first draft lottery since WW II.*
*Songs: "Leaving on a Jet Plane" by Peter, Paul and Mary; "Na Na Hey Hey Kiss Him Goodbye" by Steam*

**♥Anna Marie Hidalgo (Dennett)**
**In country: December 1969 – November 1970**
**Rank: Specialist 5, US Army**
**Duty: MACV, Combined Intelligence Center, Intelligence Data Handling System, Army Interrogations**

Anna proudly served her country, as a US Army interrogator, during the Vietnam War in Vietnam. She would later serve her community of Ventura County for 27 years as a child support officer and would later retire as a probation officer. In her retirement, Anna continued her community service as volunteer for several community organizations, such as the Red Cross and the Coalition Against Domestic Violence as a counselor. She filled her retirement days by pursuing her interests in wool spinning and genealogy research, as well as the Red Hat Society and Toastmasters. *Source: Obituary notice,* Ventura County Star*, CA, June 2013*

**Jo Anna Wilson**
**In country: December 1969 – November 1970**
**Rank: Specialist 5, US Army**
**Duty: USARV, 1ˢᵗ Logistical Command; MACV, Executive Administrative Assistant**

**Catherine "Cathy" E. Messer**
**In country: December 1969 – December 1970**
**Rank: Specialist 5, US Army**
**Duty: USARV, Special Troops, WAC Detachment, Supply Clerk;**
**Secretary of the General Staff, Administrative Specialist**

One of my memories that I have never forgotten was when about four or five of us got a rare day off and ventured into Saigon. Of course, we were not supposed to leave Long Binh but the adventure was calling us; so off we went. I don't remember if we took a bus or hitched a ride, but it was a fun day seeing the city. Kids were everywhere trying to see what we had in our pockets, and we had to watch our valuables closely. After our "big" adventure, we safely got back to the WAC Detachment. But, before we knew it, we were each called one by one to see the first sergeant. Getting a severe scolding by First Sergeant Mary Manning was not so much fun. But worse was that I had to report to Captain Shirley Ohta, our company commander! Being 19 years old, I didn't see that we were such targets while wandering about in Saigon. She clearly and succinctly outlined the unsafe position we put everyone in. Thank goodness it was just a good chewing out!

I retired from 36 years Federal Government Service, US Army and US Postal Service. Looking forward to traveling and taking care of my cat Mocha.

**Sylvia A. Johnson (Brown)**
**In country: December 1969 – June 1971**
**Rank: Staff Sergeant, US Air Force**
**Duty: 7th Air Force, 1131st Special Activities Squadron,**
**Administrative Supervisor**

**Judy D. Smith**
**Retired as a Master Sergeant**
**In country: December 1969 – July 1971**
**Rank: Specialist 6, US Army**
**Duty: MACV, J2, Executive Administrative Assistant to MG**
**William Potts**

**♥Marilyn Ann Burrow (Trainer) (Bodenstedt)**
**Retired as a Sergeant First Class**
**In country: December 1969 – July 1971**
**Rank: Staff Sergeant, US Army**
**Duty: USARV, Personnel NCO**

**Shirley P. Coppage (Wilson) (Dickerson)**
**Retired as a Command Sergeant Major**
**In country: December 1969 – December 1971**
**Rank: Specialist 5, US Army**
**Duty: USARV, G3, and 18th Military Police Brigade, Traffic Management Coordinator**

**Mary "Cathy" C. Aleshire**
**Retired as a Sergeant Major**
**In country: December 1969 – February 1972**
**Rank: Staff Sergeant, US Army**
**Duty: USARV, 1st Logistical Command, Personnel; USARV, Special Troops, WAC Detachment, Field First/Administrative NCO; USO Group**

From 1965-1968, I was stationed at Fort Myers, VA. I worked in the E1-E6 reassignment section in the Pentagon. I worked for Colonel P. J. Morseman. Colonel Shirley Barnwell also worked in the Pentagon in another section.

Later in 1968, I transferred to Aberdeen Proving Ground, MD. I handled getting assignments for trainees completing their advanced training at Aberdeen. To expedite their assignments, I would drive to the Pentagon every Monday and pick them up so that trainees shipping out did not have any delays, and we had fewer holdovers awaiting assignments. On one of my regular trips to the Pentagon, I decided to see if there were any openings in Vietnam for my grade and occupational specialty, and I lucked out. I volunteered for the assignment, and in December 1969, I left for Vietnam.

I reported to the WAC Detachment in Long Binh. After in processing I was sent to 1st Logistical Command to handle incoming assignments for E1-E6 personnel arriving in country. After 1st Logistical Command stood down, I was transferred to USARV where Colonel Shirley Barnwell was the officer in charge of the E1-E6 assignment section, and I ended up working for her, since she knew me from the Pentagon.

Later on, I was assigned to the WAC Detachment as the field first sergeant. I picked up all the new women who arrived in country, handled training, had supervision over the supply room and any other project that came up. I really enjoyed this assignment very much, because of the interaction with personnel in the unit.

One evening, a group of us went to the Chinese restaurant (Loon Foon) that was just down the road from the WAC Detachment. On the way back to the compound, we started getting incoming rockets. There was Fran Garvey, Sylvia Dobson and myself. We started running, so we could get back to the compound before the MPs (military policemen) closed and locked the gate. I was first through the gate, and then Sylvia, but she stopped and turned around to see where Fran was. It happened so fast, Fran ran right over Sylvia and knocked her down. We laughed, picked Sylvia up and headed straight for our respective bunkers.

I also had the opportunity to travel all over Vietnam with the USO. I was with a small group of men and women from Long Binh. We mainly would go to bases down south and hand out cards to soldiers who could not get off the front lines. I remember one young man crying because he got a new deck of cards for Christmas. These men were appreciative of anything they got, and most of them had not seen an American woman since they had been in country.

This was probably the trip that the most embarrassing thing to ever happen to me, happened. On the way down south on the transport plane, I got to the point I could not sit because of pain. I had no idea what was going on, so when we arrived, we had to jump out of the plane as it came down as low as it could. It could not land because of enemy fire. I went straight to the dispensary; I was starting to be very uncomfortable and in a lot of pain. I had a protruding hemorrhoid that had to be lanced. While in the dispensary, I had to drop my fatigue pants, underwear and bend over at the end of the table. While the doctor was lancing the hemorrhoid, we started getting incoming mortars. All the men started running through the dispensary heading to their post, when some of them noticed the combat boots, fatigues and pink panties. They started whistling and yelling "look at the pink panties." At least they could not see my face, because I was so embarrassed.

I kept extending six months at a time, because I wanted to stay in Vietnam until the WAC Detachment was deactivated. Unfortunately, Department of the Army would not let me extend any more since I had already been over there for 22 months.

**Laura Holguin (Pariseau)**
**Retired as a Major**
**In country: December 1969 – February 1972**
**Rank: Staff Sergeant, US Army**
**Duty: MACV, 519th Military Intelligence Battalion, Combined**
**Intelligence Center, Intelligence Data Handling System, Interrogator**

**Comments and Memories:** This is a quick story of the little things that could lift us out of the dumps while in country. Our meals usually consisted of going to the snack bar found on the compound or eating the canned foods we could buy at the post exchange. Nothing really great but it did fill the hole in our tummies. This food was definitely not something to write home about! My friend, Anna Marie Hidalgo Dennett, and I were both of Mexican descent and not accustomed to eating "American" food. We were missing our Mexican food so when my Mom or Anna's Mom sent us a care package, we were in seventh heaven! MEXICAN FOOD – beans, tortillas, salsa, hard cheese. We also always got real homemade cookies for dessert. We could get lettuce and tomatoes from the little store that was down the street from our quarters, the Medford. We always shared our goodies with the ladies in our Q. Those who wanted to participate had a 'Taco night'. Our care package only lasted the one night but it was a little bit of home given to us by the people that loved and worried about us. Those care packages were wonderful and always welcomed! *Source: Vietnam Memory Book 2000*

**Kathryn "Kathy" A. Votipka (Retzlaff)**
**Retired as a Chief Warrant Officer 4**
**In country: December 1969 – February 1972**
**Rank: Specialist 5, US Army**
**Duty: MACV, 45ᵗʰ Military Intelligence, Combined Intelligence Center, Ground Orders of Battle, Intelligence Analyst**

**Comments and Memories:** One thing I remember are the pinochle games we played. They would go on for hours into the night. The next night we'd swear we wouldn't play anymore. Then we'd start a game, but promised each other we'd quit early. Yeah! It'd be 3 or 4 a.m. again, and we'd drag ourselves to work once more.

I remember the day our maids went on strike for an increase in pay. Boy, did we miss them! *Source: Vietnam Memory Book 2000*

**Betty J. Russell**
**Retired as a Master Sergeant**
**In country: December 1, 1969 – November 30, 1970**
**Rank: Specialist 4, US Army**
**Duty: USARV, Special Troops, WAC Detachment, Company Clerk**

I was at Fort Monmouth, NJ, and volunteered to go to Vietnam. Because I was under 21 and a woman, I had to have my parents' consent. My dad had served in Vietnam, and my mom was not happy that I left college to join the Army; she was really not happy with these orders. They did sign the consent form because they knew how important it was to me. I was born in Savannah, GA, and my parents were in Columbus, GA, which is where I entered the Army.

I think I was the only woman on the plane going to Vietnam. In Guam, I ran into a high school friend and he was on his way to Vietnam to serve with the military police.

We circled waiting to land because the area was taking fire. We were rushed off the plane and into a terminal building. Everybody had to check in at the terminal building and then we were sent on to the replacement battalion.

My first sergeant was Mary Manning and my commanding officer was Shirley Ohta. My daily responsibilities included anything administrative pertaining to the women of the WAC Detachment. I did morning reports, rosters, made sure the women took the malaria pills every Monday morning; everyone had to sign the roster that they had taken their pills.

First Sergeant Mary Manning was the best leader; she was what I would describe as a soldier's soldier. She was all about her troops. She and Captain Ohta had a great working relationship and the three of us were together all day, every day. We had movie nights, hail and farewell parties, birthday celebrations; we celebrated any special event. The mess hall staff would whip up cakes and pretty much anything else we needed for celebrations. We could cook on the patio, which was a good choice because the patio was the gathering place, and there was always someone there to talk with. We had a band from Thailand perform for a WAC anniversary celebration. We had a luau once that Captain Ohta organized.

Once, on a daily distribution run, the vehicle I was in was wrecked. A lowboy truck jackknifed in front of us and my Vietnamese driver could not avoid the trailer as it wrapped around us. I was not seriously injured but did wind up at the hospital to get checked out.

When I opened the Conex (a large metal storage container) one day to get the softball equipment for the games, the largest rat I have ever seen sashayed out leisurely as I ran screaming to get some help.

For my 21st birthday – August 13, 1970 – I was in Hawaii on R&R and drank lots of Mai Tais and sang "Tiny Bubbles" and watched Don Ho perform! The layers of rum were delicious!

On the second opportunity to take some leave, I spent it on Okinawa. It was an opportunity to spend some time with some Air Force people at Kadeena Air Force Base. Hanging out with them was different. On Okinawa, the bars had to have an "A" symbol on them, or you weren't supposed to go in them.

I don't recall having a short-timer calendar. Think when I realized it was time to go home was when my replacement arrived, which was about 30 days before my departure. My replacement was Frances Black. I replaced Joyce Harker.

It was such a mixture of joy and sadness leaving Vietnam. Some had left before, some were still there and it was bittersweet.

The favorite song was by the Box Tops and you heard it endlessly – "Lonely days are gone, I'm a going home. My baby wrote me a letter." (The song had the sounds of the jet taking off.)

I arrived in Oakland, CA, and I was on my way back to Fort Monmouth, NJ. I retired in 1991 as a master sergeant.

I am excited that my son can say, "My mom served in Vietnam."

**Comments and Memories:** As we were watching the movie "The Green Berets," we didn't realize that the alarm had sounded for "incoming." We thought it was part of the sound effects from the movie. It's really funny now, but it wasn't funny then. *Source: Vietnam Memory Book 2000*

**Janice M. White Eagle (Johnson)**
**Retired as a Staff Sergeant**
**In country: December 3, 1969 – December 2, 1970**
**Rank: Specialist 5, US Army**
**Duty: USARV**

**Jacquelyn "Jackie" Kay Roach**
**In country: December 14, 1969 – December 10, 1970**
**Rank: Staff Sergeant, US Marine Corps**
**Duty: NAVFORV, Marine Corps Personnel Section, Out-Processing Administrative Clerk**

Sergeant Jackie Roach served in the US Marines for nine years and five months. In addition to Vietnam, she served at Parris Island, SC; Barstow, CA; Headquarters Marine Corps, Alexandria, VA; Iwakuni, Japan; and Camp Elmore, Norfolk, VA.

# Chapter Ten

# 1970

♥Loyce Alice Bradford
In country: 1970 – 1971
Rank: Major, US Army
Duty: Long Binh Army Depot, Adjutant

Lieutenant Colonel Bradford became ill and died while still on active duty at Fort Sheridan, IL, November 14, 1980. *Source: US Army Personnel and Dependent Casualties, Ancestry.com*

Carla R. Dixson
In country: 1970 – 1971
Rank: Specialist 6, US Army
Duty: USARV, G3, Unit Supply Specialist

♥Mary Kathryn Leath
Retired as a Colonel
In country: 1970 – 1971
Rank: Lieutenant Colonel, US Army Medical Specialist Corps
Duty: 24th Evacuation Hospital, Long Binh, Physical Therapist

♥Eleanor "Jean" Jeanne McCallum
Retired as a Lieutenant Colonel
In country: 1970 – 1971
Rank: Lieutenant Colonel, US Air Force
Duty: 7th Air Force, Personnel Staff Officer

Helen R. Nelson
In country: 1970 – 1971
Rank: Specialist 4, US Army
Assigned to: MACV, Clerk-Typist

**Geraldine F. Odom**
Retired as a Master Sergeant
In country: 1970 – 1971
Rank: Staff Sergeant, US Air Force
Duty: 7th Air Force, Management Analyst Technician

♥**Michele Robin Skipwith**
In country: 1970 – 1971
Rank: Specialist 5, US Army
Duty: MACV, US Army Security Agency, 509th Radio Research Group, Communications Center Specialist

♥**Eleanor "Ellie" Marie Strudas**
Retired as a First Sergeant
In country: 1970 – 1971
Rank: Sergeant First Class, US Army
Duty: USARV, Special Troops, WAC Detachment, First Sergeant

**Charlotte R. Tesch**
Retired as a Chief Master Sergeant
In country: 1970 – 1971
Rank: Staff Sergeant, US Air Force
Duty: Stenographic Technician

♥**M. Loretta Navik**
Retired as a Master Sergeant
In country: 1970 – January 1, 1971
Rank: Master Sergeant, US Air Force
Duty: MACV, J5, Stenographic Technician

♥**Ann Blakely Smith**
Retired as a Colonel
In country: 1970 – January 1, 1971
Rank: Lieutenant Colonel, US Army
Duty: MACV, Joint Staff, Fifth Senior Officer Advisor to the Vietnam Women's Armed Forces Corps

**Margaret H. Hernandez**
**Retired as a Sergeant Major**
**In country: 1970 – 1972**
**Rank: Specialist 5, US Army**
**Duty: USARV Headquarters, Administrative Specialist**

**♥June Elizabeth Owens Knutsen**
**Retired as a Lieutenant Colonel**
**In country: 1970 – 1972**
**Rank: Major, US Army**
**Duty: USARV, 49th Transportation Command, Personnel Staff Officer**

***Excerpt from eulogy delivered by Derek Blundell:*** June joined the Women's Army Corps and began a career in which she excelled. She rose to the rank of Lieutenant Colonel and saw service in many parts of the world. Among many other postings, she filled the post of administrative officer at the US Army Training Center, Fort Dix, NJ, and at the US Army Engineer Command, Frankfurt, Germany. For three years, she was the Special Aide to the Commanding General, US Army Materiel Command. It was during this tour of duty that she saw service in that terrible conflict in Vietnam.

Someone who was both a colleague and a friend during those days was COL Bettie Morden, who wrote of her: "She was a diligent, conscientious officer – admired and respected by her friends and Army associates. She had a keen intellect and took an individualistic approach to life and her duties. Though her methods were different, she never failed to achieve the best results on every assignment – often surpassing her peers."

With her patriotism, and her confident bearing, it is not difficult to see why she was a successful soldier.

*Reprinted with permission, Vietnam Memory Book 2000*

# JANUARY

*Memory Lane: Kansas City Chiefs defeat the Minnesota Vikings (23-7) in Super Bowl IV; Robert Altman's M\*A\*S\*H premieres.*
*Song: "Raindrops Keep Fallin' On My Head" by B.J. Thomas*

Irene Begg
Retired as a Lieutenant Colonel
In country: January 1970 – August 1970
Rank: Captain, Army Medical Specialist Corps
Duty: 3rd Field Hospital, Saigon, Dietetic Consultant

Patricia A. Morrow (Crater)
In country: January 1970 – September 1970
Rank: Specialist 4, US Army
Duty: 24th Evacuation Hospital, Long Binh, Clerk-Typist

♥Kathy J. Zeigler (Wenzelberger)
In country: January 1970 – September 1970
Rank: Specialist 4, US Army
Duty: USARV, 1st Aviation Brigade, Clerk-Typist

Erma L. Spadone (Morgan)
In country: January 1970 – November 1970
Rank: Specialist 4, US Army
Duty: USARV, Clerk-Typist

Merle Elizabeth Alvey
Retired as a Lieutenant Colonel
In country: January 1970 – December 1970
Rank: Major, US Army
Duty: USARV, Long Binh Army Depot

♥Dorothy L. Gray
Retired as a Colonel
In country: January 1970 – December 1970
Rank: Lieutenant Colonel, US Army
Duty: USARV, 1st Logistical Command, Logistics Officer

♥**Shirley "Ernie" Elizabeth Klein**
**Retired as a Chief Warrant Officer 4**
**In country: January 1970 – December 1970**
**Rank: Chief Warrant Officer 4, US Army**
**Duty: Qui Nhon, Support Command, Officer Records, Personnel/**
**Administrative Technician**

**Comments and Memories:** Always believe in doing my job to the best of my ability. . . . Kicked a football about three times when going back to my room. The next day I thought my leg had fallen off. I had used muscles that I hadn't used for years! *Source: Vietnam Memory Book 2000*

**Belen Victoria Pinon**
**Retired as a Sergeant First Class**
**In country: January 1970 – December 1970; September 1971 – June 1972**
**Rank: Specialist 4, US Army**
**Duty: USARV; 18th Military Police Brigade, S4, Clerk-Typist**

**Lucie Rivera-O'Ferrall**
**Retired as a Sergeant Major**
**In country: January 1970 – January 1971**
**Rank: Staff Sergeant, US Army**
**Duty: USARV, Central Finance and Accounting Office, Finance Team**
**Supervisor**

When I joined the US Army in San Juan, Puerto Rico, in 1961, I was so naïve that I thought I was going to be able to go on combat missions. Little did I know that I was not even going to be allowed to go overseas for years because I was a WAC. I volunteered to go to Vietnam five times before I was sent there and only because my reenlistment was up and I told them that I was going to get out if they did not send me to Vietnam.

My first night in Vietnam, January 1969, was terrifying because we had to go to the bunkers. I did

The above picture is misleading. I had to borrow the helmet and the rifle. Women were not allowed to fight nor were we given weapons to defend ourselves. ~Lucie

not know if I was more afraid of dying or being bitten by rats or roaches. After that night, it was just routine and I got used to it. Something else I had to get used to was helicopters landing next to my hootch all day, all night long since we were next to the hospital.

I remember Vietnam as the best assignment I ever had. Finally, I felt I was doing something for my country. I was assigned to the "biggest and the best" finance and accounting office in the US Army. We paid the soldiers, civilian employees and contractors. I had a large team of 20+ men to supervise who were not happy to have a female as their boss but we had the best team in the office and I earned their respect. Our team was also the team that "automated" the pay of soldiers who wanted their pay to go stateside, which saved a lot of time.

One very sad incident was Thanksgiving 1969. I decided to take a short cut through the hospital and I happened to encounter medics unloading soldiers in bags. This was the last time I went to the mess hall and Thanksgiving has never been the same since then.

Living with four roommates was a challenge, but I was very lucky. Two of my roommates were "Panama" and Ruth Pitts. Panama was also in finance, and her team paid the supply and mess hall units so, occasionally, we were able to get steaks for dinner and she was a great cook, even when we only had C-rations and ketchup. Ruth was a hoot; we laughed a lot. She came from a family of 12 and had great stories to tell. We are still very good friends after 45 years.

On one occasion, I was able to accompany a group of orphans to Vung Tau, a resort city with a beach. The bus broke down, and the nuns and I were left to guard the kids when a truckload of men in "black pajamas" unloaded (Viet Cong). We just went between the buildings and hid until they left.

After I left Vietnam in 1970, I was stationed at the Letterman General Hospital in San Francisco, which allowed me to serve soldiers wounded in Vietnam. That was the assignment where I met my husband, SGM Frederick H. Kruse, US Army retired. He passed away November 22, 2013.

I was very fortunate that I was able to get my bachelor's degree, a dual master's degree and an MBA while in the Army.

After I retired, I had other careers. I was immediately hired to oversee the European operations of the second largest community college system in the US and later on, I became the Chief Financial Officer of one of the largest nonprofit organizations in Atlanta, GA. Now, I spend my time volunteering with nonprofit organizations and working as an "extra" in movies being filmed in Atlanta.

**Annie M. Alexander**
In country: January 1970 – January 1971
Rank: Specialist 4, US Army
Duty: USARV, Administrative Specialist

**Elizabeth "Lizzie" A. Freaney**
**Retired as a Staff Sergeant**
In country: January 1970 – January 1971
Rank: Specialist 5, US Army
Duty: USARV, Central Finance and
Accounting Office, Finance Specialist

**Kay F. Hall**
In country: January 1970 – January 1971
Rank: Staff Sergeant, US Army
Duty: USARV, Materiel Control and Accounting Specialist

**Nancy E. Simmons**
**Retired as a Command Sergeant Major**
In country: January 1970 – January 1971
Rank: Specialist 5, US Army
Duty: 1ˢᵗ Signal Brigade, Telephone Service Desk, Central Office
Switchboard Operator

**Comments and Memories:** One that comes to mind in Vietnam was when the band was going to play at Bear Cat. Eleanor Strudas was First Sergeant and I don't think she approved of this smart-assed E5 traveling Vietnam playing music. Hate to tell this story, her being gone. But, what the hell, it's a good story. Our band traveled by Huey helicopter and played at the outposts. Usually no problem – and this aviation company really supported us on the trips. One day something happened to the chopper and our manager decided we would drive to Bear Cat. After all, it was only about 15 miles. He also decided that since we were running late we would change into civilian clothes and be ready to play when we got there. We were not authorized to be off post in civilian clothes. But, we were musicians and we aimed to play. Since we were running late, I had to prepare to play which usually took at least a six pack. So, off we went in that two-seater truck, five musicians in civilian clothes and our manager (a warrant officer) in uniform and all our instruments loaded in the back. Everything was great until we were on the outskirts of this village when we came under sniper fire which I mistook for someone popping chewing gum (probably had to do with my preparation to play) until I was yanked into the floorboard. That was when we discovered we only had one .45 caliber pistol, which belonged to the warrant officer, to defend ourselves. We made it past that to arrive at Bear Cat to find they were under attack and were not about to let this rag-tag bunch on to their post. Our leader, a veteran of the Korean War, explained to our manager what would happen to him if he was not successful in getting us inside the compound. He explained to him rather clearly that no way in hell were we going back through that village, that he would personally write the letter to his next of kin if he did not get us inside the compound. Guess that was the motivation our manager needed because he indeed succeeded and we waited in the lounge for the fighting to stop. We did play a few songs for them after they got through. Then came the dilemma of getting us back to Long Binh because I had a curfew and was not supposed to be there in the first place much less in civilian clothes. So they sent us back in what looked like a WWII vintage single-engine plane. We had to leave the instruments behind and finally the plane got airborne. We bounced all the way to Long Binh. That was when I had my first conversation with God and promised him if he got me safely to Long Binh he would not have to worry about me doing that again. I finally dragged myself home. First Sergeant Strudas was waiting for me because I was 30 minutes late for curfew. She was rather upset and explained to me what was going to happen to me for being late. She was not interested in my explanation. So, I figured what the hell – I told her I had been shot at, bounced around in the air just trying to get back to her, and I was going to bed. I had had a rough day – she could finish beating me up in the morning. By the way, the commander was not upset and did not bust me back to private. Just told me to try not to do it again. *Source: Vietnam Memory Book 2000*

**Mary E. Harrington (Evans)**
**In country: January 1970 – April 1971**
**Rank: Specialist 5, US Army**
**Duty: USARV, 1ˢᵗ Aviation Brigade, Personnel Specialist**

**Verneida Pinkston**
**Retired as a Master Sergeant**
**In country: January 1970 – June 28, 1971**
**Rank: Specialist 5, US Army**
**Duty: MACV, Receptionist to General Creighton Abrams**

**Jacqueline Lee Gillette**
**Retired as a Sergeant First Class**
**In country: January 1970 – July 1971**
**Rank: Specialist 5, US Army**
**Duty: USARV**

**Pamela S. Riess (Bunde)**
**In country: January 1970 – August 3, 1971**
**Rank: Staff Sergeant, US Army**
**Duty: USARV, Adjutant General, Enlisted Replacement Division,**
**Administrative NCO**

**Comments and Memories:** On a visit to a nearby orphanage – I usually worked seven days a week and so I only got to visit twice – the children of the maintenance man invited me to be their new mother. They threw in a 10-foot boa constrictor as added incentive. I declined. *Source: Vietnam Memory Book 2000*

**♥Amy Louella Carter**
**In country: January 14, 1970 – December 15, 1970**
**Rank: Specialist 4, US Army**
**Duty: USARV, G4, Maintenance, Clerk-Typist**

As I recall, we couldn't put in for a foreign assignment until we had been in our permanent duty assignment at least one year, so I put in for Germany a year in advance. When a year was up, I approached the captain about my Germany request. She told me that the request had been trapped in a Sixth Army basket and asked if I still wanted to go but that I would have to extend my enlistment. I told her I didn't want to do that. She then asked me if I'd like to go to Vietnam and get out five months early. I agreed to go. I called my Mother and told her I had come down on a levy (received written orders). She asked what that meant, and I told her I was going to Vietnam. She became very quiet. My Grandmother got on the phone, and said "It's a durn shame sending girls to Vietnam." I told her, "But Gramma, I volunteered." She said, "Then you're a durn fool."

Upon arrival in Vietnam, I was told about the bunkers. That night at 2:00 a.m., I was awakened by the lights being turned on and "Hit the bunkers." "What have I gotten myself into?" I thought. I knew there were male security guards at the guard shack. No way was I going to go out in my nightgown and curlers in my hair. I was shaking like a leaf as I hurriedly got dressed and removed my curlers. I put on my heels. The terrain was rugged, and not suitable for heels. I was shaking so bad, I fell down, bruising the top of my ankle and foot. We sat on hard benches that were very uncomfortable. I vowed to have a pillow with me next time. Then there were people smoking cigarettes and drinking beer at both ends of the bunker. I don't like the smell of either.

My foot got infected, but I didn't get it checked out. I didn't want to take time away from guys who were seriously hurt. I didn't learn 'til later that we had a Dispensary all to ourselves, and I wouldn't be taking away time to those in more serious need than a bruised, infected foot. Eventually my foot did heal. I hated my combats boots. I'd never worn any boots except snow boots. I felt like an utter clod wearing those things. I must say that my injured foot was stabilized well in those boots, though. It didn't hurt as bad when I walked.

My MOS was 71B30 or Advanced Clerk-Typist. I did secretarial work in different areas. The first time I worked for a colonel in the Maintenance Division. Although he was pleasant on the surface, it became obvious that he felt that women had no place in Vietnam. When I was first there, we had many colored tissue papers divided by carbons. We typed about weapons, tanks or things like that. It was very boring to me, and I'd fall asleep. We weren't supposed to make any errors, but I did. The only thing I got out of the colonel was that he made us type on every brand of typewriter from Executive to others. I resented it at the time, but it helped me adjust to other typewriters later. I don't remember how long I stayed in the Maintenance Division, but eventually I was transferred to POL (Petroleum, Oils and Lubricants Division).

# FEBRUARY

*Memory Lane: Jeffrey R. MacDonald kills his wife and children at Fort Bragg, NC, claiming that drugged-out "hippies" did it; Jackson 5 make TV debut on "American Bandstand."*
*Song: "Thank You for Lettin' Me Be Myself Again" by Sly and The Family Stone*

♥Beatrice Lucille Case
Retired as a Lieutenant Colonel, USAR
In country: February 1970 – February 1971
Rank: Major, US Army Medical Specialist Corps
Duty: 67th Evacuation Hospital, Qui Nhon; MACV Surgeon's Office, Physical Therapist

In July 1970, MAJ Beatrice Case transferred to MACV's Surgeon's Office to train Vietnamese rehabilitation specialists at the South Vietnamese military hospitals. Lieutenant Colonel Case died December 24, 1994.

♥Lillian Feldman
Retired as a Staff Sergeant
In country: February 1970 – February 1971 .
Rank: Staff Sergeant, US Air Force
Duty: MACV, J2, Administrative Supervisor

Patricia A. Quist
Retired as a Chief Warrant Officer 4
In country: February 6, 1970 – February 1971
Rank: Chief Warrant Officer 2, US Army
Duty: US Army International Control Commission, Long Binh; Saigon, General Supply Technician

♥Marilyn "Bobbi" B. Michaud
Retired as a Technical Sergeant
In country: February 1970 – February 15, 1971
Rank: Technical Sergeant, US Air Force
Duty: MACV, J2, Administrative Supervisor

**Dr. Janice Annette Mendelson, MD**
**Retired as a Colonel**
**In country: February 1970 – July 1971**
**Rank: Lieutenant Colonel, US Army Medical Corps**
**Duty: MACV, Chief Surgeon and Surgical and Rehabilitation Advisor**

***Carmen "Penny" Marshall (Adams):*** Janice Mendelson spent her younger years in Tientsin, China, among the military and missionaries. Her father was a medical officer in the US Army. She attended Tientsin Grammar School, but returned to the United States to finish high school and college.

She graduated from medical school at the University of Pittsburg, completed her internship there and then did surgical residencies in Lexington, KY; Nashville, TN; and Columbus, OH. She had a Fellowship in Physical Medicine and Rehabilitation at NYU, Bellevue Institute of Physical Medicine, NY. All of these programs would help her prepare for years as a surgeon in the US Army. She joined the Army during the draft days of 1955, to spare someone else who didn't want to go.

Dr. Mendelson served in various military hospitals as a general surgeon, a trauma investigator, and in surgical research. As a medical officer at the US Army Chemical Corps, Edgewood Arsenal, MD, she was the first woman ever assigned as a US Army Surgeon. During her research, she discovered that it was possible to prevent otherwise fatal infections, in severe wounds and burns, by using certain topical bacterial therapy. She was the perfect fit for a position as Chief Surgeon and Surgical and Rehabilitation Advisor in Vietnam. She spent 18 months in 1970-1971 with MACV in Saigon, as the only female Army surgeon in Vietnam.

When she returned to duty in the United States, Dr. Mendelson was appointed Director of the Military Blood Program. It was responsible for the pipeline of blood products from all military hospitals in the US to all of the triage units and military hospitals inside Vietnam and in the Far East.

After 25 years of dedicated service, Dr. Mendelson retired from the Army at Fort Sam Houston, TX, in May 1981. She continued to live in TX. In conjunction with Our Lady of the Lake College in San Antonio, she helped to found an International Folk Culture Center. She was one of the founding members of the TX International Folk Dancers, and in 2013, Dr. Mendelson received the organization's National Dance Award at the San Antonio Folk Dance Festival.

Dr. Janice Mendelson is 91 (2014) and resides at an assisted living facility in San Antonio, TX. Of her time in Vietnam, Dr. Mendelson said, ". . . Vietnam was the greatest challenge of my life!"

*~ Dr. Mendelson:* I worked mostly with the Vietnamese military medical personnel as Surgical (and Rehabilitation) advisor. Although I did go to the MACV office at least once a week, I had an office in the Department of Surgery of Cong Hoa hospital.

My mission was to help the Vietnamese military to provide the best possible surgical care and rehabilitation to the patients. At the request of their surgeon general, I started a burn unit at Cong Hoa, using techniques especially applicable to their "chronic mass casualty" situation. I do not know if the "Rehabilitation" duty was in my official job description, but I have had special training and experience in this completion of my surgical residency. I participated in the surgical procedures at Cong Hoa and helped in the training of their surgeons.

While I was working at Cong Hoa, an American TV team came for a few day, followed me around, and interviewed me. I'd been told they were documenting US military medical assistance in Vietnam, but later learned it was used for a program about "women."

The two Vietnamese military surgeons with whom I worked the most came to the United State as refugees and are serving as "family physicians" here. I've been able to be with both of them in this country.

Unlike many American military personnel, I very much enjoyed being in Vietnam with the opportunity to use all aspects of my talents and also to enjoy the extra-curricular activities, even though hazardous.

# MARCH

*Memory Lane: US lowers voting age from 21 to 18; Vinko Bogataj crashes during a ski-jumping championship in Germany – his image becomes that of the "agony of defeat guy" in the opening credits of ABC's Wide World of Sports.*
*Songs: "Bridge Over Troubled Waters" by Simon and Garfunkel; "Give Me Just a Little More Time" by Chairmen of the Board*

**Priscilla Mosby**
**In country: March 1970 – September 1970; March 1971 – April 1972**
**Rank: Specialist 4, US Army**
**Duty: USARV, 1ˢᵗ Logistical Command, TDY USO; Cam Ranh Bay and Bien Thuy, USO Show, Clerk-Typist**

*Telephone interview with Claire Starnes, 1/16/2015:* While stationed at Fort Knox, KY, I was a permanent member of the Post Chapel Choir. I love to sing. Not long after I joined the choir, I was approached to volunteer for Special Services-sponsored USO tours to Vietnam. I jumped at the chance because I would be doing what I loved to do. Thus, began a six-month revolving-door assignment to Vietnam and back to Fort Knox, where I had duty with the Post Adjutant's office. Though I enjoyed my special assignment, I grew tired of the constant traveling and requested permanent assignment to Vietnam, which eventually was granted.

In March 1971, I reported to Vietnam. I was attached to the WAC Detachment at Long Binh with assignment to Special Services, Saigon. I was assigned to a band, Phase Three, of which I was the lead singer. I had to sign a waiver permitting me to perform in a combat zone.

My band's mission was to entertain the troops, lighten the mood and bring up morale. Those were dark days for our fighting military. South Vietnam seemed to be on the verge of collapse. It was our purpose to bring smiles to those troops and make them forget for just a moment where they were.

I did a full tour, with ups and downs throughout. I finally came home with mixed emotions, having to leave my band behind. Not long after I got home, I learned that all members of my band were killed in a mortar attack. I went in a depression which I am still trying to control to this day.

Luckily, I still have my voice, and not too many years ago, I joined another band, called Rising Vision. We travel overseas and do some stateside tours. I concentrate mainly on blues, but occasionally venture into other genre. The band has been good therapy for me. But, I shall never forget what I left behind in Vietnam. That will be with me forever.

**Sandra L. Conderman**
Retired as a Captain
In country: March 1970 – March 1971
Rank: Captain, US Air Force
Duty: 7th Air Force, 377th Combat Support Group, Consolidated Base Personnel Office, Personnel Officer

♥**Patricia A. Hayes**
Retired as a Major
In country: March 1970 – March 1971
Rank: Captain, US Air Force
Duty: 7th Air Force, 1st Weather Squadron, Advanced Weather Officer

♥**Donna Lou Hollowell (Murray)**
Retired as a Master Sergeant
In country: March 1970 – March 1971
Rank: Staff Sergeant, US Marine Corps
Duty: NAVFORV, Marine Corps Personnel Section

***Adelina Dee Torres:*** I remember that Donna worked in the J5 office of MACV, downstairs from where I worked in J52. I remember her visiting the orphanage and going in-country with us to pay the marines who were out in the boondocks. Donna was a caring, lovely, energetic person – always smiling and laughing. She had a laugh that was contagious.

♥**Mary Hazel Johnson**
Retired as a Master Sergeant
In country: March 1970 – March 1971
Rank: Master Sergeant, US Army
Duty: MACV; USARV, Administrative NCO

**Norma L. K. Mokuau**
Retired as a Lieutenant Colonel
In country: March 1970 – March 1971
Rank: Captain, US Air Force
Duty: MACV, J23, Intelligence Operations, Administrative Officer

**Carol A. Ogg**
**Retired as a Sergeant First Class**
**In country: March 1970 – March 1971**
**Rank: Staff Sergeant, US Army**
**Duty: MACV, US Army Security Agency, 509ᵗʰ Radio Research Group,**
**Pacific Historical Team**

The lamplights from carefully placed lanterns, like streetlights, give off a yellow glow, lighting the way on a web of wood sidewalks. I look around, unsettled by the strange silence. I walk straight toward the building in front of me. A weather worn sign, "Incoming Personnel Report Here," hangs slightly askew.

As I walk up the wooden sidewalk, I notice what looks like a duffel bag hanging from the tripod. Printed across the duffel bag in large black stenciled letters – Potable Water. The hot blast of air splashes across my face; I scowl and continue walking.

I plunk the twenty-five cents on the counter. "Wow . . . real money. You must be new." The young soldier shoves a set of sheets, a pillow, and an army green blanket over the counter toward me. "How come they put you in the old nurses' quarters?" he asks. "I have no idea," I say hunching my shoulders. "Ain't been anyone in them barracks for months," he proclaims. "You a medic?" I shake my head.

"Just follow the sidewalk to the end." He points to my left. As I walk down the wooden sidewalks toward the building, I hear the young soldier speaking on the telephone, the sound of his voice carried on the stifling night air. "Hey, we need a guard down at the old nurses' quarters."

The screen door creaks as I open it. At the end of a long hallway, with enclosed cubicles on each side, a television crackles, as the lines rotate constantly upward. I walk down the aisle peering into several cubicles. Each one has a bed and a nightstand. I turn around and see my footprints neatly outlined on the dusty floor. I return to the first cubicle. I lay the Army blanket on top of the bed and watch the faint cloud of dust rise and settle. I write my name on the top of the nightstand.

"Hey, is there anyone in there?"

I peek outside the cubicle door and turn my head toward the front door entrance. A black silhouetted figure peers through the screen door. "Yes." I swallow.

"Okay," the silhouette growls back. "I got picked for guard duty."

I look at the toilet stall entrance. I scratch my head and wonder who designed them. Twiggy? If I use the toilet, there is no room to turn around. Guess I will have to back in, even then there is no room to reach up to pull my underpants down. I turn my back to the stall door, reach up, and pull down my underpants to around my mid-calves. Taking small backward steps, I back into the toilet stall and sit on the toilet. Looking around, I see the toilet paper holder high above on the right wall. I reach up and pull a sizable amount to use. I smile. I must first go out of the stall to use it.

No wonder they made new nurses' quarters!

*Excerpts from her book* Fields of Fire, *available at Amazon.com*

**♥Lois "Smokey" Margaret Schmoker**
**Retired as a Master Sergeant**
**In country: March 1970 – March 1971**
**Rank: Master Sergeant, US Air Force**
**Duty: 7th Air Force, 834th Air Division, Directorate of Operations, Stenographic Technician**

***Story written in tribute by Bobbie Cramer:*** To all who ever knew her, she was known as "Smokey," a Kansas gal who always had a smile and a heart of gold. A stenographer for MACV, her working hours at times were longer than the normal 12-hour day, but she didn't complain. That is, until she was unable to attend a special party. (We always saved food for her.) Smokey rotated to Ent Air Force Base, CO, then to Tyndall Air Force Base, FL, for 17 months, then back to Ent. Smokey and her heart of gold insisted my "Chinese Pug" and I live with her and her "Collie" until we found a place we liked. We both retired at Ent Air Force Base. Smokey, I miss you! *Source: Vietnam Memory Book 2000*

**Vivienne C. Sinclair (Vuosolo)**
**Retired as a Lieutenant Colonel**
**In country: March 1970 – March 1971**
**Rank: Major, US Air Force**
**Duty: 7th Air Force, Education and Training Staff Officer**

**Fannie Lee Gray**
**Retired as a Sergeant Major**
**In country: March 1970 – July 1971**
**Rank: Sergeant First Class, US Army**
**Duty: USARV, Administrative NCO**

**Mary A. Darr**
**Retired as a Sergeant First Class**
**In country: March 1970 – September 1972**
**Rank: Staff Sergeant, US Army**
**Duty: Logistics, Cam Ranh Bay Depot; USARV, 1ˢᵗ Signal Brigade;**
**USARV, Special Troops, WAC Detachment, Supply Sergeant**

I reenlisted to go to Vietnam. When I first arrived at Long Binh, there was no supply opening for me. Before I knew it, I was shipped out to Cam Ranh Bay along with Mary Parker. There I worked in Logistics at the Cam Ranh Bay Depot. In February 1971, I transferred back to Long Binh, with duty at 1ˢᵗ Signal Brigade. When I heard the WAC Detachment would need a supply sergeant, I asked for a transfer and got it. I was the unit's supply sergeant until September 1972 when I left Vietnam just before the stand-down of the unit.

My time at the WAC Detachment was a busy and interesting one. We were preparing to deactivate the detachment and move to Saigon.

The US military contracted with a Vietnamese laundry to have our sheets, blankets, pillowcases, etc., done by the locals. Thus, my duties took me into the small village near the post, and since we were not allowed to carry a weapon, those trips were a little unnerving at times.

The swimming pool was still there, but the novelty had worn off and few women used it. Besides, we were way too busy for such recreation. I was turning in beds, lockers, etc., to a civilian corporation which was also under military contract. But, all was not work. Once, a unit invited us to a party that was not in our neighborhood. I recall having to travel by helicopter to get there. The pilot wanted to show us his command of the helicopter. It was a scary experience, but fun.

I and a couple other gals thought we would take R&R in the Philippines. Wrong! The Philippines were not on the approved R&R list. We landed and were detained at the airport. They quickly deported us back to Vietnam. That probably was the shortest R&R on record.

As the war was winding down, mortar and rocket attacks were increasing. But, we continued doing our jobs the best we could. Looking back, I consider my tour in Vietnam as a good tour and a great experience.

**Barbara A. Gardner**
**Retired as a Master Sergeant**
**In country: March 3, 1970 – March 2, 1971**
**Rank: Specialist 5, US Army**
**Duty: MACV, US Army Security Agency, 509th Radio Research Group, Saigon**

**Eleanor L. Gavin (Skinner)**
**Retired as a Colonel**
**In country: March 20, 1970 – March 12, 1971**
**Rank: Major, US Air Force**
**Duty: MACV, Detachment 10, Air Force Advisory Group, USAF WAF Staff Advisor to the Vietnam Women's Armed Forces Corps**

*Darlene K. Brewer-Alexander with input from a telephone interview with Eleanor Skinner on September 19, 2014*

Major Skinner was the third WAF Advisor to the Vietnamese Air Force (VNAF). Her primary duty was to advise the VNAF Personnel officers in automating their training records, with collateral duty as the primary advisor to the head of the VNAF Women's Armed Forces Corps. In this latter capacity, she continued the work of Capt. Mary Marsh and Capt. Alice Littlejohn in the establishment of training programs for the women specifically tailored to the needs of the VNAF. She also worked with the Vietnamese Personnel Officers in the automation of training records to enhance the ability to rapidly identify those personnel with the required training to satisfy specific operational needs.

Her duties in advising the Women's Armed Forces Corps required extensive travel throughout South Vietnam to VNAF units. Many of these visits were to assess the progress of training and to update the manual records for subsequent automation. A major obstacle became apparent early on, and that was that many of the personnel she needed to evaluate were impossible to locate. These people had been at war for many years, and did not, and probably could not, consider their service in the military a full-time job. She was told not to worry, just wait until payday and they would show up and they did. That was a difficult concept for our Government to understand.

One of the things she remembers from those days in Vietnam was how very nice the people were. She also feels that, as in most conflicts, there were those of the upper class that made money off the war. Their children were still sent to France for schooling, and the war had for many years little impact on them. It was the poorer people who bore the brunt of the war. A cherished memento that she received in Vietnam was a lovely Ao Dai (Vietnamese dress) that she kept for many years. It was lost in hurricane damage.

# APRIL

*Memory Lane: Apollo 13 announces "Houston, we've got a problem!"; US troops invade Cambodia.*
*Songs: "American Woman" by The Guess Who; "Let It Be" by The Beatles*

**Carolyn L. Otey**
**Retired as a Master Sergeant**
**In country: April 1970 – February 1971**
**Rank: Staff Sergeant, US Army**
**Duty: MACV, US Army Security Agency, 509th Radio Research Group, Top Secret Control Clerk**

**Comments and Memories:** I remember riding a military bus with all the windows open, no air conditioning, back to quarters and coming to a busy intersection where we always hit a red light at this horrible smelling fish market. *Source: Vietnam Memory Book 2000*

**♥Argelis Helena Ferre**
**Retired as a Master Sergeant**
**In country: April 1970 – April 1971**
**Rank: Specialist 6, US Army**
**Duty: USARV, Central Finance and Accounting Office, Finance Specialist**

**Patricia M. Pavlis**
**Retired as a Lieutenant Colonel**
**In country: April 1970 – June 1971**
**Rank: Major, US Army Medical Specialist Corps**
**Duty: 24th Evacuation Hospital, Long Binh, Physical Therapist**

I was a physical therapist at the 24th Evacuation Hospital in Long Binh. At any given time throughout the year, there were 13 Army physical therapists in country. (One Chief, 12 Indians – a phrase I coined). When the chief was evacuated for major surgery, I was responsible for her duties also. So, I spent time in Vung Tau, Cam Ranh Bay, Hué, and a few other places. I saw the country though my primary duty was patient care.

The devastation of the country was unbelievable; much like tornado/hurricane destruction we see on TV today. The human injuries/tragedies were incredible and left an imprint upon my soul. When stationed at Fort Bragg, NC (Womack Army Hospital) and Walter Reed, 1961-1965, we thought that the Vietnam casualties looked bad upon arrival. Well, when I got to Vietnam, I realized that previously we didn't really know what "bad" really meant.

There were a few happy times. Each unit was allowed one mascot dog. I love animals and our mascot, "Christmas," attached herself to me. "Chris" was a love and brought much joy to my life. I'd save food from my mess tray to feed her and got my folks to mail me boxes of large dog cookies. Chris was passed onto other animal lovers when one of us rotated out. The other happy time: An Army Reserve warrant officer from our unit was from Washington State and belonged to an American Legion unit. They wanted to do something nice for him (us) and decided to send us a 25-foot Christmas tree. So, from June to December, we religiously started making a variety of Christmas tree ornaments out of soft drink and beer cans. A few days before Christmas and still no tree! Turns out a high ranking officer's enterprising young man had "procured" our tree. Well, our commander went to bat for us and we got our tree back and decorated for one of my most memorable Christmas celebrations.

**Edna Mae Jefferson (White)**
**In country: April 1970 – October 1971**
**Rank: Staff Sergeant, US Army**
**Duty: MACV, US Army Security Agency, 509ᵗʰ Radio Research**
**Group, Saigon; USARV, Deputy Chief of Staff for Operations,**
**Administrative NCO**

**Margaret "Peggy" K. Berry (Underwood)**
**Retired as a Master Sergeant**
**In country: April 12, 1970 – April 30, 1971**
**Rank: Staff Sergeant, US Air Force**
**Duty: 7ᵗʰ Air Force, 505ᵗʰ Tactical Support Group,**
**Administrative Specialist**

***By Margaret Underwood with edits by Colonel Darlene Brewer-Alexander:*** I was the only female assigned to the 505ᵗʰ Tactical Control Group, Tan Son Nhut Air Base, Vietnam, a group in direct support of air operations in Southeast Asia. My position was Administrative Assistant and Secretary to the Commander and Deputy Commander of the unit. The 505ᵗʰ was in harm's way, but they were a self-reliant unit using all their resources to best carry out the mission. Our Vietnamese counterparts were strong and believed in their cause. The Vietnamese Colonel liaison to the unit was from North Vietnam but was unequivocally dedicated to the South Vietnamese cause. He was a humble, respectful and educated man. In fact, he had attended our War College in the US.

Our unit was very active in sponsoring a local orphanage. We did a lot of building and repairing of the orphanage, and provided them with mosquito nets, baby bottles and clothing. All the purchases for the orphanage were made from collections from the troops. My most memorable moments from Vietnam were learning the culture, language, and adjusting to the environment. This experience made me appreciate our freedom and thank God for the United States of America.

**Shirley E. Leaverton**
**Retired as a Major**
**In country: April 12, 1970 – April 9, 1971**
**Rank: First Lieutenant, US Marine Corps**
**Duty: NAVFORV, Marine Corps Personnel Section, Administrative Officer**

*Mary Glaudel-DeZurik:* Major Shirley E. Leaverton served in Vietnam between 1970-1971. She replaced Marine CWO Lois J. Bertram. She served as Officer in Charge of the Marine Corps Personnel Section, Naval Forces, Vietnam. While there, she was awarded the Bronze Star Medal with combat "V". Her next assignment was at the Marine Recruit Depot, Parris Island, SC.

She retired in 1979 after serving 25 years in the Marine Corps. *Information provided by Shirley E. Leaverton.*

**Lyndell D. Smith**
**In country: April 13, 1970 – April 13, 1971**
**Rank: Captain, US Air Force**
**Duty: 7ᵗʰ Air Force, 600ᵗʰ Photo Squadron, Chief of Combat Documentation, Aerospace Audiovisual Service**

A small-town Georgia girl and Methodist minister's daughter, with almost two years college under my belt, I joined the Air Force on May 8, 1963, at age 21.

I was part of the largest basic training class in history to that time (close to 1,000 and basic lasted three months – not today's six-week training). In my entire Air Force career, the award of which I am most proud (beyond even Bronze Star and Presidential Unit Citations) was the American Spirit of Honor Medal for the Best Basic Trainee – the first woman ever to win that honor. To stand alongside the Basic Training School and WAF commanders as the Graduation Parade passed by was a thrill.

Happily for me, the Air Force needed Medical Corpsmen (Medics) and after training, I began my career at the 807ᵗʰ Medical Group Hospital at March Air Force Base, CA.

Accepted into the Airman Education and Commissioning Program (AECP), I graduated from Syracuse University with a Bachelor of Science degree, magna cum laude in Public Communications. After completing Officer Training School, I was assigned to the 1369ᵗʰ Photo Squadron,

Vandenberg Air Force Base, CA, where I learned my craft as a Motion Picture Production Officer.

Three years later, orders sent me to Tan Son Nhut Air Base, Vietnam, where culture shock hit as I deplaned into the terminal – stiflingly hot, with dark, crowded buildings and low, low ceilings. Could this possibly be an airport?

Assigned to the 600th Photo Squadron headquartered at Tan Son Nhut Air Base, I was the first woman to hold the position of Chief of COMDOC (Combat Documentation). Our squadron operated in trailers across from the flight line, and the workday had recently shortened to 10 hours a day, six days a week.

With three motion picture crews and six still photographers, my unit of 28 men and I were responsible for documenting Vietnamization and supporting a dozen detachments in Vietnam and Thailand. It was great working with young lieutenants, career master sergeants and airmen; almost all worked hard to do a good job and supported me both on and off duty.

Leaving aside times the Viet Cong tried to infiltrate the base, it was in many ways a wonderfully rewarding year, and I felt I was an integral part of an elite team. So, it came as a great surprise when my supervisor gave me a performance review that was just below outstanding. He said, "You should be home having babies." Honestly, I could not believe he said it out loud, and to my face.

Feeling humiliated, angry, and confused by this blatant show of discrimination, I went to the commander. He looked at my records, then said I was better at the job than COMDOC chiefs who preceded me (all male) – but those words never made it into my OER. The colonel, to my chagrin, apparently shared the major's bias against women in the military.

This open discrimination by my (heretofore highly respected) senior officers was disheartening and probably detrimental to my career in the Air Force, the service I held in such high regard.

After Vietnam, I enjoyed four years as Information Officer at the 21st Air Division in Syracuse, NY. With the Vietnam drawdown, I honorably separated from the service to complete graduate studies for a Master's degree at Syracuse University – the first time that a career change did not involve a move – what a pleasure!

**Carole J. Buss**
**Retired as a Colonel**
**In country: April 20, 1970 – April 1971**
**Rank: Major, US Army Medical Specialist Corps**
**Duty: 12ᵗʰ Evacuation Hospital, Cu Chi; 93ʳᵈ Field Hospital, Saigon,**
**Physical Therapist**

*Telephone interview with Phyllis Miller, 12/1/2014:* I graduated from college in 1956 and taught physical education and health at a school in Wisconsin. In 1960, I joined the Army. It seemed like a good fit and I came from a family of military people. My uncle was killed at Pearl Harbor.

I arrived in Vietnam and was given some indoctrination information by the MSC officer. My year was very busy. I was at 12ᵗʰ Evacuation Hospital until it closed. I did not bring home any souvenirs – in fact, I was so happy to be going home that I just had my one suitcase packed and ready. I was assigned to Walter Reed Medical Center in Washington, DC.

My retirement was mandatory – I had 30 years in service and finished as the Chief of Physical Therapy for the Army.

**Patricia "Pat" Sue Sepulveda**
**Retired as a Lieutenant Colonel**
**In country: April 20, 1970 – April 21, 1971**
**Rank: Captain, US Army Medical Service Corps**
**Duty: 71ˢᵗ Evacuation Hospital, Pleiku; 27ᵗʰ Surgical Hospital, Chu Lai,**
**Clinical Laboratory Officer**

I began in country April 20, 1970, as a Medical Service Corps Officer with a MOS of 3314, Clinical Laboratory Officer. I received two weeks of training in Saigon. My first assignment was in Pleiku: six months at the 27ᵗʰ Surgical Hospital. Hospital duties included managing the hospital laboratory (all disciplines; chemistry, urinalysis, parasitology, bacteriology, hematology, and  the blood bank), making certain the blood supply was adequate, and managing the morgue. Additional duties were serving as the payroll officer, assisting the hospitalized wounded by making runs to buy at home-type supplies (e.g. sodas) at the main post exchange, and training South Vietnamese doctors in laboratory techniques they were not familiar with. I also spent time each week helping at the leprosarium located outside of the 27th Hospital compound. Here I had the opportunity to train their laboratory technologist (Rho Pam) in the techniques for malaria diagnosis and urinalysis. The centrifuge used was hand cranked.

Now into the 7th month of my tour I was sent to my second assignment in Chu Lai at the 71st Evacuation Hospital. My duties in the laboratory were similar to Pleiku. Other duties focused on regular laboratory coverage during evenings and nights due to personnel shortages. The 71st was a larger hospital so my duties were expanded to include compound security. Since I was a Medical Service Corps (MSC) Officer, I had the privilege of having duties outside the hospital laboratory. From a personal standpoint, this made my tour interesting in ways outside of medical work.

My last transfer was to Cam Ranh Bay where I was prepared for my return to the US. On April 21, 1971, I departed Vietnam from Cam Ranh Bay. Part of our preparation for return to country was being instructed not to label any travel bags showing we were soldiers returning from Vietnam and not to wear our uniforms on the plane home. While in Cam Ranh Bay, I really did not understand fully why we were so instructed; back to this later. I left Vietnam richer in spirit, thankful for the opportunity to serve my country, thankful to have had the opportunity to train and get to know Vietnamese citizens, and with skills and memories lasting a lifetime.

It was a privilege to serve my country. The Army gave me opportunities to be found nowhere else. My administrative career was honed in Vietnam. As a female officer in a laboratory fully staffed by men, I learned quickly how to create an environment of respect and team building. We worked well together and I was grateful for the opportunity to share the experience with these dedicated, loyal and talented soldiers. There were times, particularly at the smaller 27th Surgical Hospital, where I had to create systems needed but not available in the theater of operation. These systems would not have been applicable anywhere else; a creative time for me. Serving the soldiers who gave their blood and lives was the greatest gift of all.

When we landed in the US and departed the plane entering the terminal, I understood why we received the instruction given in Cam Ranh Bay. The jeers and shouts remain imbedded in my mind. The Women's Vietnam Memorial helped soften this. For all of us who served I believe a gift we gave all soldiers who followed us was a lesson to the country; treat your soldiers with respect regardless of what you think about what they are doing. Those soldiers who followed us have, thankfully, never been treated as we were, but instead have been thanked for their service.

# MAY

*Memory Lane: Four students at Kent State University in Ohio are killed and nine wounded by Ohio State National Guardsmen, at a protest against the incursion into Cambodia; Elizabeth Hoisington & Anna Mae Mays named first female US generals.*
*Song: "The Letter" by Joe Cocker*

**♥Ethel "Hap" Elaine Apter**
**Retired as a Colonel**
**In country: May 1970 – May 1971**
**Rank: Lieutenant Colonel, US Air Force**
**Duty: 7th Air Force, Director of Administration**

Ethel Apter was a decorated Air Force Colonel, and a woman of great strength, sharp wit and keen intellect. She was the recipient of the Bronze Star, the Vietnam Gallantry Cross with Palm, and the Vietnam Service Medal with three Bronze Stars.
*Obituary,* The Hartford Courant, *May 3, 1999*

**♥Suzanne Crum**
**Retired as a Lieutenant Colonel**
**In country: May 1970 – May 1971**
**Rank: Lieutenant Colonel, US Air Force**
**Duty: 7th Air Force, Administrative Staff Officer**

**Donna "Dee" Jean Dunlap (Sams)**
**In country: May 1970 – December 1971**
**Rank: Specialist 5, US Army**
**Duty: MACV, J2, 519th Support Battalion, Combined Intelligence Center Vietnam, Translator/Intelligence Analyst**

I was at Fort Holabird, MD, when I got my orders. I was a volunteer so I was excited. I had spent 46 weeks at Defense Language Institute learning Vietnamese and I wanted to use it and see what was going on there. Although I was supposed to go to Fort Hood, TX, to translate documents, I finally got the assignment to Vietnam.

My dad didn't say much – he had been in WWII in India. I'd taken all the tests and the recruiter called the house before I got home. My mom asked me if I knew that women in the Army didn't have the best reputation. She was proud of me, though. My brother was also in the service so I knew that if I went he would not have to go.

I flew out of Travis Air Force Base, CA, to Long Binh. As soon as space was available, I was supposed to go to Saigon. It only took two days to get assigned there. I was with the 519th Support Battalion where two other women were trained Vietnamese linguists: Laura Holguin and Anna Hidalgo. I roomed with Anna.

I really felt a sense of adventure and the opportunity to see new places and things. Even the confusion about where to be when was exciting. Movie nights were weekly and the women had tight living quarters and were pretty good about sharing. I remember that even though it was hot, I frequently felt cold.

I was at MACV for nine months and it just amazed me that we had a modern air-conditioned building to work in. I spent a lot of time transcribing interviews. A young soldier came in and wanted to adopt a child and needed help translating the forms. We had 10- to 12-hour shifts. I was invited once to go to dinner with a Vietnamese family, and I remember having chopped-up chicken that was really good but the bones were in there too. The secretaries liked to practice their English on me and I would answer in Vietnamese. It was a shock to vendors that I could speak the language. After the nine months at MACV, I transferred to Combined Intelligence Center Vietnam (CICV).

I extended for six months so that I spent 18 months in country. When I returned to the States, I got out of the service and processed out, which consisted of handing over my ID card and signing a form. There was no ceremony to it and it seemed really cold and impersonal. It was about 5 a.m. when I out processed. I had no transportation so I caught a bus to Fort Ord, CA, and went to the guest house. Unfortunately, I did not have an ID card, but they were kind and let me stay for a night. The morning cannon scared me and I hit the floor. I flew home to New York State and a few weeks later went to Florida and got married. In the fall, my husband and I both enrolled in college, using the GI benefits that were one of the main reasons I signed up for the Army.

## Linda S. Little
**Retired as a First Sergeant**
**In country: May 1, 1970 – April 30, 1971**
**Rank: Staff Sergeant, US Army**
**Duty: MACV, US Army Security Agency, 509ᵗʰ Radio Research Group, S4, Administrative NCO**

I was born and raised in Parkersburg, WV, and graduated high school in 1962. On September 23, 1963, I enlisted in the Women's Army Corps. After basic training at Fort McClellan, AL, my assignments included WAC Detachment, Fort Huachuca, AZ; WAC Training Center, Fort McClellan, AL; 509ᵗʰ Radio Research Group, Saigon, Vietnam; Military Personnel Center, Alexandria, VA; US Army Hospital Vicenza, Italy; and US Army Training Center, Fort Jackson, SC. I retired as a first sergeant December 31, 1983, at Fort Jackson, SC. I later returned to my home state of West Virginia to spend time with my family.

## A. Ruth Meekins (Riggins)
**Retired as a Sergeant Major**
**In country: May 21, 1970 – May 20, 1971**
**Rank: Specialist 6, US Army**
**Duty: MACV, Office of Information; Civil Operations and Revolutionary Development Support, Executive Administrative Assistant**

## Josephine Solis
**Retired as a Sergeant Major**
**In country: May 25, 1970 – August 4, 1972**
**Rank: Specialist 5, US Army**
**Duty: USARV, 1ˢᵗ Aviation Brigade, Personnel Section, Officer Records, Personnel Specialist**

I enlisted in the Army May 25, 1968. It was my calling and I knew it in my heart. After advanced training, my first assignment was Presidio of San Francisco, CA. I was proud to be there, especially with family nearby in San Jose.

In San Francisco, it was not unusual for military members to be ridiculed and harassed in terminals and bus stops and other public locations. Therefore, military members were not authorized to wear the uniform in public. We were to blend in for our own safety. I realized we were targeted more at home in the United States than in a foreign country! I loved my assignment at the Presidio, but I was more determined than ever to serve our country in Vietnam.

I arrived in Vietnam late in the afternoon – and it was so hot. We turned in our 201 files. We were up for the night while we waited for a briefing and pending our new assignment orders to Long Binh.

The young sergeant who helped me with my bag warned me of a possible enemy attack that night. I said, "Attack! Are you joking?" He laughed and said, "I wish I was joking but the VC (Viet Cong) have a way of knowing when we have new arrivals. We call these attacks fear tactics. They use this tool to instill fear in our new soldiers." Let me tell you from my own experience that the tactic worked.

Later that night while I was trying to sleep and wrestling with my mind and body, I heard the sounds of war – it was our outgoing artillery. I jumped out of bed and looked out the window, and saw nothing except the security guard standing there looking into the darkness. He seemed unafraid. I knew then I was in good hands. But, I kept wondering what I was missing: I noticed he had a weapon. He had been trained to defend himself. I realized that I was afraid because I had not been trained to use a weapon to defend myself. I was starting my tour in Vietnam without the means to protect myself. I had my faith in God and our brave soldiers to see me through.

I would like to acknowledge the brave men and women of the 1st Aviation Brigade with whom I proudly served.

"Thanks for the memories!" as Bob Hope would say.

# JUNE

*Memory Lane: US Senate votes overwhelmingly to repeal Gulf of Tonkin Resolution.*
*Song: "The Long and Winding Road" by The Beatles*

## Nora Marie Prestinari (Burchett)
**In country: June 1970 – April 1971**
**Rank: Captain, US Army Medical Specialist Corps**
**Duty: 95th Evacuation Hospital, Da Nang; 24th Evacuation Hospital, Long Binh, Physical Therapist**

I volunteered for service in country after treating many patients who returned to the States, many patients who were training to go to Vietnam and those going back for additional tours. It was important for me to do for MY country alongside the other men and women of courage. Initially assigned to the 95th Evacuation Hospital in Da Nang, then transferred to the 24th Evacuation Hospital in Long Binh, I continued to treat patients foreign and domestic – children through adult. Since the drawdown was beginning in earnest, I returned home in April, just short of my year. I continued my military career until I was retired in 1978. It was truly the best of times and the worst of times.

## Sharon Elaine Thomas (Safford)
**Retired as a Lieutenant Colonel**
**In country: June 1970 – May 1971**
**Rank: Second Lieutenant, US Air Force**
**Duty: 7th Air Force, 12th Reconnaissance Intelligence Technical Squadron, Intelligence Photo-Radar Officer, Photo Imagery**

**Comments and Memories:** Making potato salad for church gathering – up to my elbows in mayonnaise! Remembering the services through the church, supporting local orphanages, singing in the choir that "toured" and served as background for "Christmas in Vietnam," shown on national TV. We sang "Messiah." *Source: Vietnam Memory Book 2000*

## ♥Alice Agnes Long
**Retired as a Colonel**
**In country: June 1970 – June 1971**
**Rank: Lieutenant Colonel, US Army**
**Duty: MACV, J1, Personnel Staff Officer**

**♥Edna Nester Renfroe (Fague)**
**Retired as a Master Sergeant**
**In country: June 1970 – June 1971**
**Rank: Staff Sergeant, US Army**
**Duty: USARV, Logistics Support Center,**
**Communications Center Specialist**

**Comments and Memories:** My funniest and most enjoyable memory was going to Da Nang for in-country R&R. *Source: Vietnam Memory Book 2000*

**Joan Drawdy**
**In country: June 1970 – July 1971**
**Rank: Captain, US Air Force, Biomedical Sciences Corps**
**Duty: 7th Air Force, 483rd USAF Hospital, Cam Ranh Bay, Medical**
**Food Service Officer, Dietitian/Nutritionist**

**June Walker**
**Retired as a Sergeant First Class**
**In country: June 1970 – July 1971**
**Rank: Specialist 5, US Army**
**Duty: 24th Evacuation Hospital, Personnel Specialist**

**♥Ruth Josephine O'Holleran**
**Retired as a Colonel**
**In country: June 30, 1970 – July 15, 1971**
**Rank: Lieutenant Colonel, US Marine Corps**
**Duty: MACV, Staff Historian, Administrative Officer**

# JULY

*Memory Lane: Casey Kasem's "American Top 40" debuts on LA radio; Chet Huntley retires from NBC, ends "Huntley-Brinkley Report."*
*Song: "Mama Told Me Not to Come" by Three Dog Night*

**Ruth A. Cox**
**Retired as a Lieutenant Colonel**
**In country: July 1970 – July 1971**
**Rank: Major, US Air Force**
**Duty: 7th Air Force, 2nd Aerial Port Group, 8th Aerial Port Squadron,**
**Assistant Station Traffic Officer, Group Director Aerial Port**
**Control Center**

As a major, I went from the cold to the hot! I arrived at Tan Son Nhut Air Base from Elmendorf Air Force Base, AK. Fortunately, it was July, so I didn't have to go from parka to shorts.

As a female assigned to the local transportation unit, I was exempt from sitting through the in-country briefings foisted on less fortunate GIs. It was very important to someone that syphilis and other unsavory subjects be fully explored for the newly arrived personnel. It is doubtful that much was absorbed after the 20-plus-hour flight (long since having forgotten the exact length).

Tan Son Nhut Air Base was the busiest airport in the world at the time. The job was to get the aircraft offloaded and forward the cargo to its end user. Military Airlift Command had recently developed a palletization system that greatly facilitated both loading and unloading cargo aircraft in minimum time. Unfortunately, the pallets (108"x88" aluminum sheeting, front and back, with balsa interior) were much in demand by Army in-country units. The pallets made great ceilings for bunkers. My Air Force team was run off more than once trying to recover expensive pallets.

I went TDY (temporary duty) to almost all of our airstrips in Vietnam. The one that stands out was Da Nang. The Colonel Aerial Port Commander met my aircraft and his first question was, "Where was my flak jacket and helmet?" When I told him they were in a corner of my BOQ room in Tan Son Nhut, he took me to view his "hootch" (an aluminum trailer). There was a neat row of bullet holes right through the middle. Meekly, I allowed him to take me to Supply to draw the needed equipment. It seems that a Viet Cong piper cub-type aircraft (they called him "Charlie") had been coming over every evening and firing off a few rounds. Our jets were too fast and couldn't catch him.

I was in Da Nang three nights. No piper cub. I turned in the equipment and went back to Tan Son Nhut. I had a telephone call from the colonel the next morning: Get my a\*\* back to Da Nang! Seems that as soon as I left, Charlie put in another appearance!

**Maryland L. Dorsey (Welch)**
**In country: July 1970 – July 1971**
**Rank: Staff Sergeant, US Marine Corps**
**Duty: MACV, Marine Corps Personnel Section**

**Mary Lou Fake**
**Retired as a Colonel**
**In country: July 1970 – July 1971**
**Rank: Major, US Air Force**
**Duty: 7th Air Force, Personnel Staff Officer**

**♥Virginia Lanelle Gunter**
**Retired as a Colonel**
**In country: July 1970 – July 1971**
**Rank: Lieutenant Colonel, US Air Force**
**Duty: MACV, Planning and Programming Officer**

**♥Verna Sarah Kellogg II**
**Retired as a Lieutenant Colonel**
**In country: July 1970 – July 1971**
**Rank: Major, US Air Force**
**Duty: 7th Air Force, Chief of Combat News, Information Staff Officer**

*Donna Lowery:* Verna Kellogg was given a direct commission as a first lieutenant. In her career, she was assigned to Randolph Air Force Base, San Antonio, TX, the Pentagon and the National Defense University. She was very proud of the Bronze Star she was awarded for her performance as Chief of Combat News at Headquarters Seventh Air Force in Vietnam. She enjoyed the field part of that job very much. She enjoyed a challenge and felt she could achieve anything. Stories of "Verna" were well known among her friends.

Of all of her assignments, Colonel Kellogg enjoyed her assignment as Chief of Public Information in Misawa, Japan the most. She learned how to play Mah Jong. She played at lunch daily with the Chief of Police, Mayor of the City and other officials that had concerns with the base. This was an innovative way of improving the base/community relations and another way to illustrate how incredible she was. She would go back after lunch and work on these issues. The base commander would meet with these same officials later in the day and discuss solutions to their concerns.

Colonel Kellogg enjoyed her retirement. She mentored young people, played golf, got involved with charities and played more Mah Jong. *This information was obtained from the VWV and the* San Antonio Express News *obituary.*

**Linda A. Ligon**
**In country: July 1970 – July 1971**
**Rank: Captain, US Air Force**
**Duty: 7ᵗʰ Air Force, Intelligence Photo-Radar Officer**

**Rosemary McCulley (Kitchen)**
**Retired as a Major**
**In country: July 1970 – July 1971**
**Rank: Captain, US Air Force**
**Duty: 7ᵗʰ Air Force, 3ʳᵈ Aerospace Rescue and Recovery Group,**
**Administrative Management Officer**

**♥Cecile Doreen Lanoue (Seago)**
**Retired as a Chief Master Sergeant**
**In country: July 1970 – July 1971**
**Rank: Master Sergeant, US Air Force**
**Duty: 7ᵗʰ Air Force, IG, Administrative Superintendent**

**Karen Kay King (Psimadis) (Johnson)**
**In country: July 1970 – February 1972**
**Rank: Captain, US Army**
**Duty: USARV, Command Information Officer**

**♥Dr. Clotilde O. Dent Bowen, MD**
**Retired as a Colonel, USAR**
**In country: July 6, 1970 – July 1971**
**Rank: Colonel, US Army Medical Corps**
**Duty: MACV, Office of the Surgeon Headquarters, Neuropsychiatric**
**Physician/Consultant**

In March 1971, a reporter for *The Baltimore Sun* interviewed COL (Dr.) Clotilde Bowen, US Army Medical Corps, about her experiences in Vietnam. "What is it like to be black and female in the mostly white, male US Army?" he asked. "Rough, often," she replied. "Many assume you are weak and inferior, not very capable. At best, you are patronized. At worst, there is just outright discrimination. But, it's not so much because you are black, but because you are a woman. The Army is learning, often painfully, how to accept blacks as people. But it is still uptight about women."

Traditionally, physicians have held substantial authority, and for years, the military refused to commission women doctors. They served on a temporary basis during WWII, but were not accepted as permanent members of the regular Medical Corps of the Army, Navy and Air Force until the middle of the Korean War in 1952. Very few women doctors joined the military during the 1950s and 1960s, however. During this era, women comprised only four percent of physicians in the United States, and of these, only a small number were black.

The first black woman physician to hold a military commission was Colonel Clotilde Bowen, who joined the Army in 1955. She became the first African-American female to earn the rank of colonel, to command a military hospital clinic, and to be named Chief of Psychiatry in two Veterans Administration hospitals and two Army medical centers.

By 1970, then COL Bowen, still the only black woman physician in the Army, received orders "to my surprise and dismay to go to Vietnam. We landed in Bien Hoa (Air Base) after midnight July 6, 1970, in a hail of gunfire, rockets, mortar rounds and unbearable heat," wrote COL Bowen.

Her job required frequent travel in country, and she always packed her .45 caliber sidearm. "I submitted reports about the morale and mental health of troops and civilians in Vietnam, briefed congressmen, visiting foreign dignitaries and ranking officers, and news media wanting to know what was really happening as we were losing the war." Colonel Bowen recalled her tour as being very lonely. "My position and rank precluded me from socializing with most officers or NCOs."

As the Army's chief psychiatrist in Vietnam, COL Bowen oversaw the work of 17 other physician psychiatrists, as well as nurse psychiatrists and social workers. She was also responsible for planning and coordinating the Army's drug and race relations programs in Vietnam. Colonel Bowen told a newspaper reporter that "Army psychiatry is mostly preventative – treating problems before they start. The main problem in Vietnam and in the service in general is the disaffected state of American youth today. They lack the motivation to be in the service, they certainly lack the motivation to be in Vietnam and I think they lack the motivation to do things in civilian life. This disaffection is the main reason for the use of drugs, for instance."

Colonel Bowen believed that the majority of the discrimination she encountered both inside and outside the Army Medical Corps involved not her race, but her gender. "If America became all white overnight, the most persistent form of discrimination – sexism – would still be there," she told a reporter. "Of course, when you are a colonel, discrimination is much less of a problem in the military. Even black, female colonels rate salutes in this man's Army."

Although the Army relegated most enlisted women to positions as secretaries and clerks and gave few women the opportunity to learn jobs that required mechanical or technical skills, COL Bowen believed that the Army had gone further than many sectors of society in giving women equal pay for equal work. "The Army promotes you on the basis of quality and years of service," she said. "It doesn't matter whether you are male or female; you get the same pay, the same privileges. The system is trying to be fair." Still, she said, "Changing laws and restructuring the system doesn't do much to remove the main obstacle – the male ego and the way women relate to it."

In 1977, COL Bowen was assigned to command the Hawley Army Medical Center at Fort Benjamin Harrison, IN, making her the first woman to command a US military hospital. She summarized her philosophy to a news reporter, "I know that there have been times when I have been victimized by discrimination – both racial and sexual. But, I have refused to allow the fact that people discriminate against me to defeat me or sour my judgment. Then too, I've often wondered if, when it came to assigning military physicians to new jobs, it wasn't easier for my superiors to pick me than try to deal with a pool of white men – all essentially the same. I imagine

I sort of stood out, gave them something definite to point to that made a 'reason' for them to pick me."

Colonel Bowen was honored with the Bronze Star and the Legion of Merit in 1971 for her work to set up drug treatment centers and her efforts to lessen racial conflicts during the Vietnam War. She was awarded the Meritorious Service Medal in 1974.

She retired from the US Army in 1982. Dr. Bowen passed away March 3, 2011.

**Grethe Elizabeth Wik**
**Retired as a Lieutenant Colonel, USAF**
**In country: July 17, 1970 – July 14, 1971**
**Rank: Captain, US Army Medical Specialist Corps**
**Duty: 67ᵗʰ Evacuation Hospital, Qui Nhon,**
**Physical Therapist**

"Kermit Lindgren was a burn patient of mine. He was admitted on Christmas Day 1970. Kermit went on convalescent leave at 67ᵗʰ Evacuation Hospital, Qui Nhon."

Captain Grethe Wik served in the US Army while she was in Vietnam. She later transferred to the USAF and retired as a Lieutenant Colonel.

**Nancy R. Kennedy**
**Retired as a Major**
**In country: July 26, 1970 – July 25, 1971**
**Rank: Captain, US Air Force**
**Duty: 7ᵗʰ Air Force, 176ᵗʰ Communications Squadron,**
**Communications Systems Officer**

I was born and raised in San Diego, CA. After attending San Diego State, I entered the Air Force, took my first airplane ride and went to Lackland Air Force Base, San Antonio, TX, for Officer Training School. My first assignment as a new second lieutenant was to Michigan, quite a shock for a southern Californian who had never touched snow and only seen it in pictures or topping a distant mountain. While Michigan was pretty country, after one winter of snow, whiteouts and chill factors of 40-45 degrees below zero, I volunteered for Southeast Asia. I also felt the need to do my part, however small it might be.

At Tan Son Nhut Air Base near Saigon, I was assigned to the 176th Communications Squadron, only a couple of blocks from where female officers were billeted. While I had seven communications facilities to oversee, the most important and visible was the 7th Air Force Command Post Communications Center. We were responsible for sending the daily teletype frag orders (a change to a specific part of an existing order) confirming coordinates for B-52 sorties to be flown from Thailand the next day and then receiving results and updating information. I met some great people and enjoyed the camaraderie and get-togethers in our compound. It was also interesting to live in such a different culture and environment. Of course, there were some unpleasant people and experiences, and I saw some men away from their families behaving quite badly. However, I feel fortunate that I don't suffer any ill effects from Vietnam service so far.

Once again, I was blessed because after my tour in Vietnam and leave, I went to Germany for four years, so I did not encounter the anti-Vietnam sentiment many returned to and had to deal with. I completed another overseas tour in Turkey prior to retirement. I consider myself honored to have been able to serve and am pleased to see the positive attitudes now toward our military heroes. My retirement years are now filled with some travel, volunteering and one or two mission trips a year.

**Donna Lee Giordani**
**Retired as a Master Sergeant**
**In country: July 28, 1970 – July 29, 1971**
**Rank: Specialist 5, US Army**
**Duty: USARV, 165th Aviation Group, Air Traffic Controller**

**Comments and Memories:** I was chosen WAC of the Week and had an article published in the *Army Times,* December 9, 1970, titled "On Air in Nam," Long Binh, Vietnam. The article reads: Our selection for this week is a most unusual gal in a most unusual job. Her work is up in the air and the "plane" fact is she's good at it. She used to manage an interior decorating factory specializing in custom-made draperies and now she manages air traffic control tower specializing in helicopter and airplane traffic in Vietnam. A big jump indeed, but one taken in easy stride by a multi-talented young lady with determination. Bugged on flying while decorating those interiors in civilian life back in her hometown of Pittsburgh, PA, she decided the Army was the place to learn and an air controller's job was the thing to have. Her first duty station was Crissy Army Air Field at the Presidio of San Francisco where she promptly took care of that ambition to become a flier. She earned her civilian pilot's license there while a member of the nearby Hamilton Air Force Base Flying Club. Meanwhile, Donna is in full control working in a man's field. "She does a very commendable job," says SP4 Tom Holmes, another controller at Sanford. "Some of the pilots can make it rough on a controller at times, but Donna handles them very well and they find her very capable." *Source: Vietnam Memory Book 2000*

# AUGUST

*Memory Lane: The US sinks 418 containers of nerve gas into the Gulf Stream near the Bahamas; the Women's Strike for Equality takes place down Fifth Avenue in New York City.*
*Song: "War" by Edwin Staff*

**Theresa Sanchez**
**In country: August 1970 – March 1971**
**Rank: Specialist 5, US Army**
**Duty: USARV, Personnel Specialist**

**Norma L. Holson**
**Retired as a Master Sergeant**
**In country: August 1970 – June 1971**
**Rank: Specialist 5, US Army**
**Duty: MACV, US Army Security Agency, 509th Radio Research Group, Personnel Management Specialist**

I was stationed with the Headquarters and Headquarters Company, 509th Radio Research Group, which was located on Davis Station at Tan Son Nhut Air Base in Vietnam. Davis Station was a small highly classified compound that headquartered the 509th Radio Research Group. It was where most Army Security Agency personnel processed in country and were subsequently assigned to subordinate units. The

509th Radio Research Group was covertly under the US Army Security Agency. Its primary mission was intelligence gathering. I worked in the military personnel office processing soldiers and managing their military personnel records.

Davis Station was named after the first US soldier killed in action in Vietnam (SP4 James T. Davis) assigned to the US Army Security Agency. It consisted of billeting for the male military personnel, a mess hall, enlisted men's club, armory, motor pool and medical clinic.

All the females, approximately six who were assigned to the 509th on Davis Station, were billeted at the Medford Hotel several miles away. I never encountered any enemy attacks, but we were constantly on alerts for booby traps and plastic explosives. I was more afraid of the large rats!

I was treated very well as a female soldier in Vietnam. My male counterparts treated me with respect and dignity. Many draftees could not understand why anyone would volunteer for Vietnam, especially a woman. I guess it was my sense of patriotism. I still fly the American flag every day.

I did not experience any protest against the war or for being in the army after Vietnam. It may have been because I stayed in the army and was mostly around military personnel until my retirement in 1987.

**Comments and Memories:** Carol Ogg and myself on a cyclo going downtown Saigon to a bar after the 2200 curfew. The compound guard let us back into the Medford when we returned. We laughed all the way not thinking of the dangers. *Source: Vietnam Memory Book 2000*

**Martha A. Cronin**
**Retired as a Colonel**
**In country: August 1970 – July 1971**
**Rank: Captain, US Army Medical Specialist Corps**
**Duty: 67th Medical Group, Da Nang; 3rd Field Hospital, Saigon, Dietetic Consultant**

I was assigned to the 67th Medical Group in Da Nang where I served as a consultant dietitian to eight hospitals and two air ambulance companies. My area of responsibility ran from Qui Nhon in II Corps to the DMZ in the north (I Corps) and back into Pleiku in the western part of II Corps. Because we had a lot of territory to cover, we flew whatever was available to get  to our destinations. This included any type of airplane or helicopter.

I was billeted at the 5ᵗʰ Transportation Command Compound in Da Nang where I was the only military female, though there were two or three USO females.

I retired from the Army as a Colonel after 26 years of service.

**Peggy "Peg" Lee Roberts**
**In country: August 1970 – August 1971**
**Rank: Specialist 5, US Army**
**Duty: USARV, Adjutant General, Officer Personnel**

**Comments and Memories:** One morning, still half asleep, I reached for my soap dish and trapped a lizard between my palm and the container. The louder I screamed, the harder I squeezed. I can still see everyone around me laughing as mama-san rescued the lizard. *Source: Vietnam Memory Book 2000*

**Barbara J. Aaron**
**Retired as a Master Sergeant**
**In country: August 1970 – August 1971**
**Rank: Staff Sergeant, US Marine Corps**
**Duty: NAVFORV, Administrative Clerk**

**Dorothy G. Baird**
**Retired as a Technical Sergeant**
**In country: August 1970 – August 1971**
**Rank: Technical Sergeant, US Air Force**
**Duty: MACV, J2, Administrative Supervisor**

While in Saigon, Dorothy lived in the Medford Hotel. She worked as an Administrative Supervisor.

**♥Faye Lou Beard**
**Retired as a Major**
**In country: August 1970 – August 1971**
**Rank: Captain, US Air Force**
**Duty: 7ᵗʰ Air Force, Administrative Management Officer, Cam Ranh Bay**

**Glenda Griggs (Britz)**
In country: August 1970 – August 1971
Rank: Specialist 5, US Army
Duty: USARV, 1st Aviation Brigade, Air Traffic Controller

**Nancy A. Hunter**
Retired as a Lieutenant Colonel
In country: August 1970 – August 1971
Rank: Major, US Army
Duty: USARV, Staff Judge Advocate; Saigon Support Command, 4th
Transportation Battalion, Judge Advocate

**Frances L. Black**
Retired as a Sergeant Major
In country: August 1970 – September 1971
Rank: Specialist 5, US Army
Duty: USARV, Special Troops, WAC Detachment, Company Clerk

**Carolyn "Skid" Skidmore**
Retired as a Sergeant First Class
In country: August 1970 – September 1971
Rank: Specialist 5, US Army
Duty: USARV, 221st Signal Company (Pictorial),
Southeast Asia Pictorial Center, Photographic
Laboratory Technician

♥Cynthia "Cindy" L. Baker
In country: August 1970 – December 1971
Rank: Specialist 5, US Army
Duty: USARV, 1st Signal Brigade, Personnel Specialist

♥Bridget "Ronnie" Veronica Connolly
Retired as a Master Sergeant
In country: August 1970 – April 1972
Rank: Staff Sergeant, US Marine Corps
Duty: MACV, J5, Plans Division, Marine Corps Personnel Section,
Personnel/Administrative Chief

**Gladys Berrios-Perez (Schwerin)**
**In country: August 31, 1970 – July 6, 1971**
**Rank: Specialist 5, US Army**
**Duty: USARV, Auditing Department, Clerk-Typist**

I joined the WAC in 1968 at Fort Buchanan, PR. My basic training was in Fort McClellan, AL. My advanced training was at Fort Sam Houston, TX. After finishing training, I was sent to Fort Gordon, GA, where I started Medic Training, but due to my secretarial background I was switched from medical assistant to office clerk.

In Augusta, GA, I worked in the Accounting and Editing Department/Foreign Liaison Branch. It was one of the best years of my service in the US Army. I made Specialist 5.

When the war in Vietnam was at its peak, I decided to volunteer and be of service to my country. I was not afraid to go overseas to war. As a Christian, I felt it was my mission. My faith in God gave me determination, courage and strength to undertake this task.

I arrived in Long Binh, Vietnam, in July 1970. I worked at USARV Headquarters in the Auditing Department. I was given a tour of MACV in Saigon and had the privilege of meeting General Creighton Abrams, MACV commander.

In my spare time, I visited the wounded at the 24th Evacuation Hospital in Long Binh. I volunteered with the Red Cross to provide entertainment to these soldiers. I sang in English and Spanish bringing back memories of home. I enjoyed very much putting my talents to use; I became part of the singing choir and performed as lead singer in musicals such as "The Fantastics."

I made a tape of my singing with the US Band performing nationally on Vietnamese television. This was the icing on the cake of my military service.

My three years in the US Women's Army Corps was challenging and valuable to me as a person and a female. I don't harbor any regrets. In fact, I grew as a person of character being true to my gender and to myself. My fellow men respected me because of my resilience in overcoming the odds in a world geared toward men. My faith kept me strong in the midst of hardships, but the prize was worth it! I met my future husband, made many friends, shared laughter and tears, traveled to foreign places, and had a new perspective on life – to live life at its fullest with God's blessing.

# SEPTEMBER

*Memory Lane: The first New York City Marathon begins; the Ford Pinto is introduced.*
*Song: "Lookin' Out My Back Door" by Creedence Clearwater Revival*

**Clare Price (Zens)**
**Retired as a Lieutenant Colonel, USAF Reserve**
**In country: September 1970 – December 1970**
**Rank: Captain, US Air Force**
**Duty: HQ, 7th Air Force, Intelligence Officer**

**Sandra "Sandy" M. Leino (Kaigler)**
**In country: September 1970 – July 1971**
**Rank: Specialist 5, US Army**
**Duty: USARV, Logistics**

**Comments and Memories:** Tommiie Acierno and I got the colonel's keys from the Vietnamese driver to go cruising to the post exchange. While I was waiting in the car, the colonel drove up in an old, worn-out Army-green car and parked right next to his shiny new one we had! He never said anything to us. *Source: Vietnam Memory Book 2000*

**Joan E. Barber**
**In country: September 1970 – September 1971**
**Rank: First Lieutenant, US Air Force**
**Duty: 7th Air Force, 12th Reconnaissance Intelligence Technical Squadron, Intelligence Officer**

**Sandra Britton (Jordan)**
**In country: September 1970 – September 1971**
**Rank: Specialist 5, US Army**
**Duty: USARV, Vietnam Open Mess Agency (VOMA), Clerk-Typist**

♥Sarah Chavez (Cox) (McCauslin)
Retired as a Technical Sergeant
In country: September 1970 – September 1971
Rank: Staff Sergeant, US Air Force
Duty: 7th Air Force, Directorate of Personnel, Administrative Specialist

Teresa A. Dickerson
Retired as a First Sergeant
In country: September 1970 – September 1971
Rank: Corporal, US Marine Corps
Duty: MACV, NAVFORV

Nellie Drain (Mach) (Perkins)
Retired as a Gunnery Sergeant
In country: September 1970 – September 1971
Rank: Sergeant, US Marine Corps
Duty: NAVFORV, Marine Corps
Personnel Section, Administrative Clerk

Jane Rutledge
Retired as a Major
In country: September 1970 – September 1971
Rank: Captain, US Air Force
Duty: 7th Air Force, 483rd Tactical Airlift Wing, Cam Ranh Bay,
Administrative Officer

♥Carolyn Ann Sander
In country: September 1970 – September 1971
Rank: Captain, US Army
Duty: USA Support Command, Secretary of the General Staff, Protocol
Office, Cam Ranh Bay

♥Jean W. Solomon
Retired as a Chief Master Sergeant
In country: September 1970 – September 1971
Rank: Staff Sergeant, US Air Force
Duty: 7th Air Force, Air Force Advisory Group,
Administrative Supervisor

**♥Mary Nell Turner**
**Retired as a Colonel**
**In country: September 1970 – September 1971**
**Rank: Captain, US Air Force**
**Duty: 7ᵗʰ Air Force, Administrative Management Officer**

Interest in Vietnam came in 1963 when I got a new assignment to the Tactical Air Warfare Center in Florida. They were working on plans and tactics for Vietnam. My job as a lieutenant was administrative management and that meant I shuffled papers, copied paper, printed paper, etc. In 1963, only a handful of Air Force people were in Vietnam. None were women. Later when the war heated up and the Air Force started asking for volunteers, I carefully read the requirements. There wasn't one word in there about a person having to be a man to volunteer! I ran right over to the Personnel Office to put in my volunteer statement. They laughed at me. They said, "You know women can't go into combat area." And I said, "It doesn't say a word here about Vietnam being a combat area."

The next day there was a message from the higher headquarters that said women could not volunteer for Vietnam because of the possibility of combat. A few years later, the policy changed and Vietnam was open to women in the headquarters area.

My kid brother served in Vietnam as an Army medic, been wounded and returned home. He got shot in the rear end while trying to drag another guy out of a rice paddy. After he recuperated in Hawaii he got shipped back home. No parade in Washington, DC, for him. They mailed him the Purple Heart and the Bronze Star with V for valor after he got home. He received it in the same mail as his unemployment check. I was visiting home during that time and I thought he seemed more concerned with the check than with the medals.

My firsthand knowledge of a person being wounded caused me to slack off on the desire to become a hero, but I still wanted to go to Vietnam, knowing it would probably help my career. As far as I was concerned since all the men were going to Vietnam, the women better go also if they wanted to get promoted and get good jobs. So I marched myself over to the Personnel Office to volunteer. This time they greeted me with open arms and that is how I ended up at Tan Son Nhut Air Base on September 23, 1970.

*This story is excerpts from Colonel Mary Turner's journal, writings and stories that she wrote after she retired when she was enrolled in some creative writing classes and given to SP5 Marsha "Cricket" Holder by Mary's sister-in-law, Fran Turner, to be included in this book.*

**Ruthie M. Webb**
**Retired as a Sergeant First Class**
**In country: September 1970 – September 1971**
**Rank: Staff Sergeant, US Army**
**Duty: USARV, Headquarters Support Command, Personnel NCO**

**Lois E. Weeks**
**Retired as a Master Sergeant**
**In country: September 1970 – September 1971**
**Rank: Staff Sergeant, US Army**
**Duty: USARV, G4, Materiel Control and Accounting Specialist**

**Joy J. Smith**
**Retired as a First Sergeant**
**In country: September 1970 – December 1, 1971**
**Rank: Specialist 5, US Army**
**Duty: 24th Evacuation Hospital, Long Binh, Dental Assistant**

I was the first WAC assigned to the Maxillo-Facial Team. I worked in the Dental Clinic and Operating Room treating ALL face and head injuries. I assisted the oral surgeons and plastic surgeon treating friendly and unfriendly (enemy) wounded, including civilians.

**Patricia A. Worthen (Champion)**
**In country: September 15, 1970 – September 10, 1971**
**Rank: First Lieutenant, US Air Force**
**Duty: 7th Air Force, 12th Reconnaissance Intelligence Technical Squadron, Intelligence Officer**

In September 1970, I received orders to Vietnam, where I was assigned to the 12th Reconnaissance Intelligence Technical Squadron (12th RITS), Tan Son Nhut Air Base, Saigon. I was the officer in charge of the Intelligence Library, which was the repository for all the documents, maps, photos, etc., in support of the photo interpreters and other military organizations. We worked 12-hour days with one day off per week. This was a very interesting assignment as I had the opportunity to begin to learn the South Vietnamese language as well as learn about the culture and cuisine of another country. I became acquainted with the aircrews that flew the RB-57s that took many of the films processed by 12ᵗʰ RITS, and ended up meeting a young captain who became my future husband!

During the year, I regularly volunteered to go with other squadron members to the local orphanage to interact with the children and staff, provide clothing, toys and food. I enjoyed my interaction with the native populations in spite of the language barriers. I felt safe and my duties seemed the same as my other assignments both before and following my Vietnam experience. I had an opportunity to visit both Thailand and Australia on leave or R&R.

Following my tour in Vietnam, I went on to a variety of assignments in the intelligence field, including a temporary duty assignment to Anderson Air Base, Guam, to brief and debrief the B-52 aircrews involved in the intensive bombing of North Vietnam. I was fortunate to be stationed in Hawaii when the POWs returned home, and was there on the flight line to welcome them home.

I feel fortunate to have returned home to no negative comments and no posttraumatic stress disorder. In recent days, I have met with other Vietnam veterans and have been welcomed as a comrade. My husband, who I met while in Vietnam, also has encountered no negative feedback as a result of our service. I am proud to have served.

# OCTOBER

*Memory Lane: In Los Angeles, singer Janis Joplin dies in her hotel room, from an overdose of heroin; Garry Trudeau's comic strip Doonesbury debuts; PBS becomes a US television network.*
*Songs: "Ain't No Mountain High Enough" by Diana Ross; "I'll be There" by The Jackson Five*

**Barbara L. Banks**
**Retired as a Major**
**In country: October 1970 – October 1971**
**Rank: Captain, US Air Force**
**Duty: 7ᵗʰ Air Force, Intelligence Officer**

♥Sylvia Rita Bernardini
**Retired as a First Sergeant**
**In country: October 1970 – October 1971**
**Rank: Sergeant First Class, US Army**
**Duty: MACV, Joint Staff, Sixth NCO Advisor to the Vietnam Women's Armed Forces Corps**

**Peggy Joann Erhart**
**In country: October 1970 – October 1971**
**Rank: First Lieutenant, US Air Force**
**Duty: 7th Air Force, 377th Combat Support Group, Administrative Officer**

**Sherry A. Ewan (Sieg)**
**In country: October 1970 – October 1971**
**Rank: Captain, US Air Force**
**Duty: 7th Air Force, 1876th Communications Squadron, Tan Son Nhut, Administrative Officer**

**Marie J. Gutierrez**
**Retired as a Colonel**
**In country: October 1970 – October 1971**
**Rank: First Lieutenant, US Air Force**
**Duty: 7th Air Force, 12th Tactical Recon Squadron, and 45th Tactical Recon Squadron, Intelligence Photo-Radar Officer**

**Memorable experiences:** I was in tactical aircraft maintenance, and I will forever be impressed by how dedicated and professional the young maintenance officers and enlisted people were. Maintenance has one of the toughest missions in the USAF, and maintenance people always made me proud to be in the same field.

♥Lillian Kalikolehau Maluo
**In country: October 1970 – October 1971**
**Rank: Major, US Army**
**Duty: USA Support Command, Training Center Unit, Qui Nhon**

**Joyce C. Peluso**
**Retired as a Lieutenant Colonel**
**In country: October 1970 – October 1971**
**Rank: First Lieutenant, US Air Force**
**Duty: 7th Air Force, 12th Reconnaissance Intelligence Technical**
**Squadron, Intelligence Officer**

A memorable time for me was my work with the local Vietnamese who worked on the base in the different clubs and shops. I taught them idiomatic English. Just enough so that we could all communicate better with each other. I taught about 15 men and women for an hour three times a week. Some of my students had fled North Vietnam during the war. This experience made my time there much more interesting.

**Marilyn V. Robinson**
**Retired as a Senior Master Sergeant**
**In country: October 1970 – October 1971**
**Rank: Master Sergeant, US Air Force**
**Duty: 7th Air Force, 1st Weather Squadron,**
**Weather Forecaster Technician**

**Sheila Warren (Smith)**
**Retired as a Lieutenant Colonel**
**In country: October 1970 – October 1971**
**Rank: Captain, US Air Force**
**Duty: 21st Tactical Air Support Squadron, Administration**
**Management Officer, Cam Ranh Bay**

**Maria Edna Reyes**
**Retired as a Master Sergeant**
**In country: October 1970 – February 1972**
**Rank: Specialist 5, US Army**
**Duty: 24th Evacuation Hospital, Long Binh, Administrative Specialist**

**Ella "Brooksie" L. Brooks**
**Retired as a Sergeant First Class**
**In country: October 1970 – April 1972**
**Rank: Specialist 5, US Army**
**Duty: USARV, Engineer Division, Administrative**
**Specialist**

♥**Charlene "Jamie" Ann Jameson (Seals)**
**Retired as a Command Sergeant Major**
**In country: October 1970 – May 1972**
**Rank: Sergeant First Class, US Army**
**Duty: USARV, Inventory Control Center, Administrative Supervisor**

**Joyce Evelyn Oakes (Poole)**
**Retired as a Sergeant Major**
**In country: October 1970 – June 1972**
**Rank: Specialist 6, US Army**
**Duty: USARV, 1st Logistical Command, Saigon Support Command, Staff**
**Judge Advocate's Office, Legal Specialist**

I enlisted in the US Army in January 1967 and retired as a Sergeant Major in June 1989 with 22½ years of service. Throughout my career, I served in various posts in the States to include Hawaii and overseas. My assignments were varied, busy and interesting.

I joined the Army after high school graduation and in 1970 went to Vietnam. When I arrived in country, the airport had just been shelled. We were hurried off the plane and into buses to take us to the processing station. I was sent to the WAC Detachment at Long Binh. Our WAC compound was situated down the street from the 24th Evacuation Hospital. We could hear the helicopters coming and going at all hours. It was stressful at times, but I received a lot of support from my friends in the company. Some of them I had been stationed with at other posts. We all worked hard at our various jobs. I was assigned as a legal clerk in the Staff Judge Advocate's Office of Saigon Support Command in Long Binh.

We did have company activities in our compound. Our sponsoring unit, an engineer company, would come over and we would have a barbeque or movie night. We were usually restricted to our compound except for work, but we did have several events outside the company. One time the Australian soldiers invited our detachment to visit their company at Cam Ranh Bay, up on the northern coast, for a cook out. A group of us decided to go. Of course we had to go in an armored convey of tanks and MPs – that ride was a little scary but we had a good time when we arrived. The seacoast really was beautiful, and the Australian guys were friendly. We had an uneventful return trip but our commander said never again. She worried the whole time we were gone. I think her boss was upset also. We were also allowed to visit Saigon on occasion, and we did see something of the city. The street vendors spoke multiple languages, and they sold everything you could think of. I remember the streets being very crowded, mostly bicycles and people pulling wagons. To me the city gave the impression of being old. My time in Vietnam passed fairly quickly. I had wanted to go and have always remembered it as a learning experience.

My tour ended in June of 1972. Troops had already begun pulling out. I volunteered to stay and help close our offices; afterward I was reassigned to Fort Gordon, GA. I think my tour in Vietnam gave me a greater appreciation for the opportunities and freedoms in my country. Over the years, I have never really spoken of my Vietnam service. I got into that habit upon my return due to the treatment of service members returning from tours in the Republic of Vietnam. We were briefed not to say anything or even look at the crowds of people upon arrival at the airport. We traveled in uniform so we were easy to spot. My peers could look at my uniform and tell where I had been assigned and we could talk or not, mostly not. I always felt that our women were not recognized or rewarded as they should have been. Most of us were young women barely out of our teens. I think all of us old soldiers are proud of our young women today. They have reached new heights and should be commended.

**Claudia Ann Crowley Collins**
**In country: October 7, 1970 – October 18, 1971**
**Rank: Captain, US Air Force**
**Duty: 7ᵗʰ Air Force, 12ᵗʰ Reconnaissance Intelligence Technical**
**Squadron (RITS), Officer-in-Charge, Edit and Production Control**

In a warm climate, the traditional daily uniform for a female USAF officer was a fitted, light blue, short-sleeve jacket and skirt, called polys. One morning mama-san at my quarters had just returned after taking 48 hours off to have her eighth or ninth child. She had three days of laundry stacked up and eight rooms to clean.

All my polys were dirty, so I decided to wear the slack uniform, which consisted of a light-blue blouse and dark-blue pants. As I walked into work at the 12ᵗʰ RITS, a major I barely knew stopped me in the hall. "What are you doing wearing pants to work?" he asked. "None of my polys are clean and I didn't feel like wearing heels this morning." I responded. It is important to note that we were not in the Pentagon, although the slack uniform was authorized there as well.

"Don't you girls know that you're over here for the morale of the troops? In the future you wear that skirt," he barked.

That did it. I'd been treated like something akin to the Hunchback of Notre Dame every time I'd left the building or gone to lunch in the few weeks I'd been at Tan Son Nhut. I was hot, tired, scared, lonely, and now, PISSED OFF. The thought that I'd been dragged 10,000 miles from home for troop "morale" in a Saigon office was an infuriating insult. I immediately turned around, left work and caught a hop tac (small taxi) to clothing issue. "I need two large pair of ugly green fatigues," I told the supply airman. "Yes ma'am. Will you be needing a pair of field boots?" he asked. "Why not," I said as I watched my combat uniform come together. A bush hat from a cooperative Australian soldier completed the ensemble. I was still so angry I was shaking.

Lieutenant Collins was now dressed for combat. I was in a war zone after all, but war had slightly different connotations for a woman in Vietnam. The baggy green fatigues contained dozens of pockets, thereby eliminating the need for a purse. With everything stuffed in them I looked more like Captain Kangaroo than anything female.

The jungle boots were much more comfortable than high heels, and the mesh inserts made them cooler than leather boots. I piled my too-long for

443

regulation hair under the bush hat, the complete picture of androgyny. I was going to be invisible.

Steve and I had been married for two months and I knew he would be shocked when he saw his new bride's attire, but he'd understand the reasoning behind it. My own version of "the best offense is a good defense." And, much to that demented major's dismay, I started a new fashion trend among my female colleagues.

♥**Catherine A. Brajkovich**
**Retired as a Lieutenant Colonel**
**In country: October 12, 1970 – October 1971**
**Rank: Major, US Army**
**Duty: MACV, Joint Staff, Third Junior Officer Advisor to the Vietnam Women's Armed Forces Corps**

**Barbara A. Verderber (Walker)**
**Retired as a Lieutenant Colonel**
**In country: October 15, 1970 – October 15, 1971**
**Rank: First Lieutenant, US Air Force**
**Duty: 7ᵗʰ Air Force, Tactical Air Control Center, Intelligence Officer**

If I had known that I would be stationed in Vietnam, I never would have joined the Air Force. It was ultimately a life-changing experience; and now looking back, I would not have missed it for the world. When I was assigned to Tan Son Nhut Air Base, I had no idea about what type of environment awaited me. When I got off the plane, I thought that I had been sent to the "ends of the earth." Aside from Canada and the Caribbean, I had never been outside of the United States. It was October 1970, and I was 23 years old.

**Carrie Alvine Turner**
**Retired as a Major**
**In country: October 15, 1970 – May 1972**
**Rank: Major, US Army**
**Duty: USARV, G4; Deputy Chief of Staff for Operations – Force Development**

# NOVEMBER

*Memory Lane: Democrats sweep US Congressional midterm elections; Ronald Reagan reelected governor of California; Jimmy Carter elected governor of Georgia; 37 players and five coaches from Marshall University football team are killed in a plane crash.*
*Song: "Fire and Rain" by James Taylor*

♥**Donna Ann Litehiser**
**Retired as a Lieutenant Colonel**
**In country: November 1970 – November 1971**
**Rank: Major, US Army**
**Duty: MACV, Management Analyst**

**Nancy Auerbach (Williams)**
**Retired as a Lieutenant Colonel**
**In country: November 1970 – November 1971**
**Rank: Major, US Army**
**Duty: USARV, 1ˢᵗ Logistical Command, Adjutant**

♥**Mary V. Baggan (Kelly)**
**Retired as a Colonel**
**In country: November 1970 – November 1971**
**Rank: Lieutenant Colonel, US Army Medical Specialist Corps**
**Duty: USARV Surgeon's Office, Long Binh, Dietetic Consultant**

**Elaine Lowery James**
**Retired as a Lieutenant Colonel**
**In country: November 1970 – November 1971**
**Rank: Captain, US Army**
**Duty: MACV, J2; 1ˢᵗ Military Intelligence Battalion, Air Reconnaissance Support**

### ♥Marjorie Kay Johnson
**In country: November 8, 1970 – November 7, 1971**
**Rank: Captain, US Army**
**Duty: USARV, Special Troops, WAC Detachment, Fifth Commander**

Captain Marjorie Johnson, the detachment commander, feels there is not a stabler, more mature group of women anywhere in the world. "Maybe it is because of our common bond, but all of the girls get along great. And disciplinary problems are almost non-existent."

Pacific Stars and Stripes, *November 5, 1971, National Archives Record Group 319. Records of the Army Staff, Women's Army Corps, 1945-1978*

### Shirley M. Minick
**Retired as a Major**
**In country: November 1970 – February1972**
**Rank: Captain, US Army**
**Duty: MACV, J2, Administrative Officer**

### ♥Evelyn A. Mundorff
**Retired as a Sergeant First Class**
**In country: November 1970 – February 1972**
**Rank: Sergeant, US Army**
**Duty: 24ᵗʰ Evacuation Hospital, Long Binh, Administrative NCO**

### ♥Carol Joan Tilden
**Retired as a Lieutenant Colonel**
**In country: November 1970 – May 1972**
**Rank: Major, US Army**
**Duty: USARV, 1ˢᵗ Logistical Command, Saigon Support Group**

### Yvette R. Thorne (Crutcher)
**Retired as a Senior Master Sergeant**
**In country: November 1970 – November 1972**
**Rank: Master Sergeant, US Air Force**
**Duty: 7ᵗʰ Air Force, Intelligence/Scatback, Air Operations Supervisor**

**Deborah O. Gano**
**In country: November 1, 1970 – October 22, 1971**
**Rank: Specialist 5, US Army**
**Duty: USARV, Central Finance and Accounting Office, Finance Specialist**

The year I will never forget – when I returned from Vietnam to Tampa, FL, I didn't tell anyone, other than my family, that I had served there because of the bad publicity and the way we veterans were treated on our return.

Leaving a great assignment in the Fort McPherson Finance Office, Atlanta, GA, as a Pay Disbursing Specialist, I accepted an assignment to Long Binh, Vietnam. At 19 years old, little did I know I would need to grow up fast: I wasn't prepared for the daily bombing, taking cover in the bunkers and, worst of all, the lack of any combat training.

In Finance and Accounting, USARV, I found one duty painful – processing military pay records of troops killed in action. Other duties were interesting, like the "money run" – going on a chopper to change used military payment certificates for new. (This limited the black market use by the Viet Cong.)

My brother's Vietnam tour as a cook and gunner on a ration truck began during my tour. The times I saw him on weekends helped both of us deal with our tour in country. These were also tough days for our mother as we were her only children.

On a bus outing to Cam Ranh Bay, we came under attack and the bus tires went flat – I thought this was the end for me. We had only three armed soldiers on the bus and about 20 active-duty personnel. The driver radioed for help. Still daylight, we were allowed off the bus. Finally, two Australian soldiers in a jeep invited us to wait at their base a mile away; four of us accepted. Later, a bus picked up the others, but never found us.

Day became night, and, with three gunners, we began the return on the dark, unsafe road. Vietnamese soldiers stopped our bus at a roadblock. Were they Viet Cong? They pulled their guns, and our gunners did also. To me, death was staring us in the face. Finally, they let us through. I really believe we weren't attacked because they were unprepared for our armed soldiers. Thank God we returned to Long Binh safe. I never took another outing. Later, I realized that not only had we put ourselves in danger, but also the soldiers sent to find us.

In Vietnam, I was sexually harassed at times, but have been able to deal with this over the years. Also, male soldiers asked me to help in a black market scheme to double or triple their US money. I refused.

I lost contact with the 78 active duty women at the WAC Detachment, but decades later, I still feel a bond with them.

I was involved in a short documentary film about women serving in Vietnam. I never had the opportunity to see it myself. I saw the Bob Hope Show in 1971. It was awesome. I felt so much pride knowing we were not forgotten. Since I left Vietnam, I completed college, worked for the State of Florida Department of Labor for 10 years and retired from the VA Medical Center in Tampa, FL, after working for 35 years as a Vocational Rehabilitation Specialist. It has been 43 years since I left Vietnam, and I still have mixed feelings when I talk about serving there.

**Barbara J. Thompson (Barnett)**
**Retired as a Major**
**In country: November 4, 1970 – November 19, 1971**
**Rank: First Lieutenant, US Air Force**
**Duty: 7th Air Force, 554th Civil Engineering Squadron (Red Horse), Cam Ranh Bay, Administrative Management Officer**

*Story edited by Colonel Darlene Brewer-Alexander:* I was the first female ever assigned to a Red Horse Squadron, and this squadron was the first Red Horse Squadron activated to support operations in Vietnam. Red Horse stands for "Rapid Engineer Deployable, Heavy Operations Repair Squadron, Engineer," and was one of only two units that built and repaired runways and other structures throughout Southeast Asia. The Red Horse units moved as an entire unit (300 men rotated out as 300 men rotated in) and one of my jobs was to out process the men being reassigned to another location, and to in process the men of the new squadron.

# DECEMBER

*Memory Lane: The US Environmental Protection Agency begins operations; President Richard Nixon signs into law the Occupational Safety and Health Act (OSHA).*
*Song: "The Tears of a Clown" by Smokey Robinson and The Miracles*

♥Beatrice "Betty" E. Fowler
**Retired as a Technical Sergeant**
**In country: December 1970 – September 1971**
**Rank: Staff Sergeant, US Air Force**
**Duty: 7ᵗʰ Air Force, Tactical Air Command, Tactical Air Warfare Center, Air Traffic Control, Administrative Supervisor**

♥Mary Smith (Gafney)
**Retired as a Master Sergeant**
**In country: December 1970 – September 1971**
**Rank: Technical Sergeant, US Air Force**
**Duty: 7ᵗʰ Air Force, Directorate of Personnel, Awards and Decorations, Administrative Supervisor**

**Comments and Memories:** One day while in Vietnam, I went to the restroom (outside) to find all the doors had been removed from the stalls! I went ballistic and stormed into the colonel's office 'ranting' – scared him to death! Needless to say, the doors were back in place that day." *Source: Vietnam Memory Book 2000*

♥Marie "Connie" Constance Eva Gagne
**Retired as a Lieutenant Colonel**
**In country: December 1970 – November 1971**
**Rank: Staff Sergeant, US Air Force**
**Duty: 7ᵗʰ Air Force, Contemporary Historical Examination of Current Operations, Administrative Specialist**

## Pat H. Jernigan
## Retired as a Colonel
## In country: December 1970 – November 1971
## Rank: Captain, US Army
## Duty: MACV, 525th Military Intelligence Group (Operations); J2,
## Intelligence Case Reviewer and Staff Officer

At a 525th (Military Intelligence Group) unit party, spring 1971, I wore AG brass instead of WAC brass.

I was a 28-year-old Army captain, serving in Heidelberg, Germany, when I volunteered for Vietnam in the summer of 1970. Heidelberg had been a dream assignment; the work was challenging, Germany was great, and I met my future husband (David) there.

David had gone to Vietnam in the fall of 1969, and we thought we'd both be slated for the Military Intelligence (MI) Advanced Course as we were both finishing overseas tours. We planned to get married when he finished his tour as this coincided with the end of my tour. We were upset to learn that "they" planned to send David to the advanced course and me to Korea. We decided that Vietnam was a better choice, and I volunteered to go and David volunteered to stay. I remember that I had to submit a volunteer statement specifying that I was not a sole surviving son.

I was detailed to MI but my basic branch was still WAC, and they had to approve my assignment. We didn't realize it at the time but the WAC had a policy that no married WAC would be allowed to serve in Vietnam if her husband was also there. We were glad that we hadn't told them about our plans. Once on the ground the local policy was quite different. The formal policy, in writing, was to provide quarters where possible for service members married to other service members, if they were of equivalent status.

After what seemed an endless flight, we finally arrived at Bien Hoa. I don't recall the date – only that getting off the airplane was like jumping into a hot oven or a pot of boiling water. I spent several days at the replacement depot at Long Binh where I got my fatigues, boots and equipment. I was billeted in the nurses quarters behind barbed wire, guarded 24/7 by military policemen. I was the only woman there at the time. It was a very lonely place.

Finally, someone from 525th MI Group came to pick me up – I'd been issued a boonie hat so I had it on. I was immediately told to stow the hat – they weren't allowed in the 525th. I was assigned as a division chief in the S3 office, located in the 525th MI Group Headquarters on Tan Son Nhut. For a while, I had my own jeep, but jeeps were in short supply and it was too much for the staff, all men, to have a young WAC captain with a jeep. This really wasn't a big deal for me as it was easy to get rides and there was good bus service.

After a few weeks living at the Utah BOQ, I moved to the Massachusetts BOQ located near Tan Son Nhut Air Base. The Mass (as it was called) was next to Third Field Hospital, and across the alley from another BOQ. A branch of the USO was just down the street. The closed mess (where we ate dinner) was in the BOQ across an alley. The Vietnamese Joint Staff Headquarters was located across the street.

The work wasn't difficult or challenging. It involved reading, preparing and commenting on reports, as well as giving briefings. Things seemed to be winding down and combat units were already being withdrawn. Early in 1971, there was a change of command and we got a new Group commander. He liked having a woman on his staff, and I got to travel on command visits to some of the outlying units including Da Nang, Nha Trang and Can Tho. The normal duty day was 10-12 hours long, seven days a week. We usually took a couple of hours mid-day for lunch and physical training. On Sunday mornings, we often went to the Air Force O-Club for brunch which included endless fountains of Salty Dogs and Screwdrivers. Infrequent unit parties were a real highlight. I took several night courses, one on criminal justice (that included a visit to the infamous Long Binh Jail), and one on developing color film.

Every month or two I'd pull staff duty officer (SDO) at 525th Headquarters. The SDO and the duty NCO were both armed, so I'd draw my unit .45 caliber for the duty. I had no prior training on any weapon, then or later, as this just wasn't done with WACs at the time. If anything had ever happened I'd have been a hazard to others. The major benefit of pulling SDO was you got the next day off – that was a real luxury!

One of the responsibilities of my division was to take care of "Herman" the unit's pet python. Herman was kept in a small wire cage in the yard. On weekends, the soldiers would bring Herman in and set him out on the top of several safes. It was so cold he'd just stay there, but liked to dangle his head (quite large) over the edge. One Sunday I walked in, saw Herman at eye level, and screamed. After that, they warned me that he was in the building! He often escaped, and the soldiers would usually find him in a nearby drainage ditch. Eventually he disappeared; we all figured he'd ended up in a Vietnamese stew pot.

When a major arrived in the unit, he took my job as he was senior to me. I found another job on MACV staff in a J2 office. This was a much more congenial group, though the work was still light. There were several women assigned to the MACV staff – one, in an office next to mine, became a good friend (Paula Jenkins). Sadly she died about 20 years ago from breast cancer. Another was a WAC full colonel (Betty Branch) that I'd known slightly at the WAC training center. She was the MACV historian.

David and I took two R&Rs – one to Bangkok in May 1971, the other a two-week leave to Hong Kong in October. We really enjoyed Thailand. Beautiful, friendly country! Our plane was full of male soldiers out for a good time on their R&R. The aerial port administrative NCO took us aside and gave us cold beer while the others attended a lecture on venereal disease, where to find "safe" girls and which hotels had "liberal guest" policies. Our second R&R was to Hong Kong. We probably spent four months' salary on electronics, custom clothing and cameras while there – and ate our way through some great restaurants.

By the time we got back, we were ready to out process to return to the States. We took the option of returning on a commercial flight – it was a nicer way to go. When I went to the civilian terminal at Tan Son Nhut to pick up the tickets, the lady kept telling me, "You must have return ticket." I kept telling her we weren't coming back. I guess she finally got someone who could understand our orders as we did get the tickets.

Vietnam is a distant memory now. My jobs were mundane, but I'm still glad I had the chance to go, and would like to return as a tourist. Despite the passage of time, when I run across the pungent smell of garbage on a hot summer day I'm transported back to the smells and chaos of the Saigon streets.

I stayed in the Army for another 21 years and had many challenging and rewarding jobs.

**Brenda K. Burk (Medina)**
**In country: December 1970 – December 1971**
**Rank: Specialist 5, US Army**
**Duty: 24ᵗʰ Evacuation Hospital, Personnel Records Specialist**

I'm the supervisor of five men, and I only had trouble once. He was kind of new, so the other guys took him outside and had a long talk with him. I don't know what they said to him, but I never had any more trouble.

Pacific Stars and Stripes, *November 5, 1971, National Archives Record Group 319. Records of the Army Staff, Women's Army Corps, 1945-1978*

♥Carol A. Kastensmidt (Damron)
In country: December 1970 – December 1971
Rank: Staff Sergeant, US Air Force
Duty: MACV, Administrative Specialist

♥Virginia Mary Gavin
Retired as a Chief Warrant Officer 4
In country: December 1970 – December 1971
Rank: Chief Warrant Officer 4, US Army
Duty: USARV, Personnel/Administrative Technician

♥Patricia Marie Rogers (Harlin)
Retired as a Master Sergeant
In country: December 1970 – December 1971
Rank: Technical Sergeant, US Air Force
Duty: 7th Air Force, 1876th Communications Squadron, Communications
Center Supervisor

Ann L. Hirdler
In country: December 1970 – December 1971
Rank: First Lieutenant, US Air Force
Duty: 485th Electronics Installation Squadron, Cam Ranh Bay,
Administrative Officer

Shirley A. McClendon
Retired as a Chief Master Sergeant
In country: December 1970 – December 1971
Rank: Staff Sergeant, US Air Force
Duty: 7th Air Force, Munitions

Peggy J. Starnes (Young)
Retired as a Technical Sergeant
In country: December 1970 – December 1971
Rank: Staff Sergeant, US Air Force
Duty: 7th Air Force, Personnel, Administrative Supervisor

**Mary Ardella Van Harn**
**Retired as a Colonel**
**In country: December 1970 – December 1971**
**Rank: Lieutenant Colonel, US Army Medical Specialist Corps**
**Duty: 93rd Evacuation Hospital, Long Binh, Physical Therapist**

**Yvonne Chris Young**
**Retired as a Staff Sergeant**
**In country: December 1970 – December 1971**
**Rank: Specialist 5, US Army**
**Duty: 24th Evacuation Hospital, Long Binh,**
**Physical Therapy Clinic, Noncommissioned**
**Officer in Charge**

**♥Ruth Gail Smith (Mahaffey)**
**Retired as a Senior Master Sergeant**
**In country: December 1970 – May 1972**
**Rank: Sergeant, US Air Force**
**Duty: 7th Air Force, 377th Combat Support Group,**
**Administrative Specialist**

***The story was written by her close friend, Diana Andrews, as if she wrote it:*** On my way home from work, I stopped in one of the many Vietnamese shops on base to see what they had. Spotted a really nice poster with flowers and dragonflies and thought it would look great in our cubicle. It was one of those posters that changes color when used with a black light. Also purchased a black light to add to the effect. I couldn't wait to show my roommate the picture and how it would look with the black light. When she came in from work, I proudly displayed the picture I had put up and was getting ready to turn on the black light so we could enjoy the picture. I couldn't believe my eyes when I turned on the light. There in full detail the large dragonfly transformed into the image of a nude woman. I thought we'd die laughing about my purchase. She never let me forget it. Although the figure wasn't noticeable when the black light wasn't on, you knew the image was there. We decided to leave it up but put a towel in front of the larger dragonfly to hide the nude figure. That was the last time I purchased any posters without checking them under a black light.

### Claire V. Allison
**In country: December 8, 1970 – October 4, 1972**
**Rank: Staff Sergeant, US Air Force**
**Duty: 7ᵗʰ Air Force, 377ᵗʰ Combat Support Group, Personnel Specialist**

One evening around dusk, we pulled into a gated compound in Saigon where we were met by two people in uniform. It was Martha Raye and her aide. I had been invited by Lieutenant Ethel Apter (7AF WAF Advisor) to an evening of dinner and fellowship with Green Beret soldiers who would soon be returning to the field. Martha Raye would be accompanying them.

Although unplanned, Martha Raye returned to our hootch at Tan Son Nhut (TSN). She played with our adopted puppy and visited with additional enlisted WAF who didn't mind being awakened in the middle of the night. She was genuine and caring. She even took the time to visit the women staff officers and nurses who resided on TSN.

It was an unforgettable evening with some of America's patriotic young men who believed in their country's mission. I had been at TSN about three weeks – this sure put into perspective why we all were there.

### Mary Joan Webb
**In country: December 13, 1970 – December 10, 1971**
**Rank: Staff Sergeant, US Air Force**
**Duty: 7ᵗʰ Air Force, Office of History, Administrative Supervisor**

In July 1970, I received orders to Tan Son Nhut (TSN) Air Base. I was not a volunteer and was one of 15 enlisted non-nursing Air Force women who arrived at TSN in December 1970. My husband, Austin, had a current overseas return date and did not have to go to Vietnam; but, he volunteered and spent the year at Binh Thuy Air Base.

Upon arrival, the airline quickly got the passengers off the aircraft and boarded those returning to the US. Because of the danger, they didn't want to be on the ground at TSN any longer than absolutely necessary.

Personnel pointed me in the direction of the Office of History, which had been without a clerk for three weeks, and I met Charles Rowdybush. He was in a Civil Service capacity; but this man of 60 years of age was a retired Navy Lieutenant Commander and a military historian. He had already been there 2½ years when I arrived. In his small office was one straight back wooden chair. I had a seat and the first thing he told me was he did not approve of women in the military and certainly not in Vietnam – but he would give me a chance.

Today in 2013, I remember that meeting very clearly and recall that I'm sure I wasn't breathing! In the following years, he would visit our home a few days each year, and later told me I had changed his mind about women in the military. He was very pleased with the job I had done for him.

On three occasions, I was fortunate to be able to go to the Can Tho/Binh Thuy area where my husband was stationed. We shopped at a large pottery place, enjoyed lunches at Vietnamese restaurants, and went to a local market where the men gave a boy, about 10 years of age, cigarettes for guarding the military vehicle. Because I didn't have orders, I did not travel on an Air Force plane but rather went to Binh Thuy on a small Army mail plane and various other aircraft back and forth as long as they were going the right direction! At 24 years of age, one thinks nothing will ever happen. However, if an aircraft had gone down, no one would have known I was on it!

Betty Fowler had arrived at TSN just days before I did. We shared a tiny cubicle space in a building created for the 15 non-nursing Air Force women who arrived at Tan Son Nhut in December 1970. It was a structure with screening around the top edge and we were fortunate to obtain a fan that ran all night. Betty and I have remained friends and in contact all these decades.

We enjoyed many visits to the Saigon Zoo with Austin and a friend of his. On one visit to the Saigon Zoo, a man who, in just minutes, using a broken razor blade did a silhouette picture of Austin and me. That was very special. Over the years, I often wished I could have purchased razor blades and had known how to see the man again to give them to him.

To my knowledge, none of us were volunteers. To this day, I do not know how I was chosen.

**Diana "Andy" Stack Andrews**
**Retired as a Senior Master Sergeant**
**In country: December 16, 1970 – December 15, 1971**
**Rank: Staff Sergeant, US Air Force**
**Duty: 7ᵗʰ Air Force, 377ᵗʰ Combat Support Group; Directorate of Material and Services Administration, Administrative Specialist**

One of my many duties was to take our vehicles to the Motor Pool for servicing. On my first trip there, I was wearing a wig. The motor pool had a pet monkey. The minute I stepped out of the car, that monkey made a beeline to me. Before I knew what happened he pulled the wig off and started to play with it. It took a while before the guys were able to get it away from the monkey. I never wore the wig to the motor pool again.

Another duty was to drive to the commissary in Saigon for supplies. On one trip, our colonel wanted to see the commissary and learn what it carried. During the drive, I came to a stop sign just before the entrance to the commissary compound. Before I knew it, another car bumped into our vehicle. When I got out to check for damage, the Army sergeant tried to blame the accident on the woman driver. After a short while, the colonel got out to see what the problem was. When the Army sergeant saw the colonel, the blame for the accident quickly changed to his Vietnamese driver – who was learning how to drive – or so the sergeant says.

We had mama-sans who cleaned our quarters and did our uniforms. It didn't take long for the women to learn not to give the mama-sans bleach when they did our laundry. They didn't understand how to use the bleach. After a few uniforms were ruined, the word went out to keep your bleach locked up. The mama-sans never had washing machines – they did laundry the old-fashioned way and our uniforms didn't hold up too well. We were provided with washing machines and some of the women showed them how they worked. It didn't take long for them to realize how much time they saved by using the washing machine. Just one problem, no one told them not to overload the machines. It wasn't long before the machines stopped working. Even harder was knowing that when we got home, maintaining our uniforms would again be our responsibility.

**Aida Nancy Sanchez**
**Retired as a Lieutenant Colonel**
**In country: December 25, 1970 – 1972**
**Rank: Lieutenant Colonel, US Army Medical Specialist Corps**
**Duty: 95th Evacuation Hospital, Da Nang, Physical Therapist**

Aida Nancy Sanchez, better known as Nancy, joined the Army in September 1952. After attending Army Physical Therapist School, she served at many Army hospitals until December 1970 when she was sent to Vietnam. *The information herein is based on a telephone interview and from the Aida Nancy Sanchez Collection. This remarkable collection captures LTC Sanchez's year in Vietnam and includes her 2.5-hour oral history interview, transcript and more than 250 scanned photographs, letters, newspaper articles, poems, and documents that illustrate the life of a young woman in uniform serving in a war with no front lines. The following is from an interview conducted by Kate Scott, June 29, 2004. Tape and transcript are deposited at the Women's Memorial Foundation, Oral History Program, Arlington, VA.*

One of the reasons that I received orders to go there was that a physical therapist working at the Army Hospital in Saigon needed to return to the States, and I was needed to replace her. Instead of replacing her, I was sent to the 95th Evacuation Hospital, near Da Nang. I was to establish the first Physical-Therapy Clinic in an evacuation hospital.

It was the 24th of December. We first ended up in the Philippine Islands at 4:00 in the morning, where a group of two or three American families with their kids were singing Christmas carols to us and giving us goodies such as homemade cookies and beverages. All their goodies went along with us to Vietnam.

I was the only woman in the (C-130 cargo) plane out of 75 or so soldiers that were in the plane. One of them sitting right next to me looked very worried. He had just gotten married and he said to me, "You know, this is my wedding band," and he wanted some reassurance from me when he said, "Do you think I am going to come back to my sweetheart alive?" Imagine, we were heading to Vietnam and that was the first time I started getting that "Oh-my-God" feeling.

When we first arrived in Vietnam, we were brought to the 90th Replacement Center, in Long Binh near Saigon, where every soldier went through the processing center before going to their final destination. Since I was the only female processing at that time – it was December 25 – they had me share a barrack with quite a few soldiers. My cubicle was the very last one in the barrack, with curtains around it and an MP in front of it.

We all went up a hill for a Christmas service conducted by a Catholic priest who had made a little altar out of stones, and there was me and a whole bunch of GIs ready to celebrate Christmas on top of a hill in Vietnam. I still remember so vividly, one of the GIs decided to sing and he sounded just gorgeous! I prayed, "My God, my Dear Lord (as he started to sing Silent Night that was followed by other Christmas songs) help us get out of this country alive." We all hugged each other at the end of the Mass. Some of us were in tears.

The commander of the 90th Replacement Center in Long Binh, a colonel, decided that I needed to have an MP constantly next to my bunk as a guard "to keep me safe and sound." Since there were few MPs around and not that many guys to take his place, the colonel decided that he would be a guard. Of course, every time he passed by to do his duty as an MP, the poor GIs needed to get up and stand at attention. I am sure they were a little annoyed at that especially since they had to stand at attention in their shorts. It got to be funny when I needed to go to the bathroom since he needed to follow me. It was very uncomfortable but very funny all around, indeed. We finally went on our way to our final destination; and finally I made it to the 95th Evacuation Hospital.

Since I was the only Army Medical Specialist Corps person there, and all the nurses were spread out everywhere, there was a problem in assigning me a hootch. I kept wondering what the nurses were thinking about where I would stay. But, everything came out fine and we all became good friends. That hootch was my home to come to for a little bit over a year.

The reason for my longer stay was because that during my tour in Vietnam, I was asked to go to Cambodia to see the President of Cambodia, Lon Nol. I considered that a privilege. While I was stationed at Tripler Army Medical Center, Hawaii, Dr. Dick Matterson who was then the Chief of Physical Medicine there treated him there for a severe stroke. He had written to MG (Robert) Bernstein, commander in Vietnam of all Medical Services, to send me there so that I could follow up with his treatment program. Dr. Matterson and I had worked hard at Tripler in planning a rehabilitation program for President Lon Nol.

I have to tell you, this trip to Cambodia was all very secretive. The commander of the 95th told me, "You are going to be out of Vietnam. I hope you have some civilian clothes since you must go in civilian clothes to where you are going." But, neither he nor anybody else would tell me where I was going because it was top secret, mind you.

Early in the morning the next day, I went to a landing strip near our hospital to wait for my transportation to Saigon where MG Bernstein was going to brief me about my secret mission. There was also another person waiting for transportation to Saigon. She was Colonel Katherine E. Manchester, who was the Chief of all Dietitians in the Army and was visiting the Vietnam units. We had met while we both were stationed together somewhere along the way. Anyway, she has retired but the Army asked her to be the consultant in Vietnam for food and nutrition for the soldiers. She got into a small, very small plane and I got into a helicopter. As she was getting in her plane, she said to me, "I know where you are going but I can't tell you where it is. But don't worry; it is all going to be OK."

In Saigon, General Bernstein briefed me about my mission to Cambodia to see President Lon Nol, and he told me my trip was a secret mission as a security measure. He handed me the medical records of President Lon Nol, and told me I had about one hour to review and take all the information I needed out of them. I was taken to a room; doors were closed as I read all I could read that could help me and see how far he has gone in his rehab program since I had left Tripler Army Medical Center. As I was reviewing all these records, an MP stood at attention, guarding the doors of the room.

When I landed in Cambodia that afternoon, a limousine took me directly to the hotel in Phnom Penh. The hotel was old but nicely kept, and the room assigned to me was a very lovely room with beautiful antique furniture and baskets of fruits everywhere and even wine. General Lon Nol had also assigned to me seven secret service agents from his Army. They all slept outside my room in folding chairs – yes, lounge chairs with aluminum frame. When I opened the door, they were all greeted me with a smile. I tried to speak to them in French since they right away told me they did not know or speak English. So, between a little bit of French and sign language, we got along fine.

At breakfast, I noticed two American men in civilian clothes who were also having breakfast. I didn't bother to ask who they were and I didn't know why they didn't introduce themselves. However, I noticed they were always there when I went for breakfast. The third day I finally went to them and I asked, "Do you also stay here?" Then one of them said, "Major Sanchez, we are secret agents and we have been assigned to stay with you while you are in

Cambodia. This is Lieutenant Colonel so and so. I am Major so and so. Our duty right now is to protect you. Everything you need, please, tell us, but you need to be quiet about it." There was a lot of communist infiltration in the Lon Nol government, and they were afraid that somebody would kill me if they found out the purpose of my visit to Cambodia. Being communists, they would have liked to see General Lon Nol dead rather than seeing his health improve. Of course, I was not aware of all these problems. But, the lieutenant colonel explained all of that and said, "So this is why we don't approach you. We will sit here while you have your breakfast. We will be staying in the hotel as long as you are here."

Well, the problem also was that no Americans except for me were allowed in the Palace. Americans were not allowed in the compound area of the Palace, either. At that time, I was the only American to be able to enter the palace and its surrounding areas. And because of this reason, the US Ambassador in Cambodia also got involved with my visit there. One day, the colonel came to me and said the Ambassador wanted to see me. Some of his aides showed me this big picture of the Cabinet of President Lon Nol. As the Ambassador was trying to get me to recognize members of the Lon Nol Cabinet in this big picture, I realized that to me they all looked alike. I could not distinguish their features well enough to identify separately each individual of the Cabinet that was in his bedroom while I was treating him. The only one I recognized was a doctor who had the position similar to our Secretary of Health, Education and Welfare. He was the liaison between the President and me. He was a very fine doctor, a wonderful man, and he spoke very good English. He was always there when I needed him.

The Ambassador asked me to please in my next visit to the Palace to try to pay more attention to the people who were with the President as I was treating him. What a job he was giving me! I was supposed to treat the President and at the same time keep looking at the people that were around him so that I could remember their faces. The Ambassador emphasized to me how important it was for the US government that I could recognize these people. He almost sounded desperate when he also told me, "You've got to help us." I remembered telling him, "Excuse me, please, wait a minute. I was sent here to treat the President of Cambodia; nobody ever told me that I also was going to be a spy." The Ambassador was just very tense and concerned as he told me that I was the only one who could get this information in as much as I was the only American allowed in the Palace.

So, when I went back to the Palace, while treating the President I did my best in trying to remember the faces of the people. I remembered the Ambassador telling me how important it was for him to know who they were.

The people in Lon Nol's Cabinet were very intense in seeing what I was doing. I was thinking, "This is all going to be a very difficult task." My first concern and the reason why I was there was to help the President, General Lon Nol, improve his health as it is feasible. But, you see, I'm very religious in my ways. I think now that God was there with me because somehow or other, while doing the treatment program with the President, I kept looking for those faces in his Cabinet, especially those that were showed to me in the picture at the US Embassy. Upon my return to the Embassy, the Ambassador and his aides were eagerly waiting for me. I said, "Okay, let me see the picture again." Oh, yes I kept pinpointing all the faces of the Cabinet members I had seen: this one, this one, that one, that one, and on and on. I was amazed at how many people I was able to identify. The Ambassador very excitedly said, "Oh, my God! Communist infiltration is very real now. We have got to start packing and get out of here fast." Then I said, "Wait a minute, you are not leaving me behind. Are you?" He said, "Of course NOT." Everybody in the Embassy got so excited and tense that they all started getting boxes out of shelves, all trying to get started to leave Cambodia. The Ambassador told me that the process of leaving was going to take more than just a week.

In the meantime, I went back to Vietnam, took care of business there and came back to Cambodia to see the President, two weeks or so later. At that time, he was ready to start ambulation with the help of a cane. I told the doctor (the Secretary of Health) that I needed somehow to get a cane and he said, "Oh sure, we will find you a cane. We'll find it somehow." When I returned (this was third or fourth visit there), the doctor directed me to one of the large rooms in the Palace. President Lon Nol came with me in a wheelchair. We entered a room full of canes, all of them hanging from the ceiling, from one end of the room to the other. The canes came from every nation of the world, including one from the United States. The President had his aides hang all the canes from the ceiling of the room, so that I could easily pick the one that I thought was the best for him. I wondered how my visits to Cambodia and this project had been so top secret when all the nations of the world knew, in such a very short period, that President Lon Nol needed a cane. I also have to say here that even *Newsweek* magazine had an article about the President's illness and how he was improving. That's top secret for you!

During the year that I was in Vietnam, I came back and forth to Cambodia several times but at this time, I can't remember how many.

I am very proud to say that all the physical therapists in our Army Medical Specialist Corps were well trained for the job at hand. Under any circumstances presented to us, we did what needed to be done and did it well. As for me, I was the first physical therapist of our corps to be assigned to an evacuation hospital near combat zone areas. The experience of establishing a physical therapy clinic in an evacuation hospital was an incredible, unforgettable, unique experience that I will never forget. I appreciate very much all the help I received in establishing the clinic especially from our wonderful marines and the Vietnamese. I must say that when the physical therapy clinic was finally established, it came out to be a very nice clinic. The Quonset hut where our Post Exchange used to be became the Physical Therapy Clinic of the 95th Evacuation Hospital.

Another challenge I faced was tending enemy POWs. I remember caring for a petite, but very pregnant, Vietnamese woman allegedly responsible for setting land mines that killed approximately 65 American soldiers. She had broken her right femur as she ran to escape the explosion of the land mines.

We put her in the POW ward. As I approached to treat her, she grabbed my neck and tried very hard to choke me as if she wanted to kill me. [A] Special Forces sergeant tried to get her to release her grip off my neck as I also was trying to get her hands off me. The sergeant finally gave up and slapped her. I just had to stop him. I think that knowing what she had done, killing our GIs the way she did, increased his rage. I was able to calm the sergeant by telling him that she, too, had been in the vicinity when the land mines exploded and that she could relate to his feelings. He just put his rifle straight up in front of him, put his head on top of it and he just cried and cried, almost with despair. I cannot tell you how I felt in those moments. This had to be one of the most trying times in my life. I just cried with him.

After I came back from Vietnam, I was sent to Fort Gordon, GA. I was to be the Chief of the Physical Therapy Clinic at this Army base hospital. As such, I got the duty and the task of moving the Physical Therapy Clinic from the old barracks type of hospital (it was one of those hospitals that was built in the old Army days) and established the new Physical Therapy Clinic at the new Dwight David Eisenhower Army Medical Center. It took almost six years to build the new Medical Center and to move the new Physical Therapy Clinic. Once the new Medical Center and its new Physical Therapy Clinic were established and opening ceremonies were over, I felt it was time for me to retire. After one more year of organizing and getting the new Physical Therapy Clinic going, I finally retired. (LTC Sanchez retired in 1976 after nearly 25 years of service.)

Today, I wonder how we got the "guts," the courage, the stamina, the endurance, the spiritual and physical strength to do all that we did in Vietnam to save lives, to give comfort to those who were dying from their wounds, to count the dead and try to identify them. All of these horrendous things plus all the other horrible things that happened while we were there could bring a person to the point of insanity but no, we never gave up. We never lost our faith and the reason, the purpose of our mission. We never lost our vision of what we could do for our brothers and sisters, for our fellow man. I am saying again and again that the strength of the human spirit is beyond description. It kept us going in the right direction in the worst possible times. The human spirit kept us alive so that we kept on doing our mission straight forward and without hesitation but with great hope for a better life to come, not only for us but also for all of those we were leaving behind.

# Chapter Eleven

# 1971

**Louise Delvecchio**
In country: 1971 – Date of departure unknown
Rank: Staff Sergeant, US Air Force
Duty: 7th Air Force

**♥Evelyn "Lynn" Pearl Kussman (Lindblad)**
In country: 1971 – Date of departure unknown
Rank: Specialist 5, US Army
Duty: USARV, Special Troops Personnel, Clerk-Typist

Lynn Kussman made the pages of *Army Times* as its "WAC of the Week," a featured modeled on home front news features introducing a "girl of the week." Calling her "the best thing to ever happen to a set of jungle fatigues," the report's opening paragraph contended that "petite Lynn Kussman would brighten any office anywhere, and at the Military Personnel Directorate, Long Binh, where she performs as a clerk, she is particularly illuminating." The  story went on to explain that, "Although only four-feet, eleven-inches tall, our bright-eyed gal of the week performs a man-sized job."

*From "Long Binh WACs Provide a Study in Women's Lib,"* Pacific Stars and Stripes, *November 5, 1971. National Archives Record Group 319.*

**Ruth Eva Dewton**
**Retired as a Lieutenant Colonel**
In country: 1971 – 1972
Rank: Major, US Army Medical Specialist Corps
Duty: 3rd Field Hospital, Saigon, Physical Therapist

Carol L. Witt
In country: 1971 – 1972
Rank: Captain, US Air Force
Duty: 7ᵗʰ Air Force, 12ᵗʰ Reconnaissance Intelligence Technical Squadron,
Intelligence Photo-Radar Officer

♥Wanda Mae Brechbuhler
Retired as a Lieutenant Colonel
In country: 1971 – 1972
Rank: Major, US Air Force
Duty: 7ᵗʰ Air Force, Cam Ranh Bay, Personnel Staff Officer

Ann Jane Moriarty (Gaskin)
Retired as a Lieutenant Commander
In country: 1971 – 1972
Rank: Lieutenant, US Navy
Duty: NAVFORV, Staff Personnel Officer

♥Glenda Joan Olson
In country: 1971 – 1972
Rank: Major, US Army
Duty: MACV, US Army Headquarters Area Command, Personnel Staff
Officer

Esterina Maria Vella
Retired as a Chief Master Sergeant
In country: 1971 – 1972
Rank: Chief Master Sergeant, US Air Force
Duty: 7ᵗʰ Air Force, Personnel Superintendent

Janis Lynette Waters
Retired as a Master Sergeant
In country: 1971 – 1972
Rank: Sergeant, US Army
Duty: USARV, Special Troops,
WAC Detachment, Supply Clerk

**♥Susan M. Tasca (Wright) (Gaylor)**
**Retired as a Lieutenant Colonel**
**In country: 1971 – 1972**
**Rank: Captain, US Air Force**
**Duty: 7ᵗʰ Air Force, 8ᵗʰ Aerial Port, Transportation Staff Officer**

Lieutenant Colonel Gaylor was awarded the Bronze Star with "V" for valor and the Air Force Commendation Medal in 1971. She received the Vietnamese Honor Medal first class in 1972.

*Obituary,* The Buffalo News, *September 11, 1990*

**♥Delores "Mickey" Barrett**
**Retired as a Sergeant First Class**
**In country: 1971 – May 1972**
**Rank: Sergeant First Class, US Army**
**Duty: USARV**

Sergeant First Class Delores Barrett told *The Overseas Weekly – Pacific Edition* in May 1972 that she believed in Black power to the extent that more black people should be integrated into the US government.

"I'm in favor of less segregation, more integration. I first came into the Army in 1959. I was the token Negro in many assignments. We're coming out of this. Thank God for the young people."

Barrett was waiting to rotate. Her impeccably cleaned and pressed uniform was decorated with a Bronze Star Medal, a Vietnam Campaign Medal and a Vietnam Service Medal.

"You might call me brainwashed, you might call me a lifer, but the Women's Army Corps offers a lot. Those that don't make it are those that aren't trying to make it."

*Excerpt from "The women behind the concertina barricade,"* The Overseas Weekly – Pacific Edition, *May 8, 1972, publication defunct 1975*

# JANUARY

*Memory Lane: A ban on radio and television cigarette ads goes into effect in the US; the Baltimore Colts defeat the Dallas Cowboys 16–13 in Super Bowl V; Globetrotters lose 100-99 to NJ Reds, ending 2,495-game win streak.*
*Song: "Black Magic Woman" by Santana*

## Sandra Kaye Phillips (Vandever)
**In country: January 1971 – September 1971**
**Rank: Specialist 5, US Army**
**Duty: USARV, Special Services**

My most memorable experience was while I was on R&R in Vietnam. I got a three-day pass to Phu Bai. This one night, I was walking on the pearl white sand and just listening to the gentle roll of the ocean waves. I was thinking about how torn up life was in a war and wondering if I would leave here in a body bag or walking. I was realizing just how precious time and life were when I heard something in the distance. The soothing sound was getting closer and closer. When I was finally able to make it out and see where it was coming from, I saw the singer from the band serenading me. Unfortunately, I don't remember the title of the song or his name. But, that was the first and only time I have ever had a man serenade me. After his song, he told me that he saw me walking on the beach and wanted to do something special for me. Well, he did. I will always cherish this memory.

## ♥Joyce Eloise Eslick
**Retired as a Lieutenant Colonel**
**In country: January 1971 – December 1971**
**Rank: Major, US Army**
**Duty: MACV, Joint Staff, Sixth Senior Advisor to the Vietnam Women's Armed Forces Corps**

**Comments and Memories:** In April 1950, in Knoxville, TN, my sister, Peggie, and I enlisted in the Army. Our WAC basic training company was Company C, the first integrated company. Peggie and I also pulled KP (kitchen police) in the last all-black WAC basic training company a few weeks before it graduated. I've always been proud that we were "in on the first and the last," so to speak.

Joyce Eslick initially was an enlisted woman. Later she was commissioned in the US Army Reserve on active duty; subsequently, she was appointed a Regular Army officer. Joyce served at Fort Lee, VA; Fort Sam Houston, TX; Fort McPherson, GA; Fort Jackson, SC; Yokohama, Japan; Evacuation Hospital Seattle, WA; Fort Ord, CA; Fort McClellan, AL; Oakland, CA;

Recruiting, Sioux Falls, SD; Fort Lawton, OK; Headquarters Berlin Brigade, US Army Europe; Fort Benjamin Harrison, IN; Fort Lewis, WA; Fort Sheridan, IL, and Fort Bliss, TX. Lieutenant Colonel Joyce Eslick retired after 23 years of service. *Source: Vietnam Memory Book 2000*

**♥Joan "Ski" Jodi Lesnikowski**
**Retired as a Captain**
**In country: January 1971 – December 31, 1971**
**Rank: Captain, US Air Force**
**Duty: 7th Air Force, 14th Aerial Port, Cam Ranh Bay,**
**Transportation Officer**

**Marie (Helscher) LeBlanc**
**In country: January 1971 – December 31, 1971**
**Rank: Captain, US Air Force**
**Duty: 7th Air Force, 460th Field Maintenance and Aircraft Squadron,**
**Administrative Services Officer**

While in Corona, CA, an Air Force friend who was stationed at Norton Air Force Base in Riverside gave me a tour of the base.

Captivated by the thought of being in the military, I informed my family that I was joining the Air Force. I attended Officer Training School at Lackland Air Force Base, TX, then was stationed at Hancock Field, Syracuse, NY.

In 1970, I married Rick Helscher, a Radar Officer stationed nearby. He was sent to Korea in 1971, and because I had previously volunteered, the military sent me to Vietnam in 1971.

As an Administrative Services Officer, I was not directly involved in the conflict but, because I was assigned to the 460th Maintenance Squadron (aircraft), I worked on the flight line at Tan Son Nhut Air Base and saw the results of many attacks on our aircraft. Just living with the threat of attack 24 hours a day was very stressful and I did a lot of drinking while there. I would trade my beer and cigarette rations for liquor.

Many of my memories are hazy, but one of the best memories I have was visiting the orphans at the Ky Quang Orphanage run by Buddhist monks in Saigon. One airman, Sergeant Ed Hayes, and I would "beg, borrow or steal" hot dogs, hamburgers, buns, condiments and chips from the cafeteria and surprise the children with a cookout. What a treat it was for them and a touch of home for us! We also took them on a field trip to the Saigon Zoo, such as it was.

My proudest memory is the work my two clerks and I did compiling a list of 300 soldiers per flight for 10 daily flights home on the "Freedom Birds." President Nixon had said he wanted to "bring the troops home for Christmas." We worked for two weeks straight without a break, coordinating with the Army Personnel Office responsible for scheduling the flights. On December 31, 1971, I was on the last flight that left Vietnam that year. For our efforts, my clerks and I received Bronze Stars.

To the best of my knowledge, the only residual effect of my Vietnam tour is that the sound of certain helicopters gives me goose bumps and may cause my heart to race. I attribute that to the fact that the WAF quarters were very close to the heliport, and choppers flew in and out day and night.

After Vietnam, I was stationed at Keesler Air Force Base, MS. I stayed in the Air Force one more year, and then returned to California. My drinking continued to progress and I eventually entered a recovery program. I have 29 years of sobriety; in 2000, I retired with 25 years of service for the State of California.

Thank you for giving me this "last chance" to tell my story. Since I experienced the Vietnam War on a personal level, I suppose I should share my story and be included in the history of the women who served there because I am very proud of my service and what we contributed. I am no longer using the name "Helscher" but included it since that is how I was known in Vietnam.

♥**Esther W. Weldon (Stewart)**
**Retired as a Chief Warrant Officer 4**
**In country: January 1971 – January 1972**
**Rank: CW3, US Army**
**Duty: USARV, 1ˢᵗ Signal Brigade, Cryptographic Technician**

♥**Elizabeth "Betty" Helen Branch**
**Retired as a Colonel**
**In country: January 1971 – August 1972**
**Rank: Colonel, US Army**
**Duty: MACV, Command Historian**

### Celebrating the life of Colonel Elizabeth H. ("Betty") Branch

Many adjectives can be used to describe COL Branch: patriot, leader and mentor, and friend are just a few. She was a consummate professional, a supporter of expanded roles for women in the Army, and a lover of the arts. She served on the WAC and US Army Women's Museum Foundations' Boards of Directors for over 30 years. She died February 26, 2006, after a short illness. We're very fortunate that the US Army Women's Museum has an excellent oral history done with COL Branch by COL (Ret.) Georgia Hill in May 1990. This article is based on that oral history as well as other discussions.

Betty was born in Stamford, CT, in the summer of 1917. When World War II started, she was working at Macy's Department Store in New York City, hoping to break into the fashion business. She heard that women were allowed to join the Army, and immediately applied. She entered the fourth Officer Candidate Class at Fort Des Moines, IA, in July 1942, and was commissioned a Third Officer in October.

In March 1944, then First Lieutenant Branch sailed to England on the Queen Mary. The ship had been converted for troop duty, and bunks were shared on a shift basis – when it wasn't your turn to sleep, you had to leave the area! Arriving in England, she marched through blacked-out darkened streets; later, in London, she lived with the daily menace of German buzz bombs. After D-Day, she served in France where she reported hearing the sounds of artillery each night. She returned to the US after VE day to attend a war-shortened Command and General Staff College course at Fort Leavenworth, KS.

In 1946, she went to Nanking, China, where she was the personnel officer for the Military Advisory Group headed by General George C. Marshall. She had to wait in Shanghai for a plane to be sent for her. She reported that the "Shanghai airport had one building and no plumbing. If you needed to go, you went beyond the building." She finally arrived in Nanking only to find that no one was there to meet her. Eventually a young captain took her to General Marshall's home (where he also lived) until things could be sorted out. When Mrs. Marshall learned she was there, Captain Branch was invited to join the couple for dinner. She said this gave her quite a reputation!

Betty served several tours in the Pentagon, another tour in France, and tours at Redstone Arsenal and Fort McClellan, AL. She was Commander of the Women's Army Corps Center during an early period of WAC expansion. She was one of the first six women promoted to full colonel when restrictions on promotions were lifted in 1967.

Colonel Branch's last assignment was as the Command Historian for the US Military Assistance Command, Vietnam where she spent 18 months before returning to the States to retire at Fort McClellan in 1972.

Asked during her oral history interview what she thought important about her Army service she said: "The Army expected things of me and therefore I did (them). A job is yours and you do it. The Army gave me tremendous opportunity to (travel) all over the world. It gave me a chance to give something (back) and I think that's pretty good for any citizen."

Colonel Branch lost two brothers in military service. A younger brother, Lieutenant Richard Branch, died in 1945 when his P-47 crashed during a training mission. Her older brother, Major General Irving ("Twig") Branch (USAF), was killed in 1966, also in a plane crash.

Colonel Branch continued an active life in retirement. She was instrumental in the development of The Fairfax, an Army retirement community near Fort Belvoir, VA. She volunteered at the Smithsonian and for public broadcasting fundraisers. She enjoyed the symphony, opera and plays, and was a world traveler. She was recruited to join the Norwich University Board of Trustees in 1978 to "look out for women's interests and rights" and stayed almost 20 years. She was in the first group selected to be Directors' Emeriti of the US Army Women's Foundation, but sadly died before she could be notified.

When Colonel Branch left the WAC Center in 1968, her parting words were: "May the Lord watch between me and thee when we are absent one from another." (Genesis 31:49)

*Reprinted with permission from COL Pat Jernigan (USA Ret). Thanks to Paul Bova (Norwich University), Catherine Bander, Elizabeth Saus, Betty Branch and Georgia Hill who contributed to this article.*

**Loretta Marie Morrison (Kostyn)**
**In country: January 3, 1971 – June 17, 1971**
**Rank: Staff Sergeant, US Marine Corps**
**Duty: MACV, J52 (Strategic Plans Division), Administrative Specialist**

"I volunteered for the next duty assignment: Vietnam. My position as Administrator Management for the Strategic Plans Division enabled me to enact with the Vietnamese wartime requirements. During this assignment, I was solely responsible for consolidating more than 3,000 classified files of the two divisions that combined to form the strategic plans division, receiving the Joint Service Commendation Medal." She was also awarded the Bronze Star.

# FEBRUARY

*Memory Lane: Apollo 14 returns to Earth after the third manned Moon landing; Satchel Paige becomes the first Negro League player to become voted into the Baseball Hall of Fame.*
*Song: "No Time" by The Guess Who*

**Patricia A. Seiler**
**Retired as a Major**
**In country: February 1971 – December 1971**
**Rank: Captain, US Army**
**Duty: USARV, Long Binh Army Depot, Supply Management Officer**

**Mary E. Smith**
**Retired as a Major**
**In country: February 1971 – December 1971**
**Rank: Captain, US Air Force**
**Duty: 7th Air Force, 485th Engineering Installation Squadron, Computer System Analysis, Cam Ranh Bay**

**Betty L. Griffith**
Retired as a Captain
In country: February 1971 – February 1972
Rank: Captain, US Air Force
Duty: MACV, J2, Administrative Officer

**Frances Lynne Honsowetz**
Retired as a Lieutenant Colonel
In country: February 1971 – February 1972
Rank: Captain, US Army
Duty: USARV, Adjutant General

**♥Frances Telka Stockwell**
Retired as a Lieutenant Colonel
In country: February 22, 1971 – February 1972
Rank: Major, US Army
Duty: MACV, Information Office, Information Officer

**Lena C. Duke**
Retired as a Master Sergeant
In country: February 1971 – March 1972
Rank: Sergeant, US Air Force
Duty: MACV, J3, Administrative Specialist

# MARCH

*Memory Lane: US Army Lieutenant William Calley is found guilty of 22 murders in the My Lai massacre and sentenced to life in prison (later pardoned).*
*Song: "Me and Bobby McGee" by Janis Joplin*

**♥Alice May Davis**
Retired as a Colonel
In country: March 1971 – March 1972
Rank: Lieutenant Colonel, US Army
Duty: MACV, J2, Strategic Research and
Analysis Division, Deputy Chief

**Janice Hunt (Sanborn)**
**Retired as a Major**
**In country: March 1971 – March 1972**
**Rank: First Lieutenant, US Air Force**
**Duty: 7ᵗʰ Air Force, Project Contemporary Historical Evaluation of Current Operations, Administrative Officer**

It started when I landed at Cam Ranh Bay on my way to the 504ᵗʰ Tactical Support Air Squadron at Phan Rang. I learned my orders were changed to 7ᵗʰ Air Force. I spent the night in Cam Ranh Bay sharing a trailer with another female. That night, sirens peeled announcing a sapper attack. After some thought, I figured I would stay right there. My trailer mate screeched, grabbed a helmet and ran off into the night. Never saw her again. I finally crept out to get something to eat and was spotted by someone who asked if I was Janice Hunt. Yeah, so? "We've been looking for you." I was hustled out to Tan Son Nhut to quell the panic of the person I was replacing who feared he'd be stuck there for the duration.

My office was in a row of buildings. Hop Tacs (small taxis) buzzed out front while barbed wire surrounded the volleyball court out back. My work place was a vault – file cabinets, two desks and a couple of microfiche machines. Temperature averaged cold. Who knew I'd need jackets and sweaters in Vietnam? I was assigned an M-16, but I never saw or collected it. On the other hand, the 6-foot guys were assigned pistols, which they actually had in their possession. The workday was 12 hours a days, 7 days a week. My job working on project CHECO (Contemporary Historical Examination of Current Operations) was to collect and microfilm documents of the war, which included everything from messages and official papers to personal correspondence. A female sergeant and I had blanket TDY orders and traveled extensively throughout South Vietnam and even Thailand gathering information. (Having blanket travel orders means that individual orders did not have to be issued every time the individual traveled by military transportation.) Some of the more notable places we traveled to were Pleiku, the ranger camp overlooking the Ho Chi Minh Trail, Da Nang, Phu Cat, Phan Rang and Bien Hoa.

On a regular basis, Connie (SGT Marie Gagne) and I would head out to the airport and hitch a ride to wherever and in whatever transport was available. Our transportation was usually a C-130, A-7 or helicopter. I was in

Da Nang for the elections and as we passed a bonfire celebrating the election, a lit object was thrown under our jeep. Teeth clinched, breath held and eyes wide, we all survived. On a lighter note, on another visit to Da Nang, I stayed with the nurses at the officers' quarters. We decided to build a rocket launcher. A few coke cans, gas and tennis balls. Kapow! It worked. Unfortunately, base sirens went off and the search for the launcher commenced. Two security police appeared and we invited them up to our little party. While talking to us, their rifles were stolen, and the next day there were some angry people. I left that day for Tan Son Nhut. It was time to get out of Dodge or was it Da Nang?

**Marcia C. L. Petersen**
**In country: March 1971 – March 1972**
**Rank: Captain, US Air Force**
**Duty: 377th Combat Support Group, Administrative Officer**

**Carol A. Hazzard (Waryck-McClure)**
**In country: March 1971 – June 1972**
**Rank: Specialist 5, US Army**
**Duty: USARV, Special Troops,**
**WAC Detachment, Company Clerk**

**♥Dolores "Dee" Helen Hubik**
**Retired as a Lieutenant Colonel**
**In country: March 1971 – August 1972**
**Rank: Major, US Army**
**Duty: US Army Headquarters Area Command; MACV,**
**Information Officer**

**Maralin K. Coffinger**
**Retired as a Brigadier General**
**In country: March 19, 1971 – June 1972**
**Rank: Major, US Air Force**
**Duty: MACV, Detachment 10, Air Force Advisory Group, USAF WAF**
**Staff Advisor to the Vietnam Women's Armed Forces Corps**

*Condensed extracts from the book* "Oh My! The Things That Can Happen! During An Air Force Career," *by Maralin K. Coffinger, Brigadier General, USAF, Retired*

When I arrived at Tan Son Nhut Air Base, I was told to be ready for a culture shock. It was obvious that the person who said that to me had never been to the Middle East. Saigon was a real mess; it was, after all, a war zone. But, it appeared to be more civilized than Turkey and some other countries I had visited in that part of the world. My sponsor, the one I was replacing, took me directly to the women's BOQ (officers' quarters) which was an old dilapidated, all wood, two story structure, formerly a French barracks. My room was on the second floor at the far end. It measured approximately 9'x7' and had one window. Furnishings consisted of a single bed, a small desk, a straight chair, a small chest of drawers, a metal storage cabinet that served as a closet, and believe it or not, a small refrigerator that my sponsor got for me from someone who had completed his tour. The building had community bathrooms and showers about halfway down the outside walkway. I would probably categorize it as an extremely primitive Motel 6 without the light on. On my first night in country, the Vietnamese threw me a welcoming party. They spent the entire evening teasing me about the "dog" meat they were serving. I have no idea what it was. I stuck to the rice. The folks from my office picked me up in a jeep the next day and I reported for work. My job was two-fold, Personnel Data Systems Advisor and the Advisor to the Women in the Vietnamese Air Force. On the data systems side I would be advising three Vietnamese lieutenant colonels on automating their personnel system. When we met, I knew this was going to be an interesting relationship. I'm 5'10" so I towered over them – a tall female captain advising three short male lieutenant colonels? I wondered if the Air Force bothered to really think this thing through. Moreover, the Air Force had not sent me to language school as they had done with other advisors. Communications was a challenge, but we muddled through, even though the Vietnamese Lieutenant Colonels showed little if any interest in the project. As for the women's side of the job, the officer with whom I worked was a female Major. She was very shy, but quite pleasant. Language continued to be a problem, but she understood English much better than the men did.

Although the data systems job was primary for me, I did spend several hours a week working with my female Vietnamese major on matters dealing with women in the VNAF. Most of the emphasis was on making sure the women in the VNAF were properly housed and were given meaningful duties. Recruiting was also in the mix. I traveled with her several times to Vietnamese bases, and on one occasion we stopped at the major's home for a few minutes. It was clean but had only the bare essentials. She was the mother of nine children!

At Tan Son Nhut it was not unusual to hear sounds of canons and various other kinds of exploding ammo off in the distance. Periodically, the base would be hit by a rocket attack. My biggest scare came about a week before I was scheduled to leave the country. I was at a farewell party being given for me in the BOQ when there was a rocket attack. One rocket went right over the trailer and hit just on the other side leaving a good size hole in the ground. This was by far the worst attack I had experienced and there I was just one week before leaving! The chief nurse, who was giving the party, yelled for everyone to follow her to the dispensary that was just a few yards from the trailer near the perimeter fence. We raced over to the dispensary and the chief nurse assigned each of us (none of us were nurses) to one of the immobile patients (ones that couldn't take shelter under their beds) in an effort to keep them calm and reassured. My assignment was an Army lieutenant colonel whose hand had been blown off a few days before up North somewhere. While I was standing there with him, he proceeded to show me the results of their having reattached his hand. He was wiggling his fingers! He told me that he had carried his blown off hand in his lap coming back on the helicopter a couple of days earlier. This was my kind of guy.

Once my PCS (permanent change of station) orders came through, it didn't take long to pack my bags, especially after that last rocket attack. There wasn't much that I would miss about Vietnam except for certain people in my office and my female Vietnamese lieutenant colonel (promoted before I left Vietnam). We got to be good friends and I worried about her and her family's future. When the wheels on the aircraft went up after take-off, there was a celebration throughout the plane that you wouldn't believe.

# APRIL

*Memory Lane: Supreme Court upholds busing as means of achieving racial desegregation; Samuel Lee Gravely, Jr. becomes first black admiral in US Navy. Songs: "Give Me Just a Little More Time" by Chairmen of the Board; "Just My Imagination (Running Away With Me)" by the Temptations*

**Karen S. Nagel (Adams)**
**In country: April 1971 – January 1972**
**Rank: Specialist 5, US Army**
**Duty: MACV, Comptroller; USARV, Central Finance and Accounting Office, Clerk-Typist**

**Kathryn "Kathy" Wilson (Disbrow)**
**In country: April 1971 – January 1972**
**Rank: Captain, US Air Force**
**Duty: 7ᵗʰ Air Force, 2ⁿᵈ Aerial Port Group, Administrative Officer**

**Comments and Memories:** I craved McDonald's French fries. I had many experiences that were strange, but not really funny. *Source: Vietnam Memory Book 2000*

**♥Elfriede "Elly" Bartl**
**Retired as a Sergeant First Class**
**In country: April 1971 – April 1972**
**Rank: Specialist 5, US Army**
**Duty: USARV**

**Paula V. Kerns (Woodward)**
**Retired as a Lieutenant Colonel**
**In country: April 1971 – April 1972**
**Rank: Captain, US Air Force**
**Duty: 7ᵗʰ Air Force, 600ᵗʰ Photo Squadron, Motion Picture Production Officer**

**♥Sallie Laura Elmira Carroll**
**Retired as a Lieutenant Colonel**
**In country: April 1971 – April 1972**
**Rank: Major, US Army**
**Duty: USARV, 1st Logistical Command, Inventory Control Center, Adjutant**

Lieutenant Colonel Sallie Carroll started her military career in 1952 joining the US Air Force, was commissioned as an officer in the US Marine Corps and retired in 1975 from the US Army as a lieutenant colonel. She served in Vietnam where she was the Adjutant for Inventory Control Center. Her awards include: Bronze Star, Army Commendation Medal, Meritorious Service Medal w/Oak Leaf Cluster, Vietnam Service Medal w/Four Bronze Stars, Vietnam Cross of Gallantry w/Palm, Vietnam Campaign Medal.

Lieutenant Colonel Carroll was a pioneer for women who were becoming vital members of the US Army Marksmanship Unit assigned to the Service Pistol and International Pistol Disciplines. She won numerous shooting awards on national and international level including the Distinguished Pistol Shooting Medal, Excellence–in–Competition Badge, Pistol w/Silver Oak Leaf Cluster and the US International Distinguished Shooter Medal. She was inducted into the US Army Marksmanship Unit Hall of Fame International and Service Pistol. Her fellow comrades call her a friend, mentor and a woman of a different caliber.

Lieutenant Colonel Carroll was also involved with "Sallie's Place," a collaborative endeavor for women veterans and their children. Lieutenant Colonel Carroll died September 11, 2014.

**Comments and Memories:** New Year's Eve 1971, Long Binh, WAC Detachment swimming pool area. We were shooting survival flares to welcome the New Year. The male sentry left his post and came to the swimming pool area after we shot the first flare. He wanted to know who was releasing the flare. Of course, we all faked innocence. After the second flare, he came down again, very upset, and demanded to know who did that. Again, no answer. After the third flare, he stomped to the swimming area, said a few nasty words and shined his flashlight on our nametags and rank. There were both enlisted and officers at the party. When his flashlight illuminated two majors and a full colonel, he stopped, said, "Oh, hell," and returned to his post. He never came back. *Source: Vietnam Memory Book 2000*

**Lila Jean Sharpsteen**
**Retired as a Lieutenant Colonel**
**In country: April 2, 1971 – March 10, 1972**
**Rank: First Lieutenant, US Marine Corps**
**Duty: NAVFORV, Marine Corps Personnel Section, Administrative Officer**

**Florence "Flo" I. Dunn**
**Retired as a Major**
**In country: April 9, 1971 – March 3, 1972**
**Rank: Captain, US Army**
**Duty: MACV, Civil Operations and Revolutionary Development Support, Program Evaluator**

I had tried since 1965 when I was an enlisted woman to serve in Vietnam without any success. After I was commissioned, I applied again only to be told by WAC assignment branch that I'd have to be a captain before I could go to Vietnam. So when promotion to captain came, I was more than ready for Vietnam. I reported to the Military Assistance Command Vietnam (MACV) in March 1971 and looked forward to the challenges that would help me learn about the country and its people and how the US could make a difference.

At MACV Headquarters, I was assigned to Civil Operations and Rural Development Support (CORDS), located in downtown Saigon in the US Agency for International Development (USAID) Building 2, where US Marine Corps guards provided security. I was billeted in the Meyercord Hotel in Saigon's "downtown." My first roommate was a military nurse from Thailand; we didn't communicate very well, as we didn't speak each other's language. My second roommate was a Department of the Army civilian employee, surprisingly from my home state of Virginia.

Living and working in downtown Saigon opened my eyes to the many beggars on the streets, children sleeping in cardboard boxes on the streets amid unsanitary and the poorest of conditions. With the men at war, Vietnamese women had to do jobs men would normally do such as pouring cement to pave the streets and working garbage trucks.

On the other hand, being downtown, I ate in some nice French and Vietnamese restaurants such as Cheap Charlie's, where my farewell dinner was held.

Living in downtown Saigon I didn't need a special pass; however, military from other posts, camps, or areas outside Saigon were required to have a pass authorizing them to be in the capital city. There was a curfew in Saigon from 0100 to 0500 hours. Saigon wasn't the safest place to be. In fact, I felt safer when I was traveling out in the villages and hamlets. One night a Vietnamese policeman shot and killed a Vietnamese outside my hotel.

Drugs were a big problem throughout the country. Local drugstores and pharmacies were off limits since barbiturates and amphetamines were sold without prescriptions. Thefts occurred daily in the city. One of my office workers had a dozen eggs stolen from her, another had groceries she'd purchased in the commissary rifled from her car. (Military weren't authorized to shop in the US-operated Saigon commissary without special, written permission.) "Honda" cowboys on motorcycles, with a second person riding sidesaddle on the back, would snatch purses while speeding through crowds of people on the sidewalks and narrow streets. I was a victim of one of these a month before I was to leave Vietnam and in view of a policeman watching from a police box. He did nothing, which introduced me to police corruption.

The war was winding down when I departed Vietnam in March 1972. Units were deactivating, officers' and enlisted quarters were closing, and excess supplies were being taken to a staging point. The National Training Center (NTC) was closing and one of our tractor-trailer trucks from the NTC was hijacked along part of the VC-controlled highway. In Quang Ngai Province, a jeep hit a mine wounding the civilian advisor, killing a noncommissioned officer and severely wounding another.

Upon leaving Vietnam, I felt I had contributed to helping the Vietnamese improve their way of life. I had certainly had a multitude of experiences that I could never have had anywhere else in the world, especially when it came to working with different nationalities. This was evident when Minister Lay Nuett, Minister for the Development of Ethnic Minorities, decorated several of us from the directorate with the Ethnic Minorities Medal. It's a civilian decoration and is not authorized for wear on the military uniform. Very few military have earned the decoration.

Vietnam – never-to-be forgotten experiences, memories, friends, and a greater appreciation for what I have by being a citizen of the United States.

**Comments and Memories:** Twinkies™ are one of my favorite sweets, so when I was in Vietnam my sister would send me "care" packages filled with Twinkies™. One shipment arrived covered with ants. Thank goodness my roommate had a small refrigerator in our room. She suggested putting the Twinkies in the freezer, and after the ants froze, I could just knock them off. So this is exactly what I did. They never tasted better. *Source: Vietnam Memory Book 2000*

# MAY

*Memory Lane: 1st class postage costs 8¢; Willie Mays hits his 638th home run, sets Negro League record of 1,950 runs scored.*
*Song: "Joy to the World" by Three Dog Night*

**Carol Lynn Churchill**
**Retired as a Major**
**In country: May 1971 – November 1971**
**Rank: First Lieutenant, US Air Force**
**Duty: 7th Air Force, Cam Ranh Bay, Personnel Officer**

**Glenda M. Kaufman (Lunki)**
**Retired as a Chief Warrant Officer 3**
**In country: May 1971 – February 1972**
**Rank: Chief Warrant Officer 2, US Army**
**Duty: USA Support Command, Directorate of Administrative and Troop Adjustment, Qui Nhon and Cam Ranh Bay, Personnel/Administrative Technician**

En route to Long Binh 90th Replacement Army/Air Force Personnel, I witnessed a horrific scene that made all of us aware of the reality of Vietnam. A Vietnamese man was walking along the road swinging a camera on a strap. We witnessed another Vietnamese snatch the camera and within a block saw the man and camera explode killing the thief.

My next day, I boarded a C-130 and flew to the 14th Aerial Port Cam Ranh Bay. Calling the Headquarters for transportation to report to US Army Support Command, I overheard someone shout in the background, "What in the hell are we going to do with a female warrant officer!" When the individual got back on the phone, I replied, "I'll tell you what in the hell you will do! Get me a jeep and get me to Headquarters." He replied, "Whoa! The jeep is on its way." From that day, I was nicknamed "the mean and lean warrant officer."

I can say that my duties and responsibilities and opportunity to support our American servicemen and foreign allies were the highlight of my tour in Vietnam.

My reception home was similar to many of the Vietnam veterans. Walking up steps at the Pentagon I had demonstrators toss what looked like blood on my uniform and heard negative comments.

**Sandra L. Combs**
**In country: May 1971 – March 1972**
**Rank: Captain, US Air Force**
**Duty: 7ᵗʰ Air Force, Cam Ranh Bay, Personnel Officer**

**Kathleen "Chatty" E. Wilcox**
**In country: May 1971 – March 1972**
**Rank: Specialist 5, US Army**
**Duty: USARV, G1, Personnel, Personnel Specialist**

 **Comments and Memories:** Accidentally sent to Cam Ranh Bay as a male with the first name of 'Kathleen.' Go figure! *Source: Vietnam Memory Book 2000*

**Martha D. Martinez**
**In country: May 25, 1971 – May 7, 1972**
**Rank: Corporal, US Marine Corps**
**Duty: MACV, Marine Corps Personnel Section, Administrative Specialist**

# JUNE

*Memory Lane: Ed Sullivan's final TV show on CBS; The New York Times begin publishing excerpts from the Pentagon Papers, classified documents on the long history of the US in Vietnam.*
*Song: "Brown Sugar" by The Rolling Stones*

♥**Cora D. Hunter**
**Retired as a Major**
**In country: June 1971 – March 1972**
**Rank: Major, US Air Force**
**Duty: 7th Air Force, Plans, Personnel Staff Officer**

**Ethel M. Dial**
**Retired as a Master Sergeant**
**In country: June 1971 – April 1972**
**Rank: Staff Sergeant, US Army**
**Duty: 1st Signal Brigade, Communications Center Specialist**

I was born and spent my early life in the small Georgia town of Monroe. Being a part of the military was a dream of mine during high school.

I served in the United States Navy and later I joined the Women's Army Corps. After several assignments in the US and my second tour at Camp Zama, Japan, I was granted my request for an assignment in Vietnam.

In June 1971, I landed in Saigon, Vietnam, and was assigned to Long Binh, with duty at the 1st Signal Brigade as a Communications Center Specialist (MOS 72B40). Two other women worked in another section of the communications center. I worked with all males and we worked 12-hour shifts, six days a week. Most of our incoming messages were casualty reports of the troops: KIA (killed in action), WIA (wounded in action), and their movements in the war zones.

I lived at the WAC Detachment, with meals at the 24th Evacuation Hospital mess hall. Due to the war wounds of some of the male patients, I was eventually unable to cope with eating at the mess hall. An individual could work wonders with a hot plate and grill in their living area.

I had a friend, Delores "Mickey" Barrett, who was a supply sergeant and had access to a jeep. She knew people who worked at ration breakdown. We would pick up crates of fruits and other food items and return to the detachment. Everyone was welcome to share.

We never came under attack by enemy fire and there was no hiding in the bunkers for safety. I could hear the big weapons firing far away and could hear when they stopped. I would have a strange feeling until I heard the firing begin again.

During my time at Long Binh, I was not aware of any mistreatment of the women by the men. Most weekends, we were invited to the different male companies for cookouts, softball and horseshoe games. There was a Hawaiian group with a swimming pool and they would have luaus. The boatman for one of the generals would take the WACs for rides on the Saigon River. The boat was equipped with grills, so Betty Elliott, Gabrielle "Gabe" Brancato, and I would do the barbecuing. We all enjoyed these outings and the camaraderie.

We showed respect to the men and they showed the utmost respect to us. I flew from Saigon to California with a stopover in Alaska with all males. I have nothing negative to say about them.

My intention was to extend my assignment at Long Binh, but President Nixon began the withdrawal of troops from Vietnam. Because I had made requests for Germany several times before and was ignored, I applied again on the "Wish Sheet," knowing I would be assigned to the States, or so I thought. Then I received orders – Frankfurt, Germany, here I come.

I had three overseas assignments back-to-back: Camp Zama, Japan; Long Binh, Vietnam; and Frankfurt, Germany. Before retiring, I was stationed at Osan, Korea. There are cherished memories from each place I was stationed and the people I met.

**Mary Jane Bennett (Hill) (Treadwell)**
**Retired as a Major**
**In country: June 1971 – May 1972**
**Rank: Major, US Army**
**Duty: 1ˢᵗ Aviation Brigade, 34ᵗʰ General Support Group, Aviation Materiel Management Center, Supply Branch Chief**

My job concerned the processing of supply requisitions that were received from allied forces in Southeast Asia for helicopter repair parts. The processing of requisitions is normally routine. Occasionally a requisition would require special attention for some reason but more often, the interesting part of my job concerned the people, the culture, and at that time, the few military women located in Vietnam.

The unit I was assigned to was located in Saigon, now Ho Chi Minh City. My room was located in the Massachusetts Hotel. Don't let the word "Hotel" fool you. I realize my room was luxurious when compared to how most soldiers in Vietnam lived. However, just to put it in perspective, we frequently did not have electricity, the water was always cold, big bugs that every time it rained (it poured every day during the rainy season) came up out of the drain in the bathroom and took over my room. They were on the walls, ceiling, and floor, and stayed until they felt like leaving. There was no air conditioning.

In my office there were many local national (LN) women working. They were very proud that a woman officer had arrived. But, they soon let me know that there was a big problem. The building I worked in had four small bathrooms. Each of the two floors had two bathrooms. When I arrived, the bathrooms were divided up as follows: the enlisted men had a bathroom on each floor, the officers (until I arrived, there was not a female officer) had the second bathroom on the first floor and the LN women had the second bathroom on the second floor. There were several LN men and they used one of the enlisted men's bathrooms. There were many LN women using the one bathroom. On occasion, there was a line of women waiting to get into the bathroom. Upon my arrival, several of the LN women asked me if I could speak to the colonel about the problem. The problem was quickly resolved and one of the bathrooms on the first floor was designated for women. The LN women felt uneasy speaking to a man about this problem. Fortunately, the LN women let me use their bathroom.

Often the LN women would bring me food they wanted me to try. Some of the food they had cooked at home and at other times, they had bought the food from a vendor. Not many restaurants in Saigon were on the "recommended" list of places to eat and I was always concerned about this food. However, normally the woman bringing the food would wait at my desk until I ate a bite or two of her food and appropriately raved about its merits. I had no choice but to try the food. Usually it was good, sometimes very good. Fortunately, I survived without problems.

There were LN women who attended to the rooms in the Massachusetts Hotel. One of their tasks was to wash clothes. One woman cleaned and took care of many rooms such as is the case in our motels and hotels. I soon noticed that my underwear was disappearing at an alarming rate. I had brought a sufficient amount with me because I knew the post exchange did not carry much in the way of women's clothing. One day I was in my room when the cleaning women arrived. I asked her what was happening to my underwear. She said that washed clothes were hung on a clothesline located on the roof of the building and that sometimes an American officer would steal women's underwear off the line. I knew it was possible that a man was stealing women's underwear, but I found it hard to believe. I discovered that my underwear did not disappear if I kept a very limited amount in my drawer. I believe that as long as it appeared I only had several sets of underwear the cleaning women did not take them. If I obviously had plenty, then I could afford to share with them. I stopped in Hawaii on my way home and the first thing I did was buy underwear.

♥Jennie Wren Fea
**Retired as a Colonel**
**In country: June 1971 – May 1972**
**Rank: Colonel, US Army**
**Duty: USARV, Director of Military Personnel**

**Comments and Memories:** I have great memories of outdoor cookouts (under old parachutes as canopies) and watching flares and chopper action while the fried chicken and steaks were being cooked. These cookouts were attended by officers and enlisted personnel, both male and female. Great conversation, great people and lots of jokes played on each other. All of this interaction made our 12-hour, 7-day-a-week working hours more bearable, and all of us are better soldiers for having had this experience. *Source: Vietnam Memory Book 2000*

♥Paula F. Jenkins
**Retired as a Lieutenant Colonel**
**In country: June 1971 – June 1972**
**Rank: Major, US Army**
**Duty: MACV, J2, Aerial Surveillance Officer**

Bernice J. DeSisto
**Retired as a Technical Sergeant**
**In country: June 1971 – June 1972**
**Rank: Staff Sergeant, US Air Force**
**Duty: 7th Air Force, 377th Air Base Wing, Tan Son Nhut, Administrative Specialist**

♥Colleen Margaret Ryan (Cleaves)
**Retired as a Master Sergeant**
**In country: June 1971 – June 1972**
**Rank: Technical Sergeant, US Air Force**
**Duty: 7th Air Force, 1964th Communications Squadron, Stenographic Technician**

Mary J. Smith
**Retired as a Lieutenant Colonel**
**In country: June 1971 – June 1972**
**Rank: Captain, US Army**
**Duty: MACV, J14; USARV**

♥Marilyn Jean Russell
**Retired as a Colonel**
**In country: June 1971 – June 4, 1972**
**Rank: Lieutenant Colonel, US Army**
**Duty: MACV, Personnel Staff Officer**

Lieutenant Colonel Marilyn Russell was awarded the Legion of Merit for her service in Vietnam.

**♥Rosemarie Lane**
**Retired as a Master Sergeant**
**In country: June 1971 – March 1973**
**Rank: Staff Sergeant, US Army**
**Duty: 1ˢᵗ Aviation Brigade, Administrative NCO**

Born in Brooklyn, NY, she joined the Army in 1963. In 1971, she volunteered to serve in Vietnam. While there, she worked as an administrator for the 1ˢᵗ Aviation Brigade in Saigon.

In 1973, upon leaving Vietnam, Staff Sergeant Lane worked as a drill instructor at posts around the country and Germany. In 1986, she retired at Fort Bragg, NC, as a master sergeant, having spent 23 years in the Army. It was also in 1986 that she moved to Maine and joined the VFW.

After her retirement, she went on to work for Day One Substance Abuse in Portland, ME, and the Internal Revenue Service in Lewiston, ME, where she retired in April 2008.

In June 2003, she became Maine's VFW state commander, the first female member in a New England state to achieve this distinction.

*Excerpt from the* Sun Journal, *Lewiston, ME, August 5, 2008.*

**Patricia Jane Maybin**
**Retired as a Lieutenant Colonel**
**In country: June 13, 1971 – June 10, 1972**
**Rank: Major, US Army**
**Duty: MACV, Information Office, Information Officer**

# JULY

*Memory Lane: Washington State becomes first state to ban sex discrimination; Apollo 15 astronauts take 6½ hour electric car ride on Moon.*
*Song: "It's Too Late/I Feel the Earth Move" by Carole King*

**Elsie J. Robinson**
**Retired as a Master Sergeant**
**In country: July 1971 – April 1972**
**Rank: Specialist 4, US Army**
**Duty: USARV, Administrative Specialist**

Colleen L. Brooks
Retired as a Colonel
In country: July 1971 – June 1972
Rank: Lieutenant Colonel, US Army
Duty: MACV, Civil Operations and Rural Development Support
(CORDS)

Norma Allene Goerlitz
Retired as a Sergeant First Class
In country: July 1971 – July 1972
Rank: Staff Sergeant, US Army
Duty: USARV, Central Finance and Accounting Office, Finance NCO

Kay "Casey" F. Hickok
Retired as a Master Sergeant
In country: July 1971 – July 1972
Rank: Staff Sergeant, US Army
Duty: USARV, G1; USARV, Special Troops, WAC
Detachment, Field First/Administrative NCO

♥Barbara Jean Loar
Retired as a Major
In country: July 1971 – July 1972
Rank: Major, US Air Force
Duty: 7th Air Force, 377th Combat Support Group, Air Traffic Control,
Transportation Officer

Major Loar's assignment as Traffic Management Officer was ordering
aircraft and the allocation of seats of all homeward bound military personnel.

Cheryl K. Ruff
Retired as a Captain
In country: July 1971 – July 1972
Rank: Specialist 5, US Army
Duty: USARV, USA Medical Command, Administrative Specialist

**Merline Lovelace**
**Retired as a Colonel**
**In country: July 2, 1971 – July 3, 1972**
**Rank: Captain, US Air Force**
**Duty: 7ᵗʰ Air Force, 377ᵗʰ Air Base Wing, Executive Officer**

My Vietnam story begins when I was a lieutenant and a new bride. My husband and I were married while I was stationed in Taipei and it took a while for us to work an assignment together at Carswell Air Force Base, TX. We'd barely been there six months before he got orders to Da Nang Air Base, Vietnam. I immediately volunteered to go, too, although my husband had serious concerns about me going to a war zone. At that time, family members couldn't be assigned to the same base in a combat zone, so I worked an assignment to Tan Son Nhut Air Base in Saigon.

Then some weenie at Headquarters cut orders for us to fly over on different contract flights, so I picked up the phone and called the noncommissioned officer in charge of the aerial port squadron at Travis Air Force Base, CA. The sarge said sure and booked us on the same flight. So there I was, the only woman on a Pan Am flight with 250 unhappy guys headed to Vietnam. My husband stayed with me at Tan Son Nhut for a couple days before he had to report to Da Nang. I think it really helped him to see my tiny 8x10 room at the barracks occupied by non-medical women officers and know I was settled before he flew north.

Having been married less than a year, we wrote each other every day. I also got patched through on the phone every few days. I'm sure the military operators got a chuckle (or rolled their eyes) listening in on our calls. We also got to take our three-day in-country R&Rs and two weeks of regular R&R together.

It helped so much being there in country and understanding what each was going through. Things got real hairy during the Easter Offensive of 1972, however, when the North Vietnamese launched the largest mechanized assault of the war. Overnight, more than 3,000 US marines were flown into Da Nang to counter the northern front. Another front came within a few miles of Saigon; all of us at Tan Son Nhut were issued arms and went on full alert. That's when I was so glad I insisted on being qualified on both the M-1 and .38 before I left for Vietnam. (At that time, women didn't get weapons training during basic or Officer Training School. We had classes in make-up instead!)

In retrospect, I'm proud I took part in the Vietnam war, although it breaks my heart to think of all the people – us and the Vietnamese and other nationalities – who fought and died for what time has shown was a wasted effort.

*After 23 years in the Air Force, Merline Lovelace began a second career as an author, basing many of her tales on her experiences in the service. She's since written more than 95 action-packed novels, many of which have made* USA Today *bestseller lists. More than twelve million copies of her works are in print in 30 countries. Check out her website at* <u>www.merlinelovelace.com</u> *or join her on Facebook.*

**Mary "Micki" M. Morris**
**Retired as a Senior Master Sergeant**
**In country: July 4, 1971 – July 5, 1972**
**Rank: Master Sergeant, US Air Force**
**Duty: 7th Air Force, Intelligence Division, Administrator for Division and Classified Courier**

Our hootch was surrounded by an 8- or 10-foot fence, and we fondly referred to it as Fort Round Eyes. In order to get in you had to ring the doorbell and someone from inside would go out to see if it was friend or foe. It was simple but it worked.

Our hootch and the male hootch next door were separated by a small drainage ditch so most nights we would call out to each other to say goodnight. If anything out of the ordinary happened in our area all we had to do was yell out and the men would be there immediately. They became part of our security network. I kept hitting my head on the T-Bar that held my mosquito netting up. The first time it happened I let loose with a string of cuss words that would make a sailor blush. So from then on, they would remind me to watch out for the T-Bar. It was always good for a laugh. The new ladies never quite figured it out and thought it was some kind of code.

**♥Ruth Florence Reinholz**
**Retired as a Lieutenant Colonel**
**In country: July 7, 1971 – June 20, 1972**
**Rank: Lieutenant Colonel, US Marine Corps**
**Duty: MACV, Secretary of the Joint Staff, Command Historian**

After graduation from high school in 1950, Ruth worked as a social worker for two years before being commissioned as a second lieutenant in the Marine Corps.

During her 26-year career in the Corps, she served all over the globe to include commanding the Woman Marine Training Battalion, Parris Island, SC. She was awarded the Bronze Star with combat "V" during her tour in Vietnam where she served as historian on General Creighton Abrams' staff.

# AUGUST

*Memory Lane: US President Richard Nixon announces 90-day freeze on wages, prices and rents; the US dollar is allowed to float against the Japanese yen for the first time; the unemployment rate peaks at 6.1 percent.*
*Songs: "Draggin' The Line" by Tommy James; "How Can You Mend a Broken Heart" by the BeeGees*

**Mary Frances Anderson (Shupack)**
**Retired as a Captain**
**In country: August 1971 – July 1972**
**Rank: Captain, US Navy**
**Duty: Naval Air Facility; NAVFORV, Cam Ranh Bay, Personnel Officer**

I was the personnel officer for about 260 enlisted personnel and 350 Vietnamese civilians. Because President Nixon had ordered a drawdown of US troops and the Naval Air Facility was scheduled to close in February 1972, I spent most of my time getting orders for my enlisted troops and carrying out a reduction-in-force (RIF) of the Vietnamese civilians which required going to villages to give laid-off employees their severance pay. Some Vietnamese said they were concerned for their lives and asked me to help; sadly, there was nothing I could do.

Following US RIF procedures was not the only incongruous thing I encountered. When I arrived, the question of my billeting was elevated to a "command level" decision. Despite the fact that the bachelor officers' quarters were adequate, my boss didn't think it would be appropriate for me to be billeted there because I would be the only "round eye" female. The decision was to billet me with the Air Force nurses, other female medical personnel, and the female Red Cross workers in a Quonset hut on the Air Force side of the US base. This arrangement meant that I would have to transit outside the US security perimeter to get to and from my quarters.

My job required communicating with detailers at the Bureau of Naval Personnel in Washington, DC. Since Vietnam is on the other side of the world from Washington, I had to go to my office in the middle of the night in order to reach the detailers during normal business hours. For those middle-of-the-night trips between my quarters and my office, I was given an old beat up Scout, a four-wheel drive vehicle similar to a Jeep. I was also issued a flak jacket and a helmet that I was required to wear anytime I was outside the US security perimeter. Yet, as a non-combatant, I was not issued a weapon. Often on my nightly trips, I saw gunfire and bombs exploding on the mainland across the water, but I never encountered any problems. The scariest part of my nightly excursions occurred when I turned on the lights in the office and the walls came alive with huge bugs scampering for cover.

I am very glad that I had the opportunity to serve in Vietnam. My being there meant that one less man had to go. It also gave me the chance to do one of the most important jobs in the Navy – take care of the troops.

**Nuala R. Gardner**
**Retired as a Chief Master Sergeant**
**In country: August 1971 – July 1972**
**Rank: Staff Sergeant, US Air Force**
**Duty: 7th Air Force, Stenographic Specialist**

**♥Hetty Ann Ricker**
**Retired as a Lieutenant Colonel**
**In country: August 1971 – August 1972**
**Rank: Major, US Army Medical Specialist Corps**
**Duty: 6th Convalescent Center, Cam Ranh Bay, Occupational Therapist**

While the majority of Army occupational therapy support for Vietnam casualties was provided in military hospitals in Japan, Hawaii, and the continental United States, one Army Medical Specialist Corps occupational therapist, MAJ Hetty Ricker, was assigned to Vietnam in that military occupational specialty. She arrived in country August 1971 as the occupational therapy consultant to the USARV Surgeon. Her mission was to assist in establishing a drug abuse program at the 3,000-bed convalescent center at Cam Ranh Bay, to strengthen rehabilitation programs in 13 other Army drug control treatment facilities, and to evaluate occupational therapy support and education in the medical civil assistance programs aiding the Vietnamese civilian population. Lieutenant Colonel Hetty Ricker died January 9, 2002 and is buried in Arlington National Cemetery.

*Excerpt from* The Army Medical Specialist Corps, The 45th Anniversary, *by Ann M. Ritchie Hartwick, Center of Military History, US Army, Washington, DC, 1993*

**Sharon Yamashita**
**Retired as a Lieutenant Colonel**
**In country: August 1971 – August 1972**
**Rank: First Lieutenant, Army Medical Specialist Corps**
**Duty: 3rd Field Hospital, Saigon, Dietetic Consultant**

**Virginia Kay Schooler**
**Retired as a Major**
**In country: August 1, 1971 – March 31, 1972**
**Rank: Major, US Air Force, Biomedical Sciences Corps**
**Duty: 7th Air Force, 483rd USAF Hospital, Cam Ranh Bay, Chief Dietitian, closed the hospital**

I was chief dietitian at the Cam Ranh Bay Air Force hospital from August 1971 to March 1972.

During that time, we supplied three meals a day for up to 500 patients and all of the attending medical personnel. We had a separate ward for Vietnamese patients and due to their dietary differences had to prepare meals made just for them. Food was also provided for any family members who stayed with patients at the hospital, a common occurrence.

Food orders required 5-6 months advanced planning. Someone forgot to add Thanksgiving items to the July food requisition. There was a lot of last minute scrambling to make a traditional Thanksgiving meal possible. We substituted sweet potato pie for pumpkin pie, and had candy made from family recipes.

Special diets for wounded patients had to be made from scratch. There were no pre-made liquid supplements in those days. It was a complicated procedure because we had to be certain that the correct balance of calories, protein, fat and other nutrients needed was present. We used baby food for a base. We never had any of the problems that often occurred with "homemade" oral feedings.

About Christmas of 1971, we were told that the hospital would be closing and staff would be transferred in country or sent home. Before leaving, we had to move equipment to the main dining hall on base. All remaining patients and staff would be fed from there. After our final meal at the hospital, before leaving, we even had to remove all kitchen equipment.

We had also provided medical assistance to a local Vietnamese clinic and orphanage run by French nuns. The children looked forward to our visits with fresh fruit and sometimes candy.

At the end of my dietetic internship, each student in the class was asked to tell something in particular that we wished to accomplish. Mine was "to be the last Air Force dietitian in Vietnam." My wish was granted.

**Andrea Luevon Edwards**
**In country: August 4, 1971 – August 28, 1972**
**Rank: Corporal, US Marine Corps**
**Duty: NAVFORV, Marine Corps Personnel Section, Unit Diary Clerk**

## Marlene Adele Bowen-Grissett
**Retired as a Master Sergeant**
**In country: August 5, 1971 – August 4, 1972**
**Rank: Specialist 5, US Army**
**Duty: USARV, 1ˢᵗ Aviation Brigade, Clerk-Typist**

July 3, 1972: Was sick in the afternoon at work. My boss warrant officer would not let me get off work to go back to the WAC Detachment. He didn't believe I was sick. My friend, SP5 Josephine Solis, left work early as she had CQ (Charge of Quarters) at the WAC Detachment. When I got back to the detachment after work, all I wanted was to take a shower and lie down. Later, SP5 Solis came to check on me and decided to call a medic (who happened to be my roommate).

I remember they took me in a jeep. It was raining, and they didn't have time to get other transportation.

They took me to the 24ᵗʰ Evacuation Emergency Room – no time to send me to Saigon. Next thing I knew, I was going into emergency surgery. The chaplain was there to bless me and say a prayer. I was scared, not sure what was going on. I had a bowel anomaly, Meckel's Diverticulum, so while they did surgery they also removed my appendix (appendectomy and small bowel resection). The doctor later told me I was very lucky. It was a good thing I hadn't gone to sleep and the CQ got me to the 24ᵗʰ Evac.

To this day, I remember my friend, SP5 Solis, saved my life.

Then my trouble began. They wanted to medevac me back to the States. I told them I got to Vietnam on my own two feet and wanted to return on my own two feet. After a week, I won my case only because I was in Long Binh. They told me if I had had the surgery in Saigon, I would not have had a choice. Well, I was happy.

While I was in the hospital, my unit chief warrant officer, who gave me a hard time about being sick and didn't believe me, apologized.

The unit commander awarded me my medals while I was still hospitalized because I was close to the end of my tour in Vietnam. I received the Bronze Star and Army Commendation Medal in my hospital bed in a ceremony with members of the 1ˢᵗ Aviation Brigade.

Released from the hospital, I was back in the WAC Detachment until my return to the States; they required me to have an escort for the trip.

August 4, 1972: I was escorted by my friend, SP5 Solis. We were both assigned to the Presidio of San Francisco. I got to return to the States the way I went to Vietnam, "on my own two feet." Quite an experience!

# SEPTEMBER

*Memory Lane: Ernest Medina cleared of all charges connected with the My Lai Massacre; Watergate team breaks into Daniel Ellsberg's doctor's office.*
*Song: "I Just Want to Celebrate" by Rare Earth*

**Shirley Mae McDougald**
**Retired as a Sergeant First Class**
**In country: September 1971 – January 1972**
**Rank: Specialist 5, US Army**
**Duty: USARV, 18th MP Brigade, Personnel Specialist**

**Judy Ann Martin**
**Retired as a Master Sergeant**
**In country: September 1971 – May 1972**
**Rank: Staff Sergeant, US Air Force**
**Duty: 7th Air Force, Administrative Specialist**

**Sherri "Dizzy" "PepsiKid" "Tip" A. Tipton**
**Retired as a Sergeant First Class**
**In country: September 1971 – June 1972**
**Rank: Specialist 5, US Army**
**Duty: USARV, 38th Dental Detachment, Dental Specialist**

I'm a farmer's daughter from Northwest Arkansas that suddenly found myself on the other side of the world in September 1971. I love my country, but I didn't realize how much until I volunteered to go to Vietnam as a Dental Hygienist. I wanted to make a difference and felt it was my duty to serve my country the best way I knew how.

Assigned to the 38th Dental Detachment, I worked for Colonel Sorry. He was extremely surprised to find a round-eyed woman assigned to his detachment. But, my work ethic put his mind at ease in a very short time. I would go out on Den Tact (dental activity) missions with Colonel Sorry and two interpreters. As we approached different villages to extract teeth, villagers would come from miles around to seek any kind of medical treatment. One of the most surprising things, besides lack of sanitation and running water, etc., was the fact that I was the first round-eyed woman the villagers had ever seen! That was an experience in itself.

While assigned to the 38th, I cleaned teeth for our soldiers 10 to 12 hours a day, never turning anyone away. We gave dental toothbrush kits to each patient once the teeth were clean. Much later, I found out those toothbrushes were used to clean their M-16s! Once I found that out, I started giving cases of kids' toothbrushes to any of our soldiers that came in. The dental clinic was a popular place for a while.

I had several horrible experiences from some of the Army Reserve dental officers who were assigned to the 38th to get their "combat tour." As a result I have years of anger, shame that has haunted me all my life, and I have been diagnosed with PTSD (Posttraumatic Stress Disorder). My most heartbreaking experience was landing in San Francisco coming back from Vietnam. Protesters standing outside the airport would scream "Baby killer, slut, whore; you should be ashamed of yourself." As a result, I have become much more of an introvert and withdrawn from people. My daughter asks me sometimes, if I could do it all over again would I, and my answer is most definitely!

**Nancy Geraldine Anderson**
**In country: September 1971 – July 1972**
**Rank: Specialist 5, US Army**
**Duty: USARV, 9th Medical Laboratory, Still Photographic Specialist**

**Leah L. Chappell**
**Retired as a Lieutenant Colonel**
**In country: September 1971 – July 1972**
**Rank: Major, US Army**
**Duty: Long Binh Army Depot, Adjutant**

**♥Nancy L. Rust**
**Retired as a Lieutenant Colonel**
**In country: September 1971 – September 1972**
**Rank: Captain, US Air Force**
**Duty: 7th Air Force, Support Group Personnel, Personnel Staff Officer**

**Audrey Stebenne**
**Retired as a Lieutenant Colonel**
**In country: September 1971 – September 1972**
**Rank: First Lieutenant, US Air Force**
**Duty: 7th Air Force, 12th Reconnaissance Intelligence Technical Squadron,**
**Intelligence Photo-Radar Officer**

**♥Mildred Estelle Duncan**
**Retired as a Sergeant Major**
**In country: September 1971 – October 1972**
**Rank: First Sergeant, US Army**
**Duty: USARV, Special Troops, WAC Detachment,**
**Last First Sergeant**

# OCTOBER

*Memory Lane: Walt Disney World opens in Orlando, FL; Switzerland recognizes North Vietnam.*
*Songs: "So Far Away" by Carole King; "Maggie May/Reason to Believe" by Rod Stewart*

**Sandra J. Torrens**
**Retired as a Sergeant Major**
**In country: October 1971 – October 1972**
**Rank: Specialist 5, US Army**
**Duty: USARV, 1st Signal Brigade, Executive Administrative Assistant**

According to an article in *The Overseas Weekly – Pacific Edition* from 1972, SP4 Sandra Torrens was an organizer of that year's Easter Luau.

"Captain (Constance C.) Seidemann drove out with me to pick up the pig. It was still alive so I rode in the back of the truck with it. When we stopped at the gate, the captain just gave her name and said, "And friend." The guard looked into the back and, before he could say anything, I put my arm around the pig and said, "Now don't you say anything about my date."

The article goes on to say that SP4 Torrens not only looks like Phyllis Diller, she sounds like her. "What kills me about having her body," she quipped, "is that she's getting all the money and I'm walking around with it!"

*Excerpt from "The women behind the concertina barricade,"* The Overseas Weekly – Pacific Edition, *May 8, 1972, publication defunct 1975*

**Sally L. Davidson (Creely)**
**Retired as a Colonel**
**In country: October 1971 – November 1972**
**Rank: Captain, US Air Force**
**Duty: 7th Air Force, Protocol, Administrative Officer**

# NOVEMBER

*Memory Lane: First pro golf championship at Walt Disney World; the US increases air activity to support the Cambodian government as fighting nears Phnom Penh.*
*Songs: "Theme from Shaft" by Isaac Hayes; "Gypsys, Tramps and Thieves" by Cher*

**Barbara N. Gibson**
**Retired as a Technical Sergeant, US Air National Guard**
**In country: November 1971 – May 1972**
**Rank: Specialist 4, US Army**
**Duty: MACV, Personnel Specialist**

After serving 16 years in the Army, Barbara Gibson switched to the US Air National Guard from which she retired as a Technical Sergeant.

**Welda A. Smith**
**Retired as a Lieutenant Colonel**
**In country: November 1971 – March 1973**
**Rank: Lieutenant Colonel, US Air Force**
**Duty: MACV, Joint Chief of Staff for Personnel, Information Staff Officer**

**Constance "Connie" Christine Seidemann (Ferrell)**
**Retired as a Major**
**In country: November 1, 1971 – September 1972**
**Rank: Captain, US Army**
**Duty: USARV, Special Troops, WAC Detachment, Sixth and last**
**Company Commander**

A friend of mine and I joined the Navy after high school. When my hitch was up, I left the Navy, never thinking I would return to the military. I went to school and had three years of college when I was accepted into Officer Candidate School and nine months later was commissioned as a second lieutenant in the Women's Army Corps. I later received my baccalaureate degree.

My first assignment was at Fort Rucker, AL, at the Army Aviation Center. I was the executive officer of the post WAC Detachment. I was then sent to Alameda, CA, for the first time and there I was assigned to recruiting duty. I recruited women officer candidates. I traveled a great deal to various colleges in the area and I learned something about the lay of the land in Northern California. I fell in love with it. I returned to Fort McClellan, AL, where I had my first command, Charlie Company, a basic training company.

From there, I accepted the assignment to Vietnam. For a year, I was commander of the only enlisted female detachment in country. After Vietnam, I attended the Adjutant General Advanced Course.

There were various assignments after my return, including one at Travis Air Force Base, CA, where I completed my Master's degree and was promoted to Major.

I finished my 21 years of service at Fort Knox, KY, and retired. I now know my most favorite job is retirement. The pay isn't too good but the hours are terrific.

**Laurie A. Clemons (Parkerton)**
**Retired as a Sergeant, USAR**
**In country: November 7, 1971 – November 3, 1972**
**Rank: Staff Sergeant, US Air Force**
**Duty: MACV, Office of Information, American Forces Vietnam**
**Network, Radio and TV Services**

When I arrived in Saigon, I learned that everyone except the port of debarkation and I knew that my orders had been cancelled. I was offered a transfer to the American Forces Thailand Network (AFTN), but like an ignorant twit I elected to remain in Vietnam.

It was made perfectly clear from the start that I would never be allowed on-camera. The excuse was that women did not have the "credibility" to deliver television news, especially as an anchor. I was a bit disappointed, but in truth, I really wasn't all that great on camera. However, I did excel at being technical director (TD) on the live TV newscast. TDs control everyone and everything in the studio and control room, and everything was timed to the second. It was live TV and I loved it. I was told by fellow GIs who had their degrees in the broadcast arts that I was as good a TD as any broadcast arts college graduate was.

One night, as I was running the video that announced the start of the TV nightly news, I intended to bring our sportscaster on the preview screen so I could check the camera position. I had taught our sportscaster how to use makeup to hide the circles under his eyes. The dear boy was a bit full of himself, becoming what we sarcastically called "A Saigon Star." It was an accident when I hit the "On-Air" button instead of "Preview." After a few seconds, my audio man yelled, "He's Live! YOU PUT HIM ON-AIR!" Sure enough, there was our macho sportscaster preening into my compact, squinting at his face from all possible angles. I knew I should immediately jump him back to preview but something made me hover my hand over the switch, waiting until he caught sight of himself on the in-studio "on-air" camera. When he finally realized he was live on-air and the whole country was watching him preen with pursed lips, compact in hand, I finally jumped him to "preview" – just as he was distinctly seen mouthing *"Oh F\*\*K!"* For some reason, after that, he seemed a lot less full of himself.

Then came the day that the Army staff sergeant (not so affectionately called BUFFE) – whose female Vietnamese clerk had just quit – walked into the control studio while I was directing the nightly news, pointed to me and loudly announced, "She's female. She types. She's assigned to me." No lie. That is exactly what he said. I knew of course my position as TD was secure. I would not be directing the live TV news if I wasn't very qualified, right? The next day I was doing a step above clerk work in the TV Scheduling Office, under that same staff sergeant. My control room co-workers were pissed because they had to take up the slack my leaving caused. Of course, whenever a bigwig would show up to inspect or tour AFVN, I would be dragged into the TV control room, introduced as "our TV director," then dumped back into my windowless 4'x 8' cell.

My roommate was Bridget C., an Irish immigrant with a lovely Celtic brogue who showed her love of America by becoming a career marine. One night, Bridget and I left a restaurant and went looking for a cab. I had leftovers in a bag. We passed a beggar who was sitting on the ground, his back against a wall. By then I had pretty much hardened myself to the pain and poverty that was visible at every turn. The old man held out his hand and Bridget said, "Give him your leftovers." I said "Hell no! I paid for it and I might want it later." Bridget gave me an odd look and said, very softly, "Laurie. Do you hear what you're saying?" I looked back at that gaunt, very old man, covered in rags and filth, bald headed and scrawny grey beard, eyes at half-mast. He still had his hand held out and it was trembling as if the effort was just too great. I was filled with a sense of shame I had never experienced, before or since. I put the bag in his hand. He looked a little confused as he opened the bag's contents. His eyes widened and he looked up at me, tears running down his face. He looked back down and just stared at the meager leftovers as if they were the greatest bounty he'd ever received. It hurt to watch. I just walked away. It was a lesson I pray I'll never forget.

*Author's note:* Laurie Clemons had five and a half years active service in the Air Force, eight years in the Navy Reserve, and almost 12 years in the Army Reserve, for a total of almost 26 years of military service.

**♥Judie A. Armington**
**Retired as a Lieutenant Colonel**
**In country: November 7, 1971 – November 30, 1972**
**Rank: Captain, US Air Force**
**Duty: 7ᵗʰ Air Force, 483ʳᵈ Tactical Airlift Wing, Cam Ranh Bay,**
**Protocol Officer**

When I arrived in the middle of the night in November 1971 at Cam Ranh Bay Air Base, there were flares lighting up the sky all around the plane. I was met by my boss, Colonel (later Brigadier General) Duane H. Erickson and my sponsor, Captain Sandy Combs. They were terribly concerned that I had been frightened by all the flares. Being a Southern California girl and growing up with Disneyland, I wasn't worried; it was just fireworks to me. Since I was new at protocol, Captain Sally Davidson used to come from 7ᵗʰ Air Force in Saigon to coach me.

Uniforms were a problem in those days. The only official Women in the Air Force (WAF) uniform that didn't have a skirt was a light blue blouse with dark blue slacks, called fatigues, but not really good wear for a combat zone. Fortunately, the Women's Army Corps (WAC) members that had been there before left a stash of their fatigues when they went home. I found a couple of pairs of olive drab fatigues that fit me. The pants had buttons down the sides that could easily be put on backwards in the dark or under the stress of an attack and that lead to a "gotcha" story on one new arrival. The female quarters were in the shape of an H, with single rooms down both sides and the latrine and shower area in the crossover. There was a four-foot wall down the inside of both sides of the H so that in the event of an attack we had an amount of protection. Security police were assigned to come to protect us. One of the newbies was told that she shouldn't worry about being captured, that the Security police were going to be there to shoot the women if the base was in danger of being overrun. When we did have an attack, she was in total panic, had her pants on backwards so she couldn't sit or crouch behind the wall, and wailed to the security police not to shoot her.

I worked for the 483ʳᵈ Airlift Wing Commander, and he was very protective. He said he didn't want to write a condolence letter to my mother if anything happened to me. That meant that I didn't get to go to the beach where all the nurses went, even though I drove by it daily, and I didn't get to go with the chaplain to visit the orphanage since it went through North Vietnamese territory. However, I got one trip in a helicopter before he shut that down for me, and when the social actions officer left, I commandeered his jeep for a few trips before I got found out.

At Christmas, several C-7A Caribou aircraft that were going in for scheduled maintenance were painted up as "Santa Bou." Each one had the back end loaded with a Christmas tree, portable bar, booze, sodas, candy and children's gifts. We flew into the delta of South Vietnam to fields so small that we couldn't see them till we were right on top of them. We circled a couple of times and did the short field landing that the Caribou was known for. By the time we had turned around, out of the trees came children and soldiers with bandoliers. We dropped the ramp and moved the bar into place, put the tree on top and started serving whatever was age-appropriate. It was a small touch of home a long way from home.

As we began the preparations for the turnover to the Vietnamese, the troops began to leave. For the last few weeks, I was the only non-Vietnamese female on base. I moved from my room to the chief nurse's quarters since it had its own bathroom, and the guys moved from their hootches into air conditioned comfort. When it came time to officially turn the base over to the Vietnamese, a Vietnamese captain and I wrote the dual-language ceremony and broadcast it on the public address system. I flew out right after the ceremony, and the base was attacked that night.

At the MACV/7AF Headquarters, I worked in operations plans. One day I noticed that the Vietnamese housekeeper disappeared into the bucket storage room when the classified operations briefing started and came out when ended. I went into the room and found that the sound from the operations room carried perfectly down the ductwork to the storage room. The door was locked from then on.

# DECEMBER

*Memory Lane: US President Richard Nixon commutes Jimmy Hoffa's jail term; the Libertarian Party (US) is established.*
*Song: "Family Affair" by Sly and The Family Stone*

## Elizabeth "Dee" M. Barrett
## Retired as a Commander
## In country: December 22, 1971 – March 26, 1973
## Rank: Commander, US Navy
## Duty: Director for Administration for Naval Advisory Group Vietnam

I arrived in Vietnam December 22, 1971, and assumed my assignment as Director for Administration for Naval Advisory Group Vietnam. My first berthing was the Hotel Meyercord, which was in downtown Saigon, and I walked to work to the NAVFORV Compound which was located at the intersection of Doan Thi Diem and Phan Dinh Phong. In April 1972, the Naval Advisory Group was phased out and I was transferred to the staff of Commander Naval Forces Vietnam (COMNAVFORV) in a similar capacity as assistant to the Assistant Chief for Administration COMNAVFORV. At that time, the offices were moved from the NAVFORV compound to MACV Headquarters, Tan Son Nhut. I moved from the Meyercord to BOQ1. In November 1972, I agreed to a three-month extension of tour (as we were phasing out in country operations) and I assumed the duties of Assistant Chief of Staff for Administration/Commanding Officer Enlisted Personnel for COMNAVFORV. I left Vietnam March 26, 1973. I was the first senior female Naval line officer to serve in Vietnam.

***Excerpt from* Women in the Navy, *Jean Ebbert, Former Lieutenant (Junior Grade), US Navy and Marie-Beth Hall:*** Barrett was the highest-ranking woman naval line officer to serve in Vietnam, and the first to hold a command in a combat zone. She arrived in Saigon in December 1971 and in November (1972) became the commanding officer of the 450 enlisted men in the Naval Advisory Group, a position she held until she left Vietnam in March 1973. She was 40 years old, had 19 years of naval service behind her, and knew that some of the men in her command were "not too pleased" to have a female commanding officer. "It gave them something to talk about," she said. During her 15 months in Vietnam, she had three days off: "February 2, 1972 when I went sailing at Cat Lo; March 29 when I went swimming at Vung Tau; and December 19 when I wrote Christmas cards."

**Donna Rae Bornholdt (Spaller)**
**Retired as a Master Sergeant**
**In country: December 28, 1971 – December 1972**
**Rank: Staff Sergeant, US Air Force**
**Duty: MACV, 1131ˢᵗ Special Advisory Squadron, Director of Personnel,**
**Administrative Specialist**

I arrived in Saigon December 1971. I was 20 years old, naïve, and had no idea what the world was about. I was scared spitless as I came off the plane. Every direction I looked I saw barbed wire, sandbags, and men in flak vests and helmets with M-16s. I was whisked away to an open-air "hootch" on Tan Son Nhut Air Base. My new home was surrounded by a tall, green, locked fence surrounded by piles of sand bags and guarded by a security policeman 24 hours a day. The hootch itself was divided with wooden panels leaving room at top and bottom for airflow. Blue and white plastic strips served as my door. There was a small dresser, a bed and a nightstand. Another surprise – being issued Army fatigues versus my Air Force blue fatigues, not near as feminine, but helped us to blend in. I was assigned to the 1131ˢᵗ USAF Special Activities Squadron, 1120 Support Group (Headquarters Command) with duty at Detachment 10, 1131ˢᵗ Special Advisory Squadron, Air Force Advisory Group. The Directorate of Personnel, Secretary for the Director of Personnel on Tan Son Nhut Air Base (moved to Headquarters MACV later in the year). I went into my office the next morning and believe it or not the first thing I'd noticed was the old black manual typewriter at my desk. The supply guy said electric typewriters were nonexistent in Vietnam, so I set my mind to a manual typewriter – had to cut my nails – but hey. On my third morning when I walked in to work there was an IBM box sitting on my desk and everyone was grinning. Our supply guy's smile was biggest. He said it would cost me a couple steaks and cigarettes off my ration card, small price, and since I didn't smoke or drink, my ration card became a great bartering tool. Our office sponsored the Nhut Chi Mai orphanage in Bien Hoa where we did a lot of repairs and maintenance work as well as bring in supplies. A few of the enlisted women volunteered there also. It was at the orphanage that I got my "warrior" photo actually holding an M-16. I took special training and qualified on the M-16, but when I arrived in country, the guys told me that I would not be issued or carry an M-16, that they were there to protect me.

I grew up knowing that men protect women so I had no problem accepting that statement.

About mid-year, we moved into the old nurses' quarters where we had individual rooms with doors so we could purchase air conditioners, woo-hoo. This compound, too, was surrounded by a fence, lots of sand bags and a full time security policeman. It was near Headquarters 7th Air Force and overlooked a storage area full of huge barrels. There was a central meeting area between the barracks. One night in April I had to grab my flak vest and helmet and run down to the central meeting area as the base was receiving mortar rounds. I remember being scared, but we all fell asleep on the floor the rest of the night.

As I said, I was very naïve (when I look back now, I was very stupid). I traveled around the country as often as I could to Pleiku, Nha Trang, Da Nang, Long Binh, Phan Trang, Bien Hoa, and Vung Tau – just because. I flew on helicopters, rode on a C-130 gun ship, took jeep trips – just because. I sat on a Russian tank, went out to visit a Montagnard family in their home and drank their rice wine, just because. Those adventures, the overpowering-gagging smells, the poverty, the "Hop-Tacs," "diddy mao," the dirt, the trash, the never-ending miles of barbed wire and sand bags, the people, working 12-hour days 6 days a week, waiting weeks for a letter from home and on very rare occasions getting to use "HAM" radios to "call" home – those are my memories of my tour in Vietnam.

Overall, I enjoyed my tour in Vietnam as well as the other 10 bases I was stationed at during my 20-year career. I was fortunate; I had great assignments and worked with great people. I met my husband, raised my children AND served my country well. I had a two-year break in service, and I retired in 1991 as a master sergeant E7.

# Chapter Twelve

# 1972

**Susan B. Neugebauer**
**Retired as a Colonel**
**In country: 1972 – Date of departure unknown**
**Rank: First Lieutenant, US Air Force**
**Duty: 7ᵗʰ Air Force, Cam Ranh Bay, Intelligence Officer**

I was so thrilled about a career in the Air Force after I received my commission as a Second Lieutenant in April 1971. In fact the six-month follow on intelligence specialty course at Lowry Air Force Base (CO) was a piece of cake for me. I became so confident that I badgered career personnel to send me to Vietnam for my first duty assignment. After all, there was a war going on and that's where my male classmates were going. Was this not a gender-neutral Air Force? My request was granted, and I received orders to Cam Ranh Bay Air Base, South Vietnam. During the 20-hour plane trip from McChord Air Force Base (WA) to Vietnam, with two refueling stops, I started feeling some anxiety about my zealous efforts to secure an assignment in a combat zone. However, when I gave my first intelligence briefing to the wing commander, I knew I had made the right decision. He said, "That was an excellent briefing, Lieutenant." That was all I needed to hear. This assignment was for me. I was in the middle of the action, and I loved it, even the rocket attacks. This was the first of numerous memorable experiences in a 26-year career. Would I do it again, if I had the chance? You bet I would! (*Courtesy of Women's Memorial Foundation Register*)

**♥Joan "Jo" Olmsted**
**Retired as a Lieutenant Colonel**
**In country: 1972 – 1973**
**Rank: Lieutenant Colonel, US Air Force**
**Duty: MACV, Intelligence Staff Officer**

**Susan Alinda Hallbauer (Milley) (Earl)**
Retired as a Master Sergeant
In country: 1972 – March 1973
Rank: Staff Sergeant, US Air Force
Duty: 377th Air Base Wing, Air Operations Specialist

**Arlene L. "Buzz" Mahalic**
In country: 1972 – March 1973
Rank: Specialist 5, US Army
Duty: USARV, Clerk-Typist

**♥De Ann R. Masters**
In country: 1972 – March 1973
Rank: Staff Sergeant, US Air Force
Duty: 7th Air Force, Tan Son Nhut

**Francine Tomasik**
In country: 1972 – March 1973
Rank: Staff Sergeant, US Army
Duty: USARV, Central Finance and Accounting, Finance Specialist

# JANUARY

*Memory Lane: Oil is $2.49 a barrel; Mahalia Jackson dies, Aretha Franklin sings at funeral; Super Bowl VI: The Dallas Cowboys defeat the Miami Dolphins 24–3. Song: "American Pie" by Don McLean*

**Mary A. Rives (Brillas)**
Retired as a Major
In country: January 1972 – May 1972
Rank: Captain, US Air Force
Duty: 7th Air Force, Weather Group, Administration
Management Officer

**Juanita Joyce Anglin**
**In country: January 1972 – January 1973**
**Rank: Captain, US Army**
**Duty: MACV, Secretary of the Joint Staff, Historian and Special**
**Project Officer**

My first night in Vietnam, I needed an ash tray. There was a shop across the street from where I was billeted. I purchased an elephant ashtray. When I got the ashtray back, I turned it upside down and there was an envelope, which I later learned was filled with an illegal drug. I was told that within six hours of arriving in Vietnam, my finding the envelope had helped to close down a drug ring that the Military Police has been trying to shut down for quite some time.

**Darlene K. Brewer (Alexander)**
**Retired as a Colonel**
**In country: January 4, 1972 – December 17, 1972**
**Rank: Captain, US Air Force**
**Duty: 7th Air Force, 1964th Communications Group,**
**VNAF Improvement and Modernization Plans Officer**

When I stepped off the plane at Tan Son Nhut (TSN) Air Base in January 1972 the heat and humidity was unbelievable. I'm a Southern California girl and I love warm weather, but this was like stepping into an overheated sauna. I adjusted though and was ready to face the next challenge of a visit to my new quarters for the next year. As it turns out I only stayed there a couple of months as rockets were getting closer to my dwelling, so they moved me to a trailer, a bit further out of harm's way. But, I digress, my original quarters, while I wasn't expecting the Taj Mahal, I kinda thought that I would have my own bathroom . . . nope, my quarters were in an old wooden barracks of small (really small) rooms with a communal bathroom and shower at the end of the building. While I was unpacking my duffle bag, I was introduced to my first incoming rocket attack that sounded like it was coming right for me. I dove under the bed where all manner of creatures resided and quickly decided this was a stupid idea. Just the percussion of the rocket would clearly turn my quarters into a pile of tiddlywinks, along with the bed. As it turned out the rocket hit outside the perimeter of the base, so life was good. I reported for duty the next day to the 1964th Communications Group Plans and Programs office. The Plans and Programs office consisted of one fairly good sized room in which all of us (about 15) had our desks. No one in the office, including the Lieutenant Colonel in charge had any special digs, it was same-o, same-o, regardless if you were a Staff Sergeant or Colonel – it worked well. I soon got into the seven day work week in my position as the Vietnamese Air Force Improvement and Modernization Plans Officer. Basically it was my job to oversee the training of the Vietnamese Air Force in our communications and air traffic control systems, and to formally transfer this equipment to the Vietnamese for them to operate and maintain. The job entailed taking a number of trips to our communications and air traffic control facilities scattered across South Vietnam to inventory equipment and to assess the training progress of the Vietnamese. Travel during that period was pretty exciting. To nearby facilities like those in Vung Tau we drove our jeeps in a convoy of vehicles – safety in numbers, I guess, but it wasn't unusual to run into pockets of small arms fire to which everyone took cover and returned fire in the general direction of where we thought we were being attacked. Luckily, the NVA were not good shots, so we had no serious injuries on any trips I was on, but that wasn't always the case. When I had to go up North to places like Da Nang and Pleiku, it was normally by helicopter, flying low level just over the rice fields . . . I like excitement, but this went "beyond the pale." I also made one low profile (civilian clothes only) to Phnom Penh in a C-130 with ROK (Republic of Korea) troops providing security – my one day scheduled TDY turned into several days as the capital was under attack and no planes could get out. So, I did the work I was scheduled to do and then shopped for temple rubbings for the men in my Group; met a lot of really nice Cambodians and had a fantastic time touring the city and eating gourmet Cambodian food. My trip report was a bit short on my activities after doing my official duties . . . probably not good material for an appropriate combat award. On a serious note, I was told by several seasoned combat troops before my trip that the Koreans (ROK) were the toughest fighters in country and if you're going into hostile territory you want them on your side . . . they were right. During the first couple of months in theater, my job went fairly smooth and my status briefings to the Communications division of MACV went well with most facility transfers being on schedule. There were a few problems though.

One experience I will never forget is when I briefed a Vietnamese General on a problem we were having with the Vietnamese Airmen not showing up for training classes. He told me very gently that that was a very big problem in the VNAF. He told me that the Vietnamese had been at war for decades dating back to the French occupation, and that his people did not regularly receive their pay checks from the government so they had to have another job to take care of their families. I should have known that. The General then addressed the class and sternly told them that anyone who missed another class would spend a day in the metal ammo containers, and if they missed a class after that, it would be worse. I made a course correction and decided never to complain again. After the General left I asked the class to make up a class schedule that would not conflict with their jobs. They did and we never had a problem after that. Great lesson here.

Typically throughout the day you would hear bombing going on and see fireworks in the distance. And off and on throughout the week there would be rocket attacks and if you were in the office you would take cover under your desk – not sure that did any good, but it made one feel a bit more secure. There was only once when we were under attack that we were ordered to stand by to be issued weapons. They were not issued.

As the new kid in the office, I was, as is the case in any assignment, given a number of additional duties, the majority of which my fellow office mates were only too happy to dump on me. However, there was one duty that I am so thankful I got and that was to be the liaison with a local orphanage in which the Group had adopted. Our families back in the States sent care packages of diapers, toys, clothes, candy, etc. to the Group, and I would make 1-2 trips a month to the orphanage and deliver the goodies. It was rewarding, but also very heart breaking to see little children whose eyes were filled with horror and yet they didn't cry – just blank stares. But, then I would go to another part of the orphanage where there were children who had been there for a while, and I would see happy kids that knew why I was there and I was mobbed with affection – still brings tears to my eyes.

About three months into my tour, the situation in Vietnam began to deteriorate and we began to lose a number of sites to the North Vietnamese in what is known as the Spring or Easter Offensive. Beginning in March the North Vietnamese crossed the DMZ as well as coming in from the East from Laos and from the South from Cambodia. We were getting hammered throughout the South. Then, in early May, President Nixon authorized offensive operations interdicting supply lines and hitting major logistics centers in the North – the sound of the bombing was drowned out by the cheers that could be heard throughout TSN. Needless to say the Vietnamese

Improvement and Modernization Project was discontinued and my job was now to get the communications out of country and move it to Thailand where bases like Takhli were being reactivated. One particularly memorable event was when I transferred some vital supply computers to Takhli. A few days after the computers left TSN I received a really nasty response from a Captain in the receiving communications squadron, which stated in part (note the military jargon) "what kind of crappy operation are you running over there . . . the computers have so much dirt in them that you could grow potatoes." Well, that message was from my "future husband" (that I did not know at the time). My response was, "Don't you read the papers, there is a war going on over here and we don't have the time to aspire for the 'Good Housekeeping' award." My husband is still bitching.

I do not for one moment regret going to Vietnam. It was a fantastic experience. I learned things about myself and people I worked with that I don't think one could ever learn in a less stressful or isolated environment. I also found the Vietnamese people to be lovely, hardworking, and very loyal people. While I was there, I told myself many times that I would love to return to Vietnam when there was no war . . . it is a beautiful country with beautiful people.

# FEBRUARY

*Memory Lane: Sixty million Americans tuned in to watch live TV coverage of President Nixon's arrival in Communist China; Hank Aaron becomes first baseball player to sign for $200,000 a year.*
*Song: "Day After Day" by Badfinger*

**Fannie Belle Rollins (Edwards)**
**Retired as a Staff Sergeant**
**In country: February 1972 – September 1972**
**Rank: Staff Sergeant, US Air Force**
**Duty: Headquarters, 7th Air Force, Stenographic Specialist**

**Lillie M. Rice (Smith)**
**In country: February 1972 – November 1972**
**Rank: Staff Sergeant, US Air Force**
**Duty: 7th Air Force, 377th Supply Squadron, Inventory Management Specialist**

**Mary "Kathy" Kathleen Bailey**
**Retired as a Sergeant Major**
**In country: February 1972 – December 1972**
**Rank: Staff Sergeant, US Army**
**Duty: MACV, US Army Security Agency, 509th Radio Research Group,**
**Administrative NCO**

I am honored to have served! My service in Vietnam is an experience that strengthened my love and appreciation for my country. Not only did it have a positive effect on my military career, but lasting memories. I will attempt to share, but only those who were there will truly understand. Some memories and flashbacks:

Living conditions – great compared to those living in the jungle and rice paddies. Had private room with army bed and drawer; latrine was a small room with commode that flushed by reaching up to pull a chain; and the shower water (often cold) sprayed the whole room. Ate food from the mess hall. No weight problem – returned weighing in at 80 pounds – no chocolate (smile).

B-52s – loud noise and shaking the windows. Hearing the sound of the medical helicopters flying over, watching the medics running as they carried wounded on gurneys to 3rd Field Hospital.

Incoming and outgoing artillery fire, emergency sirens – we hit the bunkers. MACV bunkers full, watching rockets hit and destroy. Tan Son Nhut Air Base taking more direct hits due to drawdown.

Small arms fire from ARVN Camp behind quarters – they were shooting large rats. During monsoon season – wading through water filled with large rats to get into the billets.

Working conditions: Duty day at least 12 hours, longer depending on mission, seven days a week. Time off – limited; one three-day pass quarterly for R&R.

Fun time: R&R at Vung Tau to visit friend, infantry soldier (now deceased due to Agent Orange); transportation there by open helicopter, gunner on each of the doors, but returning back to Saigon on Highway 1 with 1st Cavalry supply convoy in open jeep, machine guns in front and back to Long Binh, then on to Saigon on Vietnamese civilian bus. (Was told by commander never again! Only return by air!)

Taking C-130 cargo plane to various sites "Up Country" to deliver supplies. Locals staring amazed to see their first American girl (round eye); the soldiers saying, "Just let me touch you. It is so good to see an American girl!"

Watching movies on enlisted quarters' lanai – Mama-san bringing me bananas, the times she would shake me saying, "cô gái, cô gái" (girl) pointing to the clock, concerned I would be late for work when I actually had a day off.

Riding in a cyclo, wearing civilian clothes, sneaking to Saigon to tour the city and eat local food.

**Mary Ann Ehrhardt**
**In country: February 1972 – March 1973**
**Rank: Specialist 4, US Army**
**Duty: USARV, 1ˢᵗ Logistical Command, Clerk-Typist**

**Judith "Jude" L. McCurdy**
**In country: February 1972 – March 1973**
**Rank: Staff Sergeant, US Army**
**Duty: USARV, 1ˢᵗ Signal Brigade, 39ᵗʰ Signal Battalion; 1ˢᵗ Aviation Brigade, Administrative NCO**

My arrival in South Vietnam was quite the eye opener. I was immediately impacted by the amazing heat. I felt I had entered a blast furnace filled with heat and humidity. Also, I noticed how tiny the natives were. Riding through the streets of Saigon was a grand experience all in itself.

First, I noticed there were no road signs, traffic lights or directional markings of any sort. People just came at you from every direction, riding, driving, pushing, pulling anything that would roll. I never saw such mass confusion in my life. People were in a hurry to go in their own direction; they were plowing into whomever, or whatever, no matter how big or how small, in order to go a minute distance, while smiling. Whole families could be seen, a husband, wife, and two or three children on a single motor bike or moped; it was an incredible display of balance by each family member and part of the daily transportation wars on the streets of Saigon City. It made me wonder, "How could this country possibly win a war?" Truth be told, in the end they couldn't, and as we were to find out at the war's end, they really didn't care to win; they just wanted all foreigners out of their land, so they could go on their happy way.

My second observation was that the terrain of Saigon was totally flat; however, on my journey through the streets I began noticing a very large mountain atypical to the topography of the city. When I inquired, what mountain it was the driver replied, "It is not a mountain." As we got closer I realized what it truly was. It was a garbage dump, with hundreds of people, scrambling up and down the sides, rummaging through the contents of this putrid mass of debris in search of their next meal. The stench in the air was so pungent I thought I was going to be sick. As we drew closer, the driver told me to hold on tight; he then accelerated to get past the smell as quickly as possible. I saw huge rats, people and debris scatter in all directions as the driver plowed through Garbage Alley, leaving all in the wake of his tire tracks. (For what it is worth – this mountain was located directly behind US Army 3rd Field Hospital.) After a while, and much educational viewing of homes made from cola and beer cans, and with the realization of how really poor this land and its occupants were, I was very relieved when we finally crossed a river heading north out of Saigon, and on toward Long Binh.

**Georgia A. Wise**
**Retired as a Major**
**In country: February 1972 – March 1973**
**Rank: Major, US Army**
**Duty: MACV, 525th Military Intelligence Group,**
**last WAC officer to leave Vietnam**

**Barbara J. Gordon**
**Retired as a Lieutenant Colonel**
**In country: February 29, 1972 – February 12, 1973**
**Rank: Captain, US Air Force**
**Duty: 7th Air Force, 12th Reconnaissance Intelligence Technical**
**Squadron, Intelligence Photo-Radar Officer**

I spent some time with people from the Navy detachment on Tan Son Nhut, Chief Fleet Coordinating Group. In August 1972, its admiral and fleet admiral on the USS *Saratoga* cooked up a plan to bring some women for an overnight visit to the Saratoga in the Gulf of Tonkin.

I was invited, and despite feeling this was a stunt I should avoid, I couldn't pass up the opportunity. So about five of us flew out to the Carrier Onboard Delivery (COD) aircraft, made an arrested landing, had tea with the admirals (china and silver!) flew on a helicopter as it delivered mail to the support ships in the fleet, toured the carrier, observed a recovery and aircraft launch, had dinner and a movie, spent the night, and were catapulted off in the COD the next day.

I slept in the Captain's in-port cabin, quite luxurious and not used at sea. Very memorable all around!

# MARCH

*Memory Lane: Pioneer 10 was launched from Cape Kennedy; the proposed Equal Rights Amendment was approved by the Senate and sent to the States for ratification; The Godfather is released in cinemas in the United States.*
*Song: "Without You" by Nillson*

**Jo A. Pritchard**
**In country: March 1972 – November 1972**
**Rank: Second Lieutenant, US Air Force**
**Duty: 7th Air Force, Air Defense Analysis Branch, Air Intelligence Officer**

I analyzed intelligence reports on North Vietnamese air defenses, briefed aircrews on the types and locations of enemy anti-aircraft artillery, as well as enemy tactics, and provided input to the Weekly Intelligence Estimates Update. My workday began at 0400 hours, when I reviewed the intelligence reports that came in during the night and prepared the morning aircrew briefing. We worked 12-hour days Monday through Friday, 10 hours on Saturday, and 8 hours on Sunday; once in a great while I was granted half of Sunday off, but many people never had any time off in their entire tour. I was the only female in my group, and while I was always treated with respect by the men I worked with, outside of work I felt like I lived in a fish bowl; western women were a rare sight for most GIs and I was often stared at and subjected to unwanted attention or comments.

Shortly after I arrived at Tan Son Nhut, I was tasked by a superior with locating a set of little silver teaspoons with American flags on the handles for an upcoming general's visit. After a week of searching, I finally located the teaspoons, just in time for the visit. It seemed totally absurd to expend so much effort on something so seemingly insignificant during the height of war.

Once, an especially adventurous male friend of mine invited me to dinner at his Vietnamese girlfriend Mai's house. He had ordered a special dish from a local eatery, which he told Mai and I was snake soup. Neither of us believed him until the snake's head ended up in my bowl on the second serving! And yes, it did taste like chicken. When we weren't working, my coworkers and I often went out for dinner together in Saigon. It was something of an oxymoron to dine on sumptuous food on the rooftop patio of a French restaurant on a beautiful evening, laughing and talking, while artillery pounded in the distance.

I applied for an early out before the end of my tour, and returned to school for a degree in Medical Technology. After working in hospital laboratories for a number of years, I went to work in the medical device industry, where I now work as a software validation consultant.

**Ernestine "Ernie" Ann Koch**
**Retired as a Chief Warrant Officer 4**
**In country: March 1972 – March 1973**
**Rank: Chief Warrant Officer 2, US Marine Corps**
**Duty: MACV, Marine Advisory Naval Forces, Administrative Technician**

One of the memorable moments of my tour was taking a boat trip down one of the rivers with the Vietnamese Navy. Four Navy personnel and I took school supplies to a remote village school. Along the way, the Vietnamese boatmen stopped at a local village along the river for a drink. They served us with the dirtiest glasses I have ever seen, but to refuse the drink would have been an insult to their hospitality, so we drank.

We later learned that they do ALL their washing in the river we had been on.

CW4 Koch was the Personnel Officer for all in-country marines.

**Merle E. Massey**
**Retired as a Master Sergeant**
**In country: March 1972 – March 1973**
**Rank: Sergeant First Class, US Army**
**Duty: MACV, G4**

**Sharolyn K. Picking**
**Retired as a Sergeant First Class**
**In country: March 1972 – March 28, 1973**
**Rank: Specialist 4, US Army**
**Duty: USARV/MACV, Postal Group, Clerk-Typist**

I joined the Army in January 1971. There were nine brothers and sisters so the house was kind of crowded and it seems like a good idea. My mother had been in the Army in 1943, serving someplace in Georgia. I had some training at Fort Rucker, AL, and then went to the Interservice Postal School at Fort Benjamin Harrison, IN, for further training.

I volunteered for Vietnam and had a pretty interesting job there. Whenever we got inquiries about why soldiers weren't writing home, or why they were sending strange things home (an ear), one of us would travel around checking on them to find out why they wouldn't write home. I was guilty of that myself.

When the WAC Detachment closed, there were about 10 of us left but I can't remember any of them.

There was good and bad – we drank a lot. There was always something going on. I loved the nurses. They were the greatest, and they had an awful lot of stuff to deal with all the time.

A bunch of the books about Vietnam are not truthful about the way it was and it makes me mad to read some of them. I wouldn't want to do it again. Some of the veterans around Fort Rucker get together and it's okay when there are a group of us, but don't want to do too much thinking about it when I'm alone.

**♥Gloria Jean Labadie**
**In country: March 3, 1972 – November 2, 1972**
**Rank: Specialist 5, US Army**
**Duty: USARV, 1ˢᵗ Aviation Brigade, Administrative Specialist**

The Women's Army image was recently given a boost by SP5 Gloria J. Labadie, a WAC of the Week and Soldier of the Month. The 22-year-old blond who claims to like to "spread a little sunshine" more than achieved her goal when she posed in hot pants for the *Army Times*. "One

WAC who saw the story wrote to me," commented SP5 Labadie. "She said, 'Thanks for making our corps look all right!'"

Soldiers at Long Binh may be disappointed to learn that long-legged Labadie trained in track and field for the 1964-65 Olympics. She was clocked at 11.8 seconds for the 100-yard dash.

SP5 Labadie came to Vietnam one month ago. The bus she arrived on was hit by VC sniper fire. Although she confesses that "ammo dumps blowing up at night have a tendency to scare me," she was not particularly frightened under fire: "There were a lot of guys around who knew exactly what to do." She recently drove one of the trucks in a convoy from Long Binh to Saigon. "I was a mechanic for a while. I worked on a VW that won four state national championships in California . . . I used to grease and oil my XO's (executive officer) car."

Labadie's previous assignment was Letterman General Hospital in San Francisco. "In some ways I had more of an association with the war in San Francisco. I saw the physical results of war on people – on amputees . . . I would extend to keep my brothers from coming over here as draftees. I feel like I've taken their place . . . At Letterman, I passed the operating room and saw plastic bags of guys' legs and arms. It was a miniature Vietnam." She paused. "I think I'm bettering it over here. Some people say, 'You get a big kick out of this war.' Only mothers think you're doing something to help."

*Excerpt from "The women behind the concertina barricade," The Overseas Weekly – Pacific Edition, May 8, 1972, publication defunct 1975*

**Alicia Pineda**
**Retired as a Sergeant First Class**
**In country: March 4, 1972 – March 29, 1973**
**Rank: Specialist 5, US Army**
**Duty: USARV/MACV Support Command, 1ˢᵗ Aviation Brigade, Inventory Control Center, Administrative Specialist**

# APRIL

*Memory Lane: Alene B. Duerk named first female admiral in the history of the US Navy; all scheduled National League and American League games are called off by a strike over players' pensions; two giant pandas arrive in US from China. Song: "The First Time Ever I Saw Your Face" by Roberta Flack*

**♥Frances Ann Iacoboni (Krilich)**
**Retired as a Colonel**
**In country: April 1972 – February 1973**
**Rank: Major, US Army Medical Specialist Corps**
**Duty: 3rd Field Hospital, Saigon, Dietetic Consultant**

Frances Ann Iacoboni enlisted in the US Army in 1957 and was the first woman to join the newly formed Medical Specialist Corps while still in college. As a Captain, she went on to become the Chief Dietetic Consultant to the Commanding General of the 82nd Airborne Division at Womack US Army Hospital at Fort Bragg, NC. Promoted to Major she was then selected to serve as the Chief Dietitian to the US Army in Vietnam.

Upon her return from Vietnam, she was promoted to Colonel and appointed Chief Dietitian of the US Army under the Surgeon General of the United States.

Colonel Iacoboni was key in implementing and maintaining the US Medical Corp's nutritional standards. She directed the Army dietitians to implement and support the weight control program, the new field rations, key health and fitness initiatives, and field nutrition care in US Army field hospitals during ground operations against hostile forces. She also helped implement renovations in US Army Dining Facilities.

Her favorite past time was competing in the .22 small-bore prone rifle matches with her fellow members of the National Rifle Association. In 1988, she won the gold medal at the US National Championships at Camp Perry, OH, for the Prone Grand Aggregate with a telescope.

Colonel Iacoboni died May 9, 2011.

**Rebecca Harrison Shumate (Richardson)**
**Retired as Lieutenant Colonel**
**In country: April 10, 1972 – February 10, 1973**
**Rank: First Lieutenant, US Army Medical Specialist Corps**
**Duty: 3rd Field Hospital (US Army Hospital), Saigon, Physical Therapist**

As I begin my ramblings regarding my tour in Vietnam over 40 years ago, I discovered deep emotional ties to a wonderful country with exceptional people in a struggle to keep their freedom. It was a privilege to serve my country and to serve the Vietnam people.

The year I served in Vietnam was the highlight of my professional career as a Physical Therapist.

I arrived in Vietnam as a First Lieutenant to serve at 3rd Field Hospital, Saigon, as a Physical Therapist. This was the first time I had worked alone except to manage a clinic.

The patients we saw were usually severe combat injuries such as amputees, spinal injuries, burns, and general trauma involving surgical intervention. Most of the injured military soldiers were stabilized and then air-evac'ed out to Germany or Japan and back to the general military hospitals in CONUS that were close to the soldier's home. There was a Vietnamese interpreter, Ba Pham Ti Mit, who assisted as a liaison with local Vietnamese and also was trained to work as Physical Therapy Assistant. The staff included one active duty enlisted Physical Therapy Assistant and a civilian Red Cross volunteer whose husband worked for Pan America Airline. We did provide outpatient treatment for military on active duty as needed. We treated allied service members as needed as well as including more civilian patients as Vietnamization became more established and implemented. The decision by President Nixon to establish Vietnamization in country resulted in the 3rd Field Hospital being changed to US Army Hospital Saigon. Duty uniform went from fatigues to class A's.

As my patients became more local Vietnamese, injuries were more severe and required longer rehabilitation. Many of the young local Vietnamese had severe injuries by the Viet Cong from gunshots to the knee joint causing severe debility. The orthopedic clinic was next to the PT clinic, and we received many post-operative cases such as these. Montagnards were a special group from the internal highlands of Vietnam. They were rugged people and hard working. I was treating an abdominal wound for debridement and cleaning with whirlpool when I noticed this long white tissue that came from the abdominal wound area. The surgeon pointed out that this was a tapeworm. A very long tapeworm! This patient had hands that showed signs of hard work. However, on each little finger there was a very long (2"+) nail. I asked through my interpreter why such a long nail. The patient stated it showed that he was wealthy and did not have to do labor and break his nails; also, he showed that he could use it as a screwdriver and pick his nose with it!

I spent many weekends traveling to orphanages where I was able to see the devastations of polio. I was able to coordinate care for these children with the Physical Therapist at the National Rehabilitation Institute of Saigon. Many of these children who could not walk were fitted with braces and able to walk for the first time. A true blessing.

Colonel Nguyen was a senior South Vietnamese graduate of the "West Point" of Vietnam. He was a dedicated soldier who stepped on a land mine and shattered the bones in his left ankle and sustained an above-knee amputation on the right leg. He was a hard-working patient determined to walk again even if in pain. Eventually this brave man was able to ambulate with a cane. We became friends and kept in touch. I even invited him to my wedding. He sent us a gift of Vietnamese wedding dolls which I still have today.

Another privilege was when Father Joe Devlin walked into the clinic one day. He was an older priest with a "bad hip." He was a Jesuit priest who came to Vietnam to help the refugees. He had a deep compassion for the Vietnamese people. He needed crutches for an orphanage he was helping. We became friends, keeping in touch even after I rotated back to Walter Reed in Washington, DC. I was always trying to send Father Devlin whatever items he needed at the time.

Additionally, I volunteered in the evenings at the Seventh Day Adventist Nursing School in Saigon, teaching English to nursing students. My last duty as a Physical Therapist was to turn over the clinic to my capable Vietnamese assistant, Ba Pham Ti Mit, and the Seventh Day Adventist Hospital in Vietnam. The hospital is still in operation today by the Adventist Health Care System.

**Virginia "Gini" A. Griffith**
**Retired as a Senior Master Sergeant**
**In country: April 26, 1972 – March 29, 1973**
**Rank: Technical Sergeant, US Air Force**
**Duty: 7th Air Force, 377th Air Base Wing, NCOIC Manning Unit,**
**Career Control Section, CBPO; additional duty as WAF First Sergeant**

There weren't enough of us enlisted females in Vietnam to form a WAF squadron so we had an advisor. Then Captain Pat Murphy was the base Personal Affairs Officer with additional duty of WAF Advisor and I was "den mother" in the barracks. Colonel Murphy probably couldn't give you information on Murphy's Marauders because the whole thing was my idea. I had read somewhere that during WWII company clerks and others who used typewriters (apparently the military used Remington typewriters) were referred to as Remington Raiders. It only seemed natural to me that we WAF in support career fields call ourselves

Murphy's Marauders. It was all a play on words. We got together in the yard outside the WAF barracks on a Sunday afternoon, had a barbecue and took photos. After I returned to the States, I located all but one of the women in the photo, sent the photo to them and got autographs. It's fading now but is still hanging on my "I love me wall" in the living room.

What I remember the most is the camaraderie between the men in the Consolidated Base Personnel Office and the Air Force women.

A favorite memory is the Sunday evening parties at the quarters of the WAF officers. They would hold open house where all were invited regardless of rank. The Canadian International Peacekeeping Force also joined in the fun. One of the fellows brought his guitar and we had sing-alongs. Our favorite song was "Leaving on a Jet Plane" because we all looked forward to that time when we'd get on the "Freedom Bird" and head back to the World. And if I'd had enough to drink, I was known, from time to time, to launch into Janice Joplin's "Mercedes Benz." For a few hours each week the parties took us away from work, from thinking about possible rocket and mortar attacks, and from being so far away from family and friends. But, we made new friends and the fellowship in a war zone is fantastic – people working hard and partying even harder!

As for the last days in Vietnam – wow, what can I say? I left the country on the last day of troop withdrawal in 1973 (not to be confused with the Fall of Saigon in 1975). I differentiate the two because so many people, upon finding out that I left on the last day of troop withdrawal, say something to the effect that I must have been really scared what with the North Vietnamese heading for Saigon and South Vietnamese hanging off helicopters trying to get out with the last Americans to leave country.

Anyway, we Personnel folks were working our buns off trying to get everyone else processed and on their way back to the World. When the Personnel Director's civilian secretary left, I moved to his office to answer the phone. That was exciting. NOT! There were so few female officers and enlisted women left that we were all moved into one barrack, which was nicer than the one we enlisted women had occupied (concrete block as opposed to WWII wooden barracks). Since almost everyone was gone, the social scene was practically non-existent. And, that's pretty much all I remember about that.

While it would be easy to lapse into a funk about all the negatives associated with a tour in Vietnam, I choose to remember the good times and the friendships that endure to this day.

# JUNE

*Memory Lane: EPA orders an almost complete ban on the use of DDT pesticide; Atari Corporation formed to begin mass production of video games; five White House operatives are arrested for burglarizing the offices of the Democratic National Committee.*
*Song: "The Candy Man" by Sammy Davis, Jr.*

**Nancy G. Wadley (Keough)**
**In country: June 1972 – March 1973**
**Rank: Captain, US Army**
**Duty: USARV/MACV Support Command, Special Troops, Office of the Judge Advocate General**

**Mary Jane Abare**
**Retired as a Captain**
**In country: June 1972 – March 1973**
**Rank: Captain, US Air Force**
**Duty: Headquarters 7th Air Force**

**Deborah A. Godby**
**Retired as a Sergeant First Class**
**In country: June 28, 1972 – March 21, 1973**
**Rank: Specialist 5, US Army**
**Duty: USARV, Special Troops, WAC Detachment; MACV, Civil Operations and Revolutionary Development Support, Clerk-Typist**

*Interview with Pat Jernigan, 8/14/2014:* Deborah Godby enlisted in the Army February 1971. After attending basic training and a clerical training course, was assigned as a clerk at the Military Intelligence Center and School at Fort Huachuca, AZ. In early 1972, she received orders to Vietnam. At the time, women under the age of 21 could not be sent to Vietnam unless they volunteered and had their parents' permission. Specialist 4 Godby wanted to do her part, so she volunteered and got her parents to sign. When asked if she received any training in preparation for her assignment to Vietnam, she emphatically stated, "none what-so-ever." Once she was in country, she did learn to shoot with the .45 caliber pistol.

She arrived in Vietnam at the Bien Hoa Air Base June 28, 1972. She was the only woman on the flight. When the plane landed, the men were immediately given a class on venereal disease, then sent on to their units. Debbie's orders had only said "Vietnam" so it took a while to sort things out. She was assigned to the WAC Detachment at Long Binh, where she became the company clerk.

Troop withdrawals were progressing in accordance with the Paris Peace Accords that were supposed to end the war with honor; most US soldiers were already gone. USARV Headquarters, including the WAC Detachment, was being closed. Since Debbie had only been in country a few months, she was given the choice of staying for a new assignment in Saigon or going home. She chose to stay.

Once in Saigon, the women were assigned to different units and different quarters. Debbie was assigned to MACV Headquarters in the Plans, Policy, and Programs Division of Civil Operations and Revolutionary Development Support (CORDS) where her job involved personnel work at both the MACV Headquarters on Tan Son Nhut Air Base and at the American Embassy downtown.

The remaining US troops were required to depart Vietnam within 60 days of the Peace Accords signing. Debbie does not know if she was the last WAC to leave Vietnam, but she was certainly one of the last, departing March 21, 1973. She flew home in her fatigues, then, despite advice to the contrary, she changed into her Army green uniform. The extreme unpopularity of the war was very evident when she stopped in Chicago on her way home – she was spat upon.

Debbie is 100% disabled based on PTSD (Posttraumatic Stress Disorder). Despite her experiences, Debbie was then, and is now, very proud of her Army service, her service in Vietnam and her uniform. She joined the service to serve her country, fight Communism, and get an education; she believes that as an individual she has contributed to these goals. She went on to serve 20 years and retired as a Sergeant First Class.

In retirement, despite limited vision and other issues, she is active in volunteer work in the community and among her fellow veterans. She is a proud member of the WAC Veterans Association Heritage Chapter 62, and serves in the Chapter's Honor Guard.

# JULY

*Memory Lane: Actress Jane Fonda poses for photographs at a North Vietnamese anti-aircraft gun at Hanoi, and the first images are printed in a newspaper in Poland. Pictures of the actress, gazing through the gun sight of a weapon used to shoot down American planes during the ongoing Vietnam War, ran worldwide the next day.*
*Song: "Lean on Me" by Bill Withers*

**Ann H. Best (Volkwine)**
**Retired as a Major**
**In country: July 1972 – March 29, 1973**
**Rank: First Lieutenant, US Air Force**
**Duty: 7th Air Force, 377th Air Base Wing, Food Service Officer**

As the Food Service Officer (FSO) for the Air Force at Tan Son Nhut Air Base, I was tasked with feeding the Peace Keeping Forces (Canadian, Hungarians, Indonesians, Poles) after the peace treaty was signed. My FSO counterpart for the Army at MACV had the unenviable task of feeding the treaty negotiators consisting of the North Vietnamese, South Vietnamese and the Viet Cong.

He called me one evening to ask if he could sign out some C-rations as we stored the entire supply for the installation. It seemed that the first contingent of Viet Cong had arrived via two aircraft that morning. However, the South Vietnamese refused to let them off the aircraft until they produced visas which, of course, they didn't have and felt they didn't need. So, it had been a stand-off under the hot sun for the entire day. The FSO wanted to take the Viet Cong some food and water. In agreement, we processed the paperwork and loaded up his jeep. Then he asked me if I would like to accompany him and his driver on the delivery. Assuming we would just drop it off at Base Operations, I hopped in for the ride. My assumption was way off.

Approaching the security guard, the FSO explained our mission and we were waved through, headed down the tarmac directly toward the two planes. Some Viet Cong were crowded around the plane entrances pointing rifles at the South Vietnamese who were on the ground pointing rifles back. Our driver/translator explained why we were there and deposited the food and water on the steps. The Viet Cong appeared grateful and scurried to get it all into the aircraft. So far so good – around the tail to the second plane.

These guys really weren't happy; in fact they were downright angry, waving their rifles and shouting. We, of course, were sitting ducks between the two aircraft. I had the sudden image of a news headline – "WAF is last casualty of war." The supplies were again deposited on the steps and we took off. When I looked back, the VC had not made a move; I never did know if their thirst/hunger ever overcame their pride. Ah well, just another fun day in beautiful Southeast Asia.

# AUGUST

*Memory Lane: Chief of Naval Operations, Admiral Elmo Zumwalt, orders changes in the US Navy's rules to permit women to serve on ships, become aviators, and attend the US Naval Academy.*
*Song: "Alone Again (Naturally)" by Gilbert O'Sullivan*

**Patsy "Dianne" Hatley**
**Retired as a Master Sergeant**
**In country: August 1972 – March 1973**
**Rank: Staff Sergeant, US Air Force**
**Duty: 7ᵗʰAF, 377ᵗʰ Air Base Wing, Air Operations Specialist**

You have a job to do! In the early morning hours of a night shift, December 1972, at Base Operations, my Vietnamese co-worker and I were leaned back in our chairs waiting for our shift to end. Suddenly, there was a loud boom and the building started shaking. Another boom and more shaking. It was then that I realized we were probably under rocket attack. Quickly, I picked up the hotline phone to tower and asked, "Is Tan Son Nhut under rocket attack?" The person replied, "I don't think so," and I replied, "What the hell do you mean, you don't think so?" I asked again, "Is Tan Son Nhut under rocket attack?" This time he replied, "Yes, Tan Son Nhut is under attack." I grabbed the crash phone, which alerted numerous units on base, and advised, "Tan Son Nhut Air Base is under rocket attack." After alerting the base, I realized I also had to advise the officer on duty. As I started to walk back to my duty section, I froze. I was 25 years old and scared. All I wanted to do was to curl up in a ball and cry. It felt as though I stood there, frozen, for a long time. Actually, it was just for a few seconds. I told myself, "Get back to your duty station, you have a job to do."

**Darlene "Sunnie" E. Ondesko**
**In country: August 1972 – March 1973**
**Rank: Specialist 4, US Army**
**Duty: MACV, Finance and Accounting Office, Finance Specialist**

**Comments and Memories:** I was sent over to destroy top secret information at all finance offices. When I first got to Vietnam, I reported in to a colonel who asked me why I had such "sealed orders." I told him what my job involved. He actually fell out of his chair laughing because, like me, he didn't know there were any top secret documents in all of Finance. It was especially funny because he was an 11B infantry colonel who had almost been killed twice while in country. But, he hurt himself the worst by falling out of his chair the day I reported in. I only wish I had had a camera. *Source: Vietnam Memory Book 2000*

**Caroline A. Tschetter (Nuese)**
**Retired as a Master Sergeant**
**In country: August 1972 – March 1973**
**Rank: Technical Sergeant, US Air Force**
**Duty: MACV, Air Force Advisory Group,**
**Information Management Technician**

One of the things that I have never forgotten is when three of us were in a jeep going to the mailroom. On the way, we were stopped by the Security Forces personnel who told the driver something that I wasn't able to hear. I was told we were under rocket attack and we needed to get in the bunker.  I immediately asked if I could go back to my room and was told no, to please go in the bunker now. That was the first rocket attack of many.

# SEPTEMBER

*Memory Lane: The Price is Right begins a 35-year run on CBS TV; Special Supplemental Nutrition Program for Women, Infants and Children (WIC) is signed into law by President Nixon.*
*Song: "Baby, Don't Get Hooked on Me" by Mac Davis*

**Joan Frances Bence (Naylor)**
**Retired as a Master Chief Petty Officer, US Navy**
**In country: September 1972 – February 1973**
**Rank: Staff Sergeant, US Air Force**
**Duty: MACV, Deputy Commander's Office; 7th Air Force,**
**Commander's Office, Stenographic Specialist**

My assignment to Southeast Asia (SEA) began in Vietnam as a stenographer in the office of the Deputy Commander for MACV, who was also the Commander of 7th Air Force. When I arrived, it was a real cultural shock, and I remember being very scared the first week after the base experienced a rocket attack. I thought that there was just no way I could endure a whole year here, never knowing when the next attack would occur and always looking over my shoulder and being frightened. Thankfully, that was not to be, as the Peace Accords with the North Vietnamese were signed January 27, 1973; and the 7th Air Force Headquarters staff moved to Nakhom Phanom, Thailand, which is where I finished my SEA tour and my enlistment in the Air Force.

**♥Anna L. Maxwell (Bradham) (Youngblood)**
**In country: September 1972 – March 1973**
**Rank: Specialist 4, US Army**
**Duty: USARV/MACV Support Command, 1st Signal Brigade,**
**Communications Center Specialist**

**Patricia Mary Murphy**
**Retired as a Colonel**
**In country: September 1972 – March 1973**
**Rank: Captain, US Air Force**
**Duty: Headquarters 7th Air Force, Base Personal**
**Affairs Officer**

# OCTOBER

*Memory Lane: US National Security Advisor Henry Kissinger suggests that "peace is at hand;" the first female FBI agents are hired.*
*Song: "My Ding-a-Ling" by Chuck Berry*

**Catherine J. Southall**
**Retired as a Master Sergeant**
**In country: October 1972 – January 1973**
**Rank: Staff Sergeant, US Air Force**
**Duty: 7th Air Force, 377th Air Base Wing/Scatback**

**Linda A. Bellard**
**Retired as a Master Sergeant**
**In country: October 1972 – March 1973**
**Rank: Technical Sergeant, US Air Force**
**Duty: 7th Air Force, 377th Air Base Wing,**
**Administrative Specialist**

**Linda L. Liston (Katalenich)**
**Retired as a Lieutenant Colonel (USAFR)**
**In country: October 1972 – March 29, 1973**
**Rank: Staff Sergeant, US Air Force**
**Duty: MACV, Office of Information, Armed Forces Vietnam Network,**
**Radio and TV Production Specialist**

***www.macoi.net:*** Sergeant Liston arrived in Vietnam in 1972 and served as the second female assigned on-air duties at the American Forces Vietnam Network (AFVN), which operated American Forces Radio and Television in Vietnam. She hosted radio news and TV sports.

After Vietnam, she went to Carswell Air Force Base in Fort Worth, TX. Then in October 1973, she was selected for Officer Training School. With her new gold bar, she left for an assignment at Norton Air Force Base in San Bernardino, CA.

In 1982, she left active duty to take a civilian job at Offutt Air Force Base, NE. (A few years later) Linda joined the Air Force Reserve, and continued her military career with a period of active duty at the Army/Air Force Postal Service in San Francisco; as a budget analyst at US Strategic Command; and as a defense contractor at the Financial Management Board in the Office of the Secretary of the Air Force.

Over the years, Linda was elevated to the rank of lieutenant colonel in the Air Force Reserve, and GS13 in the Civil Service. She retired in 2010.

**Carol A. Urich**
**Retired as a Master Sergeant**
**In country: October 1972 – March 1973**
**Rank: Staff Sergeant, US Air Force**
**Duty: MACV, Administrative Specialist**

# NOVEMBER

*Memory Lane: President Richard Nixon wins reelection by a landslide; the Dow Jones Industrial Average closes above 1,000 for the first time in its history.*
*Song: "I Can See Clearly Now" by Johnny Nash*

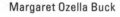

Margaret Ozella Buck     Jillian "Jill" D. Tate

**♥Margaret Ozella Buck**
**Retired as a Technical Sergeant**
**In country: November 1972 – March 1973**
**Rank: Technical Sergeant, US Air Force**
**Duty: 7th Air Force, 377th Air Base Wing, Air Operations Supervisor**

**Jillian "Jill" D. Tate**
**Retired as a Lieutenant Colonel**
**In country: November 1972 – March 1973**
**Rank: Captain, US Air Force**
**Duty: 7th Air Force, 377th Air Base Wing, Administrative Officer**

**Margaret "Marcy" Hammond (Anno)**
**Retired as a Colonel**
**In country: November 6, 1972 – February 28, 1973**
**Rank: First Lieutenant, US Air Force**
**Duty: 7th Air Force, 12th Reconnaissance Intelligence Technical**
**Squadron, Executive Officer**

**Comments and Memories:** I got my yellow fever shot in country and couldn't go back to work the next day. The senior master sergeant came to the dorm and I told him I couldn't stop throwing up. So, he went back and told the squadron commander that I was pregnant. *Source: Vietnam Memory Book 2000*

# DECEMBER

*Memory Lane: Apollo 17 launches from Cape Kennedy; Harry S. Truman, 33rd President of the United States dies; final edition of* LIFE *magazine hits the stands.*
*Song: "Papa Was a Rolling Stone" by The Temptations*

**Mary A. Curry (Murry)**
**Retired as a Staff Sergeant**
**In country: December 1972 – March 1973**
**Rank: Staff Sergeant, US Air Force**
**Duty: Headquarters 7th Air Force,**
**Administrative Supervisor**

**♥Patricia Dorothy LaRocque**
**Retired as a Technical Sergeant**
**In country: December 1972 – March 1973**
**Rank: Staff Sergeant, US Air Force**
**Duty: 7th Air Force, 377th Air Base Wing,**
**Air Operations Supervisor**

Janet Lynn Young (Held)
Retired as a Sergeant First Class
In country: December 1972 – March 1973
Rank: Specialist 4, US Army
Duty: MACV, Chief of Staff/Chief US Delegation Four Party Joint
Military Commission, Executive Administrative Assistant

# Chapter Thirteen

# ARMY AND AIR FORCE ADVISORS

No discussion of the role of military women in Vietnam can be complete without speaking of the Women's Army Corps (WAC) Advisors to the South Vietnamese Women's Armed Forces Corps (WAFC), and of the Women in the Air Force (WAF) Advisors to the Vietnam Air Force (VNAF) and the VNAF component of the WAFC.

In the early 1960s, a group of South Vietnamese women had been organized by Madame Nhu, the sister-in-law of the former South Vietnamese president, into a group called the Women's Solidarity Movement. It was a female paramilitary organization and Madame Nhu was their commander. Her desire to involve the women of South Vietnam in the defense of their country was shared by her brother-in-law, President Ngô Đình Diệm.[1] After President Diệm's assassination in 1963, the organization was briefly disbanded until President Nguyễn Văn Thiệu reconstituted it as the WAFC. The WAFC was established as part of an effort by President Thiệu to mobilize the population of the country against the Viet Cong and the North Vietnamese forces who threatened their homeland. The North Vietnamese armed forces had long before included women in their combat and support forces, and the Viet Cong routinely used women in their guerrilla forces and military. In 1964, the South Vietnamese government officially requested assistance from the United States in training and organizing the women.[2]

The US also admitted women from the WAFC to the foreign military training program in the United States and over the course of several years, 1964 to 1971, fifty-one Vietnamese women officer candidates completed the

---

[1] Langguth, A. J. (2000). Our Vietnam: The War, 1954–1975. New York City: Simon & Schuster. ISBN 0-684-81202-9.
[2] Wikipedia contributors. "Madame Nhu." Wikipedia, The Free Encyclopedia. Wikipedia, The Free Encyclopedia, 14 Sep. 2014. Web. 24 Sep. 2014.

WAC Officer Basic Course at the WAC School at Fort McClellan, AL, and one officer completed the WAC Officer Advanced Course.[3]

> *The excerpt below is part of the brochure "South Vietnam's Women in Uniform," published by the Vietnam Council on Foreign Relations, date unknown*

> Each year seven top graduates are sent to the WAC School at Fort McClellan in Anniston, Alabama. Five take the basic training course for four months and two enroll for the six-month career course. Colonel (Tran Cam) Huong, who has attended both courses, finds them very helpful. "Our girls can see the organization of the American WAC which was established 35 years ago," she says, "and being able to travel is an experience for them."

The MACV Commander, General William Westmoreland, authorized two WAC Advisors. The Director of the Women's Army Corps, COL Emily Gorman, received a letter (November 17, 1964) from BG Ben Sternberg, MACV Personnel, directing the assignment of the women and offered some friendly advice:

*"The WAC officer should be a captain or major, fully knowledgeable in all matters pertaining to the operation of a WAC school and the training conducted therein. She should be extremely intelligent, an extrovert and beautiful. The WAC sergeant should have somewhat the same qualities . . . and should be able to type as well."[4]*

*Colonel Gorman replied (November 23, 1964) they would "certainly try" and then added, "The combination of brains and beauty is, of course, common in the WAC."[5]*

---

[3] The Women's Army Corps 1945-1978, by Bettie J. Morden, Army Historical Series, Center of Military History, United States Army, Washington, DC 1990, pp 241-245.
[4] Letter from BG Ben Sternberg to COL Emily Gorman, November 17, 1964, National Archives Record Group 319 – Records of the Army Staff, Women's Army Corps, 1945-1978 (hereafter NARA RG 319), Box 50.
[5] Letter from COL Emily Gorman to BG Ben Sternberg, November 23, 1964, NARA RG 319, Box 50.

(This exchange of letters is included in most writings about the history of the WAC in Vietnam. It is amusing today, but it was a serious direction from the leadership in 1964.)

For COL Gorman, this was the opportunity she needed to improve WAC career potential and expand WAC numbers.

Major Kathleen I. Wilkes and SFC Betty L. Adams were COL Gorman's top choices as the first Advisors to help train the Republic of Vietnam WAFC. Both women had extensive experience with the US WAC in training, recruiting, administration, and command.

Colonel Emily Gorman, Director, Women's Army Corps

Major Wilkes and SFC Adams arrived in Vietnam January 15, 1965. The first year working with the WAFC was spent recruiting and establishing the training topics and standards. Training areas, uniforms, basic military skills and knowledge, and an enormous list of needed supplies kept both of them working long hours, seven days a week. One of the first recommendations for future WAC Advisors was that they receive language training before their arrival. Although the WAFC had interpreters for both the officer and enlisted Advisor, the lack of language skills presented some problems. Teaching English to the WAFC officers and recruits became an ongoing project.

## Major Kathleen I. Wilkes
### First Senior Officer Advisor to the Vietnam WAFC

Only one other American woman officer had served in Vietnam – MAJ Anne Doering in 1962. The arrival of MAJ Kathleen Wilkes in Vietnam on January 15, 1965, represented an historic event for the WAC. Major Wilkes had extensive experience in WAC training, recruiting, administration and command. Recruiting presented few problems for the WAFC as young Vietnamese women were excited to join. The challenges

involved in establishing standards for training, as well as supply lines for uniforms and equipment and even food, were far greater than in recruiting. Major Wilkes said that hundreds of young Vietnamese women volunteered for service with the WAFC. By the end of her tour, 1,300 women had been trained, and that number was set to double in the following year. More than 2,600 women were in initial stages of training.

Born in Georgia April 24, 1925, Kathleen Wilkes enlisted in the Army in 1944 as a private. She left the military at the end of WWII to attend the University of Georgia. She rejoined the Army as a Second Lieutenant in June 1950.

While in service, LTC Wilkes also earned a master's degree in economics with a focus on developing countries.

Lieutenant Colonel Kathleen Iris Wilkes died on Christmas Day in 1999 at the age of 74.

### Lieutenant Colonel Judith Christian Polk Bennett
### Second Senior Officer Advisor to the Vietnamese WAFC

Lieutenant Colonel Judith Christian Polk Bennett was assigned as Second Senior Officer Advisor to the WAFC, arriving in Vietnam February 1966. As recommended by her predecessor, she took Vietnamese language lessons. Learning the language was not easy for her. While she did score high on the exams, she told everyone that the answers were multiple choice and that she guessed well. The Vietnamese were expecting an individual who was fluent in their language. However, she spoke the language very minimally and understood the writing even less. There was no lack of Vietnamese women in the WAFC who spoke excellent English, and the interpreters received bonus pay for translating.

Lieutenant Colonel Bennett was very proud of the opportunity to serve as an Advisor to the WAFC. In a recorded interview with Specialist Mike Baker from the MACV Information Office, she talks about being able to establish the in-country Officer Candidate School, graduating 120 new officers.[6] This recorded interview has recently been posted on the website YouTube. com. The Vietnam Council on Foreign Relations also used the new training opportunity for recruiting:

---

[6] Quitney, Jeff. *"South Vietnamese Women's Army Corps (WAC) Training for Vietnam War 1966 US Army."* Online video clip. YouTube, Dec 6, 2013. Web. Sep 21, 2014

*The excerpt below is part of the brochure "South Vietnam's Women in Uniform," published by the Vietnam Council on Foreign Relations, date unknown*

In October 1966, an officer training course was started. Officer candidates first complete the basic training course, then begin the 20-week officer training class. Seventy women are now enrolled. Subjects of the basic course are covered in more depth. The future officers also learn military tactics, leadership, public speaking, and military justice. Both enlisted and commissioned women then attend military schools for advanced training in whatever field they want to specialize in - signal corps work, social welfare, etc.

Though LTC Bennett rarely talked about her experiences in Vietnam, she did write an article for the *Women's Army Corps Journal,* Jan-Mar 1971, which vividly describes the protocol, customs, ceremonies, and life of the Montagnard villagers. Following is an excerpt from that article.

"A party would be held for the 'lady colonel,' a chicken's throat cut and the warm blood poured into the rice wine we drank. . . . But, as I watched the Montagnard village chief, clad in a suit coat and loincloth, snub out a cigarette on the bamboo floor with his bare big toe, I knew I couldn't decline the honor.

"Preparations for the first part of the ceremony began as an earthenware jar about 3-feet tall was carried in and set on the floor. Moldy banana leaves covered with black, orange and other varied-colored growths were pulled from off the top of the fermenting rice. Fresh leaves then were stuffed into the jar to keep the rice from rising while water was added. Then the water — from the river where I had seen water buffalo cooling themselves and pigs rooting in the muddy banks — was added. It was a homemade, do-it-yourself brewery.

"Next, I, as honoree, was asked to take the first drink of rice wine. I was seated on a low stool before the wine jar holding a long reed straw, in my right hand. Custom required each participant to drink a pint of the brew without stopping. There could be no cheating. . . . The wine tasted somewhat like diluted vinegar, and I finished my pint a little light-headedly. However, I was careful to observe the custom and passed the straw on to the right hand of the next person before letting loose of it. I was pleased with my accomplishment and watched with interest as my fellow travelers struggled to drink their ration. My feeling of satisfaction ended abruptly as I realized with alarm that a second jar was being prepared. I learned to my distress that the first jar of wine had been judged to be improperly fermented, so we had to begin all over!

"To observe the custom, I took a long drag on the straw in the new jar and tasted what seemed to be pure gin. Swallowing the powerful stuff took some doing. . . . I asked for the rest of my pint in a glass and was grateful to have the request complied with. My plan was to gradually pour the wine through the cracks in the bamboo floor when attention was elsewhere and the clanging from drums and gongs would cover any noise I made.

"This plan worked reasonably well until suddenly the noise stopped and my wine hit the ground with a resounding splash. However, if anyone heard, they were kind enough not to notice.

"Something worse was about to happen – I suddenly realized the chicken sacrifice would be next. The effect of the wine I had already drunk, on top of my natural aversion to this unpleasantness, made me surer than ever that I had to escape. So through the interpreter, I conveyed my regrets to our barefoot host that we had to depart immediately for the airfield or miss our flight.

"The chief accepted my explanation with great regret at not having time to complete the sacrifice. As we could not stay, he handed me a large bag of rice and some thoroughly ripe eggs. Under my other arm, he placed the live, squawking chicken. . . . Once out of sight of the Montagnard village, I unceremoniously gave up my gifts to the interpreter who was as pleased to have them as I was to be rid of them."

The requirements of the Advisor job were to travel, both for recruiting and training. It was inevitable there would be trouble. While WACs were not issued weapons in Vietnam, Judy Bennett still packed a small pistol in her belt whenever she left Saigon. She did run into her share of trouble and was glad to have the pistol.

Judith Christian Polk Bennett was born April 26, 1920, in Corsicana, TX. She and her sister Grace both joined the WAAC in the summer of 1942 following Officer Candidate School. She retired on July 31, 1971. Lieutenant Colonel Bennett died December 28, 2010, and is buried at Fort Sam Houston National Cemetery in San Antonio, TX.

On occasion, LTC Bennett had the opportunity to interact with other WACs assigned in Vietnam. On June 18, 1966, she administered the oath of reenlistment to Specialist 5 Florence Woolard, the first member of the Women's Army Corps to reenlist in the Republic of Vietnam.

## Lieutenant Colonel Frances V. Chaffin (Gannon)
## Third Senior Officer Advisor to the Vietnam WAFC

***From a telephone interview:*** "When I was selected to be an Advisor to the WAFC, there was no one who could tell me what the job would entail. I was replacing LTC Judith Bennett who had already departed Vietnam.

"In Vietnam, I was introduced to COL Tran Cam Huong, the WAFC director, who was very knowledgeable and pleased to have another American WAC Advisor. My initial briefings about the Advisor role came from Colonel Huong and from the NCO Advisor, MSG Mary Phillips who had been in country for almost three months. I soon found the assignment consisted of a lot of 'make it up as you go along.'

"The WAFC director was primarily interested in setting up a standardized training curriculum, selecting the topics the women would learn to fulfill their roles. Secondary to that was where to place them after training.

"Every other week, COL Huong and I would fly to locations where their women were assigned or had been requested. Part of this was to ensure they were being properly utilized and not just placed in a kitchen somewhere. Most of the women were serving as medics to the dependents or as administrative support."

It was immediately obvious to LTC Chaffin that the Vietnamese officers did not treat COL Huong with any great respect. However, when LTC Chaffin accompanied the WAFC director, the officers' attitude was much different and gave the director some leverage.

By the spring of 1968, WAFC officers had taken over the recruiting duties and more than 2,600 women were now trained and serving as administrators, medical aids, welfare workers, interpreters, telephone operators and security checkers.

From time to time, GEN Creighton Abrams, MACV commander, would consult with LTC Chaffin on issues concerning the WACs serving in Vietnam. During the Tet Offensive, he called her in to discuss the option of arming the military women. (They were not issued weapons.)

Having had weapons training prior to their assignment to Vietnam, LTC Chaffin and MSG Mary Phillips were armed on their trips around the country. They were thankful they had qualified with the .45 pistol and the M1 rifle.

Shortly before her rotation back to the States, LTC Chaffin told a *Stars and Stripes* reporter that she regretted her lack of a working knowledge of the language and was pleased that her replacement was currently at Defense Language Institute in Monterey, CA, would have that advantage.[7]

She was the first woman selected to attend the Command and General Staff College, and was pleased when COL Shirley Heinze was also selected to attend. Colonel Frances Chaffin (Gannon) retired in 1977.

Colonel Chaffin (Gannon) has great memories of the Vietnamese people. She enjoyed meeting them. When she returned stateside, she brought home one of the tall fish baskets that she still has, along with two of the large ceramic elephants. They are a daily reminder of an interesting assignment.

Lieutenant Colonel Frances Chaffin and SFC Mary Phillips visit one of the WAFC training sites. Shown with a 4.2-inch Mortar M30 which is an American 107-mm caliber mortar originally assigned to the Chemical Corps for firing gas and smoke bombs.

## Lieutenant Colonel Lorraine A. Rossi
## Fourth Senior Officer Advisor to the Vietnam WAFC

Lieutenant Colonel Lorraine A. Rossi arrived in Vietnam in June 1968, replacing LTC Frances Chaffin as the Senior Officer Advisor to the Vietnam WAFC. She is well remembered by her NCO Advisor, MSG Evelyn Ford, who commented that she was well liked, could get things done and was pleasant to be around.

Born in 1929 in Boston, MA, she graduated from Bridgewater State College.

In 1952, she received a direct commission in the Women's Army Corps. Following training and a brief assignment at Fort Lee, VA, she was assigned to the group activating the Women's Army Corps Center at Fort McClellan, AL.

---

[7] "A Helping Hand From The Girls," by MGY SGT J. T. Frye, *Pacific Stars and Stripes*, May 18, 1968

During her service in Vietnam, the WAFC continued to expand and to graduate more women from their training centers. As a result of the growth,

MAJ Charlotte Hall, a junior Officer Advisor was assigned to assist LTC Rossi.

After her return from Vietnam and following graduation from the Army War College and promotion to Colonel, she served as the Deputy Commander of the WAC Center before replacing COL Shirley Heinze as the last Center Commander. Having worked to activate the WAC Center, she was charged with closing it on December 31, 1976. She retired June 30, 1980.

(l-r) Lieutenant Colonel Tran Cam Huong (WAFC), SP5 Charlene Kahl, SP5 Catherine Kahl and LTC Lorraine Rossi cut the cake during festivities highlighting the opening of the "new" WAC Detachment at Long Binh.

Her awards include the Distinguished Service Medal, Bronze Star Medal, Defense Meritorious Service Medal, Meritorious Service Medal, the Joint Service and Army Commendation Medals.

Retired Colonel Lorraine A. Rossi, formerly of Alexandria, VA, and Roslindale, MA, died August 7, 2010, at age 81. She is buried in the Massachusetts National Cemetery in Bourne, MA.

## Lieutenant Colonel Ann Blakely Smith
## Fifth Senior Officer Advisor to the Vietnam WAFC

Born December 19, 1930, in Quitman, GA, LTC Ann Blakely Smith was a 1951 graduate of Valdosta State University where she was subsequently named a Distinguished Alumna. Two years after graduation she went to the WAC Officer Basic Course at Fort Lee, VA, from which she graduated as a Second Lieutenant.

First assigned to the WAC Training Battalion at Fort Lee, VA., and Fort McClellan, AL, she saw additional assignments at Forts Sheridan, Riley, Eustis, at the Pentagon and again Fort McClellan, with overseas duty in Bremerhaven, Germany, and Vietnam (as Advisor to the Vietnam WAFC). She was also assigned at Redstone Arsenal, AL, and the US Army Command and General Staff College at Fort Leavenworth, KS (where she was the first woman platform instructor since 1942).

She was promoted to Colonel in 1976. Her final assignment was as Director, US Army Casualty and Memorial Affairs, Office of the Adjutant General.

Her awards and decorations include the Legion of Merit Medal, Bronze Star Medal, Joint Service Commendation Medal, and the Army Commendation Medal with Oak Leaf Cluster.

Colonel Ann Smith died September 28, 2007. Her ashes were not interred.

### Major Joyce Eloise Eslick
### Sixth Senior Officer Advisor to the Vietnam WAFC

Major Joyce Eloise Eslick was the sixth and final Senior Officer Advisor to the Vietnam WAFC. While the responsibilities of the Advisors had remained the same, many more Vietnamese women officers had been trained to handle the responsibilities and were performing well. The US involvement was drawing down, and no US Army replacement was planned.

Born in Huntsville, AL, August 31, 1929, she moved to Tennessee with her family. She originally joined the WAC as an enlisted person, and after attending Officer Candidate School, she was commissioned and rose to the rank of lieutenant colonel. Among her many career accomplishments, she was the company commander of the 14th Women's Army Corps Band. She served her country in both the Far East and in Europe during war and peace. She received the Bronze Star Medal in 1972 and the Joint Service Commendation Medal for achievement.

Lieutenant Colonel Joyce Eslick died December 31, 2010, in Seattle, WA, and is buried in Roane Memorial Gardens, Rockwood, TN.

### Major Charlotte J. Hall
### First Junior Officer Advisor to the Vietnam WAFC

In 1968, an additional WAC Officer Advisor was assigned to the WAFC training center on the outskirts of Saigon. Major Charlotte J. Hall arrived in country in November 1968.

She entered the WAC in January, 1950. She served in Germany and South Vietnam. Her awards include the

Bronze Star Medal, the Meritorious Service Medal, the Republic of Vietnam Service Medal, the Army Commendation Medal with Oak Leaf Cluster, the Joint Service Commendation Medal and the Air Service Medal, Vietnam.

She died December 22, 1974, while still on active duty and is buried at Rest Haven Cemetery, Hanover, PA.

### Major Rosemary Lee Davis
### Second Junior Officer Advisor to the Vietnam WAFC

Rosemary Lee Davis entered military service in February 1965 and retired September 1, 1985. Her awards include the Bronze Star Medal and the Army Commendation Medal with Oak Leaf Cluster.

She was born in Weirton, WV, October 9, 1938, and died in Fairfax, VA, June 11, 1993. She is buried at Bay Pines National Cemetery in Bay Pines, FL.

### Captain Catherine Brajkovich
### Third Junior Officer Advisor to the Vietnam WAFC

(*Photos courtesy of Peter Brajkovich*)

Catherine Brajkovich was born in Youngstown, OH, October 1, 1939. At some point, her family moved to Schenectady NY, and she settled eventually in Absecon, NY. Lieutenant Colonel Brajkovich retired on December 1, 1985. She was a lifetime member of Hildebrand-Davis VFW Post 1895 and VFW Post 9462. Lieutenant Colonel Brajkovich received the Army Commendation Medal for Heroism; she had alerted residents of a bachelor officers' hotel in Saigon of a fire in the building. Her other awards include the Bronze Star Medal, the Defense Meritorious Service Medal, and the Army Commendation Medal with two Oak Leaf Clusters. She died October 3, 2006, and her ashes are interred in the Atlantic County Veterans Cemetery, Estell Manor, NJ.

Captain Catherine Brajkovich poses with the school staff of the South Vietnamese Women's Armed Forces Corps

### Sergeant First Class Betty Lee Adams
### First NCO Advisor to the Vietnam WAFC

On January 15, 1965, SFC Betty Adams arrived in Saigon and stepped into her place in the history of the Women's Army Corps as the First NCO Advisor to the Vietnam WAFC.

She was born December 3, 1932, in New York. She graduated from high school in 1951 and enlisted in the US Army on May 28, 1952. In 1954, she was assigned to Fort Benjamin Harrison, IN, and completed the stenographic training course. She spent two years at Fort McClellan, AL, as a Drill Sergeant and then three years as a Personnel Specialist in the Pentagon.

In 1960, SFC Adams volunteered for recruiting duty and spent four years in Albany, NY, at the US Army Recruiting Main Station. When the requisition for an enlisted WAFC Advisor was received, she had the perfect background, including the ability to type.

While in Vietnam, she was promoted to Master Sergeant on July 30, 1965. On December 3, 1965, she left Vietnam at 5 p.m. and arrived in San Francisco at 9 p.m. the same day, her birthday. "It was the longest birthday I ever had – 38 hours long."

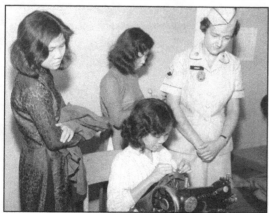

Sergeant Major Betty L. Adams, a soldier highly decorated by the US Army and South Vietnamese Army, retired May 31, 1975. She died at her home January 20, 2012, at the age of 79. She is buried at Arlington National Cemetery.

Finding uniforms to fit the petite Vietnamese women was especially difficult, but the women were quite talented at altering the fatigue uniforms to fit.

## Sergeant First Class Jane Carol Szalobryt
## Second NCO Advisor to the Vietnam WAFC

Sergeant First Class Jane C. Szalobryt served two tours in Vietnam. During her first tour as the Second NCO Advisor to the WAFC, SFC Szalobryt saw a continued rapid expansion of the WAFC. Recruiting was not an issue as there were usually more recruits than the training centers could handle.

Most of her 18-year career had focused on recruit training and she provided hands-on instruction in several areas, including basic living skills. As a drill sergeant for many years, she was well prepared to train the Vietnamese women in marching, formations, wearing of the uniform, deportment, setting up in field conditions, and other general military knowledge.

She noted that as the program expanded, the women were moved into  bare billets and quickly made them more colorful with "fancy" pillows they had made themselves. While the billets may not have had much, it was a different world for many of the women who were not used to electricity, running water, flush toilets and other modern amenities.

Sergeant First Class Szalobryt departed Vietnam in November 1966 and returned for another tour at MACV in Saigon in 1968.

She retired as a Master Sergeant.

## Sergeant First Class Mary E. Phillips
## Third NCO Advisor to the Vietnam WAFC

As the Third NCO Advisor, SFC Mary E. Phillips was in country during the time the WAFC training and recruiting goals were expanding rapidly. There were not enough hours in the day for the tasks at hand.

According to LTC Frances Chaffin, the Senior Officer Advisor, SFC Phillips was a petite woman, the size of her Vietnamese trainees who were all very small women. The Vietnamese women did not find her too intimidating. She was definitely a hands-on advisor: drilling, checking barracks, keeping an eagle eye on the details. She trained (the Vietnamese women recruits) in the US Women's Army Corps' way of doing things.

Pictured conducting inventory of food supplies and kitchen materials, it was an essential task to ensure that the recruits would be fed.

Mary Phillips was born on August 30, 1930. She entered military service in October 1949. She retired June 30, 1973, as a Master Sergeant.

She died October 19, 1999, and is buried in Anniston Memorial Gardens, Anniston, AL.

## Master Sergeant Evelyn J. Ford
## Fourth NCO Advisor to the Vietnam WAFC

During a telephone interview, MSG Evelyn Ford discussed some of the issues and responsibilities she encountered in Vietnam. "One of my main duties was to try and get supplies like uniforms and classroom materials. I was pretty good at going to the docks and finding the right person to supply whatever we needed at the time." She said that even though language school might have been recommended for the Officer Advisors, it was never suggested to her. She had two different interpreters who would accompany her whenever she was working. "We spent a lot of time each week teaching English to the Vietnamese women.

"I traveled throughout South Vietnam – anywhere that the WAFC were stationed. Lieutenant Colonel Chaffin and I visited places like Nha Trang, Da Nang, and Da Lat. I swam in the South China Sea. Vietnam had some of the most beautiful beaches. I can remember thinking, what a wonderful tourist area it could be."

Master Sergeant Ford retired in 1973 after 24 years in service and lives in Alabama.

## Master Sergeant Mary Joe Hinton
## Fifth NCO Advisor to the Vietnam WAFC

Not much is known about MSG Mary Joe Hinton. She was born in Sturgis, KY, July 29, 1933. Her home of record was South Carolina.

According to Army records, her military occupational specialty was Dental Technician so her selection as an

NCO Advisor for the Vietnam WAFC is a mystery. She remained in the Advisor slot for almost two years, from November 1968 to September 1970. Master Sergeant Hinton retired on September 1, 1980, after 26 years in service. At the time of her death March 22, 2013, she lived in Evansville, IN. She was awarded the Bronze Star Medal for achievement and two Army Commendation Medals for her service in Vietnam. She also received the Meritorious Service Medal at some point in her career. She is buried in Oak Hill Cemetery, Evansville, IN.

Major Charlotte Hall and MSG Mary Joe Hinton with the Director of the Vietnam Women's Armed Forces Corps.

WAFC classrooms were utilitarian. Shown here during a visit from the WAC Detachment members are (far left) SSG Catherine Oatman, SP5 Barbara Bacon and SP5 Linda Honor. Sitting at the desk are (l-r) MAJ Charlotte Hall; CPT Nancy Jurgevich, WAC Detachment Commander; 1SG Mary Manning; and MSG Mary Joe Hinton.

### Sergeant First Class Sylvia Rita Bernardini
### Sixth NCO Advisor to the Vietnam WAFC

No image is available of SFC Sylvia Rita Bernardini. Born February 7, 1928, in New York, little is known about her military career. She retired as a First Sergeant, and the exact dates of her tour in Vietnam are uncertain. She died November 26, 2008, in Las Vegas, NV. Her burial location is not public knowledge.

# Air Force Advisors

### Captain Mary A. Marsh
### First WAF Staff Advisor to the VNAF and the VNAF component of the Vietnam Women's Armed Forces Corps

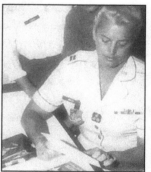

In 1968, the Vietnamese Air Force (VNAF) asked the US Air Force if they could provide a woman Advisor to help build a VNAF Women's Component of the Armed Forces. Brigadier General Jeanne Holm was the WAF Director at the time, and she selected Capt. Mary A. Marsh, who arrived in Saigon in April 1968. She was qualified with a weapon, where the WAC Advisors were not.

The question of uniforms was answered when the WAF Director told Capt. Marsh to contact the WAC Advisor and get her help. Fatigues for everyday and the summer uniform for office work.

At the time, the WAFC was a single organization, and graduates of the programs were sent to various locations and missions as needed. Captain Marsh's role was to establish a dedicated female unit for the VNAF, which was quite a challenge as she was the only US military woman assigned to the VNAF staff. Despite the language barrier, she succeeded in establishing standard operating procedures for administrative and personnel issues, designing the uniforms, and persuading the young women to accept and conform to these standards.

## Captain Alice I. Champagne (Littlejohn)
## Second WAF Staff Advisor to the VNAF and VNAF component of the Vietnam Women's Armed Forces Corps

The VNAF women were housed in a small building at the end of the VNAF compound. They had two primary training officers: a female captain who was on maternity leave and a lieutenant who spent her mornings teaching English in the MACV language school and arrived on her motorcycle in the afternoons. She was very enthusiastic about her job, explained a major concern about the adequacy of housing for the enlisted women, and became my traveling companion. Working from her excellent rapport with the VNAF officers, we examined the problem and concluded that we should travel to multiple sites. We flew with the Vietnamese from Nha Trang in the north to Binh Thuy in the south when space was available; it was usually transport provided to Vietnamese personnel making assignment moves with their families – the wives, the children and the household animals. With help from the US Army Advisor, my travel uniform became small-size male green fatigues with bloused combat boots, my required .38 weapon, and my Vietnamese insignia (Dai Uy – Captain – worn with all uniforms between the second and third buttons). I quickly learned that a "building" consisted of four walls and a roof; all other amenities, doors, shutters and especially outdoor trench latrines, were to be negotiated. Fortunately, Vietnamese base commanders were anxious to have the women on their staffs and were welcoming and helpful.

## Major Eleanor L. Skinner
## Third WAF Staff Advisor to the VNAF and the VNAF component of the Vietnam Women's Armed Forces Corps

Major Eleanor L. Skinner continued the work of Capt. Marsh and Capt. Littlejohn in instituting the training program for the Vietnamese Air Force Women. She also worked with the Vietnamese personnel officials in automating the training records so that it would be easier to identify and locate people who had already been through training. The challenge was often to actually locate these

people. The problem was solved when one of her Vietnamese officers told her that the easiest way to locate anyone was simply to wait for payday.

She advised the Vietnamese woman officer who was in charge of training women for the VNAF as needed.

Weapons training was mandatory. While she had some training with an AK-47 and a pistol, she didn't like weapons; so she put the issued pistol and ammo in the office safe and only took the pistol out when she was travelling in country and even then she gave it to the sergeant to carry.

One time a vehicle went by and threw tear gas at them; that is the only direct hostile action she encountered.

She did not volunteer for Vietnam. She had decided to leave the service as she had recently married. She got a letter that would let her leave service, but first she had to spend a year in Vietnam. After discussing it with her husband, they both concluded that if she stayed another year, it would become her career and so it did.

When asked why she decided to join the Air Force, she said she has a bachelor's degree in chemistry and had been working for about a year at a company. One payday, she and a lab pal went to pick up their checks and he saw that she was paid $50 less than he was paid. He insisted that they go to Personnel because it had to be a mistake. Someone at Personnel told them that it was not a mistake –he was paid more because he had a family (he was a bachelor) and that men just make more.

She did not like hearing that and about a month later, she saw an ad for Women in the Air Force. She filled out the form and joined in 1957. She said it might be equal pay, but you have to work twice as hard! She retired in 1983.

## Major Maralin K. Coffinger
### Fourth WAF Staff Advisor to the VNAF and the VNAF component of the Vietnam Women's Armed Forces Corps

"My job was two-fold, Personnel Data Systems Advisor and the Advisor to the Women in the Vietnamese Air Force. On the data systems side, I advised three Vietnamese officers on automating their personnel system. As for the women's side of the job, the officer with whom I worked was a female Major. She was very shy but quite pleasant. Language was a problem but she understood English much better than the male officers did.

Although the data systems job was primary for me, I did spend several hours a week working with my female Vietnamese Major on matters dealing with women in the VNAF. Most of the emphasis was on making sure the women in the VNAF were properly housed and were given meaningful duties. Recruiting was also in the mix. I traveled with her several times to Vietnamese bases and on one occasion, we stopped at the Major's home for a few minutes. It was clean but had only the bare essentials. She was the mother of nine children!"

Brigadier General Coffinger retired April 30, 1989.

A representative unit of ARVN's Women Armed Force Corps on National Armed Forces Day's parade (June 19, 1971)

WAFC (Women's Armed Forces Corps) division of the ARVN in the National Armed Forces Day parade, Saigon, Republic of Vietnam, June 19, 1971.

# Chapter Fourteen

# THE QUILT

With Love, Pride, Honoring and Healing
by Glenda "Stormy" Storni (Graebe)

Olympia, Washington, Veterans' Day, November 1999. This was the site of our First Homecoming Conference some 30 years after our service in Vietnam. With the arrival of every taxi and shuttle to the hotel, there were screams of joy, laughter, tears, hugs, lots of hugs. You had to have been there!

The pomp and ceremony was overwhelming. There were Honor Guards. There were high-ranking state officials welcoming us home. There was a Memorial Service in the rotunda of the State Capitol. There were General officers as guest speakers. There was the sharing of photo albums. It was almost too much to digest. It was like the reading of a really good book – you didn't want it to end.

Much is known about the military nurses who served, but virtually nothing is known about the many women, all services, who served in secretarial, communications, logistics, personnel and intelligence assignments. That we were there may well be the best-kept secret of the Department of Defense, and the information isn't even classified! To this day, when one of us mentions that we served in Vietnam, the retort invariably is, "Oh, so you were a nurse?" The Air Force women hear, "You were a pilot?" Because of the Olympia experience, it occurred to me that our Vietnam service could no longer go unnoticed. When I returned home, I had the idea of making a quilt that just might well be one way to convey the message that we weren't nurses or pilots. My original motivation was to illustrate my pride in the Women's Army Corps, my appreciation of our WAC leadership, love of my country and for having served it, and some of the remarkable women with whom I served. But, it was equally important to include my sisters in all branches of service. As the quilt started to take shape and more and more squares came to me, I became aware of an unexpected result – it was healing me. It was healing the wounds of being spit upon, the wounds of ridicule for having served in

Vietnam, and the wounds of having to change from the uniform I wore so proudly into civilian clothes lest I be subjected to Heaven-only-knows-what on the streets of San Francisco.

Word went out to women of all services encouraging them to send a square or photos for me to make a square on their behalf. The end result, however, exceeded my expectations. To create squares for those women in other services who wanted a square but didn't know how to go about doing it, I realized I needed some background information and photos of their branch. So, my friend Marty Contreras and I went to the recruiting station in San Luis Obispo, CA. As we were going through the brochures, one of the recruiters came up to us and asked, "Can I help you with something?" Our reply: "We want to enlist." Not to be outdone, the sergeant, with a perfectly straight face, replied, "Well, we'll need your parents' permission!" The images (on the quilt) reflect a day-in-the-life-of. . . . The viewer can see the women at work, at play, during harrowing times, and love for the local people, most especially the orphans, in their war-torn country.

Though not all women who served are represented here, their service and dedication to duty is implicit in this quilt. More than 1,000 women who served shall be remembered here for generations to come. The project was two years in the making. Many thanks go to my husband Carl, my daughter Tami, and my dear friend and Army Sister Marty Contreras who helped me with the assembly.

The close-ups of some of the squares with explanation in the pages following the entire quilt represent some special memories and what life was like for us over there – both the quilt and our First Homecoming Conference were an occasion of healing for many; but, for many others, in the words of Karen Offutt – the war goes on!

Commemorative Quilt
This quilt hangs at the US Army Women's Museum, Fort Lee, VA

The four corners, the anchors of the quilt, represent and honor the four branches of the military women who served so proudly and honorably. If the Army appears to dominate, it's because the Army had, by far, the greatest number of women there. In the six years that there was a WAC Detachment, there were approximately 600 enlisted women of the Women's Army Corps.

Left: Everyone received a copy of this Short-Timer's Calendar. The helmet and boots were divided into small sections, much like a jigsaw puzzle. Each section contained a number ranging from 364 down to 1. As a day ended, a square was colored in (it meant one less day). When #1 was colored in, finally and very happily, it meant going home the next day.

Right: Marilyn Roth (RIP) lovingly took great pains to do this cross-stitch of the Vietnam ribbon and "Vietnam" and "68," Marilyn's time in country.

This grouping of photos is intended to honor, to show respect for, and my appreciation of our leadership in the WAC Detachment during my time in country. The top photo is of our cadre, (kneeling l-r) SP5 Patty Pewitt, Mail/Supply Clerk; SP5 Rhynell "Ren" Stoabs, Company Clerk; (standing l-r) SSG Edith Efferson, Supply Sergeant; SFC Betty Benson, Admin NCO; CPT Joanne Murphy, incoming CO; CPT Peggy Ready, outgoing CO; 1SG Marion Crawford, First Sergeant.

CPT Peggy Ready, first Commanding Officer, arrived two months before the first group of enlisted women. After Vietnam, Peggy went to Law School and became a judge in St. Augustine, FL. She retired from the US Army Reserve as a Colonel.

1SG Marion Crawford was handpicked to activate the first WAC Detachment in a combat zone since WWII. In her square you see one of the two Bronze Stars she was awarded.

CPT Joanne Murphy, inset, still has her fatigue uniform cap. From time to time, she dons the cap to

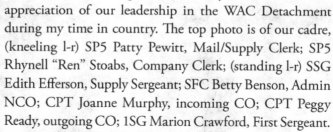

remind us she WAS the Captain. She has never explained why that cap is so important to her.

On her second tour, Anita "Jinx" Wampach concluded she needed reliable transportation. Waiting for the bus or walking was not her cup of tea. So, Jinx went to the Motor Pool and told the sergeant on duty that she needed to sign out a jeep.

What story she told the sergeant to convince him to do the paperwork, we'll never know! But a jeep she wanted, and a jeep she got. This uncovered jeep was her pride and joy. Never mind that she got soaking wet during rain storms or covered with red clay during dust storms. Just a matter of days before she was to rotate, she brought the jeep back to the Motor Pool. Curiously, the sergeant could find no record that she had signed it out. Hmmmm! That was our Jinx – one of a kind. We miss her.

Moments after Barbara "Bobbie" Cramer took the stage, the room was filled with non-stop raucous laughter. What a story-teller! Though Bobbie's assignment was with Logistics and Pacification, MACV, one afternoon she volunteered to accompany a medical team of Air Force doctors, nurses and corpsmen who were going to a remote village to render treatment to the local people. No sooner had they gotten off the Army helicopter when they realized they were under fire. The pilot told them to run for the tall grass that was next to a stream and that he'd be back for them in a little while. They hunkered down in that tall grass for what seemed like an eternity. Finally, the

helicopter came back. He circled around and around but didn't see them. Bobbie said, "I know how to get the attention of that Army helicopter." She told the nurses and doctors to face away from her. Then, she said to one of the corpsmen, "Take my jacket off and turn around, but first give me your rifle and mount the bayonet, then you turn around." Bobbie took her bra off and hooked it onto the bayonet and waved it high above the tall grass. Sure enough! The helicopter spotted them; they were rescued without incident. But, the corpsmen kept her bra!

Perhaps reminiscent of the era of Elvis velvet paintings, many of us received these velvet circles, which were wall hangings. Each was hand painted and

personalized. The tears speak to our homesickness and missing our families and friends.

From the beauty shop during the day to the bunkers at night – it happened so often that the women became desensitized to it. When the alarm sounded, well, they possibly remembered their helmets and flac jackets, but they didn't forget to bring along the frying pans, radios, bags of chips. Thiet (we called him Pierre) was our full-time hairdresser.

Deplaning are the first five enlisted Air Force women being assigned to Vietnam. They were accompanied by (l-r) Lt Col June H. Hilton, the fourth Air Force officer assigned to Vietnam, A1C Carol J. Hornick, A1C Rita M. Pitcock, SSgt Barbara J. Snavely, A1C Shirley J. Brown, and A1C Eva M. Nordstrom, June 1967.

This appliqué of a pair of helicopters was done by SP5 Rhynell "Ren" Stoabs, Company Clerk. The significance of this square is that they intruded on our daily lives, day and night. From the balconies of the wooden barracks, the tracer bullets were seen every

night. The unmistakable sound of helicopters stayed with us for years.

Not at all an unusual sight in Washington State, but this fog the morning after our Memorial Service in the State Capitol Rotunda reflected the mood of the night before. It was a time of reflection, a time to remember our departed sisters. The names of all the departed were called off by a member of each respective service.

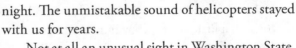

What a welcome sight! This is a photo of the front of the building we entered when we were on our way home. Our "Freedom Bird" was just beyond.

On the occasion of presenting the quilt to the Women's Museum, Fort Lee, VA, Glenda "Stormy" Storni (Graebe) proudly stands in front of the quilt which took her two years to put together. It measures 7 feet across by 10 feet long. "Murphy's Golden Girls" donated $500.00 toward the encasement of the quilt in a vitrine-paneled cabinet. The quilt is now a part of the Museum's permanent collection. The quilt was gifted to the United States Army Women's Museum at Fort Lee, VA, in May 2004.

# Chapter Fifteen

# TALES TO TELL

## *My Arrival in Vietnam-Tet 1967—Donna Lowery*

I arrived in Vietnam January 31, 1967, during the Tet holiday and a Viet Cong attack on Tan Son Nhut (TSN) Air Base. The plane could not land for more than an hour because of ground fire. I was met by 1SG Marion Crawford and SFC Betty Benson. I was a bit rattled by the time I got off the plane. I had been traveling for more than 20 hours in my Army green uniform, nylons and heels and was wrinkled. I was concerned that I would not make a good impression on whoever picked me up. I was the only woman on the plane, so it caused a lot of discussion. In fact, the pilot announced that I was not on the wrong plane, and yes, I was going to Vietnam. 1SG Crawford and SFC Benson were happy to see me but disappointed that I was the only woman on the plane; they had expected ten women. After delivering me to the barracks where I would stay for the night with a guard posted outside, they had to leave to meet the next plane scheduled into TSN. As it turns out, not another flight came for days; it could have been because of Tet.

I had long hair in those days, so I was accustomed to wearing a wig when I was in uniform. That first night I put my wig on one of the poles at the foot of my bunk, crawled under the mosquito netting, and quickly fell asleep. Not long after, I woke up to a scream. I couldn't figure out where I was. I had never been under mosquito netting, so I was frantically trying to get out. Once I was out of the netting, I saw the guard. When I asked him why he was inside instead of outside, he said he was scared because of all the firing going on. He had screamed because he saw my wig and thought something had happened to me. He asked if he could stay inside and guard me from there. I said it was fine. I was too tired to have much of a conversation, so I went back to sleep. Sometime during the night, my very efficient and brave guard left the inside of the building. I have no idea what happened to him. That was my welcome to Vietnam. I was also there for the Tet Offensive of

1968, which is when our old compound in Saigon was destroyed and Long Binh (where we had moved) was overrun by the Viet Cong.

### Don't Remember Any Explosions—Donna Lowery

I don't remember anything about the explosions in the early hours of February 18, 1968. I do remember February 17! It was the day I got promoted to staff sergeant. On my extension leave visiting my family in December 1967, I received a call from SFC Betty Benson to come back early from my leave so I could file an Inspector General (IG) complaint against the Special Troops Personnel Officer for selling drops (leave Vietnam 45 days early for a case of cognac) and other things. The IG complaint resulted in a huge investigation. The warrant officer was sent to the 9th Infantry Division.

I was at the top of the promotion list to E6 so I was moved into a staff sergeant slot on January 10, 1968, even though there were no promotions at that time. Department of Army determined that everyone on the current promotion list would get promoted. If I recall correctly, there were 252 promotions instead of 25. It took me about four hours to get from one side of the Special Troops Club to the other because everyone wanted to buy me a drink. I do not remember the explosions.

### So Much for the Paris Peace Accords—Judith McCurdy

The closer we got to the signing of the Paris Peace Accords, the closer enemy fire came to the city of Saigon, until finally, the perimeter was breeched and rocketing was upon us. This ended our stay at Truman Key (in Saigon), and it was goodbye to the Iowa BEQ, mama-san and the prostitutes. The next morning on our way to the Annex it happened; we were under a major rocket attack. Without thought, we hastily evacuated our jeep and headed for the ravines beside the Tan Son Nhut runway. I vividly remember incoming rounds whizzing over my head; I laid low and prayed for all I was worth. Stunned, scared and in disbelief of how close we came to death, it was a very quiet ride back to the BEQ. As we rode, I concluded there could never be an atheist living through a war because at some point, you would be forced to pray. A few hours later, the "All Clear" was given and we returned to the Annex. After the attack, everyone moved from the BEQ into the Annex at Dodge City and barracks life resumed.

There was little that was normal now. Security at the gate increased for all entering and exiting the Annex; all pedestrians were physically frisked and belongings searched for contraband. Mirrors were run on the underside of vehicles, seats removed and trucks thoroughly searched. Day and night we were rocketed. The ammo dump on the Annex had been hit. Sporadically, it would explode at any time day or night, and you found yourself hitting the deck.

My primary responsibility, along with congressional investigations (which deserves its own book), was receiving casualty reports. They were ever flowing and were called in via field phones. Oh, how I hated those damn crackling lines of the Army field phones! Alpha talk became the new norm and I began regretting picking up each call in fear of what was about to be reported. You must understand, at this time in the conflict 1ˢᵗ Aviation Brigade was over half the military strength in the Republic of Vietnam. Our units were flying all over, not only Vietnam, but Cambodia and Laos as well. I just wanted the casualty reporting to stop. We thought the end would certainly come after the Accords were signed – *now there was an optimistic thought!*

So, after the Paris Peace Accords were signed on January 27, 1973, the Brigade was ordered to take the M60 machine guns off their helicopters. We thought our prayers were answered; certainly now, there would be no more casualty reports. *Wishful thinking.* The enemy claimed they couldn't see that the guns had been removed and continued to shoot the choppers down. Some bright person then suggested that once the chopper complied with the removal of their weapons, an orange stripe should be painted down the middle of the chopper. *Now That Was Stupid – But It Became SOP (Standard Operating Procedure) Amazing!* With the stripes painting accomplished we knew there would be no excuse for any more casualties; however, we underestimated the enemy, who still had trouble seeing . . . and the casualty reports continued to flow. The inventor of the orange stripe theory (I guess) then decided that alternate lime green and orange stripes would be a greater indicator of compliance. *You've Got To Be Kidding Me! No!* This also became SOP. The enemy would certainly know now we were in compliance. What a joke *and* the casualty reports continued.

The indicator for leaving country on March 1, 1973, was M-1. I was scheduled to leave country on M-11, and on M-11 the enemy was still shooting choppers down. I guess we probably were still painting ridiculous stripes on our choppers on the last day. Who knows? Being on one of the last planes out of country, I reported to Tan Son Nhut AB to begin my homeward-bound journey by boarding a Pan Am flight. *Whooopeee!* As each person boarded, we all were handed a white towel—*now that was different.* In preparation for takeoff, the pilot came over the intercom and asked that we buckle up securely and place the towel up to our faces before we started down the runway. Being good soldiers, a bit perplexed and confused but never questioning, we did as we were told. Suddenly we heard a great roar from the plane engines, and we began to move very – I mean very – fast down the runway; we heard the familiar sound of artillery! *Why, the Viet Cong bastards were actually shooting at our commercial plane!* All of a sudden, it seemed we were shot straight up in the air. With this action, suddenly the blood rushed to our heads and came streaming out of our noses. We now knew the purpose of the white towels. In the aftermath of our goodbye attack, I sat there stunned, then began to chuckle, thinking, perhaps *Pan Am had not received the Orange stripe memo.*

### Memories of Vietnam—Linda Ostermeier (McDermith)

We swam in the Tent City B above-ground swimming pool. One of the GIs (Dick W.) tried on my Taylorville High School graduation ring and then dove into the pool where my ring came off his finger. We searched, but it was not to be found. How many people can say that their class ring was lost in a pool in Vietnam?

Another evening, without permission, WAC Jan C. and I slipped out in a jeep with a couple of GIs and went into Saigon. Going into an establishment with other GIs and Vietnamese patrons, Jan and I were called "round-eyed girls." The Vietnamese girls told us, "GI girls get out of here." Upon our return, Jan and I were caught, if memory serves, by 1SG Marion Crawford.

On one of my legal visits to Saigon, we visited a Vietnamese family that one of our GI friends knew. The family served us coffee with the consistency of mud but, nevertheless, I drank some.

I met a GI, John W. H., while at Tent City B. He asked me to marry him, but he was leaving for the United States. I still had time in Vietnam so under the circumstances, marriage made no sense. In the years since, we have touched base. He and his wife have stayed in my home (with my guy friend) in Springfield, IL, and we have visited them in Tulsa, OK.

At the Long Binh barracks, we had Vietnamese mama-sans helping with the "household" chores. Our barracks mama-san had a pregnant daughter. They said they were naming the baby "Donna" and wanted us to take the baby on the plane with us back to the United States.

### An Anecdote—Tanya Murphy (Hickman)

We were invited to an orphanage at Bien Hoa and from then on, I was hooked. I loved kids even more than dogs.

Sometimes, doctors and nurses would show up to doctor the children and babies who were really bad. One boy's whole back was eaten away by napalm; the doctor needed to debride the wound. He told us to wash his back in the sink, but none of us were willing because his back was raw. The doctor showed us what to do and we finished it. He then put Bacitracin on his back and bandaged it. He also lanced a cyst on his elbow. Other kids also had cysts they fixed. Two weeks later, we went to the orphanage again. The baby we called James had healed amazingly well. Much of his back was still without skin, but it was smaller and very tight. He would have to have a skin graft someday, but at least he now had a chance of leading a normal life.

One very special baby I really loved. I would have adopted her had that been possible. First, they said I wasn't old enough and second, the nuns at the orphanage said, because I was not Catholic, I would be killing the child's soul if I adopted her. Many babies there were special to us at the WAC Detachment. A planeload of kids from various orphanages were collected and sent to Holland, I think, for adoption. Faith (my baby) was scheduled for that flight. After the plane left, I was upset and didn't go to the orphanage. Finally, I couldn't stay away any longer because of the other kids. They got really excited when I arrived because Faith had not gone as we had expected. She was not allowed to go because of sores on her head. It was sad because she didn't get her family. Some of the other babies special to us did go, probably about 20 kids from the Tan Mai Orphanage.

### A Smaller Patient—Barbara Reid

My favorite child patient, Dang Bien, feeding me ice cream on a hot July day at the 67th Evacuation Hospital in Qui Nhon, 1969. She had severe burn contractures of her legs which were surgically released. By the time this photo was taken she could walk by herself to the PT clinic and be the first patient at the door giving me a hug and a kiss. Prior to July, she would scream if I got within 10 feet of her.

### *Tet Visit Brings Good Fortune—Flo Dunn*

At work, I became good friends with Lang Ha, who worked in the Ministry of Revolutionary Development. Lang, who'd worked for the American government for more than 20 years, spoke and wrote English better than some Americans. Lang became my translator and whenever I wanted to go to the beauty shop, she'd make the appointment and go with me. I'd ask her to look for a specific gift to send home, and she'd check out the various shops.

The Vietnamese custom is that the first person invited to your house on Tet (Vietnamese New Year, 1972) is to be someone who can bring you and your family good luck, good health, wealth, and happiness. I was honored when Lang Ha invited me to be the first person to visit her on New Year's. Little did I know that 20 years later, part of this tradition would come true for her family.

It took more than seven years of paperwork and phone calls; nevertheless, I was able to sponsor Lang Ha, her daughter and three small sons (ages 11, 6, 3) to the United States. They arrived at the Richmond, VA, International Airport, March 24, 1992, 20 years to the month when I last saw her. She died in February 2011. Her daughter married an American, and the family now lives in Florida. I am proud and thankful to say they are doing well; the boys are attending college and leading productive lives. So perhaps my Tet visit brought the family good fortune.

### *"Otto B," The WAC Mascot—Precilla Ann Landry (Wilkewitz)*

Otto B's mother belonged to one of the Army guys who worked nearby. I often went with our supply clerk to get IG supplies. On one supply run, I saw a very pregnant dog and asked the owner when she was due; he told me, "Soon." I really missed not having a dog, and here was an opportunity. All I had to do was convince the 1SG and WAC Commander for permission to have a dog in the compound. They, after some hesitation, agreed as long as I took full responsibility for the care of the dog. Fair enough. Otto B, *to be*, became the Detachment mascot!

The mother dog had five pups; all female we were told. I had inside information there was one male in the litter, which I (and everyone else) wanted. The guy I was dating was a friend of the guy who owned the dog, and he intervened and got me Otto B., born in October 1968. I picked him up in December after he was weaned from his mother. (I married the guy with the inside track to Otto B's owner in 1970—just a coincidence. Smile!)

Otto B was named after a lieutenant colonel in my office, Otto B. Smith, who always answered the phone with "Otto B here," not LTC Smith – it was always Otto B! A large man with a very jolly laugh, LTC Smith would tease me a lot about how he wanted to court martial me for naming my dog after him. He even brought in five IG (Inspector General) regulation books to taunt me!

We moved to the new WAC Detachment at Long Binh in January 1969. Otto B was very small and loveable, and soon captured everyone's heart, including 1SG Katherine Herney. When I was away, she would spoil him rotten with steak and let him stay in her room overnight or in the orderly room office, supposed to be off limits. She taught him how to sit, shake hands and stay – except he always found me when he heard my voice. We used to joke that Otto B looked like Ho Chi Minh with his whiskers and how skinny he was. The mama-sans, our maids, used to regularly feel him up to see if he was fat enough! Never knew if it was for his health or their next meal.

The first time Otto B heard the alarms going off – the signal to go into the bunkers because of incoming rockets – he went a little crazy. But, the 1SG got him inside a bunker, and he calmed down. From then on, Otto B was usually the first inside the bunker when the alarms sounded. The women in our assigned bunker used to say: "Landry, get your damn dog, so we can get in the bunker!" This meant for me to move Otto B so they could get in.

One day, 1SG Herney wanted to see me. She said, Landry, there has been an accident. Mama-san was washing and spilled bleach on Otto B! I looked down at the white, white dog and said that is *NOT* Otto B; that is Vagina, his sister. The joke was on the 1SG. Her mouth fell wide open at the name "Vagina!" When Otto B heard my voice, he started barking from the Mail Room. 1SG Herney was relieved, but not pleased with taking the brunt of the joke.

When I left Vietnam, I made arrangements, though costly, to take Otto B to the States. I remember well the day he arrived at the Lake Charles Airport in Louisiana. I went to pick him up and, while talking to the baggage attendant, heard Otto B barking. The man looked at me and said, "That dog must belong to you. He has been there five hours and not made a single sound nor relieved himself the entire time!"

Otto B made my time in Vietnam a whole lot less lonely! My family in Louisiana loved him, too, but he remained my dog and listened only to me!

### Gone to the dogs—Tammy gets a collar

Staff Sergeant Edith Efferson, the first supply sergeant, had a small dog named Tammy, who loved attention. It seemed appropriate that Tammy should have a pink, rhinestone collar!

### What was really important?—Donna Lowery

As I look back to my time in Vietnam, I really have difficulty with what was important to our Director. We were sent to Vietnam in Class B uniforms, heels and nylons. Approximately 99% of the Army women were not authorized to carry a weapon. The weapons familiarization course was discontinued before I entered the Army. We were given make-up and ironing classes, though. Appearance was the top priority. I made the front page of the *New York Mirror* because Mr. Daniel, a famous hairdresser, chose to come to Vietnam and do our hair. He was cutting my hair in the picture. All you could see was my rank of Staff Sergeant and my name tag. I am originally from New York. My grandma saw the paper and shared with anyone that would listen that I was on the front page – not because of any accomplishment, but, because I have very good hair.

### They Sure are Friendly—Priscilla Mosby

Specialist 4 Priscilla Mosby explains what it's like to be a WAC in Vietnam. "Well, one thing for sure, the guys sure make you feel wanted. The first day that I arrived at the detachment, I walked to the PX, about two blocks away, and before I got there I had received four ride offers, requests for nine dates, and three proposal of marriage."

Pacific Stars and Stripes, *November 5, 1971, National Archives Record Group 319. Records of the Army Staff, Women's Army Corps, 1945-1978*

### Our Holiday Celebrations in Vietnam—Gail Nelson and Jude McCurdy

I've been having a terrible time writing this story, as I wanted to include stories of all the holidays observed while in Vietnam; however, the problem is I can't remember too many holiday celebrations while there, other than our 30th WAC Anniversary.

After much pondering, I finally remembered the First Sergeant at Headquarters Company, 1st Aviation Brigade, calling me in, handing me a Santa suit and informing me I was chosen to play Santa Claus on their excursion up Route 1 (Ho Chi Minh Trail) to deliver gifts to the orphanages the next day. I do remember the ride.

The next day I dutifully donned the Santa suit, assisted in loading presents in a deuce and a half (2½-ton truck) with my comrades, and we all boarded the truck. Singing Christmas carols in 110-degree heat, we merrily proceeded up the highway to deliver gifts to Amerasian children of war. Not only did we have gifts for the children, but also, from frozen containers somewhere in the truck, ice cream bars appeared. I remember thinking, "How did this happen without the ice cream melting in this heat?" But it did happen.

Of course, the excited children all hugged Santa, and after a bit of entertainment, our group reboarded the truck and proceeded up the highway to visit more orphanages until the vehicle was empty of presents. To me it had been a worthwhile day as the spirit of giving was indeed in full bloom, and the nuns at the orphanages had kept the true meaning of Christmas intact.

For New Year's 1973, at midnight – from the roof of the Iowa billet in Saigon – we watched incoming and outgoing rounds being fired around the perimeter of the city, but I would not call this a celebration. It was more an "Oh, shit!" moment, like how much longer will the defense of the ARVNs hold up, and how much longer before they move us from the center of town into a more protected area? The hope was soon, very soon, as these rockets were getting too damn close for comfort.

When speaking with sister-soldier Sergeant Gail Nelson, who had been in Vietnam for 40 months, I asked her to recall her holiday memories. She stated her memories were also minute. She was, however, able to tell of stuffing turkeys for one Thanksgiving in a trailer at the WAC compound. She said the particular trailer had room for her to stuff the turkeys but the trailer had no oven to cook them. She took the birds over to the 24th Evacuation Hospital mess hall. It was quite an ordeal to get them stuffed, and she really hadn't given much thought to serving anything other than the turkey and stuffing. Thankfully, the 24th mess staff thought of other things to include, and when she was ready to return to the WAC Detachment not only did she have the turkeys and dressing, but all the trimmings to make a real Thanksgiving dinner for the women.

Upon further reflection, Gail remembered that at Christmas, her family sent her lights that she strung between two of the barracks. She laughed telling me that on one Fourth of July, acting silly, she hung lights out she purchased from Sears, along with an Elf, to get a rise from the First Sergeant. Throughout the holiday season packages would arrive, containing small trees and you would see them placed around the area which made the compound a bit festive. But that is about all our memories could fester up.

For myself, I do remember getting a small tree when we were in Saigon and placing it in my room. I'm sure there were the exchange of token gifts for workers and friends, but that really isn't even a memory. All that was certain is we were working 24/7. A celebration dinner, religious service or anything to honor the real meaning of the holiday was completely in our own minds' eyes and our hearts. I guess under the circumstances it was well to suppress such feelings and memories. Logistics could not permit celebrations to happen at this crucial time. The conflict was winding down and the paramount mission was to get the troops home for the holidays and out of the country as soon as possible.

### Christmas in Vietnam—Juana "Jenny" Felix

My first Christmas away from home was in Vietnam, December 1967. I had arrived in Vietnam in March. That Christmas Eve I was the CQ (Charge of Quarters) and we were allowed to call home on a two-way radio (actually it was ham radio operated through the MARS – Military Auxiliary Radio System – a group of licensed amateur radio operators). It was free!

I never knew such happiness than when I spoke to my parents, Jose and Eva Felix, may they rest in peace. We spoke in Spanish mostly although I asked them to speak in English because the operator kept saying, "English!" Not that they did not speak English – my father did speak it well, but my mother was rusty. It just seemed disrespectful not to speak to them in Spanish. Our conversation was not the greatest, because of the operator interruptions and that I had to keep saying, "Roger" each time I finished a sentence, and then had to ask them to say "Roger" every time they finished a sentence. They did not get it. At one point my mother asked, "Que le paso a Roger?" (What happened to Roger?) It was annoying then, but hilarious now and the memory makes me smile.

### 30th WAC Anniversary Luau (1972)—Gail Nelson

Gail Nelson said that when it came to the 30th WAC Anniversary she had heard no rumor of any celebration plans, so she took it upon herself to make a proposal to the Company Commander and First Sergeant and suggested the WAC Detachment hold another Hawaiian luau. Evidently the cadre thought it a good idea, monies were appropriated, wheels were set in motion, and planning for the big event began.

The Unit celebration was posted in the daily bulletin and troops were informed of the pending festivities. Volunteers could sign up and each detachment member was allowed to invite guests. The luau, in celebration of the 30th Anniversary of the Women's Army Corps, would be May 14, on the WAC patio. There would be plenty of food, drinks and a live band. All detachment members were encouraged to attend.

Sergeant Nelson was responsible for locating, purchasing, transporting, inspecting and locating someone to slaughter the pig. She was also responsible for having the pit and spit built and consulting with Veterinary Services regarding the procedures in having the pig inspected for consumption.

A pig was located at the Bien Hoa orphanage. The monies were appropriated for the purchase, and on May 11 the Supply Sergeant, Company Commander, Sergeant Nelson, and SP5 Sandy Torrens headed up Route 1 to Bien Hoa. On their arrival, they were presented with Porky the pig. Sergeant Nelson led the porker to the back of the unit's pickup truck and got it loaded. The pickup was domed in a covered-wagon-type canvas, so the porker would not jump free. Sergeant Nelson – happy with the purchase – got into the back of the truck alongside the prized pig. The Supply Sergeant drove her crew and the pig back to Long Binh to their first stop, the Veterinary Services Office, to have Porky inspected.

Arriving at the Veterinary office, they opened the tarp on the back of the vehicle. At first shocked, then stunned and finally suppressing much laughter they found not the happy little porker who had been led out to the vehicle on a leash, but a much disgruntled pig, and an even more disgruntled Sergeant Nelson, who was covered in pig poop. When the Vet saw the contents of the cargo brought his way he didn't know which to inspect first, Sergeant Nelson or the pig; however, he made the wise choice and chose the pig. He inspected the pig on the spot, and signed off on his inspection. The pig and Sergeant Nelson were reloaded into the truck and the vehicle proceeded to the Engineer Battalion where the pig was to meet its demise.

A good old farm boy had been recruited from the engineer company and agreed to slaughter and clean the animal. He then had the pig inspected by the Vet once again, and the animal was placed in one of the Engineer Battalion freezers until it could be prepped and readied for the spit.

In the interim, Sergeant Nelson returned to the WAC compound. Gail said, "I just stripped outside the shower, mama-san took the clothes away and I jumped into the shower, washed my body, my hair, became sparkling clean, and I proudly walked *au naturel* back to my room and got dressed."

The engineers had been recruited to dig a hole between the barracks and the WAC patio. The hole had to be at least one foot larger in all directions than the actual size of the pig and at least three feet deep. The addition of diced potatoes and onions wrapped in aluminum foil had to be taken into consideration when the engineers determined the depth of the hole they were digging.

Once the pit was dug, it was lined in stone to even out and hold the heat. Next, braces for the spit were put in place and the fire was built. The prepared pig was placed on the spit rod, and an apple placed in its mouth to enable the heat to go completely through the roasting pig. For 26 hours, this pig turned on the spit until it was time to serve it for dinner. Lucky there was a jeep trailer parked right beside the pit, loaded with iced beers to aid the workers in their spit-turning duties. Sergeant Nelson said, "After a while, and a few beers it was no effort at all, and the 26 hours of spit-turning just flew on by."

But that was not the only thing that flew on by. That evening we were subjected to a rocket attack, and since they had hit the electrical plant, the entire compound was left in darkness except for the glow of the pig pit. As I look back on that evening, the only vision I saw returning to my room was the silhouette of the spit turners against the light of the fire's embers in the night.

The next morning, Nancy Anderson and I had hair appointments. So off we headed to the beauty shop to look our best for the party; however, upon our arrival we were told by the beauticians all the electricity was still off. We decided to proceed with our appointments and if need be we would sit out in the sun and let our hair, set in curlers, dry out via the sun. We would deal with the rest after our hair was dry. Halfway through the drying process, the beauty shop received a call from the WAC Detachment that their electricity had been restored. So, we helped the beauticians pack up the tools of their trade and we marched on back to the WAC Detachment to be made beautiful.

Once beautified, we went to the patio, cut potatoes and onions, wrapped them in foil and placed them on the fire for the evening event. And, what an event it turned out to be!

We ate, drank and were merry for sure; many danced while Casey Cassin's Top Ten was played by a band of boys with a slight Vietnamese twang . . . actually it was quite funny. But, with each drink, their English seemed to improve. Yes, Ber-a-ma-ha was a Bull Bog. . . . Right, Gail?

### Making the Rounds in Jessie's Jalopy—Jessie Brewer

Dietitians were not included in the Table of Organization and Equipment in Vietnam. There were three of us: a Food Service Officer (warrant officer), a Food Service NCO, and my position, Dietitian. All three positions were assigned to the S4 (Logistics). When the three of us moved from the S4 office, we operated as a separate entity directly under the Executive Officer.

Of course, we had no equipment or vehicle. We only traveled to the medical units via air, but needed transportation in and around Da Nang. Warrant officers have a "brotherhood" type of relationship. My warrant visited the disposal yard and got the warrant officer in charge of the disposal unit to piece together destroyed jeeps to make a running jeep not on the "books." It was common for vehicles to have names painted on them. I decided we would have a jeep-naming contest, and the

*Major Brewer's jeep in Vietnam*

winner would receive a bottle of champagne. Jessie's Jalopy was the winner. The picture of me in the jeep is from the naming party at the 67th Medical Group Headquarters. It was the only jeep I saw with white upholstery in Vietnam. Soldiers coming to the Group Headquarters for various reasons used the jeep to go to the PX in Da Nang. Often Marines would whistle at them so they always tried to borrow one of the other jeeps at Headquarters instead of mine.

### *Chief of Pop and Beer Supplies—Joyce Harker (Saitta)*

The pop and beer runs were always challenging. When the Detachment needed pop I would go with our papa-san (Vietnamese driver) in the old Scout (SUV) that we had. We would go to all of the Base Exchanges on Long Binh to purchase the cases. I would stop soldiers and ask if they were going to buy any soda that day. If not I would ask if they would go through the line to pick up cases for me. I would hand them the money and then wait for them to bring them back. I think they could only buy one or two cases at a time, so I would have to talk to a lot of guys to buy as much as I could at each site. Poor papa-san, I drove him crazy. When we got done, the back seat and any open area was stacked to the roof with cases of soda pop. I had cases under my feet and sat on a case to hold the cases in the back from coming forward.

For the beer runs I obviously needed a larger vehicle. So after collecting everyone's ration cards, I would pick up our 4-door Dodge truck (which was in bad shape) and head out with a military driver to II Field Force to purchase the beer. We would load two pallets of beer in the back, and then stack the rest of the cases along the sides of the pallets and in the back seat. It is a wonder that the old truck made it back to the detachment, and not once did it break down.

### *Leaving Vietnam—Elizabeth "Dee" M. Barrett*

The withdrawal of Navy forces from in country after the cease-fire was relatively smooth. As we were mainly "tenants" facility-wise it was a matter of accounting for physical assets and either shipping them out of the country or turning them over to Vietnamese counterparts and rotating personnel back to the States. Those in the outlying areas went first, and the "paper pushers" in Saigon last. I was originally scheduled to depart Vietnam March 23 but was delayed when the freeze on troop withdrawal went into effect because of North Vietnam halting the prisoner exchange. I received special permission to leave on March 26 (about 10 hours before the freeze was lifted) because my father had died while I was in Vietnam and his house had to be cleared out by March 31 as it had been sold. There were only 10 people on the plane when I left Saigon (we picked up another 32 in Okinawa) so it was a very comfortable trip to Travis Air Force Base. Because of the time change, I arrived before I left!

### Long Binh to Saigon, The Last Days—Judith McCurdy

Upon my return from R&R in August 1972, I learned that Long Binh was closing and that my unit, part of 1ˢᵗ Signal Brigade, would return its colors to Korea. With this development, I was free to job hunt. What a blessing! I heard 1ˢᵗ Aviation Brigade was looking for a Congressional NCO and Personnel Actions person. Since I handled both these jobs while with the Advanced Weapons Support Command in Germany, I had only to convince the warrant officer hiring for the position that I was the person he needed. The interview went well. I was hired and transferred to Headquarters Company, 1ˢᵗ Aviation Brigade. When Long Binh closed in September 1972, I happily went to Saigon with 1ˢᵗ Aviation to work out of MACV Annex, known as Dodge City. The new living arrangements were certainly different from anything I had encountered in past assignments.

Twelve enlisted women transferred from Long Binh to Saigon after the WAC Detachment closed. We were billeted at the Iowa BEQ on Truong Minh Ky Street, not far from 3ʳᵈ Field Hospital. Sounds plush? Not quite! The rooms were adequate, with a paddle fan that produced two revolutions per minute. It was hot as hell and not as conducive to sleeping as the air-conditioned barracks we had left in Long Binh. The pollution generated by civilian and military vehicles in the city streets was everywhere, and fresh air was nowhere.

Across the street from the BEQ was a beautiful Catholic church, and right beside it was a house of ill repute. We spent free time after work on the rooftop of the BEQ where we cooked meals on a grill, played cards with our male counterparts, or just talked. I guess the women "working" across the street thought the "round eyes" were taking business away from their trade, because as we found out, they truly detested us.

When we got out of work, our practice was to purchase French bread from a mama-san who always had her pushcart positioned across the street from our BEQ. But our method of purchase would change. Rather than exiting our jeep on the street in front of the BEQ, we were forced to exit behind the wall that protected the BEQ. I would then peek out from behind the wall getting mama-san's attention by calling her and hold up the number of fingers indicating how many loaves of bread I wished to purchase. Mama-san would hold up her hand in a halting fashion and scamper off with her cart, to a new position. She would then yell, "GI girl. You come!" And with money at the ready, I would take off sprinting across the street, reaching out with one hand to pay her. And with timely precision, mama-san would take the money and place the bread in my chest so as to fall in my arms, as though I were an NFL running back. I would then sprint back, as fast as possible, to the BEQ while dodging waves of green coke bottles propelled at me from balconies by the prostitutes. At the end of my run, Truong Minh Ky Street would be littered with broken green glass. And as the crowd of onlookers cheered, I would be rejoined by my peers and we would head upstairs to prepare dinner.

Since this was a daily occurrence, spectators grew and the transaction became smoother. We could only laugh. This really infuriated the prostitutes since the white mice (Saigon police) became involved and would make them clean up the street of broken glass after each run. I was constantly asked, "If you got hit by a flying coke bottle, would that count for a purple heart?" Technically, I would have been hit by enemy fire while in a war zone. But, how would I explain the medal to my mother?

I spent New Year's Eve 1972 on the roof of the BEQ with friends watching incoming and outgoing rounds fired from around the city's perimeter. A bit scary and certainly no celebration! The Viet Cong were getting very close, and the conflict was escalating. What was going on with the Peace talks? We could only wonder.

Then, on January 27, 1973, the Paris Peace Accords were signed. The Accords included a ceasefire throughout Vietnam, agreed on and signed by the North Vietnamese and the United States. The South Vietnamese were against recognizing the Viet Cong as a legitimate participant in the discussion to end the war. Therefore, the Viet Cong were presented with a separate Accord. In addition to the ceasefire, the United States agreed to withdraw all US troops and advisors (totaling about 23,700). Further, they were tasked with dismantling all the US bases within 60 days. In return, the North Vietnamese agreed to release all US and other prisoners of war.

Our involvement in Vietnam was ending, and the 1st Aviation Brigade was now on the fast track to exit the country. Since more than half the personnel assigned in country at that time were part of my Brigade, there was much work to do, and it had to be achieved with perfection. The requirement for flawless logistical coordination to move so many troops, along with so much materials and equipment, so fast was not overemphasized.

I remember one afternoon walking to the office and seeing a small fixed-wing aircraft circling Saigon, dropping papers from the sky. I picked up one to read, but it was in Vietnamese. I immediately went to my office where a

Vietnamese National interpreted the writing. Miss Kim said the flyer was announcing to the people of South Vietnam that peace had finally come to them. It explained that the Accords had been signed and under its conditions, the majority of foreign occupants would be leaving the country within the next 60 days. She said the people of South Vietnam were encouraged to inform rogue foreigners (AWOLs) of this action and that the soldiers should be told to report to their nearest military installation or embassy for processing – to be placed on manifests to return home. The people were also asked to report the location of any AWOL US military person to the proper authorities.

This became a paramount problem for the Military Police. As I explained in my article in "Consequences of War," heroin that troops were hooked on in Vietnam was pure. If the person had no desire to get clean, they knew there was absolutely no way they could support such an intense habit stateside.

In March 1973, I said goodbye to a people who I feared were about to lose their freedoms. And, with a heaviness in my heart, I boarded the Freedom Bird that would take me to my home.

WAC Detachment members were the only American group ever allowed to tour the South Vietnamese President's Palace in Saigon (President Nguyen Van Thieu). The Palace was extremely elegant, filled with beautiful art work much like you would see in a museum.

# Chapter Sixteen

# SONGS AND POEMS

### "The Women of Vietnam"
*Music and lyrics by Claire Starnes*
*Vietnam Women Veterans Co-founder. ©May 1999*

A war was raging in a far-away land
In a country known as Vietnam
The boys out there need your help, they said.
So, we answered the call and off we went.

> *Refrain—*
> We're the women of Vietnam
> Though few know we were there
> Let's shout it out for the world to hear
> We're proud veterans of Vietnam

We arrived in country full of awe and some fear
Didn't know the battles were so near.
We gave support to our fighting men
In a hell no one else can understand.

> *Repeat Refrain—*

We served our year; some did more
Praying hard the next round wouldn't find us.
Lost more than our youth in that war
We lost brothers and sisters, most of us.

***Bootleggers of Old Long Binh*—Sarah F. Niblack, Shirley Heinze, Evelyn "Pat" Foote, Alice Hampson, and Ann Wansley (Mary Jane Grimes replaced Shirley Heinze in 1967.)**
*From the Sarah Niblack Collection, US Army Women's Museum*
*These seven songs are the entire Bootleggers' songbook.*

The five of us, Sarah F. Niblack, Shirley Heinze, Evelyn "Pat" Foote, Alice Hampson and Ann Wansley were the first WAC staff officers to be assigned to Long Binh in 1967. No BOQs were available for female personnel, so we were assigned quarters in the building formerly used for construction workers. The building was what they called "jungle construction" with its slated walls screened for ventilation. It was not a palace, but we made do with what we had. Our duty uniform was jungle fatigues and combat boots. Not long after our arrival, we determined the boots left marks on our legs and thus the term "bootleggers."

Now get ready to be entertained by talented Army women telling their stories of Vietnam in song:

# WAC Songs of Long Binh
by Evelyn "Pat" Foote and Alice Hampson

## Song # 1
***"Let's All Move to Long Binh"*** **(Tune: "Let Me Call You Sweetheart")**
Let's all move to Long Binh, it's a lovely place.
You'll get used to dust storms, and mud on your face.
Charlie flings in mortars at a furious pace,
At Long Binh, our new quarters—Life is full of grace!

USARV is moving from old Tan Son Nhut,
No one knows the time or place, or gives a hoot.
Of one thing I am certain, when we make the change.
The Long Binh ammo dump will blow—Charlie's got our range!

Long Binh ain't fit living—for this city girl.
Long Binh ain't fit living—for this city girl.

# Song # 2

***"Long Binh is Wonderful"*** **(Tune: "Glow Little Glow Worm")**

Long Binh is wonderful, how we love it.
The climate is awful, but we rise above it.
As WAC bootleggers and ladies fair,
We don't mind the dust or the rain in our hair,
Or artillery shells bursting loudly behind us,
And midnight alerts that help to remind us
A war's going on in this part of the world…
It's a great life for a girl!

# Song # 3

***"I'll Love It at Long Binh"*** **(Tune: "That Old Mountain Dew")**

I'll love it at Long Binh, you can bet.
For combat zone living, I'm set.
So I'll hone up my swords,
Don fatigues, pack my cords,
And earn that hostile fire pay that I get.

# Song # 4

***"The Royal Flush"***

General Cole, DCS (P&A),
    Answered nature's call one day.
While in the VIP latrine
    A forklift came upon the scene
It raised that john into the air,
    And to the General's great despair
Started off down the road… Started off down the road.

The forklift driver didn't know
    What he was hauling as cargo.
But many in headquarters saw
    This drama, and they watched in awe
The general's most unusual ride,
    As forklift swung from side to side
That ill-starred latrine… That ill-starred latrine.

But soon the forklift driver heard
    The anguished cries, the general's words.
He stopped his forklift, dropped latrine,
    And Cole popped out upon the scene.
Then as the general stalked away,
    The forklift driver heard him say,
Cole is Airborne all the way… Cole is Airborne all the way.

# Song # 5

**"Beautiful Long Binh" (Tune: "Beautiful Dreamer")**
Beautiful Long Binh, beckons to you.
Monsoons and dust storms and tons of mildew.
Acres of nothing. Oceans of mud.
Who picked the location sure picked us a dud.

Beautiful Long Binh, USARV's home.
With no hesitation from you I would roam,
Right back to old Saigon, the Orient's pearl.
Long Binh ain't fit living—for this city girl.
Long Binh ain't fit living—for this city girl.

# Song # 6

**"The D.T.U. Lament" (Tune: "Green Berets")**
U.S Army, Vietnam,
Has got us in an awful jam.
With Colonel Hoisington who storms,
At our damn trashy uniforms!

    *Chorus—*
    Jungle boots upon our feet,
    Baggy fatigues that don't look neat,
    We'd gladly brave the dust and boards,
    If Cole would let us wear our cute green cords.

When Colonel H. saw what we wore,
She ranted, raved, she stomped and swore.
At our fatigues and jungle shoes,
And to wear such, she did refuse.

*Repeat Chorus—*

Back at home, our leader stews,
About our OD pants and shoes.
She thinks we're ruined,
And that's a fact.
While in the job of a combat WAC.

*Repeat Chorus—*

# Song # 7
## "WACs Don't Dress Pretty" (Tune: "Cockles and Mussels")
## Dedicated to Shirley T. Heinze
In old Long Binh city,
The WACs don't dress pretty.
They all have to wear jungle boots and fatigues.
The fellows make light of
The terrible plight of
These ladies, sad ladies,
Done in by intrigues.

~~~~

Yet the Red Cross and DACs *
Do not wear OD slacks.
They wear dresses or skirts,
Heels and hose, use cologne.
But to us Tabor said,
Feminity's dead,
WACs are one of the boys
While in this combat zone!

~~~~

The inequity of it
Makes all of us covet
The different status of Red Cross and DACs.*
But we will persevere
Col Heinze, never fear.
Baggy pants, muddy boots,
We're still proud to be WACs

~~~~

585

At the Army War College,
Colonel Heinze will excel.
She'll convince all them fellers,
She knows strategy well.

~~~~

Multilateral treaties,
Militarily viewed,
Will not scare this WAC leader.
They'll be cranial food.

~~~~

For she loves knotty problems,
Controversy adores.
Likes to bait stodgy thinkers,
Can expound on all wars.

~~~~

She's conversant on Russia,
China, Poland and France.
All those fellers won't snow her,
With their male song and dance.

~~~~

They'll be awed by her wisdom,
Overcome by her charms.
Sure, they'll make her a member,
Of their own combat arms.

~~~~

And, when she's graduated,
I'm sure no one will laugh.
When she's quickly appointed
FIRST-WOMAN-CHIEF-OF-STAFF!

* DACs – Department of Army Civilians

# Poem Collection

Many of the women wrote poetry, some while they were in country and some many years later. Dealing with memories and issues that are with them every day can be overwhelming and the poetry is one way they can find an outlet. Here are a few of the many submitted.

## Reflections from a WAC

by Cheranne "Cheri" Asmus (Halsey)
Written while at Long Binh, 1967

The combat zone is far from home.
There is a job for you alone.
Courage in the midst of fear
Never knowing if you'll see next year.
A newfound friend to share the day.
Loneliness just a breath away.
Mortar firing in the night.
Flares that light the sky so bright.
Mama-sans to shine your shoes.
For time is precious, there's none to lose.
There's always something to be done
But, even here, there's time for fun.
The path for you will not lead North
But, still the WAC must prove her worth.
And if I do nothing else worthwhile today,
At least I pray
That all who pay the final price
Make freedom closer come tomorrow's day.

## The Other World

*by Donna M. Loring*

I stepped off the "Freedom Bird" into another world.
A world of profound beauty and yet a world of desolation and despair.

Just as a new born babe comes into the world so came I...
into a world I knew nothing of unto a people I knew nothing of.

Why was I here?

I walked down the war-torn streets of the village
not knowing the answer.

As I walked, I looked down and saw the tattered remains of a newspaper...
and on the front page a picture of a man holding
the lifeless body of his infant son.

There was emptiness in his eyes as tears of a lifetime flowed down his face.

In that instant I knew the answer.

I was here to help save this country--
this other world

And in so doing,
**save mine...**

## I Forgot
*by Doris "Lucki" Allen*

The longer I waited for the reunion conference, the more I remember just how much I forgot. I forgot because of my road-blocked brain. My Vietnam-time brain-road had so many stopovers.

I FORGOT...
The reason I went to Vietnam.

I FORGOT...
For just a moment, to thank God for my safe return from that combat zone.

I FORGOT...
How I actually enjoyed working from sunup to sundown.
Sometimes, working for 18 or 22 hours a day was so rewarding.

I FORGOT...
How much it mattered whether a Viet Cong soldier was killed,

Or whether it was an American soldier who lost his battle.
All dead people are dead!

I FORGOT...
How many of my acquaintances and a few of my friends left me at the "office" – never to return.
Some were caught in ambush. Some were wounded by sniper fire.
A 122mm rocket blew up the hootch of five of my guys.
Some were wounded and never returned to my road-blocked brain.
My Vietnam-time brain-road had so many stopovers.

I FORGOT...
How many times I went to the bunker; it was supposed to get me out of harm's way.
I forgot the time the CO had to come to my room, shake me awake
And remind me that whenever the incoming alarm sounded, I was to go to the bunker.
(I remember that I remembered to take my cigarettes and bottle even though I forgot my flak jacket.)
I even forgot who brought me that fifth of Crown Royal every day!

I FORGOT...
So much. I've even forgotten what I forgot.

*But, wonder of wonders!*

I NEVER FORGOT...
My friends. I know that those friendships were forged in the heat of battle.

I NEVER FORGOT...
Grendel and Joanne and Mickey and Effie and Marion C and Betty B and Mary Jo and Betty T.

I NEVER FORGOT...
The Shirleys, the Marys, the Joanies, the Donnas, the Claires, the Pats, the Annas, nor the Lauras.
They are forever here in my heart. They help me through the nightmares and PTSD.

And the very moment that I recognize a sad period approaching, I call on my Vietnam sisters who help me through my Vietnam time. And, at least one or two of you were always at one of those stopovers on my Vietnam-time road.

And now I get a chance to offer my sincere thanks to all of my sisters. Thanks for listening when I tried to be "mama," and thanks for ignoring me when you thought it best.
Thanks for inviting me to enjoy a swim with you in our little backyard pool.
Thanks for being my friend. THANKS for being my friend!

## And the War Goes On
*by Karen Offutt, ©1999*

Don't show them you're afraid.
Smile - get on the plane.
Go on over there, wherever "there" is.
You'll probably come back.
I don't feel like I'll come back.
I'm scared 'cause ahead is the unknown.
My family is crying. They're making this worse.
Go home. Let me do this. I have to.
Long flight. I'm tired.
Already miss my brother - my best friend.
I'll show my parents I am strong and brave
And I can do anything a boy can do.
Plane full of men - no women.
What am I doing?
What am I trying to prove?
You know it won't be good enough anyway.
You'll die and it still won't be good enough.
They'll say, "We told her not to go.
We told her to marry, stay home and sew,
Raise babies and take care of a man."
Act like a girl! What's wrong with you?
Finally, I am here, but I don't know where.
I want to go home, but I can't.
Need to sleep, try to figure this out.

Pick a bed, any bed, not that bed, this one.
Monsoon rains pouring outside and in the room.
Hitting metal pans with giant "plunk, plunk, plunks."
Everything is hot and the earth as red as blood.
Click your heels together and you'll be home.
You are home, silly girl. Rest now.
What's wrong?
Being hit with powerful concussions
As though a giant's fists are pounding.
My bed is shaking and I'm afraid,
More afraid than I've ever been.
There is nowhere to hide or run.
Someone says there's a bunker somewhere.
What's a bunker? Where is it?
I'm lost and new here. Why won't anyone help me?
I am paralyzed in my little bed.
It continues all night.
I wait to die. Well, this is why you came.
Give your life for your country.
Make them proud, as they drape the flag
Over your empty casket, because you're in pieces
Somewhere, in a place far away from home.
Pray. Tell God to let your family know you loved them.
Prepare to die. I am 19. I haven't learned how to live. And
I don't know how to die.
How do I do this right? Can't I do this one thing right?
Fall asleep from the drumbeat. It pounds steadily.
It's louder than my heart. What music is that?
It's rocket and mortar - a symphony
It's the music of war.
How can I sleep while someone is trying to kill me?
This is insane.
I awake and it's morning. The music has stopped.
I am alive. I am dead. I am a kid. I am old.
Home EC, Honor's Biology, Basic Training -
All worthless. No class prepared me for this.
Naked children playing in mud.
Beer can and cardboard houses.

Children selling their sisters to soldiers.
Working 6 A.M. to 6 P.M.
What a way to make a living!
Children touching my skin,
Teenage girls feeling my eyelashes,
GIs taking my picture.
Strange sounds, penetrating smells that will never leave.
Snipers firing, barely missing my head.
Don't flick your lighter – it'll explode.
Don't pick the kids up - they may be booby-trapped.
Claymores and barbed wire, mama-sans and black pajamas.
Time to go home. But, I am home.
I don't want to leave. I'm on the edge of life and death.
Fear and excitement mix. Pride and guilt intermingle.
I'm confused again - still.
Parents meet me at the airport. Seems they think
I've been on vacation. They have suffered they say.
Mom shows me her white hair and her limp
Caused by a tumor pressing on her uterus.
I feel guilty. I have failed again,
I haven't brought them honor - only pain.
Why didn't I die there?
Maybe I can go back and try again.
What am I afraid of? Of not measuring up?
Of not doing life right, even though there
Seems to be no "right" way of doing it?
Afraid to die, but wishing I could, quickly, painlessly.
Scared of not being loved. Frightened of the dark
When all the bad people out there
Wanted to hurt someone with their war toys and evil hearts.
Afraid of myself and the rage inside.
Afraid of the dark side of myself,
And the war words that can come from within
To push others away so that I am alone
As I deserve to be. Alone and afraid.
Afraid to live, afraid to die.
That year of war changed me.
Made me see the evil in mankind.

Took my youth and trust and naivety
Grounding them into the red mud of Vietnam.
You can't see the scars. I look as good as new.
But the scars are there - within.
Vietnam is alive.
And the war goes on . . .

## A Healing Time
*by Patricia Babcock (Schmauch), ©May 30, 1998*

Since July 3, 1965, the beginning
There have been tears and sorrow.

Since March 28, 1973, the end
We hoped to dry the tears
and lessen the sorrow.

A war of purpose holds honor
In the tears and sorrows,
and never to be forgotten.
A war of failure
there is only "Why?"
and "Let it be forgotten."

We will never forget, we can't.
Our tears and sorrows are so deep.

We gave honor and duty and all that we had
We wished only for honor in return.

"Time will heal." That's what some say
Time for healing will someday be.

One decade, two decades, we wait.
Three decades, will it take?

A dream of a dedication has begun
That dream has a date.

"The Wall That Heals" has been built
For all the souls, and tears and sorrows.

And now, we are so honored
To share our tears and be healed.

## Memories
*by Nora H. Lebron*

Memories are so vague,
I can't remember what happened yesterday,
But, there are memories that last to your dying day

On 4 February 1970 I went to Vietnam
And, for the life of me I don't know why, except to say
That I wanted to see firsthand what so many people
were talking about

While there I cried and cried
When I saw the dead bodies of young men go by

I did my work, and I did it well
I worked so hard, so that I could sleep at night.

Feelings of loneliness were the hardest to bear is all I can say
But they were worse when I arrived in the USA
No one to talk to, to tell how I felt
No one to share my memories with

No one cared

## Youth in Asia
*by Peggy Roberts*
**Dedicated to Aida "Rootzie" Ruiz**

Grey-white smoke
Slips and slides
Out from under big bellied planes
Forming crescent shaped markers
Filling a once blue sky

## Ten Thousand Eagles
*by Donna M. Loring*

Ten thousand eagles flew that day across the bright blue sky
to meet the spirits on their way from fiery smoke filled tombs.

They soared above the dark, black clouds billowing from the earth
and hovered for a moment there and saw the face of doom.

Ten thousand eagles gathered and swooped down beneath the clouds.

They found the spirits one by one and plucked them from their plight.
They carried each new spirit through the black and hate-filled clouds.

They gave them each a shelter wrapped in warm wings oh so tight.
They gave them strength and comfort too on their unexpected flight.

On swift wings they flew towards their final destination where each spirit
knew without any hesitation there would be peace and love and harmony.

They would forever be wrapped
within the eagles' wings through all eternity.

Ten thousand eagles flew that day as all the world stood still
and watched in shock and horror as the tragedy unfurled.

Now we are left here on this earth to face the billowing clouds
and our eyes search for the eagles as we say our prayers out loud.

May our spirits soar on eagles' wings above the dark black clouds
of hatred, murder and revenge that keep us hatred bound.

Ten thousand eagles flew that day as all the world stood still.
The eagles flew above those clouds. Perhaps someday...we will.

# Chapter Seventeen

# VIETNAM WOMEN VETERANS
# CONFERENCES

*Compiled by Betty Jean Stallings and Donna A. Lowery*
*Images provided by Vietnam Women Veterans, Inc.*

## 1999: Olympia, Washington

November 10-13, 1999: Olympia, WA, hosted the first-ever Vietnam Women Veterans (VWV) conference for military women, recognizing that many who served were not nurses. The 124 women who gathered for the conference represented four services: Air Force, Army, Marine Corps and Navy.

November 10: A large group representing VWV participated in a ceremony honoring veterans at the Vietnam Memorial on the Capitol grounds. Though it was pouring, our women stood proudly throughout the event as they were recognized as Vietnam veterans for the first time.

The conference officially began the evening of November 10 with a Joint Opening Ceremony. Brigadier General Sherian Cadoria, US Army Retired, gave the opening speech. Her message that we "have a special bond which should never be severed" was well received with cheers from the women. Following were greetings from 24 representatives from Washington State and local governmental and service organizations and a Vietnamese delegation. This marked the first time this group of women was officially told "Thank you" and "Welcome Home."

November 11: Because of the constant rain, the state Veterans Day event was moved inside the Rotunda of the Capitol building. At 11 a.m., the VWV took its place for the first time as an official organization among other veterans groups to honor all veterans.

That afternoon, the VWV held its own Memorial Service inside the Rotunda. This was probably the most emotional event of the conference as we remembered those who had died since Vietnam. The Candlelight Tribute was performed by representatives of the four armed services.

Following the Memorial, the Ladies Auxiliary of VFW Post 318 hosted dinner for more than a hundred of our women and their guests.

November 12: Joan Furey, director of the Center for Women Veterans, Department of Veterans Affairs, Washington, DC, opened the seminar portion of the conference. Concurrent with the seminars were the Health Care Fair, VA registration, and domestic violence one-on-one counseling. Also on hand was a VA expert on PTSD.

That evening was time to relax and have fun. The barbecue took place in the hotel's ballroom. With no agenda to follow, the evening was free-flowing. Many memories were shared and new ones made. Several participants took to the podium in impromptu sessions.

November 13: Sightseeing day, and time to reminisce, share photos and just have fun.

The Closing Banquet was held in the hotel's ballroom. Throughout the conference, emphasis was placed on including young people. They were runners and escorts. They helped the women with assigned tasks, to include setting up the ballrooms. This night was no different. Civil Air Patrol cadets and US Naval Sea cadets presented the colors then took their seats among the women for the dinner. Guest speaker was BG Evelyn "Pat" Foote, US Army Retired, who shared her personal recollections of her time in Vietnam. Most everyone in the audience identified with her experiences – some hilariously funny, others tragically sad. After several other speakers, toasts, and presentations, the conference ended with the Colors retired for the last time of this historical conference.

This conference's success was due in large part to the efforts of the WA State Department of Veterans Affairs Deputy Director, Command Sergeant Major John E. Lee (USA, Ret) and Tom Schumacher, USAF veteran, PTSD expert, WA State Department of Veterans Affairs.

# Reflections

*by Linda S. Earls*
*Written for the First Vietnam Women's Homecoming Conference, Olympia, WA,*
*November 1999*

Our gathering here today is long overdue.
We're finally seeing old friends and making new.

We the women who served in Vietnam
Have a special understanding, a special bond.

We must not allow history to forget
The sacrifices we made, the challenges we met.

Some remember with smiles, some with tears
Those difficult times, those tumultuous years.

The nights spent in the bunkers very hot and damp
With spiders, rats and roaches we did camp.

The long days of work though we were tired,
The scream of sirens, the sound of machine guns, the rockets being fired.

For the R&R in Penang, Bangkok, Hong Kong,
Sydney, Singapore or Hawaii we did long.

Waiting for mail call with hope in our hearts
For a letter or package from those far apart.

Hitching rides on choppers, watching bombs in the valley below
These things we did for entertainment, you know.

The sights and sounds, the experiences we had
Are now only memories whether good or bad.

As we look around at faces here today
We see some are missing, some have gone away.

They may be gone but their spirits live on,
We'll make sure they do even after we're gone.

Each of our lives has been changed in some way
By our service and the debt we chose to pay.

We served with dignity, bravery and pride,
We remember now with nothing to hide.

## 2001: San Antonio, Texas

September 25-29, 2001: San Antonio – one of America's most historic cities – was a fantastic backdrop for the second conference. Noted for its famed Riverwalk, five Franciscan missions, the five-time NBA Champion San Antonio Spurs, five universities, and four community colleges, San Antonio is a mecca for tourists from around the world.

Shortly after the horrific events of 9/11, there was talk of cancelling it, but contracts had been let, plane tickets had been purchased, and about 90 enthusiastic attendees were coming and were looking forward to renewing friendships.

The historic Sheraton-Gunter Hotel had been selected. Because of the events of 9/11, only two weeks earlier, some women cancelled, but the hotel staff and management appreciated having the conference take place as scheduled and were generous about adjusting costs. The Riverwalk provided an entertaining and relaxing experience for conference attendees, momentarily setting aside thoughts of 9/11.

The Opening Ceremony featured Major General Daniel James III, Air National Guard, Texas Adjutant General. We did not know at the time he accepted the invitation to be our key speaker that he was the son of General "Chappie" James, the famous Air Force fighter pilot.

One of the key events was an all-day health fair/workshop. Panel discussions included information on Agent Orange, Posttraumatic Stress Disorder (PTSD), Hepatitis C and other service claims.

Dr. Linda Spoonster Schwartz, chair of the Vietnam Veterans of America Committee on Health and an Air Force nurse in Vietnam, led a discussion on Agent Orange effects and veterans' entitlements. Counselors from the Veterans Center were on-hand and available to talk with members.

The only female surgeon in Vietnam, Dr. Janice Mendelson, AMC, Colonel, US Army Retired, told of her experiences in Vietnam, and Brigadier General Wilma L. Vaught reported on the status of WIMSA (Women in Military Service for America).

Many items were donated for a Silent Auction from members and local businesses, including the River Art Group Gallery of San Antonio. Proceeds from the auction helped defray expenses. The Silent Auction has become a regular event at each of the conferences.

## 2003: Washington, DC

November 9-11, 2003: With part of the ceremonies at Arlington, VA, and part in Washington, DC, the attendees stayed busy. Most of the events took place in conjunction with the celebration of the 10th Anniversary of the Vietnam Women's Memorial. Vietnam Women Veterans set up a table on the East Knoll along Constitution

Wreath Laying Ceremony: (l-r) Sandra Spatz Wiszneauckas, Maryna Misiewicz, Cheranne Asmus Halsey, Marsha "Cricket" Holder, Precilla Landry Wilkewitz, Claire Brisebois Starnes

Avenue in Washington, DC, and members spent the day educating people about the role military women who were not nurses played in Vietnam. Many people were unaware that there had been other military women in Vietnam and did not realize the extent of their numbers and roles in country.

Sunday, November 9, included a non-denominational Memorial Service at the National City Christian Church in celebration of the service of women during the Vietnam era.

After the VWV business meeting, our women had the opportunity to attend the play "A Piece of My Heart" presented at the Women in Military Service for America (WIMSA) Memorial.

On November 10, our women were invited to give interviews as part of the Library of Congress Veterans History Project Oral History. These oral histories became part of the collection of the American Folklife Center of the Library of Congress.

A celebration luncheon featured veterans from all services, from all eras. The Keynote Speaker was Ms. Cokie Roberts, noted journalist and author of "We Are Our Mothers' Daughters."

Later there were readings at the Wall, sponsored by Circle of Sisters, and a Candlelight March and Ceremony followed by a Native American Round Dance by the Navajo Nation at the Vietnam Women's Memorial. The evening concluded with "A Rock 'n' Roll Reunion" DMZ to Delta dance.

The highlight of the conference was on Veterans' Day when the VWV, for the first time, participated in events that previously were attended only by other veterans groups. Throughout the day, stories of the women represented by the Vietnam Women's Monument came to life as Vietnam veterans shared their experiences in their own voices. Our members also took part in the Reading of the Deceased while three of our women laid a wreath at the monument. In addition, for the first time ever, the women took part in the parade of female veterans to the Vietnam Women's Monument. Our group

Laura Pariseau and quilt

marched under our own banner and had our own color guard. Later, that afternoon, one of our members helped lay a wreath at WIMSA, ending the conference.

There was discussion of dissolving the organization but the majority voted to continue and officers were elected. Marty Misiewicz was elected president.

On display was a colorful, storyboard Vietnam Women's quilt, made by Glenda Storni Graebe. The quilt, which honors women Vietnam veterans, is on display at the US Army Women's Museum at Fort Lee, VA. Chapter 14 explains several of the panels.

# 2005: Biloxi, MS

The conference was scheduled for Biloxi, MS, in 2005. However, Hurricane Katrina caused extensive damage to the area and the conference was cancelled.

# 2008: Branson, MO

VIETNAM WOMEN VETERANS CONFERENCE
BRANSON, MISSOURI · MAY 23, 2008

May 22-24, 2008: Speakers at the fourth conference included Dr. Betty Moseley-Brown, Associate Director of the Center for Women Veterans with the Veterans Administration; Sherril Sego, MSN, FNP-C, Lead Women's Program Manager with the Department. of Veterans Affairs in Kansas; and retired Vice Admiral Patricia A. Tracey, first female Vice Admiral.

The conference attendees had an opportunity to talk with all the speakers who were there for at least one meal with time before and after.

Officers were elected for the next two years: Marty Misiewicz, President; Nancy Jurgevich, 1st Vice President; Aurora Toth, 2nd Vice President; Ren Stoabs Karr, Secretary; and Precilla Wilkewitz, Treasurer. Handouts included a special edition of the VFW magazine titled "Women at War – from the Revolutionary War to the Present," dated March 2008.

There were probably fewer than 50 people registered for the VWV events but everything was well planned and all attendees enjoyed the festivities.

## 2010: Branson, MO

April 29 – May 2, 2010: The Conference site was the Grand Plaza Hotel and 51 people attended. There was a permanent Hospitality room just off the lobby that was well stocked with snacks, beer and wine. Each attendee received two tote bags filled with goodies.

Elected officers present

VIETNAM WOMEN VETERANS REUNION
BRANSON, MISSOURI · MAY 1, 2010

were Acting President Nancy Jurgevich, 2nd Vice President Aurora Toth, and Secretary Ren Karr. Other officers (President Marty Misewicz, 3rd Vice

President Nancy Keough, and Treasurer Precilla Landry Wilkewitz were excused). Nancy Jurgevich was elected President for the following term.

A representative from the Veterans Administration helped anyone with a DD214 to register with the VA. Various fundraisers were held to defray costs of future VWV events.

The Keynote Speaker was Dr. Irene Trowell-Harris, Director of the VA Women's Center.

## 2012: Biloxi, MS

Vietnam Women Veterans Conference
Biloxi, MS. 2012

April 26-29, 2012: Biloxi, MS: The Keynote Speaker was again Dr. Irene Trowell Harris, Director of the Veterans Administration Women's Center, who gave a detailed presentation on support from the VA, what support is available, and health benefits. She stayed two full days and many women were able to discuss individual concerns with her.

Other activities included an all day trek to New Orleans and the WW II Museum, a visit to the Mississippi Armed Forces Museum at Camp Shelby, and a tour of the Jefferson Davis home on the waterfront in Biloxi. While at Camp Shelby, the women ate with the soldiers at their mess hall. Evenings were spent visiting local jazz pubs and reminiscing.

The following officers were elected: President, Nancy Jurgevich; 1st Vice President, Mary Hay Wilson; 2nd Vice President, Carole "Teddi" Gittman; 3rd Vice President, Aurora Toth; Secretary, Pat Jernigan; and Treasurer, Precilla Wilkewitz.

Speakers included:

- Fred Wesley, Department of Louisiana VFW State Commander and his wife, Pat Wesley, who reported that the VFW now welcomes women and supports women's efforts.
- Yvonne Schilz, Chief, Commemorative Partner Program and POW/MIA Liaison with USA Vietnam War Commemoration.

- Sallie Carroll spoke on Cancer Awareness and her experience in dealing with Carcinoid cancer.
- Dr. Kathryn Magruder, although not present, sent a report on the Vietnam Era Women Veterans Study Update. Phase III is now underway to interview 900 women who have completed both the mail survey and telephone interview.

## 2014: Concord, NC

May 1-4, 2014: Officers present were President, Nancy Jurgevich; 1st Vice President, Mary Hay Wilson; 2nd Vice President, Teddi Gittman; Secretary, Pat Jernigan; Treasurer, Precilla Wilkewitz. Dianne Hatley was conference coordinator and Frances Crawford led the transportation committee. Aurora Toth, 3rd Vice President was not present. Fifty-one members were present. With guests, total attendees were 77 individuals.

The business meeting included adoption of revised bylaws. The election of officers was conducted by Mary Hay Wilson. The following were elected: President, Laura Pariseau; 1st Vice President, Carol Ogg; 2nd Vice President, Penny Adams; 3rd Vice President, Aurora Toth; Secretary, Pat Jernigan; Treasurer, Precilla Wilkewitz. The new officers assume their duties October 1, 2014.

Speakers for the conference included Concord Mayor Scott Padgett; Major General Janet Cobb, USAR, Assistant Deputy Chief of Staff, G4, an individual mobilization augmentee; Penny Greer-Link from the VA; Alfie Alvarado-Ramos, Director, Washington State Veterans Affairs; Donald Owens from the National Cemeteries; Dr. Kathy Magruder from the Vietnam Era Women Veterans Study; Dr. Françoise Bonnel from the

Outgoing President of VWV, Nancy Jurgevich, presents award to ♥Frances Crawford for enthusiastic support of the conferences and events. Although not a Vietnam veteran, Frances was a staunch supporter of the Vietnam Women Veterans. Frances passed away late in 2014.

US Army Women's Museum, and Yvonne Schilz, Chief, Commemorative Partner Program and POW/MIA Liaison who made a presentation from the 50th Vietnam Anniversary celebration.

Eight reunions have been held by the women who served in Vietnam. It has been fun to celebrate and revisit former coworkers and feel that we know what is meant by "Service Together; Friends Forever."

# Chapter Eighteen

# All-Service Listing of Women Vietnam Veterans

While researching for this book, one of the most important questions we asked was, "Who else do you remember?" It was wonderful to have so many women pull names out of their memories and give us new information to continue the search. We found that many of the women extended their tours or went home and then came back for a second and even a third time. It was a challenge to assign the proper dates to some of the women.

In this chapter, arranged by oldest Service to newest Service, we have included lists of who was there and when for the Army, and made a special effort to indicate who was serving as cadre for the WAC Detachment. Many of these Army women had overlap with two or more Detachment cadre. Where we could find the information, you will see asterisks and notes at the end of the lists. For the Marine and Navy women, the lists are alphabetical and include ranks. Their numbers were much smaller.

The Air Force section describes the effort to get women assigned to Vietnam and lists the women who were in country. There is a special section for the medical women who were not nurses, including the four women who served aboard the hospital ships.

## ARMY

### Recollecting the Notable Service of WACs in Vietnam:
### A Short Narrative
*By Dr. Françoise B. Bonnell, PhD & Amanda J. Strickland*
United States Army Women's Museum

Women have served with the Army since the founding of our nation. Although their numbers are seemingly small in some conflicts, their contributions are nonetheless extremely important. The service of members of the Women's Army Corps (WAC) in Vietnam is one historical example of this phenomenon. The significance of the work of these women cannot be over stated. Lieutenant General Engler, former Deputy Commander, United States Army Vietnam (USARV) wrote in a letter to Brigadier General Hoisington in 1981 that WACs conducted their work in "...an outstanding manner. It would have been a serious mistake not to use their skills. The decision to deploy the WAC's to Vietnam was correct." The WAC presence began with Major Anne Doering's assignment in March 1962 to the United States Military Assistance Advisory Group-Vietnam and ended with the last two WACs', Major Georgia Wise and Captain Nancy Keough, departure in March 1973. The number of women assigned to Vietnam changed in direct correlation to the overall mission. WACs served side-by-side with their male counterparts as the situation and environment in the theater evolved. There is no doubt that the service of hundreds of WACs in Vietnam would forever change the role of women in the Army.

The Women's Army Auxiliary Corps (followed by the Women's Army Corps) was created in 1942 "for the purpose of making available to the national defense the knowledge, skill, and special training of the women of the nation." During the course of World War II over 120 military occupational specialties were open to women – "freeing a man to fight" – and they served on every continent. Although they were designated as non-combatants, the 140,000 WACs found themselves stationed in combat zones. The Women's Army Corps (which replaced the WAAC in July 1, 1943) was to last for the "duration of the war plus six months" but the selfless service and sacrifice of this all-volunteer force of women proved beneficial to the war effort and the Women's Armed Services Integration Act was signed into law in 1948, making the WAC a permanent part of the Army. The ranks of the Women's Army Corps were expanded twice in the following decades: first, beginning in 1951 and again, beginning in 1968 – both periods when the nation was at war. Unlike World War II, the WACs in Vietnam, regardless of their utilization, were "interchangeable . . . that is, either men or women can and do handle them, depending on who is available." Colonel Hoisington, as the WAC Director, added, "We are not replacing any men in Vietnam. We are part of the Army's regular table of distribution and, as such, are handling Army jobs rather than feminine jobs."[8]

---

[8] Tom Tiede, "Army Seeks WAC Role in Vietnam," *Jackson Citizen Patriot*, (October 1968).

This statement is evident when one examines how women were assigned in Vietnam.

There were several groups of WACs working for different headquarters in varying capacities in Vietnam between 1962 and 1973. Some women were assigned directly to the WAC Detachment between 1966 and 1972: first at Tan Son Nhut Air Base near Saigon and then at Long Binh, the largest military base in the Pacific. Others were assigned directly to units located throughout Vietnam. Some WACs were isolated from other women, an experience that could be trying. For

(l-r) COL Graham, 1SG Marion Crawford, SFC Betty Benson and SGM DeVilla, USARV HQ, Long Binh, circa 1968

example, Major Florence Dunn had orders assigning her to Headquarters (HQ), Military Assistance Command-Vietnam (MACV) and duty with HQ, Civil Operations and Rural Development Support. She was the only WAC assigned to that command. The list of WAC assignments is too long to include in its entirety, but a few are: 12th Evacuation Hospital, 4th Psychological Operations Group, 69th Signal Battalion, 1st Logistical Command, 9th Medical Laboratory, 1st Signal Brigade, 525th Military Intelligence Group, 509th Radio Research Group, and 165th Aviation Group.

CPT Joanne Murphy administers reenlistment oath to SP5 Juliette Dortch, circa 1967-1968

Service in Vietnam for the WAC was mostly voluntary; however, the WAC Director was advised to send the very best, so surely there were some women who were asked to go. Colonel Hoisington reported that there was a long list of women waiting to be called upon for service in Vietnam; many WACs extended their tour of duty.[9] In 1968, WACs were given the option of reenlisting with a guarantee of serving in Vietnam if they wanted. Some took advantage of these offers.[10]

The majority of WACs on duty in Vietnam were enlisted and between the ages of 19 and 24 years old.[11] Their reasons for volunteering for this duty

---

[9] Ibid.

[10] "WAC Reups For Vietnam Under New Army Program," *The Armored Sentinel*, (February 2, 1968).

[11] Bettie Morden, *The Women's Army Corps 1945-1978* (Washington D.C.: Center of Military History, 1990), 246.

varied. Specialist 4 Joyce Harker said "I thought it was a chance to serve my country . . . I didn't feel I was doing enough in the States" – a sentiment echoed by Staff Sergeant Maryna Misiewicz.[12] Specialist 4 Geraldine Young said, "I wanted to see what it was like, and I knew it was a chance to do a lot of good."[13] Sergeant Margaret Gold, one of those WACs recruited in the expansion in 1951, stated, "I wanted to see firsthand what was going on. When I first came into the service, I worked with Korean casualties, and that gave me an interest."[14] Not surprisingly, many of these sentiments resemble those given by women who served before and after them.

Prior to WACs being assigned in Vietnam there were 44 officers and 300 enlisted WACs stationed in the Pacific. Major Anne Doering was the first WAC assigned to Vietnam, joining over 5,000 American male soldiers in Vietnam in 1962.[15]

She was born to a French father and German mother, Vietnamese was her first language, and she lived in Vietnam until she was 15. As a World War II veteran, she was stationed in New Guinea, Leyte and the Philippines and was undoubtedly familiar with the Pacific theater.

SFC Betty Adams trains members of the WAFC on how to salute, circa 1965, WAFC Headquarters, Saigon

Two years later, in 1964, General Westmoreland commander of MACV, requested that one officer and a noncommissioned officer be assigned to his headquarters as advisors to assist the Army of the Republic of Vietnam in the planning and development of training for Vietnamese women in the Women's Armed Forces Corps (WAFC). Colonel Emily Gorman, Director of the WAC, approved the new positions; and in January 1965, Major Kathleen Wilkes and Sergeant First Class Betty Adams became the first advisors to the WAFC. They worked directly with MAJ Tran Cam Huong, director of the WAFC, and her assistant MAJ Ho Thi Ve. Originally, the WAC stayed in the Embassy Hotel but would later move to various local Saigon hotels. Their days and weeks were long – 10 to 15 hours a day

---

[12] Carol Johnson, "A Chance to Serve," USARV Information Office, (1969).

[13] Ibid.

[14] Ibid.

[15] "No April Fools For Dogfaces," *The Houston Chronicle*, (June 11, 1962).

for seven days a week. As a liaison, they also arranged for members of the WAFC to attend training at Fort McClellan, AL; between 1964 and 1971, 51 Vietnamese women officer candidates finished the WAC Officer Basic Course.

Soon after, General Westmoreland requested 15 enlisted WAC stenographers and 12 WAC officers be assigned to fill personnel, administrative, logistics, intelligence, military justice, and other positions in the MACV Headquarters and Tan Son Nhut Air Base. The first contingent of WACs assigned to MACV totaled 25 enlisted and 8 officers.

The WACs with MACV in Saigon typically chose to wear their "cords" (a nickname given to a uniform consisting of a blouse, skirt, and pumps or oxfords) until the launch of the Tet Offensive in 1968. The WACs then switched to fatigues (comprised of an olive drab blouse, pants, and black boots) because of the frequent alerts.

Aerial photo of Tan Son Nhut Air Base, Vietnam. The WAC Detachment area is outlined and USARV Headquarters is on the far right side of the photo, circa 1966-1967

LTG Jean Engler with CPT Peggy Ready at Ribbon Cutting of the WAC Detachment at Tan Son Nhut Air Base, Saigon, circa 1967

It became evident throughout the various commands that the work of the WACs was outstanding and that women with the correct skill sets could in fact create efficiencies for not only MACV but also USARV. In April 1966, LTG Jean Engler (later General), Deputy Commanding General of USARV, requested a WAC Detachment to be assigned to his headquarters in Tan Son Nhut. In response to LTG Engler's request, the Chairman of the Joint Chiefs of Staff, GEN Earle Wheeler, approved the use of WACs at USARV Headquarters. Major Ann Fisher was immediately sent and assigned to the headquarters. Orders activating the WAC Detachment in October 1966 designated it as a direct reporting unit to United States Army Vietnam Special Troops.[16] Within a few months, five WACs, led by CPT Peggy Ready and 1SG Marion

---

[16] Shelby Stanton, *Vietnam Order of Battle* (Mechanicsburg: Stackpole Books, 2003), 62.

Crawford, were sent to USARV to "stand up" the WAC Detachment.[17] The first group of WACs assigned to the USARV WAC Detachment arrived early January 1967 and celebrated with an open house on 21 January 1967. They lived in Quonset huts at Tan Son Nhut Air Base. In July of the same year, the WAC Detachment moved with USARV Headquarters to Long Binh where they were integrated into the Headquarters staff working in the G1, G2, G3, G4, Command Information Office, and Judge Advocate General's Office to name a few. Prior to the construction of new billets in 1968, the USARV commander, Brigadier General John Norton, allowed WACs to wear fatigues because their living and working conditions were so austere – no windows, lots of red dust and extreme heat. The size of the WAC Detachment grew throughout 1967 and by the end of that year, over 80 WACs were serving at the USARV WAC Detachment.

WAC Detachment in formation at Long Binh, Vietnam, circa 1969-1970

The detachment commander established standing operating procedures (SOP) that created a routine Army environment.[18] Rules for the barracks were established – no vulgarity or cursing, overhead lights out at 2200 hours, visiting over at 2330 hours. Rules for personal appearance and conduct were set – could not eat, drink or smoke while walking outside, military headgear is to be worn squarely on the head. The First Sergeant put all in the grade E6 and below on detail for charge of quarters (CQ) duty. Monthly inspections of barracks areas were conducted. Wear of the uniform was designated – black or olive drab socks only, no low quarters in fatigues, no "pegging" the trousers or cutting off the sleeves were allowed. Mail call, pay call, sick call, leaves, passes and R&R were all outlined. All personnel were required to read the unit bulletin board every day. Everything seemed rather routine, except they were in Vietnam! One paragraph in the SOP reminds one of this: "Piaster Spending: In the efforts being made to stabilize the economy of the RVN, you are encouraged to spend as few piasters per month as possible . . . it hinders the Vietnamese economy through inflation."[19]

---

[17] "USARV in Action Press Release," USARV Information Office, 1967.

[18] WAC Detachment Commanders (in order): CPT Peggy Ready, CPT Joanne Murphy, CPT Nancy Jurgevich, CPT Shirley Ohta, CPT Marjorie Johnson, CPT Constance Seidemann

[19] "Standard Operating Procedures" WAC Detachment, USARV, November 1971.

The launch of the Tet Offensive in January 1968 only solidified what the WACs already knew – Vietnam was a dangerous place for American service members.

They were subjected to multiple mortar attacks and increased threat levels. Nevertheless, WACs were non-combatants and therefore not given weapons. However, some WAC officers were issued a sidearm to protect themselves as they travelled back and forth to work. Duty in Vietnam held no special privileges for the WACs. They were treated equally with their male counterparts in many ways to include one-year tours and received $65 a month in hostile fire pay.[20] The tribulations of war did not stop Army women from wanting to serve.

SSG Sylvia "Dobbie" Dobson shows where her desk was hit during a shelling of Long Binh, March 1970

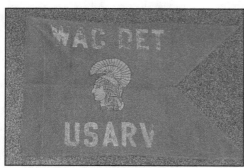

WAC Detachment, U.S. Army Vietnam guidon from the collection of the U.S. Army Women's Museum

The number of women serving in country continued to increase through 1971. This coincided with plans for an enormous expansion of women in the Army. Colonel Elizabeth Branch and Colonel Jennie Fea were the two highest-ranking WACs stationed in Vietnam at the time; the former was the Command Historian at Headquarters MACV, the latter as the Military Personnel Director, Headquarters USARV.[21] However, once the drawdown of US forces began, vacancies created by WACs departing Vietnam were not filled. In September 1972, the WAC Detachment was "stood down" and the remaining members moved to Saigon before redeploying to the United States. A handful of WACs

---

[20] Sandi Olson, "… In Vietnam," *WAC Journal* no.1 (January 1970): 8-10.
[21] "WAC Officer Rosters," US Army Pacific (USARPAC), (June 1970-December 1971).

remained at the MACV Headquarters; by March 1973, the last two WACs left Vietnam.

In the ensuing years, the Women's Army Corps was called upon to shore up the Army as it transitioned to an all-volunteer force when the draft was discontinued in 1973. The number of women serving increased exponentially from 10,000 in 1968, to 17,000 in 1973, to 53,000 by the end of the WAC era in 1978. The numbers continued to expand from 65,000 in 1980 to 72,000 in 1984.[22] Much was proven by Army women by their service in Vietnam. They were courageous, professional and dedicated. These women did what was asked of them with pride and selfless service. Many experienced firsthand the horrors and stresses of the war zone; some continue to bear these scars and burdens today. The women who serve today in the Army owe a great debt of gratitude to these Vietnam veterans; they helped ensure equality and opportunity for future service women.

The contributions of WACs to the war effort in Vietnam are significant. Approximately 700 WACs served in Vietnam (and another 1,600 WACs served in the Pacific in support of the war).[23] So why is it that we do not know

Vietnam Women Veterans Conference attendees, Concord, NC, May 2014

more about the history of these extraordinary veterans? It is difficult to say, but undoubtedly, it is because so little is written about them and people do not know about their experiences.

The painstaking work of the Vietnam Women Veterans organization to attempt identifying every WAC who served in country is a noble beginning. Oral histories need to be collected, veterans need to share their memories, and their history needs to be preserved in reputable repositories so that the service of these women can be studied and written about. Colonel (Ret) Bettie Morden wrote *The Women's Army Corps 1945-1978*

---

[22] All Statistics are from: Bettie Morden, *The Women's Army Corps 1945-1978* (Washington D.C.: Center of Military History, 1990), 409-410.

[23] Bettie Morden, Article *The Women's Army Corps During the Vietnam War*, (date and publisher unknown). These numbers are approximations. After extensive research the authors have found conflicting reports of numbers regarding WAC strength throughout the Pacific and specifically in Vietnam. The authors continue to research to gather greater clarity of the statistics.

which was published by the Center of Military History in 1990.[24] Chapter IX, titled "Vietnam; WAC Strength; WAC Standards," is 40 pages long and does an excellent job of recounting WACs involvement in Vietnam. It weaves together the historical context in which women's assignments to Vietnam took place; this short narrative relies heavily on her book. However, Morden examined the WAC history from an internal perspective – internal to the Office of the Director of the WAC. What is missing is the history as seen through the lens of the rest of the Army. This will take greater research and study. Documents need to be found; many of the references Morden uses in her book are unaccounted for now, but undoubtedly are somewhere. Archival holdings need to be examined; records for USARV and MACV will have to be combed through. Collectively the history of the service of Army women in Vietnam can and should be written so as to interpret and better understand our nation's own history.

---

[24] A digital copy of the book can be found on line at http://www.history.army.mil/html/books/030/30-14-1/index.html

# USARV, Special Troops
# WAC Detachment

## 1ˢᵗ Commander – Captain Peggy E. Ready
### October 31, 1966 – October 27, 1967

### WAC Detachment Cadre, USARV, Saigon, VN
Located on Tan Son Nhut Air Base, Saigon
Moved to Long Binh July 13, 1967

**1SG Marion C. Crawford**
First Sergeant

**SFC Betty J. Benson**
Field First/Admin NCO

**♥SSG Edith L. Efferson**
Supply Sergeant

**SP5 Rhynell M. Stoabs (Karr)**
Company Clerk

**SP5 Patricia C. Pewitt**
Mail Clerk

Doris I. Allen *

Cheranne Asmus (Halsey)

Christine Baker

Delores A. Bala (Liederbach)

Rosario Bermudez (Tinsley)

Loretta J. Bohlke (Meredith)

♥Roberta Bozman

Donna K. Bramley

Patricia L. Brooks (Hildebrand)

Linda M. Bruns (Moore)

Emma Jean Clark

Lauren F. Collins

Faye S. Conaway

♥Janice Gwen Curtis

Donna J. Dear

Phyllis J. DeLong

Juliette A. Dortch (Coleman-Hallman)

Marie I. Dube (Gross)

Virginia P. Dubics

Martha Duncan (Jackson)

Barbara A. Ebel (Flaaen)

♥Gwendolyn K. Faught (Wakolee)

Juana C. Felix

Anita Flores (Massey)

Pamela J. Forbing

♥Penny A. Freeman (Choiniere)

Ruth M. Fulton

Linda Jean Garrigan

Sheron L. Green

Gloria J. Grenfell (Fowler) (Leigh)

Joeann Harris (Burr)

Mary E. Hay (Wilson)

Vicki Ann Heydron

♥Jo Ann Hoyer *

♥Bernice A. Kearschner (Guion)

Anne M. Lally

♥Shirley Larsen

Penelope L. Lewis (Wilcox)

Donna A. Lowery

♥Janet Elise Lupher *

Barbara M. Maine *

Joanne B. Manger (Willaford)

♥Carol J. Matisz (Miller)

Michele T. McCarthy

Anna A. McPherson

Hester E. Miller

Carolyn L. Mitchell (Wiggins)

Reya Monte

Carolyn A. Moore

Beverly Mounter (Evans)

Tanya L. Murphy (Hickman)

Judith D. Nickloy (Jones)

Patricia A. Ogg

Carmen E. Oliveras (Martinez)

Linda K. Ostermeier (McDermith)

Mildred A. Park

♥Edith A. Powell

Linda S. Pritchard (Woolm)

Judith L. Rathman

Diana M. Reed

Sharon A. Ridout

Ruth E. Riter

Mary E. Rutledge (Fish)

Lillian Sampson (Grasham)

Sherry E. Saunders (Howard)

Mavis D. Schmidt *

Margaret M. Sigley (D'Onofrio)

Janet F. Singer

Dorothy Smith (Gardner)

Holly A. Smith

Janet A. Smith

Mary A. Stedman (Vasas)

Susie Mae Stephens (McArthur)

Kathleen E. Stoner (DeCollo)

Glenda E. Storni (Graebe)

Luretha Taylor

Emma L. Thornton (Henderson)

Dianne P. Tipton (Turbyfill)

Margaret T. Trapp (Jones)

Joyce P. Trumpet

♥Donna K. Van Deventer (Turpen)

Phylis A. Wahwasuck (Thomas)

♥Gloria A. Walker

♥Anita M. Wampach *

Patricia A. Wilcoxon

Carol A. Williams (Harris)

Nancy M. Wooten (Thorne)

* In the listings of the WAC Detachment, names marked with the asterisk transferred to or from MACV or had a second tour at MACV or other locations in Vietnam

## 2<sup>nd</sup> Commander – Captain Joanne P. Murphy

October 27, 1967 – October 16, 1968

### <u>WAC Detachment Cadre, USARV, Long Binh, VN</u>
**1SG Marion C. Crawford**
First Sergeant
replaced by
**♥1SG Katherine E. Herney**
First Sergeant
**SFC Betty J. Benson**
Field First/Admin NCO
replaced by
**♥SFC Margaret E. Gold**
Field First/Admin NCO
**♥SSG Edith L. Efferson**
First Supply Sergeant
replaced by
**♥SFC Velma M. Calcio**
Supply Sergeant
**SP5 Rhynell M. Stoabs (Karr)**
First Company Clerk
replaced by
**SP5 Patricia C. Pewitt**
Mail/Company Clerk

Emma F. Rides Bear Adams (Core)
♥Harriet G. Albers
Varina A. Albers
Christine Almanza (Sampley)
♥Wanda Lee Baker
Linda M. Barnes (Poole)
Ida Imani Betts
Margaret F. Bevill
♥Gabrielle Brancato
Cathy L. Brock
Fannie M. Brooks

Carol F. Bruckerhoff (Reynolds)
Janet M. Brusseau (Munger)
♥Marjorie Ann Brzozowski
♥Carolyn A. Carmack (Robinson)
Barbara F. Chorak (Ballas)
Judith K. Chorak (Greathouse)
Patricia K. Coder (Humeumptewa)
♥Susan M. Commons
Lidia M. Contreras
Zulma I. Cruz (Martorell)
♥Betty Mae Davis (Smith)

♥Karen J. Dillaman (Scott)

♥Annette M. Drumming (Douglas)

Earnestine Dumas (Barkers)

Linda S. Earls

Olivia J. Ellis (Favre)

Emily E. Embree

Regenia Feltner (Sizemore)

Betty J. Ferguson

Judith A. Fisher

Henrietta E. Florido

♥Betty Jane Fuller (Legleiter)

Betty F. Gant (Kinney)

Carole A. Gittman

Patricia A. Givens

Esther M. Gleaton

♥Margaret Elizabeth Gold

Sonia B. Gonzalez Mendez *

♥Gabrielle M. Goulet

♥Christa Maria Grayer

Virginia S. Green

Madelene L. Hall (Showers)

Norma S. Hamm

♥Virginia E. Hanley

Rosemary Hanson (Miller)

Therese E. Harnden (Peters)

Paulette B. Hill

Penelope Hill (Radebaugh)

Peggy R. Hilton

Mary L. Himes

Marsha D. Holder

Julie E. Hollis (Bumpas)

Janis G. Horvat

Grendel Alice Howard

♥Barbara J. Ivey (Riddle)

Rose M. Jackson (Johnson) *

Judy A. Jacque

Linda D. Jankowiak (Pride) *

♥Nancy Jolene Johnson

Glenda F. Jones (Hamlin)

Patricia E. Keefe (Miyaji)

Kathleen E. Kennedy (Fontana)

Janice A. Kluge (Fountain)

Mary Constance Koster

Precilla Ann Landry (Wilkewitz)

♥Victoria Lapinski (Lennert)

Carrie M. Latimer

♥Mary E. Pritchard Lennon *

Doris L. Lewis (White) *

Karen S. Linley (Kamm)

Donna M. Loring

Pilar L. Magallon *

Christine Matthews (Blocksidge)

Karen McClung (Feher)

Ruth A. McKenney

Patrice M. McKeone

Maryna L. Misiewicz

Natalie E. Moody (Summers)

Ladina L. Moore

Sally J. Moore

Marsha L. Mossing

Mary J. Nicholls

Doris Olheiser (Davison)

Penny A. Ormes (Price)

T. Elaine Palmer

Patricia C. Patterson (Smith)

♥Joan A. Peck *

Sandra F. Phipps

♥Patricia Kay Powell

Patricia M. Powell

Peggy Pruitt

Dorothy J. Rechel

Judith L. Roberts

♥Marilyn Roth

Constance Sue Schungel (Delk)

Eileen T. Seelman (Meredith)

♥Betty M. Stone

Diana J. Symanowicz (Reedy)

Willella T. Taylor (Williams)

Sandra E. Wainwright (McGowan)

Marian J. Wells

♥Phyllis Arlyne Williams (Palmer)

Lee N. Wilson

Nancy K. Wiltshire

Michele A. Yacura (Fennimore)

Nancy C. Young

# 3rd Commander – Captain Nancy J. Jurgevich

October 16, 1968 – November 12, 1969

## WAC Detachment Cadre, USARV, Long Binh, VN

### ♥1SG Katherine E. Herney
First Sergeant
replaced by

### ♥1SG Mary E. Manning
First Sergeant

### ♥SFC Margaret E. Gold
Field First/Admin NCO
replaced by

### ♥SFC Bernice A. Myhrwold
Field First/Admin NCO

### ♥SFC Velma M. Calcio
Supply Sergeant
replaced by

### ♥SSG Rena D. Hurley
Supply Sergeant

### SP5 Patricia C. Pewitt
Mail/Company Clerk
replaced by

### SGT Joyce I. Harker (Saitta)
Company Clerk/Supply Clerk

### SP5 Barbara D. Bacon
Part-time Mail Clerk/Supply Clerk

Sharon Thomasina Acierno
Lawanda E. Allen
Velma A. Anderson (Davis)
♥Dorothy Jean Artioli
♥Apolonia Patricia Atayde
Patricia V. Babcock (Schmauch)
♥Phyllis J. Bertram
♥Linda M. Brackett (Grasso)

Claire M. L. Brisebois (Starnes) *
Beverly L. Brooks
Janie M. Brown (Cole)
Rebecca R. Carlson (Gardner)
Susie L. Carter (Houston)
Gloria M. Chicoine
Lana H. Clark (Majewski)
Verna M. Clark

Connie F. Conlin

Ruth A. Conrad

Idalia E. Correa

Doris A. Denny *

Kathleen Deschamps (Poole)

♥Sylvia M. Dobson

♥Barbara Ann Duerkop (Biermeier)

Kathryn A. Dwyer (Feltz)

Linda J. Eagleson (Dodge)

Frances A. Earle

Brenda S. Eichholz (Caldwell)

♥Betty Jean Elliott

Frances Ernestine Ellwanger

♥Rosalie Ann Fleshman

♥Marjorie Jean Freeman

♥Jo Ann Fremont (Patterson)

♥Doris D. Fuller

♥Ellen Frances Garvey

Jo Ann Gasmund (Dowdy)

♥Louise Jenny Giacomuzzi *

♥Vera I. Gordon

Virginia Grant *

♥Carrie M. Gray (Richmond)

♥Jessie A. Gregory

Susan J. Haack

Oneta A. Harrington

Louise J. Hartley (Rather)

Rhoda C. Hay (Blitch)

Edith I. Hayhurst

Susan C. Hicks (Franklin)

♥Linda Camille Honor

♥Pinkie Bell Houser

Lynda K. Jacobs (Michalik)

Carol F. Johnson *

♥Mary Ellen Johnson

Mary J. Johnson

Augustina R. Jones (Foster)

Kathleen Kabler *

Catherine M. Kahl

Charlene M. Kahl (Kennedy)

Julianne Kubeczko (Viduya)

Nora H. Lebron (Encarnacion)

Linda A. Lesser (White)

♥Melba Sue Lindsey

♥Evelyn L. Lozano (Roussos)

Paulette S. Luxford (Isabell)

Catherine A. Martin

♥Christine M. Marx (Head)

Marjorie D. McLain

Carol A. Mellen (Lincoln)

Gwendolyn L. Mitchell

♥Elizabeth E. Moore (Jones)

♥Linda Sue Neblock (Plumm)

Ruth M. Neeley (Cremin) *

Gail Nelson *

Queenola Nelson

♥Catherine Louise Oatman *

Karen Offutt *

♥Lillian Ruth Ogburn

Doris Oliveras

Mary Virginia Parker *

Peggy Lou Patterson

Carmen M. Perez

Ruth E. Pitts

Delores E. Reid

Marjorie T. Rinke

Karie L. Ennis (Clark) (Robertson) *

Teresa M. Romero

Barbara J. Rubenstein (Acee)

♥Aida Ruiz

♥Adrienne Lee Schamp *

Eva B. Schmaing (Pederson)

D. Ann Sims (Antomattei)

Donna L. Stephens *

♥Betty Grace Claus (Teager) *

Rejeanne C. Tellier (Ridgeway)

Norma Jean Thelen
Marcella F. Trujillo
♥Margaret E. Walker
Iva J. Wallace *
Sharon Dawn Weikel

♥Patricia Jane Whalen
Frances D. White (Marks)
♥Betty Frances Whitmire (Freeman)
Geraldine Young

## 4th Commander – Captain Shirley M. Ohta

November 12, 1969 – November 8, 1970

### WAC Detachment Cadre, USARV, Long Binh, VN

**♥1SG Mary E. Manning**

First Sergeant

replaced by

**♥SFC Eleanor M. Strudas**

First Sergeant

**♥SFC Bernice A. Myhrwold**

Field First/Admin NCO

replaced by

**SFC Marjorie T. Rinke**

Temp Field First/Admin NCO

**♥SSG Rena D. Hurley**

Supply Sergeant

**SGT Joyce I. Harker (Saitta)**

Company Clerk

replaced by

**SP4 Betty J. Russell**

Company Clerk/Mail Clerk

**SP5 Catherine E. Messer**

Temporary Supply Clerk

**SP5 Edith "Nikki" Hayhurst**

Supply/Mail Clerk

| | |
|---|---|
| Mary C. Aleshire | ♥Marilyn Ann Burrow (Trainer) |
| Annie M. Alexander | (Bodenstedt) |
| Nancy G. Anderson | ♥Amy L. Carter |
| ♥Cynthia L. Baker * | Shirley P. Coppage (Wilson) |
| ♥Delores Barrett | (Dickerson) |
| Audrey M. Bergstresser | Mary A. Darr * |
| Gladys Berrios-Perez (Schwerin) | Carla R. Dixson |
| Sandra Britton (Jordan) | ♥Argelis Helena Ferre |
| Ella L. Brooks | Elizabeth A. Freaney |

Jacqueline L. Gillette

Donna Lee Giordani

Fannie Lee Gray

Glenda Griggs (Britz)

Kay F. Hall

Mary E. Harrington (Evans)

Margaret H. Hernandez

♥Mary Hazel Johnson *

Sandra M. Leino (Kaigler)

Linda J. McClenahan

Patricia A. Morrow (Crater)

Priscilla Mosby

Joyce Evelyn Oakes (Poole)

Belen Victoria Pinon

♥Edna N. Renfroe (Fague)

Maria Edna Reyes

Pamela S. Riess (Bunde)

Lucie Rivera-O'Ferrall

Peggy L. Roberts

Theresa Sanchez

♥Charlene Ann Jameson (Seals)

Nancy E. Simmons

Carolyn Skidmore

Joy J. Smith

Josephine Solis

Erma L. Spadone (Morgan)

June Walker

Ruthie M. Webb

Lois E. Weeks

Janice M. White Eagle (Johnson)

Jo Anna Wilson *

♥Kathy J. Zeigler (Wenzelberger)

## 5th Commander – ♥Captain Marjorie K. Johnson

November 8, 1970 – November 7, 1971

## WAC Detachment Cadre, USARV, Long Binh, VN

### ♥SFC Eleanor M. Strudas
First Sergeant
replaced by
### ♥1SG Mildred Estelle Duncan
First Sergeant
### SFC Marjorie T. Rinke
Temp Field First/Admin NCO
replaced by
### SSG Mary C. Aleshire
Field First/Admin NCO
replaced by
### SSG Kay F. Hickok
Field First/Admin NCO
### ♥SSG Rena D. Hurley
Supply Sergeant
replaced by
### SSG Mary A. Darr
Supply Sergeant
### SP4 Betty J. Russell
Company Clerk/Mail Clerk
replaced by
### SP5 Frances L. Black
Company Clerk
replaced by
### SP5 Carol A. Hazzard (Waryck-McClure)
Company Clerk
### SP5 Edith "Nikki" Hayhurst
Supply/Mail Clerk

♥Elfriede Bartl
Marlene A. Bowen-Grissett

Brenda K. Burk (Medina)
Ethel M. Dial

Deborah O. Gano

Norma Allene Goerlitz

Edna Mae Jefferson (White)

♥Rosemarie Lane

♥Evelyn Lynn Kussman (Lindblad)

Shirley Mae McDougald

♥Evelyn A. Mundorff

Sandra K. Phillips (Vandever)

Elsie J. Robinson

Cheryl K. Ruff

Sherri A. Tipton

Sandra J. Torrens *

Kathleen E. Wilcox

Yvonne Chris Young

# 6th Commander – Captain Constance D. Seidemann (Ferrell)

November 7, 1971 – September 21, 1972

## WAC Detachment Cadre, USARV, Long Binh, VN

Deactivated September 21, 1972

### ♥1SG Mildred Estelle Duncan

First Sergeant

### SSG Kay F. Hickok

Field First/Admin NCO

### SSG Mary A. Darr

Supply Sergeant

### SP5 Carol A Hazzard (Waryck-McClure)

Company Clerk

replaced by

### SP5 Deborah A. Godby

Company Clerk

### SP5 Janis L. Waters

Supply Clerk/Mail Clerk

Mary Ann Ehrhardt

♥Gloria Jean Labadie

♥Anna L. Maxwell (Bradham) (Youngblood)

Judith L. McCurdy

Alicia Pineda

Sharolyn K. Picking

Francine Tomasik

**September 21, 1972 – the deactivation of the WAC Detachment**

In a May 8, 1972 article, titled "The women behind the concertina barricade," in the *Overseas Weekly* – Pacific Edition, CPT Constance Seidemann, WAC Detachment Commander, said there were 41 women in the detachment of which 12 remained at its closing on September 21, 1972. We know of 33 women who were at the unit (two of which we have not found), while the remaining eight women are unknown. They most likely are on the Search List. Since there doesn't seem to be any record of this unit in its final days, we have reconstructed, to the best of our knowledge, the last WAC Detachment to ever be in a combat zone.

**Left country prior to Detachment closing**
SSG Mary Darr, Supply Sergeant
SP5 Carol A. Hazzard, Company Clerk
SSG Kay Hickok, Admin NCO
SGT Janis Waters, Supply/Mail Clerk
Nancy G. Anderson
♥Delores "Mickey" Barrett
Marlene A. Bowen (Grissett)
♥Gabrielle Brancato
Ruth A. Conrad
Norma Allene Goerlitz
♥Evelyn Lynn Kussman (Lindblad)
Joyce Evelyn Oakes (Poole)
Belen V. Pinon
Cheryl K. Ruff
Josephine Solis
Sherri A. Tipton

**Left country when Detachment closed**
CPT Constance Seidemann, Commander
♥1SG Mildred Duncan, First Sergeant
♥Jessie A. Gregory
♥Gloria Jean Labadie
Arlene L. "Buzz" Mahalic
Francine Tomasik

## Went to Saigon

♥Anna L. Maxwell (Bradham) (Youngblood)
Mary Ann Ehrhardt
Deborah A. Godby
♥Rosemarie Lane
Judith L. McCurdy
Gail Nelson
Sharolyn K. Picking
Alicia Pineda
Sandra J. Torrens
Iva J. Wallace

Despite months of calling, researching and writing letters, it was difficult to reconstruct the last six months of WAC service in Vietnam.

Staff Sergeant Judith McCurdy agreed to describe those last months, from her perspective:

The deactivation of the WAC Detachment, USARV Special Troops, on September 21, 1972, turned out to be a non-event, unlike when the WACs arrived in country in 1967. There was no fanfare, no retirement of the unit guidon, a formal protocol of closing a unit – an event I had experienced several times in my military career.

The women had been given the choice of reassignment to Saigon or leaving immediately for the States to be reassigned there or separated from the military. For those of us choosing to remain, arrangements with our new units were made to pick up our belongings at the WAC Detachment, and off we headed down Route 1 to Saigon on our way to the Iowa BEQ, our new home in the Republic.

I remember a few days before I left Long Binh, I arrived at the detachment to find that our First Sergeant had loaded a flatbed truck with beds, lockers, dressers and other barrack items. I knew she was not one who was staying in country, but was surprised to learn she was taking leave and staying in Saigon. She had rented a villa where these items were being taken. What in the world was she really going to do with all these things in a villa in Saigon? I just never knew and still wonder to this day. By the time I saw her again, she had dementia and didn't recognize me, so I was unable to ask her this vital question which I was, and still am, curious about.

As for CPT Seidemann, our Company Commander, who knows when she left? There was no good-bye letter posted on the bulletin board. Hell! The bulletin board was gone. There was no ceremony, no party or thank you of any kind from anyone. Some of the women got together the evening prior to leaving for a small in-house drinking party. I guess it was the sign of the times. No one really thanked us for our service, not even those for whom we served.

**Fast forward:** I had an occasion to revisit Long Binh in December 1972 or early January 1973. Driving on the installation was a real eye opener as it was worse than visiting Tombstone, AZ, on its worst day of abandonment. What we found in Long Binh was a shadow of its former self. Locals had pillaged the WAC Detachment buildings. All hardware and glass, boards, flooring, tin, anything portable or detachable had been carted off, probably on their way to the black market. Their profits, for a while anyway, would provide for their families, since many would surely be losing significant wages due to the withdrawal of American troops. The WAC Detachment itself was unrecognizable. The once jungle-free, gravel-covered grounds were a mess, the Agent Orange no longer effective. Trash and weeds and rubble – a heart-breaking sight and I was happy to leave it behind.

# SPECIAL WOMEN AMONG MANY
# IN MY UNIT IN VIETNAM

*~ 1SG Marion Crawford*

I've been asked to write a story about my feelings about the women who were in the first and second groups assigned to the WAC Detachment in Vietnam. My friends would say about now "don't get her started." Well, I have told everyone since being there and since returning that I was the luckiest First Sergeant in the Army. As my Field First/Admin NCO, Betty Benson, and I stood waiting for the first large group of women to come in, we were so excited! We were told that they would be "all volunteers" so we had no idea what we'd see. They were sharp as a tack and you couldn't convince us that they had not been hand-selected. Even though they had been traveling for two days, they were happy but very concerned that they were so wrinkled and there were photos being taken.

They were happy to be on solid ground after the 22-hour plus flight from California. They were anxious because the first thing they saw upon arriving in Vietnam was men, both American and Vietnamese, carrying weapons. The heat was terrible and the landscape definitely not luxurious. BUT, they smiled as we met them and from that day on, my commander, cadre and myself tried to keep that smile on their face.

I will pick are a few of the women and tell you why they were so special. *CHERIE ASMUS HALSEY and GLORIA FOWLER LEIGH* were two who were selected by the WAC Detachment commander and me when dignitaries came and we needed someone to show them around. They were both very attractive and had personalities to match. Cheri was from Ohio, and Gloria was from California. Cheri met her husband Dave in Vietnam; Gloria met Fred before she went to Vietnam. Both of the husbands were military policemen and both husbands became police officers upon getting out of the Army. Sadly, both died while police officers.

It was many years before Gloria married again and Cheri never married anyone else.

*ANNE MARIE LALLY:* Over there she was very quiet, well-liked and a tiny blonde. None of us were too surprised when we were told that she is now Sister Anne Marie, C.S.J. in Brooklyn, NY. She has been in this admirable profession for more than 30 years and is very happy.

*PRECILLA "PAT" LANDRY WILKEWITZ:* Then there is Precilla "Pat" Landry Wilkewitz. She was my Cinderella troop. She was either so good or was so good at covering her tracks. The next time I saw her was more than 30 years later, and she was now an accomplished and beautiful red head who had married a nice guy and lived in Zachary, LA. She was the State Adjutant/Quartermaster, Department of Louisiana, VFW, Administrator and Finance Officer. She was one of the founders of the Vietnam Women Veterans organization and is the glue that holds the group together.

*FAYE CONAWAY:* What can I say? She was a wonderful, attractive, very talented troop whom I told once before I left that country "don't waste your talent, Faye, do something with it." She came up to me at the first reunion and said, "Sergeant Crawford, I did what you wanted me to do. I went to college and became a music teacher." Her signature song was "Under the Board Walk." She could really sing that one. This is one woman who has done well, and I am very proud of her.

*MILDRED "MOTH" PARK:* This troop, obviously, was special from the beginning. She was the driver for our Director of WAC, Colonel (Elizabeth) Hoisington, before getting orders for Vietnam. On the way over, her group got lost and needed transportation. She called back to her boss and they were soon on their way. "Moth" stood out from the average woman, and it was a "given" that she would do well whatever she did after this assignment. She stayed in the Army and like myself became a First Sergeant. She also married and is retired from the Army, living in Oklahoma.

*GLENDA STORNI GRAEBE:* Let me tell you, she did not like her First Sergeant at all while in Vietnam (me) because she was what the Army referred to as "overweight for her height." We had to call her in once a month for weighing in. She hated that. She almost didn't come to the first reunion because of me. BUT, I wrote to her, explained the Army policy, etc., and she finally agreed to come. At the reunion, she looked at me and she slowly started to grin. I was chubbier than she was. We got reacquainted through humor and finally she and I became fast friends. Another troop came along as weight was being discussed and sent us into hysterics by tapping me on my stomach and saying, "Suck it in, Sarge." That was *CAROLE "TEDDI" GITTMAN.* The troops don't let me live it down.

*DONNA A. LOWERY:* This woman was always exceptional. She has an outgoing personality, always happy and smiling, easily liked by everyone. Her career was similar to my own. In fact, I was the youngest 1SG at 23 in Germany in 1953. Many years later, Donna would be the youngest 1SG in the Army outside of combat and she was only 21. She was a 1SG at many installations, as I was. But, one of the funniest times we had together was at the first reunion in Olympia, WA, in 1999. The first time we ran into one another was at the hotel as I entered, she was in the midst of an interview with a reporter. When she looked up and saw me come in, she knocked him over getting out of her chair and yelled really loud, "Oh my God, my First Sergeant" and ran and grabbed me in a tight hug. Everyone sure laughed. This is the same Donna who worked so hard to get a team together to make our book a reality.

*SONIA "SUNI" GONZALEZ MENDEZ:* What a special woman this one is! She was always a ray of sunshine no matter the day you were having. She was also one of these Army women who walked out of the unit to go to work looking like a million bucks; and when she came home 12 to 14 hours later – LOOKED THE SAME. I loved to step out of the Orderly Room and give her a big hug to wrinkle her uniform. Years later, she would come to visit me many times and I've unofficially adopted her. She is like a daughter to me.

# ARMY WOMEN NOT ASSIGNED TO THE
# WAC DETACHMENT

♥Betty Lee Adams
Merle E. Alvey
Juanita J. Anglin
Nancy Auerbach (Williams)
♥Imogen Elaine Averett
♥Betty J. Bailey
Mary K. Bailey
Carol J. Baker
♥Lillian Emily Baker
♥Maxene M. Baker (Michl)
Donna P. Baldwin
Joan L. Barnes (Barco)
♥Shirley M. Barnwell
♥Mary Van Ette Bender
♥Judith C. Polk Bennett
Mary Jane Bennett (Hill) (Treadwell)
♥Sylvia R. Bernardini
Carolyn K. Boston (Bright)
♥Loyce Alice Bradford
♥Catherine A. Brajkovich
♥Elizabeth H. Branch
Colleen L. Brooks
♥Deloris Lee Browning
Norma V. Busse
Sherian G. Cadoria
Doris L. Caldwell
Agnes M. Carlin
♥Sallie L. E. Carroll
Theresa A. Catano
Frances V. Chaffin (Gannon)
♥Jacqueline R. Chappell
Leah L. Chappell
Charlotte Clark
Ida E. Colford (Willis)
♥Joan M. Crawford (Blakeley)

Mary Louise Curry
♥Alice M. Davis
♥Rosemary Lee Davis
Alice J. Delgado
Barbara J. Devlin
♥Anne Marie Doering
June P. Dohnal
Donna Jean Dunlap (Sams)
Florence I. Dunn
Donna Dutton
Phyllis R. Egermeier
Janet May Ellis (Ziegler)
♥Joyce E. Eslick
♥Louise M. Farrell
♥Jennie Wren Fea
Audrey A. Fisher
Evelyn P. Foote
Evelyn J. Ford
♥Rebecca Jurel Fourth
♥Anne S. Frantz
Marcia A. Galbreath
Barbara A. Gardner
♥Virginia M. Gavin
Barbara N. Gibson
Helen Ruth Gilmore
♥Dorothy L. Gray
♥Mary Jane Grimes
♥Charlotte Josephine Hall
♥Alice I. Hampson
♥Joann Hastings
♥Shirley M. R. Heinze
♥Anna Marie Hidalgo (Dennett)
Patricia L. Hill (Shoum)
♥Mary Joe Hinton
Laura Holguin (Pariseau)

Norma L. Holson

Frances L. Honsowetz

♥Mary L. Hootman

Beatrice Ashley Howard

♥Dolores Helen Hubik

Nancy A. Hunter

♥Barbara J. Wilson (Jack) (Norman)

Joy J. Jacob (Kent)

Elaine L. James

♥Margaret Mary Jebb

♥Paula F. Jenkins

Pat H. Jernigan

Carol L. Johnson

Glenda M. Kaufman (Lunki)

Nancy G. Wadley (Keough)

Rayneta Diane Kinne

♥Shirley E. Klein

♥Marie Sylvia Knasiak

♥June Elizabeth Owens Knutsen

Judith P. Lewis

Renee Estelle Lippman (Priore)

♥Donna Ann Litehiser

Linda S. Little

♥Alice A. Long

Lois A. Main

♥Lillian K. Maluo

♥Shirley Jane Marney

♥Miriam G. Marsh (Felty)

♥Carol Anne Martin (Timar)

Merle E. Massey

Patricia Jane Maybin

Connie McDonald

♥Ann M. McDonough

♥Agnes S. McLennan

♥Bonnie Jean McWilliams

A. Ruth Meekins (Riggins)

♥Thelma Alberta Merrill (Morse)

Elizabeth G. Meyer (Tullis)

Janie R. Miller

♥Madeline V. Miller

Shirley M. Minick

Ruth C. Minutoli

Karen S. Nagel (Adams)

Helen R. Nelson

Betty L. Nemyer (Shellenberger)

♥Sarah Fairly Niblack

Carol A. Ogg

♥Glenda J. Olson

Gloria A. Sondra Olson

Darlene E. Ondesko

Carolyn L. Otey

Joan G. Pekulik

Charlotte E. Phillips

♥Mary E. Phillips

Verneida Pinkston

♥Martha Jane Provo

Karen K. King (Psimadis) (Johnson)

Phyllis Arlene Puffer

Patricia A. Quist

♥Betty Eloise Reid

♥Beverly Eileen Ridley

Marcia Lou Rinkel

♥Lorraine A. Rossi

Helga I. Rubnich

♥Marilyn Jean Russell

Beverly A. Salisbury (Suafoa)

Jacqueline M. Salisbury

Lillian Sanchez

♥Carolyn Ann Sander

♥Patricia L. Schlaht (Ernst)

Patricia A. Seiler

♥Michele Robin Skipwith

♥Ann Blakely Smith

Judy D. Smith

Mary J. Smith

Betty Jean Stallings

Ruby Rose Stauber
♥Dorcas A. Stearns
♥Lois May Steelman
♥Frances Telka Stockwell
Jane Carol Szalobryt
Barbara A. Tarczynski
♥Carol Joan Tilden
Carrie A. Turner
Kathryn A. Votipka (Retzlaff)
♥Ann Wansley
♥Nana B. Wathaw (McDaniel)

Frances Weir
♥Esther W. Weldon (Stewart)
Lois L. Westerfield
♥Kathleen I. Wilkes
Pauline D. Wireman (Edison)
Georgia A. Wise
Florence I. Woolard (Lovensheimer)
Grace J. Wright
Susan E. Wudy
Janet L. Young (Held)

# MARINE CORPS
*~ Mary Glaudel-DeZurik*

Women Marines have served with pride in many of our nation's conflicts. During World War I, World War II and Korea, the Women Marine Reserves were called upon to take on positions that would free a man to fight in the war. Mainly these duties were administrative jobs but also included such positions as radio operators, photographers, parachute riggers, drivers and mechanics. It was not until the Women's Armed Forces Integration Act in 1948 that women were accepted into the regular component of the Marine Corps. In all these past conflicts the duties were performed stateside or in Hawaii. In September 1966 General Wallace M. Greene, Jr., Commandant of the Marine Corps, directed that Women Marines be permitted to volunteer for service in Southeast Asia. Vietnam was the beginning of a change for Women Marines. This time they lived and worked in a combat theater. Many worked at Headquarters MACV in such divisions as Planning, Intelligence Production, Strategic Plans, Military History and the Adjutant General office. Others worked in the Marine Corps Personnel Office/NAVFORV attending to the records and administrative functions for the 700-800 Marines who were not specifically attached to a unit.

While living in Saigon, we were fully aware of the risk when venturing out in the city and were advised to travel in pairs but this was often impossible given the varied work schedules. Hotels were bombed, so were restaurants. Anything could happen on the crowded streets. Some experienced the Tet Offensive of 1968 and subsequent attacks. Despite the circumstances and long hours with few days off, many found time to help at orphanages, a prenatal clinic and to volunteer in civic action programs. The total number of Women Marines who served in Vietnam was eight officers and 27 enlisted. We were, and are, "The Few, The Proud, The Marines."

Marine officers who served in country in the Republic of South Vietnam with final or last known rank.

Bertram, Lois J., Chief Warrant Officer 4
Filkins, E. Elaine (Davies), Colonel
♥Jones, Vera M., Colonel
Koch, Ernestine A., Chief Warrant Officer 4
Leaverton, Shirley E., Major
♥O'Holleran, Ruth J., Colonel

♥Reinholz, Ruth F., Lieutenant Colonel
Sharpsteen, Lila J., Lieutenant Colonel

Marine enlisted who served in country in the Republic of South Vietnam with final or last known rank.

Aaron, Barbara J., Master Sergeant
♥Connolly, Bridget V., Master Sergeant
Denton, Doris L., First Sergeant
Diaz, Adelina (Torres), Master Sergeant
Dickerson, Teresa A., First Sergeant
Dorsey, Maryland L. (Welch), Sergeant
♥Dulinsky, Barbara J., Master Sergeant
Edwards, Andrea L., Corporal
Francoeur, Jeanne L. (Bell), Sergeant
Glaudel, Mary E. (DeZurik), Sergeant
Gonzales, Frances I. (Shore), First Sergeant
Hensley, Jeanette I. (King), Sergeant
♥Hollowell, Donna Lou (Murray), Master Sergeant
Ivy, Alaine K. (Thomas), Sergeant
Lester, Carol E., Gunnery Sergeant
Mach, Nellie D. (Perkins), Gunnery Sergeant
Makinster, Nola E. (Wilcox), Sergeant
Martinez, Martha D., Corporal
Morrison, Loretta M. (Kostyn), Staff Sergeant
Netherton, Ella L., Sergeant
Potter, Diane L., Sergeant
Roach, Jacquelyn K., Sergeant
Salazar, Ermelinda (Esquibel), Staff Sergeant
Spatz, Sandra (Wiszneauckas), Sergeant
Varden, Helen J., Sergeant
♥Walsh, Mary P. (McDermott), Gunnery Sergeant
Wilson, Pauline W., Corporal

# NAVY
*~ Mary Glaudel-DeZurik*

With Vietnam turning into a prolonged engagement, the Navy was in need of more ships and therefore, more manpower. The Dillon Board in 1962 had determined and recommended an overhaul of the Navy's administrative structure. While this reorganization was taking place, the Women of the Navy waited to see how they would fit into this new structure and how they would be utilized in this expanding war. Wartime service was not new to the Women of the Navy. The need for additional personnel to fill positions formerly held by men occurred in both World War I, World War II and Korea allowing women to enlist in the US Navy Reserve. Like the other members of their sister services many were released from active duty, which was typical of all post-war trends, once the wars had ended.

Captain Viola Brown Sanders, Assistant Chief of Naval Personnel for Women, issued a fact sheet in April 1965 stating the need for Navy women in peacetime and for a centered foundation from which to expand in case of war or a national emergency. In late 1966, the Navy, along with the other branches of the service, agreed it was time to enlarge their women's positions within the military. Although not entirely receptive to the idea of sending female Navy personnel to Vietnam, Captain Rita Lenihan, who was the Director of the Navy Women and Assistant Chief of Naval Personnel (1966-1970) along with Vice Admiral, Benedict J. Semmes, Jr., Chief of Naval Personnel, relented in early 1967 and allowed one WAVE to go to Saigon. The work and dedication of Lieutenant Elizabeth G. Wylie so impressed her commanding officer at NAVFORV that he wrote and requested additional well-qualified Navy female officers be sent. The Navy set a policy that only female Navy officers requested by a commanding officer by name would be allowed to go to Vietnam. Seven more Navy officers followed, but no enlisted would be allowed to go. Their positions included Command Information Center; Resources management analyst; Historian; and Naval Support Activity, under the Commander NAVFORV. One Navy officer, Lieutenant Ann Moriarty, in 1971 became the first female naval advisor to help Vietnamese Navy dependents become self-sufficient by operating various businesses. Commander Elizabeth M. Barrett was the highest ranking female line officer to hold a command in a combat zone. After the disestablishment of the Naval Advisory Group in early 1972, Commander Barrett was transferred to Commander Naval Forces Vietnam where she was first assigned as the Assistant Chief of Staff for Administration and then Chief of Staff for Administration/Commanding Officer Enlisted Personnel COMNAVFORV, giving her the judicial authority to convene Summary or Special Court Martials and to hold Captain's Mast. She served in Vietnam for 15 months.

While the Navy was the last military branch to send their women to Vietnam and sent the smallest number of women, there can be no doubt that their dedication and service opened the doors for future generations of women serving in the Navy.

It is known and recorded that eight female Navy officers served during the Vietnam War. No female enlisted Navy personnel were in Vietnam. Their stories (those that were available) are contained in the chronological chapters of this book.

♥Adsit, Carol Alpha, Captain
Anderson, Mary A. (Shupack), Captain
Barrett, Elizabeth M., Commander
♥Bole, Barbara, Commander
Bostwick, Sally L., Lieutenant
Hamilton, Susan F. (Cusson), Lieutenant Commander
Moriarty, Ann J. (Gaskin), Lieutenant Commander
Wylie, Elizabeth G., Captain

Four female Navy Medical Technicians also served during the Vietnam War on the USS *Sanctuary* and USS *Repose* not as nurses, but in the Medical Service Corps. They also earned the Vietnam Service Ribbon. Their names will now be a part of the history of women who served in the Republic of Vietnam. Their stories are also presented in this book.

## USS *REPOSE* (AH-16)

On October 16, 1965, the USS *Repose* was recommissioned for service in Vietnam after being in reserve for nearly 11 years. On January 3, 1966, the *Repose* was permanently deployed in Southeast Asia serving mainly in the area of I Corps (northernmost part of South Vietnam). Known as the "Angel of the Orient," she treated more than 9,000 battle casualties and 24,000 inpatients until she permanently left the area on March 14, 1970.

♥**Lieutenant Commander Paula Cecelia Towle** served on the USS *Repose* from October 1966 until October 1967 as the *Repose* Pharmacy Operator. Lieutenant Commander Towle also served during World War II and the Korean War. On July 1, 1970, she retired from the US Navy after 25 years of dedicated service. She passed away June 27, 2003, and is buried at the Massachusetts National Cemetery in Bourne, MA.

♥**Lieutenant Commander Edna E. "Mickey" McCormick**, a native of Ohio, enlisted in the US Navy Reserves in October 1942, released to inactive duty in 1945, then recalled in October 1950. Lieutenant Commander McCormick served aboard the USS *Repose* as the Blood Bank Specialist for 18 months starting in 1965. She was a registered Medical Technologist with the American Society of Clinical Pathologists. She retired from the Navy May 1, 1968, after a long and distinguished career. Lieutenant Commander McCormick passed away July 19, 2003, in Albuquerque, NM.

**Lieutenant Carmen P. Marshall (Adams)** enlisted in the US Navy Reserve in July 1964 after graduation from St. Mary of the Springs College in Columbus, OH, and completion of her year of training as a Medical Technologist, American Society of Clinical Pathology (MT ASCP) at Mt. Carmel Hospital, also in Columbus. Her first duty station was in the Blood Bank at Naval Hospital Bethesda, MD, where Lieutenant Commander Edna McCormick was her supervisor. Lieutenant Marshall extended her active duty service for duty on the USS *Repose*, but was first transferred to Balboa Naval Hospital, San Diego, to work in the Blood Bank there. In November 1967, she was assigned to the Laboratory and Blood Bank on board the USS *Repose* and served there until November 1968. In addition to her medical duties, she rotated on Watch as Administrative Duty Officer for the hospital. She returned to the Blood Donor Center, Naval Hospital, San Diego, to finish her contract. Lieutenant Marshall resigned her commission in July 1969 to return to civilian life. She worked for 45 more years as a Medical Technologist. She retired in 2009.

## USS *SANCTUARY* (AH-17)

The USS *Sanctuary* was also a recommissioned ship, having spent five years from September 1, 1966, berthing with the National Defense Reserve Fleet, until March 1, 1966 when it was towed to the Avondale Shipyards for modernization. The official recommission was November 15, 1966. She now was equipped with 20 wards, four operating rooms, a helipad, three x-ray rooms and other modern conveniences. On April 2, 1967, she joined the 7th Fleet at Subic Bay, and on the 10th she arrived at Da Nang, South Vietnam. The USS *Repose* mainly operated in the I Corps area including not only Da Nang but also Phu Bai, Chu Lai and Dong Ha as needed. After March 16,

1970, the USS *Repose* was the only Navy Hospital ship off Vietnam. On April 23, 1971, she departed from Da Nang for the last time.

**Lieutenant Commander Patsy J. Robinson** served on the USS *Sanctuary* from 1967 – 1968 working as a Medical Technologist in the Laboratory/Blood Bank. She entered the US Navy in 1964 and retired in July 1983.

# AIR FORCE
*~Darlene Brewer-Alexander*

## The Struggle to Enter the War

This story must begin with the Air Force woman who cleared the way for all of us to serve in Vietnam. Then Colonel Jeanne M. Holm, Director of Women in the Air Force (WAF) from 1965–1973, knew without a doubt at the onset of the war in Vietnam that AF women expected to be deployed right along with the men. But that didn't happen. Nurses and female civilians deployed, but WAF volunteers were turned down. Complaints came pouring in to her office. "In early 1966, a plainspoken master sergeant, a veteran of World War II, demanded to know why she had been told by a 'fresh-faced' lieutenant in the base personnel office that he would not accept her request for duty in Southeast Asia (SEA). 'He wouldn't know one end of an M-16 from the other,' she exclaimed in exasperation, pointing to her triple rows of ribbons. 'I served in North Africa and Italy – I can sure as hell serve in Vietnam.'" "A young sergeant clerk-typist in the Pentagon was more philosophical about having her request for assignment to SEA turned down until she learned to her chagrin that a civilian typist who worked across the hall had volunteered and was soon on her way to Saigon. 'Why not me?' she wondered aloud."

It was a complicated time – on the one hand harassed assignment officers had jobs to fill in SEA and piles of volunteer statements from WAF who could fill them, but their hands were tied because of an unwritten policy that AF women would not be assigned to a combat zone. Excuses were made about the conditions and lack of accommodations for women. Finally, trip reports started filtering back to the Pentagon that WAF skills were needed in SEA and that Wing Commanders had said they could accommodate them. Colonel Holm took that opening and made a trip to SEA to gain firsthand knowledge of the situation in order to advance the argument that would allow AF women to be assigned to SEA. She visited bases in Vietnam and Thailand and the various headquarters in Saigon, Bangkok and Hawaii. Her conclusions mirrored the reports of others that women could be accommodated and there was a critical need for their skills.

It didn't happen overnight or in just one battle, but by June 1967 AF women were being assigned to the Republic of Vietnam. Between 500 and 600 WAF served in the Southeast Asia theater, of which over 200 served within the Republic of Vietnam. Women in the Air Force had become an essential and integral part of the Air Force effort.

Colonel Holm was promoted to Brigadier General in 1971, the first woman ever to hold that rank in the Air Force, and in 1973 the first woman of any Service to be promoted to the grade of Major General. She was an extraordinary woman and was the driving force behind expanding the roles and opportunities for Women in the Air Force – it began with the Vietnam War.

## WAF Enter the Vietnam War

Excerpts from General Holm's article below, Air Force Women in the Vietnam War, tells a story of struggle and triumph for these women.

"At the time of the Vietnam War military women in the United States Air Force fell into three categories: female members of the Air Force Nurse Corps (AFNC) and the Bio-medical Science Corps (BSC) (all of whom were officers). All others, officers and enlisted women, were identified as WAF, an acronym (since discarded) that stood for Women in the Air Force." It is this latter group of women whose stories are included in this book.

"When one recalls the air war in Vietnam, visions of combat pilots and returning prisoners of war come easily to mind. Rarely do images emerge of the thousands of other dedicated Air Force women and men who performed the support roles essential to the overall success of the air operations, or the flight crews who daily risked their lives to pick up casualties from the battlefield and transport them to medical facilities in country and to hospitals outside the war zone, or the people who participated in the repatriation of our prisoners of war. Nor does one generally think of the dedicated members of the Air Force Reserve and Guard aeromedical evacuation units who were called upon to put aside civilian pursuits to fly missions into Southeast Asia to bring the wounded home.

"By the time U.S. forces were withdrawn from the Southeast Asia (SEA) theater of war, hundreds of Air Force women had served tours in South Vietnam and neighboring Thailand. Working side-by-side with their male comrades, they faced the same challenges and were exposed to the same risks and hardships as the men in the same units. And, like the men, many received wartime citations and decorations. One gave her life (Capt. Mary Therese Klinker, a flight nurse killed in the "Babylift" crash, the last casualty of the Vietnam War by some accounts). Many other Air Force women volunteered for duty in the combat zone but because of a lack of a coherent Air Force or Defense Department policy on the wartime deployment of women, their requests were denied.

"Because women had no military obligation, either legal or implied, all who joined the Air Force during the war were volunteers in every sense. Most were willing to serve wherever they were needed. But, when the first American troops began to deploy to the war in Vietnam, the Air Force had no plans to send its military women. It was contemplated that all USAF military requirements in SEA would be filled by men, even positions traditionally considered 'women's' jobs. This was a curious decision indeed considering the Army Air Corps' highly successful deployment of thousands of its military women to the Pacific and Southeast Asia Theaters of war during World War II.

"When the U.S. became involved in Vietnam, many Air Force women saw no reason why they should not take their fair share of duty in the war zone wherever their skills were needed and insisted they were capable of coping with the combat theater environment. Commanders, however, expressed practical concerns about having to divert precious resources and energy to provide for the women's safety, housing and other special needs. While most of these concerns were without merit, they might well have foreclosed on the deployment of Air Force women to SEA had it not been for growing shortages of men in some fields and for the persistence of women volunteering for SEA tours.

"In reality, female officers required little or no special arrangements. They could easily be accommodated in bachelor officer quarters (BOQs), as were the female officers of the other services and the civilian women (civil service employees, Red Cross workers, librarians) working in the theater. However, Air Force policies dictated that lower-grade enlisted women be quartered in separate all-female dormitories supervised by a WAF squadron, commanded by a female officer. (The Air Force did not want to set up a WAF squadron in Vietnam, so only a limited number of enlisted women were assigned to Vietnam at any one time). As a result, (many) enlisted women with skills needed in the combat theater war were exempted from tours . . . (while) many men in the same fields (were faced) with involuntary second and third tours. . . .

"With the successful deployment of female nurses (to the combat theater) the policy of excluding other military women from SEA duty became moot. In June 1967, at the request of the Military Assistance Command, Vietnam (MACV), the first WAF, a lieutenant colonel and five enlisted women arrived for duty with the headquarters in Saigon. Others soon followed for duty in the Saigon area in MACV and 7th Air Force headquarters and Tan Son Nhut air base on the outskirts of Saigon. A few officers were subsequently assigned to duty at Bien Hoa and Cam Ranh Bay air bases.

"Because of the requirement for WAF squadrons and separate dormitories, only a limited number of enlisted women were stationed in South Vietnam at any one time. Most enlisted women served in Thailand assigned to units of the 13ᵗʰ Air Force at Korat, Udorn, Ubon, Nakhon Phanom, Takhli, and Don Muang. They also served with the Military Assistance Command Thailand (MACTHAI) in Bangkok and at U-Tapao.

"WAF officers and enlisted women were assigned as routine replacements for male personnel with the same skills who were rotating out at the end of their one-year tours. Unlike the nurses, who were in a field still dominated by women, the WAF were something of an anomaly because they were assigned to jobs normally filled by men. WAF officers were in a wide variety of noncombatant fields including supply, aircraft maintenance, public affairs, personnel, intelligence, photo-interpretation, meteorology, (communications-electronic) and administration.

"Except for living in all-female officers' quarters, WAF officers were fully integrated in the units to which they were assigned as replacements for male line officers and, in general, they adapted to the combat environment as well as the men they replaced. Nevertheless, they were always aware of their status as female officers in what was still regarded as a male world and were conscious of living under a microscope 24 hours a day.

"Each WAF in SEA realized that she was on trial. In addition to adapting to the combat theater environment, she was conscious of living in a fishbowl where her professional competence, her personal character and her courage were always subject to critical scrutiny . . .

"Despite the initial reluctance to deploy women to SEA, by the end of the U.S. involvement in the war, the proportion of WAF officers serving in SEA was comparable to that of the male line officers, Air Force-wide. But, because of their more limited assignment options, the proportion of enlisted WAF who served SEA tours remained relatively small. They were employed chiefly in traditional jobs, such as: administration, clerical, personnel, data processing, supply and data processing . . .

"By law and policy, all military women were noncombatants. Nonetheless, in recognition of the ever-present danger of enemy infiltration and attack, Air Force women receiving orders to SEA were given weapons familiarization training, including the M-16 rifle. Flight nurses on air evacuation missions in country often carried side arms for their own protection and that of their patients. But, the need for all women to be able to handle weapons took on new meaning with the Tet offensive. If any proof was needed that modern American women were capable of performing under fire, the Tet offensive provided it. Even though they were noncombatants and were generally confined to the well-protected Saigon area and Cam Ranh Bay, Air Force women in country were as much at risk of enemy fire as their male comrades in the same units. Certainly, gender was no protection when the Viet Cong launched the coordinated attack on U.S. installations in January 1968. The mortar rounds, rockets and sniper fire that came in did not discriminate by occupation or sex. . . .

"The conduct and performance of the women were attested to by many observers, male and female. A male senior master sergeant reported to the Chief Master Sergeant of the Air Force 'What impressed me the most, with respect to the conduct of our personnel during the Tet offensive was the calm (with which) female service members went about their duties. That belief that the frail (or fair) sex will tremble at the first sign of trouble is not true,' he wrote. 'I observed female military members performing their duties no different than anyone else. If they had fears . . . they did a terrific job of concealing them,' adding that 'Air Force women are doing an outstanding job here.'

"Nevertheless, shortly after the first Tet attack, some Air Force command officials proposed to USAF Headquarters in Washington that, for their own protection, all WAF officers and enlisted women be evacuated from Vietnam. But with few exceptions, the women would have none of it. 'I want to stay and finish my tour,' a WAF major insisted. 'I'm not a fool and I'm not saying this because I'm patriotic. I feel we have a job to be done and we'd best get on with it.' A female staff sergeant echoed the same sentiments in a letter to the WAF director in the Pentagon: 'Don't let them send us home. I came here to do a job and I want to see it through.' Air Force personnel officials agreed – the policy would be the same for male and female military personnel.

"No one has ever compiled a list of the military citations and decorations awarded to women who served in SEA during the war. In fact, there are no data that accurately reflect the number of Air Force women who actually served in the Southeast Asia theater of operations during the Vietnam War. The question is academic in any case since the air war was not waged in isolation from the rest of the Air Force. It was an integral part of a vast organization of commands and a worldwide network of installations staffed by dedicated men and women of all ranks and skills.

"Many Americans have wondered why women, for whom there was no legal or implied obligation to serve their country in peace or war, would volunteer for duty in Vietnam. Most of those who volunteered felt it was their patriotic and professional duty to serve wherever their skills could be used. Some wanted the challenge and the obvious career benefits of serving in a combat zone. Others wanted to go where the action was. For many of the more senior officers and noncommissioned officers there was a determination not to be denied their right to serve in any assignment they were qualified to fill, whatever the risks. One female major intelligence officer put it bluntly: 'I have the same training (as the men). I get the same pay. I signed the same oath. I should take the same risks.'

"Whatever originally motivated women to volunteer for duty in Southeast Asia during the Vietnam War, they had very little idea of what they would experience or how profound an impact that year would have on the rest of their lives. They had done more than their country had expected of them without asking for special treatment or favors. The war experiences left an indelible imprint on each of their lives; they would never be the same again. They would continue to share a special bond, often unspoken, with other women and men who shared that experience. And they would always carry a special private grief for those who did not make it home alive."

### Sources

*Women in the Military: An Unfinished Revolution,* by Brig. Gen. Jeanne M. Holm, Presidio Press, 1982. All quotes in the Introductory Section are from this book.

*Air Force Women in the Vietnam War,* by Jeanne M. Holm, Major General, U.S. Air Force, Retired, and Sarah P. Wells, Brigadier General, U.S. Air Force Nurse Corps, Retired. The full article is available at the Women in Military Service for America Memorial Foundation (WIMSA) and the Vietnam Women Veterans Organization websites. This article is from a booklet produced for the dedication of the Vietnam Women's Memorial and published in the commemorative booklet, titled: *Celebration of Patriotism and Courage: Dedication of the Vietnam Women's Memorial,* November 10-12, 1993, Washington, D.C., pages 45-49. Vietnam Women's Memorial Project, 1993.

Maj. Gen. Jeanne M. Holm was Director of the Women in the Air Force (WAF), Headquarters, USAF, from 1965 to 1972. From 1973 to retirement in 1975, she served as the Director of the Air Force Personnel Council. Maj.

Gen. Holm retired with four years in the United States Army Air Force and 27 years in the United States Air Force.

Brig. Gen. Sarah P. Wells served from 1968 to 1972 in the Office of the Command Surgeon, Military Airlift Command, two years of which were as the command nurse. From 1979 to 1982, she served as Chief of the Air Force Nurse Corps, Office of the Surgeon General, Headquarters, USAF.

# Air Force Women in Vietnam

Mary Jane Abare
Maria M. Abrahante
Claire V. Allison
Alice F. Anderson
Diana Stack Andrews
♥Ethel E. Apter
Norma A. Archer
♥Judie A. Armington
Dorothy G. Baird
Mary E. Baker
Barbara L. Banks
Joan E. Barber
♥Faye Lou Beard
Linda A. Bellard
Joan F. Bence (Naylor)
Margaret B. Berry (Underwood)
Carol S. Bessette
Ann H. Best (Volkwine)
Ruth M. Black
Donna R. Bornholdt (Spaller)
♥Wanda Mae Brechbuhler
Darlene K. Brewer (Alexander)
Shirley J. Brown
♥Margaret Ozella Buck
Martha A. Cessna
Alice I. Champagne (Littlejohn)
♥Sarah Chavez (Cox) (McCauslin)
Carol L. Churchill
Katie Mozelle Clark
Laurie A. Clemons (Parkerton)
Maralin K. Coffinger
Claudia Crowley Collins
Sandra L. Combs
Nancy L. Comer (Lesher)
Sandra L. Conderman
Cheryl L. Connor (Ainsworth)

Juanita R. Cox
Ruth A. Cox
♥Barbara Ann Cramer
♥Mary Lavinia Crosby
♥Suzanne Crum
Mary A. Curry (Murry)
♥Carol A. Kastensmidt (Damron) *
Sally L. Davidson (Creely)
Patricia M. Dean (Rourk)
♥Frances Juanita DeLee (Taylor)
Louise Delvecchio
Bernice J. DeSisto
♥Catherine Louise Dismuke
♥Mary Elizabeth Dowd
Mary F. Draisker
Lena C. Duke
♥Sophia Adele Dziadura
Fannie Belle Rollins (Edwards) *
Ruth M. Ellis (Anderson)
Peggy J. Erhart
Sherry A. Ewan (Sieg)
Mary Lou Fake
♥Lillian Feldman
Bessie L. Fickel
Dale Ford (McGlynn)
♥Beatrice E. Fowler
Meredith L. Freeman (Nakabayashi)
♥Mary Smith (Gafney)
♥Marie Constance Eva Gagne
Nuala R. Gardner
Aurora Gibson (Toth)
Barbara J. Gordon
Lynn F. Gormley (Christian)
Helene Gotch
Wera F. Grammer (Damhauser)
Betty L. Griffith

Virginia A. Griffith

♥Virginia Lanelle Gunter

Doris W. Gustafson

Marie J. Gutierrez

Margaret M. Hammond (Anno)

♥Patricia M. Harlin

Sara N. Harris

Louise Haselrig

Patsy Dianne Hatley

♥Patricia A. Hayes

♥Ann Bernardette Healy

Jane Helms (Vance)

Marie L. (Helscher) LeBlanc *

Dona R. H. Hildebrand

June H. Hilton (Augustine)

Ann L. Hirdler

Carol J. Hornick (Gilmour)

Beverly K. Huber (Roberts)

Janice Hunt (Sanborn)

♥Cora D. Hunter

♥Ann R. Johnson

Clara Chris Johnson

Sylvia A. Johnson (Brown)

♥Verna Sarah Kellogg, II

Nancy R. Kennedy

Paula V. Kerns (Woodward)

♥Cecile Doreen Lanoue (Seago) *

♥Patricia Dorothy LaRocque

♥Rita A. Lawler

♥Joan Jodi Lesnikowski

♥Lillian Mildred Lewis

Linda A. Ligon

Linda L. Liston (Katalenich)

Cynthia H. Little

♥Barbara Jean Loar

Merline Lovelace

Catherine J. MacBride

Mary A. Marsh

Judy Ann Martin

♥De Ann R. Masters

Diane R. Matthews

Grace M. McAlister (Gallo)

♥Eleanor Jeanne McCallum

Shirley A. McClendon

Rosemary McCulley (Kitchen)

♥Jessie Marguerite McGraw

Regina M. McGuiness

Constance L. McVey

♥Marilyn B. Michaud

Susan A. Hallbauer (Milley) (Earl)

Norma L. K. Mokuau

Mary M. Morris

Patricia M. Murphy

Sharon M. Murry

♥M. Loretta Navik

Gayle B. Neave

Susan B. Neugebauer

♥Eva Marie Nordstrom

Geraldine F. Odom

♥Joan Olmsted

♥Yvonne C. Pateman

Betty A. Patterson (Pope)

Dorothy Peek

Joyce C. Peluso

Marcia C. L. Petersen

Linda L. Pilcher

Rita Pitcock (Gilchrist)

♥Barbara M. Sweeney

(Pratt-LeMahieu)

Clare Price (Zens)

Jo A. Pritchard

♥Velma Frances Reid

Lillie M. Rice (Smith)

Mary A. Rives (Brillas)

Marilyn V. Robinson

♥Nancy L. Rust

Jane Rutledge
♥Colleen Margaret Ryan (Cleaves)
♥Kathleen Frances Sabo (Grassmeier)
Elizabeth A. Schattner
♥Lois Margaret Schmoker
♥Neely Elizabeth Scott
Vivienne C. Sinclair (Vuosolo)
Eleanor L. Gavin (Skinner) *
Jean M. McLintock (Smith)
Lyndell D. Smith
Mary E. Smith
♥Ruth Gail Smith (Mahaffey)
Welda A. Smith
Barbara J. Snavely
♥Jean W. Solomon
Catherine J. Southall
Martha N. Stanton
Peggy J. Starnes (Young)
Audrey Stebenne
Loretta Jane Struthers
Frances Talley (Symes)

♥Susan Tasca (Wright) (Gaylor)
Jillian D. Tate
Kimberly Y. Taylor (Johnson)
Charlotte R. Tesch
Sharon E. Thomas (Safford)
Barbara J. Thompson (Barnett)
Yvette R. Thorne (Crutcher)
Caroline A. Tschetter (Nuese)
♥Mary Nell Turner
Carol A. Urich
Wilma L. Vaught
Esterina Marie Vella
Barbara A. Verderber (Walker)
Camilla L. Wagner
Eileen C. Ward (Rossi)
Sheila Warren (Smith)
Mary J. Webb
Annie E. Whitman (White)
Kathryn Wilson (Disbrow)
Carol L. Witt
Patricia A. Worthen (Champion)

In the Air Force section above, names marked with * indicate the WAF was using her married name while serving in Vietnam.

# Medical Specialist Personnel in Vietnam
*~ Carmen P. Marshall (Adams)*

Whenever I mention that I served in Vietnam, the response is always, "Oh, you were a nurse." I was never a nurse and though I admire and respect the profession, it was never a career that I wanted for myself. I chose laboratory medicine, along with education and administration in that field and spent many years following that path in the military and civilian life.

Like me, there were many women who chose other medical fields and took their professional training into all branches of the military. They served active duty personnel and their families, the sick and the wounded. They were physical therapists, dietitians, laboratory technologists, occupational therapists and pharmacists. They were in military facilities all over the world. When told that their area of medical expertise was needed in Vietnam, they willingly stepped forward as volunteers. They were in Vietnam as early as 1965 at the request of Command surgeons and physicians. They were among the last to leave in 1973.

They went to work in Convalescent Centers, Evacuation Hospitals, Field Kitchens, MAST units, Command Centers and Hospital Ships. They were in Saigon, Tan Son Nhut and Cam Ranh Bay, Cambodia and Laos. They sailed up and down the coast of I Corps from Da Nang to the DMZ taking care of the military and civilian casualties (I Corps being the northernmost segment of South Vietnam). They helped train ARVN (South Vietnamese Army) nurses and therapists to care of their wounded military personnel. They acted as consultants to Vietnamese officials who wanted to establish rehabilitation programs for civilian and military wounded. At Vietnamese hospitals and clinics, they assisted men, women and children who had been injured in the war. They prepared nutritional food to help with healing, and to feed the myriad personnel supporting the combat troops. They even volunteered at orphanages and schools, helping the Vietnamese people in whatever ways they could.

These women went where they were needed. They flew in helicopters and cargo planes, rode in jeeps and trucks to get there. They lived in tents and barracks with wood floors. They hid in bunkers when the mortar fire came their way. They walked by the leaking drums of Agent Orange and breathed the humid air and red dirt of Vietnam. They celebrated birthdays and holidays thousands of miles from home, because they were doing a job they loved. They cried with their friends when mail didn't come, because they could not cry about their patients. They were trained professionals serving their country as they had promised and giving the highest quality care possible, even under the most trying circumstances.

Today, as a group or individually, they will tell you that even though they might not remember what they had for lunch, they will never forget the time in Vietnam. The experience was memorable, in some cases life changing, definitely rewarding; but tears still come when they talk about it. Each one expresses pride at being a veteran who served their country and thankful to be asked about their experiences for this publication. Some of these women are no longer with us, but those with whom they served will never forget them. None of us have forgotten Vietnam. Now the rest of the world will know what we can't forget.

Every branch of the military has different designations for their medical specialty professionals.

**ARMY:** *AMSC* is Army Medical Specialist Corps. This division is for Physical Therapists, Dietitians, and Occupational Therapists, and just recently Physician Assistants. *MSC* is the Medical Service Corps, which is a combined group of Healthcare Scientists, Healthcare Administration and Clinical Care Providers. Medical Laboratory Technologists, Medical Supply and Administration, Psychologists and Physiologists (PhD, not MD) are included in this group.

**NAVY:** *MSC* is a combination of all of the above professionals, including Pharmacists.

**AIR FORCE:** *BSC* is the Biomedical Sciences Corps. All of the science-related careers: Physical Therapists, Dietitians, Medical Laboratory Technologists, Occupational Therapists, etc., are included. *MSC* is Healthcare Administration. These professionals are in charge of a department or facility in the Air Force Healthcare System, e.g. hospital, clinic, research facility, etc.

We owe this differentiation to an Act of Congress. In August 1947, the government made medical science professionals within the military equivalent to line officers, with all of the attending benefits. This was the first Medical Service Corps, whose officers were to take over the medical administrative, technical, and research duties from the physicians, so that the doctors could concentrate on taking care of their patients. Originally, the Medical Service Corps was MEN only.

The Army Women's Specialist Corps was established by this same Act of Congress; it was for Physical Therapists, Dietitians and eventually for

655

Occupational Therapists. This was for WOMEN only. These women had been serving in the military medical system (since WWI) as civilian contract workers, and later received temporary officer status similar to the nurses, but only for the duration of the war, and only within the medical department.

When the Women's Specialist Corps was disbanded and Women's Army Corps was integrated with the Army, these professions became AMSC or MSC. Since 1955, the Medical Service Corps had men and women serving together, so with this new designation, men were allowed in the AMSC.

Some of the AMSC women joined the Air Force at this time, and the BSC was started by the Air Force for their medical professionals in these designations.

*Source: Wikipedia on Army, Navy and Air Force Medical Service Corps History*

♥Patricia L. Accountius
Judith M. Adelman (Eason)
♥Mary Armstrong (Kelso)
♥Mary V. Baggan (Kelly)
Irene Begg
♥Clotilde O. Dent (Bowen)
Jessie S. Brewer
Carole J. Buss
Mary M. Cartwright
♥Beatrice L. Case
Gwendolyn E. Caton (Doty)
Martha A. Cronin
Ruth E. Dewton
Joan Drawdy
Mary P. Dwyer
Joanne E. Fenninger
Ann D. Fritsch
Jane E. Gierhart
♥Priscilla K. Gilchrist
Barbara Dickinson Gray
Mary S. Hall (Van Bebber)
♥Elizabeth J. Hamilton
♥Frances A. Iacoboni (Krilich)
Janet P. Jolin

Marcia B. Jones (Snow)
Joan B. Kyllo
♥Estill V. Latimer
♥Jacqueline M. Lavin
♥Mary Kathryn Leath
Mary P. Lowery
Carmen P. Marshall (Adams)
Sally Ann McCandless
♥Edna E. McCormick
Janice A. Mendelson
Nancy A. Meyer (Elliott)
Rita C. Minogue
Jeanne R. Moran (Gourley)
Bonnie G. Moscatelli
Mary Sue Ozburn
Patricia M. Pavlis
Nora M. Prestinari (Burchett)
♥Mary Rachel Preston
Barbara C. Reid
♥Cora Dexter Reynolds
Ida Richard
♥Hetty Ann Ricker
Patsy June Robinson
Sylvia Maria Rodriguez

♥Julia A. Rosengreen
Aida Nancy Sanchez
♥Marilyn J. Schmechel
Virginia Kay Schooler
Grace E. Scruggs
Patricia Sue Sepulveda
Rebecca H. Shumate (Richardson)
♥Barbara Jean Stearns
♥Bonnie J. Stewart (Hurst)
♥Beatrice Elizabeth Thompson
♥Marian E. Thompson

Jolene Kay Tomlan
♥Paula Cecilia Towle
Marcia Lou Turpin (Beasley)
Mary A. Van Harn
Jane C. Vickery
Mary Lee Welch
Mary Frances Westhoven
Grethe E. Wik
Barbara Wirth (Colon)
Sharon Yamashita

# Chapter Nineteen

# CONSEQUENCES OF WAR?

Every war, every conflict that our nation has fought has left its share of broken and damaged men and women who served. With today's social media and the worldwide reach of the internet, there are dozens of Facebook pages and websites that are by and for Vietnam veterans. Veterans are sharing their hearts, their stories, their nightmares, their health problems and an overwhelming sorrow and frustration with the medical care they have received. The national news has recently uncovered scandals at the Veterans Administration in several States and there are Congressional investigations ongoing. And it is nothing new.

The lingering effects of Agent Orange on military and civilian personnel who were in Vietnam prompted the creation of a Health Registry through the Department of Veterans Affairs to specifically examine and address the issues. It took decades to bring this about. The Registry starts with a comprehensive health exam which includes an exposure history, medical history, physical exam, and any tests if needed. For more information about this Registry, visit the Department of Veterans Affairs website.

*http://www.publichealth.va.gov/exposures/agentorange/benefits/registry-exam.asp*

Beyond Agent Orange issues, our veterans have drug and alcohol problems, mental issues that include Posttraumatic Stress Disorder and more recently, Military Sexual Trauma, both men and women. Many veterans speak openly about the increasing number of suicides of their friends. The Department of Veterans Affairs released "Suicide Data Report, 2012" that states there are approximately 22 veteran suicides a day. These numbers were mostly for older veterans.

At the Vietnam Women Veterans Conference held in Concord, NC, in May 2014, one guest speaker was Lourdes E. Alvarado-Ramos (Alfie), the Director of Washington State Veterans Affairs and a retired US Army Command Sergeant Major. She commented that women veterans, especially those who served during the Vietnam War, are an enigmatic group. "We served with distinction and ventured into unknowns that paved the way for those currently serving. Still, many have not found their earned place as a veteran nor claimed their benefits for many reasons. A veteran is anyone who served and was released with any type of discharge except dishonorable. My fellow WACs who were discharged for pregnancy still think they are not veterans. Our WWII veterans who did not deploy and served at home have not yet claimed their veteran status. Our gay sisters who were discharged do not think they are veterans. Many women who were unable to meet weight or physical training standards but did their job with honor and were discharged under chapters do not think they are veterans. If you served, you deserve! It is our hope that this book will wake the dormant warrior in all of us so that we can claim what is rightfully ours."

It should be noted that on January 16, 2014, S.1956 – Restore Honor to Service Members Act – was introduced in the Senate. It requires appropriate military record correction boards or discharge review boards to review the discharge characterization of any former members of the Armed Forces requesting a review who were discharged because of their sexual orientation, and it permits such boards to change a characterization to honorable if such characterization is any characterization except honorable.

Among the stories collected for this book, there were many that discussed these types of problems, and some of those stories are collected in this chapter for added emphasis and information. These are stories far too prevalent amongst women veterans. Many of the women interviewed were still unable to share or discuss their problems and told us they would only share the "good" things. They just don't talk about their time in Vietnam much.

***Judith McCurdy:*** When I got to Long Binh, I was sent for assignment to Camp Gerry, Headquarters Company, 39th Signal Brigade, as Administrative NCO and Drug Counselor. The company commander explained there was a massive heroin problem within the unit because of the infestation of "taxi" girls, a term with which I was unfamiliar. He explained "taxi" girls were prostitutes whose main purpose in life was to get the troops hooked on drugs. At first, the girls would give free heroin. Once the soldier was hooked, she would begin charging for the drugs along with her sexual services.

He further explained that the heroin in Vietnam was pure. This meant a three-vials-a-day habit in Vietnam would be equivalent to a 30-vials-a-day habit in the States. It was imperative for unit drug counselors to get these soldiers through the Crossroads Rehab Center before they rotated stateside. It was evident that a returning soldier with this kind of habit would not be able to support his needs once in the States. I was further informed that no records were to be kept of the soldier's addiction or his rehabilitation, and that the soldier had to volunteer for rehab. No one could be forced into the program. We were there to support the soldiers' rehab efforts. In addition, I was to be available for all "taxi" raids.

Now that the conflict was ending, it was the commander's number-one priority to get the drugs out of his compound and get his troops cleaned up before they were sent home. Therefore, since many of the "taxi" girls had long lived with their selected GI, Military Policemen were task with coming into the compound, unannounced, during evening hours to raid the hootches. I had to be available, to frisk the girls and confiscate their drugs. Once relieved of their drugs, the girls were loaded into military vehicles, and the MPs escorted them off the installation. The raids seemed futile since most times the "taxi" girls had returned to the barracks before the MPs had even returned their vehicles to the motor pool. This became a nightly exercise in patience and endurance, until the post was closed and the troops were either reassigned or sent home.

I wasn't prepared for what I saw on the first "taxi" raid. I was sitting in the NCO lounge with the unit's first sergeant and company commander when the announcement of the raid was made. We immediately went to the orderly room to find an MP had lined up maybe 25 women, ready to be frisked. My thought was, "No problem, they probably have some drugs taped to their ankles under their silk pajamas." WRONG! The first "taxi" girl I searched had vials of heroin taped at one-inch increment, up and down on the inside and outside of her legs. THIS WAS CRAZY! Her street value had to have been in the thousands of dollars, as was that of the next girl, and the next, etc. I was flabbergasted. The ensuing days were even worse.

The soldiers knew they were soon to receive orders to return stateside and that's when the reality of their situation hit them hard. THEY HAD TO CLEAN UP THEIR ACT! That's when my job as a Drug Counselor started. A young soldier would enter my office, eyes glazed, usually with a silly, bashful smile on his face. I knew exactly what his request was going to be. He would sit atop my desk and say, "Sarge, I need help. Can you take me there?" My answer? "Sure." I would make a call to his work section and informed them of their soldier's unexpected vacation plans. My next call was to Crossroads to inform them I was on my way.

During our journey to rehab, my conversation with the soldier was to reinforce the fact that his decision to go into rehab was a wise one. Then, I would be straight with him and tell him withdrawal was no Sunday school picnic, but was painful and required incredible strength. I would assure him that he was a strong man with the rest of his life ahead of him and that he could endure anything. I would tease him and tell him that after rehab, he would go home, have a bunch of kids, and if his wife could go through labor with his children, drug rehab was going to be a piece of cake. We would both laugh, and with a scared expression, the request was usually, "Please don't leave me alone." I would pat his hand, smile and reassure him that I would honor his request. I then appealed to his spiritual nature letting him know that if he called upon God for help, I was sure even God would be there with his loving embrace for assistance.

These "men" were actually boys, barely out of their teens. Yes, they had done something wrong. However, in my mind, they had been enticed by real pros in doing wrong and our military had taken a blind eye to the situation until they were due to go home to mama. And, yes, the young man beside me just wanted to be a clean, fit man going home to his mother. During those times, I had mixed emotions. I was bitter toward the "taxi" girls and the military system I loved.

There were also troops who were unable to face facts and were busy thinking up creative ways to smuggle drugs home, while hoping and praying not to be caught by inspectors. They would make room for drugs by taking apart their stereo speakers. Hollowing ceramic art figures was another method. Anything that could conceal heroin vials that would be shipped home became a purchase of choice.

On the streets of Saigon, one could buy huge ceramic elephants that were used as end tables by many Americans. The troops called them BUFFE (Big Ugly Fat F------ Elephant). Because these elephants were fired ceramics, their center was hollow, and it was common for brave/dumb(?) smugglers to put as many drugs as they could within the beast. However, this exercise was in vain, as the inspectors had long been on to this trick. The fact was they could never smuggle back enough dope to support a habit acquired in Vietnam. Eventually, the soldier had to face reality and go through rehab, if not in Vietnam, somewhere in the States.

To understand the magnitude of this problem let me jump forward to after the Paris Peace Accords were signed and the last planes began leaving the country. Military Policemen were given the relentless task of rounding up AWOLs, mostly soldiers who were so hooked on drugs they didn't want to leave the country. I remember seeing an MP pick up a soldier and handcuff him. En route to Tan Son Nhut Air Base, the soldier leaped from the jeep causing the MPs to chase him through the streets of Saigon. The MPs at this point had a very hard job. I told an MP friend about this incident and was surprised when he said it was quite common. With relief, I was told that once the soldier was taken to Tan Son Nhut, he was placed on a Medevac flight back to the States where he was taken to a military or VA hospital for proper rehabilitation.

I concluded that ALL soldiers in a combat environment do some dumb things thinking they can get away with it.

***Karen Offutt:*** Vietnam was a life-changing experience for me. Yes, I am proud that I went and that I made it home, but I had a lot of guilt about even surviving. I cried all the way home and wanted to do another tour. I was told I'd have to come home for a year and then go back. Vietnam changed the way I feel about trust, about people's ability to be cruel, about our involvement in wars, about my faith in our government. It destroyed my ability to just have fun. I have PTSD and cannot handle loud noises, people in my face, fireworks, etc. I never sleep all night. I'm constantly on guard. I used to be such a happy-go-lucky girl, but at 19, I grew old, quickly.

In addition, III Corps, where I mostly was, got sprayed the most of all the years of the war, in 1969. We weren't told anything about Agent Orange, although our government knew what the consequences would be. As females, we are born with all the eggs we will ever have. My eggs were damaged in Vietnam by Agent Orange. I got married and had twin sons in 1971. One son was born with cancer of the kidney, which I found when he was 15 months old. His fraternal twin had ADHD (Attention Deficit Hyperactivity Disorder), and bone and teeth deformities. My daughter, born three years later, was born with grand mal seizures and learning disabilities. I still knew nothing about Agent Orange (AO). It was years later that I finally learned of similar birth defects from AO. I testified at a Congressional Hearing to pass a bill for women Vietnam veterans who had children with birth defects. I was told that it would be in our families for seven generations! The bill passed, but I have yet to hear of any of our children receiving compensation, as the guidelines are ridiculously narrow. My son who had cancer of the kidney, just had heart procedures and he is 42. One of my granddaughters has had seizures and one of my grandsons was diagnosed with Type 1 Diabetes at 8 years old. What a legacy!

I was willing to go to Vietnam. I was willing to die for my country. To make it home and then be told we have a death sentence, from something we weren't informed of, is not something I would have been willing to risk. I've watched my friends die from Agent Orange and many from suicide because we had no mental health assistance when we returned. Yes, I'd like to forget about Vietnam, but no one can tell me how. The nightmares, the sights and smells will be with us forever. The war came home inside our bodies and our minds. And, the war goes on . . . ©2014 Karen Offutt

***Linda "Sgt. Mac" J. McClenahan:*** In the summer of 1970, I experienced three traumatic events which changed my life forever. The first involved a wounded orphan who I met when one of the orphanages came to the WAC Detachment to visit for a day of fun. The second was seeing a severely burned soldier come in to the 24th Evacuation Hospital while on my way to our mess hall. The third was being gang-raped by a friend of mine named Tony and two friends of his who were with the 212th Military Police. Afterwards I was dumped out the jeep Tony was driving like garbage discarded on the roadside and walked in a great deal of pain back to the WAC Detachment and told Captain Shirley Ohta, my unit commander, about what had happened. She was wonderful. However, the men's commander refused to cooperate and nothing came of it. He had threatened to ruin my military record and besides, "What did you women expect trying to be part of a *man's* war?" After that time, I started drinking very heavily, kept myself away from people, and just waited out my time to leave. I even stopped going to Mass because I no longer believed in God.

Coming back home was miserable. People were rude at best and violent at worst. Someone once called out, "Hey look, there goes one of Uncle Sam's whores." I was also with a paraplegic veteran friend who was pushed over in his wheel chair one day. I truly believed I was crazy because of the thoughts and emotions I had and the fact that I was angry all the time. But I didn't want anyone to know so I acted okay during the day at work (although I was written up for "anger issues" more than once) and at night would drink myself into oblivion. When the term PTSD came on the scene, I was relieved to know I wasn't crazy. I became part of a women veteran's therapy group at the Vet Center in Concord, CA, which helped greatly as well as individual counseling. It took a LOT of years and tears for me to feel somewhat "normal." I also found my way back to God. Actually, I formed a new relationship with God as I realized that it wasn't that I no longer believed in God, I just didn't believe in the God of my childhood. My own spiritual relationship with God is good.

I still thought about becoming a Sister at times but thought that no convent would want me with what I had done and what I had been through.

I was wrong; and in 1992 joined the Dominican Sisters of Racine, WI, an order known for its work with justice issues. I have been a co-facilitator of free retreats for veterans on healing from Posttraumatic *Spiritual* Disorder since about 2003, and give speeches on "Women in Military Service: from the American Revolution to Afghanistan and still forgotten in history."

I still suffer from PTSD, but am much better at responding to triggers and am at some peace with it all. I am proud to have served my country in a very difficult time and proud to be a Vietnam Veteran. I do, to be honest, still hold a little bit of resentment for how we were treated, but mostly I am okay.

***Deborah Godby:*** Debbie is 100% disabled based on PTSD (Posttraumatic Stress Disorder). Despite her experiences, Debbie was then, and is now, very proud of her Army service, her service in Vietnam and her uniform. She joined the service to serve her country, fight Communism, and get an education; she believes that as an individual she has contributed to these goals. She went on to serve 20 years and retired as a Sergeant First Class.

In retirement, despite limited vision and other issues, she is active in volunteer work in the community and among her fellow veterans. She is a proud member of the WAC Veterans Association Heritage Chapter 62, and serves in the Chapter's Honor Guard.

***Carol Bruckerhoff (Reynolds):*** My children paid for my service over there. Both of them have suffered debilitating abnormalities that are a direct result of my exposure to Agent Orange.

***Natalie Moody Summers:*** I remember one of the times when the ammunition dump blew up. I looked around and everyone was acting unusually uneasy. I decided to go to bed. In the morning, everyone was shocked that I slept through the whole thing. I now have a loss of high pitch hearing from Vietnam.

***Charlotte E Phillips:*** There were very significant moments when the combat units were firing on locations near our installation. The tracer rounds made a display I will never forget. It looked like every round was red but actually every hundredth shot was a tracer round. It was always scary because even in the bunkers, we still were subject to enemy fire – like the gentleman who just arrived in the country and was in the bunker with a flack vest on when a ricocheted round hit him in the chest between the vest. He was DOA (dead-on-arrival).

***Linda M. Barnes (Poole):*** I remember thinking what about all of those guys I was on the plane with; did any of them get killed on their first night in Vietnam? Yes, their base camp had incoming and I found out that some of the men were killed.

Things happen when you have been in a war zone. I have been going to VA counseling and have been diagnosed with PTSD. I could go on with more incidences while I was in Vietnam, but at this point in my life, my VA counselor is the one helping me to adjust.

***Joyce I. Harker:*** One of my worst memories is from the chopper landing site where the medics would cut the bloody clothing off the guys – there was a huge pile of clothing and it didn't seem to get smaller. And, I remember the triage stations – not good memories.

***Edith "Nikki" Hayhurst:*** Our Sundays (only day off), we would go to the orphanage hospital to care for the little children. I remember cleaning this little girl (just a few days old) when the Nun told me not to waste my time because the child wasn't going to make it.

I kept cleaning up this little girl – holding her close. Not long after I finished cleaning this special little girl, she died. It was such a hard time for me because she was part American.

***Marie L. (Helscher) LeBlanc:*** As an Administrative Services Officer, I was not directly involved in the conflict but, because I was assigned to the 460th Maintenance Squadron (aircraft), I worked on the flight line at Tan Son Nhut Air Base and saw the results of many attacks on our aircraft. Just living with the threat of attack 24 hours a day was very stressful, and I did a lot of drinking while there. I would trade my beer and cigarette rations for liquor.

To the best of my knowledge, the only residual effect of my Vietnam tour is that the sound of certain helicopters gives me goose bumps and may cause my heart to race. I attribute that to the fact that the WAF quarters were very close to the heliport, and choppers flew in and out day and night.

After Vietnam, I was stationed at Keesler Air Force Base, MS. I stayed in the Air Force one more year and then returned to California. My drinking continued to progress and I eventually entered a recovery program. I have 29 years of sobriety; in 2000, I retired with 25 years of service for the State of California.

***Sherri A. "Dizzy" "Pepsi Kid" "Tip" Tipton:*** I had several horrible experiences from some of the Army Reserve dental officers who were assigned to the 38th (Dental Detachment) to get their "combat tour." As a result I have years of anger, shame that has haunted me all my life, and I have been diagnosed with PTSD. My most heartbreaking experience was landing in San Francisco coming back from Vietnam. Protesters standing outside the airport would scream "Baby killer, slut, whore; you should be ashamed of yourself." As a result, I have become much more of an introvert and withdrawn from people. My daughter asks me sometimes, if I could do it all over again would I, and my answer is most definitely!

***Faye Conaway:*** One night during monsoon season, I was running to the outhouse and lost my way. I tried running toward voices I heard, but fell into a ravine and hurt my neck and back. (I began to show signs of this accident about 10 years ago – bulging discs and pinched nerves.) I'm currently in the medical program at the Veterans Administration in Kansas City, MO. My benefit is for Agent Orange Diabetes.

***Judith Diane Nickloy (Jones):*** It took me 15 years to get enrolled with the Veterans Administration. For the past 20 years, I have been trying to get the VA to test me for Agent Orange. I get boils on my face and tailbone (three or four at a time) and so does my 28-year-old son. He is totally blind in one eye due to Agent Orange. His father (my ex) also came in contact with Agent Orange.

***Nancy Wooten (Thorne):*** I'm dealing with PTSD and the effects of cancer, but I am grateful I'm still here. I am proud to have served my country – even my Vietnam experience.

***Alice "Baby" J. Delgado:*** Then there was a fire in my hotel. I still suffer from that experience. Worst of all: the picture in my mind of a truckload of dead bodies, from our own headquarters people –remains with me and will forever. Every day was awful after that. It was hard to laugh; we just drank a lot more. My heart is heavy; my mind and soul are numb. It's hard to write anything else. . . . The BAD was VERY BAD.

***Evelyn J. Ford:*** I can remember going to the Vietnamese headquarters where they had the pine box coffins of those killed. They were not airtight. To this day, I can still smell the odor of rotting bodies lined up in the hot sun. There were other smells, that, after all these years, I can still remember – the stink of the open fish market and the piles of trash in the streets.

***Christine Almanza (Sampley):*** The sound of helicopters coming and going was ceaseless. We spent many a night in bunkers. One night in particular after we had incoming, I went to work the next morning and was informed that one of the officers in the office next to ours had been killed. Readjustment to life stateside was not easy; for months, I had trouble sleeping and kept hearing the thumping sound of helicopters in my sleep.

I didn't realize that so much of life had passed me by. I was 20 years old going on 40! My perspectives on life had changed so much. My friends at home hadn't changed. Vietnam was just something they saw on TV. I did go out with them once, but left realizing that we didn't have anything in common anymore. So, I put in to go back to Vietnam.

***Brenda Sue Eichholz (Caldwell):*** To get to a meal, I had to walk to the nearest hospital where the mess hall was located. The best route was walking next to the helipad where the wounded were brought in. I had to walk through the emergency room. After a battle, the wounded were brought in groups for Triage, a medical strategy that determines the level of care to the wounded. Quick assessments were made, and those who would not survive were pushed aside on a gurney.

The average age of a soldier was 19, my age at the time. I walked past these gurneys and most soldiers would be moaning in pain. Many wanted to talk . . . so I stopped . . . and listened. Many times, I tried to comfort them by holding their hand. I watched many die. When I came back to the World, I brought these men back with me. Every day they flash before my eyes. They were my comrades. Someone needs to remember them.

***Barbara C. Reid (Physical Therapist):*** As I write this in January 2015, I am now 71 years old. I departed Vietnam 46 years ago. I am grateful for the fact that I volunteered to go to Vietnam and served my country and our wounded soldiers. I received a Bronze Star for meritorious service. I retired in 1985 with 20 years of service and obtained the rank of Lieutenant Colonel. I believe war is a horrible way to address conflict between countries. It destroys lives and wounds our service men and women both mentally, emotionally, spiritually and physically. It saddens me to this day that our veterans of Afghanistan and Iraq wars were repeatedly sent for multiple deployments and every day someone resorts to suicide. One deployment is difficult enough to recover from and I often wonder if one ever does completely recover. War changes one's life. We return different from when we went.

***D. "Dee" Ann Sims (Antomattei):*** After being in Vietnam for several months, stress began to take a toll on me physically and mentally. Whenever I became distraught or deep depression set in, I pulled on my hair and rubbed the edges of my temples often until I made my head bald in that area. I knew I had to get away to somewhere, anywhere, before I completely lost my mind.

***Frances "Frankie" Ann Earle:*** No doubt I had led a sheltered life, but even with the bad things, I remember how wonderful the Vietnamese people I met were and I don't regret that tour. It was a great experience but it has left me with some serious health issues. I have high blood pressure, chronic depression, and I am being treated for PTSD (Posttraumatic Stress Disorder).

667

You can't see people get their faces blown off and not keep seeing it. I also had to have a hysterectomy, and I heard that several of the women who served there had them. In addition, I have vitiligo – a loss of skin pigmentation – affecting mostly all the skin on my legs.

*Anonymous:* I have suffered most of my life since I left Vietnam. I have been diagnosed with PTSD and I am on the Agent Orange Register. I have developed large boils all over my body. I have difficulty sleeping at night. I never sleep more than two hours before I awaken from a nightmare. I feel as if I am back in Vietnam and am going to die. I see myself being attacked and I have NO means to protect myself. I have this nightmare every night. I am afraid to sleep because I know what I will be dreaming about. I suffer from depression related to my service in Vietnam. This is just no way to live.

*Anonymous:* It has been more than 45 years since I returned from Vietnam. I don't consider myself a hero, but I have been called that by some. I worked at the General Officer level. I saw and heard things that sicken me to this day. I cry from the time I wake up until the time I go to bed. It is so painful to me to relive those times. I have lived a very sheltered life since I have been home. Things happened to me that I can't express. Some of the things that happened to Sister Linda McClenahan happened to me. I have never gone to get any care – from anyone. I am afraid that once I share the smallest piece of what happened to me, I will completely fall apart and need intensive psychiatric care.

# Chapter Twenty

# STILL SEARCHING

*Marsha "Cricket" Holder:* Since the first conference in Olympia, WA, in 1999, there has been a search list of women we are trying to locate. I was probably on that list for a short time because no one remembered my real name. All they remembered was "Cricket." It was Hester "Peanut" Miller, who worked down the hall from me during my first 11 months in country, who remembered my first name and that I was from Mississippi. With that information, I got a phone call one day from Claire Brisebois Starnes and she asked, "Are you Cricket and did you serve in Vietnam?" Other than the lack of records for all women who went to Vietnam, two of the biggest obstacles in finding them have been the frequent use of nicknames and married names.

When we started this book, I looked at the Sister Search list on the Vietnam Women Veterans website; using genealogical research websites, I found addresses for 10 on the list and sadly found death records for 12 more. The names that still remain on that list are in this chapter. Any military records found online that confirm the woman served in Vietnam have been included. Some of those online military records indicate service in Vietnam, but because they are deceased or because we have not been able to locate them, we don't know when or where they were in country. I find new names almost daily and hope to continue this search until all are found and their service recognized in some way, even if it is only me telling them "Welcome Home."

I want to acknowledge the websites I use on a daily basis while searching for not only our deceased sisters but also those unknown women who served in Vietnam.

**Archives:** http://www.archives.com provides military records such as Vietnam Veterans Personnel Records, Retirements Records and Burial Records. These tell me when the women enlisted or retired; and based on the enlisted dates, I can estimate when they were born. The Archives site also has addresses for the living as well as birth, death and marriage records that have proved to be helpful. Sadly, the military records are not complete and the Vietnam records cannot be separated from all other records when searching.

**Nationwide Grave Locator:** http://gravelocator.cem.va.gov/ a free-to-use website from the Veterans Affairs to locate burial locations for those with a veteran's headstone.

**Ancestry:** http://www.ancestry.com This site has social security death index (SSDI), public records that sometimes give dates of birth and addresses, military burial information that gives service dates and some Vietnam veteran's awards and decorations information.

**Genealogy Bank:** http://www.genealogybank.com has obituaries from 1976 to present from major newspapers across the United States, plus news articles and the Air Force, Army, Navy and Marine Registers from the 1960s that provided dates of birth for the officers. GenealogyBank also has SSDI listings from the beginning of Social Security; but because of recent changes in the privacy laws, deaths from the latest three years cannot be posted.

**Find a Grave:** http://www.findagrave.com also a free-to-use website, where as a contributor, I created three Virtual Cemetery lists:

- http://goo.gl/yTjo9t for my deceased military sisters listed in this book
- http://goo.gl/wCVcDk for the Sister Search list of deceased women who <u>may</u> have served in Vietnam but for whom we have no dates in country
- http://goo.gl/jL2Sm9 for all women veterans to honor their service

Knowing year of birth and home of record has been all that was needed to find some of our women. Finding women veteran for all wars, especially Vietnam Veterans, has become a lifetime commitment for me. Please visit these virtual cemeteries for biographical information, and if you have information that can be added to a memorial, use any of the active links of my name: Marsha Holder.

Contact us if you can provide any additional information about the women listed above.

By EMail: **Women.Vietnam.Veterans@gmail.com**
By mail: **Vietnam Women Veterans (VWV)**
          **PO Box 54**
          **Acton, ME 04001**

# Gone, But in Our Hearts

These women served in Vietnam according to the records available, but no dates of service were found. They are listed in a separate Virtual Cemetery at http://goo.gl/wCVcDk

♥Peggy Ann Aldrich (Merschiem) / In country: UNK / Rank: Specialist 5, US Army / Duty: WAC Detachment, Administrative Specialist

♥Karen A. Clarke (Oldsen) / In country: UNK / Rank: Specialist 5, US Army / Duty: Executive Administrative Assistant

♥Patricia P. Delsman / In country: UNK / Rank: Major, US Air Force / Duty: 7th Air Force, Administrative Staff Officer

♥Terry Lynn Doubledee / In country: UNK / Rank: Specialist 4, US Army / Duty: Personnel Specialist

♥Delma Gray George / Retired as a Lieutenant Colonel / In country: UNK / Rank: Lieutenant Colonel, US Army / Duty: G4, Supply Staff Officer

♥Gwendolyn I. Pall / Retired as a Lieutenant Colonel / In country: UNK / Rank: Lieutenant Colonel, US Air Force / Duty: Transportation Staff Officer, Saigon

♥Lynda Ruth Horner / In country: UNK / Rank: Specialist 4, US Army / Duty: Clerk-Typist / Service dates: May 1969 – May 20, 1972

♥Letha Rosalee Whaley / In country: UNK / Rank: Specialist 5, US Army / Duty: Administrative Specialist

♥Elaine T. White / Retired as a Staff Sergeant / In country: UNK / Rank: Staff Sergeant, US Army / Duty: Food Service Specialist

♥Anne Merle "Sandy" Whitman / Retired as a Major / In country: UNK / Rank: Major, US Army / Duty: Personnel Staff Officer

♥Diane Victoria Wilson / In country: UNK / Rank: Specialist 5, US Army / Duty: Administrative Specialist

♥Thelma J. Wright / In country: UNK / Rank: Specialist 5, US Army / Duty: Administrative Specialist

# All-Service Sister Search List
*Names on this list **may or may not** have served in Vietnam.*

Many books are works-in-progress long after they have been published and this one is no different. As more information becomes available on the internet and through social media, the names on the following lists may catch the notice of someone who can fill in the blanks. If the reader can supply this information, please use this contact information:

By EMail: **Women.Vietnam.Veterans@gmail.com**
By mail: **Vietnam Women Veterans (VWV)**
**PO Box 54**
**Acton, ME 04001**

**Names in bold lettering** have partial military records available from Archives.com research.

Peggy Abbly / In country: UNK / Rank: UNK / Duty: most likely in Long Binh

Barbara Agee / In country: UNK / Rank: UNK / Duty: most likely in Long Binh

**Shirley A. Agee /** In country: UNK / Rank: UNK, US Army / Duty: Material Control & Accounting Specialist / Service dates: July 1971 – April 1972

**Barbara J. Allen /** In country: UNK / Rank: Specialist 5, US Army / Duty: Communications Center Specialist / Service dates: September 1968 – February 1982

**Barbara N. Allen /** In country: UNK / Rank: Specialist 5, US Army / Duty: Medical NCO / Service dates: September 1969 – July 1971

Loriann Allen / In country: UNK / Rank: Specialist 4, US Army / Duty: most likely in Long Binh

**Beverly U. Babcock /** Retired as a Staff Sergeant / In country: UNK / Rank: Staff Sergeant, US Army / Duty: Recruiter and Career Counselor (after Vietnam) / Service dates: September 1958 – September 1978

**Karen L. Beck /** Retired as a Master Sergeant / In country: UNK / Rank: UNK, US Army / Duty: Personnel Specialist, most likely in Long Binh / Service dates: July 1971 – May 1972

**Maxine M. Berg /** In country: UNK / Rank: Specialist 4, US Army / Duty: most likely in Long Binh, Clerk-Typist / Service dates: June 1967 – September 1971

**Karen Lu Bower (Sulheim) /** In country: UNK / Rank: Staff Sergeant, US Air Force / Duty: most likely in Saigon, Administrative Specialist / Service dates: November 1968 – August 1975

Helen Brewster / In country: UNK / Rank: UNK / Duty: most likely in Long Binh, Administrative Clerk

Muriel C. Bricker / In country: UNK / Rank: Specialist 4, US Army / Duty: most likely in Long Binh, Clerk-Typist

**Bertha M. Broyles /** In country: UNK / Rank: Senior Airman, US Air Force / Duty: most likely in Saigon, Administrative Specialist / Service dates: March 1968 – October 1977

**Mary L. Delinko /** In country: UNK / Rank: Specialist 4, US Army / Duty: most likely in Long Binh, Clerk-Typist / Service dates: October 1969 – July 18, 1972

**Mary A. Douglas /** In country: UNK / Rank: Specialist 5, US Army / Duty: most likely in Long Binh, Clerk-Typist / Service dates: March 1968 – January 27, 1971

**Frances Ellis /** In country: UNK / Rank: Specialist 4, US Army / Duty: most likely in Long Binh, Clerk-Typist / Service dates: August 1968 –January 1970

Juanita Ellis / In country: UNK / Rank: UNK / Duty: most likely in Long Binh

**Karen S. H. Fischer** / In country: UNK / Rank: Captain, US Air Force / Duty: most likely in Saigon, Administrative Management Officer / Service dates: July 1967 – August 1971

**Betty R. Freeman** / In country: UNK / Rank: Specialist 5, US Army / Duty: Medical NCO / Service dates: April 1970 – August 1976

**Mary L. Gant** / Retired as a Staff Sergeant / In country: UNK / Rank: Specialist 5, US Army / Duty: Administrative Specialist / Service dates: August 1966 – September 1986

**Barbara A. Gardner** / Retired as a Master Sergeant / In country: UNK / Rank: Staff Sergeant, US Air Force / Duty: most likely in Saigon / Date of Retirement: February 1988

**Linda J. Gonsalves** / In country: UNK / Rank: Specialist 4, US Army / Duty: most likely in Long Binh, Clerk-Typist / Service dates: June 1968 – September 24, 1971

**Alice B. Goodrich** / In country: UNK / Rank: Specialist 4, US Army / Duty: most likely in Long Binh, Administrative Specialist / Service dates: December 1966 – June 7, 1969

Michelle "Mitch" Goodwin / In country: UNK / Rank: Specialist 5, US Army / Duty: most likely in Long Binh

Harriet Gray / In country: UNK / Rank: UNK / Duty: most likely in Long Binh

Gloria Greeks / In country: UNK / Rank: UNK / Duty: most likely in Long Binh

Karen A. Green / In country: UNK / Rank: Specialist 5, US Army / Duty: 24th Evacuation Hospital, Medic

Victoria Green / In country: UNK / Rank: E5 / Duty: most likely in Long Binh

**Elaine M. Henning /** In country: UNK / Rank: Captain, US Air Force / Duty: most likely in Saigon, Intelligence Officer / Service dates: January 1969 – September 1982

**Patricia J. Hill (Baker) /** In country: UNK / Rank: Senior Airman, US Air Force / Duty: most likely in Saigon, Administrative Specialist / Service dates: February 1970 – December 1977

Vicki Horn / In country: UNK / Rank: UNK / Duty: most likely in Long Binh

**Karen L. Johnson /** In country: UNK / Rank: Specialist 4, US Army / Duty: Patient Administrative Specialist / Service dates: April 1970 – April 1972

**Patricia A. Johnson /** In country: UNK / Rank: First Lieutenant, US Air Force / Duty: Saigon, 12th RITS, Intelligence Officer / Service dates: May 1970 – September 1972

Amelia J. Kendall / In country: UNK / Rank: UNK / Duty: most likely in Long Binh

Evelyn Kezane / In country: UNK / Rank: UNK / Duty: most likely in Long Binh

**Karen King /** In country: UNK / Rank: Specialist 4, US Army / Duty: most likely in Long Binh, Medical NCO / Service dates: February 1970 – February 1973

**Mary L. Laird /** In country: UNK / Rank: Captain, US Air Force / Duty: most likely in Saigon, Intelligence Photo-Radar Officer / Service dates: August 1967 – August 1971

Jane Larsen / In country: UNK / Rank: UNK / Duty: most likely in Long Binh

**Barbara J. Lilly /** In country: UNK / Rank: Specialist 5, US Army / Duty: Long Binh? Medical NCO / Service dates: March 1968 – May 1971

Helen Lindsey / In country: UNK / Rank: UNK / Duty: most likely in Saigon

**Elaine J. Maczka /** In country: UNK / Rank: Specialist 4, US Army / Duty: most likely in Long Binh, Clerk-Typist / Service dates: March 1971 – April 1972

Mary Martin / In country: UNK / Rank: UNK / Duty: most likely in Long Binh

**Beverly J. Mathews /** In country: UNK / Rank: Specialist 5, US Army / Duty: most likely in Long Binh, Personnel Specialist / Service dates: March 1969 – March 1972

Deborah McCabe / In country: UNK / Rank: Specialist 5, US Army / Duty: most likely in Long Binh

**Karen K. McConnel /** In country: UNK / Rank: UNK, US Army / Duty: most likely in Long Binh / Service dates: August 1968 – June 1975

Judith E. McLain / In country: UNK / Rank: Staff Sergeant, US Air Force / Duty: most likely in Saigon

**Charlotte M. Miller /** In country: UNK / Rank: Senior Airman, US Air Force / Duty: most likely in Saigon, Administrative Specialist / Service dates: March 1970 – March 1974

Charlene Moody / In country: UNK / Rank: Specialist 4, US Army / Duty: most likely in Long Binh

**Elaine Doris Morgan /** Retired as a Master Sergeant / In country: UNK / Rank: Staff Sergeant / Duty: Recruiter/Career Counselor (after Vietnam) / Service dates: October 1963 – November 1983

Rose Marie Oksewsju / In country: UNK / Rank: UNK / Duty: most likely in Long Binh

**Billie J. Oliver /** In country: UNK / Rank: Specialist 5, US Army / Duty: Personnel Specialist / Service dates: July 1965 – July 1969

Joanne Paluski / In country: UNK / Rank: UNK / Duty: most likely in Saigon

**Karen K. Penney /** In country: UNK / Rank: UNK, US Army / Duty: most likely in Long Binh, Dental Specialist / Service dates: September 1971 – April 1972 (only record found)

Mary Petrosino / In country: UNK / Rank: UNK / Duty: most likely in Long Binh

**Patricia Pritchard /** In country: UNK / Rank: Specialist 4, US Army / Duty: most likely in Long Binh, Medical Corpsman / Service dates: October 1971 – March 1972 (only record found)

Cynthia Reddig / In country: UNK / Rank: UNK / Duty: most likely in Long Binh

**Deborah A. Reid /** In country: UNK / Rank: UNK, US Army / Duty: most likely in Long Binh / Service dates: December 1971 – April 1972 (only record found)

**Eloise L. Reid /** In country: UNK / Rank: Staff Sergeant, US Army / Duty: most likely in Long Binh, Practical Nurse / Service dates: September 1968 – April 1971

**Carol M. Rice /** Retired as a Sergeant First Class / In country: UNK / Rank: Staff Sergeant, US Army / Duty: Journalist / Service dates: July 1956 – February 1980

**Jackie C. Roberts /** In country: UNK / Rank: Specialist 5, US Army / Duty: most likely in Long Binh, Personnel Specialist

**Suzanne G. Roberts /** In country: UNK / Rank: Specialist 5, US Army / Duty: most likely in Long Binh, Pharmacy Specialist / Service dates: September 1968 – June 1972

**Sandra J. Robertson /** In country: UNK / Rank: Specialist 4, US Army / Duty: most likely in Long Binh, Communications Center Specialist / Service dates: September 1968 – June 1972

**Lorraine D. C. Sherwood /** In country: UNK / Rank: Staff Sergeant, US Air Force / Duty: 377th Combat Support Group, Personnel Specialist / Service dates: February 1968 – October 1973

Diane Siebert / In country: UNK / Rank: UNK / Duty: most likely in Saigon

**Mary C. Sims /** In country: UNK / Rank: Specialist 5, US Army / Duty: Finance Specialist / Service dates: September 1969 – May 1972

**Janet E. Smith /** Retired as a Technical Sergeant / In country: UNK / Rank: Senior Airman, US Air Force / Duty: most likely in Saigon, Administrative Specialist / Service dates: August 1968 – July 1990

**Joyce E. Smith /** In country: UNK / Rank: Specialist 5, US Army / Duty: most likely in Long Binh, Administrative Specialist / Service dates: September 1967 – October 1970

**Judy P. Smith /** In country: UNK / Rank: Specialist 5, US Army / Duty: most likely in Long Binh, Medical NCO / Service dates: October 1968 – September 1974

Patricia Smyth / In country: UNK / Rank: Specialist 4, US Army / Duty: most likely in Long Binh

**Patricia Anne Spalding /** In country: UNK / Rank: Specialist 4, US Army / Duty: most likely in Long Binh, Clerk-Typist / Service dates: November 1969 – May 1973

**Norma J. Spangler /** In country: UNK / Rank: Specialist 5, US Army / Duty: Administrative Specialist / Service dates: June 1969 – September 1974

**Elizabeth E. Spann** / In country: UNK / Rank: Specialist 4, US Army / Duty: most likely in Long Binh, Information System Operator / Service dates: November 1969 – May 1972

Kathy Sparata / In country: UNK / Rank: UNK / Duty: most likely in Long Binh

Theod Stapert (first name is probably Theodora) / In country: UNK / Rank: Master Sergeant, US Air Force / Duty: most likely in Saigon

**Christy Staples** / In country: UNK / Rank: UNK, US Army / Duty: most likely in Long Binh, Administrative Specialist / Service dates: August 1969 – July 1971

**Mary I. Sutherland** / In country: UNK / Rank: UNK / Duty: most likely in Long Binh, Clerk-Typist / Service dates: November 1970 – May 1972

**Karen L. Syates** / In country: UNK / Rank: UNK, US Army / Duty: most likely in Long Binh, Clerk-Typist / Service dates: November 1969 – March 1972

**Kim E. Taylor** / In country: UNK / Rank: Specialist 5, US Army / Duty: most likely in Long Binh, Personnel Specialist / Service dates: May 1967 – May 1970

**Karen F. Thompson** / In country: UNK / Rank: Specialist 4, US Army / Duty: Clerk-Typist / Service dates: March 1971 – February 1974

**Tina M. Wentzel** / In country: UNK / Rank: Specialist 5, US Army / Duty: most likely in Long Binh, Practical Nurse / Service dates: September 1969 – April 1972

Carol D. Williams / In country: UNK / Rank: UNK / Duty: most likely in Long Binh

Karen Willis / In country: UNK / Rank: UNK / Duty: most likely in Long Binh

**Barbara M. Wilson /** In country: UNK / Rank: Specialist 4, US Army / Duty: most likely in Long Binh, Clerk-Typist / Service dates: July 1968 – July 1988

Betty J. Wilson / In country: UNK / Rank: UNK / Duty: most likely in Long Binh

**Victoria L. Wilson /** In country: UNK / Rank: Specialist 5, US Army / Duty: most likely in Long Binh, Stenographer / Service dates: September 1969 – May 1972

Sherry Wren / In country: UNK / Rank: UNK / Duty: most likely in Long Binh

## Possible Service in Vietnam (Deceased)

In the search for the women we knew had served in Vietnam, these women were found, some by chance, others provided by the Women's Memorial Foundation Register and the Army Women's Foundation Bronze Memorial Plaques. These women have partial records on Archives.com that include Vietnam but the archives contain **both** Vietnam and Vietnam-Era veterans.

The deceased are listed first, alphabetically, followed by the presumed still living. If the reader has information about these women, please see the Contact Us information at the end of this list. Additional information about the deceased women is located in a virtual cemetery on Find-a-Grave.com at this address: http://goo.gl/wCVcDk

**Names in bold lettering** have partial military records available from Archives.com research.

♥Beverly Jo Boyle / Retired as a Sergeant First Class / In country: UNK / Rank: UNK, US Army / Duty: UNK

♥Margaret S. Browne / Retired as a Sergeant First Class / In country: UNK / Rank: UNK, US Army / Duty: Unit Supply Specialist

♥Ruth L. Butler / In country: UNK / Rank: Sergeant First Class, US Army / Duty: Unit Supply Specialist

♥Grace C. Clymer / Retired as a Master Sergeant / In country: UNK / Rank: UNK, US Army / Duty: Food Service Supervisor

♥Dolores I. Dolan / In country: UNK / Rank: Sergeant First Class, US Army / Duty: Unit Supply Specialist

♥Elizabeth E. Drexler / Retired as a Command Sergeant Major / In country: UNK / Rank: MSG, US Army / Duty: Administrative NCO

♥Angel M. Duty / In country: UNK / Rank: Specialist 5, US Army / Duty: Medical NCO

♥Sonia Kay Epley / Retired as a Master Sergeant / In country: UNK / Rank: Sergeant First Class, US Army / Duty: Administrative NCO

♥Mary Kathryn "Miki" Evans / Retired as a Major / In country: UNK / Rank: Captain, US Air Force / Duty: Administration Management Officer

♥Teatta G. Farmer / Retired as a Staff Sergeant / In country: UNK / Rank: Sergeant, US Army / Duty: Administrative NCO

♥Phyllis Caroline Foley / Retired as a Sergeant First Class / In country: UNK / Rank: UNK, US Army / Duty: Administrative Specialist

♥Pamela K. Fox / Retired as a Master Sergeant / In country: UNK / Rank: Sergeant, US Army / Duty: Administrative NCO

♥Linda M. Golden / In country: UNK / Rank: Specialist 4, US Army / Duty: Communications Center Specialist / Service dates: April 1970 – March 13, 1972 – died in an auto accident in Coral Gables, Florida while still on active duty

♥Barbara Jean Hile / Retired as a Sergeant First Class / In country: UNK / Rank: Staff Sergeant, US Army / Duty: Unit Supply Specialist

♥Helen Joann Hoback (Allen) / Retired as a Command Sergeant Major / In country: UNK / Rank: Master Sergeant, US Army / Duty: Personnel Specialist

♥Edith W. Kingsbury / Retired as a First Sergeant / In country: UNK / Rank: Sergeant First Class, US Army / Duty: Personnel Specialist

♥Ethel L. Lane / In country: UNK / Rank: Sergeant First Class, US Army / Duty: Computer Systems Operator

♥Daphney Mary Melson / In country: UNK / Rank: Sergeant First Class, US Army / Duty: Administrative NCO / Assigned to the Defense Language Institute, Presidio of Monterey, CA, when she died suddenly. She was 42 years old and had more than 22 years of service.

♥Olive Marie Miller / Retired as a Sergeant First Class / In country: UNK / Rank: Sergeant First Class, US Army / Duty: Administrative NCO

♥Judy Ann Money (Finn) / In country: UNK / Rank: Specialist 5, US Army / Duty: Ear, Nose and Throat Specialist / Service dates: September 1969 – August 1976

♥Marsha Jo Morris / Retired as a Sergeant Major / In country: UNK / Rank: Sergeant First Class, US Army / Duty: Personnel Specialist

♥Virginia Mercedes Musselman / Retired as a Sergeant First Class / In country: UNK / Rank: Sergeant First Class, US Army / Duty: Administrative NCO

♥Betty Nelson / Retired as a Master Sergeant / In country: UNK / Rank: UNK, US Army / Duty: Administrative Specialist

♥Patricia Kay Powell / In country: UNK / Rank: Specialist 6, US Army / Duty: USARV, Occupational Therapy Specialist

♥Phyllis J. B. Pryse / In country: UNK / Rank: Staff Sergeant, US Army / Duty: Administrative NCO / Service dates: November 1965 – January 1986

♥Anne Lucille Reidlinger (Gresham) / In country: UNK / Rank: Specialist 4, US Army / Duty: Clerk-Typist

♥Bernadette Rice / In country: UNK / Rank: Sergeant, US Army / Duty: Medical NCO

♥Lamona O. Rivers / Retired as a Sergeant Major / In country: UNK / Rank: UNK, US Army / Duty: Legal Specialist

♥Beulah Mae "Pat" Scheidt / Retired as a Master Sergeant / In country: UNK / Rank: UNK, US Army / Duty: Administrative Specialist

♥Mary Katherine Sheehan / Retired as a Sergeant First Class / In country: UNK / Rank: Staff Sergeant, US Army / Duty: Personnel Specialist

♥Susan Hope Smith / In country: UNK / Rank: Specialist 5, US Army / Duty: Medical NCO / Service dates: July 1969 to June 1972, died in auto accident 6/27/72 while still on active duty

♥Dorothy Louise Williams / In country: UNK / Rank: Specialist 5, US Army / Duty: Medical NCO

♥Virginia Ray Worthington / Retired as a Master Sergeant / In country: UNK / Rank: UNK, US Army / Duty: Food Service Supervisor

## Possible Service in Vietnam (Presumed Living)

**Mary L. Bailey /** In country: UNK / Rank: Specialist 4, US Army / Duty: Administrative Specialist / Service dates: November 1968 – October 1985

**Mary R. Connelly /** In country: UNK / Rank: Specialist 5, US Army / Duty: Unit Supply Specialist / Service dates: April 1969 – April 1972

**Mary A. Davis /** In country: UNK / Rank: Specialist 4, US Army / Duty: Traffic Management Coordinator / Service dates: September 1969 – March 1972

**Ramona L. "Mickey" Flynn /** In country: UNK / Rank: Specialist 5, US Army / Duty: most likely in Saigon, Administrative Specialist / Service dates: June 1967 – June 1974

**Carolyn S. Freeman /** In country: UNK / Rank: Specialist 4, US Army / Duty: Medical NCO / Service dates: September 1970 – May 1972

**Mary K. Freeman /** In country: UNK / Rank: Specialist 4, US Army / Duty: Clerk-Typist / Service dates: September 1970 – June 1972

**Barbara F. Gardner /** In country: UNK / Rank: Specialist 5, US Army / Duty: most likely in Saigon, Recruiter/Career Counselor after Vietnam / Service dates: June 1967 – March 1973

**Mary A. Herman /** In country: UNK / Rank: Specialist 5, US Army / Duty: Medical NCO / Service dates: August 1969 – March 1972

Costella Hicks / In country: UNK / Rank: Staff Sergeant, US Army / Duty: MACV, Chief of Staff for Logistics, Personnel NCO

**Patricia A. Hill /** In country: UNK / Rank: Specialist 5, US Army / Duty: Personnel Specialist / Service dates: October 1970 – December 1972

**Mary E. Johnson /** In country: UNK / Rank: Sergeant First Class, US Army / Duty: Radiology Specialist / Service dates: April 1957 – December 1976

**Patricia E. Johnson /** In country: UNK / Rank: Captain, US Air Force / Duty: Administrative Management Officer / Service dates: September 1968 – August 1974

**Glenda J. Jones /** In country: UNK / Rank: Specialist 5, US Army / Duty: Medical NCO / Service dates: December 1969 – June 1976

**Virginia Anne Kiewra /** Retired as a Sergeant First Class / In country: UNK / Rank: Specialist 4, US Army / Duty: Behavioral Science Specialist (probably after Vietnam) / Service dates: January 1971 – February 1991

**Sharon K. Kinne /** Retired as a Master Sergeant / In country: UNK / Rank: Specialist 5, US Army / Duty: Medical NCO
Service dates: July 1969 – January 1992

**Jyll Pontaine Maddox /** In country: UNK / Rank: Staff Sergeant, US Army / Duty: Administrative NCO / Service dates: July 1967 – July 1970

**Mary A. McQueen /** In country: UNK / Rank: Specialist 5, US Army / Duty: Optical Laboratory Specialist / Service dates: May 1969 – April 1972

**Mary W. Parker /** In country: UNK / Rank: Specialist 4, US Army / Duty: Medical NCO / Service dates: September 1969 – March 1972

**Margaret M. Roberts /** In country: UNK / Rank: Captain, US Air Force / Duty: Weather Officer / Service dates: September 1965 – June 1971

**Mary A. Smith /** In country: UNK / Rank: Specialist 5, US Army / Duty: Personnel Specialist / Service dates: October 1969 – April 1972

**Mary Sue Smith /** In country: UNK / Rank: Specialist 5, US Army / Duty: Medical NCO / Service dates: April 1969 – July 1989

**Patricia A. Smith /** In country: UNK / Rank: Specialist 4, US Army / Duty: Clerk-Typist / Service dates: August 1970 – June 1972

**Annie L. White /** In country: UNK / Rank: Specialist 4, US Army / Duty: Medical NCO / Service dates: June 1970 – May 1972

**Ruth M. Young /** Retired as a Master Sergeant / In country: UNK / Rank: UNK, US Army / Duty: Administrative Specialist / Service dates: March 1950 – May 1974

# Chapter Twenty-One

# WHAT THE AUTHOR HAS TO SAY

Now that you have read this incredible book, there are some things that I would like to share with you. I have always worked hard, whether it was in the Army or for Washington State or in my many volunteer endeavors. In 2013, at the age of 66, I decided to make 2013 a year of travel and personal endeavors and I named it "The Year of Me." My first stop was to visit Precilla Landry Wilkewitz and her husband, Ken in Louisiana. I introduced them in Vietnam and they have been married more than 44 years.

Precilla is the co-founder of the Vietnam Women Veterans, Inc., (VWV), a non-profit organization for military women who served in Vietnam. During that visit, we talked about a proposed book that had been a topic of discussion with several of the women members of the VWV over the past two decades. For many reasons, it hadn't really gotten underway, and Precilla said to me, "Many of our women are already dead, and more are dying all the time. It has to be written soon or it never will get done." She looked right at me and suggested that "The Year of Me" could wait and I should get moving on this book.

So, where to start? I wrote to President Obama and Vice President Biden, requesting that they locate or assign someone who could find the WAC records. My letter was hand-carried to the White House and received no response. I am disappointed and surprised at the lack of response.

The government can tell you how many men and how many female nurses served in Vietnam. They can even provide you names, but they know little about the other military women who served. The Pentagon used to provide an estimate; now we're told they have no accurate count. The majority of the military women in Vietnam were WACs. The other services sent far fewer women.

Meticulous records were supposedly maintained for the WAC but, NO ONE knows where those records are today. We were told the WAC Detachment records from USARV, Special Troops, were packed up and sent to storage at Hickam Air Force Base in Hawaii. From there, no one knows where they were sent. Over the years, several writers have suggested that a search should be made for this paperwork. One is Colonel Bettie

Morden, author of *The Women's Army Corps 1945-1978* that was published by the Center of Military History in 1990. Chapter IX, titled "Vietnam; WAC Strength; WAC Standards" is 40 pages long and does an excellent job of recounting WAC involvement in Vietnam. Many of her references are unavailable or their location is unclear. It is embarrassing that no office in the government has felt it important enough to locate these records. Additionally, requests for search and retrieval of the records have been ignored.

I agreed to put this book together because if we don't tell our stories, our history will be lost. I did this for women like my friends, Gloria Grenfell (Fowler) (Leigh) and Cheri Asmus (Halsey). They were in the initial group of enlisted women assigned in January 1967 to the WAC Detachment in Saigon, Vietnam. They served their country honorably. When they returned home, they were spit at, called Uncle Sam's whores and other vile names from our countrymen who were protesting the war. Until recently, that was the last memory they had of their service.

When I took on this project, I decided that to do it properly the book would have ALL military women that served in Vietnam, except the nurses, who have their own organizations and stories, as well as the memorial in Washington, DC. This book includes women from the Army, Marine Corps, Navy and Air Force.

The dedication of the Vietnam Women's Memorial in 1993 was greatly anticipated by many of us. We looked forward to seeing "our" memorial and participating in the Veterans Day activities. I remember approaching the memorial and immediately seeing a nurse caring for a male patient. I walked around and saw the other two figures and thought, "This isn't about me. What am I doing here?" Looking at the memorial, it is obviously about nurses.

*"The Vietnam Women's Memorial was established not only to honor those women who served, but also for the families who lost loved ones in the war, so they would know about the women who provided comfort, care, and a human touch for those who were suffering and dying." ~ Vietnam Women's Memorial Foundation webpage*

There have been additions to the information about the memorial that make it more inclusive of the other women veterans. In fact, I found reading "Moving a Vision: The Vietnam Women's Memorial" by Diane Carlson Evans very interesting. This group did an incredible job of making sure that they were recognized. I am very proud of all of their hard work. What an accomplishment they achieved! But after reading this article, it is my opinion that leaving the other women veterans out was an intentional oversight by the nurses. I no longer go to what I believe is the "Nurses" Memorial. The Vietnam Wall is my memorial.

The source document I used to start this book was a 56-page paper copy of an email with 570 women on it dated September 14, 2001, from Claire Starnes, the co-founder of the VWV, Inc., to Frances Crawford. Frances had many friends within the VWV, and although she was not a Vietnam Veteran, she was always an active participant at the reunion conferences. She was recognized at the 2014 conference in Concord, NC, and she passed away later that year.

I knew that to accomplish this huge task, I would need help. The names of the book team members are in **bold** in the following paragraphs.

As anyone who knows me will tell you, I simply do not possess the computer skills for this project. I knew that my friend of 40 years, **Phyllis K. Miller,** did. She was the first one I called. When I explained what I wanted to do, she immediately agreed because although not a Vietnam Veteran, she wanted to honor those of us who are. She could remotely connect to my computer, 2,600 miles across country, to see what I had done with a file, or fix a problem. She helped any of the team members who had computer issues, edited stories and assembled the many pieces into the final product. I am glad her talents were available for this project. This book would not have been possible without her.

My friend Precilla Landry (Wilkewitz) told me that **Patty Babcock (Schmauch)** was still handling the VWV database. I called Patty and she, too, was happy to help.

I took the list and put the women in chronological order. Those that had no dates were put in a separate search list. I wanted to tell the story of the war from the arrival of the very first military woman to the departure of the last one. The chronological order of the women allows the reader to see the similarities and differences of the experiences, especially between the services.

I knew from the start that I wanted the commemorative quilt in the book. I decided to visit **Glenda "Stormy" Storni (Graebe)** in Indiana. She invited her close friend, the second company commander, **Joanne "Murph" Murphy,** who lives nearby, to join in this project. Glenda's friend, **Marsha "Cricket" Holder,** came up from Mississippi to join us.

There was so much excitement about having the opportunity to get our history recorded, especially since we've all been asked many times if we were nurses. In my 26 years in the Army, I don't think it is an exaggeration to say that I have been asked that question at least 1,000 times.

When **Cricket Holder** said that her interest was in honoring the deceased, I cried. I had been worried about how we would honor our deceased women – we have so many of them. She created our Virtual Cemetery which is on the internet website www.FindAGrave.com and can be found by using this shortcut URL: http://goo.gl/yTjo9t. She has done a tremendous job on this project, and it remains her cherished and continuing goal to find and honor all of our deceased women veterans. She is certainly our Guardian Angel of the deceased. There is a second Virtual Cemetery for the women we could not definitely place in Vietnam: http://goo.gl/wCVcDk, and it has our Sister Search women.

Organizing a team of people to work on this project was another challenge. The most obvious members were the cadre of the WAC detachment, and **Joanne Murphy** had already agreed to work on finding the women who served under her command. I gave her the list of women that she was responsible for. In addition, she writes very well so she was initially assigned to edit the early stories. She is a professional photographer so we were blessed to have her be able to turn the initial old blurred photos into some of the ones you see in the book.

**Marion Crawford** was also an immediate and obvious choice. She is a snowbird and lives in Georgia part of the year and Florida the rest of it. She is a hero of mine who loves "her troops" and we love her back. She wrote many of the stories in this book and has been a wonderful resource. She contacted the women who served under Peggy Ready, who was not able to work on the project. Marion Crawford is 85 and is the only surviving first sergeant from the Vietnam WAC Detachment cadre. She continues to be full of life and everyone really enjoys spending time with her. She is the first person I will be visiting when I finally start "The Year of Me" in 2015.

For a long time, we did not have anyone to research and contact the group of Army women who had served in Saigon. **Carol Ogg** called me one day to ask where she should send her information. When I told her that we had no one to search for and contact the Saigon group, she immediately volunteered. Carol is extremely efficient and did a wonderful job locating and contacting the women who were not at the WAC Detachment during their tour.

**Nancy Jurgevich** was the third detachment commander. She is a snowbird who alternates her time between Florida and Kentucky. She was President of the VWV for five years. I have had many interactions with her and all of them have been terrific! **Shirley Ohta,** from Indiana, was the fourth commander. The fifth commander was Marjorie K. Johnson, who is deceased. **Pat "PJ" Jernigan,** from Virginia, stepped up and took on the task of locating and contacting Marjorie Johnson's women. PJ is the researcher and historian on the team and has saved me from making mistakes more than once. All of us in the first group of women in 1967 were told that we were in the first

WAC Detachment to ever serve in a combat zone. As PJ pointed out, that was not true. We had been repeating an error for over 40 years. We now know, thanks to PJ, that we were the first WAC Detachment in a combat zone since WWII, not the first one ever. She also helped by correcting an issue about a unit award, and she was the one who told me we would need a Consent and Release form from the women, along with their stories and pictures. Constance "Connie" Seidemann (Ferrell) was the last commander.

We were fortunate to have **Mary Glaudel-DeZurik** as our US Marine team member. In May 2013, she was doing a web search for Women Marines in Vietnam and came across the VWV web page. She looked at the "Sisters" list and recognized two of the women that she knew quite well – Nola Makinster and Polly Wilson. She contacted Nancy Jurgevich, President of the VWV, who referred her to me. I really enjoyed working with Mary.

Joanne Murphy volunteered to write all of the Air Force women to see if anyone was interested in joining the book team to locate and contact their women. **Darlene Brewer-Alexander** wrote and shared with Joanne that she could donate some time to this project. Darlene wrote to me, "Joanne Murphy sent me a beautiful letter, and her entreaty was so earnest and compelling that I just couldn't refuse, so I joined up so to speak. And, I am glad that I did." I am glad that she did also!

When the Vietnam Women Veterans organization was initially formed, **Claire Brisebois (Starnes)** and Precilla Landry (Wilkewitz) made the decision to invite the AMSC, AMC, MSC, and BSC women (medical fields but not nurses) to join as there was no separate Vietnam Veterans organization for them. The first AMC woman to join the VWV was Dr. Janice Mendelson, MD. There were also four Navy MSC women who have been overlooked in previous histories about the service of women in Vietnam because these four served aboard the hospital ships, USS *Repose* and USS *Sanctuary:* **Carmen "Penny" Marshall (Adams)**, who helped include the stories of these women; Lieutenant Commander Paula Cecelia Towle; Lieutenant Commander Edna E. "Mickey" McCormick; and Lieutenant Commander Patsy J. Robinson. Penny Marshall Adams did much of the research and located many of the AMSC, MSC and BSC women on the list in the All-Services chapter.

The first Homecoming Conference in November 1999 was held in Olympia, WA. The cities of Olympia, Tumwater and Lacey, the Washington State Department of Veterans Affairs (WDVA), with significant contributions from CSM John Lee (USA Ret), who was the Deputy Director and Tom Schumacher, who ran the PTSD Program, and the State of Washington made me very proud! It was the most moving tribute I have seen for any veteran's group, and I was delighted that I had "volunteered" the location and support. Everyone truly rolled out the red carpet for us.

I wanted to have the conferences memorialized. The name that came up from everyone I talked to was **Betty "Jean" Stallings**. I called Jean and asked her to do this. She readily agreed.

**Alfie Alvarado-Ramos** is the current Director of the Washington State Department of Veterans Affairs. I knew we were going to need some serious support in order to get any assistance from the various organizations we wanted to interact with. She is an exceptional leader and well respected in the veteran community. She has shared our history with many people, is a strong advocate for us and is one of my closest friends.

Washington, DC, was high on my list of research destinations. I thought it would be a wonderful time to reconnect with one of my former bosses as well as a friend of mine, **Dee McWilliams.** I was her Sergeant Major when she was a Major. She loves to tell people that I did such a great job of training her she was promoted to two-star general. We both know that's not true but, I sure love having her say it! I knew that she was very involved in the veteran community and would be willing to help me. Dee McWilliams and Pat Jernigan took me to the Women in Military Service for America (WIMSA) Memorial Foundation Headquarters in Virginia and to the WIMSA Memorial itself, at the Arlington Cemetery. I was introduced to Marilla Cushman, LTC, USA Retired, who is the Director of Public Relations and Development for WIMSA. I needed copies of registrations and pictures from their records, which were willingly provided. On another research trip, I spent three days at Fort Lee, VA, and was able to get an appointment with the Director and Archivist of the US Army Women's Museum, **Dr. Françoise B. Bonnell** and **Amanda Strickland**. They were both very excited about this project. The museum displays **Glenda Storni Graebe's** commemorative quilt in the main Briefing Room so it gets lots of attention. I invited Françoise and Amanda to join our team and write the piece on the Army, which is in the All-Service Listing, Chapter Eighteen. The museum bookstore will carry this book.

There were a number of things I really had not anticipated on this project:

- The computer issues – the women range from 63 to 92 years old. Many women did not have computers. Many of the women had computers, but had limited skills. Scan and attach a picture? Not going to happen. Converting files from one software program to another was another challenge.

- In the research process for this book, we have accumulated a tremendous amount of transcriptions, photographs, newspapers, and other miscellaneous documentation. These items represent all Branches of the Armed Services. The Vietnam Center and Archive at Texas Tech University in Lubbock, TX, will be the repository for items used in publishing this book. The Vietnam Center and Archive will receive all originals, except for Army materials of which the Archive will receive copies. Donated materials will be available to future researchers under the current Vietnam Women Veterans (VWV) Collection. Army originals will be deposited at the United States Army Women's Museum, Fort Lee, VA. In addition, a digitized copy of all materials will be presented to the Women in Military Service for America (WIMSA) for inclusion in its Women's Memorial Foundation Office of History & Collections.

Vietnam Center and Archive, Texas Tech University
  http://www.vietnam.ttu.edu/
US Army Women's Museum
  http://www.awm.lee.army.mil/
WIMSA Foundation
  http://www.womensmemorial.org/H&C/h&cwelcome.html

- We had eight frauds, which surprised us – women who said they were Vietnam veterans and yet they are not. Pat Jernigan has become somewhat of an expert in this fraud area. I believed one "wanna be" and felt personally hurt that she lied to us.
- I was very unhappy to see so many of our women still suffering from their war experiences. I talked to one woman who cried the entire 40 minutes. She said her story was similar to Sister Linda McClenahan's. She said her experience in Vietnam was so painful that she did not want to relive it. She said she had never gone to the VA to seek treatment because at the time she came home it was unbearable. Forty years later and she still felt too traumatized to seek help. This veteran died recently. We know where she lived. We found nothing on her death but two signatures on a paper in a funeral home. It sickens me to see the physical and mental issues our women and their families are still suffering. One of the women was a happy-go-lucky young woman in Vietnam but has turned into a recluse because

she worked in the Evacuation Office and found out there was no evacuation plan for our unit. She has not been able to accept that her country sent her to a war zone in Class B uniform, heels, and nylons but no weapons and no plans to evacuate us.

Phyllis Miller and I went to the VWV Conference, which was held in Concord, NC, May 1-4, 2014. **Lyndell Smith** joined the book team just before the conference and came to meet with us.

**Claire Starnes** had a break in her busy schedule and helped us with the editing beginning in summer 2014. It was perfect timing – she is one of the two women who started this adventure and now will get to see this book to completion. Precilla Wilkewitz continues to advocate for veterans working for the Veterans of Foreign Wars.

I know we will have errors and omissions but it is not from lack of trying. There is still hope that someone will locate the WAC records so errors and omissions can be corrected someday. Someone out there must know where they are. The Marine records are complete. And, because of the comprehensive research by Carmen "Penny" Marshall Adams, we have added four Navy women who served aboard the USS *Sanctuary* and the USS Repose during the Vietnam War.

As our Air Force expert, Colonel Darlene Alexander-Brewer (USAF, Ret) has said, "The Air Force kept records on all those assigned to Southeast Asia, with their dates in country, unit of assignment, position, etc. . . .The biggest problem is that the records have not been automated, so extracting figures of the number who served in Vietnam as versus Thailand has to be done manually. The point is that at this time we cannot confirm the exact number, period."

It is sad that this year (2015) we are commemorating the 50th Anniversary of the Vietnam War, and it seems no one has taken the time to manually check the records of these USAF women so we could honor them in this book.

As I look back at this, I am amazed at all of the hard work that this all-volunteer team did to make this book a reality. It took us more than two years from start to submission. We started with 570 names on the list I used and have more than 1,000 women listed in the current database because everyone kept looking. We are still looking. The Sister Search List has contact information for any updates our readers can provide.

We want these incredible women to take their place of honor with the rest of the Vietnam veterans.

# IMAGE INDEX

Front Cover
Army: 1SG Marion Crawford and WAC Detachment Drill Team, US Army photo
Navy: CDR Elizabeth Barrett, US Navy photo
Air Force: First enlisted WAF arrive in Vietnam, US Air Force photo
USMC: Mary Glaudel-DeZurik, personal photo

MAJ Sherian G. Cadoria, personal photo

108    SP4 Emma L. Thornton (Henderson), personal photo

SP5 Cheranne Asmus (Halsey), personal photo

110    SP5 Christine Baker, Vietnam Memory Book 2000

SP5 Martha Duncan (Jackson), Vietnam Memory Book 2000

111    SP5 Gloria J. Grenfell (Fowler) (Leigh), personal photo

113    SP5 Carol J. Matisz (Miller), Vietnam Memory Book 2000

114    SP5 Carolyn L. Mitchell (Wiggins), Vietnam Memory Book 2000

SP4 Carolyn A. Moore, Vietnam Memory Book 2000

SP5 Beverly Mounter (Evans), personal photo

115    SP5 Lillian Sampson (Grasham), personal photo

SP5 Holly A. Smith, photo by Glenda Storni Graebe

SP5 Dianne P. Tipton (Turbyfill), US Army photo

116    SP5 Patricia L. Brooks (Hildebrand), Vietnam Memory Book 2000

SSG Janet F. Singer, Women's Memorial Foundation Register

SSG Reya Monte, Vietnam Memory Book 2000

SP4 Loretta J. Bohlke (Meredith), photo by Glenda Storni Graebe

117    SP5 Penelope L. Lewis (Wilcox), Vietnam Memory Book 2000

SP5 Juliette Anita Dortch (Coleman-Hallman), Vietnam Memory Book 2000

119    SSG Donna J. Dear, personal photo

120    SP4 Linda K. Ostermeier (McDermith), Vietnam Memory Book 2000

121    SP4 Sharon A. Ridout, Vietnam Memory Book 2000

122    SP5 Linda S. Pritchard (Woolm), Vietnam Memory Book 2000

123    SP5 Janice Gwen Curtis, US Army photo

124    SP5 Joeanne Harris (Burr), Vietnam Memory Book 2000

SP5 Patricia A. Wilcoxon, personal photo

125    SP5 Rosario Bermudez (Tinsley), Vietnam Memory Book 2000

SP5 Faye S. Conaway, Vietnam Memory Book 2000

126    SP5 Mary Ann Stedman (Vasas), personal photo

127    SSG Donna Ann Lowery, personal photo

129    SP5 Anne Marie Lally, Vietnam Memory Book 2000

130    SP5 Penny Arlene Freeman (Choiniere), Vietnam Memory Book 2000

131    SP5 Hester E. Miller, Vietnam Memory Book 2000

132    SP5 Donna K. Bramley, personal photo

SP4 Patricia A. Ogg, Vietnam Memory Book 2000

133 SP5 Ruth E. Riter, US Army photo

134 SSG Janet A. Smith, Vietnam Memory Book 2000

SP5 Kathleen E. Stoner (DeCollo), Vietnam Memory Book 2000

SSG Margaret T. Trapp (Jones),Vietnam Memory Book 2000

135 SP5 Phylis A. Wahwasuck (Thomas), personal photo

136 SP4 Joyce P. Trumpet, Vietnam Memory Book 2000

SP5 Margaret M. Sigley (D'Onofrio), US Army Women's Museum

SP5 Joanne B. Manger (Willaford), Vietnam Memory Book 2000

137 SP5 Nancy M. Wooten (Thorne), personal photo

138 SP5 Dorothy Smith (Gardner), personal photo

140 SP5 Glenda E. Storni (Graebe), personal photo

141 SP5 Anita Flores (Massey), Vietnam Memory Book 2000

LT Patsy June Robinson, US Navy photo

142 CPT Jolene Kay Tomlan, US Army photo

144 LTC Imogen Elaine Averett, Vietnam Memory Book 2000

145 SP5 Juana Christina Felix, personal photo

146 SP5 Susie Mae Stephens (McArthur), personal photo

148 SP5 Gwendolyn Kay Faught (Wakolee), Vietnam Memory Book 2000

SSG Anita Marie Wampach, Vietnam Memory Book 2000

149 CPT Joanne E. Fenninger, personal photo

MSgt Barbara Jean Dulinsky, Women's Memorial Foundation Register

151 MAJ Norma V. Busse, personal photo

SP5 Ida E. Colford (Willis), personal photo

152 Capt Kathleen Frances Sabo (Grassmeier), US Air Force photo

SP5 Patricia C. Pewitt, Vietnam Memory Book 2000

153 SSG Barbara M. Maine, Vietnam Memory Book 2000

SP5 Linda Jean Garrigan, Vietnam Memory Book 2000

SP5 Mary Eliza Hay (Wilson), personal photo

154 CAPT Elizabeth Gordon Wylie, US Navy photo

155 Capt Vera Mae Jones, US Marine Corps photo

156 SP5 Marie I. Dube (Gross), personal photo

SFC Mary Louise Cook (Curry), personal photo

157 Lt Col June Hilton with first five enlisted WAF assigned to Vietnam, US Air Force photo

LTC Sarah Fairly Niblack, US Army Women's Museum
190 Sgt Nola Evon Makinster (Wilcox), personal photo
191 SP5 Betty Mae Davis (Smith), Vietnam Memory Book 2000
192 SP5 Therese E. Harnden (Peters), Vietnam Memory Book 2000
SFC Mary Elizabeth Pritchard (Lennon), courtesy of Glenda Storni Graebe
195 CPT Bonnie G. Moscatelli, Women's Memorial Foundation Register
197 Lt Col Bonnie Jane Stewart (Hurst), photo courtesy of RAFDA
200 SSG Cathy L. Brock, Vietnam Memory Book 2000
SP5 Barbara F. Chorak (Ballas), Vietnam Memory Book 2000
201 Capt Camilla L. Wagner, Airman, May 1969
SP4 Sandra Emily Wainwright (McGowan), personal photo
202 LT Sally Louise Bostwick, personal photo
203 SSG Gabrielle Brancato, courtesy of Marion Crawford
204 SP5 Lee N. Wilson, Vietnam Memory Book 2000
SP5 Esther M. Gleaton, Vietnam Memory Book 2000
205 SSG Maryna Lee Misiewicz, personal photo
207 SFC Grendel Alice Howard, personal photo
209 SP5 Precilla Ann Landry (Wilkewitz), Vietnam Memory Book 2000
210 SP5 Ladina L. Moore, personal photo
211 SP5 Lidia M. Contreras, personal photo
212 SFC Margaret F. Bevill, personal photo
213 SSG Judy Ann Jacque, personal photo
215 SP5 Annette M. Drumming (Douglas), courtesy of Douglas family
SP5 Julie E. Hollis (Bumpas), Vietnam Memory Book 2000
LTC Priscilla Katharine Gilchrist, photo by Gordon D. King, The Citizen, Laconia, NH, February 18, 2000
217 LT Susan F. Hamilton (Cusson), personal photo
SP5 Nancy Jolene Johnson, US Army Women's Museum
218 SSgt Doris L. Denton, personal photo
219 SP5 Marsha Dale Holder, personal photo
221 SP5 Sonia B. Gonzalez Mendez, personal photo
223 SFC Dorothy J. Rechel, personal photo
LTC Marie Sylvia Knasiak, US Army Women's Museum
224 SFC T. Elaine Palmer, personal photo

MAJ Charlotte Josephine Hall, US Army Women's Museum

287 MAJ Lois L. Westerfield, personal photo

288 Maj Clara C. Johnson, Airman, May 1969

SSgt Maria M. Abrahante, Airman, May 1969

289 SP5 Geraldine Young, courtesy of Nora Lebron

290 SP5 Phyllis J. Bertram, courtesy of Penny Ormes

LCDR Barbara Bole, US Navy photo

SP5 Beverly L. Brooks, Women's Memorial Foundation Register

291 SFC Ellen Frances Garvey, Vietnam Memory Book 2000

SSG Pinkie Bell Houser, Vietnam Memory Book 2000

292 CW2 Barbara J. Wilson (Jack) (Norman), Vietnam Memory Book 2000

293 SP5 Marjorie D. McLain, US Army photo

294 SFC Lillian Ruth Ogburn, US Army Women's Museum

SSG Rena Darlene Hurley, Vietnam Memory Book 2000

296 SP5 Susan J. Haack, personal photo

299 SSG Catherine Mary Kahl (l) and twin, SSG Charlene Mary Kahl (Kennedy), personal photo

301 MAJ Jessie Stuart Brewer, personal photo

302 SSG Eva B. Schmaing (Pederson), Vietnam Memory Book 2000

SP5 Lawanda E. Allen, Women's Memorial Foundation Register

303 CPT Barbara C. Reid, personal photo

307 LTC Frances Weir, US Army Women's Museum

SP4 Evelyn L. Lozano (Roussos), US Army Women's Museum

308 SP6 Susan E. Wudy, Vietnam Memory Book 2000

SSG Claire M. L. Brisebois (Starnes), personal photo

311 SSG Catherine Louise Oatman, Vietnam Memory Book 2000

312 SP5 Nora Hilda Lebron (Encarnacion), personal photo

313 SP5 Lana H. Clark (Majewski), personal photo

SSG Brenda Sue Eichholz (Caldwell), personal photo

314 SSG Ruth Marleen Neeley (Cremin), personal photo

316 SSG Sharon Dawn Weikel, Vietnam Memory Book 2000

Sgt Ella L. Netherton, Vietnam Memory Book 2000

317 GySgt Adelina Diaz (Torres), personal photo

318 SP5 Idalia Edna Correa, courtesy of Nora Lebron

319 Capt Alice I. Champagne (Littlejohn), personal photo

| | |
|---|---|
| 382 | SP5 Anna Marie Hidalgo (Dennett), Vietnam Memory Book 2000 |
| 383 | SP5 Catherine E. Messer, personal photo |
| 384 | SSG Mary C. Aleshire, personal photo |
| 386 | SSG Laura Holguin (Pariseau), Vietnam Memory Book 2000 |
| 387 | SP5 Kathryn A. Votipka (Retzlaff), Vietnam Memory Book 2000 |
| | SP4 Betty J. Russell, Vietnam Memory Book 2000 |
| 389 | SSgt Jacquelyn Kay Roach, personal photo |
| 391 | SFC Eleanor Marie Strudas, US Army Women's Museum |
| 392 | MAJ June Elizabeth Owens Knutsen, Vietnam Memory Book 2000 |
| 393 | CPT Irene Begg, personal photo |
| 394 | CW4 Shirley Elizabeth Klein, Vietnam Memory Book 2000 |
| | SSG Lucie Rivera-O'Ferrall, personal photo |
| 396 | SP5 Elizabeth A. Freaney, courtesy of Penny Ormes Price |
| | SP5 Nancy E. Simmons, Vietnam Memory Book 2000 |
| 398 | SSG Pamela S. Riess (Bunde), personal photo |
| | SP4 Amy Louella Carter, personal photo |
| 401 | LTC Janice Annette Mendelson, MD, courtesy of Carmen Adams Marshall |
| 403 | SP4 Priscilla Mosby, US Army Women's Museum |
| 404 | SSgt Donna Lou Hollowell (Murray), Vietnam Memory Book 2000 |
| 405 | SSG Carol A. Ogg, personal photo |
| 406 | MSgt Lois Margaret Schmoker, Vietnam Memory Book 2000 |
| | Maj Vivienne C. Sinclair (Vuosolo), Women's Memorial Foundation Register |
| 408 | Maj Eleanor L. Gavin (Skinner), personal photo |
| 409 | SSG Carolyn L. Otey, personal photo |
| 410 | MAJ Patricia M. Pavlis, personal photo |
| 411 | SSgt Margaret K. Berry (Underwood), personal photo |
| 412 | Capt Lyndell D. Smith, personal photo |
| 414 | CPT Patricia Sue Sepulveda, personal photo |
| 416 | SP5 Donna Jean Dunlap (Sams), Vietnam Memory Book 2000 |
| 418 | SSG Linda S. Little, personal photo |
| | SP5 Josephine Solis, personal photo |
| 420 | CPT Nora Marie Prestinari (Burchett), personal photo |
| | 2d Lt Sharon Elaine Thomas (Safford), courtesy of Claudia Crowley Collins |

Sgt Ruth Gail Smith (Mahaffey), courtesy of Diana Andrews

455 SSgt Claire V. Allison, personal photo

SSgt Mary Joan Webb, personal photo

457 SSgt Diana Stack Andrews, personal photo

458 LTC Aida Nancy Sanchez, Women's Memorial Foundation Register

465 SP5 Evelyn Pearl Kussman (Lindblad), US Army photo, National Archives

466 SGT Janis Lynette Waters, US Army Women's Museum

468 SP5 Sandra Kaye Phillips (Vandever), personal photo

MAJ Joyce Eloise Eslick, Vietnam Memory Book 2000

469 Capt Marie (Helscher) LeBlanc, personal photo

471 COL Elizabeth Helen Branch, US Army photo

473 SSgt Loretta Marie Morrison (Kostyn), personal photo

474 LTC Alice May Davis, Vietnam Memory Book 2000

475 1st Lt Janice Hunt (Sanborn), personal photo

476 SP5 Carol A. Hazzard (Waryck-McClure), US Army Women's Museum

477 Maj Maralin K. Coffinger, personal photo

479 Capt Kathryn Wilson (Disbrow), Vietnam Memory Book 2000

480 MAJ Sallie Laura Elmira Carroll, photo by Jerri Parness

481 CPT Florence I. Dunn, personal photo

483 CW2 Glenda M. Kaufman (Lunki), personal photo

484 SP5 Kathleen E. Wilcox, Vietnam Memory Book 2000

485 SSG Ethel M. Dial, personal photo

487 MAJ Mary Jane Bennett (Hill) (Treadwell), personal photo

488 COL Jennie Wren Fea, Vietnam Memory Book 2000

490 SSG Rosemarie Lane, US Army photo

491 SSG Kay F. Hickok, US Army Women's Museum

492 Capt Merline Lovelace, personal photo

493 MSgt Mary M. Morris, personal photo

494 CAPT Mary Frances Anderson (Shupack), personal photo

498 SP5 Marlene Adele Bowen-Grissett, personal photo

499 SP5 Sherri A. Tipton, Vietnam Memory Book 2000

501 1SG Mildred Estelle Duncan, US Army Women's Museum

SP5 Sandra J. Torrens, US Army Women's Museum

| 503 | CPT Constance Christine Seidemann (Ferrell), US Army Women's Museum |
|---|---|
| 504 | SSgt Laurie A. Clemons (Parkerton), personal photo |
| 506 | Capt Judie A. Armington, personal photo |
| 508 | CDR Elizabeth M. Barrett, US Navy photo |
| 509 | SSgt Donna A. Rae Bornholdt (Spaller), personal photo |
| 512 | SSgt De Ann R. Masters, Vietnam Memory Book 2000 |
| 513 | Capt Darlene K. Brewer (Alexander), personal photo |
| 517 | SSG Mary Kathleen Bailey, personal photo |
| 518 | SP4 Mary Ann Ehrhardt, Women's Memorial Foundation Register |
| | SSG Judith L. McCurdy, personal photo |
| 519 | Capt Barbara J. Gordon, personal photo |
| 520 | 2d Lt Jo A. Pritchard, personal photo |
| 521 | CWO2 Ernestine Ann Koch, personal photo |
| 522 | SP4 Sharolyn K. Picking, personal photo |
| | SP5 Gloria Jean Labadie, Overseas Weekly Pacific Edition, May 8, 1972 |
| 524 | MAJ Frances Ann Iacoboni (Krilich), Women's Memorial Foundation Register |
| | 1st Lt Rebecca Harrison Shumate (Richardson), personal photo |
| 526 | TSgt Virginia A. Griffith, personal photo |
| 531 | SSgt Patsy Hatley, personal photo |
| 532 | TSgt Caroline A. Tschetter (Nuese), personal photo |
| 533 | SSgt Joan Frances Bence (Naylor), personal photo |
| | Capt Patricia Mary Murphy, Vietnam Memory Book 2000 |
| 534 | TSgt Linda A. Bellard, Vietnam Memory Book 2000 |
| | SSgt Linda L. Liston (Katalenich), www.macoi.net |
| 535 | SSgt Carol A. Urich, Vietnam Memory Book 2000 |
| | TSgt Margaret Ozella Buck, Vietnam Memory Book 2000 |
| | Capt Jillian D. Tate, Vietnam Memory Book 2000 |
| 536 | 1st Lt Margaret Hammond (Anno), personal photo |
| | SSgt Mary A. Curry (Murry), Vietnam Memory Book 2000 |
| | SSgt Patricia Dorothy LaRocque, Vietnam Memory Book 2000 |
| 540 | COL Emily Gorman, Director, WAC, US Army photo |
| | MAJ Kathleen I. Wilkes, US Army Women's Museum |
| 541 | LTC Judith Christian Polk Bennett, US Army photo |

# Name Index

# B

Babcock, Beverly U., 674
Babcock, Patricia V. (Schmauch), xii, xiv, 335, 593, 621
Bacon, Barbara D., 332, 354, 552, 621
Baggan, Mary V. (Kelly), 445, 656
Bailey
    Betty J., 252, 635
    Mary Kathleen, 517, 635
    Mary L., 684
Baird, Dorothy G., 431, 651
Baker
    Carol J., 350, 635
    Christine "Cookie", 110, 616
    Cynthia L. "Cindy", 432, 624
    Lillian Emily, 331, 635
    Mary E., 273, 651
    Maxene Monetta (Michl), 74, 635
    Wanda Lee, 192, 229, 618
Bala, Delores A. (Liederbach), 119, 616
Baldwin, Donna P., 364, 635
Banks, Barbara L., 438, 651
Barber, Joan E., 434, 651
Barnes
    Joan L. (Barco), 198, 635
    Linda M. (Poole), xii, 254, 618, 664
Barnwell, Shirley M., 280, 384, 635
Barrett
    Delores "Mickey", 467, 485, 624, 629
    Elizabeth "Dee" M., 10, 13, 508, 577, 641
Bartl, Elfriede "Elly", 479, 626
Beard, Faye Lou, 431, 651
Beck, Karen L., 674
Begg, Irene, 393, 656
Bellard, Linda A., 43, 534, 651
Bence, Joan Frances (Naylor), 533, 651
Bender, Mary Van Ette, 178, 635

Bennett, Judith Christian Polk, 77, 541, 635
Benson, Betty J., 7, 13, 29, 47, 50, 53, 86, 89, 119, 122, 128, 147, 212, 225, 560, 564, 565, 616, 618, 632
Berg, Maxine M., 674
Bergstresser, Audrey M., 380, 624
Bermudez, Rosario "Rosie" (Tinsley), 125, 616
Bernardini, Sylvia R., 439, 553, 635
Berrios-Perez, Gladys (Schwerin), 433, 624
Berry, Margaret B. (Underwood), 411, 651
Bertram
    Lois J., 318, 412, 638
    Phyllis J., 269, 290, 621
Bessette, Carol S., 237, 651
Best, Ann H. (Volkwine), 530, 651
Betts, Ida Imani, 262, 618
Bevill, Margaret F., 212, 618
Black
    Frances L., 432, 626
    Ruth Marie, 351, 651
Blocher, Terry, xiv
Bohlke, Loretta J. (Meredith), 116, 616
Bole, Barbara, 9, 290, 641
Bonnell, Françoise, xiii, xiv, 607, 692
Bornholdt, Donna Rae (Spaller), 509, 651
Boston, Carolyn K. (Bright), 289, 635
Bostwick, Sally Louise, 202, 641
Bowen, Clotilde O. Dent, 9, 425, 656
Bowen-Grissett, Marlene Adele, 22, 498, 626, 629
Bower, Karen Lu (Sulheim), 674
Boyle, Beverly Jo, 681
Bozman, Roberta "Robby", 152, 616
Brackett, Linda M. (Grasso), 357, 621
Bradford, Loyce Alice, 390, 635